The Female Pen

THE FEMALE PEN

Women Writers and Novelists
1621–1818

by
B.G. MacCARTHY

with a preface by JANET TODD

CORK UNIVERSITY PRESS

First published by Cork University Press in two volumes: Women Writers: Their
Contribution to the English Novel 1621–1744, in 1944 (reprinted 1945 and 1946),
and The Female Pen: Women Writers and Novelists 1744–1818, published in 1947.
Both volumes © Cork University Press.

This edition published in 1994 by Cork University Press
University College, Cork, Ireland.

© Cork University Press 1994

British Library Cataloguing in Publication Data
A CIP catalogue record for this book is available from the British Library.

ISBN 0 902561 97 9 paperback
1 85918 022 1 hardback

Typeset by Seton Music Graphics, Bantry, Co. Cork
Printed in Ireland by ColourBooks, Baldoyle, Dublin

'But his misfortune was to fall in an obscure world that afforded only a female pen to celebrate his fame.'

Aphra Behn, *Oroonoko*, 1688

'Nay, even my own sex, which should assert our prerogative against such detractors, are often backward to encourage the female pen.'

Susannah Centlivre, Dedication to *The Platonic Lady*, 1707

'You know how female writers are looked down upon. The women fear and hate, the men ridicule and dislike them.'

Elizabeth Hamilton, *Letters to a Hindoo Rajah*, 1791

'Men have had every advantage of us in telling their own story. Education has been theirs in so much higher a degree; the pen has been in their hands.'

Jane Austen, *Persuasion*, 1818

Contents

Contents

B.G. MacCarthy (1904 - 1993)

Preface

A fascination for early women writers is a minority emotion, which is, happily, growing more general. B.G. MacCarthy's work, out of print since its initial publication in the 1940s, has for us workers in this vineyard the kind of status achieved in feminist theory by Simone de Beauvoir's *Second Sex* or Virginia Woolf's *A Room of One's Own* — which MacCarthy took as her own starting point.

Writing during the Second World War when women assumed unusual roles, MacCarthy prefaced her work not with the common apology for its existence but with the assertion that she needed much space to treat her subject; if the War prevented her fom publishing in full, she would not respond by condensing but would divide her work into two volumes. She intended to quote expansively. Although she did not anticipate a time when many of the books she treated would be in print, she none the less made it clear that she valued these forgotten works and wished them to be sampled in her pages and then read in full. She did not, like Julia Kavanagh in *English Women of Letters* (1862) and so many other critics of the nineteenth and early twentieth centuries, describe only to dismiss.

B.G. MacCarthy is one of a generation of stalwart women who read extensively and then wrote authoritatively, having acquired confidence in their judgements which they assumed to be correct — women such as J.M.S. Tompkins, Joyce M. Horner and Edith Birkhead. Tompkins published her *Popular Novel in England, 1770–1800* in 1932; it brought into focus the huge mass of popular fiction, sensational gothic novels and sentimental romances, often by women, that had been largely ignored by critics in favour of the major male writings. Horner published *The English Women Novelists and their Connection with the Feminist Movement* (1688–1797) in 1930 setting the claims of the women she chose to treat, such as Mary Wollstonecraft, against the conventional expectations of the women for whom they wrote. Edith Birkhead brought out her influential essay 'Sentiment and Sensibility in the Eighteenth Century Novel' in 1925; it describes the growth of the cult of sensibility often overlooked by early twentieth century critics with their eyes firmly on Romanticism. To this group of historical critics can be added Joan Riviere whose 'Womanliness as Masquerade', first published in 1929 in the *International Journal of Psychoanalysis* (X), influenced the conception of woman as masquerade, a notion that would be turned into a strategy for destabilizing patriarchal history and literature by modern feminist literary critics. These and many other women, including the social historians Alice Clark, Ivy Pinchbeck and Dorothy George, wrote vigorously and informatively and all prepared the way for the explosion of study that occurred from the late 1960s onwards. MacCarthy's and Tompkins' work on literary figures would be continued, in very different mode, in the encyclopaedias of early women's writing in the 1970s, in the histories of female fiction which came out in the 1980s, to be in turn succeeded by the more detailed, intricate studies of particular themes and individual authors of the 1990s. MacCarthy's legacy is the growth of the subject itself.

MacCarthy, Tompkins and Horner were academic in their research but their tone was inviting and conversational. They were secure in their views and they did not need to mystify an audience into respect by jargon or unnecessary notions taken from contemporary psychoanalysis and philosophy. They conversed with their readers, rather than dominating them with gnomic utterances and opinions which they could not test. They wrote cheerfully and well and made the reader feel comfortable in their work. *The Female Pen* breathes of an earlier age before academic literary specialization. The first few pages alone refer to Homer, Milton, Fielding, Emily Brontë, Marie de France, and George Elliot. MacCarthy weaves her way through criticism, manuscripts, collections and novels, making what must have been great labour easy for her reader. But she expects that reader to have a mind well-stocked with the major literature of Europe.

To read MacCarthy is to become acquainted with her. She is there on every page of her book in opinion and in style, but she never succumbs to what she calls the 'dogmatism of the everlasting "I"'. Although close to Virginia Woolf as essay-writer, she lacks Woolf's occasionally overbearing quality. She takes the reader along with her, but then lets her read enough to judge. She surveys and generalizes and quotes from material in criticism and fiction that she has made her own. She does not, like so many of us now when academic criticism has been professionalized, give the impression of writing with a dictionary of quotations and a stack of new paperbacks on the latest theory. So she makes some mistakes in reference — as one would expect from someone conversing and eager to make her points.

MacCarthy has a definite sense of literature as an imaginative construction. She is a literary critic, not a modern cultural historian and she makes claims for her women in the context of her belief in values in art. She has no interest in the women writers who do not pretend to Literature, but who have come to prominence in recent years in accordance with new theories such as New Historicism or Cultural Materialism. So she ignores Ann Trapnel, Ann Collins and Anne Wentworth and the many other Quaker and Dissenting women of the seventeenth century, the aristocratic letter writers of the eighteenth century like Lady Mary Coke, and the cookery book and conduct book makers such as Hannah Wolley and Anna Laetitia Barbauld. This allows some judgements that we would now dispute: for example she can note that pre-Restoration women writers were mainly upper class because she overlooks those who were not and she asserts that women had no truck with the picaresque or rogue biography because she has little interest in the female rogues. Mary Carleton and Moll Cutpurse do not feature in her story. But her omissions are due to her view of art rather than to any moralistic scruples and she gives a spirited reading of Aphra Behn, 'the first and greatest of the literary swashbucklers'.

MacCarthy's thesis concerning women and the novel is a bold one. Virginia Woolf in *A Room of One's Own* had imagined a sister for Shakespeare, one just as gifted and profound as William. This woman, Woolf argued, would not have made it to London, where she would in any case have found the theatre a male-only affair both in acting and in writing, since she would have been raped and silenced long before she reached the city. To counter this thesis MacCarthy advances a far more positive and daring notion: that women are peculiarly associated with realism and verisimilitude.

In which case their long (relative) silence before the beginnings of the novel resulted not only from their imprisonment in ignorance but from their indifference to the dominant genres of men: the heroic epic, the saga or the pastoral. Shakespeare's sister failed to write not only because she was maltreated by men but also because she did not much care for her brother's sort of plays.

MacCarthy has none of the modern anxiety over identity and she gives no hint of the dispersed subject or of woman as a rhetorical position and strategy. The woman authors she treats were real and realized women who, like MacCarthy herself, were a little separate from sources of academic and literary power, but both she and they are empowered by the existence of that literary power. The women are often excused for their defects as artists by some personal detail: if the seventeenth-century biographies they wrote lacked irony, it was because of their grief. But the explained failure does not obliterate the notion of literary excellence itself which women are quite able to understand. In MacCarthy's pages we get to know the combative and litigious Anne Clifford, Duchess of Montgomery, of whom Donne wrote, 'She knew well how to discourse of all things, from predestination to slea-silk' and Margaret Cavendish, Duchess of Newcastle, whose mind was like a chaos of the firmament: 'comets, meteors, fireballs, planets, stars — a blazing world, an astounding coruscation of dazzling confusion', a woman who none the less was convinced of her 'infallibility as an author'. Because her writers are real people, MacCarthy can enter into their frustrations and hopes. Assuming some fixed female identity, she can make comparisons across the centuries, aligning Fanny Burney with Mary Davys, not worrying about inroads that culture makes in that identity.

As well as being recognizable human beings, MacCarthy's women are also writers. What they wrote was often 'art', defined as 'experience realized in a special way and expressed in a corresponding medium'. She has little time for that aesthetic transcendental claim with which men, especially in the nineteenth century, sought to evict women from the highest Literature. She keeps her amazement not for the alleged poor quality of women's writing through the ages, but for women's ability to write at all considering that they were so excluded from education and so crammed with prejudices about their feeble capacity. Because a few women writers can stand judgement in male terms, she is not content to bypass the others who, she insists, must be judged in relation to their opportunities as well as to literary standards.

Like Virginia Woolf, MacCarthy fixes her women with an image: 'the Duchess of Newcastle was a diamond of the first water . . . uncut save for a facet or two which sent out a fitful and ill-balanced brilliance'. She imagines them in a revealing moment in action, high spirited and witty, always with their feet on the ground and their eyes open to the details of life, the feel of cloth or the texture of a fruit's skin. She illuminates her subject with metaphor and simile: women writers are like a visiting team in a hostile country; innovative women resemble hockey players using crochet hooks; women writers'of the past are the common soldiers in a great campaign. Occasionally she overdoes it, mixing her metaphors with the ebullience of her full mind or making comparisons that overshadow her meaning. But, even then, she conveys excitement.

As with women, so with genres and movements of history. Fiction in the English Renaissance is a disowned foundling pining in the cellar. The Restoration is conveyed by the statement that 'the learned sock' was off and Shakespeare's granddaughter could come into her own with the 'comfortable buskin' of domestic intrigue. Historical changes are rendered through the psychology of individuals: the woman's entry into literature makes her solitary; she stops looking up to her man and so is condemned by him as loose or eccentric.

Although MacCarthy genuflects to Art and often takes major male writers as her model, such as Henry Fielding, she can be as astringent with canonized men as with little known women. Admitting that Lady Mary Wroth's *Urania* is dull and tedious except in the sub-plots, she asks daringly, 'Who will say that it is not wearying to plough through the *Arcadia* . . . ?', the influence of which is 'entirely to be deplored'. Even Samuel Richardson does not pass muster. Famed as he was for his 'marvellous insight into the female heart', he becomes in MacCarthy's pages an absurd fabler deluding men and women alike about the nature of women. In his heroines she sees an unpleasant self-consciousness which, despite being necessary for the epistolary method, is also distasteful.

She counters the absurdity displayed by men interpreting women by taking the male images and running with them towards the real women she knows. So she delightedly quotes

Addison's consumerist description of the lady living to be ornamented by furs and feathers, ores and silks. Then she allows the image to self-destruct in its confrontation with the gifted Brontës, for whom not even a moulting parrot would cast a feather, with poor ugly Harriet Martineau at whose feet no self-respecting lynx would cast his skin, and with George Eliot whom no furs, nor gems nor silks could adorn.

She also takes issue with silly male critics like Ernest Baker or T. Longueville to whose 'bad-tempered book' we 'need not refer . . . again'. As for Horace Walpole, his judgement is marred by his 'finicking celibacy' as he sits in his 'little pseudo-Gothic stronghold at Strawberry Hill'. The work of such a man becomes a 'miasma of malicious preciosity'.

Like Ian Watt, whose influence on the study of male fiction has been so influential, MacCarthy has a teleological sense of the novel. So it has its muling infancy and awkward adolescence as it moves towards the triumphant maturity of nineteenth-century realism. She shares with Bakhtin a preference for the people over their rulers, elevating folk tales, chap-books and popular fiction above the artificial and intricate literature of the upper orders. In one of her characteristically luxuriant metaphors, the latter becomes an unnatural fungus beside the fresh sunny fruit of the lower ranks who value character and story-telling, the essence of the novel.

Clearly MacCarthy enjoys exuberance. But she has a stern morality as well. Often she justifies her writers' naughty freedoms by the standards of their age, but her notion of virtue and vice prevents her celebrating this freedom. So the early eighteenth-century writers, Manley and Haywood, become inhabitants of a noxious swamp and debauchers of the novel. MacCarthy tries to explain her morality in artistic terms: the depiction of vice is monotonous. But, then, as she clearly reveals, so is the depiction of virtue — at least the depiction provided by the majority of eighteenth-century women writers. But although she does not generalize on virtue as she does to the detriment of vice, on the whole she cannot be accused of prejudice in favour of the virtuous writer and she has some tart remarks on Katherine Philips, the 'Matchless Orinda' whose morals were famous. For MacCarthy she is a 'fine example of what may be achieved when a facile talent is exploited by a pose so convincing that it is even self-hypnotic.' The pious Mrs Rowe is dismissed in an adjective: 'the excrutiating Mrs Rowe'.

Clearly, whatever her expressed opinion, MacCarthy's writing suggests a preference for the 'school of female desperadoes', which includes Aphra Behn and the *risqué* Delarivier Manley, to the 'legions of . . . expostulating, explaining, defending' ladies of the eighteenth century. She found in these latter a 'distasteful sex-consciouseness'. However she might condemn the wicked 'swash-buckling' women, like Milton she appears to have been on the side of energy, giving especial life to what she herself avowedly dis-approved. Indeed she is closest in her authorial self-image to the Restoration women writers whose intellectual vigour she mem-orably portrays: 'They could not shelter behind a coat of arms, or a sermonizing mediocrity, or a *precieux* classicism, nor lap them-selves about with the facile and soothing adulation of a select coterie'.

MacCarthy has none of the trepidation of modern female critics before the male noun and pronoun, no need for the tortuous plurals that her descendants have to employ to avoid mention of 'man' and 'his' world. She also lacks fear of the slippery words such as 'classicism', 'romanticism' and 'symbol' on which later critics have expended so much labour. She defined them in a straightforward and useful way, sufficient for her purpose. Her aristocrats are given their titles in contrast to the rather bizarre modern practice of denying such women as Margaret Cavendish, Duchess of Newcastle, her much-loved rank.

There is no denying that the first volume sparkles more than the second. The writers she treats in volume II are better known on the whole than those of volume I and her method of plot summary followed by speedy assessment can become tiresome when the works are familiar. This is especially so with the section on Jane Austen where summary is followed by rhapsody. But MacCarthy makes some useful points with these late writers none the less. She sees the literary ambition behind the eighteenth-century woman writer's necessary pretence of humility and she insists on the neglected female contribution to the epistolary form which Richardson is so often seen as inventing. And there are still the fresh judgements and asides: Mrs Haywood never learned 'the value of moderation'; Clara Reeve, writing a Gothic novel, calls up the picture of 'a maiden lady in elastic-sided boots, endeavouring to control a mustang' and 'Miss Knight (Ellis Cornelia Knight who continued *Rasselas*) evidently felt that two marriages would produce a greater amount of happiness than one, and gracefully ignored the question of ratio.'

Between the two volumes MacCarthy seems to have become more nationalistic — or perhaps the second volume allowed her more scope for expression. We are told whenever a writer has any possible link with Ireland: Fanny Burney's Irish ancestors on her father's side and Mary Wollstonecraft's Irish mother are both mentioned, although even her distant Irish heritage cannot save Fanny Burney from contempt and MacCarthy gleefully quotes her dreadful sentences. Maria Edgeworth is found unworthy of an Irish connection: although it seems for a paragraph or two that her Irishness might be approved, she is in the end taken to task for her Ascendancy social position which will not let her write what MacCarthy wishes to read. Her Irish stories therefore carry conviction only to those who do not 'fully know Ireland'.

Inevitably MacCarthy's book lacks the intricate theory that came to mark much criticism on women from the 1970s onwards, the sort that can only occur when many scholars work in the same area and inspire each other to greater discrimination and subtlety. Early women writers now inhabit an expanding universe and a growing body of scholars push deeply into the texts of the recently canonized writers and bring into prominence characters which MacCarthy would have judged irredeemably minor.

Inevitably, too, scholarship has marched on and left some of her assumptions, opinions, and facts behind. Take, for example, the case of Aphra Behn. MacCarthy accepts Montague Summers' belief that Behn was the Afara Amis born at Wye in 1640, unaware that the Burial Register indicated her death two days later. Behn's background is even now insecure, but it seems more likely that she was the Eaffrey Johnson born to a barber in Harbledown in Kent. When she interrupts her rapid production of plays in 1682, MacCarthy assumes this is because she was arrested for defaming the Duke of Monmouth. She was indeed taken to task for her epilogue to *Romulus* but the offence does not seem to have been regarded very seriously. The main reason for Behn's switch from play-writing to prose fiction and translation was the amalgamation of the two licenced London theatres and the decreased need for new plays that affected all the dramatists of the time; in the harsh years that followed, Behn was especially fortunate in having more of her plays revived than most playwrights. As to her works, the one most praised by MacCarthy is now generally thought not to be by her: *The Ten Pleasures of Marriage* which appears to be written by a man, to contain the kind of rollicking misogyny that Behn rarely reveals, and to depict a bourgeois life that she only touches on in her other works. Because MacCarthy has dismissed the extraordinary achievment of *Love-Letters between a Nobleman and His Sister* as 'libellous effusions' and indeed seems not to have read the original but rather a verse edition of Part I, not written by Behn, she needs to find something other than this extraordinary novel to occupy Behn's fertile pen during the time of its writing. The dates she gives for *The Unfortunate Bride: or, The Blind Lady a Beauty, The Dumb Virgin: or, the Force of Imagination, The Wandring Beauty* and *The Lucky Mistake* were based on Vita Sackville-West's errors; the first three were in fact posthumously published and the final one (in 1689) may well have been likewise.

These changes in opinion and developments in research do not invalidate MacCarthy's general treatment of writers such as Behn or her overall thesis. If one cannot take *The Female Pen* as her contemporaries could, as 'a standard work of reference for the period' (*The Standard*) it is still possible to echo the sentiment of the *The Irish Times*, that for the reader 'in search of something witty, interesting and astringent it is a real treasure-trove'.

B.G. MacCarthy had a long career. She was born in Cork in 1904, experienced the struggles for Irish independence, struggles which no doubt contributed to her fervent nationalism in later life. She took her BA at University College, Cork, in 1925 and an MA two years later, distinguishing herself in both degrees. She then took a Ph.D. in Cambridge, finishing in 1940, her thesis forming the basis of what became *The Female Pen*. As a teacher at the Craiglockhart RC Training College in Edinburgh, later as a lecturer in the Department of Education in Cork, and still later as a professor in the English department in Cork, her style of teaching appears to have been similar to that of her written works: her referees write much of her vigour and enterprise.

Nothing in her life, however, quite prepares one for the two volumes of *The Female Pen*, vol. I coming out from Cork University Press in September 1944 for 10s. 6d. and vol. II from Cork and Blackwells in Oxford just after the war in 1947. Having made this dazzling academic beginning in a subject quite alien to most of her colleagues, she seems to have preferred teaching to writing, subsequently authoring only a couple of plays, some essays on Irish male writers, one or two on Irish women, and one on the cinema, all published in *Studies: An Irish Quarterly Review* and *The Dublin Magazine*. Many of these breathe pride in her religion, her country, and in the city of Cork round which many of her articles revolve. Even the two that might seem to avoid this generalization — on Emily Brontë and Thackeray — concern the relationship of these to Ireland, and, in Thackeray's case, to Cork. To her successors it might seem disappointing that she did not follow her groundbreaking work with further studies of women writers, but one should remember the context in which she wrote. To her contemporaries she caused surprise that someone of her calibre should waste energy on women novelists at all.

The outer events of her personal history are quickly told. She married but lived with her husband only for a short time before she separated from him. In this situation she resembled many of the woman novelists she disapproved, such as Eliza Haywood and possibly Aphra Behn. After her years in Edinburgh she moved back into her childhood home with her mother. When her mother died, she lived with her aunt to whom she dedicated the second part of *The Female Pen* (the first being dedicated to her parents). She retired — very thoroughly — in 1966, giving away her extensive library to her friends and declaring she had 'had enough'. She left a memory of an abrasive temper and an exhilarating style.

Like so many women of her generation she disliked modern American-influenced feminism; she thought it 'silly' and was aghast that she and Virginia Woolf should ever be classed as 'feminists'. Again one should remember her context. It was in 1947 that Ferdinand Lundberg and Marynia Farnham published *Modern Woman: The Lost Sex* in which the eighteenth-century feminist Mary Wollstonecraft was displayed as a severe case of penis envy, the epitome of the modern degenerate woman who mistakenly thought to equal man despite her possession of distinct sexual organs — which, to clinch their case, Lundberg and Farnham list in detail. It is also salutary to note that the *Times Literary Supplement* in 1945 felt the need to defend MacCarthy from 'aggressive feminism' because of her subject;

happily the reviewer could assure her potential readers that there was 'no ground for that suspicion — no trace of "sex-antagonism" or other such nonsense'. The review in *Studies* again suggests her uneasy context when it takes her to task for some of her claims for women, though it does agree that she has discovered 'amid much rubbish in these forgotten books, gleams of true feminine observation of life . . . '.

I never met Professor MacCarthy. I was planning to visit her in Cork in the summer of 1993 but, sadly, she died in April. Probably it was as well that the meeting did not take place. Like so many high-achieving women who came to maturity between the wars, who faced the dilemmas of marriage and career and the often conflicting demands of family and of the self, she was stridently anti-feminist. If she did not take kindly to modern feminists, I in turn am not attracted to nationalism; so a real-life conversation might have been tense. This way I know her entirely through her book and can renew my acquaintance at any time. Thus I can enjoy her wit without needing to combat the astringency and the security of opinion. I hope new readers will treasure the acquaintance as much as I do.

Janet Todd
Norwich, 1993

VOLUME ONE

Women Writers:
Their Contribution to the English Novel
1621–1744

Foreword

If Shakespeare had had a sister endowed with literary powers, could she have won to success in that early period? What factors would have impeded her development as a writer? These questions, raised by Virginia Woolf in her penetrating essay, *A Room of One's Own*, seemed to me well worth answering. They were the starting point of a long journey backwards through the years — a journey which had for its object a consideration of those forces which affected women writers during the sixteenth, seventeenth and eighteenth centuries; and an evaluation of these women's contributions to the development of the novel. Their contribution and the influences which conditioned it have been traced from 1621 until 1817. The present volume represents the first half of the work. It is hoped to publish the second volume in the near future.

It might perhaps have been possible to condense these researches into a single volume, but only by omitting or shortening most of the passages quoted from the writings of these women-novelists. It seemed essential to retain the copious quotations, since they have been taken from books so rare as to be difficult of access to the interested student.

B.G. MacCarthy

Chapter I

Cogent Influences

Women's contribution to literature is no arbitrary or artificial distinction. However much the reformer may welcome, or the conservative lament, the growth of a harmonious sharing of ideals between men and women, that growth has been a hard-fought struggle. It has been an escape from a prison, which, when it did not entirely shut out the greater world, at least enclosed a little world of education meant for women, a literature adapted to the supposed limitations of their intellect, and a course of action prescribed by the other sex. To show how the literary efforts of women developed and justified their claims to free activity is the purpose of this book.

When women at last began to seek after literary expression, it was inevitable that they should attempt to tell a story. There has always been, and there always will remain, deep-rooted in the human heart a desire to hear something told of the world without us and within. From these roots in varying forms and often strangely transmuted grew all education and the arts. For men it was a transition from telling to writing, and for women the transition was no less long, and like their opportunities for literacy, took place far later. Women as listeners influenced the art of storytelling long before they actually shared in it, and naturally the growth of the novel gained in variety and verisimilitude when women were given a place in the subject-matter. The novel is a very improbable development of the *Odyssey*, but it is an inevitable development of *Daphnis and Chloe*. Beowulf and his firedrake are almost as far from the art of fiction as they are from probability, and such sagas could be of no interest to women. It is not the titanic figure, with his death-dealing sword, invincible in his destiny, that a woman loves, in fact or in fiction — or at any rate, not until he has

1

shown himself vulnerable to human emotions. Victorious Perseus, flying through the clouds, does not win a woman's interest until he sees Andromeda and comes down to earth. This descent from free fancy to actuality is, in a word, the evolution of the novel.

Women make their entrance into fiction with the development of the short tale such as the *novella*, which had love-interest as its pivotal point. Marie de France, writing in England in the twelfth century, found in her episodic lays exactly the mould which suited her, and she used it with such ease that she had scope to develop her technique and to create from the oft-told tales of the minstrels works of art which not only endured, but served as an inspiration to later writers. Margaret of Navarre, writing in prose, found the short tale equally suited to her powers; and in her case also, ease in technique allowed her genius to express itself with a power perhaps not surpassed by Bandello or Boccaccio. These women excelled because they were, for the most part, retelling stories they had heard, but most of all because they had for subject-matter themes and events most familiar, if not in their own lives, then certainly in the lives of those about them.

But alas for the women writers! Daphnis and Chloe, neglected on their pastoral slope, were growing up and developing a stultifying artificiality. Their simple idyll was now to be complicated by rival lovers, perfidy, royalty incognito, shipwreck, and chivalrous emprises, into a superfluity of characters endlessly involved in a maze of tedious events. And where Sir Philip Sydney led, what could an ambitious niece do but follow? It could not be expected that Lady Mary Wroath would escape the quagmire of the Pastoral Romance, and in fact, she overpassed its pitfalls with far more success than might have been expected. If women were daring even in attempting to write, it is not to be expected, at that stage, that they would have the extreme audacity to become innovators as well. If only, instead of being satisfied with diligently copying the headline set by men, they could have bridged the great gap between romantic and domestic fiction, then not only would the development of the novel have been hastened by hundreds of years, but women would have been able to exert their talents on exactly the subject-matter which they knew best, and consequently there would have been far more women writers. It is obvious that creative imagination, no matter how individual and how varied its power of synthesis, must have material to synthesize, and this material may be real life, or some artistic reproduction of life, or, as is most usual, both. This does not mean that because women's actual experience of life was limited to only one aspect, therefore they could not exercise creative imagination. Certainly they could have done so, as did, for example, the two gifted women already mentioned, and if we wish to understand why women were not at that time actively creative, we must consider the education at their disposal, and we must remember that an ability to read and write is not education, though it may be a means thereto. Such education as women received was nominal, and creative imagination without education is not productive. One must either admit this fact, or else assert that women in bygone ages lacked the kind of imaginative power which later women most obviously possessed. Any view which claims variation in the mental capacity of women at various epochs is quite untenable. On the other hand, any view which explains the dearth of early women-writers by reference to their limited experience, does not need to be disproved. It simply collapses of itself, because it is illogical in theory, and its invalidity is proved by the evidence of the great women-writers who, despite a human sphere as circumscribed as that of their ancestresses, later achieved fame. We know that the material on which creative imagination may work can be found in daily life no matter how limited in extent. Experience need not be wide for human or literary fulfilment, but it must be deep, and, for literary purposes, it must be artistically realized, and it must be expressed. Depth of experience implies depth of character, but does not connote the power of artistic realization or artistic expression, and it is precisely in this relation that the question of education arises. Creative imagination transforms experience into a work of art, but it can only give artistic form when it is familiar with such forms, and can manipulate the chosen form with ease. It requires training and familiarity with many aspects of one's art before one masters technique, or develops individuality in technique. Nor can one even say that we achieve a work of art merely by giving artistic form to experience, for the truth is that the artist apprehends experience in a fashion which is partly the result of his mental characteristics, but also the result of his artistic training. Perhaps we may say that art is experience realized in a special way and expressed in a corresponding medium. Emily Brontë's experience of actual human life was unusually limited, and yet she produced not only a work of art, but one of unusual power.

If it were possible to analyze her genius, one might suggest that it consisted in intensity of experience, in her case mainly imaginative experience, which she realized in literary terms, and embodied in the artistic form she knew best — the art of fiction. But it is worth noting that not only was Emily Brontë endowed with natural genius, but was, for that period, very well educated and very widely read. Yet despite these advantages, which enabled her to use language in a plastic, even in an intuitive way, *Wuthering Heights* is structurally clumsy, because, of course, a literary education is merely a way by which we recognize and evaluate literary technique, but only by literary experiment can we develop such technique in ourselves. *Wuthering Heights* also shows that imaginative experience is not in itself a sufficing material for realistic fiction, for it is clear that, though Emily Brontë knew hell and heaven, she did not know how farm-hands talk.

In judging the average woman's chance of success in the writing of fiction, it seems, perhaps, a digression to speak of Emily Brontë, whose genius must always entitle her to be judged apart, but we deliberately choose her, because we wish to show that even such genius cannot arrive at technique without an apprenticeship, and that even such genius cannot safely depend on imaginative intuition, cannot dispense with the necessity for everyday experience. Writing of the essential characteristics of a great novelist, Fielding states the necessity for *Genius, Learning, Conversation,* and *'a good heart.'* By *Genius* he means 'that power or rather those powers of mind, which are capable of penetrating into all things within our reach and knowledge, and of distinguishing their essential differences.' These powers he distinguishes as *Invention* and *Judgment* under the collective name of *Genius*. By *Invention* Fielding means, not the creative faculty, but quite literally the power of discovery — 'a quick and sagacious penetration into the true essence of all the objects of our contemplation. This, I think, can rarely exist without the concomitancy of judgment; for how we can be said to have discovered the true essence of two things, without discerning their difference, seems to me hard to conceive. Now this last is the undisputed province of Judgment.'[1]

Of the necessity for learning, Fielding finely says: 'Nature can only furnish us with capacity . . . or the tools of our profession; learning must fit them for use, must direct them in it, and lastly must contribute part at least of the materials. A competent

4

knowledge of history and of the *belles-lettres* is here absolutely necessary; and without this share of knowledge at least, to affect the character of an historian (i.e., a novelist) is as vain as to endeavour at building a house without timber or mortar, or brick or stone. Homer and Milton, who though they added ornament of numbers to their works, were both historians of our order, were masters of all the learning of their times.'

Conversation, by which Fielding meant experience of life, he held to be absolutely indispensable to a novelist: 'However exquisitely human nature may have been described by writers, the true practical system can be learnt only in the world.' People who write without experience of life are only making a 'faint copy of a copy . . . which can have neither the justness nor spirit of an original. Now this conversation in our historian must be universal, that is with all the ranks and degrees of men, for the knowledge of what is called high life will not instruct him in low, nor, *è converso* . . . and though it may be thought that the knowledge of either may sufficiently enable him to describe at least that in which he hath been conversant, yet he will even here fall greatly short of perfection: for the follies of either rank do, in reality, illustrate each other.'

But *Genius, Learning,* and *Conversation* do not dispense a great novelist from the necessity of having a *Good Heart*, by which Fielding means humanity.

Applying Fielding's words to women-novelists, their handicaps at once become only too apparent. Genius and a good heart they might have as natural endowment, but learning and 'conversation' were beyond their reach long before and long after Fielding's time. These facts prepare us for the low standard very often observable in the novels written by women, but they do not prepare us for the inexplicable way in which women persisted in proving that they could rise above their limitations. It is not feminism, but the merest common-sense to insist that women's contribution to fiction can only be judged in relation to their opportunities. That this standard of judgment is not sufficiently remembered is, perhaps, because so much that women contributed, by its own merit claims equality with the best attainments of men-novelists, and appears to dispense with the special consideration which is actually its due.

That the writing of fiction becomes clumsy hackwork in the hands of the uneducated is proved in the works of large numbers of the women whom we shall discuss, but we must remember that the art of fiction evolved so slowly and with so many digressions of form and content that there was not, for a long time, any clearly defined standard of what fiction ought to be. This was one reason why women were brave enough to attempt such writing. Women enjoyed stories (particularly love-stories which confirmed their personal view of the focal point of life) and, unlike poetry, unlike essays which called for a cultural mould and commerce in abstractions, a story could be told by anybody who had sufficient gumption to sandwich a middle between a beginning and an end. 'To the composition of novels and romances,' says Fielding, bitterly, 'nothing is necessary but paper, pens, and ink, with the manual capacity of using them.'[2] George Eliot, passing judgment, after several centuries, on the large brood of incapable women-novelists of her day, gives the reason thus: 'No educational restrictions can shut women out from the materials of fiction and there is no species of art which is so free from rigid requirements. Like crystalline masses, it may take any form and yet be beautiful, we have only to pour in the right elements — genuine observation, humour, and passion.' But pour them into what? George Eliot does not discriminate between the lack of a cultural mould and the lack of the novelist's technique. However, she expresses very well the danger which lay for women in the very looseness of the fictional medium:

> It is precisely this absence of rigid requirements which constitutes the fatal seduction of novel-writing to incompetent women. Ladies who are not wont to be very grossly deceived as to their power of playing on the piano; here certain positive difficulties of execution have to be conquered, and incompetence inevitably breaks down. Every art which has its absolute technique is, to a certain extent, guarded against the intrusions of mere left-handed imbecility. But in novel-writing there are no barriers for incapacity to stumble against, no external criteria to prevent a writer from mistaking foolish facility for mastery.[3]

If this could be said in the middle of the nineteenth century, how much less formulated was the form of the novel, three centuries earlier! And yet one cannot fail to observe that, according as the art of fiction became (as it did) more exigent with advancing years, women continued not only to maintain the required standard, but often to surpass it, and even to contribute to the development of new genres.

It might have been imagined when Elizabethan fiction developed along the lines of the Pastoral Romance, the picaresque novels, and the guild-tales, that women writers would have retired from the lists, despairing of ever achieving the pseudo-Greek note, the pot-house experience, or the tradesman's touch so necessary respectively to these three types of fiction. Of the three, the Pastoral Romance was the easiest, because though one might not progress with classic grace, one could, at any rate, undulate pleasantly through mazes sufficiently intricate to defy detection. Since pre-Restoration women writers were of the upper-classes, it was not likely that they would choose such plebeian realism as the guild-tales for their literary medium, even if they felt competent to portray that aspect of life, and it was not to be imagined that any female pen would then dare to follow, or could successfully follow a rogue, whether Spanish or English, into the unimagined dens of his villainy. The picaro's swashbuckling attitude to women could not be changed unless by reforming the picaro, and a reformed picaro is a contradiction in terms; therefore, with a delicate flutter, the female pens took refuge in gentle valleys, beside murmuring brooks, where shepherd and shepherdess anticipated the poses of Dresden. Thus Lady Mary Wroath and still later Anne Weamys, both with more success than might be expected in so artificial a type of fiction, and, in the case of the *Urania*, with realism staring out from the courtly inanities like a pair of honest eyes from a mask.

But although the Pastoral novel was moribund with the passing of the Elizabethan age, its mummified form obtruded itself for long upon the attention of the reading public, and its ghostly accents continued to echo in the style of subsequent prose fiction for a century and a half. The persistence of the Pastoral tradition and the delay in the development of realistic fiction is more easily understandable when we recall that people of the sixteenth and seventeenth centuries preferred to find life represented before the footlights than in the pages of a book. Women in Shakespeare's time did not write plays, because the blank-verse form called for a technique in language which they did not possess,[4] but with the Restoration period came a spate of women-dramatists, most notably Aphra Behn, Mrs Centlivre, Mrs Manley, Mrs Pix and Mrs Trotter. These were highly successful in this new medium for story-telling, mainly because drama had taken a different turn, and instead of tragedies in conception too lofty and in form too difficult for women who lacked learning, now the learned sock was off, and the comfortable buskin which had only to find its way through domestic intrigue, fitted the women beyond any possibility of limping. Not only was the subject-matter more congenial, but the prose dialogue most generally used required only the power of brilliant verbal fencing which would be instinctive in a witty woman. Background and dialogue were rudimentary as yet in the novel, and characterization was so rare as to be almost non-existent. Still, in a prose story it was necessary to sketch some sort of background, to describe the passage of events and to interpolate conversations, or at least to report them. It was necessary to indicate the passage of time, and in all this there was no very clear precedent for one's procedure. Such freedom was an advantage to the original, but the tendency of the more average person would naturally be to imitate a form which had clear rules for guidance. In drama women found such a form, because, though one could transcend certain of the unities, yet they always remained as a reliable framework of construction. These points, no doubt, served to encourage women, and partly account for the increase in women-writers at this period.

But there was another consideration which, from the beginning of women's literary adventuring had loomed large, and greatly affected their work and their status. This was the condemnatory attitude of the reading public towards women-writers. Masculine condemnation of women's quill-driving was 'compounded of many simples' but chiefly of a double fear: fear that women's new occupation might change their attitude towards domestic and social duties, and fear that women's achievements might eclipse those of men. For countless ages women had been given the sort of education which fitted them to become wives and mothers in this world, and saints either here or hereafter. These activities were conducive towards man's happiness, and were no encroachment on the territory he was accustomed to consider as peculiarly his own. But if women were to realize themselves in some separate way if they, like men, should have an intellectual life, which, of necessity, must be led alone and which, as man knew, was richly self-rewarding, might not women become intolerable from the man's point of view? That is to say, not merely preoccupied with other than domestic details, but no longer looking up to man as the arbiter of her fate.

'While thou keepest always looking up at me, and I down at thee, what horrid obliquities of vision may we not contract?'[5] — obliquities not to be quickly cured, capable of distorting all one's impressions, and very painful if readjusted too suddenly. 'I imagine,' says the Duchess of Newcastle, 'that I shall be censured by my own Sex; and Men will cast a smile of Scorne upon my Book, because they think thereby, Women incroach too much upon their Prerogatives; for they hold Books as their Crowne, and the Sword as their Scepter, by which they rule and governe. And very like they will say to me, as to the Lady that wrote the Romancy,

> Work, Lady, Work, let writing books alone
> For surely wiser women nere wrote one.'[6]

And she continues:

> Spinning with the Fingers is more proper to our Sexe, than studying or writing Poetry, which is spinning with the Braine, but I, having no skill in the art of the first (and if I had, I had no hopes of gaining so much as to make me a garment to keep me from the cold) make me delight in the latter . . . which made me endeavour to Spin a Garment of Memory, to lapp up my Name, that it might grow to after Ages. I cannot say the web is strong, fine, or evenly spun, for it is a course piece; yet I had rather my Name should go meanly clad, than dye with cold.[7]

Mean indeed was the reputation of women-writers, when they were so fortunate as to have any reputation at all. The reading public and the general public (those widening circles in the pool of opinion, obedient to the stones cast by the critics) divided women writers into three chief classes, each of which received a different judgment. First, there were the women-writers, who not only escaped condemnation, but were never even put on trial. These were the dilettante ladies, the literary dabblers, who wrote polite verse, translated plays and pious treatises, and kept their eyes well averted from the roaring pageant of life. Always they were of the privileged classes. Often they were the relatives of literary men, and won an amused tolerance or a degree of kindly commendation for their precocity. In the case of Sir Philip Sydney's sister and niece, they might have written the *Heptameron*, and not the slightest murmur of disapproval would have disturbed the paeans of loving praise

which enveloped that illustrious family. Amongst its many virtues was a profound generosity in literary patronage, and so it
was that the Countess of Pembroke was accounted a notable
success in literature. Yet her works, so lavishly eulogized, consist
of a play translated from the French,[8] (never acted, and never
even read by the critics who extolled it); a poem whose sole claim
to recognition was that Spenser published it with his *Astrophel;*
and a metrical version of the Psalms, in which she was helped by
her brother and her chaplain. Nash, Spenser, Nicholas Breton,
Whincop, Osborn, Langbaine and many others were loud in her
praise, and her epitaph was written probably by Ben Jonson.

   Let us compare the case of Marie de France, who made so
notable a contribution to French literature:

> Tous, à l'exception de Denys Pyramus, qui en a dit peu de
> chose, ont gardé un profound silence sur cette femme fort
> supérieure à son siècle par ses lumières, par ses sentiments,
> et par le courage qu'elle eut de dire la vérité a des oreilles
> mal disposées ou peu accoutumées a l'entendre.[9]

What is the explanation of this silence? It is, apparently, that Marie
belonged to the great company of women-writers who were condemned by their own generation. They were condemned because
they were suspected either of looseness or eccentricity. If they were
suspect on moral grounds, absence of evidence did not acquit them
and the best they could hope for was the grudging Scottish judgment of 'Not Proven.' The third class, those who were obviously
above moral reproach but were still suspect of some abnormality,
was labelled 'Queer.' For whatever cause, it is clear that Marie was
attacked, for she says:

> Indeed, wherever there is a man or a woman of great fame,
> those who are envious of her good work often slander her,
> and with the intent to lessen her fame, play the part of a
> wretched cowardly dog, a cur that bites folk stealthily. But I
> will not leave off for this, even though backbiters and false
> flatterers work mischief against me — for to speak ill is their
> nature.[10]

   That the Duchess of Newcastle was considered queer is confirmed by all the criticisms of her own time. Queer she undoubtedly
was, but she had sufficient genius to justify her eccentricity, a fact

recognized by Disraeli. And though she showed a fine disregard for her critics, male and female, yet she was very conscious that current opinion was opposed to literary pursuits for a woman. She appeals endlessly for her right to be an author. Is it not better for her to occupy her time in writing than to behave loosely as so many Court ladies do? Is her occupation really less useful than painting and embroidery, or 'the making of Flowers, Boxes, Baskets with Beads, Shells, Silke and Strawe?'

> I hope you will spare me [she says to her readers] for the Harthe is swept cleane, and a Bason of Water with a cleane Towell set by, and the Ashes rak'd up; wherefore let my book sleep quietly, and the Watch-light burning clearly . . . and let it be still from your noise, that the feminine Cat may not Mew, nor the masculine Curs bark nor howle out railings to disturb my harmless Booke's rest.

The feminine Cats, however, continued to mew, as they had done from the beginning of women's literary efforts. Again and again the women-writers comment on this feminine attack upon them. 'Nay, even my own sex, which should assert our prerogative against such detractors, are often backward to encourage the female pen.'[11] And writing long afterwards (1791) another woman says: 'You know how female writers are looked down upon. The women fear and hate, the men ridicule and dislike them.'[12]

Still, it must be allowed that, apart from the prejudice and even the possible envy with which the non-literary woman regarded her more gifted sisters, there was very often a legitimate reason for objecting on moral grounds to the women who wrote fiction, and to the kind of fiction which they wrote. Men had created the standard of literary taste, and if women were to write at all they had to compete with men on their own ground. It was not considered improper that men should write loosely for a reading public (or for an audience) composed of women as well as men, nor even that they should write lewdly for women's particular instruction, as for example, did Jacques d'Amiens, whose *L'Art d'Amors* was merely one of many such works during the Middle Ages:

> Chez Jacques d'Amiens les femmes ne sont pas considerées que comme des joujoux qui sont là uniquement pour le plaisir des hommes: il ne considère jamais le côté moral des choses; il n'a pas de sens moral.[13]

It seems surprising that women might consume such literary repasts in the privacy of their bowers, but emphatically might not cater for such tastes in others. There is indeed a moral distinction in culpability, but it was not this consideration which inspired the general condemnation of women-writers. It is not for us to determine whether women-writers should have wished or attempted to evangelize the reading public. In any case, they could not possibly have done so. The fact that they entered into literary competition meant that they accepted the code established by the majority of writers in accordance with popular demand. Literary fame and, later, financial success depended on playing the game at least as well as their masculine adversaries, and playing a game involves the acceptance of definite rules and the developing of a particular technique. Women who wrote according to a standard of their own would have had as much hope of success as if they decided to play hockey with a crochet-hook. Playing even in the accepted way, they had to take it for granted that the umpire-critics would always be prejudiced, and that the public would howl them down at every opportunity. They were like a visiting team in hostile country where their every effort would be adjudged offside. If they were ever to win approval, they needed to be not merely as good as, but better than their opponents, and the difficulty of this was evident, when one reflects that they were heavily handicapped from the beginning. That they did adapt themselves to the rigours of the contest, that they did score so early in the game was a triumph — unpopular, and not without its price. Wounded reputation was to be expected, and at one period was really deserved, although even then the public put the cart before the horse. The literary women of the Restoration were not loose because they were writers. They were writers because they were loose. They were adventuresses before they adventured into literature. In a word, they were driven by circumstances to drive a quill, and they had the only equipment by which a woman of that time could succeed in letters — a great intellectual vigour and an absence of scruples. It was nothing much to them that, as women-writers, they lost caste. They had lost caste already. Mrs Behn, Mrs Centlivre, Mrs Manley, Mrs Pix, Mrs Haywood and the rest of the battered crew, came to the profession of writing with no illusions, almost no education, a wide though ill-balanced experience of life, and an immense vigour of mind and body. They asked, and they got, no quarter, and they stamped their names defiantly into the minds of their contemporaries and into literary history. It is no mean feat at any time to make a living by free-lance writing. In the sixteenth, seventeenth and eighteenth centuries it was incredibly difficult. It was easier to starve than to eat by the sweat of one's brow, as even men-writers, from the days of Nash, Dekker, Fox and Drayton knew to their cost. To be a genius was no guarantee against the gutter or imprisonment for debt. It was necessary to find patrons and to keep them from tiring; to cultivate anyone who might have influence; to ingratiate oneself with editors and booksellers; to flatter the critics; to be hail-fellow-well-met with all sorts of people, in all sorts of places; to be ready to turn one's hand to anything — play-patching, 'ghosting,' political propaganda, rudimentary newspaper work; to haunt the greenrooms, and 'keep in with' the players; to write plays for a small circle of loose-livers at a time when no decent woman would go to a theatre, and even the courtesans went masked. It will be admitted that no conventional woman could do all this, and if a group of unconventional women did it, then we must evaluate the gain entirely from the literary point of view. Nobody can contest the literary contributions of Mrs Behn, Mrs Centlivre, Mrs Haywood, and even of Mrs Manley. With the exception of Mrs Centlivre (who excelled exclusively as a dramatist), these women wrote not only plays (which had an indirect but definite influence on the growth of fiction) but notably aided the development of the novel, both by using accepted forms, and by helping to initiate other forms. In their own time (and even now) women-writers of that particular period were strongly censured for their loose writing. One might as well blame an Arctic fox for changing his colour in the winter. He lives by adaptation, and so did they. From amongst the innumerable evidences that a double standard of criticism was exercised on a single standard of writing, we may perhaps mention one example. Aphra Behn, as brilliant as any writer of her generation, was loaded with obloquy for plays which, compared to those of Dryden and Congreve, might almost be considered pure. Dryden, writing to Mrs Elizabeth Thomas in 1699, expressed his certainty that she would avoid the license which Mrs Behn allowed herself 'of writing loosely, and giving, if I may have leave to say so, scandall to the modesty of her sex. I confess I am the last man who ought in justice to arraign her, who have been too much a libertine in most of my poems; which I should be well contented I had time either to purge, or to see fairly burn'd.'[14]

13

He was, indeed, the last man who should have attacked licentiousness in any writer, and he should have abstained from casting a stone at one of his few direct imitators. 'I should be inclined,' says Nicol, 'to think that it is almost entirely the influence of Dryden which has led this authoress away from the comparatively pure plots to this of most immodest intrigue. "Mr. Limberham" could contaminate a whole shoal of writers; and Dryden with his immodesty was showing to the playwrights of his time exactly what the audiences of the time desired.'[15] An interesting sidelight on the single standard of popular taste is given by Sir Walter Scott. He says that an aged lady, a relation of his, 'assured him that in the polite society of her youth, in which she held a distinguished place, the plays and novels of Mrs Aphra Behn were accounted proper reading'; and, 'she added, with some humour, it was not until a long interval, when she looked into it at the age of seventy that she was shocked with their indecorum'[16] — shocked, that is, only in retrospect and when influenced by the more correct moral standards of a later age.

This anecdote to the contrary, there is no room for doubt that even in a grosser period the type of women-writers to which we have referred could not avoid ostracism. It is worth considering whether their equivocal position had any effect on their writing, apart from what we have already discussed. There is little question that it had, and there are gains and losses to be computed. It was a gain that declassed and plebeian as they were, they could not shelter behind a coat of arms, or a sermonizing mediocrity, or a *précieux* classicism, nor lap themselves about with the facile and soothing adulation of a select coterie. They were in no danger of being praised for powers they did not possess. On the contrary, they had to fight for recognition, and the only compliment they received was that of being treated as responsible writers, able to take and to give blows, and with no privileges at all. The struggle to find and to retain a place for themselves, led them to realize and, so far as they could, to remedy their deficiencies. Sometimes, as in the case of Mrs Manley, they made the mistake of endeavouring to achieve by slanderous salacity what they could not achieve by literary ability, but this recourse to mere licentiousness for a *tour de force* is rare. The chief women-writers of that period had enough real literary power to have succeeded in a happier age. That they had a wide though unfortunate experience of life meant something on the credit and on the debit side. In losing an idealized view of existence, they found a measure of reality, and they encountered a multiplicity of human types, reacting characteristically to a variety of circumstances — sufficient in number and diversity to enable them to see a pattern in the confusion and a unity in complexity. They could see that heroes and villains had much in common, and that characterization deals with material far less easily recognizable than virtues and vices. It is better to see a courtesan as she really is, than to imagine a shepherdess as she never really was. One cannot doubt that for realism in literature it is better to write with one eye on the object, but an idealized representation of life is not more unreal than life depicted as entirely without ideals. Realism must take into account that ideals are actual forces intermingling with the stuff of events, sometimes shaping and sometimes merely interpreting them, but in either case by no means to be discounted. And this is exactly where the Restoration women writers, following the rules laid down by their stronger brethren of the pen, lost the authentic touch in interpreting and expressing human life. But their own experiences made it all the easier for them to concur in a view of life which mocked at ethical conventions, and it was natural that they should carry off their ostracism by laughing loudly at the unco guid, whose prudery caused them to miss all the fun. It was easier to go a step further, and to believe self-justifyingly that all of life was as they knew it, and that virtue at best was merely a seductive perfume, an alluring patina; at worst a hypocritical veil for the subtle. In the writings of these women this added impetus of experience is often detectable:

> Mrs Behn, perhaps, as much as any one, condemned loose scenes and too warm descriptions; but something must be allowed to human frailty. She herself was of an amorous complexion; she felt the passions intimately which she describes, and this circumstance added to Necessity, might be the occasion of her plays being of that cast.[17]

Sometimes added to the impetus of personal experience is the impetus of personal spite, a desire for vengeance on that society, which drew its skirts aside. This is one reason why Mrs Manley and Mrs Haywood took to the *histoire scandaleuse* like a duck to water. In Mrs Haywood's case, it was not lack of ability to do good work in a superior genre of fiction, as is proved in her authorship of *Miss Betsy Thoughtless* and *The History of Jemmy and Jenny Jessamy*. When Defoe[18] and Mrs Haywood[19] both used the life of the deaf and dumb fortune-teller, Duncan Campbell, as material for fiction, their respective points of view are very evident. Defoe was interested in recounting the wonders of Campbell's powers, and specifically mentions that he omits tales of Mr Campbell's women consultants, because they were so numerous that, if included, the work would be endless. Mrs Haywood, however, 'was evidently more interested in the phenomena of passion than in the theory of divination,'[20] and she also utilizes the opportunity of revealing scandalous secrets, and opening old wounds. In fact, she makes her material serve the purpose of the *histoire scandaleuse* — an erotic arrow dipped in poison.

The point to be observed is that in the already ill-balanced literature of that period, any added impetus which further disturbed the balance, was artistically inadmissible. Measure, balance, symmetry — these are in life, and no matter how brilliant, vivid and witty the literature of a period may be, a fault in emphasis is a fault in art, and must lead to the decay of that genre. In this case, the emphasis was on an aspect of life which allowed, after all, very little variety. Few things are less capable of variation, and therefore few things are more monotonous than the representation of vice. The conventions of immorality in drama and fiction are really more stultifying than the conventions of virtue.

But even at worst, such drama and such fiction were alive, and it was easy to see how they might develop when they had outgrown the excesses of youth. In its immature state, however, because it was, perhaps, of more mixed ancestry than the accepted forms of writing, and because it was, at that stage of its evolution, very lacking in art, fiction was regarded as a raggle-taggle sort of composition. Sir Philip Sydney claimed that the *Arcadia* was poetry, and later Fielding speaks of *Tom Jones* as 'this heroic, historical, prosaic poem.' Poetry had a high and ancient tradition, and its female devotees, thus chaperoned by the muses, were regarded with much indulgence.[21] Such a one was Catherine Philips, and though she did not write fiction and therefore does not enter our field of consideration, she serves to show that, by adherence to a classical genre, a mediocre woman could win a literary reputation without sacrificing either her good name or her reputation for good sense. Nothing could be more fantastic than the legend of the Matchless, the Incomparable Orinda. Speaking of the 'celebrated scribbling women' of the seventeenth century, Sir Edmund Gosse says:

> Among all these the Matchless Orinda takes the foremost place — not exactly by merit, for Aphra Behn surpassed her in genius, Margaret, Duchess of Newcastle, in versatility, and Catherine Trotter in professional zeal; but by the moral eminence she attained through her elevated public career and which she sealed by her tragical death. When the seventeenth century thought of a poetess, it naturally thought of Orinda; her figure overtopped those of her literary sisters; she was more dignified, more regal, in her attitude to the public than they were, and in fine she presents us with the best type we possess of the woman of letters in the seventeenth century.[22]

Even if 'the best' meant simply the most moral, she could claim no pre-eminence over Lucy Hutchinson or the Duchess of Newcastle. It is clear that 'the best' does not mean the most gifted, versatile or zealous. 'The best type' cannot mean the most typical of seventeenth century England, because Orinda is really not even representative, and would have claimed France as her spiritual country.

This incredible *précieuse*, born of honest, middle-class Cockney parents, is a fine example of what may be achieved when a facile talent is exploited by a pose so convincing that it is even self-hypnotic. Catherine Philips, neé Fowler, used her pen as a vaulting-pole into society, and was never so happy as when, by her imagined poetical genius, she edged her way into a higher social stratum. She wrote a considerable quantity of artificial poetry, translated two of Corneille's plays *(Pompée* and *Horace)* into wooden verse, and carried on an epistolary correspondence with Sir Charles Cotterel (Poliarchus). These works are the apparent basis of her literary reputation, and her passport to the friendship of such men as Cowley and Jeremy Taylor. Her patrons and associates were such people as the Earls of Orrery and Roscommon, the Countess of Cork, and the Viscountess of Dungannon. When the Countess of Cork caused *Pompey* to be acted, the Earl of Roscommon spoke the prologue. Orinda was lauded to the skies, and critics like the sycophantic Langbaine said that she far surpassed Corneille.[23] Her death left *Horace* unfinished and it was completed by Sir John Denham and acted at Court by 'Persons of Quality' fourteen years later, the Duke of Monmouth speaking the prologue. What was the secret of that extraordinary furore which has not withstood the impartial judgment of posterity? It is, simply, that Catherine Philips's greatest creation was Orinda and she, alas! was subject to mortality. She was the first sentimental writer in the English language.[24] She created a cult of sentiment and classicism, and loved to imagine that she was the leader of a salon which she called the Society of Friendship. Her house in Wales was a kind of Hotel de Rambouillet, or rather hers was a peripatetic salon, following her peregrinations among the houses of her patrons. Honest English names offended her sensibilities, and her friends were obliged to masquerade under such titles as Poliarchus, Palaemon, Lucasia, Valeria. She averred that she read English books with patience, but French ones with pleasure. She indulged in an endless series of sentimental friendships with young women, and was always mortally offended when they abandoned classicism for marriage. The patient and unassuming Mr Philips (alias Antenor) quietly continued to eat roast beef and Yorkshire pudding, and to live his own life outside the Society of Friendship. One imagines him smiling in humorous resignation on reading his wife's poems, and discovering that she is 'dying for a little love.'

Writing eight years after Langbaine, Charles Gildon scornfully contradicts his statement that Orinda is a better writer than Aphra Behn, and accuses him of snobbish bias. He says 'I must confess I cannot but prefer Mrs Behn infinitely before her; she seems to be a very cold Writer, while you may find in Aphra both Fire and Easiness, which Mrs Philips wanted.'[25] By 1747 the myth of Orinda, which needed the support of her living personality, had so far faded, that Whincop, under the blunt heading: 'C. Philips,' records all that remains: 'She was commonly called the Matchless Orinda, on account of an Epistolary correspondence carried on between her and Sir Charles Cotterel, under the feign'd names of Orinda and Poliarchus.'[26] Then follow, without comment, the names of those plays which surpassed Corneille.

The case of Catherine Philips illustrates the fact that a woman of mediocre mind and a veneer of education could, by adherence to an accepted genre of writing, not only secure powerful patrons, and an immediate success, but also an immunity from that criticism which ever pursued the women who wrote fiction, and which persisted even in the days of Jane Austen and the Brontës. 'Orinda' was a *nom de panache,* but 'Ellis Bell' was a guilty expedient, and it is strange to reflect that though, with the lapse of centuries, the novel increasingly proved its claim to be recognized as a particular form of art, and the world became increasingly familiar with the ability of women-novelists, yet the old stigma remained, and drove even genius to conceal itself under a pseudonym.

But there was a kind of literary composition, other than poetry, which even in the sixteenth and seventeenth centuries was considered legitimate for female pens. This was the biography or autobiography, and it is interesting to note in how far it shaped towards fiction in the hands of those women who employed it. Anne Clifford, Countess of Pembroke, the Duchess of Newcastle, Mrs Lucy Hutchinson, and Lady Fanshawe wrote their biographies, the first so as to clarify her daughter's claims in a legal dispute; the Duchess and Lucy Hutchinson, as it were, *en passant,* their particular interest being centred in writing their husbands' biographies. Lady Fanshawe more evenly develops her own life-story with that of her husband.

Biography had for women the advantage of giving them a chance to write on a subject they really knew, but the necessity for authenticity which was the object, and to them the justification of their compositions, crippled their imaginative powers. Their very familiarity with the people and the events in these works made it difficult for them to realize the necessity for describing them fully for other people. Thus, with the exception of Lady Fanshawe (the most vivid and detailed of the female biographers), they do not essay descriptions of domestic events, nor attempt to sketch in, however roughly, the backgrounds they knew so well. One does not often find in the biographical writings of Anne Clifford, the Duchess of Newcastle, or Lucy Hutchinson a realistic and full presentation of such events as are described, though frequently one is conscious of emotion flowing, with awakened memory, into their narratives. Still, they do not recreate happenings by the illumination of subsequent experience. They do not show much perspective. There is no dramatic irony. There is an entire lack of humour, due, no doubt, to the fact that when these women wrote they were worn out by many griefs. Their unrelieved seriousness must also be ascribed to an excessive anxiety. They are determined to present their husbands, their families and themselves in the best possible light and it is hard to smile with one's teeth clenched. With all four women there is a definite effort to achieve character-portraits, and not much notion of how to proceed. For the most part, they simply enumerate the ineffable virtues and bodily characteristics of those whom they wish to describe. Apart from the self-consciousness and difficulty in perspective which are obvious disadvantages in recording one's own life or that of a near relation, these women were also confronted with another serious handicap, namely, the necessity of showing the development of their family fortunes in relation to a complicated background of political events. Anne Clifford simply presumes such knowledge, as well she might, since she wrote only for her daughter. Lucy Hutchinson and the Duchess, forced to deal with the maze of the Civil War, and aware of their inability to do so, depend on others for their account of political and military events, the Duchess with her usual frankness, and Lucy Hutchinson without acknowledging her sources. As is only to be expected, both fail to control this extremely complicated mass of material, and they are very much at a loss as to how best it might be introduced into their narratives. The result is clumsy, and no wonder, seeing that the genre of the historical novel, shadowed faintly forth in their compositions, was yet almost a century and a half from its full evolution. When, about fifty-five years later, Defoe published, in 1722, the *Journal of the Plague Year* and *Colonel Jacques*, we see that despite the power and realism which characterized his works, he also failed to manage the historical background which his circumstantial method of composition forced him to introduce. Actually he should have experienced less difficulty in mastering his historical material, since, as his aim was really fiction, he had naturally no hesitation in juggling with historical data. In the *Journal of the Plague Year* this lack of technique is clearly evident. 'Large parts of the book are cast into statistical form: they read more like a Blue Book than anything else.'[27] This goes to show that even the freedom of fiction in the hands of a genius could not yet give ease in the interweaving of historical and personal material, and gives us moreover a true idea of what might reasonably be expected from the Duchess and Lucy Hutchinson. Lady Fanshawe makes no attempt to sketch in a comprehensive background of the Civil War — a wise abstention on the whole, although it often leaves the causes of the great Fanshawe Odyssey too obscure. Whatever the short-comings of these biographers, it was a step in the right direction that they were endeavouring to tell a story which was part of their lives, and much of which came within their personal experience; but it is amusing to reflect that while these women, pen in hand, endeavoured to marshal troops, to take castles, to summon and dismiss Parliaments and to discuss treaties, Mr Pepys was committing to an undreamed immortality the colour (and price) of his wife's dresses; the furnishings of their house; the sort of dinner one might expect on washing-day; the servant problem; the latest play; his outings with his wife, their friends, their quarrels, their reconciliations — in fact all the fabric of daily life, the fabric of domestic fiction, which had never yet been attempted by any writer, man or woman.

Mrs Manley's efforts at disguised autobiography came later than the *Life of William Cavendish* and the *Memoirs*, and went much nearer to direct fiction. In the new *Atalantis* she had introduced in a spasmodic and vagrant way some account of herself under the name of Delia, and this idea evidently developed in her mind, and claimed fuller expression in *Rivella*. The fact that *Rivella* is a biography in the form of a key-novel gave Mrs Manley a great advantage over her more forthright predecessors. The thin cloaking of reality in the key-novel gave just the necessary amount of freedom for the exercise of imagination and individuality. When Mrs Manley wrote *Rivella* she stood outside her life and contemplated its happenings in the light of after-knowledge, and this detachment, this escape from the hairsplitting responsibility of authenticity, from the dogmatism of the everlasting 'I,' was exactly what was needed for the development of biography into fiction. The close analogy between Defoe's *Roxana* and *Rivella* shows how two genres, originally separate, eventually became telescoped, and for opposite and corresponding reasons. Defoe veiled his fictions under the appearance of fact; Mrs Manley veiled her facts under the appearance of fiction. The point to be made is briefly this: that though women-writers were more successful in fiction than in any other type of writing, because their bent and their abilities alike indicated that medium of expression, yet convention decreed that, if they must write at all, then they ought to limit themselves to authenticated compositions; if they must feign, then it must be the sort of feigned writing called poetry. If a woman had written the life of Mrs Manley, thoroughly authenticating every fact, suitably deploring her immoral adventures and drawing elevated lessons from every lapse from grace, she really might have managed to escape severe popular censure; at any rate, she would have a much better chance of doing so than if she enlivened her subject by giving it, as Mrs Manley did, the form of a novel.

Nevertheless, and despite the passing of the Restoration school of female desperadoes, women continued to write fiction. What else could they do, if they were to write at all? In the words of Mary Davys:

> The Pedant despises the most elaborate Undertaking, unless it appears in the World with Greek and Latin Motto's; a Man that would please him, must pore an Age over Musty Authors till his brains are as worm-eaten as the books he reads . . . I have neither Inclination nor Learning enough to hope for his favour, so lay him aside.
>
> The next I can never hope to please, is the Dogmatical Puppy, who like a Hedgehog is wrapt up in his own Opinions . . . I leave him therefore . . . I confess the Royal Exchange, Southsea with a P-x, Exchange Alley, and all trade in general, are so foreign to my understanding that I leave 'em where I found 'em and cast an oblique glance at the Philosopher, who I take be a good clever fellow in his way. But I am again forced to betray my ignorance. I know so little of him that I leave him to his, *No Pleasure, No Pain*; and a thousand other Chimera's while I face about to the Man of Gallantry. Love is a very common topic, but 'tis withal a very copious one; and wou'd the Poets, Printers, and Booksellers but speak the truth of it, they wou'd own themselves more obliged to that one subject for their Bread, than all the rest put together. 'Tis there I fix.[28]

Mary Davys, a clergyman's widow, was typical of a new kind of woman-writer — the respectable woman who, forced for some reason to support herself, could find no other way of doing so save by writing or keeping a school. Sometimes, like Harriet and Sophia Lee, women did both, and even then found it difficult to exist on their earnings. One of these writing-women gives a description of herself which might easily be taken to designate her kind: 'Resident not very far from the market-place, immersed in business and in debt; sometimes madly hoping to gain a competency; sometimes justly fearing dungeons and distress.'[29] They appear to be overwhelmed by doubts as to the legitimacy of fiction, and of a female authorship. If they have any real impulse to write, any real conviction of ability, or any real literary ambition, they hasten to disclaim them so that they may propitiate their public:

As I never was ambitious of the Name of Author, nor even design'd to indulge my inclinations in writing any Thing of this Nature, more than for my own Amusement. I have printed this Manuscript (which otherwise I never had done) with a View to settling my self in a Way of Trade; that may enable me to master those Exigencies of Fortune, which my long illness had for some time past reduc'd me to suffer: That I may be capable of providing for my now ancient, indulgent Mother; whom Age, and the charge of many Children hath render'd incapable of providing for herself; As I shall directly sell Paper, Pens, Ink, Wax, Wafers, Black Lead Pencils, Pocket Books, Almanacks, Plays, Pamphlets and all manner of stationary goods. I must humbly beg the Favour of my honourable Subscribers (who are not already engag'd) to be so very good as to be my Customers.

E. Boyd.
March 2, 1732.

N.B. — Be Pleas'd to send to me in George-Court, in Prince's Street near Leicester-Fields, the First House on the Right Hand.[30]

There were legions of such women, a few with real ability, most of them without; all protesting, expostulating, explaining, defending their having dared to write. Not all, however, were as humble as Mrs Boyd: Mary Davys says in justification of her writing: 'Let them [her critics] consider that a woman left to her own endeavours for Twenty-seven Years together, may well be allowed to catch at any opportunity for that Bread, which they that condemn her would very probably deny to give her.'[31]

But, fortunately for the quality of women's literary work, it was not merely external necessity which continued to drive women to authorship. There was sometimes an inner compulsion of genius which neither ignorance nor convention could stifle; and it is useful to recall in this connection that women of the eighteenth and early nineteenth centuries still received no education worthy of the name. This was true even of those women who came of cultured families, and this lack of education was to a great extent deliberate, so that we may say without exaggeration that the ignorance of woman in those days was an effect of the prevailing convention. 'It was not the fashion for young ladies to be literary; a woman who wrote or read much was thought to be a HALF-MAN![32] To be a half-man was an infinite disaster, because it was the business of every young lady to catch a husband, and what man would wish to marry a blue-stockinged hermaphrodite? It was the business of women to be all that men admired, and they naturally did not admire a counterpart of themselves. No, the ladies, God bless them, must be lovely, gracious, gay, arch, inconsequent, diffident in weighty matters, sure only of their own beauty, bent only on pleasing, the dear, delightful fairies! 'I consider woman,' says Addison, 'as a beautiful, romantic animal that may be adorned with furs and feathers, ores and silks. The Lynx shall cast its skin at her feet to make her a tippet; the peacock, parrot and swan shall pay contributions to her muff: the sea shall be searched for shells and the rocks for gems; and every part of Nature furnish out its share towards the embellishment of a creature that is the most consummate work of it.' But since woman was not a study in still life, some rules were necessary, lest she might forget her role of charming vacuity. They were glibly supplied by Hannah More:

> *The animated silence of sparkling intelligence* with an occasional modest question which indicated at once rational curiosity and becoming diffidence is in many cases as large a share of the conversation as it is decorous for feminine delicacy to take.

This being the case it does not surprise us that Fanny Burney was so badly educated that at eight years old she did not know the alphabet; nor does it appear at all unnatural that Frances Sheridan's father disapproved of women being taught to read, and was vigorously opposed to their being taught to write. But the child who at eight years did not know the alphabet was scribbling stories, odes, plays and songs two years later, in hieroglyphics which only she herself could read; and the child who was forbidden to read or write secretly prevailed on her brother to teach her, which, recognizing her intelligence, he did, thus saving from illiteracy the author of *Miss Sydney Bidulph*, the mother of one of our finest dramatists. At fifteen, Fanny Burney became overwhelmed with a sense of guilt at her passion for writing, and thought it her duty to subdue it, so, taking advantage of her parents' absence from home, she made a bonfire of all she had written. This holocaust included *The History of Caroline Evelyn* — a tale which she found it impossible to forget, and which later she was again to commit to paper, under the title of *Evelina*. After her decision not to go on writing she commenced to keep a diary which she dedicated 'TO NOBODY.' 'To whom must I dedicate my private opinions, my wonderful, surprising and interesting adventures? To whom dare I reveal my private opinions of my nearest relations? My secret thoughts of my dearest friends? My own hopes, fears, reflections, and dislikes? — Nobody.' But she could not stifle her impulse towards literary expression, and like Jane Austen, she wrote on scraps of paper, alone when she could escape her vigilant family, in the common living room when escape was impossible — making a pretence of occupying herself with her needle. Ah! those deceptive needles of the female scribblers! How zealously they flashed, what ground they seemed to cover, and how curiously little they achieved! Jane Austen knew that trick too — Jane, that frightful warning to young ladies of her day of the price one paid for secretly plying the pen. Miss Mitford's mother describes her as 'the prettiest, silliest, most affected, husband-hunting butterfly she ever remembers,'[33] and the next thing we hear is that 'she has stiffened into the most perpendicular, precise, taciturn piece of "single blessedness" that ever existed . . . no more regarded in society than a poker or a firescreen.'[34] As for the motherless Brontës, they missed, alas, the training that young ladies ought to receive, and really behaved in the most unsuitable way. Wolfing books and scribbling among the gravestones could lead only to such unnatural works as *Wuthering Heights* and *Jane Eyre*. For such women not even a moulting parrot would cast a single feather.

Harriet Martineau, perhaps, was less to be blamed, for the poor thing was really very ugly. She never received but one civil speech about her looks, which accounts, no doubt, for the fact that she always looked glum. As she showed every sign of being a superfluous woman, it was perhaps just as well that she took to her pen. She also, however, had to pay tribute with her needle. 'She was at the work table regularly after breakfast, making her clothes or the shirts of the household, or engaged on fancy work. She studied almost by stealth, meeting her brother James at seven in the morning to read Latin with him or translating Tacitus, that she might compress her thoughts.'[35] When she became deaf and penniless, she had to earn her living. No doubt it was because she was so plain that she wrote didactic tales on various aspects of political economy, but possibly, however, she may have been influenced by the fact that the Reform Bill was pending and that cholera had begun to rage. Harriet Martineau published by subscription, and she got reasonably generous terms, in view of the fact that she was quite destitute, and deaf, and only a woman: five hundred copies were to be taken before her book came out, and if one thousand copies were not sold in the first fortnight, the publication would be stopped. She accepted the proposition and took the prospectus into town, then stunned by the certainty of failure, and half-starving, she walked the four and a half miles back to her lodgings. 'On the road, not far from Shoreditch, she became too giddy to stand without support. She leaned over some dirty pailings, pretending to look at a cabbage-bed, but saying to herself with closed eyes ' my book will do yet.' She wrote her preface that evening, and finished it as the Brewery clock struck two. At four o'clock she went to bed and cried herself to sleep, but at 8.30 she was up again, preparing and sending out her circulars. Thin, yellow and coughing with every breath she returned to Norwich.'[33] She was self-sufficient and self-assertive. Her stories were dry and heavy; she was obviously a woman at whose feet no self-respecting Lynx would cast his skin.

And what of George Eliot, sprung from the tradesman class, who, when the women of cultured families had had little hope of education, still could not repress her ambition for learning, and could not stifle in her mind the impulse to clothe in fiction a whole philosophy of life? We watch her acquiring knowledge, withdrawing into a world of her own fashioning, experimenting in literary form, doggedly driving upwards out of the stultifying mediocrity of her surroundings, until she becomes the assistant editor of a highly intellectual London review; the friend of Spencer; the author of novels which led Lord Acton to say that she was greater than Dante, and Herbert Spencer to exempt her works, as if they were not fiction, when he banned all novels from the London Library. She was guilty, however, of an unforgiveable lack — she had no charm: 'In fiction where so much of personality is revealed, the absence of charm is a great lack, and her critics who have been, of course, mostly of the opposite sex, have resented, half consciously perhaps, her deficiency in a quality which is held to be supremely desirable in a woman. George Eliot was not charming; she was not strongly feminine.'[37] She was at the same time condemned for being an errant woman, and for being too masculine, for being depressingly equine and for being, in the words of George

Meredith, 'a mercurial little showman.' And yet she wrote at least one immortal novel, this strange dark soul, whose gloom was rent by the lightnings of genius — this butt for youthful derision — a woman whom neither furs, nor ores, nor gems, nor silks, nor tippets could adorn.

Whether women novelists wrote from genuine inspiration or from mere financial necessity, certain it is that they did not do so to win fame. Novels were a more likely source of notoriety than of fame even in Jane Austen's time. Writing at the end of the eighteenth century Fanny Bumey had to say: 'In the republic of letters there is no member of such inferior rank, or who is so much disdained by his brethren of the quill, as the humble novelist.'[38] And Robert Bage, in proof that even the didactic school of novelists were not exempted from popular censure, says: 'Novels are now pretty generally considered as the lowest of the human productions.'[39]

Writing in 1798, Jane Austen, in her defence of the novelist's art, shows how contemptuously it was regarded even by the novelists themselves:

> I will not adopt that ungenerous and impolitic custom, so common with novel writers, of degrading, by their contemptuous censure, the very performances to the number of which they are themselves adding: joining with their greatest enemies in bestowing the harshest epithets on such works, and scarcely even permitting them to be read by their own heroine, who, if she accidentally take up a novel, is sure to turn over its insipid pages with disgust. Alas! if the heroine of one novel be not patronised by another, from whom can she expect protection and regard. I cannot approve of it. Let us leave it to the Reviewers to abuse such effusions of fancy in threadbare strains of the trash with which the press now groans. Let us not desert one another; we are an injured body. Although our productions have afforded more extensive and unaffected pleasure than those of any literary corporation in the world, no species of composition has been so much decried. From pride, ignorance, or fashion, our foes are almost as many as our readers and while the abilities of the nine-hundredth abridger of the History of England, or of the man who collects and publishes in a volume some dozen lines of Milton, Pope, and Prior, with a paper from the Spectator, and a chapter from Sterne, are eulogised by a thousand pens, there seems almost a general wish of decrying the capacity and undervaluing the labour of the novelist, and of slighting the performances which have

only genius, wit, and taste to recommend them. 'I am no novel reader; I seldom look into novels; do not imagine that I often read novels; it is really very well for a novel.' Such is the common cant. 'And what are you reading, Miss — ?' 'Oh! it is only a novel!' replies the young lady; while she lays down her book with affected indifference, or momentary shame. 'It is only Cecilia, or Camilla or Belinda' , or in short only some work in which the greatest powers of the mind are displayed, in which the most thorough knowledge of human nature, the happiest delineation of its varieties, the liveliest effusions of wit and humour, are conveyed to the world in the best chosen language.[40]

One of the most striking proofs of the attitude which a sensible and discreet person might take towards seeing his name on the title page of a novel lies in the fact that Sir Walter Scott at first published under a pseudonym. If a man shied away from such publicity, a woman had an added reason for doing so, since her defiance of conventionality would be so much greater than his. Thus it is that the student of women's works of fiction needs a pretty wit in resolving the mysteries which they have woven about their author-ship. Even literary success did not always lure them into declaring their identity as we see, for example, in the case of Jane Austen. Her novels were published anonymously after they had mouldered in a drawer for years. *Pride and Prejudice,* completed in 1797, was published in 1813; *Sense and Sensibility,* completed in 1798, was published in 1811. *Northanger Abbey* was sold to a publisher in Bath for £10 in 1803. He did not venture to print it, and was glad to take back his money and return the manuscript to one of her brothers a few years later, not realizing until the bargain was complete that the writer was also the author of four popular novels. Though the authorship of the novels was an open secret to Jane Austen's friends during her lifetime, it was not made public until after her death, and while she lived she remained in obscurity. It has been said that Fanny Burney 'forced the superior sex to acknowledge a woman's wit and grant her the right, never before admitted, to think for herself and express her own opinions, *without loss of respectability or caste.*'[41] If such had been the case, Jane Austen and her works would not so long have remained unknown; and there are not wanting many other examples to prove that the prejudice against women-novelists persisted after Jane Austen's day. Fanny Burney, in addition to a small group of women-writers, was so fortunate as to win the praise and encouragement of Dr Johnson, and it would have needed a stout heart indeed to have attacked the protégées of so doughty a champion of morality and learning.

But, with the coming of Jane Austen, a new note appears in the attitude of women-novelists. Criticism and indifference had until then driven them to expostulate, to cringe, or to defy, in accordance with their particular temperaments or circumstances. Jane Austen does neither. Her only apologia was a defence, not of women-novelists, but of the art of fiction, and she showed that neither fear nor opportunism could deflect her from her particular *métier*. She was fully aware of the artistic value of her work, and equally conscious of her limitations. Not even the patronage of a Prince Regent could persuade her to relinquish the right of keeping her own literary conscience. This is a milestone in the story of women-novelists, and though, there being only one Jane Austen, many women after her were to wheedle or to flout their public, the miracle had been accomplished, the miracle of a woman-novelist who was not conscious of inferiority, and whose work was not influenced in any way by what Fielding inimitably calls 'a little reptile of a critic.'[42]

Looking back over the long years since 1621, during which women persisted in writing fiction, we see, rising above the flood of mediocrity, certain names which connote something of value, which mark some definite contribution to the development of English fiction. In fact, so consistently did women keep step with the advance in novel-writing that to trace their progress is to trace the progress of the novel itself. To trace women's contribution to fiction is somewhat like tracing the contribution of a common soldier in a great campaign. It looks, at first, as if no one should ever hear of this undistinguished fighter, his tireless energy, endurance and good humour, of his dogged refusal to go under without giving a good account of himself. It seems as if, granted these qualities, his natural limitations and an invidious convention would keep him in the ranks. But nothing in life is surer than that real ability coupled with ambition must find its own level, and as the common soldier, indispensable even in his normal sphere, often by a stroke of genius so natural that it appears merely an impulse, saves the situation and turns the tide, so also women-writers not only shared all the dust and heat, but often by a culmination of originality and technique initiated a new genre of fiction. There is no kind of novel which they did not attempt, and there are few kinds which they did not enrich. The pastoral novel, the novella, the picaresque, the satire, the novel of authenticated realism, the novel of sensibility, of manners, of domesticity, of social purpose, the Gothic novel, the Oriental novel, the epistolary novel, in all these genres they were active, many of them they helped to initiate, and in some of them they showed genius.

What is literary initiation? It is easier to show what it is not. It is not to give birth to an entirely new type of fiction which leaps fully armed like Pallas Athene from the head of Jupiter. Literary initiation is the result of a slow development of certain literary tendencies which, almost unconsciously, come into being, and which await the mind which will recognize their value, and which by experiment will unify them and give them a recognized place among mature literary genres. This Mrs Radcliffe did for the Gothic novel, exerting an immense influence on the writers of the Romantic Revival; this Fanny Burney and Jane Austen did for the domestic novel and the novel of manners, revolutionizing completely the conception of realism in fiction; this Charlotte Lennox did for the Anti-Romantic satire; this Mary Manley did for the epistolary novel; this Mary Shelley did for the pseudo-scientific tale of wonder; this George Eliot did for the philosophic novel; this Charlotte Brontë did for the subjective novel — the novel which shows life chiefly as it is reflected in an isolated soul. Emily Brontë did far more than all this in her novel which, without ancestors or progeny, by one superb explosion of genius defies criticism and classification.

And it is not only in strength and patience, marching side by side with the men-writers who disowned them, nor in leadership to which they did not aspire, but to which their inspirations carried them, that women contributed to the English Novel. They contributed to it also by giving to it a new conception of women. This they could not do for a long time, impeded by the Heroic tradition in accordance with which men and women writers alike purveyed to an apparently satisfied public women-characters who bore not the slightest likeness to reality. Not indeed that these heroic beauties, without passions or any characteristic of humanity, were more fantastic than the heroes whom they spurred on to terrific feats of devotion and valour. Both the authors and their public knew these fictional characters to be as completely outside nature as their background was outside geography. They were not aiming at reality, but at heroism which, fortunately for human comfort, does not much invade every-day life. Still, if the disguised princes subscribed to an amazing code of life, it was chiefly the incognito princesses who formulated it, and it does not surprise us to see, as time progressed, that these heroines, under the strain of such lofty sentiments, tended to an extreme delicacy of mind and body. No doubt another contributory cause of the lack of stamina in these ladies was that throughout an entire novel, running into many folio volumes, they never ate or drank. The men are almost as ethereal. Sir George Bellmour, romancing after the style of such knights so as to win the interests of Arabella, The Female Quixote, describes the hardships he endured for the love of his fair mistress (Polly Acorn, the milkmaid). His sufferings include ten months of melancholy sojourning in a forest:

> 'Give me leave,' said Sir Charles [the voice of common sense], 'Give me leave to ask, If you eat in all this Time.'
> 'Alas! Sir,' replied Sir George, 'Sighs and Tears were all my Sustenance.'[43]

By the time Charlotte Lennox wrote her burlesque, the heroic tradition was dead, but the era of sensibility was an established fact. That is to say, women in fiction now ate and drank, rode in coaches and went to balls like ordinary mortals; but whereas before they had wandered elegantly through an unreal world, now their surroundings were real, and the unreal world was within their breasts. If it had not been put there by Richardson, it had certainly been confirmed and licensed by him and never surely did a more absurd fable delude the public, than that fable of Richardson's marvellous insight into the female heart. But so great was Richardson's vogue with his woman-readers that, had it been possible for them to abjure nature, and regulate their cardiac activities according to the Richardsonian scheme, they would have done so. Alas! this was beyond even feminine adaptability. It must have been with mingled feelings of regret and relief that they found in the pages of Fanny Bumey and Jane Austen just such women as themselves, women whose beauty, wit and wisdom were subject to decay; whose virtue was not infallible; who could suffer without histrionics, and who could love without illusion. Then this had all been clothed in language

31

a very long time before by the writer of the *Portuguese Letters*, but whether or not that authorship is to be ascribed to the nun of Beja, certain it is that English fiction had to await the coming of Emily Brontë to hear the authentic accents of love and grief.

And so at last we find women writing with confidence, for men and women alike, in a way both knew to be true, in language which they could mould to the technique of their art; and supported by a tradition of literary achievement which was so necessary for the free exercise of the female pen. Courage and self-respect are the necessary ballast of any fine endeavour. George Eliot, who withers with her scorn the silly and pretentious school of women-novelists, quietly turns away from them to show that women's achievement in fiction is so firmly established that it cannot be degraded by the fatuous female scribblers: 'Happily we are not dependent on argument to prove that Fiction is a department of literature in which women can, after their kind, fully equal men. A cluster of great names, both living and dead, rush to our memories in evidence that women can produce novels not only fine, but among the very finest; novels too that have a precious speciality lying quite apart from masculine aptitudes and experience' — no mean record this, as we shall realize when we consider more fully their contributions.

Notes and References

1 Henry Fielding, *Tom Jones* (1749), Preface to Book ix.
2 Ibid.
3 R. Brimley Johnson, *Novelists on Novels* (1928), pp. 226 ff. (Extract from George Eliot, 'Silly Novels by Silly Novelists,' *Westminster Review*).
4 Mary Herbert, Countess of Pembroke, rendered into blank verse Robert Garnier's French tragedy of *Antonie*. For date of publication *D.N.B.* gives 1592: *Biographic Dramatica* gives 1595.
5 Robert Bage, *Mount Henneth* (1781).
6 The Duchess of Newcastle, *Poems and Fancies* (1653); an address '*To all Noble and Worthy Ladies.*'
7 Ibid., dedication to Sir Charles Cavendish.
8 Mary Herbert, Countess of Pembroke, *Antonie*. (For date of publication see note 4 above).
9 *Works of Marie de France* (ed. de Roquefort), introductory note.
10 *Works of Marie de France* (ed. Rickert), p. 1. The beginning of *Guigemor*.
11 Susannah Centlivre, dedication to *The Platonic Lady* (dedicated to

'All the generous encouragers of female ingenuity').

12 Elizabeth Hamilton, *Letters to a Hindoo Rajah*, (1791), ii, p. 328.

13 Alice A. Hentsch, *De la Littérature Didactique du moyen âge s'adressant spécialement aux femmes* (Cahors, 1903), pp. 68 f.

14 *Dryden's Works* (ed. Scott and Saintsbury), xviii, p. 166.

15 Allardyce Nicol, *Restoration Drama, 1660–1700* (2nd edn. 1928), p. 211.

16 *Dryden's Works* (ed. Scott and Saintsbury), xviii, p.166n.

17 Theophilus Cibber, *The Lives of the Poets* (1753).

18 *The History of the life and adventures of Mr Duncan Campbell* (1720). There seems reason to ascribe part authorship to Defoe.

19 *A Spy upon the Conjurer* (1725). Ascribed by Dr G. B. Wicher to Mrs Haywood, in *The Life and Romances of Mrs Eliza Haywood* (Columbia University Press, 1915). Similarly ascribed by Mr E. A. Baker, *History of the English Novel* (1929), iii, p. 178.

20 G. B. Baker, *The Life and Romances of Mrs Eliza Haywood* (Columbia University Press, 1915), p. 80.

21 Of these, in Elizabethan and Jacobean days, there was a fair number, notably Catherine Killigrew, Jane Weston and Mary, Countess of Pembroke.

22 E. Gosse, *Seventeenth Century Studies* (1885): Essay on 'The Matchless Orinda.'

23 Langbaine, *An Account of the English Dramatic Poets* (Oxford, 1691), pp. 403 f.

24 See E. Gosse, *Seventeenth Century Studies* (1885).

25 Gildon's Langbaine, *The Lives of the Poets* (1699), pp. 110–11.

26 T. Whincop, *Scanderbeg* (appendix).

27 E. A. Baker, *History of the English Novel* (1927), iii, pp. 201 f.

28 Mary Davys, *The Reformed Coquet* (1724), pp. 2 f.

29 Mrs Mary Latter, *The Miscellaneous Works in Prose and Verse* (1759), Introduction.

30 Advertisement in front of E. Boyd's *The Female Page* (1737).

31 Mary Davys, *Collected Works* (1725), Preface to vol. 1.

32 Catherine Hamilton, *Women Writers and their Ways* (1893), ii, 'Harriet Martineau'.

33 *Life of Mary Russell Mitford* (ed. L'Estrange, 1870), i, p. 305. J. E. Austen-Leigh flatly contradicts 'this strange misrepresentation of my aunt's manners' (see last pages of *Memoir of Jane Austen*, Oxford, 1926). Nevertheless, although Mrs Mitford evidently could not have gained it by heresay, which is not, after all, a bad guide to the more obvious aspects of behaviour. Jane Austen's letters show that she took a lively interest in finery and balls.

34 Quoted by Virginia Woolf, *The Common Reader* (1925), 'Jane Austen.'

35 Catherine Hamilton, *Women Writers and their Ways*, (1893), ii, 'Harriet Martineau.'

36 Ibid.

37 Ibid., 'George Eliot.'

38 Fanny Burney, *Evelina* (1778), Preface.

39 Robert Bage, *Hermsprong* (1796).

40 Jane Austen, *Northanger Abbey*, ch. 5.
41 Brimley Johnson, *Novelists on Novels* (1928), pp. xxvi f.
42 Henry Fielding, *Tom Jones* (1749), Introduction to Book IV.
43 Charlotte Lennox, *The Female Quixote: Or, The Adventures of Arabella* (Intro. Sandra Shulman, 'Mothers of the Novel', Pandora, London, 1986), Bk. vi, p. 267.
44 R. Brimley Johnson, *Novelists on Novels* (1928), p. 236 ff. (Extracts from George Eliot 'Silly Novels by Silly Novelists', *Westminster Review*).

Chapter II

The Pastoral Romance

And when in Sydney's death, Wit ebbed in men,
It hath its spring-tide in a Female pen.

(Vaughan, *A Continuation of Sir Philip Sydney's Arcadia*)

In 1621, in the person of Lady Mary Wroath, woman made her first contribution to English prose fiction. Having barely mentioned the name of the first English woman-novelist, we must at once retrogress after the manner of a writer who introduces his heroine only to leave her standing while he laboriously sketches in the background. But truly it would be quite impossible to judge the work of Lady Mary Wroath without at first considering briefly the state of Elizabethan and Jacobean prose fiction of which her novel was an integral part.

The main point to be observed in regard to the prose fiction of the Elizabethan age is that on the whole it did not recognize itself as a separate literary medium. Narrative had undergone many changes in aim and in form, since the days of the old epics which had for their object the recital of certain events. This uncomplicated aim led to a direct form, to a treatment which Heine rightly called a classic treatment.[1] This treatment was classic because the form of that which was portrayed was identical with the idea of the portrayer. The wanderings of Ulysses, for example, represented merely the wanderings of a man who was the son of Laertes and the husband of Penelope. There was no wider meaning, no esoteric significance, and for this reason there was complete harmony between the idea and the form. Classic art aimed only at representing the finite, and it succeeded by direct means. But this simplicity of aim and medium did not last. Man began to be troubled by subjective views of life. He realized that direct descriptions would not express what he now wished to say, and he attempted to convey his thoughts by parabolic means. This new treatment of the subject-matter was romantic; that is to say that the form did not reveal the idea through identity, but suggested what was beyond literal expression. To attain their effects the narrators changed and adapted the material of their tales, thus departing from the classic ideal of authenticity. But the fictional nature of these tales appeared to them a sign of decadence; deliberate fiction appeared too much of a pretence, and so we find, for long ages, a persistent effort to give authenticity to feigned stories.

From the epic to the cycles of romance, from classicism to romanticism, was the natural transition. It was held by some that romanticism was merely the decadence of classic art. But this would be to arraign also the realm of poetry, and particularly of lyric poetry. Romanticism grew from taking thought, from finding in life a depth of meaning below the surface. Romanticism either endeavoured to suggest such meaning through the agency of language, or else attempted to escape this subjective reality by taking refuge in literary compositions as far as possible unlike the world around them. This was the starting-point and material witness of their mental state. The ideal of the ancients was the man of action, and they feared for the man of action who might lose his manliness and become thought-sick. It is to be observed that with the Greeks romanticism did not arise until a period of national deterioration had set in. With the humiliation of Athens, the destruction of the Macedonian monarchy and of Asiatic Greece, political liberty was lost, and the main activities of the Greek people were rendered henceforth impossible. Disillusionment led to scepticism in religious and other forms of thought. Prose fiction grew from the decadence of poetry at this time. It was far from being an introspective kind of writing. On the contrary, it was merely an objective record of imaginary events which never had been, and which never could take place in the mortal world. This unreal, this romantic fiction was of different kinds; the short story, the imaginary journey to incredible countries, the romance of adventures, and the love intrigue; the Milesian tale — a particular type of amatory short story — and the Pastoral romance. These tales were a refuge from the life which pressed too sorely upon men: and to escape more fully from reality, writers not only depicted unreal events, but projected them against a background which had no identifiable locus. The *Golden Ass* of Apuleius, the first romance of antiquity, was to have a strange and varied posterity, but, though the symbolic presentation of truth or beauty was often obscured, the escapist characteristic always remained, frequently with dire effect.

In common with every other literary movement the Romance of Chivalry had established itself abroad before reaching England. *Amadis de Gaul*, published in 1508, was available in manuscript and in oral recitative since about the year 1300. The Pastoral Romance, a sub-development of the Romance of Chivalry, had its originator in Longus, who was to pastoral prose fiction what Theocritus had been to pastoral poetry, but the fine simplicity of *Daphnis and Chloe* did not survive, and the pastoral novel really began its sophisticated course in the *Arcadia* of Sannazzaro. This work was surpassed in interest by Montemayor's *Diana Enamorada*, which was translated into English in 1583. Sidney's *Arcadia* was a fusion of the main characteristics of the Amadis cycle of chivalric romance, and of the pastoral romance.

Sidney was not aware that in his *Arcadia* he was adhering to a moribund form. The astonishing fact is that the Pastoral Romance which had first arisen in a decadent period was received in England with great enthusiasm at a period of re-birth. There were several reasons for this anomaly. In the first place, English prose fiction was in a very undeveloped state. It was too young to know its own nature or its bent, and not only so, but it was suffering from under-nourishment. Men's attention and abilities were focused on the drama and on poetry. These Siamese twins, considered really as one, were carefully nurtured and exhibited with pride, while fiction, that disowned foundling, pined in the cellar. The coming of the Pastoral Romance, with its pseudo-poetic style, made it possible for the poets to redeem the rickety outcast from inferior darkness, and to give it a place in the family circle. Under the protection of the poetic tradition, the Pastoral Romance, though always sickly, persisted in living for a long time. It was, for example, primarily because Sidney was a poet that he wrote the *Arcadia*. He maintained always the fallacious contention that all imaginative creation was poetry. This obsession which he shared with the established, conservative, literary forces of his period serves to show all the more clearly that the slow and painful transition from prose to poetry had not yet become an established fact in English story-telling.

In 1400, Chaucer had written an excellent story in verse. Although it owed much to Boccaccio, *Troilus and Cresseyde* showed at one stroke a remarkable power of construction and characterization, and much subtlety in narrative device. But at least two hundred years elapsed before English fiction profited by this example, simply because it was impeded by the transition from verse to prose. Prose had an obvious advantage in story-telling. It was more economical than verse, and it could represent life more closely and more fully. Furthermore, the invention of printing gave to prose works a certainty of remembrance which until then had been possible only in verse. The trend towards prose was thus greatly hastened. But as verse had taken time to perfect itself as a medium for story-telling, so prose had now to be forged into a fit instrument for the writer of prose fiction. It had to become clear, ample, vivid, flexible and yet strong, capable of expressing the entire gamut of human experience. And while prose was thus evolving, the writers of prose fiction were endeavouring to clothe their stories in a kind of prose not yet suited to the purpose. The Elizabethan novel at its best was a living entity, with endless possibilities of thought and action, but unable yet to speak or act freely. Not only was the medium of expression lacking in resilience, but the very method of telling a story was as yet only glimpsed. The lesson of Chaucer's technique in story-telling was lost to succeeding prose writers, because they were confused by the change in medium, and seemed unable to apply to prose tales the methods which Chaucer had employed in verse-form.

This transition period gave to the prose story-teller a choice between two schools of writing, radically different in every respect. On the side of the privileged class, and springing from the poetic tradition, there was the Heroic Romance and the Pastoral Romance (the elements of which were often fused, as in the *Arcadia)*; there was also, as a sub-classification, the sort of romance initiated and typified by Lyly's *Euphues* which for a long time had a great success, and which, strangled in an impossible style, contained portents of future developments in fiction. On the popular side, and chiefly of prose origin, there were the short, pithy, unpretentious stories which found their best expression in the form of the Italian *novelle,* and which were available in the collections of Painter, Whetstone, Fenton, and others; there were the moral tales, closely allied to the *novelle* and typified in the *Gesta Romanorum;* [2] there was popular satire which Langland's verse had established long before and which was now developed vigorously by such men as Nash and Greene; there were the stories of low life, such as the gest books, the picaresque tales, the cony-catching pamphlets; there were semi-fictious and real biographies; there were Deloney's guild tales; and there was much letter-writing to imaginary people (an activity which later became a very important development in form). This popular school presented the realistic trend in fiction, which, because it had its roots in actual life, became increasingly alive, and held its ground through succeeding centuries to develop triumphantly into the modern novel.

Between the extreme right wing and the extreme left wing in fiction there was the simple prose romance of the burgher class, which later became the chap-book of the seventeenth and eighteenth centuries, as for example, *Guy of Warwick* and *Huon of Bordeaux*. These last were offshoots of the medieval cycles of romance which had found new life in homely soil, and which lived, therefore, when the larger cycles had passed from the memory of the people.

The popular school had its origin in folk-tales which had always existed orally side by side with the elaborate stories of the privileged classes. Its prose tradition and its unambitious aim saved it from an involved form. In fact, in identity of form and idea it might almost be called classic. It was direct, simple and all the more vital because it did not dissipate its energies in devious symbolism or elaborate intricacies. It was spontaneous, but often crude. The romantic kind of writing had its origin in poetry, but it had also found copious expression in prose. In the use of this prose medium it was, however, hampered by the conviction that its mission was poetic, and it therefore expended its energies on a mistaken object. It contained a diffused beauty and a deliberate melodiousness which were not evident in the people's tales, but it was cumbersome, artificial and in no way a representation of life. Indeed it intentionally aimed at the portrayal of a world unconnected with reality. It is clear that the modern novel could not develop from such a school of fiction, because such writing could not become real. And it is equally clear that the novel could develop from the popular school of fiction, because the realistic writing of the ordinary people *could* become aesthetic and *could* find artistic devices to suit its purposes. The reality on which the novel must feed, if it were to grow, was the main virtue of this popular fiction, and time would enable it to achieve artistic form. When Sidney wrote, the Pastoral Romance was dying. To save it there would have been needed a transfusion of common blood, rich and varied food, great draughts of wine, fresh air and sunshine, and a complete change of scene. An inbred parent-stock, and a thin and rarefied existence had produced anaemia not more pernicious, however, than its posthumous influence. But it was not to die yet awhile. Unnatural fungus that it was, it was to draw new life from Sidney's death. When Sidney died at Zutphen, he established a tradition for romantic heroism which prolonged the life of the heroic romance, and which perpetuated its repute. It would have been well for subsequent fiction if Sidney had not been as noble in character as in lineage. To be young, gifted, and heroic, to love with passionate austerity, and coin one's heart into lyrics; to die with an immortal sentence on one's lips — this is to create a legend, and the dazzling legend of Sidney blinded even the critical to the grave defects of the *Arcadia*.

Published in 1590, the *Arcadia* had an immense success. By 1600, there had been four editions. There were fourteen editions during the seventeenth century. In 1725 a three-volume edition appeared, and was reprinted in Dublin in 1739. From that time until 1907, only abridgements were printed. In 1725 appeared Mrs Stanley's modernized version, with which Richardson was doubtless familiar, and from which he took the name of his heroine Pamela.

The *Arcadia* attracted a great number of imitators, who wished either to continue the story or to use it as a model for similar themes. In 1606, John Day wrote *The Ile of Guls:* 'A little string or rivulet drawn from the full stream of the Right Worthy gentleman, Sir Philip Sidney's well known *Archadea*.' Shirley dramatized many episodes in his *Pastoral called the Arcadia* (1640). Shakespeare may have embodied in the scenes between Gloster and his son, in *King Lear*, the story of the dispossessed king of Paphlagonia. Mr C. Crawford has found traces of the *Arcadia* in *The Duchess of Malfi* and other plays by Webster. Francis Quarles, author of the *Emblemes*, made the story of Argalus and Parthenia the subject of a long poem (1622). Many writers linked their works to the fame of Sir Philip Sidney by mentioning his name on their title-pages, and one writer in particular found in her near relationship to this idolized man the courage to emerge into the world of letters under the protection of his glory.

In 1621, years after the first appearance of the *Arcadia*, Lady Mary Wroath published her stout folio, the *Urania*. This attempt at Pastoral Romance has for the most part been buried in oblivion. Very occasionally some searcher among the minutiae of literature brushes aside the dust of ages, and glances inside her book. The elaborate frontispiece does certainly justify Mr E. A. Baker's remark that Lady Mary made great play with her pedigree on the title-page. The title runs:

The
Countesse
of Montgomeries
URANIA
Written by the right honourable the Lady
MARY WROATH
Daughter to the right Noble Robert
Earle of Leicester
And niece to the ever famous and renowned
Sr. Phillips Sydney, Knight. And to
The Most exelet Lady Mary Countesse of
Pembroke late deceased.

Lady Mary Wroath grew up within a charmed circle, in an atmosphere of social and literary impeccability. Sir Philip Sidney was not only a true poet himself, but an extremely generous literary patron. The centre of all that was best in Elizabethan poetry, and with his house and purse ever open to needy writers, it was only natural that he should have been beloved, and that he and his family should have been liberally praised by the best poets of the day. Sidney himself was indeed worthy of the encomiums lavished upon him as a poet and as a man, but, as we have already shown, the Countess of Pembroke merely shone in a reflected glory which her literary talents did not deserve. It is not surprising that Lady Mary Wroath should trust that the spell would hold in her case also. Yet she did not determine to write until she was driven to it as a last expedient.

The eldest daughter of Robert Sidney, first Earl of Leicester, she married Sir Robert Wroath in 1604, at the age of eighteen. She was often at court after her marriage, and King James frequently visited her husband's estate at Durrants. She was a liberal and

41

sympathetic patroness of literature, and as such was honoured by many of the chief poets of the age. It is recorded that on Twelfth Night, 1604–05, she acted at Whitehall in Ben Jonson's *Masque of Blackness.* Jonson dedicated to her his play *The Alchemist* (1610), as well as a sonnet and two epigrams. Chapman addressed to her a sonnet which was prefixed to his translation of Homer's *Iliad* (1614). George Wither and William Gamage offered similar tributes to 'the most famous and heroike Lady Mary Wroath.' But these pleasant circumstances came to an end with the death of her husband in 1614. She was left with an infant son, an income of £1,200 a year, and an estate swamped in debt. Nor had death ceased to ravage her happiness. Two years later her son died, and then her father. This last blow led to the complete wreck of her financial affairs, because, ignoring the trustees whom her father had appointed to administer her small possessions, she insisted on managing them herself. She soon proved her inability to do so, and her financial embarrassment became so serious that, in 1623, she was forced to petition the King for protection from her creditors for the space of one year. Prior to that date, however, she had determined on authorship as a solution of her difficulties.

The Countess of Montgomeries Urania was modelled on the *Arcadia.* As this literary venture was a financial speculation, it was to be expected that Lady Mary Wroath would adhere to the form which had already been received with acclamation, and which, to judge by sedulous imitators, was in the main stream of literary development. No doubt, she also hoped that a descendant of Sidney, using the pastoral medium, would strike home to the hearts of the reading public. It is quite possible, too, that she believed that she might be an inheritor of poetic gifts, and the fact that she was a woman would not deter her, in view of her aunt's reputation as a writer. Prolonged adulation is apt to destroy the critical faculty, and Lady Mary was not likely to judge aright either her aunt's talents or her own.

The *Urania* is an exceedingly complicated pastoral romance, after the Sidneian pattern. The scene is laid partly in the island of Pantaleria, governed by the Lord Pantalerius who, because of a grievance, is self-exiled from his own country. The heroine is Urania, apparently a shepherdess, but really a princess, daughter of the King of Naples. The hero is also of noble blood, Parselius, Prince of Morea. Minor characters linked to the main plot are

Amphilanthus, brother of Urania, and heir to the throne of Naples; and Leonius, the younger brother. There are various sub-plots very slenderly connected with the main plot. The story of the king of Albania and his children is dull and digressive. There are other inset stories which are equally digressive, but so far from dull that we must make particular mention of them, when the main plot of *Urania* has been outlined.

The beginning of *Urania* is a good example of the style in which the book is written:

> When the Spring began to appear like the welcome messenger of Summer, one Sweet (and in that more sweet) morning, after Aurora had called all careful eyes to attend the day, forth came the faire shepherdesse URANIA (faire indeed; yet that farre too meane a title for her, who for beautie deserved the highest stile could be given by best knowing Judgements). Into the Meade she came, where usually she drave her flocks to feede, whose leaping and wantonesse showed they were proud of such a guide. But she, whose sad thoughts led her to another Manner of spending her time, made her soon leave them and follow her late begun custom: which was (while they delighted themselves) to sit under some shade, bewailing her misfortune; while they fed to feed upon her owne sorrow and teares, which at this time she began again to summon, sitting down under the shade of a well-spread Beech; the ground (then blest) and the tree with full and fined leaved branches growing proud to beare and shadow such perfection. But she, regarding nothing in comparison of her woe, thus proceeded in her grief: Alas, Urania, said she, (the true servant of misfortune) of any misery that can befal a woman, is not this the most and greatest which thou are falne into? Can there be any neare the unhappinesse of being ignorant, and that in the highest kind, not being certain of my owne estate or birth? Why was I not still continued in the beleefe I was, as I appeare, a Shepherdes, and Daughter to a Shepherd?[3]

Other shepherds and shepherdesses having come into the plain, the unhappy Urania endeavours to avoid them. She climbs a hill and comes to a cave, the first of these subterranean recesses mentioned in the story, but unfortunately not the last. A jaundiced reader might be forgiven for thinking of the *Urania* as a succession of caves, all full of royal personages, bemused and forewandered, who sit about endlessly narrating their misfortunes. On entering this, the first cave of the series, Urania penetrates to an inner chamber, and discovers a sonnet (newly written) lying on a stone table. A more remarkable discovery, however, is a young man, lying on a bed of boughs, raving with love and anguish of Limena. The Sidneian sentence is rather an involved medium for delirium, and we learn, only after much circumlocution, that this miserable wight is Persissus, nephew of the King of Sicilie. He recounts the story of Limena whom he believes murdered, and Urania very sensibly suggests that she may not be dead. If not, let him find her. If so, let him avenge her. Having thanked her in a speech of some thousand words, Persissus leaves the cave to follow her advice, and Urania drives home her flock.

Next day, Urania encounters a wolf, which is slain by two beautiful youths, who are seeking food for their aged father. Urania gives them for their food a lamb to which she has been confiding her troubles a few minutes before. They all repair to a sea-cave which shelters the aged father of Urania's rescuers. Having bewailed their respective fates in the loftiest language, they exchange mutual compliments, and Urania bids farewell to the old man (who is, in fact, the exiled King of Albania) and to his sons. She has not proceeded far when she meets still another beautiful youth: Parselius, Prince of Morea. He has left that country with his great friend and kinsman, Amphilanthus (heir to the Kingdom of Naples), with the object of finding the lost sister of Amphilanthus, who was stolen when an infant. It has been re-vealed to her father by divination that she is still living. (The reader immediately smells a rat, but alas! it takes hundreds of pages, a wilderness of misunderstandings and oceans of tears before it becomes perceptible to Urania.) Arrived in Sicily, Amphilanthus and Parselius go in different directions in their search, arranging to meet a year later at the court of the King of Naples. Parselius, while talking to Urania, sees in her a resemblance to Leonius, a younger brother of Amphilanthus, and he suspects her identity. He accompanies her to the cave where the King of Albania and his wolf-slaying sons have taken up quarters. Parselius engages to restore him to his rights, and the aged man dies of joy. Unfortunately, his sons are less susceptible to strong emotion. Parselius then goes to see Persissus (the distraught adorer of Limena) and Urania goes home, in love with Parselius.

It would serve no good purpose to continue to outline so complicated, repetitive and extravagant a plot. The scene shifts in kaleidoscopic fashion, and we find ourselves now in Pantaleria, now in Morea, now in Constantinople, Rhodes, Delos, Negropont, Pamphilia or Mytilene. But in fact the scene is always Arcadia, and the blue-blooded shepherds and shepherdesses remain ever faithful to the heroic-pastoral code. After many wanderings, exploits, and sufferings which serve merely to discover their enduring constancy, all the lovers are united, all the kings reinstated, and all the mysteries are resolved.

Since we have shown that Lady Mary devotedly copied the romantic characteristics of Sidney's novel, it is only just to show that like him she sometimes gives us beautiful little passages which are quite free from exaggeration. She has been describing a disputatious, angry man who has deafened the company with his talk, and she says:

> When he was gone, the Roome was like a calme after a storme, or as after foule weather the Aire is silent, and sweete; so all being quiet, they pleased themselves as Birds in the Spring with their own tunes.

It has been maintained by such critics as have thought it worth while to mention Lady Mary Wroath, that the *Urania is* only a slavish imitation of the *Arcadia*, and that in her novel Lady Mary Wroath 'copies and outdoes Sidney's utmost extravagances, both in the story and in the mode of telling it.'[4] Certainly the *Urania is* 'tedious . . . awkward and longwinded,'[5] but is it really more so than the *Arcadia?* One sometimes suspects the *Arcadia* of being so sacrosanct that it is not judged on its own merits even now. Horace Walpole had the courage to judge the *Arcadia* apart from the aura of its author. It was a critical honesty never displayed before and seldom since in this connection. Who will say that it is not wearying to plough through the *Arcadia*, or how many do so conscientiously, even in the cause of literary research? Indeed, it is so sacred that it is not often approached. The claims of the most learned commentators are not based on the intrinsic worth of the *Arcadia* — a question which they pass over almost in silence — but are entirely concentrated on its position in the development of English fiction, and on its influence on succeeding generations. Its position is said to emphasize the period of poetic invention which came between the period of traditional writing, and the development of realism. This is true, but it is perhaps more cogent to note that the *Arcadia* copied a mode of fiction which was passing, if not already past, and that, in consequence, the *Arcadia* is simply a digression in the development of the English novel. Its direct imitators were therefore splashing about in a backwater, while the main river and its tributaries flowed on surely to the open sea. As for the influence of the *Arcadia*, it is entirely to be deplored, and its occasional poetic beauties do not compensate for the fact that for long centuries English fiction was cursed with this heritage of artificial sentimentality. Certainly the French Heroic Romance was a most powerful influence in perpetuating this sort of writing in England, but it could not have had such a ready reception if Sidney had not already prepared the English mind for these extravagances, and established the Heroic Romance by force of his own personal and literary prestige.

The *Urania* sedulously copied, and possibly exaggerated, all the defects of the *Arcadia*, and if it could claim nothing individual it would simply not be worth mentioning. But this work of Lady Mary Wroath's does contain an individual feature of great interest and significance from the standpoint of fictional development; that is, the introduction of minor stories in subject and manner of the type of the *novelle*. These sub-plots are attached by very slender filaments to the main theme of the *Urania* and they are not ambitious in quality, but they give to the *Urania* the significance of uniting the realistic and the romantic genres. In a word, the *Urania* is not merely, like the *Arcadia*, representative of a decadent and retrogressive kind of fiction. It is also symptomatic of the way in which realism was developing in its own genre and was henceforth to obtrude itself in alien territory.

The best of these stories is that of Limena and Persissus. It is simple, direct, vivid. When the characters speak, they do so without circumlocutions. Limena is the daughter of a duke, who before departing for the wars in support of his king, bestows her in marriage on 'a great Lord in the Country,' named Philargus. This he does to ensure her safety and protection, but he does not take into account that Limena and a noble youth called Persissus are deeply in love with each other. Persissus, indeed, does not know that Limena loves him until he visits her some time after her marriage, in the home she shares with her husband and her father. They see each other frequently though innocently, but the husband is suspicious. 'That night,' says Persissus, 'I saw her, but spake not to her, so curiously her husband watched us, yet could he not keepe our eies, but by them we did deliver our soules.' The next day Philargus in his jealousy takes her away with him from their home; 'And so went all worth with this odd man to have her delicacy like a Diamond in a rotten box.' Persissus, however, takes the opportunity of seeing her on his way to camp, and she tells him of her husband's jealousy. Persissus had observed her paleness.

> Desirous to know the cause, I remain'd almost impatient not venturing to speak to her before her husband for hurting her; but he going out of the roome, after we had supped, either to cover the flames which were ready to break out in huge fires Of his mistrust, or to have the company fitter for him, affecting still to be chiefe: his absence, however, gave me opportunitie to demand the reason of her strangeness; she sigh'd to hear me call it so: and with tears told me the reason, concluding; and thus do you see my Lord (said she) the torments I suffer for our love; yet do you more torture me with doubting me, who have no happiness left me, but the knowledge of my faith to you, all afflictions being welcome to me, which for your sake I suffer. Between rage and paine, I remain'd amazed, till she, taking me by the hand, brought me more woefully to myselfe with these words. And yet am I brought to a greater mischiefe; with that fixing her weeping eyes upon mine . . . I must my Lord (said she) entreat you to refraine this place since none can tell what danger may proceed from mad, and unbridled jealousie; refraine your sight? Command me then to die (said I) have I deserved to be thus punished? Shall this brutishness undoe my blessings? Yet this place I will, since you will have it so, hoping you will find some means to let me know Philargus house is not in all places. That I will doe, or die (said she).

Persissus departs the next day. He gets news from Limena that her husband intends to murder her. Persissus gives the following description of the interview between husband and wife:

> After my departure from his house to the Citie, and so to the Campe, the Jealous wretch finding my Ladie retired into a Cabinet she had where she used to passe away some part of her unpleasant life; coming in, he shut the dore, drawing his sword and looking with as much fury, as jealous spite could with rage demonstrate, his breath short, his sword he held in his hand, his eyes sparkling as thick and fast as an

> unperfectly kindled fire with much blowing gives to the
> Blower, his tongue stammering with rage bringing forth
> these words; thou hast wrong'd me wild creature: I say thou
> hast wrong'd me; she who was compounded of virtue and
> her spirit, seeing his wild and distracted countenance guest
> the worst, wherefore mildly she gave this answere:
> Philargus, saide she, I know in mine owne heart I have not
> wrong'd you, and God knows I have not wrong'd myself.

There was no dialogue in the *Arcadia*. There is breathless dialogue here. There is dramatic urgency in the abrupt sentences, in the emphatic repetition, in the suspense which awaits violence. The simple dignity of the wife's reply makes the husband's fury seem all the more savage. This is how the scene might be described orally, by one who was actually present, and its spontaneous rightness, its realism is in complete contrast with the flowery Arcadian style. Space does not permit further quotation, so we must content ourselves with recounting briefly the remainder of the story. The husband is not depicted as a complete villain. We are shown love struggling in him before finally, through jealousy, it turns to hatred. He gives his wife two days in which to decide whether to lure Persissus to death or to die herself. She chooses to die, and Philargus takes her into a nearby wood. There he intends to murder her, but having inflicted some minor wounds, changes his mind. He takes her with him then into a distant retreat, and continues daily to torture her until she is rescued by a passing knight, who engages Philargus in combat and slays him. At that moment Persissus chances to pass that way. Philargus gives his blessing to the lovers before expiring, and they live happily ever after.

Limena's account of her sufferings is not in as realistic a style as Persissus's narrative, but although the end of the tale is rather romantic in language, it is quite just to say that this minor story is in substance and manner reminiscent of the *novelle*. Other stories worthy of mention in the same connection are that of Belizia which is good but brief, and the story of Bellamira which is also illustrative of the same trend.

It is not for a moment suggested that Lady Mary Wroath deliberately aimed at realism in those parts of the *Urania* which we have described. On the contrary, we know that she did everything in her power to imitate the style of the *Arcadia*. But apparently there were times when the strain of the Arcadian prose proved too great, and Lady Mary took a short respite to draw breath, before returning to her precarious and exhausting performance. It has been excellently said that 'Sidney in the "Arcadia" is like the coryphée in some elaborate ballet, swimming indefatigably through the mazes of an intricate dance.'[6] Lady Mary's weaker muscles craved relief from the exquisite agony of unnatural posturing, and in the intervals she became her real self. Perhaps, also, she was more at home in some of her tales, simply because she was drawing on events within her experience.

One cannot at this late date assert that Lady Mary's realistic little stories were those founded on the amorous adventures of some of her contemporaries. It is not possible now to identify the details of age old scandals, but we know that the book had, to some extent, a satiric intention and that it set Jacobean society by the ears. On December 15th Lady Mary wrote to Buckingham, assuring him that she had never intended her book to offend anyone, and stating that she had stopped its sale.[7] On March 9th, 1623, Chamberlain wrote to his friend Carleton, enclosing 'certain bitter verses of the Lord Denny upon the Lady Mary Wroath, for that in her book of *Urania* she doth palpably and grossly play upon him and his late daughter, the Lady Mary Hay, besides many others she makes bold with: and, they say, takes great liberty, or rather license to traduce whom she pleases, and thinks she dances in a net.' Chamberlain adds that he has seen the answer by Lady Mary to these verses of Lord Denny, but that he did not consider it worth the writing out.[8] These proofs make it clear that Lady Mary's declaration of innocence was disingenuous, and it is a sobering thought that the first woman-novelist in English literature could not refrain from that kind of veiled slander which later developed into the *histoire scandaleuse*. There was a vast moral and social gap between a Lady Mary and a Mrs Manley. Why did Sir Philip Sidney's niece stoop to besmirch a family record of nobility which so recently had been a national glory? Perhaps she had observed that, though the dead Sidney moved the hearts of men 'more than with a trumpet,' those same hearts were quite impervious to the misfortunes of his nearest descendant. Perhaps she realized that though the Countess of Pembroke was revered for literary feats which were either puerile or supposititious, the Lady Mary

Wroath could expect no indulgence from the literary world of which she was no longer the patron. It was precisely because she anticipated cold criticism that she larded her title-page with the names of those who had died at the zenith of fame, before they could commit the social solecism of becoming poor. The satiric intention in the *Urania* was not without antique precedent, for the Eclogues of Baptista Mantuanus satirized allegorically in pastoral dialogues the social and moral vices of fifteenth-century Italy. No doubt, in attacking her contemporaries, she aimed at making her book more saleable. Veiled slander, however, is not a passport to fame, however productive it may be of immediate notoriety. Even if the *Urania* were as good a book as John Barclay's *Argenis* which appeared in the same year, it would have had less permanent success, and less influence, because while political or social satire is sufficiently wide in aim to save it from an appearance of spite, personal satire always creates a revolution of feeling in its own time, and falls into oblivion when the earth lies heavily alike on the slanderer and the slandered.

It is unnecessary to comment on the fact that Lady Mary copied, in the Urania, the practice of introducing verse into the romance. This custom, to which Sidney adhered in the *Arcadia*, was of Italian origin, and was certainly no advantage to prose fiction. Most of Lady Mary's poetry is facile and superficial. In dismissing it, however, one may mention some verses which combine sincerity and grace: chiefly 'Love, what art thou?' 'Come, merry Spring, delight us,' and 'Who can blame me if I love?' She used the sonnet with little depth, but with great mastery of form. The perfect Italian form of sonnet 4 is worthy of note.

It is a paradox that Lady Mary Wroath's best claim to remembrance lies in her accidental realism. Two other women wrote Arcadian novels. In 1651, Anne Weamys published *A continuation of Sir Philip Sydney's Arcadia*, which had its second edition in 1690. When she wrote it a king had been beheaded, and England had been convulsed in political revolution and civil war; when it was republished, a king had returned, bringing with him a new era in national and literary history — a curious proof, if proof were needed, of the divorce between the Pastoral and the real, of the difficulty of killing a romantic school of writing, and of its escapist nature. Between the two editions of the *Continuation* appeared Mlle de la Roche Guilhem's *Almanzor and Almanzaida. A Novel written by Sir Philip Sidney, And found since his Death amongst his Papers.* This work merits no particular attention, but it will not be out of place to comment on the novel of Anne Weamys.

The full title of this novel defined the particular subject-matter of the narrative:

> *A CONTINUATION of Sir Philip Sydney's Arcadia*
> *wherein is handled the Loves of Amphialus and Helena*
> *Queen of Corinth, Prince Plangus and Erona*
> *With the Historie of the Loves of Old Claius and*
> *Young Strephon to Urania*
> *Written by a young Gentlewoman*
> *Mtis A.W.*

Thomas Heath, the bookseller, woos the 'ingenious Reader' in an introductory letter. He begs him not to marvel that heroic Sidney's renowned fancy should be pursued to a close by a feminine pen. Here is 'Sir Philip's fantasie incarnate: both Pamela's Majestie and Philoclea's Humilitie exprest to the life in the person and style of this Virago. In brief, no other than the lively Ghost of Sidney, by a happie transmigration, speaks through the organs of this inspired Minerva.'

It is to be feared that the lively ghost of Sidney would not endorse Heath's volatile words. In fact, if it were possible for lively ghosts to tear their hair, then indeed Sir Philip's locks would fall thick as autumnal leaves. Granted that a continuation always lacks cohesion with the original work, at least it should aim at artistic unity, and it should have for its object the same aesthetic principles. Sidney was guided by the principle that all imaginative invention was poetry, and to this end he evolved a prose style which was intended to be poetic, and which in its billowing, emotional prolixity was in itself a figure of the romantic complications which it expressed. Though Anne Weamys continues the adventures of some of Sidney's characters, she does not do so in Sidneian prose. Lady Mary Wroath imitated Sir Philip Sidney's style with more or less success, and occasionally lapsed into everyday language. Anne Weamys never lapses into everyday language, and never attempts Sidneian prose. She never attempts it — not because she could not. Her writing has a consistent style of its own which shows her ability to govern language. She tells her story in a pastoral manner, but she avoids the swaying garrulity of Sidney's style, and expresses herself in a style which, though certainly romantic, is clear, straightforward and economical. Let us for a moment ignore the story which has really nothing to do with our contention, and support our argument by comparing certain characteristic manners of writing. Here is Sir Philip Sidney's description of the love of Pyrocles for Philoclea:

> Pyrocles, who had that for a law unto him, not to leave Philoclea in anything unsatisfied, although he still remained in his former purpose, and knew that time would grow short for it, yet hearing no noise, the shepherds being as then run to Basilius, with settled and humble countenance, as a man that should have spoken of a thing that did not concern himself, bearing even in his eyes sufficient shows that it was nothing but Philoclea's danger which did anything burden his heart, far stronger than fortune, having with vehement embracing of her got yet some fruit of his delayed end, he thus answered the wise innocency of Philoclea: 'Lady, most worthy not only of life, but to be the very life of all things; the more notable demonstrations you make of love so far beyond my desert, with which it pleaseth you to overcome fortune, in making me happy: the more am I, even in course of humanity, to leave that love's force which I neither can nor will leave, bound to seek requital's witness that I am not ungrateful to do which, the infiniteness of your goodness being such as I cannot reach unto it, yet doing all I can and paying my life which is all I have, though it be far, without measure, short of your desert, yet shall I not die in debt to my own duty.[9]

'Faire Mistress' (says Nicholas Breton, once in the service of Sir Philip Sidney, and on Sidney's death devoted to the service of the Duchess of Pembroke):

> Faire Mistresse, to court you with eloquence were as ill as to grieve you with fond tales: let it therefore please you rather to believe what I write, than to note how I speake . . . I could commend you above the skies, compare you with the Sun, or set you among the Stars, figure you with the Phoenix, imagine you a goddesse, but I will leave such weak praising fictions, and think you only yourself, whose vertuous beauty, and whose honourable discretion in the care of a little kindnesse is able to command the love of the wise, and the labours of the honest.[10]

Anne Weamys gives the following description of the love-sick Plangus:

> In this sweet place, he sat himself down, with an intention to rest his wearied limbs under a branched tree, whilest his servants refreshed themselves and baited their horses, but no ease could be harboured in his disquieted heart, his eys being no sooner closed, but that he saw Erona burning in their unmerciful fire: at which sight he staringly opened them, and determined with himself, that since sleep would procure no comfort to him, other than Tragical scenes, he would never enjoy any contentment before he had settled Erona in her throne in safetie.[11]

One observes that Anne Weamys' style is neither as flowery as Sidney's, nor as direct as Breton's. If, however, we compared her with Breton alone, her pastoral romantics would seem emphasized. She thus describes a summer morning:

> At last he entered the pleasant country of *Arcadia*, which was adorned with stately woods: no cries were heard there but the lambs, and they in sport too sounded their voices to make their playfellow lambs answer them again in imitation of the like. And the abundance of shadie trees that were there, were beautiful with the sweet melodie of birds.

But Breton exclaims, in his *Merry Dialogue*:

> Oh, to see in a faire morning, or a Sunnie evening the lambes and Rabbits at bace, the birds billing, the fishes playing, and the flowers budding. Who would not leave the drinking in an Alehouse, the wrangling in a dicing house, the Lying in a market, and the cheating in a fayre; and think that the brightness of a faire day doth put down all the beauties of the world.[12]

This world of Breton's is the real world, and he wrote in the springtime of realism, when the sap was running free in the youthful stock and showing its energy in proliferation. Anne Weamy's style was very far from this, but it was far also from the style of Sidney. She could steady herself to write with dignified incisiveness such passages as the following:

> It is Justice to bring murderers to their deserved punishments. And because you Prince Plangus testifie yourself to be such an affectionate friend to my dear children, shew

53

yourself one in their revenge; you I will entrust to be the General of my Armie; prove as valiant now as you have ever done; let all your aim be at Plexirtus; and, if possible, convey him hither alive, that he may die a publick spectacle of shame and terror before all the People.[13]

As for the plot of the *Continuation,* it is complicated, but well constructed. It is a noticeable fact that, in a period of literary long-windedness, and in a medium which has always connoted prolixity, Anne Weamys tells her involved story without a single digression, and without a single ambiguity. No doubt there are parts which are too synoptic, and which might have pleased more if they had been elaborated, but this is the fault of her very good quality of verbal economy. Anne Weamys subscribes to the Pastoral convention, but she keeps one eye on real life. Her heroes and heroines (and there are about ten of them) show energy and common sense in achieving their purposes, and never evince the slightest inclination to confide their troubles to lambs. They pursue a life which contains love and adventure — too much love and too much adventure to be realistic, but also too much realism to be truly pastoral. Anne Weamys' book is at the parting of the ways. Mopsa, in the *Continuation* is presented with humour. Her fairy-tale of the King's daughter is really funny, and is told with all the deviousness and love of proverb one would expect in such a narrative.

To conclude, the works of Lady Mary Wroath and of Anne Weamys are of value, because of their position in regard to the romantic and the realistic schools. The social position of these writers made it inevitable that they should choose the aristocratic medium. Had a woman of a lower social stratum wished to write a novel, she would, no doubt, have gravitated towards the realistic fiction of her class, but in point of fact no such woman could have written a book at that period, because she would have lacked the necessary education. Women of the upper classes, in Elizabethan and Jacobean times, had such 'education' as permitted them to read romances. They had no education in the real sense of the word. Naturally, the books they read were those written for their own social class, and very often dedicated actually to their sex, for in that period well-bred women assumed an important position as readers of fiction. Such works, for example, as Lyly's *Euphues* were dedicated to feminine readers. If a female were actually entreated to read such works, then a female, greatly daring, might write one — if she could. But to begin one's career in fiction with no choice but the Pastoral medium might well have daunted the stoutest feminine spirit. Lady Elizabeth Carew, for example, wrote a play,[14] but the drama with its acts, and scenes, gave, as it were, a neat form into which one might pour one's ideas, and this form was far shorter and required less of a sustained effort. The construction of the pastoral novel, and the exigencies of the style were such feats for these first women-novelists, that one can only liken it to a child who achieves an *entrechat* before he has learnt to stand. Both women are best in their more realistic vein — so that however small their contribution it was in accordance with the vital trend in fiction. 'Be eloquent in plainness' said Nicholas Breton, 'You must not speak in the clouds to them that are acquainted with the moon.'[15] We shall see in the following chapter whether other women writers were able to comply with this injunction.

Notes and References

1 See *The Prose Writings of Heinrich Heine* (1887), 'Religion and Philosophy in Germany,' p. 163 ff.
2 Published by Wynkyn de Worde, 1577.
3 Lady Mary Wroath, *Urania* (1621), i, p. 1.
4 E. A. Baker, *History of the English Novel* (1929), iii, p. 88.
5 *D.N.B.*
6 E. A. Baker, *History of the English Novel* (1929), iii, p. 88.
7 Hist. MSS. Comm. 2nd Rep., p. 60.
8 *Court and Times of James I*, ii, p. 298; Calendar of State Papers. Dom. 1619–23, p. 356; Hist. MSS. Comm. 3rd Rep., p. 179. Hatfield. MSS.
9 Sir Philip Sidney, *Arcadia* (ed. Baker, 1907), Book IV, p. 545.
10 *The Works in Verse and Prose of Nicholas Breton* (ed. Grosart, 1879): 'Letter of Love to a Gentlewoman' (No. 19).
11 Anne Weamys, *The Continuation of Sir Philip Sydney's Arcadia* (1651), pp. 10, 11.
12 *The Works in Verse and Prose of Nicholas Breton*, (ed. Grosart, 1879): 'A Merry Dialogue,' originally published in 1603.
13 Anne Weamys, *Continuation* (1651), p. 288.
14 *Marianne, or the Fair Maid of Jewry*.
15 *The Works in Verse and Prose of Nicholas Breton* (ed. Grosart, 1879): 'A Post with a Packet of Mad Letters,' (No. 19).

Chapter III

Biography

There is nothing I dread more than Death, I do not mean the
Strokes of Death, nor the pains, but the oblivion in Death.

Tears are apt to flow especially from moist brains. But deep
sorrow hath dry eyes, silent tongues and aching hearts.

(Both from the *Sociable Letters* of the Duchess of Newcastle)

From the Arcadian shepherdesses to the representation of real
women in fiction was a great transition, and it was long before this
gap was bridged. In the meantime however, we are not without
testimony as to the manner in which women of flesh and blood
acquitted themselves in the environment in which it was their fate
to live. We may listen to their voices endeavouring to relate how
they fared in the complicated adventure of life. Such records remain
in biographical form.

In the second half of the seventeenth century, four women
wrote biographies. They were the Countess of Montgomery, the
Duchess of Newcastle, Mrs Lucy Hutchinson and Lady Fanshawe.
Their narratives are simply the written testimony of actual fact,
but nevertheless they are significant in the development of
prose fiction.

The biography is a form of writing which is analogous to fiction
and which became a recognized fictional form. It requires sound
construction and the sustained power of telling a story. In structure,
therefore, its kinship with the novel is obvious. In treatment, both
genres require imagination, with this fundamental difference that
the biographer may not invent or adapt his material as the novelist
does. But in the biography, as in the novel, the imagination is exercised by the need for selectivity, artistic emphasis and vivid

56

presentation. These characteristics give the biography a quality not easily distinguished from fiction of the simple narrative form. This parallelism is extremely important, as it paved the way for the pseudo-biographies which from very early times had been presented as truthful narratives. Such literary imposition arose from the necessity of disarming the suspicions with which the reading public regarded fiction. Readers continued to be haunted by the old classical tradition of authenticity, and they enjoyed their feigned stories with a freer conscience if they were assured that these stories were veracious accounts of actual happenings. The biography was a type of prose narrative which originally was its own guarantee of truth, so it was natural that writers of fiction, who wished to give plausibility to their narratives, should take advantage of this self-authenticating form. The biographical form was indeed so much used as a passport to credulity that it became difficult to distinguish a true narrative from mere fiction. Now, it is clear that to have an appearance of authenticity, a narrative should record credible events, and should depict them in a convincing manner, that is to say, in a realistic manner. Thus, this pseudo-authentic kind of writing was a powerful agent in the development of realistic fiction. Finally, as we have already remarked, the real and the invented telescoped, and facts presented as fiction seemed ultimately to belong to the same genre as fiction which was circumstantially vouched for as fact. Realistic fiction was served by pseudo-authentic biography, which in turn, was modelled on real biography. We cannot therefore adequately review the work of women in prose fiction without examining their earlier efforts as biographers. It should be remembered that biographies written by women, after prose fiction had established its right to independence, have a separate existence, and therefore do not come within our scope. The most immature biography, at this elementary stage of fiction, is of more significance than the most perfect biography at the period when biography and prose fiction had established themselves as distinct genres of writing — the reason being that women who tried to tell a story of real events were in the main stream of realistic story-telling, whether or not their stories were true.

Because of their sex, it was daring of Lady Mary Wroath and Anne Weamys to write, but they had employed a form which was considered to be poetry, and which, furthermore, was sanctified by its greatest exponent in England. Had they attempted a *Jack of*

Newberie or some other form of democratic fiction, it would have been considered an outrage. The four women whose writings we are about to consider also chose a safe medium, because, although biography cannot naturally be considered as poetry, neither is it a feigned tale. Not indeed that the Duchess of Newcastle would have given a fig for such conventions if she had chosen to write a romance, but actually she had the most complete scorn for 'romanceys,' which she stigmatizes as the adulterous offspring of History and Poetry — a significant remark. To Lucy Hutchinson, as a rigid Puritan, romances were anathema. Whatever were the views of Lady Fanshawe, her wanderings gave no leisure for writing. The Countess of Montgomery's life was not of a kind to give her much faith in romance, and in addition, hers was the sort of mind which prefers facts not softened by illusion.

Anne Clifford, fourth Countess of Montgomery, was more redoubtable as a woman than as a writer. In fact, she never aimed at a literary production, and her biography is little more than a summary of the main events of her life. Probably she undertook it to verify for the benefit of her children her claim to the Clifford possessions in the North of England, which had been the object of litigation for thirty-eight years of her life. There are touches in the narrative however, which show that it was to her something more satisfying than a mere deposition of facts that might be useful to her legal heirs. The manuscript in the first person, as written by the Countess, has never been published. It was copied by Henry Fisher (1737), and this copy is available in the British Museum. *The Proceedings of the Archaeological Institute at York,* edited by Hailstone in 1846, contains a third-person version of the autobiography. This account was taken from a small quarto volume containing an abstract of the great volumes of records which were 'collected by the care and painfull industry of Margaret Russell, Countess Dowager of Cumberland, out of the various offices and courts of this Kingdom, to prove the right title which her only childe, the Lady Anne Clifford, now Countess of Pembroke, had to the inheritance of her ancestors.' The original first-person account is naturally more vivid and more authentic, and has therefore, been used by the present writer. It is part of a manuscript entitled: *A summary of the Lives of the Veteriponts, Cliffords and Earls of Cumberland, And of the Ladye Anne, Countess Dowager of Pembroke, Dorsett, And Montgomery, and Daughter and Heir to George Clifford Earl of Cumberland, in whom ye name of the said Cliffords determined! Copied from ye original manuscript ye 29th of December 1737 by Henry Fisher.* Then follows the heading: *A summary of the Records, and a True memorial of the life of me the Lady Anne Clifford.* Her titles are fully appended.

Anne Clifford began to write her autobiography when she was sixty-three years old. Twenty-four years later the narrative was broken off by her death, but it was practically complete then, enumerating all the main events of her life from the moment of her birth. Enumerating but not describing — that is the main characteristic of Anne Clifford's writing — for nothing which she records is as astounding as her omissions. This woman lived under six reigns — Elizabeth, James I, Charles I, the Commonwealth, Charles II, and James II, and yet she contrives to say nothing at all about the great fluctuations in government, in religion, in social life, and in literature which constituted the background of her life. She has nothing to say of Elizabeth's court, nothing to say of Jacobean times or of the Mayflower's sailing; nothing to say of Cromwell, or of the beheading of Charles. She makes two references to the Civil War one being that, as it were 'very hot,' it was necessary for her to change her residence; the other, a remark that her estates in the north were for a time rendered profitless by these disturbances. She does not profess herself an adherent of either party. Of the extraordinary event of the Restoration, of the surprising marriage of James II, and of the insecurity of his rule she has still nothing to say. She never refers to a single literary work, out of all the poems, plays, romances, polemics, and multiform writings which deluged England during her lifetime, and many of which she certainly read. She is silent as to the changing social customs which she saw arise and decline within her span. Only once does she designate a friend, and an enemy. Certainly it is true that she dictated her narrative to a secretary, and that it would therefore be necessary for her to keep her own counsel as to private matters, but there are many omissions and reticences which discretion did not require, and one is at a loss to explain them. Perhaps she believed that commentary should not be included in a biography. Perhaps she was so busied in performing all that she deemed necessary before death snatched her away, that she saw little value in recording her thoughts. She was a practical woman, and when she wrote she was already old.

What was she doing for the eighty-seven years of her life? She was involved in a tedious law-suit. Her mother died. She had two worthless husbands and seven children. She gained possession of her estates, and restored them. But this is merely the framework of a life, within which the mind and character would demonstrate themselves. Not from her utterances, but from her reticences are her mind and character revealed, and it needs the external testimony of her contemporaries to fill in the outline of her personality: 'She had a clear soul shining through a vivid body,'[1] said Dr Rainbow, who preached her funeral sermon. 'She knew well how to discourse of all things, from predestination to slea-silk.'[2] testified Dr Donne. 'Her house was a school for the young, and a retreat for the aged; an asylum for the persecuted, a college for the learned, and a pattern for all.'[3] It is characteristic that this woman who never refers to Spenser, had a monument erected to him in Westminster Abbey. Neither did she mention the poet Daniel, her tutor, nor the verses he dedicated to her in her youth, but the memorial to him in Beckington Church is the material testimony of her affection.

Anne Clifford was of a strong and undemonstrative character, not imaginative, quite free from sentimentality, but capable of deep feeling. She was inflexibly tenacious of her rights, meticulously observant of the rights of others; frugal in her own way of living, extremely generous to her friends and dependants. Her benevolence and her sense of justice rose above her sense of injury, as is well seen in the fact that she even educated and portioned the illegitimate children of her first husband. She never was, however, a sweet, suffering saint, but was strongly combative of any infringement of her proper prerogatives. However dubious the authenticity of the letter she is supposed to have sent to Sir Joseph Williamson, in style and sentiment it is very characteristic. Williamson, then secretary of state to Charles II, had written to the Countess, naming a candidate for her pocket borough of Appleby. The following answer is ascribed to her:

> I have been bullied by an usurper, I have been neglected by a Court, but I will not be dictated to by a subject. Your man sha'n't stand. — Anne Dorset, Pembroke and Montgomery.

Anne Clifford was born at Skipton Castle on the 30th January, 1590. The woman of sixty-three looks back over the years, and thus describes the childish self she remembers:

I was very happy in my first Constitution both in mind and body, both for internal and external endowments, for never was there child more equally resembling both father and mother and my self, ye color of mine Eyes were black like my father, & ye form and aspect of ym was quick & lively like my Mothers, the hair of my head was brown & very thick, & so long yt it reached to the calf of my legs, when I stood upright, with a peak of hair on my forehead, & a Dimple in my Chin, like my father full Cheeks & round face like my Mother, & an exquisite shape of body resembling my father, but now time & age hath long since ended all those beauties, which are to be compared to the grass of the field. Isaiah 40.6.7.8. 1 Pet. 1.24. for now when I caused those memorables to be written I have passed the 63d year of my Age. And tho I say it, the perfection of my Mind, were much above those of my body; I had a strong and copious memory, a sound Judgment and a discerning Spirit, and so much of a strong imagination in me, as that many times even my Dreams & apprehensions before hand have proved to be true.

Her father died when Anne was about sixteen years old, and by his will all his castles, lands and honours were left to his brother, Francis, who succeeded him in the earldom, and to Francis' male heirs, but all these possessions were to revert to Anne if the male heirs failed. Anne chose as legal guardian her mother who at once began 'to sue out a Livery in the Court of Wards for my right to all my fathers lands by way of prevention to hinder . . . the livery which my Uncle of Cumberland intended to sue out in my name, without either my consent or my mother's.' Thus the great law-suit began its tortuous course.

Anne Clifford was married in 1609 to Richard Sackville, afterwards second Earl of Dorset. By him she had three sons, all of whom died young, and two daughters: Margaret, who married the subsequent Earl of Thanet, and Isobel, who married the third Earl of Northampton.

In 1616, Anne's mother died, about six weeks after Anne had visited her for the last time:

And the 2nd of that April 1616, I took my last leave of my Dear & blessed Mother with Many tears & much sorrow to us both. Some quarter of a mile from Brougham Castle in ye open Air after which time she and I never saw one another.

Of all the afflictions which beset Anne Clifford this was the heaviest, and again and again she recurs to this focal point of pain. In fact, in no other point was she very vulnerable, as she later explains.

After she had been married for fifteen years, her husband died. Her life with him had made her averse to marrying again, and this disinclination was confirmed by an attack of small-pox, which destroyed her good looks. She did marry, however, in 1630, and it seems probable that she was influenced in this decision by her feeling that a powerful connection would strengthen her legal claims: 'This 2nd Marriage of Mine was wonderfully brought to pass by ye providence of God, for the crossing and disappointage, ye envy, Malice, & Sinister practices of my Enemies.' This husband was Philip Herbert, Earl of Pembroke and Montgomery, Lord Chamberlain of the King's Household, and Knight of the Garter. He was the son of Mary Herbert, second Countess of Pembroke, the nephew to Sir Philip Sydney, and the first cousin of Lady Mary Wroath.

To the third Countess of Montgomery Lady Mary had dedicated the *Urania*, but Anne Clifford stood in no danger of dedications from the Sydney family. In disposition she was quite unpoetic, although she exerted a pastoral care over all her belongings. Philip Herbert, however, vied with her in business acumen, and it was not long before he brought pressure to bear on his wife so that she should force her younger daughter Isobel to marry one of his younger sons. This was but the starting point of their differences, and after four and a half years, Anne lived apart, having left the Court at Whitehall on 18th December, 1634, 'by reason of some discontents.' This discreet explanation was no doubt worded thus so as to keep her secret from the secretary who wrote at her dictation. The true explanation appears in a letter to her uncle, Edward, Earl of Bedford,[4] in which she entreats him to obtain her husband's consent that she may go to London to transact some business. She says: 'I dare not venther to come upe witheoutt his leve, lest he shoulld take that occasion to turne mee out of this howse, as he did outt of Whitehall, and then I shall not know wher to put my hede.'

In 1647, Isobel married James Compton, Earl of Northampton, 'but I was not yr present at ye Marriage for many reasons' — obviously to avoid further friction with her husband, or because he compelled her to absent herself. She had succeeded to all the disputed property on the death of her first cousin without male issue in 1643, and so was in a position to defy her husband if she had so wished, but she did not intend to expose her matrimonial troubles by openly ignoring her husband's wishes. That she was on friendly terms with Isobel is clear, since on June 3rd, 1649, she went to visit her at Islington prior to travelling north to enter into her possessions. Before going to Islington she took leave of her husband 'in his lodging in ye Cockpit' — a last farewell, actually, since he died seven months later. She was at Appleby when the news reached her, and she did not return to London for the funeral. She had never been a hypocrite.

She did not remember either of her husbands with bitterness, and speaks of that part of her life with justice and restraint. She had never submitted to a husband in the management of her own personal affairs. She might have been a happier woman if she had been weaker, but suffering is invariably the price of strength.

> I must confess [she says] with inexpressible thankfulness that tho' through the goodness of Almighty God, & the mercies of my Saviour Christ Jesus Redeemer of the World, I was born a happy Creature in Mind, body & fortune, & that those 2 lords of mine to whom I was afterwards by the Divine Providence marryed, were in their Several Kinds worthy Noblemen as any then were in this Kingdom, yet was it my misfortune to have Contradictions and Crosses with them both, with my first Lord, about the desire he had to make me sell my Rights in ye lands of my Antient inheritance for Mony, which I never did, nor never would Consent unto, insomuch as this matter was the cause of a long Contention betwixt us, as also for his profuseness in consuming his estate & some other extravagancies of his; and with my 2nd Lord, because my Youngest Daughter, the lady Isabella Sackvill, would not be brought to marry one of his younger sons, and that I would not relinquish my Interest I had in 5000 pounds, being part of her portion, out of my lands in Craven, nor did there want diverse malicious illwillers to blow & forment the Coals of Dissention betwixt us, so as in both their lifetimes, the Marble Pillars of Knowle in Kent, & Wilton in Wiltshire were to me oftentimes but the gay harbour of Anguish, insomuch as a wise man yt Knew the insides of my fortune, would often say that I lived in both these My Lords great familys as the River of Roan or Rodamus runs through the lake of Geneva, without Mingling any part of its Streams with that lake, for I gave myself wholly to retiredness as much as I could in both those great families, & made good books and virtuous thoughts my Companions, which can never discern affliction, nor be

daunted when it unjustly happens, and by a happy Genius I
overcame all those troubles . . . the prayers of my blessed
Mother helping me therein.

Anne Clifford was fifty-three years when she gained her estates;
six years later she entered into the north, and the joy that attended
her gives vivid life to the narrative. This happiness is expressed
mainly in computing how long it has been since she last saw
these childhood scenes. She stays from July to August 7th at
Skipton Castle where she was born, and most of which had since
been destroyed by order of Parliament as it was used as a Cavalier
stronghold during the Civil Wars. She says: 'I was never till now
in any part of ye castle, since I was 9 or 10 weeks.' From there she
visited the old Tower at Barden for the first time. On August 8th,
1649, she goes to stay at Appleby Castle:

> I came into Appleby Castle, ye most antient Seat of my Inheri-
> tance & lay in my own Chamber there, where I used formerly
> to lye with my Dear Mother & there I continued to lye till
> about ye 13th of Feb. following, this 8th of Aug. being the 1st
> time yt I came into ye sd Appleby Castle ever since I went out
> of it with My Dr. Mother ye 8th day of October in 1607.

There had been an interval of forty-two years. Time has no
power over a loving heart, but love ever seeks some defence
against oblivion. So it was that Anne Clifford erected a memorial
pillar at the very place on the road between Appleby and Penrith
where she and her mother had their last parting.

That Christmas of 1649 she held at Appleby, as she had done
the previous year at Skipton. Through many storms she had won
to peace, and there was fulfilment in her old age which her youth
was denied. She had endured much, and the litigious struggle
was at the root of all her great contentions. In maintaining her
rights, she adhered to her mother's parting counsel, and so
achieved a double fidelity.

> From Many Noble progenitors I hold Transmitted lands,
> Castles & Honours which they swayed of old . . . And in
> this settled abode of Mine, in these 3 antient houses of mine
> inheritance Appleby Castle & Brougham Castle in Westmore-
> land, and Skipton Castle . . . in Craven, I do more and
> more fall in love with ye Contentments & Innocent pleasures

> of a Country life, with humor of mind, I do wish with all my
> heart . . . may be confirmed on my posterity, yt are to suc-
> ceed me in those places, for a wise body ought to make their
> own home ye place of self fruition, & ye comfortablest pt of
> their life.

Her happiness lasted twenty-seven years, and she died at the age of eighty-seven, having worn out all her troubles by sheer longevity.

A biography which merely chronicles events is not a good biography. It is the infrequent glimpses of Anne Clifford's mind which render her manuscript worth reading, and it is strange to notice that, despite her complete discretion, her strong personality impresses itself upon her measured words. The three motifs in the narrative represent the three main forces which went to the moulding of her life: religion, love for her mother, and deter-mination to succeed to the Clifford possessions. Her particularity in regard even to unimportant dates, her reminiscent discoveries of odd coincidences as to time and place, and her continual repe-tition of facts show the senescent mind. She died before the manuscript was completed, and she does not appear to have made any effort to revise it. Hence many facts which might have been incorporated in the narrative hang raggedly about its fringe.

Her secretary writes the final page, in which he describes very simply her last few days of life. The closing words stress that ances-tral note which was most fitting to the death of such a woman.

> After she had endured all her pains with a most Christian
> fortitude, always answering those that asked her how she did,
> with I thank you, I am very well, which were her last words
> directed to mortals, she with much cheerfulness in her own
> chamber in Brougham Castle in Westmoreland wherein her
> noble father and her blessed mother died, yielded up her
> precious soul into ye hands of her Merciful Redeemer.

In the brilliant days of the Restoration, when Anne Clifford was finding such deep happiness in Cumberland, an extraordinary woman might very occasionally be seen in London. Her rare visits were one of the sights of the town, and never failed to arouse the vociferous delight of the populace, the tittering amusement of the fashionable, and the puzzled disgust of conventional citizens. The Count of Grammont thought he saw one evening:

As I was getting out of my chair, I was stopped by the devil
of a phantom in masquerade . . . It is worth while to see
her dress; for she must have at least sixty ells of gauze and
silver tissue about her, not to mention a sort of pyramid
upon her head, adorned with a hundred thousand baubles.
'I bet,' said the king, 'that it is the Duchess of Newcastle.'[5]

Pepys really saw her one April day, and records the event
with all the gusto of a child describing a circus:

Met my Lady Newcastle going with her coaches and
footmen all in velvet; herself (whom I never saw before), as I
have heard her often described, for all the town talk is now-
a-days of her extravagances, with her velvet cap, her hair
about her ears, many black patches . . . about her mouth,
naked-necked, without anything about it, and a black just-
au-corps. She seemed to me a very comely woman, but I
hope to see more of her on May-day.[6]

He saw her again on May 30th, as she went to attend the Royal
Society, and this time, the novelty having staled, he did not like her
at all and feared she might make the Royal Society ridiculous, 'as
her dress was so antick and her deportment so ordinary.'[7] Evelyn,
received with great kindness at the Newcastle house at Clerkenwell,
stresses, although with pleasure, 'the extraordinary fanciful habit,
garb, and discourse of the Duchess.'[8] Such was the universal judgment of her contemporaries on Margaret Cavendish, Duchess of
Newcastle — commonly called 'Mad Madge.'

Who could depict with a mere pen's point this dear, delightful,
opinionated, child-like, fantastic genius? One may draw a rhombus
to represent a diamond, and sketch in some radiating lines to suggest the effulgence of light, the depth, the colours, the fluctuating
radiance. But such a sketch would only be a crude diagram, unless
the mind which knows the quality of the precious stone evokes
from memory its dazzling light. The Duchess of Newcastle was a
diamond of the first water, partly obscured by its original covering
of clay, uncut save for a facet or two which sent out a fitful and ill-
balanced brilliance. Her genius was so productive and so various,
her ideas so original and so ill-regulated, her vision so exalted, her
ignorance so profound, her style alternately so preposterous and so
perfect, that one despairs of ever reducing to the cold canons of
criticism the inspired confusion of her works.

Of the many women whose intellectual powers were rendered ineffectual by a want of education, the Duchess of Newcastle is an outstanding example. Like other well-bred women, she had had her tutors, who were paid to give a semblance of schooling, but who were not even supposed to exact the discipline of study. A young lady could read, write and cipher, she could chatter a foreign language, dance, and play the virginals, embroider and make bead bags. In the name of common sense what more could any one expect? Let her carry her 'education' as she would a handkerchief — in case she should need it. It were unnecessary, and indeed rather ill-bred to make great play with either or flourish them about. But Margaret Newcastle was haunted by a dual hunger — for knowledge and for fame. She wanted to know 'whether it be possible to make men and other Animal creatures that naturally have no wings, flie as birds do?' 'Whether the Optick Perception is made in the Eye or Brain, or in both?' 'Whether there could be self-knowledge without Perception?' 'Whether snails have a row of small teeth orderly placed in the gums?' Such knowledge was not forthcoming, and the undisciplined and voracious mind raced on to other fields of enquiry. There was not time enough in eternity to know all she wished to know, or to write all she felt impelled to write. She writes so fast that she cannot stay to format the letters properly. She never revises. She fills twelve folio volumes, and the more she writes the more her readers tap their foreheads significantly, and rock with laughter. She knows, but she does not care. If writing is a disease, then countless great men have been at death's door. 'All I desire is fame,' she says; and again: 'I have an Opinion, which troubles me like a conscience, that 'tis a part of Honour to aspire to Fame.'[9]

> As for learning, that I am not versed in it, no body, I hope, will blame me for it, since it is sufficiently known, that our Sex is not bred up to it, as being not suffer'd to be instructed in Schools and Universities; I will not say, but many of our Sex may have as much Wit, and be capable of Learning as well as Men; but since they want Instructions, it is not possible they should attain to it; for Learning is Artificial, but Wit is Natural.[10]

Writing over two centuries later, Sir Egerton Brydges says:

> That the Duchess was deficient in a cultivated judgment; that her knowledge was more multifarious than exact; and that her

powers of fancy and sentiment were more active than her powers of reasoning, I will admit; but that her productions mingled as they are with great absurdities, are wanting either in talent, or in virtue, or even in genius, I cannot concede.[11]

Disraeli supports the same view:

Her labours have been ridiculed by some wits, but had her studies been regulated she would have displayed no ordinary genius . . . Her verses have been imitated even by Milton.[12]

And finally in the following criticism we find the same judgement more fully expressed:

There are [in the writings of the Duchess] the indisputable evidences of a genius as highborn in the realms of intellect as its possessor was in the ranks of society: a genius strong-winged and swift, fertile and comprehensive, but ruined by deficient culture, by literary dissipation and the absence of two powers without which thoughts are only stray morsels of strength, I mean Concatenation and the Sense of Propor-tion. She thought without system, and set down everything she thought. Her fancy turning round like a kaleidoscope changed its patterns and lines with the most whimsical variety and rapidity. Nevertheless, I believe, had the mind of this woman been disciplined and exercised by early cul-ture and study, it would have stood out remarkable among the feminine intellects of our history.[13]

Happily, however, two of the Duchess of Newcastle's works are free from those fixed ideas and exaggerated fancies which distort her other writings. These are the two biographical works which we are about to consider. In them, the turgid current of her thought flows clearly and surely to the end she had in view.

In 1656,[14] appeared *Natures Pictures drawn by Francie's Pencil* . . . which contained, as the eleventh and last book *The True Relation of My Birth, Breeding and Life*. It preserves, as all autobiographies should, the quintessence of the writer's individuality.

Anne Clifford had presented a chain of events with few com-ments. Margaret Newcastle presents thoughts in which events are caught like flies in amber. She does not lose her way in the tangled happenings of her career, because external events never constituted her life. Life to her was thought. Well might she say: 'I have made a world of my own.'[15] Out of the press and hurry of the years she gathered something timeless — a conception of values which took its nature from her own personality. She might have been embittered by her misfortunes, intoxicated by her powers of endurance, made querulous by her poverty, or disillusioned by that spiritual weariness which always follows the triumph of a political cause. But she had an inner existence against which the tide of external events beat in vain. She does not particularize her backgrounds, and yet she gives sufficient to convey a feeling of vivid intimacy. The depth of her judgements, the unpretentious sincerity of her story and the steady undercurrent of emotion which carries it onward give this biography an unforgettable pathos and beauty.

In 1667, the Duchess published *The Life of the Thrice noble, high and puissant Prince, William Cavendish, Duke . . . of Newcastle*, a book 'both good and rare' for which, says Lamb, 'no binding is too good: no casket is rich enough, no casing sufficiently durable, to honour and keep safe such a jewel.'[16] Since husband and wife shared the same fortunes, it is best to consider these biographies together, thus avoiding a wearisome repetition of background.

Margaret Lucas was the youngest daughter of Sir Thomas Lucas of St John's, Colchester, a gentleman of sound reputation and estate, who died when she was still an infant. She and her brothers and sisters were reared by their mother with great affection and care. It was a very happy home at St John's, in those days, before the storm of the Civil War bore furiously down upon the Lucas family, scattering and slaying. Eight children played there of whom any mother might justly be proud, they were all so spirited and so good. They must have made a very pleasant picture, they were so properly proportioned, and so 'well-featured', with their 'clear complexions, brown haires, but some lighter than others, sound teeth, sweet breath, plain speeches and tunable voices.' Lady Lucas was the kind of mother every fortunate child remembers: lovely, loving and brave.

> My mother was of an heroick spirit, in suffering patiently where there is no remedy, or to be industrious where she thought she could help: she was of a grave behaviour, and had such a majestic grandeur, as it were continually hung about her, that it would strike a kind of an awe to the beholders, and command respect from the rudest of civilised people,[17] I mean not such barberous people as plundered her, and used her cruelly, for they would have pulled God out of

heaven, had they had the power, as they did royaltie out of his throne: also her beauty was beyond the ruin of time, for she had a well-favoured loveliness in her face, a pleasing sweetness in her countenance, and a well-tempered complexion, as neither too red nor too pale, even to her dying hour, although in years, and by her dying, one might think death was enamoured with her, for he embraced her in a sleep, and so gently, as if he were afraid to hurt her.[18]

Margaret Newcastle gives a delightful account of the young Lucases. She describes their clannishness, their mutual affection, their mother's careful training, their education, their amusements and much more.

As for tutors, although we had for all sorts of vertues, as singing, dancing, playing on musick, reading, writing, working, and the like, yet we were not kept strictly thereto, they were rather for formality than benefit, as my mother cared not so much for our dancing and fidling, singing and prating of severall languages, as that we should be bred virtuously, modestly, civilly, honourably, and on honest principles.[19]

Even when they were growing up they were little inclined to go outside the family circle for companionship. There were enough of them to make a merry party when in winter the river froze and they skimmed over the ice, their laughter ringing in the frosty air; or when they went to London to visit a play-house and to see the thronging life of the busy streets. In the fine weather there were expeditions to Hyde Park, or Spring Garden, and there were long summer days upon the water, 'when they would have music and sup in barges.' When it was not high-holiday, the boys had still such pastimes as fencing, riding and shooting; the girls had country walks, embroidery, the making of simples, and all the pleasant arts of housewifery. But there was one of the Lucas family who did not take part in these diversions. She was too shy, too withdrawn, and too self-absorbed. She took her pleasure in reading or scribbling. Whether the trees were afoam with blossom, or the trout leaped in the weir, or the snow fell hissing an invitation to merriment, Margaret Lucas's pen scribbled over the paper, in mad pursuit of the ideas which ever sped faster than hand could follow. She set down what she could catch in hasty, frantic hieroglyphics which took their erratic course among huge mountains of blots. Where are now the sixteen books which this ambitious child felt impelled to write — those curious effusions which were such a mixture of 'sense and no sense, knowledge and ignorance?' She tells us herself that they were not worth reading. At any rate, they vanished as surely as her youth.

The young Lucases were very tolerant of their youngest sister's shyness. One would not say that they understood her (except perhaps her sister Pye, whom she loved 'with a supernatural affection'), but they were good natured, and sheltered her from the necessity of those social contacts which caused her such awkward misery. Picture then, their amazement when this bashful Margaret suddenly declared that she wished to go to Court. She had heard that the Queen, Henrietta Maria, had now fewer maids of honour than formerly, and either a sense of loyalty to the Stuart cause, or an impulse to conquer her anti-social habits led her to volunteer for this service. With much difficulty she obtained the consent of her mother and family, who feared lest her excessive timidity and inexperience might make her miserable among so many strangers. Still, they let her go, and miserable she was for two years. She lacked the power to adapt herself to Court life, and was soon the laughing stock of the women, whom she could not understand, and of the men, whom she avoided. They could make nothing of this fantastic maid of honour who was so awkward and so naive.

In 1645, the Queen moved to Paris, and Margaret Lucas was one of those who accompanied her. In Paris she met the Duke of Newcastle, then a widower of fifty-three. He was just the sort of man to appeal to a young girl's hero-worship — good-looking, kindly, whimsical, cultivated, a Royalist refugee who had lost almost everything in the King's cause. She says:

> My Lord the Marquis of Newcastle did approve those bash-
> ful fears which many condemned, and would choose such a
> wife as he might bring to his own humours, and not such an
> one as was wedded to self-conceit, or one that had been
> tempered to the humours of another; for which he wooed
> me for his wife and though I did dread marriage, and
> shunned men's companies as much as I could, yet I could not,
> nor had not the power to refuse him, by reason my affections
> were fixed on him, and he was the only person I ever was in
> love with; neither was I ashamed to own it, but gloried
> therein. For it was not amorous love, I never was infected
> therewith, it is a disease. or a passion, or both, I only know by
> relation, not by experience; neither could title, wealth, power,

or person entice me to love. But my love was honest and honourable, being placed on merit, which affection joyed at the fame of his worth, pleased with delight in his wit, proud of the respects he used to me, and triumphing in the affections he profest for me, which affections he hath confirmed to me by a deed of time, sealed by constancy, and assigned by an unalterable decree of his promise; which makes me happy in despight of Fortune's frowns.[20]

They were married in Sir Richard Browne's Chapel in Paris, in 1645, Margaret being at that time twenty years of age.

Then began the extraordinary career of the exiled Newcastles. Not the least thing they had in common was their poverty, for as the Duchess says, both the family to which she allied herself and the family from which she sprang were ruined in the Civil War. It was very fortunate that she and her husband shared a magnificent indifference to worldly possessions and a child-like ignorance of money matters. If either had been of an anxious disposition, it would have been a very unhappy marriage. As it was, they were ideally suited, and displayed what one might call a reckless common sense in ignoring the impecuniosity for which they had no cure. Their creditors, however, were not likely to be convinced by such logic, and though very long-suffering, did not by any means share the facile optimism of these Micawbers. In Paris, a short time after the marriage, the Duke found himself at bay. His creditors, no doubt disgusted at the levity with which he added a wife to his other liabilities, refused absolutely to trust him any longer:

> My Lord, being always a great master of his passions, was — at least showed himself — not in any manner troubled at it, but in a pleasant humour told me that I must of necessity pawn my clothes to make so much money as would procure a dinner. I answered that my clothes would be but of small value, and therefore desired my waiting-maid to pawn some small toys which I had formerly given her, which she willingly did. The same day in the afternoon, my Lord spake himself to his creditors, and both by his civil deportment and persuasive arguments, obtained so much that they did not only trust him for more necessaries but lent him money besides to redeem those toys that were pawned.[21]

About two years afterwards, when the Duke had again prevailed upon his creditors, the first thing he did was to move out of lodgings into a house which he rented and furnished on credit, and withal, resolving for his own recreation and divertisement, in his banished condition, to exercise the art of manage . . . bought a Barbary horse for that purpose, which cost him 200 pistoles, and, soon after, another Barbary horse from the Lord Crofts, for which he was to pay him £100 when he returned to England.[22]

Some time later, the Queen mother being security for their debts in Paris, the Newcastles followed their Prince to Rotterdam, lived there for six months at a great charge, keeping an open house and a noble table for all comers. Thence, having spent £3,000 of borrowed money, they retired to live quietly at Reubens' house, which they rented from his widow. The two Barbary horses died, but though the Duke

wanted present means to repair these his losses, yet he endeavoured and obtained so much credit at last that he was able to buy two others, and by degrees as many as amounted in all to the number of 8. In which he took so much delight and pleasure, that though he was then in distress for money, yet he would sooner have tried all other ways, than parted with any of them; for I have heard him say that good horses are so rare, as not to be valued for money.[23]

The Duke acted in accordance with this principle, foiling alike the would-be purchasers of his horses and his desperate creditors. The Duchess, so far from being enraged at his irresponsible behaviour, was happy to think that he could squeeze even this much pleasure from life. Finally, however, the situation became so serious that the Duchess and her brother-in-law, Charles Cavendish, returned to England to effect a composition for the sequestered family estates. They were in such dire straits that they had not even enough money to carry them to London, and Sir Charles had to pawn his watch in Southwark to pay for their night's lodgings. Even here they were pursued by the frantic entreaties of her Micawber husband whose Augean stable of debt was none the less fearful for that it contained eight prancing Barbary steeds. By heroic efforts they scraped together £200, which they sent him.

But in the meantime, before the said money could come to his hands, My Lord had been forced to send for all his creditors, and declared to them his great wants and

> necessities where his speech was so effectual and made such
> an impression in them that they all had a deep sense of My
> Lord's misfortunes and instead of urging the payment of his
> debts, promised him that he should not want anything in
> whatsoever they were able to assist him; which they also
> very nobly and civilly performed.[24]

This indeed was a very strong proof of the Duke's persuasive-
ness and amiability.

After eighteen months in England, Margaret heard that the
Duke was ailing and returned to Antwerp. His brother remained
behind and died soon afterwards. There is no doubt that the
Newcastle family was greatly to be pitied, their estates not only
being seized and sold, but many of their houses deliberately pulled
down. They lost in all about £10,000. The Lucas family also paid
dearly for their loyalty, and Margaret had many deaths to lament.
Her eldest sister died first, then her mother, then her two brothers,
one of them being executed during the war. If poverty did not
matter greatly to the Duchess of Newcastle, she had enough of
other sorrows to break the strongest heart. Her only joy was in her
husband, and her loyalty to him during their bitter years of exile
makes a story in which the epical and the humorous are
inextricably entwined. She loves to show that there was grandeur
in the Duke's life abroad. She relates incidents to prove that their
house was visited by all the people of quality who came to
Antwerp, even by the entire court of Don John of Austria. Every
civility shown to her husband, every compliment, every kind word
from the King is treasured by this loving woman, 'onely to declare
My Lord's happiness in his miseries.'

At last the Restoration, so long and so vainly awaited, becomes
a fact. The Duke is invited to come to England in one of his
Majesty's ships, but begs leave to hire a vessel for himself and his
company. He crosses to England in 'an old rotten frigate that was
lost the next voyage after . . . At last, being come so far that he was
able to discern the smoke of London, which he had not seen in a
long time, he merrily was pleased to desire one that was near him,
to jog and awake him out of his dream, for surely said he, I have
been sixteen years asleep, and am not thoroughly awake yet.'[25]

Alas for the Duchess! That indomitable woman was left behind
as a pawn for her husband's debts. Nothing daunted, she busied
herself in her writings, and quietly awaited her release. Soon she

had the joy of returning to her own country, when she and the Duke retired to their ruined estate, and devoted the rest of their lives to each other and to their particular pursuits. The Duchess died thirteen years later at the age of forty nine. Her husband survived her by three years, and was buried with her in Westminster Abbey. Their tomb, on which lie two life-size images in white marble, bears the following epitaph:

> Here lies the loyal Duke of Newcastle and his Duchess, his second wife, by whom he had no issue. Her name was Margaret Lucas, youngest sister to the Lord Lucas of Colchester, a noble family, for all the brothers were valiant, and all the sisters virtuous. This Duchess was a wise, witty and learned Lady, which her many books do well testify: She was a most virtuous and loving and careful wife, and was with her Lord all the time of his banishment and miseries; and when they came home never parted from him in his solitary retirements.

The biography of the Duke of Newcastle ran into three editions even within the life-time of the subject. The first edition, in 1667, was followed in 1668 by a Latin version,[26] translated by Walter Charlton, subsequently well known as President of the College of Physicians. The third edition was in quarto, published in 1675. There was a reprint of the first edition in 1872, and various other editions and extracts have been published since then. *The True Relation* is generally appended.

There have been diverse opinions as to these biographical works of the Duchess. Pepys was very forthright in his condemnation. On March 18th, 1667, he writes: 'Staid at home reading the ridiculous History of my Lord Newcastle, wrote by his wife; which shows her to be a mad, conceited, ridiculous woman, and he an asse to suffer her to write what she writes to him and of him. So to bed my eyes being very bad.'

His myopia, however, was nothing to that of Horace Walpole, who fulminates against the Newcastles 'with less taste and justice than are commonly to be found in his censures, and with more than his usual spleen.'[27] Disraeli dismisses as mere levity Walpole's criticism which in brief is as follows:

> Of all the riders of [Pegasus] perhaps there have not been a more fantastic couple than his Grace and his faithful

Duchess who was never off her pillion. One of the noble Historian's finest portraits is of the Duke: The Duchess has left another more diffuse indeed but not less entertaining. It is equally amusing to hear her sometimes compare her Lord to Julius Caesar, and often to acquaint you with such anecdotes as in what sort of coach he went to Amsterdam.

Having jeered at the Duchess's claims to genius and at her peculiarities, he ends thus:

> What a picture of foolish nobility was this stately poetic couple, retired to their own little domain, and intoxicating one another with circumstantial flattery on what was of consequence to no mortal but themselves. [28]

And what a picture of finicking celibacy was Walpole himself, retired into his little pseudo-Gothic stronghold at Strawberry Hill, surrounded by an arid collection of artistic curiosities, and drawing his life-breath from the sterile eulogies of his select coterie! Whereas the Newcastles left a memory of faithful love, this doyen left a miasma of malicious preciosity. Before he sneered at Margaret Newcastle's literary absurdities, he should have wiped the bloody drop from Alfonso's nose. [29] Before he stigmatized a childless woman as a 'fertile pedant,' he should have considered for a moment his own barren existence.

Happily, however, there have been few such critics. The general consensus of opinion has always emphasized the profound value of *The True Relation* and the *Life of William Cavendish.* To the worth of the latter biography, Firth has finely testified:

> The special interest of the book lies in the picture of the exiled Royalist, cheerfully sacrificing everything for the King's cause, struggling with his debts, talking over his creditors, never losing confidence in the ultimate triumph of the right, and on his return, setting to work uncomplainingly to restore his ruined estate. It lies . . . in the portrait drawn of a great English nobleman of the seventeenth century; his manners and his habits, his domestic policy, and his alliances with neighbouring potentates, all are recorded and set down with the loving fidelity of a Boswell. [30]

The Duchess of Newcastle was not the only woman biographer in the north of England. While she was writing *The Life of William*

Cavendish — or more probably after it had been written, another woman was committing to paper the memoirs of her husband. This was Lucy Hutchinson, widow of Colonel Hutchinson of Owthorpe, whose family had for generations been near neighbours of the Newcastles in Nottinghamshire. The Hutchinsons belonged to an old and respected family, and were on amiable terms with the Newcastles, but the two families differed entirely in political and religious outlook. They took opposing sides in the Civil War, and consequently their fortunes soared and fell for opposite reasons. The Battle of Marston Moor ushered in for each family a widely different era — for the Newcastles exile, poverty, and sorrow; for the Hutchinsons success and security. The Duke of Newcastle lost all but life for the cause of Charles I; Colonel Hutchinson was one of the regicides. Nevertheless, the Duke did all he could to protect Colonel Hutchinson and his family when the Restoration demanded vengeance on its enemies. These facts are cogent to the problem presented by Lucy Hutchinson's biographical works.

Lucy Hutchinson's writings remained unpublished for well over one hundred years after they had been written. During this interval, they remained in the careful possession of the Hutchinson family. Thomas Hutchinson, who held the family estates at the end of the eighteenth century, had refused to permit publication of these works, but when his nephew, The Revd Julius Hutchinson, succeeded to a part of the property, he showed himself of a different mind. He found in the library of Hatfield Woodhall (the Hertfordshire house) the following manuscripts:

1. The Life of Colonel Hutchinson.
2. A book without a title in which Lucy Hutchinson recorded certain events, and which she used when she came to write her husband's Life.
3. A fragmentary account of Lucy Hutchinson's own life.
4. Two books dealing exclusively with religious subjects.

Of these manuscripts, numbers 1 and 3 were published by The Revd Julius, in 1806, under the title of *The Memoirs of Colonel Hutchinson;* number 4 was published by him in 1817, under the title of *Principles of the Christian Religion;* number 2 is in the British Museum (Add. MSS. 25, 901), but only a fragment of it, as part was lost or destroyed.

Before we give any detailed account of *The Memoirs of Colonel Hutchinson*, it would be well to discuss the interesting contention of Mr A. H. Upham in regard to the spontaneity of this work.[31] Mr Upham considers it very probable that Lucy Hutchinson modelled the fragmentary account of her own life on the Duchess's *True Relation of my Birth, Breeding and Life*, and planned *The Memoirs of Colonel Hutchinson* on *The Life of William Cavendish*. Mr Upham's argument has as its starting-point the similarities to be found in these works, and he reinforces his view by pointing out striking parallels in the fortunes of these two women.

Externally, there were many coincidences in the circumstances of the Duchess and Lucy Hutchinson. Both sprang from families which were staunchly Royalist in the Civil War, although Lucy Hutchinson subsequently adhered to her husband's Roundhead principles; each had lost a brother fighting on the Royalist side; both had married widowers; both had made heroic exertions, Lucy Hutchinson to save her husband's life, and the Duchess to save her husband's possessions; both lived in neighbouring estates in Nottinghamshire, and ordered their lives upon similar lines, the Duchess a voluntary exile from the corruption of the Court, Lucy Hutchinson forced to go into seclusion which, however, well suited her Puritan mode of life; both had such educational possibilities as the age offered, and were given to unregulated reading, and no study; both had a bent towards writing. There had never been any enmity between their families, even when party feeling was at its highest. On the contrary, the Duke had several times tried to protect the Hutchinsons. All these points, taken in conjunction with the fact that each woman wrote her own life and that of her husband, and there are similarities to be observed in these works, lead one to suspect that one woman imitated the other. The Duchess had been writing all her life, and was to the fullest degree original. She was already an established literary figure when her *True Relation* and her husband's *Life* appeared, and these works were written before Mrs Hutchinson began hers, so there is no doubt at all that, if there was imitation, Mrs Hutchinson was the culprit.[32]

Now the work which Mrs Hutchinson most obviously and clearly modelled on that of the Duchess is the fragmentary account of her own life. Upham has collated parallel passages in proof of Lucy Hutchinson's indebtedness, and to the present writer, at any rate, he has proved this point quite conclusively.[33] Lucy Hutchinson's autobiography is, like all her manuscripts, undated, and all one can really say is that it must have been written sometime after the Duchess's *True Relation of my Birth, Breeding and Life* which appeared in 1656 (some copies in 1655).[34]

In regard to *The Memoirs of Colonel Hutchinson,* the question of imitation is more troubled. Convincing internal evidence need not be expected, as the lives of Colonel Hutchinson and the Duke differed widely in incident, and the only parallels which could have been made were those which might appear in the portrait presented of each man and his pursuits. These parallels are actually to be found in the *Memoirs,* and can be classified under such headings as personal appearance, recreation, self-control, foresight, humility, etc.[35] Moreover, the *Memoirs* are in plan similar to the *Life of William Cavendish.* The Duchess divided her biography and her husband thus:

1. His birth, breeding and his
   share in the Civil War   } Strictly biographic
2. The story of his exile   }
3. Description of his person,
   disposition and habits   } A character study
4. Notable sayings of the Duke   }
5. (Appended) *The True Relation of
   my Birth, Breeding and Life*

The Memoirs of Colonel Hutchinson follow in general the same plan, although the parts are not set out in the same order:

1. The Life of Lucy Hutchinson,
   written by herself (a fragment)
2. To my children
   (Mrs Hutchinson to her   } A character study
   children concerning their father) }
3. The Life of Colonel Hutchinson   } Strictly biographic

The greatest complication in this entire question is the impossibility of assigning a definite date to any of Mrs Hutchinson's manuscripts. The most we can say as to the date of the *Memoirs* is that they were written at some time between the death of the Colonel in 1664, and the release of certain of his fellow-prisoners on July 7, 1671.[36] Since Mrs Hutchinson appears to have been influenced by *The Life of William Cavendish* which was published in 1667, it would be reasonable to suppose that she wrote, or at any rate completed the *Memoirs* after that date. Her biography, however, contains a passage which seems to suggest that she began the *Memoirs* very soon after her husband's death. She says:

> But I that am under a command not to grieve at the common rate of desolate women, while I am studying which way to moderate my woe . . . can for the present find out none more just to your dear father nor consolatory to myself than the preservation of his Memory.[37]

The passage is ambiguous, and the interpretation of it as an immediate expression of grief is based on the idea that sorrow is lessened by time. So it is, but not in every case, and besides, a widow writing the life of her husband may not have been inclined to admit time's softening qualities. Indeed, the narrative flowing from her pen may have revived all her first grief, and the foregoing passage may have been written in that frame of mind, although years afterwards. The Revd Julius Hutchinson did accept the *Memoirs* as 'a simple unstudied utterance,' the immediate expression of the widow's first unmoderated woe, but in this acceptance he entirely overlooked the significance of manuscript number 2, and of other facts to be mentioned later.

Manuscript number 2 was not a diary of events in the Colonel's life. If it had been, the events would have been dated. Actually, spaces were left for dates which were to be filled in later. It is, then, an account of events, written a considerable time after they had occurred, and written for a specific purpose. Surely that purpose obviously was the deliberate marshalling of facts, preparatory to writing the *Memoirs.* Manuscript number 2 was a rough sketch of these political happenings which Mrs Hutchinson knew she must accurately reconstruct as the background of her husband's life. Manuscript number 2 disproves the theory of the 'simple unstudied utterance,' but it does not disprove the theory that the *Memoirs* may have been begun soon after Colonel Hutchinson's death, that is, at some time before *The Life of William Cavendish* appeared in 1667.

Accepting the evidence that the *Memoirs* were modelled on *The Life of William Cavendish,* we must adhere to either of two alternative views:

1. That the *Memoirs* were not begun, or not completed until after 1667, when Mrs Hutchinson would have the opportunity of studying the published *Life of William Cavendish*.
2. That the *Memoirs* were begun soon after Colonel Hutchinson's death in 1664, and that Mrs Hutchinson had access to *The Life of William Cavendish* which existed in manuscript as early as 1665.

Upham makes out a case in support of both theories, but his case for view b is not at all convincing. Taking the similarities in the circumstances of the Duchess and Lucy Hutchinson, and the fact that they were neighbours, he builds up an intimacy between the two women, makes it appear that they exchanged visits, and that the Duchess showed her unpublished manuscript to Lucy Hutchinson. Apart from the slender nature of these arguments which rest upon pure surmise, they are untenable because they were highly improbable. Similarity of external circumstances does not connote or induce similarity of outlook, and the world is full of people in whom similarity of circumstances does not awaken the slightest mutual sympathy. Furthermore, though the Duchess and Lucy Hutchinson shared an aversion to society, and were characterized by high ethical principles, the difference between the Duchess and Lucy Hutchinson is the difference between rectitude and righteousness. The Duchess disliked the Puritan sisterhood, as many of her letters show. She considered them extremely boring and presumptuous. Again, as to the intimacy between these women, it should be remembered that they became neighbours only after the Restoration. Prior to that time, the Duchess lived abroad except for one hurried visit to England. This gave no opportunity for deep roots of friendship to grow. In fact, although Lucy Hutchinson in the *Memoirs* highly praises the Duke of Newcastle for his kindness to her husband, she makes one remark which surely she would have omitted, had she been truly a friend of the Newcastles. She says that no man in the North of England was a greater prince 'till a foolish ambition of glorious slavery carried him to court where he ran himself much into debt to purchase neglects of the King and Queen and the scorn of the proud courtiers.'

This sort of gibe would certainly have prevented Lucy Hutchinson from showing *her* manuscript to the Duchess, whatever the Duchess might have shown to her. And really, nothing is more utterly improbable than that the Duchess showed her manuscript to Lucy Hutchinson, even if they had been sister spirits. The dearest of friends show a distinct reserve as to their unpublished manuscripts. Literary emulation is a deterrent, not a spur, to such exchanges. Since the theory that Lucy Hutchinson began the *Memoirs* soon after 1664, and before 1667, involves the belief that she had access to the unpublished manuscript of *The Life of William Cavendish*, we must abandon it. It is far more probable that she knew the Duchess was engaged on the Life of her husband, determined to do likewise, wrote manuscript number 2 as a necessary first sketch of background, studied *The Life of William Cavendish* when it appeared in 1667, modelled the *Memoirs* on this fair pattern, and completed it in due time.

Upham finds not only a marked similarity of plan and detail, but also a close resemblance in the literary style of these two women. With this criticism it is not easy to agree. One can really see no similarity in the style of the Duchess and of Lucy Hutchinson, except such general traits as characterized the prose of the period. Within these limits, there is a vast difference in the styles of Mrs Hutchinson and of the Duchess. That of Mrs Hutchinson is clear, smooth-flowing, firm and uninspired; that of the Duchess is vivid, turgid, choked with metaphor, impeded by a plethora of ideas, startling with sudden patches of sheer beauty. One is the style of an intelligent and systematic mind; the other is the style of an erratic genius.

Lucy Hutchinson was born about the year 1620. She was the daughter of Sir Allen Apsley, Lieutenant of the Tower of London, by his third wife, Lucy St John. Her parents, considering her beautiful and unusually intelligent, spared no pains with her education. She had at one time eight tutors for such subjects as 'languages, music, dancing, writing and needlework,' but she had no interest in anything but reading. She was taught French by her nurse, and Latin by her father's chaplain. Her writings show that she also knew Greek and Hebrew, and was well read in classical and theological learning.

Like the Duchess she praises her mother's beauty. The Duchess says:

I dare not commend my sisters, as to say they were handsome. But this I dare say, their beauty, if any they had, was not so lasting as my mother's. Time making suddener ruin in their faces than in hers.[38]

Lucy Hutchinson says:

There were not in those days so many beautiful women found in any family as these, but my mother was by the most judgments preferred before all her elder sisters, who something envious at it, used her unkindly.[39]

Firth refers to the extraordinary mistake Lucy Hutchinson made as to her mother's age.[40] She alleged that her mother was married at sixteen years, and yet she enumerates incidents in her mother's earlier life which would seem to indicate that she was so ardently wooed by suitors at the age of nine, that she was forced to take refuge in Jersey from her sisters' jealousy. This was no mistake on Lucy Hutchinson's part, but a stupid effort to have her cake and eat it. She wished to show the devastating effects of her mother's beauty, and yet to hide the fact that her mother did not marry until she was twenty-seven.[41]

Lucy Hutchinson may have imagined that there was a great similarity between her disposition and that of the Duchess. Let us compare what each has to say of her young days:

For I [says the Duchess] being addicted from my childhood to contemplation rather than conversation, to solitariness rather than society, to melancholy rather than mirth, to write with the pen rather than to work with a needle, passing my time with harmless fancies, their company being pleasing, their conversation innocent, in which I take such pleasure, as I neglect my health, for it is as great a grief to leave their society, as a joy to be in their company . . . . Likewise in playing at cards, or any other games, in which I neither have practised, nor have I any skill therein; as for dancing, although it be a graceful art, and becometh unmarried persons well, yet for those that are married, it is too light an action . . . and for revelling I am too dull a nature.[42]

Mrs Hutchinson says:

As for music and dancing, I profited very little in them, and would never practise my lute or harpsichords but when my masters were with me; and for my needle, I absolutely hated it. Play among other children I despised . . . and kept the children in such awe that they were glad when I entertained myself in elder company; to whom I was very acceptable . . . and very profitable discourses being frequent at my father's table and in my mother's drawingroom, I was very attentive to all, and gathered up things that I would utter again, to the great admiration of many that took my memory and imitation for wit.[43]

These characteristic accounts mark a great difference in the mental traits of the little Margaret Lucas and the little Lucy Apsley. The one was unobtrusively contemplative, a shy and awkward child feeding on thought; the other was a self-assertive prodigy, feeding on the praise which her facile parroting won from her elders. As women, both were convinced of their mental powers, and they were right, but the difference still remained between creative vision and very intelligent imitation.

Lucy Apsley married Colonel Hutchinson, then a widower, in 1638. The story of their meeting and courtship is very pleasantly and gracefully told. It stresses the fact that, like the Duchess, she was very bashful, and that none but this particular suitor could have persuaded her to marry. Her life with her husband was very happy, and he seems to have been tolerant of her literary ambitions. She found it possible during the early days of her married life to unite the care of her children with her translation of the six books of Lucretius' *De Rerum Natura*, which, long afterwards, she dedicated to the Earl of Anglesea, at a time when her views in regard to the doctrines of Epicurus and the atomic theory had suffered regeneration:

> 'Tis a lamentation and a horror [she says in 1675] that in these days of the gospel men should be found so presumptuously wicked to study and adhere to his and his masters ridiculous, impious, execrable doctrines, reviving the foppish, casual dance of the atoms, and denying the Sovereign wisdom of God in the great design of the whole universe.[44]

'This dog,' she calls Lucretius finally, and she speaks of all worldly learning as 'Those walks of wit which poor vainglorious scholars call the Muses' groves, enchanted thickets . . . While they tipple at their celebrated Helicon, they lose their lives, and fill themselves with poison, drowning their spirits in their puddled waters, and neglecting the healing spring of truth.' And this is the intimate confidante of the Duchess, to whom 'Atomes' were dearer than life, who drank so deep of Helicon and wandered so long among the thickets that the sober were always shocked by the intoxicated dishevelment of her mind!

That Lucy Hutchinson came to share not only her husband's moral principles but his political outlook, is abundantly clear in the *Memoirs*. These convictions made it inevitable that the Hutchinsons should take the Puritan side in the Civil War, and it must be said that, except for one somewhat pardonable vacillation, they adhered to their chosen path in the face of misery and death.

When the Duchess was confronted with the task of building up the political background of her husband's life, she relied on the sound information of the Duke's Secretary, John Rolleston. Lucy Hutchinson derived her background from May, but, unlike the Duchess, did not acknowledge her indebtedness. She sometimes objects to May's impartiality, but follows him rather closely nevertheless. In some respects, however, she was better informed than May. For example, she gives the true reason for the dissolution of the Long Parliament. May does not. For the account of the warfare in Nottinghamshire she revised manuscript number 2, but was careful to omit certain facts which, on mature consideration, appeared to reflect unfavourably on her husband's conduct — such as the story of Colonel Hutchinson's insulting message to Sir Roger Cooper, and his torturing of the spies from Newark. Sometimes, like the Duchess, she is apt to exaggerate the part played by her husband, and when she deals with the Colonel's escape from the immediate vengeance of the Restoration, she conceals and misrepresents much of the truth. As a regicide, Colonel Hutchinson's life was forfeit in 1660. He escaped by eating humble pie. His recantation was embodied in a letter to the Speaker in Parliament, and 'no more humbling and dishonouring petition for life could be uttered.'[45] Lucy Hutchinson says that she wrote that letter and signed it with her husband's name. This fact has been confirmed. But Colonel Hutchinson did not trust merely to his wife's expedient. He sent a second petition to the House of Commons six weeks later. He was regarded as a renegade by his old comrades, and this, coupled with the reproaches of his own conscience, made him repent his apostasy. When, after a few years of active Royalist enmity he was again arrested, he greeted the prospect of his imprisonment with relief.

From the moment that Colonel Hutchinson was arrested and taken to London, there is a different tone in the *Memoirs*. The style throughout has been admirably clear and forceful, but now there is a restrained emotion which raises it to a different level. We should be glad to claim this as Lucy Hutchinson's best writing — her own literary style vivified by deep feeling, and owing nothing to the compositions of any other writer. But the truth is that Colonel Hutchinson himself wrote an account of his arrest and imprisonment while he was in the Tower of London, and succeeded in getting it printed before he was removed to Sandown. It was reprinted in the *Harleian Miscellany* and is therefore accessible for comparison with this part of the *Memoirs*. It is quite clear that Lucy Hutchinson owed much to her husband's narrative. Some parts of it she copied with merely verbal changes. She did, however, incorporate Colonel Hutchinson's account in the *Memoirs* with such success that, were it not for evidence to the contrary, one would ascribe this part of the narrative entirely to her, and one would be inclined to explain the increased vitality of her style by the gathering force of the tragedy she is about to describe. It is an important fact that though her husband's account ends before he was removed to Sandown, she continues the story to its conclusion, with no observable change of style, or diminution in force or imaginative insight. Despite all her imitations, she did not need help to describe her husband's death. She did the only thing which could have been of the slightest use — she poured out that part of the story from her heart.

Throughout the *Memoirs* Lucy Hutchinson speaks of her share in events always in the third person. This gives a peculiar dignity and grief to the latter part of the narrative. There is a detailed account of the political atmosphere prior to Colonel Hutchinson's arrest: the threats, the consciousness of impending danger, the insults, the raids on their house. No wonder that before the opening of the final stage the Colonel has a dream of ill-omen:

> He dreamt one night that he saw certain men in a boat upon the Thames, labouring against wind and tide, to bring their

boat, which stuck in the sands, to shore; at which he, being
in the boat, was angry with them, and told them they toiled
in vain, and would never effect their purpose; but, said he,
let it alone and let me try; whereupon he laid him down in
the boat, and applying his breast to the head of it, gently
shoved it along, till he came to land on the Southwark side,
and there, going out of the boat, walked in the most pleasant lovely fields so green and flourishing, and so embel-
lished with the cheerful sun that shone upon them, as he
never saw anything so delightful, and there he met his
father, who gave him certain leaves of laurel which had
many words written in them which he could not read. The
Colonel was never superstitious of dreams but this stuck a
little in his mind.[46]

Finally he is arrested, despite all the Duke of Newcastle can do
in his favour, and having been illegally imprisoned for four days,
is taken to London. The long journey begins on October 28, 1663.

They were forced to stay a day at Owthorpe [the Colonel's
own house] for the mending of the coach and coming in of
soldiers where the Colonel had the opportunity to take
leave of his poor labourers, who wept all bitterly when he
paid them off, but he comforted them and smiled, and
without any regret went away from his bitterly weeping
children, and servants, and tenants, his wife and his eldest
son and daughter going with him.[47]

He was imprisoned in the Bloody Tower. His repeated
examinations, the efforts to make him incriminate himself in
conversation with his guards and fellow prisoners, the attempts
to involve and to browbeat Mrs Hutchinson are all excellently
described. Robinson, the Lieutenant of the Tower, is a fine portrait of a scoundrel. Every deceit, every effort to extort money,
every detail of his petty persecutions are recorded. Robinson
refuses Mrs Hutchinson access to her husband who is ill, and
who is deliberately confined in the worst possible room because
he cannot afford to bribe Robinson into more bearable treatment.
Finally, Mrs Hutchinson threatens to publish an account of
Robinson's behaviour which the Colonel has committed to paper:

The next day, being the Lord's, he sent one of the warders
to entreat her to come to her husband, and the *blood-hound*
Cresset, met her at the gate and led her to her husband, and

left her all the day alone with him, which they had never
before done . . . and in the evening Sir John Robinson sent
for her, and partly expostulated and partly flattered.[48]

It must have been very strange for Lucy Hutchinson to find
such suffering in the Tower of London where she was born, and
which was bound up with the happy memories of her childhood.

At last, the Colonel is sent to Sandown Castle where his quarters and his treatment are even worse. The castle is dilapidated,
and he is kept in a room with unglazed windows, a room with
five doors, used as a thoroughfare, and swept by such damp
winds from the sea that even in summer the walls and the
wretched pieces of furniture are covered daily with mould. The
walls ooze with damp, and salt lies like a perpetual sweat upon
them. Notwithstanding all this, the Colonel is cheerful and
endeavours to cheer his wife and daughter, who lodge at Deal
and come to and from every day to visit him.

> His wife bore all her own toils joyfully enough for the love
> of him but could not but be sad at the sight of his unde-
> served sufferings; and he would very sweetly and kindly
> chide her for it, and tell her that if she were but cheerful,
> he should think this suffering the happiest thing that ever
> befel him.[49]

One day she tells him that despite all his courage, she knows
he will die in prison. He replied:

> I think I shall not, but if I do, my blood will be so innocent I
> shall advance the Cause more by my death, hasting the
> vengeance of God on my unjust enemies, than I could do by
> all the actions of my life. Another time when she was telling
> him she feared they had placed him on the seashore but in
> order to transport him to Tangier, he told her, if they had,
> God was the same God at Tangier as at Owthorpe; Prithee
> said he, trust God with me; if he carry me away, he will
> bring me back again.

Not long afterwards, Colonel Hutchinson died, while his wife
was gone northward in an effort to raise enough money to secure
him better treatment in prison.

> From London he was brought down to Owthorpe, very
> seriously bewailed all the way he came along by all those

who had been better acquainted with his worth than the strangers amongst whom he died, and was brought home with honour to his grave through the dominions of his murderers, who were ashamed of his glories, which all their tyrannies could not extinguish with his life.[50]

We have seen that the *Memoirs* written by Lucy Hutchinson were very far from being 'a simple, unstudied utterance;' that they were, on the contrary, the result of long planning, steady labour and much imitation. We have noted that she modelled her work on that of the Duchess of Newcastle, based her political background on May, and relied on her husband's account for much of the latter part of her story. Even her character-portrait of her husband she wrote twice over, so earnestly was she studying how best to express what she had in mind.[51] But it would be a mistake to imagine that because Lucy Hutchinson used borrowed threads as well as those from her own distaff, and because she tried to imitate an existing pattern, that therefore she did not weave a sound reliable fabric. It is certainly no mean feat to recount in an interesting, thorough and systematic manner the events of forty-eight years.[52] A woman who could thus recount the complicated happenings of real life is well worth mentioning as a portent in the evolution of fiction. Julius Hutchinson showed some wisdom when he said of the memoirs that the book 'carries with it all the interest of a novel, strengthened with the authenticity of a real history.'[53]

In 1643, when Margaret Lucas, awkward and unhappy, was striving to adapt herself to Court life in Oxford, another girl (one year younger than herself), lodging in a back-street in the same town, was striving to adapt herself to poverty. This was Anne Harrison, eighteen years old, fated also to lose everything in the Royalist cause, to be a wanderer in far countries, to cleave to her husband through thick and thin, and to record her adventures in a biography.

Anne Harrison was the elder daughter and the fourth child of Sir John Harrison of Balls, Hertfordshire. She was born in 1625, in Hart Street, St Olave's, London, and although her education gave her all the advantages that the time afforded, her interest in accomplishments was formal. Needlework, 'French, singing, lute, the virginals and dancing' were well enough,

Yet was I wild to that degree, that the hours of my beloved recreation took up too much of my time, for I loved riding in the first place, running, and all active pastimes; in short, I was   that which we graver people call a hoyting girl; but to be just   to myself, I never did mischief to myself or people, nor one immodest word or action in my life, though skipping and activity was my delight, but upon my mother's death, I then began to reflect, and, as an offering to her memory, I flung away those little childnesses that had formerly possessed me, and, by my father's command, took upon me charge of his house and family, which I so ordered by my excellent mother's example, as found acceptance in his sight.[54]

When Anne became the mistress of her father's house she was fifteen — not a great age at which to assume the responsibilities of a woman. It was not long before her endurance and courage were fully tried. In 1641 her father, who had held a post in the customs, lent King Charles a large sum of money. In 1642 he was imprisoned by the Parliament and deprived of his property. Again at liberty, he attended the Court at Oxford in 1643, and sent for his children so that they might be near him. The Harrison family was then in such financial straits that Anne and her sister had to make shift as best they could.

From as good a house as any gentleman of England had, we came to a baker's house in an obscure street, and from rooms well furnished, to lie in a very bad bed in a garret, to one dish of meat, and that not the best ordered, no money, for we were as poor as Job, nor clothes more than a man or two brought in their cloak bags: we had the perpetual discourse of losing and gaining towns and men; at the windows the sad spectacle of war, sometimes plague, sometimes sicknesses of other kind, by reason of so many people being packed together, as, I believe, there never was before of that quality; always in want, yet I must needs say that most bore it with a martyr-like cheerfulness. For my own part, I began to think we should all, like Abraham, live in tents all the days of our lives.[55]

The beautiful and high-spirited Anne Harrison did not remain long in her garret. On May 18, 1644 (the year following her arrival in Oxford, and shortly after her brother William's death) she was married with her mother's wedding ring to Richard Fanshawe, her third cousin. Marriage to Prince Charles's Secretary of War could not mean 'settling down.' It involved every kind of uncertainty and danger, hardship and privation. It meant a restless and fugitive existence, home being merely wherever one happened to pause for a breathing space. In Anne Fanshawe's life only one thing was permanent — the faithful love between her and her husband. When, thirty-two years later, she set down the crowded events of her married life, her husband had been dead ten years; at fifty-five she was worn out by many griefs; poor, lonely and ignored; of her fourteen children born in various parts of England, Spain and France nine were dead; and yet her devotion to her husband, ardent as ever, revived every detail of those strenuous years which were to her supremely worthwhile. Indeed she wrote the *Memoirs* so that her only surviving son, Richard, might properly appreciate his father's character and achievements.

The *Memoirs* were written in 1676, either by Lady Fanshawe herself or else at her dictation.[56] This manuscript was copied in 1776 by Charlotte Colman, said to be a great-granddaughter. Charlotte Colman's manuscript was copied in 1786, and this third manuscript was published in 1829. In 1830 there was a new edition with corrections and additional notes. One would expect mistakes in the second copy of a manuscript, particularly since Charlotte Colman was not a careful copyist, but even in Lady Fanshawe's manuscript[57] the dates are not reliable, partly because she wrote from memory, partly because she sometimes used the old and sometimes the new style of computation. Occasionally, too, she mentioned events out of their proper sequence. The arrangement of the *Memoirs* is as follows:

1. A portrait of her husband, Sir Richard Fanshawe.
2. An account of his ancestors.
3. A reference to their marriage, together with the names of their children alive and dead. Of the dead she mentions the burial places.
4. A few pages dealing with the family of Sir Thomas Fanshawe of Jenkins, who was a near relative of her husband.
5. An account of her own birth; of her mother and her mother's death; and of her own brothers and sister.
6. An account of her father's second marriage; of his birth and relatives.
7. An account of her own childhood, and upbringing.

8. A long and detailed account of the adventures which befell her husband and herself during their married life.

It is true that parts 1 to 7 are badly arranged, but this does not greatly matter, as, from the fictional point of view, the main interest is centred in the long narrative which constitutes section 8.

To the composition of the *Memoirs* Anne Fanshawe brought a most energetic, vivid and individual mind. She was a woman of great courage and directness, with a knack of adapting herself to any circumstances and of rising to any situation. We see her, fine and bejewelled, sweeping her curtsey to the Queen, or standing squarely on deck in the tarry clothes of a cabinboy to meet the attack of Turkish pirates; gracing the brilliance of ambassadorial banquets, or gnawing a hunk of rotten cheese when shipwrecked off the coast of France; defending her husband's house from robbers, outwitting the passport authorities at Dover, fleeing through the streets of embattled Cork, or with her hair standing on end at the sight of a fearful ghost. She never wearies. She takes what comes with the simplicity and verve of a child. She remains always the spontaneous and gallant Anne Fanshawe. She retains her tremendous gusto for living. In the minuteness of her observation, in her interest in clothes, customs, food, she is very much a woman. When her husband goes as English ambassador to the Spanish court, she can tell us exactly the width of his coat-lacing, the colour of his shoe-strings and the sort of ribbon which trimmed his gloves. When she flees from Bristol to Barnstaple to escape the plague, she notes (with delightful inconsequence) that 'near Barnstaple there is a fruit called a masard, like a cherry, but different in taste, and makes the best pies with their sort of cream I ever eat;' also that at the merchant's house where she lodged there was a parrot a hundred years old. Such Pepysian particularity adds greatly to the realism of the narrative. Like the great diaries she has an insatiable appetite for curious facts. For example, the Spanish women 'all paint white and red, from the Queen to the cobbler's wife, old and young, widows excepted, who never go out of close mourning, nor wear gloves, nor show their hair after their husband's death;' and again, that in Spain 'they have a seed which they sow in the latter end of March, like our sweet basil; but it grows up in their pots, which are often of china, large, for their windows, so delicately, that it is all the summer as round as a ball and as large as the circumference of the pot, of a most pleasant green, and very good scent.'[58] She loves also anything that is traditional or mysterious, and tells with great relish how the prophecy written over the entrance gate of the Alhambra came to be fulfilled.[59] She describes further that through an iron grate fixed in the side of a hill near the Alhambra, one could distinctly hear the clashing of swords, and she adds that, according to a legend, it could never be opened since the Moors left, and that all perished who attempted it.

But although Anne Fanshawe's attention to detail gave a particular vividness to her narrative, she had a power of natural realism quite independent of such touches. The vigorous simplicity of her style, and its worth as an expression of personality can best be shown by extracts; and a brief resume of the principal events will show the ability of this biographer to tell a gripping and at times, a very moving story.

Anne Fanshawe's marriage to Richard Fanshawe was in itself an adventure, for though he was the Prince's Secretary for War, and had the King's promise of future reward, the young couple were practically penniless. Both had large fortunes in expectation, and empty pockets for their present needs:

> We might truly be called merchant adventurers, for the stock we set up our trading with did not amount to twenty pounds between us; but, however, it was to us as a little piece of armour is against a bullet, which if it be right placed, though no bigger than a shilling, serves as well as a whole suit of armour; so our stock bought pen, ink, and paper, which was your father's trade, and by it, I assure you, we lived better than those that were born to £2,000 a year as long as he had his liberty.[60]

When her first child was dying very soon after its birth, Anne Fanshawe's husband had to go to Bristol in performance of his duty. Three months later he sent for her to join him, and she, leaving her sick-room for the first time, set off for Bristol a few days afterwards, with a high heart; 'but little thought I to leap into the sea that would toss me until it had racked me.' When she arrives her husband greets her lovingly, and gives her a hundred pieces of gold saying:

'I know thou that keeps my heart so well, will keep my fortune which from this time I will ever put into thy hands as God shall bless me with increase.' And now I thought myself a perfect queen, and my husband so glorious a crown, that I more valued myself to be called by his name than born a princess, for I knew him very wise and very good, and his soul dotes on me.

Though his love for her is indeed great, she is very happy to prove that he loves honour more, and relates a vivid little story in proof thereof. Another lady, with whom she is very friendly, suggests that she should have a knowledge of state affairs, like other wives, and urges her to find out from her husband the contents of a packet that came from the Queen in Paris that night.

I that was young and innocent, and to that clay had never in my mouth what news, began to think there was more in inquiring into public affairs than I thought of, and that it being a fashionable thing would make me more beloved of my husband, if that had been possible, than I was. When my husband returned from Council, after welcoming him, as his custom ever was, he went with his handful of papers into his study for an hour or more; I followed him; he turned hastily and said, 'What wouldst thou have, my life?' I told him, I heard the Prince had received a packet from the Queen, and I guessed it was that in his hand, and I desired to know at was in it; he smilingly replied, 'My love, I will immediately come to thee, pray thee go, for I am very busy.' When he came out of his closet I renewed my suit; he kissed me and talked of other things. At supper I would eat nothing; he as usual sat by me, and drank often to me, which was his custom, and was full of discourse to company that was at table. Going to bed I asked again, and said I could not believe he loved me if he refused to tell me all he knew; but he answered nothing and stopped my mouth with kisses.

She cries herself to sleep and refuses to speak to him even on the following day, but he takes her in his arms and explains his position in these words:

'My dearest soul . . . when you asked me of my business it was wholly out of my power to satisfy thee, for my life and fortune shall be thine, and every thought of my heart in which the trust I am in may not be revealed, but my honour is my own, which I cannot preserve if I communicate the Prince's affairs; and pray thee with this answer rest satisfied.'

Such goodness makes her realise her folly and she never again troubles him so.

From Bristol she goes in her husband's (and the Prince's) train to Cornwall, and at Truth she defends the house against robbers in her husband's absence. Thence they proceed to the Scilly Isles, where they have almost no food, clothes, or fuel, and where their lodgings are so wretched that, when she wakes in the morning her bed is 'near swimming in the sea.' Three weeks later they go to Jersey, where a second child is born; from there, after fifteen days, to Caen, and then Anne Fanshawe returns to England to raise some money for her husband. He is allowed to join her, and for some time they live very privately in Portugal Row. During this time they visited King Charles, who was imprisoned in Hampton Court. Anne Fanshawe thus describes the last visit:

> I went three times to pay my duty to him, both as I was the daughter of his servant, and wife of his servant. The last time I ever saw him, when I took my leave, I could not refrain weeping: when he had saluted me, I prayed to God to preserve his Majesty with long life and happy years; he stroked me on the cheek, and said, 'Child, if God pleaseth, it shall be so, but both you and I must submit to God's will, and you know in what hands I am.'

Soon they were in France again with letters from the King for Prince Charles and Queen Henrietta. In September of the same year (1648) Sir Richard was ordered to embark in Prince Charles's ship in the Downs, to act as Treasurer of the Navy under Prince Rupert. Later he joined Prince Charles in Holland, and was sent to Ireland to raise money. There he was joined by Anne. She landed in Youghal, and for six months they lived in Cork very happily, in Red Abbey, a house of Dean Boyle's. They were on excellent terms with the Boyle family, as also with Lord Inchiquin, whose daughter Elkenna was christened by Anne. But this pleasant interlude was soon to end. Lady Fanshawe had only just got news of the death of her second son when Colonel Jeffries seized Cork on behalf of Cromwell. Lady Fanshawe was most unhappily circumstanced at the time of this occurrence. Sir

Richard was in Kinsale, and she was in bed with a broken wrist and an impending childbirth when the trouble began. It was the 16th October, 1649.

> At midnight I heard the great guns go off, and thereupon I called up my family to rise which I did as well as I could in that condition. Hearing lamentable shrieks of men, women and children, I asked at a window the cause; they told me they were all Irish, stripped and wounded, and turned out of the town, and that Colonel Jeffries with some others, had possessed themselves of the town for Cromwell.[61]

She at once determines to escape and writes a message to her husband, to tell him that she is securing his papers. With this letter a faithful servant is lowered over the garden wall of Red Abbey, and he makes his escape in the darkness of the night. She packs up her husband's papers and all the valuables that can be carried, 'and then, about three o'clock in the morning, by the light of a taper, and in that pain I was in, I went into the market-place, with only a man and a maid, and passing through an unruly tumult with their swords in their hands, searched for their chief commander Jeffries.'[62] Jeffries who, while he had been loyal, had been well disposed towards the Fanshawes, gives her a pass.

> With this I came through thousands of naked swords to Red Abbey, and hired the next neighbour's cart, which carried all I could remove; and myself, sister and little girl Nan, with three maids and two men, set forth at five o'clock in November,[63] having but two horses amongst us all, which we rid on by turns. In this sad condition I left Red Abbey . . . We went ten miles to Kinsale, in perpetual fear of being fetched back again; but, by little and little, I thank God, we got safe to the garrison where I found your father.

Thence the Fanshawes went to Limerick where they were received with great kindness. They stayed three nights with the Lady Honor O'Brien, the youngest daughter of the Earl of Thomond. There Anne Fanshawe saw a ghost:

> About one o'clock I heard a voice that wakened me. I drew the curtain, and, in the casement of the window, I saw, by the light of the moon, a woman leaning into the window, through the casement, in white, with red hair and pale and

> ghastly complexion: She spoke loud, and in a tone I had
> never heard, thrice, 'A horse,' and then, with a sigh more
> like the wind than breath she vanished, and to me her body
> looked more like a thick cloud than substance. I was so
> much frightened, that my hair stood on end, and my night
> clothes fell off.[64]

She wakens her husband and they both observe that the window
is still open. Next morning Lady Honor comes to tell them that a
cousin of hers, whose ancestors owned the house, died during
the night. She fears that they may have been disturbed, because
whenever a member of the family was dying the apparition of a
woman always appeared at the window. It was a woman who
had been wronged and murdered ages before by the owners of
the house. Very naturally the Fanshawes left at once.

They are ordered to Spain, and sail from Galway — a Galway
ruined by war and plague: 'this disconsolate city, where now
you see the streets grown over with grass, once the finest little
city in the world.' As the ship gathers way before the wind Lady
Fanshawe puzzles over the unending misfortunes of the 'brave
Kingdom' of Ireland. But soon the threat of personal danger
rouses her. A Turkish galley is sighted, and it draws nearer every
moment. An engagement seems inevitable. The captain locks
Lady Fanshawe in the cabin, but she has no intention of
remaining there while her husband fights on deck. She beats on
the door until the cabin-boy comes. Then

> I, all in tears, desired him to be so good as to give me his
> blue thrum cap he wore, and his tarred coat, which he did,
> and I gave him half-a-crown, and putting them on and
> flinging away my night clothes, I crept up softly and stood
> upon the deck by my husband's side, as free from sickness
> and fear, as, I confess, from discretion; but it was the effect
> of that passion, which I could never master.[65]

Her determination is not put to the final test, because the
Turks, seeing the other vessel prepared, sail off.

Arrived in Spain they go from Malaga to Madrid by way of
Granada, and are most kindly received, but the Spanish King
shows no desire to help Prince Charles, and the Fanshawes leave
Spain. Crossing to Nantes they are almost shipwrecked, and of
this, as of everything else, Lady Fanshawe gives an excellent

description. A terrible storm arises in the Bay of Biscay. Sails and mast are swept away, and the ship drives wildly on, while the crew 'ran swearing about like devils,' and finding all efforts useless, 'ran into holes and left the ship drive as it would.' On the third evening there comes a great calm, but they are still in peril of their lives, because the compass is lost.

> Thus, between hope and fear we passed the night, they protesting to us they knew not where they were, and truly we believed them; for with fear and drink I think they were bereaved of their senses. So soon as it was day, about six o' clock, the master cried out, 'The land! the land!' but we did not receive the news with the joy belonging to it, but sighing said God's will be done! Thus the tide drove us until five o'clock in the afternoon, and drawing near the side of a small rock that had a creek by it, we ran aground.[66]

Anne Fanshawe well remembers their good cheer then. How (as no beds were to be had) they sat up all night around roaring fires regaling themselves with butter, walnuts, eggs, milk and some very bad cheese. 'And,' she says, 'was not this enough, with the escape of shipwreck to be thought better than a feast.'

Having seen the Queen mother in Paris, the Fanshawes return to England. Sir Richard is captured at the Battle of Worcester and kept in solitary confinement in Whitehall 'in a little room yet standing in the bowling-green', often examined, and all the time in expectation of death. He falls ill and nearly dies of scurvy .

> During the time of his imprisonment, I failed not constantly to go, when the clock struck four in the morning, with a dark lantern in my hand, all alone and on foot, from my lodging in Chancery Lane, at my cousin's Young's, to Whitehall in at the entry that went out of King's Street into the bowling-green. Then I would go under his window and softly call him: he, after the first time excepted, never failed to put out his head at the first call: thus we talked together, and sometimes I was so wet with the rain, that it went in at my neck and out at my heels.[67]

Finally Fanshawe is released on bail, and subsequently secures his full freedom. After a few years they go to France — Sir Richard first, but soon joined by Anne, who manages to escape the English authorities. They are at The Hague in May, 1660, and sail back to England triumphantly in the King's ship.

The king embarked at four of the clock, upon which we set sail, the shore being covered with people and shouts from all places of a good voyage, which was seconded with many volleys of shot interchanged: so favourable was the wind that the ships' wherries went from ship to ship to visit their friends all night long. But who can sufficiently express the joy and gallantry of that voyage, to see so many great ships, the best in the world, to hear the trumpets and all other music, to see near a hundred brave ships sail before the wind with vast cloths and streamers, the neatness and cleanness of the ships, the strength of the commanders, the vast plenty of all sorts of provisions, but above all, the glorious majesties of the King and his two brothers, were so beyond man's expectation and expression! The sea was calm, the moon shone at full, and the sun suffered not a cloud to hinder his prospect of the best sight, by whose light, and the merciful bounty of God, he was set safely on shore at Dover in Kent, upon the 25th[68] of May, 1660.[69]

Although the Fanshawes gloried in the return of the King whom they had served so faithfully, they had not much cause for personal satisfaction. Charles had promised to make Sir Richard one of his Secretaries of State, but this office he gave instead to a Mr Norris. Lady Fanshawe ascribed this reverse to Clarendon whom she heartily disliked. S. L. Lee says[70] that her dislike was unreasonable, since Clarendon always spoke of Fanshawe's abilities and services in flattering terms. However that may be, Lady Fanshawe had ample cause later to complain of the treatment meted out to her. In 1662 Fanshawe was appointed Ambassador to Portugal, and he and his wife remained in Lisbon for a year. Back in England, they were graciously received by the royal family, and in January, 1664, Sir Richard was appointed Ambassador to Spain. He and his wife were in high favour at the Spanish court when the King of Spain died, on September 17th, 1665. They were present at the proclamation of the new infant King, Charles II, and Lady Fanshawe most vividly describes all these events, as well as the general background of their life in Spain.

But now her husband entered into the final phase of his fortunes. For some time he had been trying to negotiate a treaty between Spain and England, and at length a draft treaty was prepared by the Spanish council granting favourable terms to English merchants, but it was presented to Fanshawe with the proviso that it should either be confirmed by his sovereign within a fixed period or withdrawn. Fanshawe considered it right to sign the protocol without communicating with his government. On March 26th he was notified that Sandwich had been sent as Extraordinary Ambassador to supercede him. Clarendon said that Fanshawe's failure to communicate the terms of the Treaty to his home government while pledging it to confirm the articles stipulated therein, constituted so grave a breach of his duty that the English Council could not do otherwise than recall him. Fanshawe received his successor very kindly, introduced him to the King on June 10th, and sixteen days later was seized with a fatal illness. He died on June 26th, 1666, and was embalmed on the following day.

Fanshawe's recall was doubtless justified, but nothing can justify the attitude of the English authorities towards his widow. The Fanshawes had never had more money than was sufficient for their immediate needs, and very often not even that. On her husband's death, Lady Fanshawe was stranded in Spain without the money necessary for the journey to England, and she had to transport thither her husband's corpse and her family of five children. The home government gave her no help whatever.

> Much less found I that compassion I expected upon the view of myself, that had lost at once my husband, and fortune in him with my son but twelve months old in my arms, four daughters the eldest but thirteen years of age, with the body of my dear husband daily in my sight for near six months together, and a distressed family, all to be by me in honour and honesty provided for, and to add to my afflictions, neither persons sent to conduct me, nor pass, nor ship, nor money, to carry me one thousand miles, but some few letters of compliment from the chief ministers, bidding, 'God help me!' as they do to beggars and they might have added, 'they had nothing for me,' with great truth. But God did hear, and see, and help me, and brought my soul out of trouble.[71]

In this, the nadir of her fortunes, Anne Fanshawe acted with her usual fortitude. She sold more belongings to raise money, and left Spain owing not one shilling there or at home ('which every Ambassador cannot say'). Back in England, she found that the commissioners, by the instigation of one of them, Lord Shaftesbury ('the worst of men'), did all they could maliciously to oppress her in money matters. She withdrew into the country where, under straitened circumstances, she reared her family. She died in 1680, after fourteen years of poverty and loneliness quietly endured.

> How far that was from a reward, judge ye, for near thirty years' suffering by land and sea, and the hazard of our lives over and over, with the death and beggary of many eminent persons of our family, who when they first entered the King's service, had great and clear estates.[72]

No more is needed to attest the excellence of Anne Fanshawe's *Memoirs*. They are characterized not only by her complete realism and narrative power, but also by the sincerity of feeling. Had she written fiction it could never have been Pastoral or Heroic. To her the world around her was so colourful and so vitally interesting that she could never have found self-expression in fashioning a pale world of shepherds and knights. She knew an exiled Prince and a slain King: she had experienced real wars, real shipwreck, real love, and real grief. She had a firm grip on facts. If she were to create a story, one feels sure that she could never have subscribed to literary conventions which bore no relation to actual life.

As biographers Anne Fanshawe and the Duchess of Newcastle are immeasurably superior to Anne Clifford and Lucy Hutchinson. It is not so easy to compare Anne Fanshawe's work with that of the Duchess. In the construction of a narrative, in realism, in vivid descriptiveness, Anne Fanshawe was the superior, but the Duchess of Newcastle had — how shall one phrase it? — moments of greatness which somehow set her apart. This aspect is most clearly seen in *The True Relation*. It is a subjective aspect, the value of which in the development of fiction is not perhaps so strikingly apparent as the more external qualities of Anne Fanshawe's writing. Nor would it be just too greatly to stress Lady Fanshawe's objectiveness, lest one should seem to deny her that sensitive rightness of feeling so evident in many of the passages we have quoted. One cannot weigh different qualities against each other. It is best to think of the Duchess and Lady Fanshawe as two halves of a future whole — as contributing towards that mastery of narrative form and that expression of the inner being which finally fused in the modern novel.

Our female biographers were alike in one thing: they defied mortality. They were determined that not all of them should die, that they would erect a monument more lasting than brass to those events which were their pride and their heartbreak, which had devoured the years of their lives and demanded all their love, their faith and their endurance. Naturally it was essential for them to show that these sacrifices had been worth while, and so we find them exercising selectivity — not artistic, but merely human selectivity — in the use of their material. Anne Clifford never doubts that the lawsuit was worth the contentions of a lifetime, and she clenches her teeth on the humiliations of her married life; the Duchess ignores the slanders on the Duke's hasty exile; Lucy Hutchinson omits the details of the Colonel's lapse from valour; Anne Fanshawe refuses to consider that her husband's recall from Spain might have been deserved. Anne Fanshawe was nearest to the technique of fiction, but each woman told the story which she had lived in fact. Thus our female biographers' writings represent a phase in the evolution of the English novel which cannot be ignored.

Notes and References

1   *Funeral Sermon of the Countess of Pembroke*, preached by Edward Rainbow, Bishop of Carlisle, 1677.
2   Ibid., p. 38.
3   Dr Whitaker, in his *History of Craven*.
4   *The Harleian Collection*. Letter dated January 14, 1638.
5   *Memoirs of the Count of Grammont*, p. 134.
6   *Pepys' Diary*, April 26, 1667.
7   Ibid., May 30, 1667.
8   *Evelyn's Diary*, April 18, 1667.
9   The Duchess of Newcastle, *Poems and Fancies 1653* (Scholar Press, Yorkshire, 1972), 'To All Noble and Worthy Ladies', p. 3; 'An Epistle to Mistris Toppe', p. 4.
10 The Duchess of Newcastle, *Observations on Experimental Philosophy* (1666): 'Reader's Preface.'
11 *A True Relation of the Birth, Breeding and Life of Margaret Newcastle, Duchess of Newcastle* (ed. Lowers, 1872). Critical Preface by Sir E. Bridges, pp. 255 f.
12 Isaac Disraeli, *Curiosities of Literature* (1849), i, p. 365.
13 *The Cavalier and his Lady* (ed. Jenkins, 1872): Introductory essay, p. 8 f.
14 Some copies appeared in 1655.
15 Prefatory letter to *The . . . Blazing World* (1666).
16 Charles Lamb, *Last Essays of Elia*: 'Detached thoughts on Books and Reading.'

17 Not from Mr T. Longueville, who in his bad-tempered book (*The First Duke and Duchess of Newcastle-on-Tyne*, 1910) shows an active dislike towards the subject of his research. He considers it extremely cogent to mention that Lady Lucas's great-grandfather had been townclerk in Colchester, and that the eldest son of Sir Thomas and Lady Lucas was born before the marriage of his parents. 'For this trifling confusion of dates,' says Mr Longueville, 'the excellent Lady Lucas endeavoured to atone by the prudishness upon which she insisted in her children' (pp. 174. f.). Mr Longueville considers it highly amusing that the Duchess of Newcastle omitted to record this part of her mother's life. This is merely one example of the regrettable attitude which this most ungenerous biographer brings to his task. In speaking of Margaret Newcastle's estimate of the Duke's first wife, Mr Longueville says 'The Duchess is condescending enough to say that "his first wife was a very kind, loving and virtuous Lady," which, in most cases, might be taken to mean about the worst that one lady could politely say of another' (p. 11). The spirit of this work renders it valueless as an honest biography, and we need not refer to it again.

18 'The True Relation of My Birth, Breeding and Life' in *The Life of William Cavendish* . . . (See note 21 below), p. 290–91.

19 Ibid., p. 279–80.

20 Ibid., pp. 195 f.

21 *The Life of William Cavendish, Duke of Newcastle, to which is added The True Relation of My Birth, Breeding and Life* (ed. C. H. Firth, John Nimmo, London, 1886), pp. 88–89.

22 Ibid., p. 90.

23 Ibid., p. 100.

24 Ibid., p. 110.

25 Ibid., pp. 126–27.

26 *De Vita et Rebus gestis G. ducis Novo-Castrensis commentarii* (Fol Londini, 1668).

27 Edmund Lodge, *Portraits of Illustrious Personages of Great Britain* (1835), viii, pp. 8 f.

28 Horace Walpole, *A Catalogue of the Royal and Noble Authors of England* (2nd edn., 1759), ii, pp. 12 ff.

29 'The Castle of Otranto' (*Works of Horace Walpole*, 1798), ii, pp. 76 f.

30 *The Life of William Cavendish* . . . , op. cit., p. x.

31 A. P. Upham, 'Lucy Hutchinson and the Duchess of Newcastle,' Anglia, xxxvi (1912).

32 Upham presents all these arguments in the article already mentioned.

33 The reader is referred to A. P. Upham's treatment of this point in the article already indicated. He deals with the matter in a way which is too long to quote and which cannot be improved.

34 Upham suggests that Lucy Hutchinson's autobiography was written three years after the Duchess's *Life of William Cavendish*, i.e. about 1670. There is no reason to accept this date.

35 Upham has done this very effectively.

36 When Colonel Hutchinson was arrested, Capt. Wright and Lieut. Franck were arrested also, and brought to Newark 'where,' says Mrs Hutchinson in the *Memoirs*, 'they are yet prisoners, and to this day, know not why' (p. 345). Mr Baily, in his *Annals of Nottinghamshire*, pointed out that, as Capt. Wright was arraigned before Judge Hale at the King's Brench, on July 7, 1671, and then discharged for want of evidence, the *Memoirs* could not have been written after that date.

37 Lucy Hutchinson, *Memoirs of the Life of Colonel Hutchison with the Fragment of an Autobiography of Mrs Hutchinson* (ed. James Sutherland, Oxford University Press, London, 1973), p. 1.

38 'The True Relation of my Birth, Breeding and Life', op. cit., p. 293.

39 *Memoirs of the Life of Colonel Hutchinson* . . . , op. cit., p. 284.

40 This point was raised, but left unexplained in Notes and Queries. July 19, 1884.

41 Lucy St John's father died on September 20, 1594 according to the inscription on the outside of two large doors at the north side of the altar in the village of Lydiard Tregooge (see *Notes and Queries*, July 19, 1884); Lucy St John was five years old when her father died (according to her daughter, Lucy Hutchinson, in her autobiography) therefore when she married twenty two years later, in 1616, she must have been twenty-seven years.

42 'The True Relation of my Birth, Breeding and Life', op. cit., p. 307–08.

43 *The Memoirs of Colonel Hutchinson* (ed. Firth, 1885), p. 25.

44 Dedication to the Earl of Anglesea, quoted by Firth (1885), Appendix 37 to the *Memoirs*, p. 454.

45 *The Memoirs of Colonel Hutchinson* (ed. Firth, 1885), Introduction, p. xv.

46 *Memoirs of the Life of Colonel Hutchinson* . . . , (ed. Sutherland, 1973), op. cit., p. 243.

47 Ibid., p. 248.

48 Ibid., p. 261.

49 Ibid., p. 264.

50 Ibid., pp. 274–75.

51 The character-portrait itself came into possession of The Revd Julius Hutchinson in two MS versions, of which he rejected the second as much more laboured and much less characteristic (A. H. Upham, op. cit.)

52 1616–1664.

53 *Memoirs* (ed. Hutchinson, 1810), Introduction, p. xxviii.

54 *The Memoirs of Anne, Lady Halkett and Anne, Lady Fanshawe* (ed. John Loftis, Claredon Press, Oxford, 1979), p. 110.

55 Ibid., p. 111.

56 S. L. Lee in *D.N.B.* speaks of 'The original in Lady Fanshawe's hand-writing.' The writer of the preface to the 1830 edition (one N.H.M.) says 'The original . . . was written *under her Ladyship's inspection.*'

57 This, the original manuscript, was never published, and remains or remained, in the possession of the Fanshawe family. See *D.N.B.*

58 *The Memoirs of Anne, Lady Halkett* . . . , op. cit. p. 173.

59 Ibid., p. 100.

60 Ibid., p. 112.
61 Ibid., p. 123.
62 Ibid, pp. 123–24.
63 Lady Fanshawe is mistaken as to the month.
64 *The Memoirs of Anne, Lady Halkett* . . . , p. 125.
65 Ibid., p. 128.
66 Ibid., p. 131.
67 Ibid., p+p. 134–35.
68 Actually on 26th May.
69 *The Memoirs of Anne, Lady Halkett* . . . , op. cit. pp. 140–41.
70 See *D.N.B.*, article on Sir Richard Fanshawe.
71 *The Memoirs of Anne, Lady Halkett* . . . , op. cit. p. 189.
72 Ibid., p. 189.

Chapter IV

Living Restoration Trends

I have heard that some . . . say my Wit seemed as if it would overpower my Brain, especially when it works on Philosophical Opinions.

(Duchess of Newcastle, *Natures Pictures*, Book xi, Epistle)

1st Gentleman: But if a woman hath wit, or can write a good [tale] what will you say then?
2nd Gentleman: Why, I will say nobody will believe it, for if it be good they will think she did not write it, or at least say she did not . . . the very being a woman condemns it.

(*Duchess of Newcastle's Plays*, Final Introduction)

'Thoughts [says the Duchess of Newcastle] are like stars in the firmament; some are fixed, others like the wandering planets, others again are only like meteors.' By this simile the mind of the Duchess was like a chaos of the entire firmament; comets, meteors, fireballs, planets, stars—a blazing world, an astounding coruscation of dazzling confusion. There were, in particular, two fixed stars which shed a baneful influence upon her writings. One was her conviction of infallibility as an author. She was 'Margaret the First,' benevolent autocrat, subject to no laws of thought or of composition save those which she formulated for herself. Happy in the security that all she wrote would endure, she never revised her manuscripts. She considered it fairer to posterity not to waste valuable time in priming her utterances, but to continue to pour out all her ideas exactly as they occurred to her. It is not surprising, therefore, that most of her writings are spoiled by this lack of judgment.

She considered originality to be the most important literary virtue. Every idea, every fancy, every whimsy, every metaphor was swept into the current of her style, as flowers, weeds and all sorts of flotsam are swept onward by a cataract. She undoubtedly had that concomitant of genius, a lofty and high confidence in herself, but she lacked an infinite capacity for taking pains. She did not even know that there were pains in authorship. She was an instinctive believer in the myth of continuous inspiration. She had no self-critical powers, and she was indifferent to the criticism of others. Her attitude to her readers is summed up in the nonchalant challenge:

> I hope you'll like it, if not, I'm still the same,
> Careless, since Truth will vindicate my Fame.[1]

The other fixed star which distracted the Duchess is best described by the one word 'Atomes.' Hobbes (of *Leviathan* fame) was at least in part responsible for this obsession. He was one of the Duke's friends. He visited at Welbeck, where extraordinary views on scientific and philosophical subjects were discussed without any poor-spirited hesitancies in regard to proof. In the *Treatise on Optics* (dedicated to the Duke) and in the *Decameron Physiologicum* the Duchess found the basis for her scientific poppycock. What she did not know she felt free to invent. The only sanction she ever needed for her scientific and philosophic pronouncements was the sanction of her own approval. She did not feel daring when she published, in 1655, her *Philosophical and Physical Opinions.* She was sure that truth lay in her subconscious mind, and that the cream of such intuitions must rise naturally to the surface, and could therefore be enunciated with perfect safety. There was always more of artlessnesss than of arrogance in the Duchess.

If her literary egotism, her belief in the divine right of authorship, had remained quietly in the background, if her sciento-philosophic propositions had confined themselves to her treatises, we could ignore them here. But these *idées fixes* disturb the balance of all except her biographical writings, and it is better to prepare ourselves for their intrusion.

In 1666, while the twin stars to which we have alluded were in the ascendant, the Duchess conceived a fictional work which in its nature gave free scope to her idiosyncracies. This was

The Description of a New Blazing World which shared a volume with *Observations on Experimental Philosophy*. It was exactly the sort of invention which evoked all that was fantastic, exaggerated, and unstable in the mind of the Duchess. It conformed to a definite literary genre which had its origin in antiquity, and which has endured to the present day, but it was out of harmony with what is best in Margaret Newcastle's work. So little, indeed, does it conform to the most valuable trend in new writings, that we feel justified in ignoring chronology, and treating it at the beginning of the chapter, leaving until the end a volume which preceded it by ten years, but which we shall need as a sobering draught when we reel out of the *Blazing World.*

Since the days of Lucian, and even previous to that time, supposed journeys to imaginary countries had appealed greatly to the readers of feigned stories. In the beginning of the seventeenth century this vogue drew new life from the influence of Fontenelle. There was a variety of Lucianic writings in England, any one of which might have been the fuse to the Duchess's rocketing imagination. There was, for example, the essay of Francis Godwin, Bishop of Hereford, *The Man in the Moon, or a Discourse of a voyage thither by Domingo Gonzales, the speedy Messenger, 1638,* and that same year John Wilkins, Bishop of Chester, contributed *A Discovery of a New World in the Moone, with a discourse concerning the possibility of a passage thither.*

The Duchess sets out with the most sensible intentions, as she explains in her prefatory letter. She resolves to keep her fancy in check, to write a work of fiction that will embody some of her views on Experimental Philosophy. She is determined to set on paper a description of a New World, 'Not such as Lucian's, or the French-man's World in the Moon,' but a world of her own, a Blazing World which is situated at the North Pole. Let us not enquire why the Duchess should insist on a situation involving such a contradiction in temperatures. She did so in accordance with her own laws of ratiocination, and it is for us to suspend our disbelief. Suspicion does dawn upon us, however, when we hear that the first part of the work is to be 'Romancical,' the second philosophical, and the third 'merely Fancy.' We know Margaret Newcastle's attitude to romanceys, and we are not deceived by this leafy camouflage. We are to be lulled by security, coaxed to draw near, and then riddled by a fatal volley of 'Atomes.'

The story begins in a very promising manner as follows:

> A Merchant travelling into a foreign Country fell extremely in Love with a young Lady; but being a stranger in that Nation and beneath her both in Birth and Wealth, he could have but little hopes of obtaining his desire; however, his love growing more and more vehement upon him, even to the slighting of all difficulties, he resolved at last to steal her away; which he had the better opportunity to do, because her Fathers house was not far from the Sea, and she often using to gather shells upon the shore, accompanied not with above two or three of her servants, it encouraged him the more to execute his design. Thus coming one time with a little light vessel . . . mann'd with some few Sea-men, and well victualled, for fear of some accidents, which might perhaps retard their journey, to the place where she used to repair, he forced her away: But when he fancied himself the happiest man of the World, he proved to be the most unfortunate;— for Heaven frowning at his theft, raised such a Tempest, as they knew not what to do, or whither to steer their course; so that the Vessel, both by its own lightness, and the violent motion of the Wind, was carried as swift as an Arrow out of a Bow, towards the North-pole, and in a short time reached the Icy Sea, where the wind forced it amongst huge pieces of Ice; but being little and light, it did by assistance and favour of the Gods to this virtuous Lady, so turn and wind through those precipices as if it had been guided by some experienced Pilot, and skilful Mariner: But alas! those few men which were in it, not knowing whither they went, nor what was to be done in so strange an adventure, and not being provided for so cold a Voyage, were all frozen to death, the young Lady onely, by the light of her Beauty, the heat of her youth, and Protection of the Gods, remaining alive: at last, the Boat still passing on, was forced into another World.[2]

She is rescued by the Bear-men, who live in the land of snow, and is carried to the Emperor of the Blazing World. He is overwhelmed by her loveliness and marries her, whereupon she is metamorphosed into Margaret the First, and holds endless conversations with her wise men as to the nature of Atomes, spirits, snails, air, lice, nettles, the sun, sight, and innumerable other problems. The arguments are somewhat enhanced by the appearance of the disputants:

> The Bear-men were her Experimental Philosophers, the Bird-men her Astronomers, the Fly-worm—and Fish-men—her

Natural Philosophers, the Ape-men her Chymists, the
Satyrs her Galenick Physicians, the Spider-and-Lice men her
Mathematicians, the Jack-daw-Magpie and Parrot-men her
Orators and Logicians, the Gyants her Architects . . . They
were of several Complexions not white, black, tawny,
olive—or ash-coloured; but some appear'd of an Azure,
some of a deep Purple, some of a Grass-green, some of a
Scarlet, some of an Orange-colour, etc. Which Colours and
Complexions, whether they were made by the bare
reflection of light, without the assistance of small particles,
or by the help of well-ranged and order'd Atomes; or by a
continual agitation of little Globules; or by some pressing
and reacting motion I am not able to determine.

The young Empress is also very much exercised as to the
nature of spirits, and she wonders whether everything in the
world is 'soulified' and toys with the idea of soul transmigration.
She seeks a spiritual scribe to write down the esoteric mysteries
divulged by the spirits. None of the ancient or modern philosophers would deign to perform such an office for a mere woman,
'"But, [said the Spirit] there's a Lady, The Duchess of Newcastle,
which although she is not one of the most learned, eloquent,
witty and ingenius, yet she is a plain and rational Writer, for the
principle of her Writings, is Sense and Reason, and she will
without question, be ready to do you all the service she can" . . .
"You say well, replied the Empress; wherefore I pray you send
me the Duchess of Newcastle's Soul."' The exponent of sense and
reason at once arrives. Then follows a Tweedledum-and-
Tweedledee conversation between the disseevered halves of the
Empress-Duchess. Finally the soul of the Empress follows the
soul of the Duchess on a journey to this earth. They visit a theatre
and the Court, and then set off for Nottinghamshire, one
hundred and twelve miles from London, to visit the Duke of
Newcastle. The Empress deplores so greatly the loss of his
property that she decides to hear his grievance against Fortune.
Each side is represented, the Duchess pleading for her husband
and the Empress acting as judge. Ultimately the sister-souls part,
the Empress returning to the Blazing World and the Duchess
remaining in Nottinghamshire except when summoned by her
majestic friend to confer on matters of state. During her periodic
absences, the Duchess is still mindful of her husband's happiness. To show her devotion and to divert his mind from his

misfortunes, she is careful to bring him back from the Blazing World just the very information he would like best:

> She . . . related to her Lord what Magnificent Stables and Riding-Houses the Emperor had built, and what fine Horses were in the Blazing-World, of several shapes and sizes, and how exact their shapes were in each sort, and of many various Colours, and fine Marks as if they had been painted by Art . . . Were there but a passage out of the Blazing-World into this, said she, you should not onely have some of these Horses, but such Materials, as the Emperor has, to build your Stables and Riding-Houses with.[3]

We have omitted to mention many of the wonders which exist in the Blazing World. There is a youth-restorer, which is far more effective than monkey glands. A certain rock produces a gum which takes one hundred years to reach its full perfection. When heated, this gum melts into an oil which, swallowed in small quantities daily, changes the most ancient man into a youth of twenty. The treatment lasts nine months and causes, during that time, such a complication of bodily misery that none but an ancient lunatic could think the game worth the candle, unless indeed, he were fond of eagles' eggs and hinds' milk, which constitute the entire diet during rejuvenation.

There are many Utopian touches in the Duchess's description of her imagined world. She shows a country with few laws (because many laws lead to dissensions); a country which has only one form of religion, and which cannot have more because the people have 'all but one opinion as to the Worship and Adoration of God.' In such ways *The Blazing World* shows kinship with *Gulliver's Travels*.

During the Restoration period novelists and playwrights continued to be inspired by notions of imaginary worlds, but, as we have seen, this was already an established genre of writing, which gained nothing particularly characteristic from Restoration hands. The Duchess of Newcastle did not conform to Restoration fashions in prose fiction, and it is for that reason that we are justified in mentioning here separately not only *The Blazing World*, but also those other forms in which she contributed to the growth of the novel.

The Duchess of Newcastle kept clear of the entire school of the Heroic Romance. It offended her by its artificiality and by its false emphasis on the rodomontade or the whining of lovers. She believed in love, but with a difference, and she assigned it a different value in the scheme of existence. She wrote feigned stories, but she made the distinction that they should not contain feigned estimates of life. She was a realist, not drawn towards the kind of realism in the *novelle*, but to a typically English expression of English life. She would have disowned allegiance to any school but that of Margaret the First; nevertheless, certain of her efforts at fiction show the same kind of native realism as we find in the writings of Greene, Nash, Breton and Deloney.

In 1656 appeared *Nature's Pictures drawn by Fancie's Pencil to the Life*. This work contains ten books consisting of moral tales, fables, dialogues, and some stories of varied length in which the moral is not explicit. At the end is 'a true story in which there is no feigning', i.e. *The True Relation* . . .

The frontispiece of the volume containing *Experimental Philosophy* and the *Blazing World* prepares us somewhat for the contents. The Duchess there confronts one with a rakish air, her coronet askew to give place to the wreath of laurels with which she is being crowned by four fat cherubs. Literary and noble insignia thus precariously perched give an air of ill-balanced and ambitious distinction to the wearer. But if a frontispiece is symbolic of a book, then more normal entertainment awaits us in *Natures Pictures*. Diepenbeck's very rare engraving shows us the Duke and Duchess of Newcastle, crowned with bays, sitting comfortably before a roaring fire, surrounded by their relations—all the children, wives and husbands—who are listening spellbound to the stories which the Duchess relates. Underneath is the verse:

> Thus in this Semi-Sircle wher they sitt,
> Telling of Tales of pleasure and of witt,
> Heer you may read without a Sinn or Crime
> And how more innocently pass your tyme.

We soon perceive, however, that even this fireside group is no sanctuary from Margaret Newcastle's abstractions. When the philosophic sock is on the Duchess proves herself without heart or conscience, scrupling nothing to attract us with a very good beginning and then to cheat us of the tale. For example, *The Schools Quarrels, or Scholars Battles* commences thus:

112

A man travelling, and being very weary, seeing a large house, alighted, and went to the Gates, which he found open for any to pass without any opposition; and entering therein, he came into a large paved Court; and walking about it, he heard a noyse or sound like a great Wind whereat he looks up towards the Clouds, and seeing the Air not much agitated, he wondered at it; at last he looked in at a Door that was open, but there was such a mist, that he could see no further than the entrance . . .[4]

But, alas! when he enters, he merely sees a library in which a number of old men in tattered gowns are turning the leaves of books, with a loud noise, and arguing about Grammar, Logic, Moral Philosophy and kindred subjects.

Sometimes the Duchess's philosophizing takes the form of a witty conversation which much enlivens her didacticism. For example:

There was a grave Matron, who came to visit a young Virgin, whom she asked why she did not marry, since she was of marriageable years. Truly, said she, I am best pleased with a single life.

What! answered the Matron, will you lead Apes in Hell? The young lady said, it was better to lead Apes in Hell, than to lie like Devils on Earth, for, said she, I have heard that a married Couple seldome or never agree, the Husband roars in his drink and the Wife scolds in her Choler, the Servants quarrell, the Children cry, and all is disorder, than 'tis thought Hell is, and a more confused noise.

Said the Matron, such are onely the poor meaner sort of people that live so; but the noble and rich men and their wives live otherwise; for the better sort, as the noble and rich, when they are drunk are carried straight to bed and laid to sleep, and their wives dance until their husbands are sober. Said the Lady, if they dance until their Husbands are sober, they will dance until they are weary; so they do, replied the Matron.[5]

It is of course the Duchess who speaks through the lips of the Discreet Virgin. The action of the story is permanently suspended while the Virgin delivers a diatribe on men and their manners. We are not surprised to find that the Virgin eschews matrimony altogether, her final denunciation running into two folio pages. This is only one example of Margaret Newcastle's habit of using her characters as mouthpieces for her own opinions. She herself is her favourite heroine, and she stalks through all her plays and most of her stories, talking common sense about life or nonsense about philosophy, challenging all comers to argument, fencing according to a wild and whirling fashion of her own. Her opponents always leave their guard open, and she drives her blade home to the very hilt. They are not dead, however. They turn up again under a different label to be further reduced to mincemeat. Often these debates end in the opposers rolling the whites of their eyes heavenwards in astounded appreciation of this female prodigy who is invariably—the Duchess.

The supreme example of this kind of 'story' is *The Anchoret*.[6] Once upon a time there was a young woman who, after her father's death, vows herself to a secluded and single life, but gives leave to any to speak to her through the grating of her cell. She has not long been enclosed when she grows 'as famed as Diogenes in his tub.' All sorts of people come to converse with her, or rather to listen to her. The face is the face of the Anchoret, but the voice which discourses breathlessly of 'Atomes' could belong to nobody but the Duchess. The rest of the story is a mere recital of the inspired replies made by the Anchoret on a variety of subjects:

> Then they asked her what the moon was?
> She answered a body of Water . . .
> Then they asked her what Snow, Hail, Ice and Frost was.
> She answered, that Snow was curded water . . .
> As for Frost, said she, that is candied, or crusted vapour.
> Then they asked her what caused sleep in Animal figures.
> She said the tiredness or weariness of sensitive innated matter, which are called sensitive spirits, as of that part of the innated which works more to the use than to the consistence . . . for though the sensitive spirits doth not desist from moving in any part, as to the consistence, or dissolution of the figure, yet all the sensitive spirits doth not work one and the same way . . . but as some of the innated matter or spirits work in several parts of a figure on the dull part of matter to the consistence or dissolution of the figure, so others and sometimes one and the same degree works to the use, consistence, or necessities of the figure.

This inquisition continues for fifty-nine folio pages, and embraces all possible and impossible subjects. Finally, the fame of the Anchoret reaches the ears of a wicked monarch who comes to see her and immediately becomes 'a desperat Lover.' He has a wife, but when a man decides to marry an encyclopaedia all flesh is grass. Encyclopedias however, are best on the shelf, and sometimes they recognize their proper place. The Anchoret scorns the tender passion. She makes an oration to a convenient multitude, and swallows poison before anyone can prevent her, whether they would have done so being a controverted point.

We have deliberately shown that the Duchess and her pseudo-philosophy spoiled between them many of the tales in *Natures Pictures*. There remains however, more than sufficient material to prove that when the Duchess alights from her hobby-horse and directs her attention to the world about her, she is beyond gainsaying, a very good story-teller.

Let us take first *The Matrimonial Agreement*. The characters have no names; indeed, they are simply types, but it is nevertheless a very convincing story of real life. The events move rapidly and clearly. There is not one redundant word. If the Duchess could more often have written thus nobody could deny her ability to fashion excellent, flexible prose, and to describe with humour and sincerity. It is a pity that space does not permit us to quote the tale in its entirety, but we must limit our wishes.

It is the story of a handsome young man and a fair young lady. He comes a-wooing, but she distrusts the permanency of love in matrimony. She agrees finally to marry him, but as a proof of good faith, she asks that he settle on her part of his estate, so that, should he prove a false husband, she may be in a position to leave him. Confident of his fidelity, he agrees. They marry, and for some time all goes well. Then, after two years, the wife falls very ill, and recovers very slowly. At first, the husband is kind and sympathetic; then he becomes weary. Business calls him abroad and he embraces the opportunity. Henceforth he spends as much time as possible from home, and evades all his wife's questions as to the business (now entirely mythical) which so engages his attention:

> The Husband returning home one day from jolly Company, whose discourse was merry and wanton, he met with his Wife's Maid at the door, and ask'd her how her Mistris did; she said, not very well; thou lookest well, said he and chucks her under the chin; she proud of her Masters kindness, smerks and smiles upon him, insomuch that the next time

he met her he kiss'd her. Now she begins to despise her Mistris, and onely admires her self, and is allways the first person or servant that opens her Master the door; and through the diligence of the Maid, the Masters great affair abroad were ended, and his onely employment and busy care is now at home.

In the meantime his wife grew well, and his Maid grew pert and bold towardes her Mistris; and the Mistris wondered at it; began to observe more strictly what made her so; for perceiving the Wench came oftener than accustomed where her Husband and she were; also she found her Husband had allwayes some excuse to turn his head and eyes to that place where she was; and whenever the Wench came where they were, he would alter his discourse, talking extravagantly.

The wife realizes her husband's infidelity, but nothing is said. He is sent on State affairs into another country, and lives there in a profligate manner: 'Like a Horse that hath broken his reins, when he finds himself loose, skips over Hedges, Ditches and Pales . . . so wildly he runs about untill he is wearied.' His wife goes to visit him while he is abroad. He feigns a welcome, shows her the sights, and hurries her home again: 'So she, good woman, goeth home to care and spare, whil'st he spends.' When he returns home at last, 'Custom making Confidence, and Confidence Carelessness, [he] begins to be less shy, and more free, insomuch as . . . his Maid, whom he did hut eye, and friendly kiss, now he courts in every room; and were it not for his Estate he made over, even before his Wife's face; but that made him fawn and flatter, and somewhat for quietness sake.'

At last, however, the wife has ocular proof of his back-sliding. She finds a letter from one of his mistresses. He cringes and promises amendment.

No, said she, I never will trust in a broken Wheel; do you know what is in my power, said she? Yes, said he, a great part of my Estate. O how I adore Dame Nature, said she, that gave me those two Eyes, Prudence to foresee and Providence to provide; but I have not onely your Estate, but your I honour and Fame in my power; so that, if I please, all that see you shall hiss at you and condemn whatever you do.

For if you had the beauty of Paris, they would say you were but a fair Cuckold.

If you had the Courage of Hector, they would say you were but a desperate Cuckold.

> Had you the Wisdom of Ulysses, or Salomon, they would
> laugh and Say, there goes he that is not so wise as to keep
> his wife honest.

With these words she embarks on a course as dissipated as her husband's, nor can he say her nay, because she has his example before her and his money to give her independence. 'So they play like Children at bo-peep in Adultery; and face it out with fair looks, and smooth it over with sweet words, and live with false hearts and die with large Consciences. But these repenting, when they dyed, made a fair end.'

Plain words for plain facts. Cupid does not aim his dart, Philander's soul does not burn, Elismonda does not languish, and pen grandiose epistles before yielding the last favour. The Duchess knows the jargon, but she will have none of it. In that loose age of sham and tinsel she knows the unequivocal English word for 'Gallantry,' and she does not hesitate to use it. Until we examine the contemporary Restoration literature we cannot estimate at its full worth the moral and literary realism of this highly individual woman.

But it is not always plain words which the Duchess gives us. When she feels beauty, then words flock to her like seraphs dropping from heaven. It is in words like these she relates *The Tale of the Lady in Elysium.* There was a Lord who made suit to a lady. She agrees to marry him and then hears a false report which wounds her to the heart. She falls into a swoon and for an hour is believed dead. When she recovers, she describes the country where she has lingered. She was not dead, "twas onely the sudden and violent passion which hurried my soul to Charon's Boat in a distracted Whirlwinde of Sighs, where in the Crowd I was ferried over to the Elyzium Fields . . . such a place the Poets had described, pleasant green Fields, but as dark as a Shady Grove, or the dawning of the Day, or like a sweet Summer's evening when the Nightengale begins to sing.'

We have referred to Margaret Newcastle's English realism and compared her in that respect to the best of the popular school. *The Marriage Contract* supported this claim, and *The Tale of the Traveller* definitely establishes it. This is the story of a man who tries many ways of life in succession, only to find that happiness was waiting for him always in the place from which he first set out. His education is described from horn-book to University, and it is continued in travel abroad. His observation of distant countries and the various aspects of life, civil governments, peace and war, military glory, all merely serve to convince him that country life on his own estate is best. Then follows a truly excellent description of the country squire, an ancestor from whom Sir Roger de Coverley would be very proud to have descended:

> Well, said he, I will now return to my native Soil again, leaving the flattering and dissembling Courts, the deboist cities, the Cruell Warrs, and never take up Arms more, but when my King and Country sends me forth, but I will lead a Countrey life, study husbandry, follow my plows, sell my cattell and corn, butter and cheese at markets and faires, kisse the country Wenches, and carry my Neighbours Wife to a tavern when market is done, live thriftily and grow rich; then . . . he returned to his own Countrey, where after he had visited his friends, who had joyed to see him, and had welcomed him home, he put himself into one of his Farm houses; stocking his grounds, taking men-servants, and maid-servants to follow his business, and he himself would oversee and direct, clothing himself in a frize Jerkin, and a payre of frize breeches, a frize pair of mittins and a frize mountier-cap, to keep out sharp cold in Winter mornings, when the breath freezes between the teeth; industrious to call up his servants, before day light, and was the last a bed when their work was done. And in Summer time he would be up, with the Lark, to mow down his hay, to reap down his harvest, to see his Carts loaded, riding from cart to cart; and at noone would set down on his sheafs of corne or hay-cocks, eating bread and cheese, and young oynions with his regiment of Work-men, tossing the black leather-bottle, drinking the healths of the Country Lasses and Good wives, that dwelt thereabouts; and after his harvest was brought into his barnes; and his sheep-shearing-time done, make merry, as the custome of the Countrey was, with good cheer, although Countrey-fare, as Goose-pyes, Pudding-pyes, Furmity, Custards, Aples, and march-beere, dancing to the horne-pipe, with the lusty lasses and merry good Wives, who were drest in all their bravery, in their stammell petticoats and their grey Cloth wascoates or white-wascoats wrought with black worsted, and green aprons.
>
> The men with cloth-breeches and leather doublets, with peuter buttons, these and the like recreations the Countrey people hath mixt with their hard labours; when their stomacks were full and their leggs weary with dancing, or rather with running and leaping; for their dances hath no nice and difficult measures to tread, they disperse every one

118

to their severall houses, which are thatch, and only holes cut
for windows, unless it be the rich farmers, and they most
commonly have a chief room which is glazed yet the poorer
sort are seldom without bacon, cheese, and butter to entertain
a friend at any time.

Then giving thanks to the gentlemen for their good
cheere, and he shaking them every one by the hand, took
their leave.[7]

Now follows his search for a suitable wife, which is described
with great simplicity and vividness. A young lady is found with
all the necessary qualities. Their first interview passes off very
well, and each retires to consider the situation and to come to a
decision. The Squire confides in his man, Jack, and the lady in
her maid, Joan. There is much humour and raciness in these
touches, but alas! there is space to quote only a little more:

. . . Thus while the Master was trimming himself up, his
man and he discoursed.

In the meantime, the young lady was gone into her
Chamber; and calling her Maid to bring her the Glass, and
to view if the curls of her hair were in order. Lord, said she,
Joan, how red my face is! I seem as if I were drunk, my
cheeks burn like fire. You told me the other day I was in the
Green-sickness, you cannot think so now.

They are married, and 'Whilst he governed his outward Affairs,
she governed the Family at home, where they lived plentifully,
pleasantly and peaceably, not extravagantly, vaingloriously, and
luxuriously; they lived neatly and cleanly, they loved passionately,
thrived moderately, and happy they lived and piously died.'

The fable was another kind of feigned story which the Duchess
of Newcastle considered worth writing. From 1484, when Caxton
published the first English translation, Aesop's Fables had been
extremely popular, and that they continued to be so is proved by
the great number of translations and paraphrases which constantly appeared up to the nineteenth century and beyond it.
Before 1656 there had been numerous editions, and the Duchess
therefore, had ample opportunity to grow familiar with this
literary form. It was natural that she should have a lively interest
in this kind of story-telling. There was within her an irrepressible
spring of simplicity, wonder and imagination—her secret of
eternal youth—and she regarded Nature with the loving

familiarity of a child. Like a child, she liked nothing better than to endue animals and birds with human personalities, to create conversations between them, and to record their supposed thoughts and adventures. Indeed, sometimes, she goes further and distinguishes their characters with circumstantial quirks and quiddities. Even in her poems, published in 1653, three years before *Natures Pictures*, there is clear evidence of this disposition. Wat the Hare is not simply any member of the hare family. He is himself and none other. Whether he is lying, chin on paws, between a furrow, or sitting on his hindlegs washing his ears, or gazing obliquely out of his great grey eyes, or fleeing wildly before the pack, or dying without a cry—still he is Wat to the very last whisker. So it is with the Sparrow, that Bolshevik bird who piles up his arguments against human tyrants with the most ruthless and cocky logic. So it is with the 'Oake Tree in the Grove,' that mild and noble veteran. The Duchess had the power of making such characters live.

It is not surprising then that her fables, which constitute Book 4 of *Natures Pictures*, are all very good. They are four in number: three moral tales of the Ant and the Bee, and the moral tale of the Woodcock and the Cow. Since we have already described what the Duchess made of this sort of writing, there is no need to dissect these fables. Each exemplifies a moral truth which is however, so skilfully interwoven that it never obtrudes itself dryly. The characters are spirited and are presented with humorous insight. Sometimes we are given a sudden revelation of style, as for example in *The Woodcock and the Cow*. The two are comparing their lives. One enjoys the freedom of the air; the other the security of the earth. Each envies the other. The Woodcock complains that in the air there is no food, whereas:

> You sit here all day chewing the Cud . . . and in the Summer you are put to rich Pasture, or lye in green Meadows growing thick with Cowslips and Daisies; or else for change, you walk up to the Mountain-tops to brouse on wilde Time or sweet Margerum; and yet you rail against our good Mother Earth from whose Bowels we receive life, and food to maintain the life she gives us; she is our kinde Nurse, from whence we suck out of her springing Brests fresh Water, and are fed by her Hand of Bounty, shaded under her spreading Boughs land sheltered from Storms in her thick Groves.

Surely it was a happy portent that a woman could, with inspired realism, bring to her narrative such strong, simple and melodious praise.

We cannot close an account of the Duchess's contributions to prose fiction, without commenting on her *Sociable Letters*.[8] It will be necessary later to discuss the growth of the Epistolatory Novel, and to show that Richardson was by no means an innovator in form or in idea. Among those who anticipated him were several women, and it is to such a discussion that the *Sociable Letters* are most cogent. Let us here content ourselves in remarking with Jusserand: 'She too may be credited with having anticipated Richardson in her *Sociable Letters* in which she tries to imitate real life, to describe scenes, very nearly to write an actual novel.'[9]

Speaking still of the Duchess of Newcastle, Jusserand says: 'Among the mass of her writings . . . ideas are scattered here and there which are destined to live, and through which she anticipated men of true and real genius.' Yes, but that is only a part of the truth. It is not only by embryonic ideas that the Duchess contributed to the development of the novel, but also by such definite means as we have illustrated—in a word, by avoiding the decadent, and by showing in many forms her adherence to the living trend in story-telling.

Notes and References

1 *Natures Pictures drawn by Fancie's Pencil to the Life* (1656). Dedication to Pastime.
2 *Description of a New Blazing World* (1666), pp. 13 f.
3 Ibid., p. 31.
4 *Natures Pictures* . . . Book ii.
5 Ibid., Book ii, 'The Discreet Virgin.'
6 Ibid., Book x.
7 *Natures Pictures* . . . Book ix, 'The Tale of the Traveller.'
8 *CCXL Sociable Letters* (1664).
9 J. J. Jusserand, *The English Novel in the time of Shakespeare* (1890), p. 378.

Chapter V

Main Restoration Genres Contrasted

Love in fantastic triumph sate
While bleeding hearts around him flowed,
For whom fresh pains he did create,
And strange tyrannic power he showed.

(Aphra Behn, *Abdelazar*)

Sixteen sixty: fanfare of trumpets! Ring up the curtain on the literary tragi-comedy of the Restoration period. To describe the period from the literary point of view one would need the antithetical pen of Carlyle. Then one might say—it was an age of brilliance and an age of squalor; an age of vitality and an age of paralysis; an age of genius and an age of servile imitation. For drama it was a period of intense activity; for the novel it was a period of stagnation. It was an age when a large number of women forced their way into both fields, and at least held their own. Before we judge their work, let us consider the public they had to serve and the possibilities of developing prose fiction at that time.

The Restoration, coming after long years of bloodshed and rancour, found a certain section of the English people drained of idealism and sentiment. Events had made them cynics. They had seen England rebel against kingship only to groan under the heel of common men; now they heard the cry 'Long live King Charles,' and their minds sardonically revived the memory of one frosty morning in Whitehall. They had seen a revolt against what was termed licence in life and art, and had watched life being narrowed down to a mere preparation for death: for their part they were sick of death, coldly determined that life should pay them their arrears. For twenty years there had been too much dying, too much whispering, too much canting, too much wrestling with the spirit. It would take more than three score years and ten to wipe out the memory of those starved years of poverty and exile, to press into one lifetime all the luxury, the licence, the love, wit, beauty, shapes, colours, perfumes, sounds—all the richness of life to satisfy senses and brain—not heart nor conscience— those painful and demoded organs were no longer necessary to life. Necessary to happiness, whines the Puritan? Happiness— what thing is that? It is a word like so many other words that mean nothing—like love, for instance, or honour, or fidelity or fortune. When a man has seen governments rise and fall, love debased, honour shift with every wind, fortune crumble overnight, he cannot really be expected to regard them seriously, in the manner of good simple folk of twenty years ago. It is, after all, more amusing and more sensible to take the world with careless elegance like a pinch of snuff.

This, in effect, was the philosophy which Charles II and his courtiers shared alike. It was by no means the philosophy of all England. The Puritans stood apart. Middle class citizens, steadily growing in power, regarded the new era with a suspicious or an indulgent eye, according to their dispositions, or their chance of worldly success. Dissenters from the Restoration spirit had no power to check it, or to moderate its effect on the literature of the age, and though they did express themselves in one immortal book, they cannot be considered in our present scheme.

At the Restoration, the people of England were passing through a phase of disillusionment and spiritual exhaustion. They might show energy in literary work, but it was not likely that they would show much initiative. It was, in fact, a time when imitation of French literary fashions reached a height unparalleled since the days when, between the Conquest and the rise of Chaucer, England forgot that she had a native genius and accepted the literary dominance of France. English drama, which absorbed the main interest and activity at the Restoration, was to a great extent modelled on the French, although, indeed, France was not responsible for the depravity which became its peculiar characteristic. In fiction English writers gave to the French more than predominance: on the whole, they did not even compete, preferring to let French prose fiction satisfy the needs of English romance-readers. Drama was strangling prose fiction, and English writers had practically no interest at all in averting its doom.

123

Prior to 1660, English imitation of French Drama had been rendered impossible owing to Puritan oppression of the theatre, but for a considerable time before the Restoration (from the year 1647 onwards) a particular kind of French prose fiction had invaded England. This was the French Heroic Romance. Gomberville's *Polexandre* was the advance guard soon to be followed by the works of La Calprenède and Mlle de Scudéry. Battalions continued to arrive even until the year 1677 when Mlle de Scudéry's *Almahide* made its appearance. It is difficult now to understand how these ponderous romances, dragging on their wearisome and complicated narratives through tome after tome (sometimes through a dozen folio volumes), could possibly have won and retained the interest of the reading public. Apart from the unreality of their subject-matter, one would have supposed it no small inconvenience to wait long years to discover whether the hero and heroine are finally united. For example in *Clélie*, published by Madeleine de Scudéry in January, 1649, the tale begins: 'There never shone such a fine day as the one which was to be the eve of the nuptials between the illustrious Aronce and the admirable Clélie.' The marriage is delayed until the end of the tenth and last volume in September, 1654.

These heroic romances grew from the popularity of d'Urfé's *L'Astrée*, which was, however, like the *Arcadia*, a union of the pastoral and the chivalric romances. The pastoral trend of d'Urfé's romance was not much imitated, but the chivalric trend grew into the French Heroic Romance. *L'Astrée* bequeaths to the heroic romance three very important characteristics: authentication of background; the sovereignty of love, and a new conception of the relationship between men and women, whereby women were made the centre of society and the objects of respectful devotion.

These French Heroic Romances all had for their theme the love of a great hero for a lovely and discreet lady. He might be a Frenchman, a Roman, a Merovingian or a Turk, he might be the conqueror of the entire world, but he was still the captive of love. His love, the mainspring of all his actions, was of the most idealistic kind. He would endure for twenty years the most tremendous onslaughts of fate, perform the most heroic feats of valour, and then think himself mightily rewarded by one glance from the pure eyes of the fair one. A single favour, such as a ribbon from the lady's wrist, or a scarf from the ivory column of her neck, was enough to spur him on there and then to another twenty years' hard labour. As the imagination of the authors, who were, after all, human, sank before the prospect of inventing sufficient exploits and obstacles to fill the customary succession of folio volumes, they adopted the device of making their characters write innumerable letters to each other, and constantly recount the stories of their lives. Sometimes, says Jusserand, we see them go to bed in order to listen more comfortably. In *Cassandre*, the eunuch Tireus has a story to tell Prince Oroondates: '"The prince went to his bedroom and put himself to bed; he then had Tireus called to him, and having seats placed in the ruelle, he commanded us to sit," and then the story begins and it goes on for pages; and when it is finished we observe that it was included in another story told by Araxe; wherefore instead of finding ourselves among the actors of the principal tale, we alight among those of Araxe's narratives. These stories are thus enclosed in one another like Chinese boxes.'[2]

It is perhaps incredible, but it is none the less true, that even during the Civil War these French Heroic Romances were greedily devoured by the upper and the bourgeois classes in England. Charles I, on the eve of his execution, distributing some of his books as souvenirs, left *Polexandre* to the Earl of Lindsay. Dorothy Osborne, against the background of a convulsed England, constantly exchanges with Sir William Temple volumes of *Cleopâtre* and *Le Grand Cyrus*. Mrs Pepys, somewhat later, was an insatiable reader of French romances. Despite her husband's avowed disapproval, he not only bought them for her as a peace offering when he had been too attentive to Pierce or Knipp, but actually stayed up late at night to read them himself. No doubt the immediate popularity of these romances was due to the fact that they were a refuge from grim reality, but it must be remembered that the *Arcadia* had left in England a definite susceptibility to such fiction.

Whatever the attitude in England towards the Heroic Romance up to 1660, one would not have expected the Restoration public to tolerate such tedious accounts of a kind of love quite alien to their cynicism. Probably they would not have done so if these romances had been their only form of fictional amusement, but in fact the main interest of the public and the main energies of the best writers were all devoted to the drama. It is true that the two London playhouses were the only ones in England, and that they were attended only by the corrupt, courtly clique and the riff-raff of the town. But this did not limit the influence of the drama. Plays were printed and widely circulated, and they furnished a depraved eroticism far more titillating than the meek pruderies of heroic love. We have nothing to do with the heroic tragedies which were partly modelled on French Tragedy and partly a distortion of Shakespeare, but Restoration Comedy, although at the time it stunted the writing of prose fiction, nevertheless enriched it in the long run. It was based on imitation of Ben Jonson, but more particularly on Molière, and though it was a depraved offspring of these sources, its brilliance cannot be denied. It was a comedy of manners, and even if it represented the scavengings of human nature it represented them in a very realistic way. It developed a flexible, lifelike prose, graphic description, excellent dialogue and minute characterization—*minute,* not deep. It is interesting to note how rapidly Restoration Comedy gained that verisimilitude which was denied to the novel. This was because the novel was being ignored as a vehicle for storytelling, but also because a story in action compels realism. A novel though utterly untrue to life, may by the very number and extravagance of its episodes or by its style make us forget that we are being cheated of reality, or at least make us willing to be so. With a play it is far otherwise. However much our imagination is willing to be imposed upon, it is continually being checked by the senses, which insist that the little world on the stage must represent the world we know. Comparing even in length the Heroic Romance and the drama, the reversal of aim is apparent— one endeavouring to concentrate action and the other incredibly to prolong it. It was no wonder that Congreve, in his *Incognita* tried to enclose a written story within the dramatic unities.

But it was really quite unnecessary to seek in the drama some clue towards the concentration of action in prose fiction. The astounding fact is that over a hundred years previously England had been flooded with short, vivid, realistic stories—true novels in miniature—and yet, although they proved a wonderful inspiration to English drama, they were not accepted as models by English writers of fiction. The *novelle* may be said to have flowered simultaneously in France and Italy during the Middle Ages. Italy hit on the form of the *novella*. France, meanwhile, had been embodying similar material in the *fabliaux*, which when made into prose, stood side by side with the Italian prose tale as belonging to the same genre—that genre known as the *novella*.[3] In 1566 and 1567, Painter and Fenton published their collections of translated *novelle*,[4] but even before then, in 1563, Roger Ascham had fulminated against the translation of such harmful and 'ungratious bookes.'[5] England welcomed with delight these pictures drawn from real life, these apparently authentic stories which displayed 'the possibilities of action to which men and women, in pursuit of any passion, might be driven by that force or virtu of the will, restrained neither by law nor conscience.'[6] But neither Bandello, Cinthio, Boccaccio, Margaret of Navarre, Straparola nor Fiorentino could induce the English to imitate their example and to write such stories as the *novelle*. Possibly this was because a strong bent towards the drama caused English writers to ignore prose fiction, and to embody the influence of the *novelle* in dramatic form. There was also the very important fact that prose writers had to please their powerful patrons, and that the aristocratic taste was entirely in favour of the Chivalric and the Pastoral Romances and their modifications. England of the Elizabethan period was about two hundred years behind Italy in culture and in sophistication. The English people had banished dragons from their romances, but they still preferred to live in a world of illusion which was merely an echo of medieval chivalry and Greek idylls, and which was a complete contrast to the surging life about them. Also, they were not attracted by the intrigues which were the pivotal point in the *novelle*. They preferred to adhere in fiction to the idea of constancy in love, a central theme which they had adopted from the Greek and Spanish romances. From free fancy to realism is the road of development in fiction. The Italians had arrived. The English refused to be hurried, chiefly because they did not know where they were going. They preferred to linger on the way, indulging in prolonged and complicated daydreams. Indeed they were benighted, for when they had almost escaped from Arcadia they lost themselves again in the *pays du tendre*.

Suddenly, after this long period of quiescence, the *novelle* once more sprang into activity. From about the year 1670 onwards it again commenced to attract attention. From 1640, when they were first translated as a whole by Mappe, Cervantes' *Exemplary*

Novels had engaged the interest of the reading public. They were reprinted in 1694, 1708 and 1728.[7] In these Spanish tales the subject was generally the struggles of two lovers to be united in spite of cruel parents; or the determination of the deserted girl to pursue her recreant lover. Both the Spanish and the Italian short stories were alike in the stratagems and surprises in which the plot worked itself out. Both had also the great attraction of brevity. This was one reason for the revival of interest in the *novelle* after 1670. Another and very powerful reason was that they were erotic, and in this respect the Italian *novella* far outdid the *Exemplary Novels*. The Italian *novella* had for its central theme sensual love— all the subterfuges and scheming of infidelity. No wonder that in the Restoration period, the *novella* had a new lease of life, and that this time its influence was not indirect. It aroused imitators. The reading public was not only beginning to weary of the tortuous prolixity of the Heroic Romance, but was at last beginning to realise that, like the sandpiper in the proverb, it could not fish both strands at once. Gallant and fine lady could not equally enjoy the intrigues of the drama (or of their own experience) and the mawkish *naïveté* of Oroondates and Cassandra. They did not speak the same love language as these elevated spirits, and they preferred a tale which echoed their own views and which was full of highly coloured adventures: 'Come near us,' says Congreve, 'and represent to us intrigues in practice, delight us with accidents and odd events, but *not such as are wholly unprecedented*, such which *not being so distant from our belief*, brings also the pleasure nearer us. Romances give more of wonder, novels more delight.'[8]

This seems most promising. One would suppose that the day of the Heroic Romance was ended, and that tales after the realistic style of the *novelle* would now be written, tales which would depict the London hurly-burly, the roystering brilliance of the court, the stout adventures of merchants and their wives— life in short, however much interwoven with love intrigue. But alas! the Heroic Romance had not yet loosened its grip. The short tales which now appeared were so sicklied over with the romantic cast that they were not really imitations of the *novella*, but actually sentimental novelettes. These novelettes were a strange mixture of the worst elements in the *novella* and in the Heroic Romance. From the *novella* was borrowed its central theme that passionate love justifies every means to its end. From the Heroic

Romance was borrowed its blue-blooded characters, its grandiose sentimentality and its emotional exaggerations. The result was often farther than ever from reality and the best point in favour of the majority of these productions was their brevity. The Heroic Romance, however unreal, had a certain dignity—a quality which the romantic novelette frequently lacked. The effect which Restoration life and tastes had on most writers is well seen in Roger Boyle. His *Parthenissa,* a clumsy Heroic romance, appeared in six tomes, which were published separately at intervals from 1654 to 1669. In 1676, when court life and a desire to conform to the new fashion in novel writing had changed his outlook, he published a novel called *English Adventures.* It was a medley of the picaresque, the pastoral, scandal veiled as history, and sensual intrigue, all 'related with . . . debauched cynicism.'[9]

It was to be expected that the romantic vogue would produce a reaction. In France it had done so as early as 1627, when Sorel made fun of *L'Astrée.* Passing from satire he struck a blow for bourgeois realism in his *Francion.*[10] Scarron, Molière, Antony Hamilton, Subligny and Furetière all carried on the anti-romantic campaign. In England, although translations of the French anti-romantic works appeared, they did not inspire imitations until the day of the Heroic Drama was nearly over. And even then readers were still so enmeshed in romantic fiction that they ignored two really notable attempts to disillusion them.

Nor was there wanting a precedent for a finer sort of fiction. In 1678, in the same year as the *Pilgrim's Progress* (which had no influence on the output of the literary period which it so completely surpassed), there appeared Mme de la Fayette's *Princesse de Clèves.* This had for its theme renunciation, and it concentrated in its short form a reality, an insight and a power of characterization which had never before shown themselves in French prose fiction. But neither in France nor in England had this any immediate effect.

The picaresque, coney-catching realism, and the imaginary journey drew a feeble life from the writings of Head and Kirkman. Popular fiction awaited the realism of Defoe to develop its powers.

Such were the genres of fiction which existed at the Restoration and in the days of James II. When we come to the women novelists and consider them against the social and literary background which it has been necessary to describe, several points at once suggest themselves. First, that no women unless under financial compulsion would write in such an age; secondly, that a woman hard pressed for money would not be content to sit and starve while she turned out a dozen volumes of Heroic romance; thirdly, that women would write plays as the most popular and paying concern, and write them like men for the depraved tastes of the period; also, that they would excel in the comedy of manners aided by the feminine power of minute observation, and perhaps of repartee; fourthly, that, if they wrote fiction at all (and the first woman writer of the age was possibly forced to it because she was 'warned off' the stage), then they would concentrate on the romantic novelette, because it would exactly suit their public, and because it represented their outlook, and was within their literary scope; and, further, one would expect that their experience as dramatists would help them as fiction writers. All these facts are true of the women we shall discuss in this and subsequent chapters.

Aphra Behn was the first and the greatest of the literary swashbucklers who swept into prominence in Restoration and Post-Restoration days. She was one of a band of women early left to fend for themselves either because of moral transgression or lack of money. Many of them were of good family, a few (for example, Mrs Trotter) led honest private lives. But their origin had nothing to do with their career as writers (Mrs Pix, the author of the filthy *Spanish Wives*, was a clergyman's daughter). The reason was obvious. If one decides to be a miner one expects to be blackened from head to foot in the course of one's work. A fastidious miner in kid gloves and immaculate suiting, withdrawing delicately from contact with a coal seam, would at once find that tension and starvation were the sole rewards of this particularity. So it was in the business of writing in Restoration days. The motto might have been 'Get dirty or get out,' and the women could not get out. They were writing to earn their bread. Their success depended on writing as the men wrote, and the men wrote to please the lewd and cynical tastes of the rich and leisured. The influential public wanted in plays or in stories a representation of life as they knew it, and life as they knew it stank to heaven. Theirs was a world hinging on open sexuality; a world which was, indeed, bored with ordinary immorality, and which insisted on themes of incest and perversion to relieve the monotony; a world in which men and women, even supposedly decent women, talked in an incredibly licentious manner; a world in which women considered it amusing to be mistaken for prostitutes, and in which certain diseases were considered a joke or a boast. Allardyce Nicol says:

> All sorts of moral ties, all sense of decency had gone. Women had become as libidinous as the men. 'Common women' were 'public grown . . . in this damn'd lewd town.' 'What a lewd world we live in!' says Aphra Behn, 'Oh, London, London, how thou aboundest in iniquity! Thy young men are debauched, thy virgins deflowered, and thy matrons are turned bawds . . .' Nothing was left to occupy the minds of this circumscribed clique but intrigue and sensuality. Every name and title given to a woman came, during this period, to have an evil significance. 'Lady' as Pepys shows us, had become debased in meaning, as had 'mother' and 'Madam,' 'Miss' and 'Mistress.' The utter filth that marks many of the lyrics contained, for example, in such a collection as the *Poems on affairs of State* is but the ordinary speech of women of this type and of their men companions, made a trifle more 'poetical.' It is evident from the dialogue in the comedies that the conversation of men with men or women with men, reaches a freedom seen at no other period of our history. If we listen to the words of a couple of lovers of the time we wonder sometimes whether our ears be not deceiving us. Turn even to a work of one of the geniuses of the age, turn to John Dryden's *Secret Love*, and read the words of Celadon and Florimel; in spite of the wit we stand aghast. That such a conversation as appears in the fifth act of this play—and it was evidently realistic—could ever have taken place between two cultured persons in a civilised society, or that it could have been presented on the stage to a general audience shows us probably as clearly as anything the peculiar temper of the age with which we are dealing.[12]

That is the point we wish to drive home—the peculiar temper of the age, and the fact that it characterized women as well as men. Moral decadence is never confined to the male members of a community. If it were, it could not possibly persist unless there were segregation of the sexes. It is necessary to emphasize another fact. Aphra Behn and her followers wrote in the Restoration fashion, because the were Restoration women. To listen to the criticisms levelled at them not only by elegant vipers like Pope, but also by kind and serious critics from that time to the present day, one would suppose that these women could have had the moral principles of Alice Meynell or Elizabeth Browning, but wilfully perverted their natures to write obscenely. Actually they wrote obscenely because their minds were already obscene, and their minds were obscene because they made no effort to resist the spirit of the time. Could they have withdrawn from infection as did the Duchess of Newcastle? Certainly, if they had had the Duchess of Newcastle's financial independence. It is a vicious circle. Let us, in the name of common sense, judge them as the product of that age, and not as if they could have been the product of the Hannah More era. Madonna lilies did not flower in the literary London of Aphra Behn. Tiger lilies did. All novelists, women included, express some tendency of their period. Many modern women write salacious fiction with far less external compulsion.

Aphra Behn was the first woman to earn her living by her pen. The details of her life have been the subject of a controversy upon which a question in regard to her literary creativeness is supposed to hinge. Since the problem makes itself felt in *Oroonoko*, one of her last works, we shall defer until then a discussion of the conflicting arguments, and here limit ourselves to the humble statement that as she really was born, she must have had parents, and must have had a birthplace. She maintained that she spent part of her youth in Surinam. She was certainly engaged in secret-service work in the interests of Charles II. It is believed that she had been married to a Dutch merchant in London. There is proof that she had also been in a debtor's prison. We find her, after the Restoration, established in London as a writer of plays, holding her own with the best dramatists of her time. She took the Tory side against the Whigs and attacked them roundly in her plays. In revenge, the Whigs succeeded in getting a warrant issued against her, and she was forced to abandon the theatre in 1682. She may before then have experimented in novel writing, but circumstances now made it, for a while, her legitimate literary outlet, and though in 1688 she again took to plays, she continued to write prose fiction of several kinds up to the time of her death.

When Mme de la Fayette wrote her short novel *La Princesse de Clèves* the way to popular taste was indicated. But already in England Aphra Behn had brought to the writing of short novels the power of her personality and her literary prestige. She

created a new vogue which paved the way to important developments in prose fiction. Not only did the short form give fresh
possibilities to story-telling, but in the hands of Aphra Behn it
showed distinctive trends which were of the utmost value in the
subsequent history of the novel. Mrs Behn as a novelist, says
Jusserand, can only be studied with the authors of the middle of
the eighteenth century.[13] In her thirteen novels these trends are
sometimes distinct, but more often mingled curiously. There is
the influence of the Heroic Romance, there is the influence of the
continental *novelle*, and there is the urgent prompting of everyday
life. Chronological classification of Mrs Behn's stories is very
doubtful, and so it is not really necessary to review them in the
order in which they are supposed to have been written, nor
would it be easy since these dates vary so much. It will be more
helpful to consider them as far as possible in relation to their
most predominant trend. Even this, however, is not easy, since
romance and realism are often so interwoven as to defy classification, and also since it is not always possible to define whether
Aphra Behn's realism is imaginative or genuine.

It seems very probable that Aphra Behn's first novel was *The
Adventures of the Black Lady*.[14] This tale has signs of immaturity
not observable in her other novels. It is original not only in its
brevity, but also in its subject-matter which shows clearly that
Mrs Behn had been browsing on anti-romantic literature. *The
Black Lady* is one of the three novels to which Aphra Behn gave a
London background and which truly represent the world in
which she lives.

The story begins: 'About the beginning of last June (as near as
I can remember) Bellamora came to town from Hampshire and
was obliged to lodge the first night at the same inn where the
stage-coach set up.' She wishes to spend about six months with
Madam Brightly, a kinswoman of hers, undiscovered, if possible,
by her friend in the country. She seeks Madam Brightly all over
St Anne's parish, but in vain. And she is so foolish as to entrust
her trunk to a porter she saw in the street. She is behaving like
the typical country bumpkin; she wanders about, expecting everyone she meets to know the whereabouts of her relative. She is
exasperating, but we are sympathetic, and our curiosity is aroused.
How will she extricate herself from this predicament? She does
so by a surprising stroke of what we can only call fool's luck. She

seeks Madam Brightly in the house of a decayed gentlewoman, and encounters there a lady who knows her, but whom she herself does not know. Next morning she reveals that she came to town to conceal the disgrace brought on her by one Mr Fairlove who loves her, but whom she refuses to marry. The lady who recognizes her is Fairlove's sister. She and the decayed gentlewoman concoct a benevolent plot. They summon Fairlove to town, and, to detain Bellamora until his arrival, they pretend that her trunk (which has been safely delivered) has been lost. By the time Fairlove appears Bellamora is so distracted with anxiety and misery that she is willing to marry him — and does.

The story is told in a simple, conversational style. It is not of intrinsic value. Its significance is in its background of London life, and in the fact that it was to the familiar scenes around her that Aphra Behn instinctively turned when she decided to write a novel.

When struck (no doubt) by the realism of *The Black Lady*, some friends of Mrs Behn's challenged her to imitate Scarron, she wrote *The Court of the King of Bantam*. *As* it was based on the *Roman Comique*[15] one would naturally expect to find it an anti-romantic, witty tale of London life. This exactly what it is. The story, which is excellently told, hinges on an elaborate practical joke. It plunges us directly into the fortunes of the principal characters:

> This money certainly is a devilish thing! I am sure the Want of it had like to have ruined my dear Philibella in her love to Valentine Goodland; who was really a pretty deserving Gentleman, Heir to about fifteen hundred Pounds a Year; which however did not so much recommend him, as the Sweetness of his Temper, the Comeliness of his Person, and the Excellency of his Parts. In all which Circumstances my obliging Acquaintance equall'd him, unless in the Advantage of their Fortune. Old Sir George Goodland knew his Son's passion for Philibella and tho' he was generous and full of a Humour sufficiently complying yet he could by no means think it convenient that his only Son should marry with a young Lady of so slender a Fortune.

Here with admirable directness, economy and spirit we have the key to the situation which arises. Philibella lives at Charing Cross with an uncle on whom she is dependent, and is adored by a wealthy nincompoop called Mr Would-be-King. Although married, Mr Would-be-King is a happy-go-lucky Lothario, and in addition suffers from a *folie de grandeur* which leads him to shower expensive presents on his feminine acquaintances, not however, in the spirit of pure philanthropy. Philibella steadily ignores his advances, but he continues to visit at her uncle's house. On a particular evening, Sir Philip, his niece and her lover, Valentine Goodland, sit playing cards, with Sir Philip's wife and Lucy, his former mistress — a juxtaposition which would amaze anyone given to straining at gnats. Mr Would-be arrives to find them 'very merry, with a flask or two of Claret before 'em and Oranges roasting by a large fire for it was Christmas time.' They win a considerable sum of money from him, and Sir Philip urges him to come again on Twelfth Night to renew the famous and ancient solemnity of choosing king and queen. This invitation is given in furtherance of a scheme which Sir Philip has devised, by which Would-be shall be parted from £3,000, and Philibella shall be united to Valentine. Valentine is instructed that on Twelfth Night he shall pick a quarrel with Would-be, and Lucy is to pretend that she is simply a niece to Sir Philip. On the appointed evening, Would-be-King arrives, and is entertained most royally. In fact, so that nothing shall be lacking in his splendid illusion, it has been arranged that by the lots in the cake, he shall be chosen king. To the surprise of the household, he has brought musicians who play all the more merrily for the money he lavishes on them 'for gold and wine doubtless are the best rosin for musicians.' In comes the mighty cake 'teeming with the Fate of this extraordinary Personage.' Would-be discovers the bean which indicates that he is King of the revels, and Lucy (by a similar pre-arrangement) is the Queen. Healths are drunk amid laughter and applause, and the dupe becomes intoxicated, chiefly with magnificence. He gives costly presents to Lucy and Philibella, and incautiously offers Valentine enough money to marry whomever he likes. He is enraged to hear that Lucy is 'that not impossible she,' and turns furiously on Valentine, thus relieving him of the necessity of picking a quarrel. They exchange insults, Valentine playing his role with a zest derived from Would-be's attentions to Philibella. After an eruption of rodomontade he departs, breathing vengeance. 'Let him go', cries Would-be, 'like a pragmatical captious, giddy fool he is! I shall take a time to see him.' Sir Philip ingeniously points out that

Valentine cannot fail to have the upper hand as he is to be married to Lucy before Easter. Would-be falls into the trap, and led by amorousness, vanity and spite, reacts exactly as Sir Philip had hoped he would. This worthy knight explains that Lucy has a fortune of £3,000, and that accordingly Valentine means to marry her although he loves Philibella. But how diverting it would be if Lucy could be induced to become Would-be's mistress before becoming Valentine's wife! The King of Bantam is enchanted at the prospect. That it is to be achieved by giving Philibella a fortune of £3,000 does not deter him, because, as Sir Philip points out, he can recover the sum in gaming with her future husband, a young fop appropriately called Sir Philip Flygold. In fact, this is a doubly useful scheme because it will give him future power over Philibella. To while away the time until morning the intriguing pair play piquet, and Sir Philip, with unaccountable luck, wins three thousand two hundred guineas, for which Would-be gives him a bond witnessed by Will Watchful and Sim Slyboots, Sir Philip's servants, 'a couple of delicate beagles,' as Mrs Behn inimitably calls them. The next day Sir Philip receives Valentine, reports progress and instructs him now to make his peace with Would-be, which he does to the great relief of that regal personage, who, in contemplation of a duel, has already died a thousand deaths. Sir Philip returns the bond to Would-be on condition that he pays £3,000 to Philibella. This is done. A few days later Would-be achieves his supposed vengeance only to discover that Philibella and Valentine have married on the strength of the money he has so obligingly provided.

The *King of Bantam* is surprisingly modern in form, and we see in it a proof of what Aphra Behn could have achieved had she been brave enough to abandon more frequently and more fully the Heroic tradition, and to depict life as she knew it. Here we have a glimpse of Restoration London, not an edifying glimpse, but if we are to walk with Aphra Behn we must be prepared to take things in our stride. How real it is, how completely alive — the jostling crowds, the eating houses, the plying coaches, the theatre (described with authentic particulars of the very plays being acted at the time and with familiar references to the King's box), not to mention the ways of the reckless gallants, the drinking-bouts, the gaming, the balls! We know so well already all these people to whom we are introduced: 'The Lady Flippant, the Lady Harpy, the Lady Crocodile, Madam Tattlemore, Miss Medler, Mrs Gingerly, a rich Grocer's wife, and some others besides Knights and gentlemen of as good humours as the ladies.' There can be no mistaking Madam Tattlemore with a secret: 'How wondrous hasty was she to be gone, as soon as she heard it! It was not in her power, because it was not in her nature, to stay long enough to take a civil leave of the company, but away she flew . . . proclaiming it to every one of her acquaintance.'

The Unfortunate Happy Lady is the third one of these novels that reflect a London background. It is less characteristic of this background than are *The Adventures of the Black Lady* and the *King of Bantam*, and it is more like an Italian or Spanish *novella*. The ironic style is rather in the manner of Scarron. The story begins

> I cannot omit giving the World an account of the uncommon villainy a Gentleman of a good Family in England practis'd upon his sister, which was attested to me by one who liv'd in the Family, and from whom I had the whole truth of the story. I shall conceal the unhappy Gentleman's own under the borrow'd Names of Sir William Wilding, who succeeded his father, Sir Edward, in an estate of near 4,000 a Year, inheriting all that belong'd to him, except his Virtues.

To avoid paying his sister, Philadelphia, her portion of £6,000 (which he cannot afford owing to his extravagance) he takes her to London and under the pretence of putting her under the protection of a friendly old lady, he puts her into a brothel. To the old beldame he pretends that Philadelphia is his cast-off mistress. The sardonic tone of the narrative is well seen in the following description of the relations between the harridan and the as yet undeceived girl:

> Not long after, they went to Dinner; and in the Afternoon, three or four young ladies came to visit the Right Reverend the Lady Beldam; who told her new Guest that these were all her Relations, and no less than her own sister's Children. The Discourse among 'em was general and very modest, which lasted for some Hours: for, our Sex seldom wants matter of Tattle. But, whether their Tongues were then miraculously wearied, or that they were tir'd with one continual Scene of Place, I won't Pretend to determine: but they left the Parlour for the Garden, where after about an Hour's Walk, there was a very fine Desert of Sweetmeats and Fruits brought into one of the Arbours. Cherbetts Ros Solis, rich

and small Wines, with Tea, Chocolate, etc., completed the Old Lady's Treat; the pleasure of which was much heighten'd by the voices of two of her Ladyship's Sham-Nieces, who sung very charmingly. The Dear, sweet Creature, thought she had happily got into the Company of Angels; but (alas!) they were Angels that had fallen more than once.

Fortunately Philadelphia's character is realized by a young man called Gracelove. He removes her to the protection of an honest family, and calls the wicked brother to account. Sir William goes abroad hastily, and changes his name. Philadelphia refuses to marry Gracelove until her fortune has been paid. He also has to cross the seas. When he returns Philadelphia has been married and widowed. She is now very rich. At the same moment her brother reappears in the story. Debts drive him back to England and finally into prison, 'where he learnt the Art of Peg-making, a Mystery to which he had been a Stranger all his Life long 'till then.' Philadelphia now buries the wicked William under an avalanche of coals of fire, paying all his debts to the extent of over £2,000. She marries Gracelove, William marries an heiress, and all ends with a deplorable lack of poetic justice.

We now come to a group of novels in which Heroic sentiment makes a strange veneer for the intrigues so dear to Restoration tastes. In her more usual code of sexual morality, the divine Astrea was a true child of her epoch. Her two main principles she thus defines:

> Conscience: a cheap pretence to cozen fools withal.
> Constancy, that current coin for fools.[17]

She has read her Bandello, and she shows sometimes that she has benefited by his example, but for the most part she is satisfied to smother the dramatic directness of the *novella* in a suffocating jargon of gallantry. It is interesting to note that she is not really at ease with the sophisticated roués and demi-rips whom she so often depicts. Her muse was more direct and colloquial. She is certain that love and sexual indulgence are the same thing, and she is comfortably determined that every Jack shall have his Jill. But she spreads a smoke screen, in the fashion of the day. Desire must not be too crudely naked. It must say:

> 'Tis you deny me life: 'tis you that forbid my flame; 'tis you will have me die, and seek my remedy in my grave, when I

complain of tortures, wounds and flames. O Cruel Charmer!
'tis for you I languish.[18]

The Heroic Romance showed the mighty champions of the
world as the slaves of their pure goddesses. The romance of
gallantry showed every man and woman the slave of passion.
Oroondates with high-souled ecstasy cherished the hope of one
kind look. Lysander languished, and cherished the certainty of
obtaining all he desired. If he did not obtain it, he, like Oroondates,
went to death's door, but first he was careful to exhaust every
means of success. It was the law of Love that all obstacles could
be removed and that the end justified every possible means.
Seduction, abduction, murder, were not criminal nor even blame-
worthy if only they were undertaken in the service of the sacred
flame. Lysander was as one devoted — no more responsible for his
excesses than a dervish or an epileptic. The God of Love inspired,
justified and rewarded all the actions of its helpless victims.

Mrs Behn wrote three stories in which the heroine was a nun.
In this, as in her *Love Letters between a Nobleman and his Sister
(1683)*, she was influenced by the *Portuguese Letters*, which
appealed to the public. It was not to be supposed that the essential purity and dignity of these letters would at that time be
understood. It was characteristic of Restoration writers that they
depraved all they touched. Their ideas in regard to convents are
so ludicrously ignorant that we can but laugh. Generally the nun
is an incredibly immoral woman, and the convent a kind of
elegant brothel with the added piquancy of a grille. Occasionally,
however, the convent is a retreat for harassed damsels fleeing
from a plethora of lovers. They take the veil for a few days merely
while they get their second wind, and then proceed to repel the
naughty villian and to encourage the true adorer from the top of
the garden wall. Soon they are off again into the world which
their fatal loveliness makes so perilous.

In The Fair Jilt, or Tarquin and Miranda,[19] we have the more
sinister view of convent life. Mrs Behn begins with a preamble
which puts us in mind of the argument with which Bandello
prefaces his *novelle*. Only in this case there is no moralizing, but
instead an excellent little disquisition on love and lovers, which
could well stand alone as a miniature essay in which complete
truth is presented with mordant wit, in which every word

expresses vividly a close observation of life and manners. But to the story: Miranda is a member of a religious community in Antwerp, a curious community whose inmates coruscate with diamonds, and who spend their time coquetting with their languishing admirers. This nun is young, wealthy, witty, accomplished and beautiful. 'She was admirably shaped: she had a bright hair and hazel-eyes, all full of love and sweetness.' She conceals under a modest exterior an insatiable lust, which, weary of too easy conquests, finds provocation in the purity of a young friar called Hendrik. Her interest is all the stronger when she hears Hendrik's story from her maid.

Hendrik's story is a complete digression, and in fact Hendrik himself is more of a hindrance than a help to the main narrative, but Aphra wished to show a nun trying to seduce a friar and would not be deprived of this artless pleasure. It is unnecessary to recount Hendrik's sad past. Suffice it to say that he once loved innocently, was robbed of his betrothed, and narrowly escaped being murdered by a wicked rival. He then decided to become a monk. He repels the foul Miranda's advances without the slightest difficulty, and she is so infuriated that she accuses him of the evil he has refused. He is cast into prison and condemned to be burned, but there is a delay in his execution.

Meanwhile Miranda, cured of her love and triumphing in her revenge, secures in marriage the great Prince Tarquin, whose title and fame have attracted her, and who is so besotted with love for her that neither the Bishop nor the nobles of Antwerp can dissuade him from his ruin. The married pair live in great splendour, partly supported by the embezzled fortune of Alcidiana, Miranda's young sister. But soon Alcidiana wishes to marry, and a gulf yawns at Miranda's feet — because the necessity of a marriage portion will reveal her theft. She does everything in her power to discourage her sister's suitors, but finally Alcidiana invokes the aid of a powerful kinsman who arranges a marriage for her. The day is appointed, the portion is demanded, and Miranda sees only one way out of the impasse. She sets on to the murder of her sister a young page who is her adoring tool. His ingenuity, however, is as deficient as his morals, and he bungles his attempt to poison Alcidiana. Condemned to death, he reveals the complicity of Miranda who is apprehended. However, with her genius for being saved by every situation, she throws all the blame on the page, makes a triumph of her imprisonment, and so far from slinking in chains, surrounds herself with royal pomp, and uses Tarquin as a buttress for her prestige. Still, she is forced, with a halter around her neck, to witness the page's execution and to see him for the last time hanging on her words. But her final release does not relieve the situation because Alcidiana's suitor is still intent on the marriage, undeterred by the fact that his future bride has 'lost the finest hair in the world, and the complexion of her face ever after,' not to mention that her eyes are 'starting out of her face black and all deformed.' Completely cornered, Miranda, woman-like, seeks refuge in bed. She refuses 'to eat, or sleep or see the light.' The Prince, raving with love and compassion, implores that she will suffer herself to live. She graciously consents, on condition that the Prince will assassinate Alcidiana. Seeing the reasonableness of this request, Tarquin puts two bullets into his pistol and later into Alcidiana's petticoats. She escapes without a scratch. Tarquin is captured and sentenced to be beheaded. Miranda, under pressure, confesses all her wickedness. Tarquin escapes death, through an error on the part of the headsman. He is pardoned and goes to Holland, where presently he is joined by the indefatigable Miranda and they live happily ever after. Aphra Behn is not content to omit Hendrik the friar from the final unity of action. During his long imprisonment we lost sight of him, but he influences the denouement. Tarquin's pardon is secured by the confession of Miranda, and Miranda confesses only under compulsion, Hendrik's fellow monks insisting that she shall clear him and all the others whom she has implicated.

This story is an excellent example of Aphra Behn's amoral romanticism. It is really more than immorality: it is a complete absence of moral sense. Throughout the narrative her sympathy is entirely with the evil-doers. It is as if she believed them to be the hypnotized slaves of love. Sometimes in listening to her observations, we can hardly believe our ears.

Having described Miranda's effort to seduce the friar in the confessional, Mrs Behn comfortably refers to her as 'the charming wanton.' Later, when Miranda's false accusation has condemned Hendrik to death, Mrs Behn, with an indulgent cluck, calls her 'the implacable beauty.' Prince Tarquin, after his attempted murder, is spoken of as 'the poor unfortunate gentleman' and his imprisonment is described as follows:

141

> In an hour's Time, the whole fatal Adventure was carried all
> over the City, and everyone knew that Tarquin was the
> intended Murderer of Alcidiana, and not one but had a real
> Sorrow and Compassion for him. They heard had bravely
> he had defended himself, how many he had wounded
> before he could be taken, and what numbers he had fought
> through. And even those who saw his Valour and Bravery
> and who had assisted at his being seiz'd, now repented
> from the Bottom of their Hearts their having any Hand in
> the ruin of so gallant a Man . . . He was eternally visited
> by his friends and acquaintance and this last action of bravery,
> had got him more than all his former conduct had lost.

This attitude to murder seems entirely fantastic, until we
remember that since Tarquin's attempt at crime was prompted
by his passion for Miranda, he was not a murderer but a martyr
to the sacred flame. Similarly, in describing the execution of the
page, Aphra recounts how he approached the scaffold 'fair as an
angel but languishing and pale;' and when Miranda joins her
husband in captivity, both criminals are referred to as 'the
amorous prisoners.'

Even in this artificial tale certain characteristics are apparent—
characteristics which are of the first importance in our final
assessment of Aphra Behn as a novelist. Passing over the
influence of heroic sentiment, we observe first the influence of
the drama, sometimes exaggerated to melodrama, sometimes
more rightly displayed in the focusing of attention on a dramatic
situation for which she carefully sets the scene. Witness the stage
directions for Miranda's love-making: 'On one side of him, she
kneel'd down, over-against a little altar where the priests' robes
lye, on which were placed some lighted waxcandles . . . which
shone full upon Miranda.' Another noteworthy point is Aphra
Behn's occasional aptness of phrase. When Hendrik is unjustly
suspected by a jealous husband, who plots to murder him, it is
unfortunate that he persists in his innocent visits for 'every visit
more and more confirmed his death.' And when the murderers
came on Hendrik in a wood: 'One of the men advanced, and cried
"Prince, you must die—I do believe thee (reply'd Hendrik) but
not by a Hand as base as thine."' And when Miranda is beguiling
Tarquin to murder Alcidiana, 'She kissed him to an oath, a
solemn oath to perform what he had promised.' This aptness is

part of a pithy colloquialism which breaks now and then through the rococo style of her hyper-romantic stories, and of which we shall find much more later on. Aphra Behn could not maintain her high-flown artificialities for long. The real woman, the woman of racy, vigorous diction was forever tearing her way through the tinsel. Even when Prince Tarquin's heroics are at their height, he must come down to take water. When, loaded with debt and summoned to pay Alcidiana's fortune he sought for bail among his friends, he could get none for 'Every one slunk their heads out of the Collar when it came to that.'

Not only in this, but in all Aphra Behn's novels we observe her determined effort to make them appear the records of real events. It is that same trick which Defoe afterwards used so lavishly and in which he was certainly anticipated by Aphra Behn. There is no length to which she will not go to render her stories credible. She is forever telling us that the characters were known to her personally, and that she was present at the time of the occurrence, and that she saw the correspondence to which she refers; or, at the very least, that the tale was recounted to her by one who could vouch for its authenticity. In *The Dumb Virgin* she takes the greatest pains to prove that, although she herself knew only English, yet by a lucky accident the heroine's sister (a Venetian) spoke English also, and thus the narrator got a first hand account of all that happened. One of the most amusing of Mrs Behn's efforts at authentication occurs in *The History of the Nun, or the Fair Vow-breaker*. Supporting her views on the seriousness of taking the veil she says: 'I once was design'd a humble Votary in the House of Devotion, but fancying myself endued with an obstinacy of Mind great enough to secure one from the Efforts and Vanities of the World, I rather chose to deny myself that Content I could not certainly promise myself, than to languish . . . in a certain affliction.' If she had been describing the hunting of elephants she would have written as a former elephant-hunter. Such was her particular technique. It was an important part of her efforts towards realism, which we shall have to analyze more fully at the end of this chapter. And it was not only by her persistent claims to first-hand information that Mrs Behn achieved verisimilitude. She did so by a thousand tricks of detailed description. Witness Prince Tarquin's execution:

When he came to the Market-Place, whither he walked on foot, follow'd by his own Domesticks, and some bearing a black Velvet Cohn with Silver Hinges; the Head's-man before him with his fatal Scimiter drawn, his Confessor by his Side . . . he mounted the Scaffold; which was strewed with some Sawdust, about the place where he was to kneel, to receive the Blood: the scaffold had a low Rail about it that every body might more conveniently see . . . He was some time in Prayer, and a very short time in speaking to his Confessor; then he turned to the Head's-man, and desired him to do his Office well, and gave him twenty Louis d'Ors; and undressing himself with the Help of his Valet and Page, he pull'd off his Coat and had underneath had a white Sattin Waistcoat: He took off his Periwig, and put on a white Sattin Cap, with a Holland one done with Point under it, which he pulled over his Eyes; then took a cheerful Leave of all, and kneel'd down, and said 'When he lifted up his Hands the third Time, the Head's-man should do his Office.' Which accordingly was done, and the Head's-man gave him his last stroke, and the Prince fell on the Scaffold . . . and murmurs and Sighs were heard from the whole Multitude, who scrambled for some of the bloody Sawdust, to keep) for his Memory.

Such passages support Macaulay's view that Roxana, Moll Flanders or Colonel Jack would have been well within the scope of Aphra Behn.

Another tale of a coiffed adventuress is *The Nun or the Perjured Beauty*[20] Two friends, Antonio and Henrique love the same woman—Dona Ardelia, a miracle of beauty and falsehood. Antonio loved her first, but her family forbade the marriage, so Don Henrique plays John to Antonio's Miles Standish, and with the same result. Ardelia falls in love with the eloquent newcomer, but he, torn between love and friendship, resolves to sacrifice Ardelia to Antonio, and Ardelia agrees to marry Antonio as proof of her adoration for Henrique. This seems devoid of sense or meaning, but we presume that it must have appeared logical in the days of high romance. The fatal charmer points her generosity by telling Antonio why she is marrying him. Antonio recoils as if stung, as indeed he has been. All three rant for the length of three pages, their hearts burn, their eyes start and they give every sign of mental disturbance. Finally the rivals escort Ardelia to a convent where she is to remain for a few hours. They then retire, still ranting, and fight a duel. Antonio is slain, and having kissed his cheek Henrique withdraws from the scene as he is himself bleeding to death. He decides to bleed in the house of Ardelia's father, who, delighted that Antonio is dead, receives him cordially and permits him to stay there in hiding until he has recovered.

Meanwhile, Ardelia has fallen into a high fever, and no wonder. She continues to languish until Henrique's wounds are healed, and then, because she loves Henrique and they are now free to marry, she decides to become a nun. No sooner has she donned the veil, however, than she wishes to doff it again. Accordingly she and Henrique plan an elopement. But an enemy out of Henrique's past now comes on the scene — Don Sebastian, whose sister Elvira, Henrique had wronged. By a surprising coincidence this sister is now a nun in the same convent as Ardelia. When Sebastian comes to the convent Ardelia remembers that when she was ten years old she loved him to madness, and now this tender feeling revives. Sebastian's sister warns Henrique that her brother intends to slay him, but Henrique, persuaded that Ardelia still loves him, comes to the convent with high hopes and a rope ladder. Ardelia descends, confident that Sebastian awaits her at the other side of the wall. Actually both her lovers are there in concealment. They fight, and the sword passes 'quite through Ardelia's body.' With great presence of mind, but singular inappropriateness, she says: 'Alas, poor maid!' In a final access, Henrique and Sebastian stab each other, and they all die simultaneously and with suitable farewell speeches. Elvira dies also (of a violent fever in twenty-four hours) and the moral is — but we are too dazed to find a moral. We only know that nothing in life became any of them like the leaving of it. Aphra Behn described this as 'a true novel.' Mr Baker calls it 'a debased novella.'[21]

For a long time it was supposed that this story, *The Nun, or the Perjured Beauty* was the source of Southerne's tragedy, *The Fatal Marriage, or the Innocent Adultery*. In the dedication to Antony Hammond with which Southerne prefaced his play, he acknowledged his indebtedness to 'a novel of Mrs Behn's called *The Fair Vow-breaker*.' It seemed to be accepted[22] without further question that this was the same story as *The Nun, or the Perjured Beauty*. It was pointed out that Aphra Behn had muddled her titles in one definite case, i.e., in the 1689 edition of *The Fair Jilt*, the title-pages bore the double title: *The Fair Jilt, or the history of Prince Tarquin and Miranda*, whereas the half-title of the same was: *The Fair Hypocrite, or the Amours of Prince Tarquin and Miranda*. In view of this, and because people did not appear to remember that Aphra Behn had really written two tales called *The Nun*, opinion concentrated on the better known tale of the two, i.e., *The Nun, or, the Perjured Beauty*, which we have just summarized. In 1909, however, Dr Paul Hamelius of Liége pointed out that the plot of Southerne's *Fatal Marriage* was not at all like Aphra Behn's *Perjured Beauty* which was supposed to be its source. Dr Hamelius however, took it for granted that the two novels were one and the same, only under two different names.[23] It was The Revd Dr Montague Summers who in 1916 elucidated the mystery.[24] Aphra Behn wrote two tales both of which had as the main title: *The Nun. The Nun, or, the Perjured Beauty*, published in 1697, was not the source of Southerne's play, which he really derived from *The Nun or the Fair Vowbreaker*[25] published in 1689.

This last mentioned work is greatly superior to *The Perjured Beauty*. Although liberally coated with heroics, it does convey the impression that Aphra Behn had in mind some genuine Italian *novella*, which however, has not been identified. In the introductory passages she is on the side of the angels and she maintains this attitude in the tale that follows: In Iper lived Count Hendrick de Vallery, who, on the death of his wife, decides to be a Jesuit and arranges that his daughter Isabella shall be reared in a convent, with the proviso that at the age of thirteen she shall decide whether to marry or to become a nun. Despite the just efforts of the Abbess who counsels her to think carefully before renouncing the world, she takes the veil, thereby dooming to misery her many suitors, one of whom is Villenoys. He goes to the wars. She becomes so holy a nun that her name becomes a proverb.

In this same convent was a young nun, Sister Katherina, Isabella's dearest friend. Katherina's brother Henault, when visiting the convent falls in love with Isabella, and despite all her efforts to resist, she returns his love. Katherina pleads with Isabella that she remember her vows. Henault's father threatens to disinherit him. All is vain; Henault plans an elopement and after an inward struggle Isabella agrees, her father's death removing one obstacle from her path. Henault's father however, is in flourishing health, and ready to cut him off with a shilling at the least breath of scandal, so the sensible creature bridles his impetuosity, and suddenly points out that one cannot live on air. Isabella is wounded by his mercenary thoughts. She says: 'I thought of living in some lonely Cottage far from the noise of crowded busy Cities, to walk with thee in Groves, and silent shades . . . my Monarch thou, and I thy Sovereign Queen.' They do elope finally. They change their names, marry and live on a farm near the Rhine. They write for pardon. Henault is duly disinherited; bad luck dogs them; crops fail, cattle die; for a while they appear to be under a curse. Then they are pardoned by church and state. Henault's father offers to forgive him if he will leave Isabella and go to the wars. To the wars Henault goes, but merely to humour his father. He has no notion of abandoning Isabella. During the campaign he meets Villenoys, Isabella's old suitor, and shortly after he falls in battle entrusting Villenoys with a dying message to Isabella. Villenoys delivers the message, and later prevails on Isabella to marry him. They live happily for some years, and then one day a ragged man comes to the door. One glance is enough for Isabella. Henault has returned.

Throughout the story Mrs Behn has shown clear insight into the workings of a woman's heart, but at this point her imaginative power raises the narrative to a far higher level. Her style is now no longer sentimental. It is grimly realistic. We are shown Isabella's horror on finding that she has quite innocently committed bigamy. Amid the whirling confusion of her mind one thought prevails: she now loves Villenoys, and she will not return to Henault. She meditates on killing herself, but that will not mean happiness for Villenoys and herself, so in a sudden fit of despair she smothers Henault in his sleep. Villenoys comes in at that moment, and filled with remorse and horror, she tells him that Henault has returned and has died of shock on learning that she had remarried. Villenoys sees that they will be suspected of foul play, although he does not realize that it has actually taken place. He puts the body in a sack with the intention of throwing it into the river:

> Isabella all this time said but little, but filled with thoughts all black and hellish, she ponder'd within, while the fond and passionate Villenoys was endeavouring to hide her shame, and to make this an absolute secret: she imagin'd, that could she live after a deed so black, Villenoys would be eternal reproaching her, if not with his tongue, at least with his heart, and embolden'd by one wickedness, she was the

readier for another, and another of such a nature, as has, in my opinion, far less excuse than the first; but when fate begins to afflict, she goes through stitch with her black work.

Through stitch—that is the secret of the denouement, because when Villenoys has the sack on his back, ready to bear it to the river, Isabella bids him tarry a moment while she tucks in some of the corpse's clothes which, she says, are sticking out. To make all sure, she will sew them inside the sack. With a packing needle and strong thread she sews the sack to the collar of Villenoys' coat, and bids him go now 'and when you come to the bridge,' said she, 'and that you are throwing him over the rail, which is not above breast high, be sure you give him a good swing, lest the sack should hang on anything at the side of the bridge, and not fall into the stream.' 'I'll warrant you,' said Villenoys, 'I know how to secure his falling.' At the bridge he gives one mighty swing and, carried over by the weight of the dead body which is sewn to his coat, he is borne down to drown with Isabella's other victim. She is so tortured by remorse that she brings suspicion on herself and is executed.

This story is remarkable in that it is not merely shot through with realism as are so many of Mrs Behn's romantic tales. It shows an abrupt change of style. This change comes at the point where the dramatic interest is heightened, at the point where the author really lived her subject. The result is valuable, as might be expected, and it proves that Aphra Behn turned to realism when she was most in earnest. It was her natural medium.

It was not often, however, that Mrs Behn, in high-falutin' vein, so completely deviated into reality. In *Agnes de Castro, or the Force of Generous Blood*,[26] she is again on the side of morality, but her adherence to the convention of aristocratic characters and romantic attitudinizing is once more evident. *Agnes de Castro* is based on the true story of Ines de Castro, who lived in the earlier part of the fourteenth century. That her life was a very popular subject with writers is seen in J. de Araujo's huge *Bibliographia Inesiana* (1897). Aphra Behn, no doubt, borrowed the tale from Peter Ballon's translation[27] of Mlle de Brillac's *Agnes de Castro, nouvelle portugaise*.[28] Mrs Behn's novel is far better than her source.

The story begins in the reign of Alphonso IV of Portugal. Although, on the whole, the construction is sound, Aphra Behn again repeats her mistake of concentrating interest on unimportant preliminary details. First we see Don Pedro, the Prince of Portugal, marry Bianca, Princess of Castile. After a short time Bianca is afflicted with the palsy, the marriage is dissolved, and Bianca departs to languish in a melancholy retreat. We never hear of her again, and there is really no reason why we should have heard of her at all. A marriage is then arranged between Don Pedro and Constantia Manuel, daughter of Don John Manuel, a prince of the blood of Castile, and famous for the enmity he has towards his king. But this marriage is scarcely more fortunate, because although Constantia is devoted to her husband, he is secretly interested in Agnes de Castro, his wife's maid of honour. Agnes is quite unconscious of the Prince's love for her; indeed, she is the faithful friend of the Princess, and the Prince's love might well have remained a secret but for the spiteful interference of Elvira Gonsalez, who had hoped to become his wife. Elvira discovers the Prince's secret to the Princess, who, although deeply grieved, blames neither her husband nor Agnes de Castro. In fact, she herself tells the innocent Agnes of the Prince's love for her. But Elvira is determined to revenge herself on the Prince for his indifference to her charms, so she determines that the king shall learn of his infatuation. This she achieves through her brother Don Alvaro, the king's favourite, but she is enraged to discover that her brother also is in love with Agnes de Castro. 'Don Alvaro was one of those ambitious men, that are fierce without moderation, and proud without generosity: of a melancholy, cloudy humour, and of a cruel inclination; and to effect his ends he found nothing difficult or unlawful.' He hates the Prince because he considers him his rival in the affections of the king, but particularly in the love of Agnes. The king learns of his son's unwise devotion, and promises to help Don Alvaro in his courtship. To please his favourite he orders a tournament and commands that everything shall be magnificent. The rival lovers enter the lists. The Prince, out of respect for his wife, abstains from wearing Agnes's colours, but though Don Alvaro has almost as little right to them, no scruples withhold him. Don Alvaro 'appear'd there all shining with gold mix'd with stones of blue, which were the colours of Agnes; and there were embroider'd all over his equipage, flaming hearts of gold on blue and velvet, and nets for the snares of love with abundance of double A's.'

However, we find with some pleasure that 'the pride of Don Alvaro was soon humbled at the feet of the Prince of Portugal, who threw him against the ground with twenty others.' But Don Alvaro is not a whit deterred from his pursuit of Agnes. She desires to leave the court, but is dissuaded by the Princess who loves her dearly:

> 'What ails you, Agnes? (said the Princess to her, in a soft tone, and with her ordinary sweetness). And what new mis-fortune causes that sadness in thy looks?' 'Madam (reply'd Agnes, shedding a rivulet of tears) the obligation and ties I have to you, put me upon a cruel trial. I had bounded the felicity of my life in hope of passing it near your highness, yet I must carry to some other part of the world this unhappy face of mine, which renders me nothing but ill-offices.'

She is persuaded to remain, but still has some scruples as to the effect of her presence on the Prince. What if he should speak to her of his flame? The tale goes on to show the Princess and Agnes treating the love-lorn Prince as if he were an infant to be kept from crying by any means, and we are asked to believe that the wife bids the young girl not to repulse her husband's avowals of love. That this is not lovers' psychology nobody should have known better than Aphra Behn, but if it is a faulty portrayal of women in love, it is entirely consistent with Aphra's philosophy. Elvira unsuccessfully plots against Agnes's abduction, and then forges a guilty note purporting to be from the Prince to Agnes. The handwriting would not deceive a child, but nevertheless it deceives the Princess who now dies of grief at a supposed infidelity which but a short time before she appeared willing to overlook. Before she expires she advises and blesses the future marriage of Agnes and the Prince, and with relief we feel that the web is broken. By no means; Agnes has serious scruples, and considers that in respect of Constantia's memory they should part forever. 'Go, Madam,' replied the Prince, growing pale, 'go and expect the news of my death . . . I will go seek it in those wars which reign among my neighbours . . . Follow the motions which barbarous virtue inspires you with . . . enjoy the glory of having cruelly refused me.' For a moment Agnes considers marrying Don Alvaro because she loves the Prince. Then she decides to leave the court. But alas! the king insists that she shall remain and marry Don Alvaro, which does not at the last moment appear so romantic a solution of the tangle. The Prince is now falling into a decline from thwarted love, so Agnes finally agrees to marry him secretly. Their joy is brief. Don Alvaro's passion leads him to discover the truth. His fury is unbounded, and one night in the absence of Don Pedro, and abandoning all hope of otherwise touching the heart of the fair Agnes, he pierces it with his poignard. Don Pedro's vengeance leads him to wage a terrible war against the assassin, but with what success we are not told. He succeeds to the throne of his fathers, and, one supposes, reigns in single blessedness. With such a matrimonial record a fourth marriage would have been a proof of demented optimism.

Space makes it impossible to deal fully with more than one other novel—*Oroonoko*, and therefore we can only refer in passing to five equals of Mrs Behn's as yet unmentioned. Three of these are in the romantic tradition: sentimental in tone, and based on stock themes of intrigue. These are: *The Unfortunate Bride;*[29] *The Unhappy Mistake, or, The Impious Vow Punished;* and *The Lucky Mistake*. There is a tendency towards real life in *The Wandering Beauty*, which is noteworthy as the sort of tale that in some form or other, appears to have pleased the public long before Richardson immortalized it. Mrs Behn shows a beautiful girl, Peregrina, who, to escape marriage with an aged suitor, leaves home and becomes a servant in a far-off country. She is sought in marriage by a young gentleman whose lack of snobbishness is later rewarded by the discovery that Peregrina's family is as good as his own. A clergyman appears also, but unlike Richardson's clergyman, this divine considers it beneath him to contemplate marriage with a servant, however much her beauty attracts him. He is well punished by having to perform the marriage ceremony which unites her to one far more important than himself. *The Dumb Virgin* is a very close approach to the real Italian *novella*. It is told with much power and dramatic intensity. Incest is the theme.

We now come to Mrs Behn's great novel *Oroonoko*, which carried her far beyond all the novelists of the age. Published in 1688, it is unique in being the apotheosis of her three main characteristics as a novelist, and yet in possessing also something which differed essentially from all else she wrote. In her other novels she is the romantic; the realist deriving her power from the drama, from the continental *novella* or from the life about her; the fanatical fabricator of evidence calculated to prove the truth of her stories. In *Oroonoko* these three qualities are very marked. Indeed as for authentication, never did Mrs Behn so whole-heartedly vouch for every fact, to the immense satisfaction of her immediate public and to the despair of modern critics.

In 1696, just after Aphra Behn's death, appeared Charles Gildon's *Account of the Life of the Incomparable Mrs Behn*,[30] to be followed in the same year by *The Life and Memoirs written by one of the Fair Sex*.[31] The *Memoirs* state that Mrs Behn's maiden name was Johnson, that her father was a gentleman of good family in Canterbury, that when she was a young girl her father was appointed lieutenant-general of Surinam and that she, with her parents and family, went to Surinam, where although her father had died on the outward voyage, they settled in the best house in the colony. She returned to England, and married a Dutch merchant; she went to court and diverted King Charles II with her descriptions of Surinam and of one Oroonoko. On the death of her husband she went on a secret service mission to Holland, and actually warned the English authorities of De Witt's intended attack on the Medway. She was neither thanked nor paid for her services, returned to England in a destitute condition, saw the inside of a debtors' prison, and took to writing so as to earn her living. In 1884 Gosse struck the first blow at the truth of the above biographical details. A note by Lady Winchilsea in a volume in his possession (to the effect that Aphra Behn was born at Wye and that her father was a barber) led him to seek confirmation of these remarks from the vicar of Wye. The vicar undertook the examination of the parish register, and verified Lady Winchilsea's statements.

In 1913, Dr Ernest Bernbaum[32] not only discovered glaring inconsistencies in the accepted facts of Aphra Behn's life, but endeavoured to show that his discoveries definitely proved certain facts about her powers as a writer. In another article[33] published that same year he concentrated his discoveries to prove that, as Mrs Behn had never been to Surinam, certain claims could no longer be made for her as a narrator. Before we discuss the bearing that Dr Bernbaum's conclusions might have on Aphra Behn's status as a novelist, it is as well to show that his dogmatism as to her putative visit to Surinam is quite baseless.

If Dr Bernbaum had possessed all available information on the Surinam question, that is to say if he had known and adduced the evidence later offered by The Revd Dr Montague Summers[34] and Miss Sackville-West,[35] it would still have been impossible for him to prove by honest logic that Aphra Behn had never been to Surinam. A complete review of this matter which has engaged the attention of Gosse, Dr Bernbaum, The Revd Dr Montague Summers, and Miss Sackville-West proves only that all the evidence adduced so far on either side is insufficient to establish any final decision. In 1913 Dr Bernbaum accepted unquestioningly the statement that Aphra Behn's father was a barber named Johnson, and stated that, as such an individual could not have been made lieutenant-general of Surinam, Aphra Behn most certainly could not have accompanied him there. In 1915 The Revd Dr Montague Summers, by the simple process of examining for himself the parish register at Wye, discovered there an entry recording the baptism of Ayfara, the daughter of John and Amy Amis, July 10, 1640; and he noted the fact that so far from there being proof that Ayfara's father, was a barber, there was actually no column in the register for 'Quality, Trade and Profession.' Some years later Miss Sackville-West, although on the whole satisfied by the evidence of the parish register, referred[36] to a surprising passage in James Rodway's *Chronological History of the Discovery and Settlement of Guiana*, 1493–1668 (Georgetown, Demerara, 1888). Rodway makes the curious statement that Aphra Behn was the adopted daughter of the man (a relative of Lord Willoughby's) who was sent as lieutenant-governor to Surinam; and further states that this lieutenant-governor died on the outward voyage, and that Aphra and the rest of the family continued their journey to Surinam, and lived there for two or three years. One might, in view of Rodway's remarks, try to reconcile these conflicting pieces of evidence by deciding that Aphra really was a barber's daughter and that she was adopted by Lord Willoughby's relative, but whatever the barber's name may have been, Rodway states definitely that the lieutenant-governor's name was — Johnson! This brings us back again to Lady Winchilsea's marginal note, and it is clear that this vicious circle cannot solve the question of Aphra's visit. The same confusion exists as to the date when Aphra Behn went to Surinam and returned therefrom. Dr Bernbaum makes out an interesting case here, but not a conclusive one. He begins by noting that if Aphra Behn returned from Surinam at eighteen years (as she claimed) she must have returned in 1658, and he finds this an impossible date. Actually there is no need to accept Aphra Behn's statement as to her age, as women's accounts of their age generally err on the side of youth. Dr Bembaum says that if Aphra Behn was right in claiming that she knew certain officers in Surinam, then she must have been there within the period 1665 to 1666, because this was the period during which these officers served in Surinam. Aphra Behn also said that the Dutch took over the colony immediately after Oroonoko's death. Therefore, Dr Bernbaum argues, in consideration of these facts, Aphra Behn could not have returned to England earlier than December, 1665; but, he continues, State Papers prove that she went to Holland in August, 1666, so it is necessary to believe that in the intervening eight months she was married, widowed, and had her famous interview with King Charles II. Dr Bernbaum, says it is impossible to believe that such a programme could be crowded into eight months. It is improbable, but it is not impossible. These contentions do not disprove Aphra Behn's visit to Surinam. The Revd Dr Summers believes that Aphra Behn returned to England in 1663, despite the question of the officers. Miss Sackville-West also agrees that Aphra Behn returned to England earlier than 1664, and supports this view by dates given in Rodway's *Chronological History . . . of Guiana*. It is clear that these irreconcilable arguments as to the dates of Aphra's journey to Surinam and her return therefrom do not point to any definite conclusion. Leaving the realm of attempted chronology, Dr Bernbaum, because the background of *Oroonoko* resembles George Warren's *Impartial Description of Surinam*, 1667, is certain that she was never in that country, and that she depended on Warren for her facts. He piles up a marvellous accretion of alleged evidence: Mrs Behn's descriptions are correct only when she imitates Warren; the moment she raises her eyes from *The Impartial Description* she introduces white marble cliffs where they do not exist, and omits the twenty-eight waterfalls. Mr Baker agrees with Dr Bernbaum in this (and indeed is inclined to believe that Mrs Behn never did go to Surinam). However, The Revd Dr Summers and Miss Sackville-West point out that as Mrs Behn was about fifty years when she wrote *Oroonoko* it was quite natural that she would revive in Warren's book the background which had grown dim. It is stalemate again. And when Miss Sackville-West and Dr Summers point out the unanimous opinion of Aphra Behn's contemporaries, and the peculiar coincidences of testimony which however confused, do indicate Mrs Behn's visit to Surinam, the anti-Surinamians may reply that these hypotheses do not constitute proof.

We have mentioned some of the pros and cons of this argument simply to show that Dr Bernbaum's conclusions on Aphra Behn's kind of realism are based on no decisive proofs. But this problem does not arouse one's enthusiasm, because even if the fundamental proofs were decisive, Dr Bernbaum's inferences therefrom, so far as they concern Aphra Behn's powers as a novelist, are altogether incomplete and faulty. Dr Bernbaum delighting in his excavations, insists on investing them with excessive and disorientated literary significance, and this is quite in keeping with the distinct lack of balanced judgement which both of his articles on Aphra Behn display. Dr Bernbaum is not really concerned with the literary value of *Oroonoko*. He merely uses it as a stick to beat Sir Walter Raleigh and any others who may share Raleigh's belief that 'realistic fiction in this country was first written by way of direct imitation of truthful record.' In his anxiety to disprove Raleigh's theory, he sets himself to show that the pseudo-biographies of the seventeenth century, which, he says, were generally accepted as fact, are, on the contrary, fiction. His work on the *Mary Carleton* narratives is interesting, but discretion should have kept him from the quagmire of Aphra Behn's works. His insistence that *The Fair Jilt* is not a record of facts would seem to indicate that Dr Bernbaum has a genius for the obvious, but unfortunately the obvious conclusions of his Surinam arguments escape him utterly. Dr Bernbaum is like some amateur archaeologist who having dug up shards, coins and knives, cannot arrive at any estimate as to their value or significance. When, in regard to *Oroonoko*, he outlines the effect which his discoveries may have on future estimates of Aphra Behn's art as a novelist, then it is that he so curiously stops short of those final conclusions towards which his basic arguments inevitably direct themselves. To explode a myth means so often the discrediting of its oiginator that exploding the myth of *Oroonoko*'s 'genuine' realism has blinded Dr Bernbaum to the true significance of his discoveries in relation to Aphra Behn's powers. He claims to show that *Oroonoko* was not the result of Aphra Behn's personal experiences; from that it follows that she was not what Dr Bernbaum calls a genuine realist, and therefore he erroneously concludes that whatever she substituted for genuine realism must be inferior to it. There his conclusion ends. But it cannot end there. On the contrary, that is only the first link in the chain of conclusions which cannot be broken if Dr Bernbaum's Surinam claim is correct. He says Mrs Behn was not a genuine realist. Very well; let us say that she was not. We must still take into account: that, despite the romantic tinge in *Oroonoko*, it contained a particular kind of realism which carried conviction to readers and critics for two hundred and twenty-five years. This was not merely the sort of verisimilitude attempted by the pretence that a narrative was a record of real events, because, although Aphra Behn made this claim in almost all her novels, it is *Oroonoko* alone which carried conviction to the critics. Assuming that Aphra Behn was not in Surinam, what is this realism which for so long completely hoodwinked everyone? Since it is not genuine realism it must be then a sort of realism at which she arrived by using her imagination on collected facts and ideas—it must be imaginative realism. What is the difference between these two kinds of realism? Genuine realism, that is reproductive realism, regurgitates experiences as they have occurred; imaginative realism builds up from a thousand scenes, hints, emotions and concepts something which appears convincingly real. The genuine realist is a mere narrator. The imaginative realist is a creator. It is surely unnecessary to indicate which is the superior kind of realism, and yet Dr Bernbaum seems to consider that somehow in abolishing the Surinam visit, he detracts from Aphra Behn's status as a novelist. On the contrary, he establishes it on a far higher plane—so much so that no true friend of the Divine Astrea should dream of contesting Dr Bernbaum's claim that she invented *Oroonoko* and her trip to Surinam. When Dr Bernbaum raised this hare (and a long-lived, prolific animal it will prove) he really should have trained it to run in the right direction.

When Raleigh said that realistic fiction in England was first written by way of direct imitation of truthful records he never meant that fiction was the better for being a mere narration of real events, but merely that (in common with the majority of literary authorities) he believed that this was a stage in the development of realistic fiction. It seemed natural to suppose that, as an infant cannot walk alone at first, so in the beginning story-tellers might have needed the support of actual events. This was considered to be a phase in the development of realistic prose fiction pending the evolution of a superior growth of novelists who could spin reality out of imagination plus experience, instead of merely describing experience seriatim or with slight embroideries. If, as Dr Bernbaum appears to claim, realistic fiction did not pass through this phase, then the writers of realistic fiction in the seventeenth and early eighteenth centuries deserve nothing short of reverence for dispensing with the slow process of evolution.

Speaking of Congreve's romantic[37] novel *Incognita*, Mr Baker says: 'It *does not detract* a whit from its ingenuity if the plot is based on actual experience as Congreve himself avers. His biographer of 1730, the *Biographica Briannica*, and Mr Brett Smith himself, the recent editor of *Incognita*, make unnecessary fuss about this point.'[38] So? It does not detract from the *Incognita* that its plot is not original, and yet (in Dr Bernbaum's view) it does detract from *Oroonoko* that its plot is original. Again, speaking of Green's cony-catching pamphlets of which the avowed object was to show up scandals, Mr Baker says: '*From the literary point of view, however, we are concerned solely with his success in painting a realistic picture . . . It is, of course, no business of the realistic painter of life to provide any evidence save that of verisimilitude.*'[39] Since Mrs Behn provided that to an unusual extent, why are we concerned with anything except her success as a realistic painter of life? Would Jane Austen be a better kind of novelist if it could be proved that she knew Elizabeth Bennet, Darcy and Mr Collins in real life, and that she had actually lived at Longbourne and visited Rosings? Is Charlotte Brontë superior to Jane Austen because we can identify segments of her life in *Villette, Jane Eyre* and *Shirley*? Mrs Ann Radcliffe is praised by literary critics for her ingenuity in creating convincing backgrounds of travel and letting her imagination play around them.[40] Mrs Aphra Behn is not in the least praised for doing the same thing one hundred years before. When it is found that Mrs Radcliffe for her descriptions in *The Mysteries of Udolpho* and *The Italian* took as a basis Mrs Piozzi's *Journey through France and Italy* and de Carbonières' *Observations faites dans les Pyrénées*[41] her imaginative power is rightly commended. When it is found that Mrs Behn drew on Warren she is treated like a child who has been found stealing jam. Is there, after all, any reason why literary criticism should not be consistent? Dr Bernbaum's researches are interesting, but he seems to have been more engrossed in making them than in determining their use or pursuing his inferences to their conclusion.

Oroonoko was published in 1688. It was written by an Aphra Behn with whom we are not familiar—not the woman whose bawdy dialogue kept the pit in a roar, not the woman who deified the passions—and yet the same, so many soul-sides have we all. Aphra Behn had a lyrical genius, and a generous nature. Her profession showed her at her worst, but, as Gosse said, she was 'not degraded although she might be lamentably unconventional.'[42] Within the rombustious Aphra Behn there was the woman who wrote: 'He began to tell her how short life was and how transitory its joys; how soon she would grow weary of vice and how often change to find repose in it, but never arrive to it;'[43] and who wrote in her paraphrase of the Lord's Prayer:

> Oh that this grateful, little Charity,
> Forgiving others all their sins to me,
> May with my God for mine atoning be,
> I've sought around, and found no foe in view,
> With whom the least revenge I would pursue,
> My God, my God, dispense thy Mercies too.[44]

This is the Aphra Behn who shows herself in *Oroonoko*.

In her other novels Mrs Behn does no more than indicate the background of the action, but in *Oroonoko* she takes pains to show us the country in which this tragedy is enacted. Her initial description of Surinam is in the nature of an inventory. She tells us of 'marmosets, a sort of monkey, as big as a rat or a weasel, but of a marvellous and delicate shape, having face and hands like a human creature . . . then . . . little parakeets, great parrots, mackaws and a thousand other birds and beasts of wonderful and surprising forms . . . rare flies . . . various excellences, such as art cannot imitate.' But later on, when the emotion of her story has kindled her imagination, she situates as follows the house in which she claims to have lived in Surinam:

> It stood on a vast rock of white marble, at the foot of which the river ran a vast depth down, and not to be descended on that side; the little waves still dashing and washing the foot of this rock, made the softest murmurs and purlings in the world; and the opposite bank was adorned with such vast

quantities of different flowers eternally blowing, and every day and hour new, fenced behind them with lofty trees of a thousand rare forms and colours, that the prospect was the most ravishing that fancy can create. On the edge of this white rock, towards the river, was a walk, or grove, of orange and lemon trees, about half the length of the Mall here, whose flowery and fruit-bearing branches met at the top, and hindered the sun, whose rays are very fierce there, from entering a beam into the grove; and the cool air that came from the river made it . . . fit to entertain people in, at all the hottest hours of the day . . . and it is a marvel to see how such vast trees, as big as English oaks, could take footing on so solid a rock, and in so little earth as covered that rock. But all things by nature there are rare, delightful and wonderful.

In this description we see very clearly the romantic and the realistic struggling for supremacy. That the romantic strain should appear is not surprising when we consider the age in which it was written and the idyllic nature of the story. Let us observe also the vivid and circumstantial precision of the details given.

To this paradise, as a slave, came Oroonoko, the Prince of Coramantien. In his own country he had loved and married the beautiful Imoinda, but by an evil chance the king, his grandfather, demanded her for his harem. Oroonoko, despite great difficulty, succeeded in visiting Imoinda. He is discovered, and, certain that she can mollify the king, Imoinda bids him return to camp. He obeys her, and in his absence the vengeful king sells Imoinda into slavery. Oroonoko believes her dead. Some time later he is lured aboard an English ship and brought as a slave to Surinam. Although he is nominally a slave, his captors and all the people who see him are so impressed by his princely air that he is treated like a free man. By a remarkable coincidence he finds again in Surinam the beautiful and chaste Imoinda, and for a little while they are happy together. But soon it becomes clear that the white rulers of the colony have promised them freedom only to secure their submission. Oroonoko tries to escape. He is overtaken, and he surrenders on the condition that he shall not be punished. He is tortured, but greater far than any bodily suffering is the knowledge that a dreadful fate awaits his unprotected wife. He wins free for a little time; he kills Imoinda so that she shall not fall into the hands of the white men. He is recaptured and put to death by being hacked to pieces.

Such is the story and we can see that there are several ways in which it could be treated. Mrs Behn's way is half heroic and half realistic. For example, Oroonoko loses some of his reality by being presented as a lofty hero. Miss Sackville-West very well describes the impression we receive: 'Oroonoko resembles those seventeenth century paintings of negroes in plumes and satins, rather than an actual slave on a practical plantation. She dresses him, it is true, in a suit of brown hollands; but none the less the plumes continue to wave in the breeze and the satins to glisten in the sun. She could not wholly escape from ' Le Grand Cyrus.'[45] Very unlikely also is the picture of Oroonoko sitting at meat with the white men and even with the white women in those days of racial prejudice; and the fact that he was, if only nominally, a slave makes the improbability all the greater. Still, that Mrs Behn should have written thus of a negro proves very thoroughly her novel point of view. It is novel in our age, not to mention hers, because even in this century we are assured of white superiority. It would be interesting to discover why she chose a negro as her hero, but this is a point entirely beyond proof. It is also note-worthy and very characteristic of Aphra Behn that, having chosen him, she did not by the fraction of a shade abate his negritude, as Mrs Kavenagh believed Mme de la Fayette or Mlle de Scudery would have done.[46]

Many critics have said that this is the first novel which champions the emancipation of the coloured races. This is true in effect, but (as the present writer believes) not in intention. If Mrs Behn intended her story as a polemic against slavery she would hardly have shown her hero in agreement with the practice. In contrast with Oroonoko's leadership of his fellow slaves in an attempted escape we must set his offer to deliver many of his countrymen into bondage in exchange for his own freedom and that of Imoinda: 'He was every day treating with Trefry for his and [Imoinda's] liberty, and offered either gold, or a *vast quantity of slaves,* which should be paid before they let him go, provided he could have any security that he should go when his ransom was paid.' This offer is refused and Oroonoko's slavery con-firmed, so he incites his fellow prisoners to escape. Then he uses arguments which, however incontestable, did not deter him from making his previous offer to Trefry:

[Oroonoko] having singled out these men from the women and children, made a harangue to them of the miseries and ignominies of slavery; counting up all their toils and sufferings, under such loads, burdens and drudgeries, as were fitter for beasts than men . . . He told them, it was not for days, months or years, but for eternity; there was no end to be of their misfortunes. They suffered not like men, who might find glory and fortitude in oppression; but like dogs, that loved the whip and bell, and fawned the more they were beaten; that they had lost the divine quality of men, and were become insensible asses, fit only to bear: nay, worse; an ass, or dog, or horse having done his duty, could lie down in retreat, and rise to work again, and while he did his duty, endured no stripes; but men, villainous, senseless men, such as they, toiled on all the tedious week till Black Friday, and then, whether they worked or not, whether they were faulty or meriting, they, promiscuously, the innocent with the guilty, suffered the infamous whip, the sordid stripes, from their fellow-slaves, till their blood trickled from all parts of their body; blood, whose every drop ought to be revenged with a life of some of those tyrants that impose it . . . 'And why,' said he, 'my dear friends and fellow-sufferers, should we be slaves to an unknown people? Have they vanquished us nobly in fight? Have they won us in honourable battle? And are we by the chance of war become their slaves? . . . No, but we are bought and sold like apes or monkeys, to be the sport of women, fools and cowards; and the support of rogues and runagates, that have abandoned their own countries for rapine, murders, theft and villainies. Do you not hear every day how they upbraid each other with infamy of life, below the wildest savages? And shall we render obedience to such a degenerate race who have no human virtue left, to distinguish them from the vilest creatures?'

And again:

[Oroonoko] told him [Byam] there was no faith in the white men, or the gods they adored; who instructed them in principles so false, that honest men could not live amongst them; though no people professed so much, none performed so little: that he knew what he had to do when he dealt with men of honour and with them a man ought to be eternally on his guard, and never to eat and drink with Christians without his weapon of defence in his hand; and, for his own security, never to credit one word they spoke.

161

These are the vehement words of one deeply moved by a grievous wrong. They are the words of Mrs Behn, speaking through Oroonoko. But if she had wished to launch an attack upon the slave trade would she not have considered Oroonoko's offer to Trefry as a serious lowering of his character? One is inclined to believe that Mrs Behn's feelings are entirely centred in her hero, that it is, primarily, *his* enslavement which arouses her sympathy. Then the depth of her feeling for her own creation leads her, in denouncing his oppressors, to denounce the entire abomination of slavery. She brings to her story a strong conviction that civilization is a curse which achieves only degeneracy, and which connotes only misdirected cleverness, hypocrisy, avarice, cruelty and lip-religion. Her proofs are all about her in the society of her time, and suddenly the life she knows nauseates her, a stench rises from its corrupt heart, its teeming life seems to feed only on decay, and from this aggregation of evil she recoils, and she escapes into a different world. Here is a purer air; here is 'eternal Spring, always the very months of April, May and June; the shades are perpetual, the trees bearing at once all degrees of leaves, and fruits.' Here are people who have retained innocence and dignity because their desires are no more than their needs:

> These people represented to me an absolute idea of the first state of innocence, before man knew how to sin: And 'tis most evident and plain, that simple Nature is the most harmless, inoffensive and virtuous mistress. 'Tis she alone, if she were permitted, that better instructs the world, than all the inventions of man: religion would here but destroy that tranquillity they possess by ignorance; and laws would but teach 'em to know offences, of which now they have no notion.

It is interesting to note how in this story Aphra Behn's emotion mounts with the action. Here she finds her spiritual centre; she speaks deeper truths than she knows; she overleaps time; she anticipates the theories of Rousseau, the fierce satire of Swift, the abolition of slavery, and she does all this because the gap between her experience and her idealism, realized suddenly with deadly clarity, wrings from her something nobler than she guessed. *Oroonoko* is as far above the rest of her writings as the real Aphra Behn was above the stamp life put upon her. How often in her other novels and in her plays, are our feelings shocked, not even so much by the lack of morality, as by her deviations from aesthetic taste, her inability to hit the truth! But in *Oroonoko* all this is changed. Some excess of romanticism there may be, but since it is expended on an epical subject it does not offend our sense of probability. Nor is it a sterile romanticism; it is really the effect of an enthusiasm which raises the theme to the height of ideality.

Where now is her trolloping muse, her cynical materialism? One would have thought that she could not resist the chance of erotic writing offered by that part of the story which deals with the harem of the King of Coramantien, but even that she invests with considerable dignity. Thereafter, transformed for once in her life by a noble inspiration, she exercises on her subject an instinctive measure. Most notable as a proof of this is Oroonoko's farewell to Imoinda, whom he is about to kill. We have had so many ranting farewells in Aphra Behn's stories that we may be pardoned for suspecting one here. It is the fatal climax of many misfortunes; it is the end of a great love. How will she describe it? What words can she possibly ascribe to them which will not offend one's sense of fitness? Listen:

> It is not to be doubted, but the parting, the eternal leave-taking of two such lovers, so greatly born, so sensible, so beautiful, so young, and so fond, must be very moving, as the relation of it was to me afterwards. All that love could say in such case being ended . . .

No more. Mrs Behn has faced her problem with the ease of sincere feeling, and in her refusal to intrude on that scene she achieves her finest artistic effect. Dr Bernbaum has taken much trouble to point out the impossibilities and improbabilities in *Oroonoko*. The story of the electric eel is unlikely, the healing of the hero's abdominal wound is possible, but not probable, and we are told this on the authority of a doctor whose opinion Dr Bernbaum has sought to reinforce his own; the natives of Surinam must have known how to tell a lie because their language at that time had five distinct words meaning falsehood— these are but a few of Dr Bernbaum's objections. Since they add nothing to the Surinam question and have no bearing on literary criticism, it is unnecessary to consider them. We have in *Oroonoko* a story which is universally judged to be of worth. It seems a pity to destroy, for the sake of mental gymnastics, something of permanent worth in the history of the novel.

Similarly, because in this story we are concerned with the hero's personality, we do not trouble to ask ourselves whether Oroonoko could actually continue to smoke while his body was being hacked to pieces. That is what Oroonoko would have wished to do, and therefore it does not ring false. It is a truth in art. Thus Aphra Behn describes Oroonoko's end:

> And turning to the men that had bound him, he said 'My friends, am I to die, or to be whipt?' And they cried 'Whipt! no, you shall not escape so well! And then he replied, smiling, 'A blessing on thee!' and assured them they need not tie him, for he would stand fixed like a rock, and endure death so as would encourage them to die: 'But if you whip me,' said he, 'be sure you tie me fast.'
>
> He had learned to take tobacco, and when he was assured he should die, he desired they would give him a pipe in his mouth, ready lighted; which they did. And the executioner came, and first cut off his members, and threw them into the fire: after that, with an ill-favoured knife they cut off his ears and his nose, and burned them; he still smoked on, as if nothing had touched him; then they hacked off one of his arms, and still he bore up and held his pipe; but at the cutting off of the other arm, his head sunk, and his pipe dropped, and he gave up the ghost, without a groan, or a reproach . . . They cut [Oroonoko] into quarters, and sent them to several of the chief plantations: one quarter was sent to Colonel Martin; who refused it, and swore he had rather see the quarters of Banister, and the Governor himself, than those of [Oroonoko] on his plantations; and that he could govern his negroes, without terrifying and grieving them with frightful spectacles of a mangled king.
>
> Thus died this great man, worthy of a better fate, and a more sublime wit than mine to write his praise. Yet, I hope, the reputation of my pen is considerable enough to make his glorious name to survive to all ages, with that of the brave, the beautiful and the constant Imoinda.

Southerne in his dedication of the dramatized version of *Oroonoko* expressed his amazement that Mrs Behn, having so great a command of the stage, 'would bury her favourite hero in a novel, when she might have revived him in the scene. She thought either that no actor could represent him, or she could not bear him represented; and I believe the last, when I remember what I have heard from a friend of hers that she always told his story more feelingly than she writ it.'[47]

Charles Gildon however, in comparing Southerne's version with the novel *Oroonoko* makes an illuminating remark which hints at a reason for Mrs Behn's choice of medium, and which shows that the essential difference between the drama and the novel was commencing to be understood: 'But as to this play *Oroonoko*,' says Gildon, 'you find our poet [Southerne] has allowed the Plot of it to Mrs Behn; for on that Prince she has composed the best of her novels: and as it must be confess'd that the Play had not its mighty Success without an innate Excellence; so in my Opinion, the necessary regularities a Dramatick Poet is obliged to observe, has left many Beauties in the Novel which our Author could not transfer to his Poem.'[48]

It is necessary to sum up what we already know of Aphra Behn's prose fiction if we are to judge the value of her contribution. So far we have seen that she was influenced by the Heroic tradition and that she sought to escape from it; that she alternately subscribed to and rejected the code of gallantry; that she anticipated the method by which Defoe vouched for the truth of his narratives; that she could create backgrounds of natural scenery when nobody else attempted it, foreshadowing, even though feebly, as Mr Baker says,[49] the prose epics of Chateaubriand; that she wrote the first eulogy of the Natural Man—a subject which was later to become a distinct genre of literature, and a cult in the hands of Bernardin de St Pierre and Rousseau; that she wrote the first novel which anathematized the slave trade, and that her savage indignation taught her to write as scathing a satire as any of Swift's. We have seen something also of her realism. Sometimes we know that it is imaginative realism (as in the case of the latter half of *The Nun; or, the Fair Vow-breaker)*; sometimes, as in the novels with a London background, we see, not 'genuine realism' but the weaving of Mrs Behn's actual surroundings into invented tales. On this very subject Miss Sackville-West says: 'It is a pity that Mrs Behn, as a novelist, thought her London experiences beneath the dignity of her pen. She had that gift of God, a free, rapid, and colloquial style, and she neglected to turn it to its best advantage.'[50] We shall see that she did turn it to excellent advantage in that ruthlessly realistic satire: *The Ten Pleasures of Marriage*.

Notes and References

1 *Cassandre*, i, Book v.
2 J. J. Jusserand, *The English Novel in the time of Shakespeare* (1890), p. 362.
3 'The fabliaux or fableaux were "unrhymed" (i.e. made into prose) and made their appearance in the famous form of the novelle or novella, in regard to which it is hard to say whether Italy is most indebted to France for the substance or France to Italy for form.' G. Saintsbury, *History of the French Novel* (1917), p. 32.
4 William Painter, *The Palace of Pleasure*, i (1566); ii (1567); additions made in 1575. Geoffrey Fenton, *Certaine Tragical Discourses* (1567). There were many other collections of translated *novelle*.
5 The *Scholemaster*, begun in 1563, left unfinished at Ascham's death in 1568.
6 Lord Earnle, *Light Reading of our Ancestors* (1921), p. 112.
7 Individual tales appeared much oftener in collections, such as *The Four Tragicomical Histories of Our late Times* (1638), *The Annals of Love* (1672), and the *Spanish Decameron* (1687).
8 Congreve, Preface to *Incognita*.
9 E.A. Baker, *History of the English Novel*, iii, p. 102.
10 Published 1622–1641.
11 *The Adventures of Covent Garden* (1699); and *Zelinda* by T. D. Gent (1769). (T. Duffet, Jusserand suggests.)
12 Allardyce Nicol, *Restoration Drama, 1660–1700* (2nd edn. 1928), pp. 21 f.
13 J. J. Jusserand, *The English Novel in the time of Shakespeare* (1890), pp. 416 f.
14 Miss Charlotte Morgan (*The Rise of the Novel of Manners*, Columbia University Press, 1911, p. 78) says that *The Little Black Lady* appeared in 1663. No doubt she means that it was then published. She gives no reasons for assigning this very early date, and facts connected with Aphra Behn's biography make it appear improbable. The Calendar of State Papers proves that she went to Holland in August, 1666, on her secret mission, and returned in the following December or January. It was after her return to London that her plays began to be acted and her works published. No doubt, as in the case of *The Young King*, some of them may have been written earlier, but nobody except Miss Morgan has claimed that Aphra Behn published a work of any kind as early as 1663. Could this possibly be a misprint for 1683—a very probable date, since Mrs Behn had been obliged to abandon the stage temporarily in 1682, and then turned to fiction as her *Love Letters between a nobleman and his sister*, 1683, testifies? Gosse (in *D.N.B.*) gives 1684 as the date of *The Adventure of the Black Lady*. It is all the more probable that Miss Morgan's date is a misprint, since, on page 76, there are two similar mistakes, i.e. 1671 (instead of 1670) as the date of Aphra Behn's first play; and 1691 (instead of 1689) as the date of Aphra Behn's death.
15 (a) Scarron, *Roman Comique* (Paris, 1651). (b) *Scarron's 'Comical Romance: or a facetious history of a company of strolling stage-players*

(London, 1676). The latter was not merely a translation, but also an Anglicized version of the *Roman Comique*. The translator substituted London where Scarron spoke of Paris, etc. This work was available at the time when Aphra Behn wrote.

16 These three novels are *The Black Lady; The Court of the King of Bantam;* and *The Unfortunate Happy Lady*. All three were published together in 1697, eight years after Aphra Behn's death.

17 Miss V. Sackville-West quotes these lines in this connection in *Aphra Behn* (1927).

18 *The Works of Aphra Benn* (ed. Montague Summers, 1967), vol. v, *The Fair Jilt*, pp. 91–92.

19 Published in 1688. Ten years earlier there is advertised for R. Tonson *The Amorous Convert; being a true relation of what happened in Holland*. Summers believes that this may have been the first sketch.

20 Not published until 1697, eight years after Aphra Behn's death.

21 E. A. Baker, *History of the English Novel*, iii, p. 97.

22 By such critics as the following: Ward, *History of Dramatic Literature* (1899), iii, p. 42, and Article on '*Southerne*' in *D.N.B.*; Charlotte Morgan, *Rise of the Novel of Manners* (Columbia University Press, 1911); *Cambridge History of English Literature* (1912), viii, ch. 7 (by A. T. Bartholomew); Joseph Knight, *David Garrick* (1894).

23 Dr Paul Hamelius, 'The Source of Southerne's Fatal Marriage,' *Modern Language Review* (1909), vol. iv, p. 352.

24 The Revd Dr M. Summers, 'The Source of Southerne's Fatal Marriage,' ibid., April, 1916.

25 C. E. Morgan had been of opinion that *The Fair Vow-breaker* (1689) was the name of the *editio princeps* of *The Nun, or, The Perjured Beauty*. See *The Rise of the Novel of Manners* (Columbia University Press, 1911), p. 83, note 63.

26 Published in 1688, dramatized by Mrs Trotter in 1690.

27 P.B.G., *Two New Novels* (1688).

28 Charles Gildon says that Aphra Behn's *Agnes de Castro* was a translation from 'the French Lady's' novel, but this is incorrect. See Gildon's Langbaine (*The Lives and Characters of the English Dramatic Poets*, 1699) under Mrs Trotter.

29 *The Unfortunate Bride, or the Blind Lady a Beauty, The Dumb Virgin, or the Force of Imagination* and *The Wandering Beauty* were published in 1687; *The Lucky Mistake* was published in 1688. These dates are given by Miss V. Sackville-West, *Aphra Behn* (Representative Women Series, 1927). E. A. Baker simply says that they were written between 1671 and *Oroonoko* which was published in 1688. (See E. A. Baker, *History of the English Novel*, iii, p. 86).

30 Prefixed to *The Younger Brother* (1696).

31 Prefixed to *The Histories and Novels* (1696). *The Life and Memoirs* was probably also written by Charles Gildon, and gives a more detailed account.

32 E. Bernbaum, 'Mrs Behn's Biography a Fiction' (*Modern Language Association of America*, xxviii).

33 E. Bernbaum, 'Mrs Behn's Oronooko,' *Anniversary Papers by Colleagues and Pupils of G. L. Kittredge* (1913).

34 *Aphra Behn's Works* (ed. Summers, 1915), i, *Memoir of Mrs Behn*.

35 V. Sackville-West, *Aphra Behn, 1640–1689* (Representative Women Series, 1927).

36 V. Sackville-West, *Aphra Behn, 1640–1689* (Representative Women Series), Apppendix I.

37 Although anti-romantic in purpose, *Incognita* is romantic in tone.

38 E. A. Baker, *History of the English Novel*, iii, p. 104, footnote. The italics are the present writer's.

39 E. A. Baker, *History of the English Novel*, iii, p. 144, footnote. The italics are the present writer's.

40 See C. F. McIntyre, *Anne Radcliffe in relation to her time* (New Haven, 1920), ch. 2.

41 Also other sources mentioned in J. S. M. Tompkins' excellent article, 'Raymond de Carbonnières, Grosley and Mrs Radcliffe,' *Review of English Studies* (July, 1929).

42 *D.N.B.*

43 *The Works of Aphra Benn*, op. cit., vol. v, *Oroonoko*, p. 130.

44 *The Works of Aphra Behn* (ed. Janet Todd, William Pickering, London, 1992), 'A paraphrase of the Lord's prayer', p. 173.

45 V. Sackville-West, *Aphra Behn, 1640–1689* (Representative Women Series, 1927), p. 74.

46 Julia Kavenagh, *English Women of Letters* (1863), chapter on Aphra Behn.

47 Southerne, Dedication of *Oroonoko*.

48 Gildon's Langbaine (*The Lives of the Poets*, 1699), p. 136.

49 *Aphra Behn's Novels*, (ed. E. A. Baker), p. xxiii f.

50 V. Sackville-West, *Aphra Behn, 1640–1689* (Representative Women Series, 1927), p. 72.

Chapter VI

Satire — English Realism

If there be nothing that will lay me in my Tomb till Love
brings me thither, I shall live to all eternity.

(Aphra Behn, *Lycidas, or, the Lover in Fashion*)

Some years ago in an antiquarian bookseller's shop in the heart
of London was found a book which the Navarre Society considered
well worth publishing. This was *The Ten Pleasures* of *Marriage and
the Second Part, the Confession of the New Married Couple*. On the
title page appears the name A. Marsh, Typogr. It has not been
possible to trace the identity of A. Marsh, nor is the book included
in the Stationers' Register for the period, i.e., 1682–1683. It has
been suggested that Marsh may have thought the book too licentious for registration, but this explanation does not seem probable
in view of the material which poured from the printing presses
in Restoration times, and more particularly since, in 1682, there
was registered a book of the same parent-stock as *The Ten Pleasures*,
and at least as loose in tone. It is thought that *The Ten Pleasures* of
Marriage was published abroad—probably, Hazlitt thinks,[1] at The
Hague or Amsterdam. In the very first page of the original
edition there appears one of several hints of Batavian origin:
'younger' is printed 'jounger.' But the mystery of this book is not
confined merely to its printer. No author's name appears on the
title-page of *The Ten Pleasures of Marriage*. There is, however, a
clue as to its authorship: a letter in the first part is signed A.B.,
and in view of many facts which seem to support the contention,
the work (including both first and second parts) is ascribed to
Aphra Behn. Before we examine the arguments in favour of her
authorship let us glance at the ancestry of this book.

The Ten Pleasures of Marriage, a vigorous satire on marriage and women, springs from an ancient root. It is based on *Les Quinze Joyes de Mariage,* attributed to Antoine de la Salle, but he in turn must have been acquainted with three important satires against women which were published in France in the thirteenth and fourteenth centuries. The earliest and most influential writing of this kind was that part of the *Roman de la Rose* written by Jean de Meun, who attacked the idealized conception of women so dear to the hearts of the troubadours. Another anti-feminist work was *The Lamentations of Mathieu* (1295–1300) written in Latin verses, and translated *c.* 1370 by Jean Le Fevre. A third important French satire against women was *Le Miroir de Mariage* by Eustache Deschamps.[2] *Les Quinze Joyes de Mariage* was written between 1448–1456. The idea of the title was irreverently borrowed from one of the prayers which terminated the Book of Hours—a pious composition entitled *Les Quinze Joyes de Notre Dame, Mere de Dieu.*

> Les Quinze Joyes de Mariage ou la Nasse forment une suite de litanies dans laquelle sont longuement enumerées avec le repons, le final invariable
> > Ainsi vivra en languissant tousjours
> > Et finira miserablement ses jours
> > Les tribulations infinies de l'homme marié.[3]

The first English translation of *Les Quinze Joyes de Mariage,* printed by Wynkyn de Worde in 1509, was entitled: *The Fifteen Joyes of Maryage.* It was a poor verse rendering of de la Salle's excellent prose work. Other translations and adaptations followed. In 1599 Adam Islip's *The XV Joyes of Marriage* was burnt at Stationers' Hall. For the greater part of the seventeenth century the popular translation of *Les Quinze Joyes de Mariage* was *The Batchelars Banquet*[4] which is generally ascribed to Dekker, but which may have been the work of Robert Tofte.[5] The earliest extant edition of *The Batchelars Banquet* was published in 1603 and the last in 1677. In Restoration times it is not surprising to observe that *Les Quinze Joyes de Mariage* took a fresh lease of life. In 1682 there appeared a new translation: *The XV Comforts of Rash and Inconsiderate Marriage or select Animadversions upon the Miscarriage of the Wedded State. Done out of French.* 'In this the Frenchman's delicate irony is here debased to a broad leer, the dialogue is mean and slovenly, though in places pert and lively.

The grossest passages in *Les Quinze Joyes,* omitted in *The Batchelars Banquet,* are given with advantages.'[6] It is not surprising, therefore, that *The XV Comforts* ran into three editions in one year, and continued to be reprinted up to 1760. It gave rise to a spate of pamphlets for and against women. For example, *The Fifteen Real Comforts of Matrimony, by a person of Quality of the Female Sex,* 1683. In 1682 appeared *The Ten Pleasures of Marriage* mentioned above, followed in 1683 by its second part *of the Confession of the New Married Couple.* We believe that both parts were written by Aphra Behn.

Some of the arguments which support Aphra Behn's authorship can be briefly stated. Others require more lengthy consideration. First, it is remarkable that *The Ten Pleasures* was published in 1682 — that very year when Aphra Behn had been obliged to intermit the writing of plays. We know that she turned to prose fiction between 1682 and 1688, when she resumed her dramatic work. Indeed, in 1683 she published *Love Letters between a Nobleman and his Sister,* and it is natural to suppose that she did not allow a year to elapse before trying her hand at this new kind of work which could be essayed without peril of the law. Presuming that Aphra Behn wrote *The Ten Pleasures and the Second Part, the Confession* why did she not acknowledge her authorship? In the first place, there appears to have been a tradition of anonymity connected not only with all the translations and modifications of *Les Quinze Joyes,* but also with *Les Quinze Joyes* itself, and we have seen that these writings had always been regarded as daring and disreputable, as the fate of Adam Islip's book amply demonstrates. But, it will be argued, Aphra Behn was not a squeamish author, and she was writing for a debauched age, therefore there was no reason why she should not have published *The Ten Pleasures* boldly over her own name. On the contrary, there was a most urgent reason for her anonymity. In 1682 she had been summoned for her dramatic writings, and debarred from continuing such work. *The Ten Pleasures* could not shock the Restoration public. Indeed, to tell the truth, it was more broad than salacious. Still Aphra Behn had already been condemned, and knew herself an object of suspicion. She could not risk a further embroilment with the law, particularly within the selfsame year. It is easy, therefore, to understand why she preferred *The Ten Pleasures* to be anonymous. She could nevertheless give a clue as to the authorship, to stir the interest of the reading public, and perhaps to mock slyly the very authorities she feared. Possibly it was for these reasons that we find the letter at the end of *The Ten Pleasures* signed A.B. In Restoration times there was only one writer of note whose initials were A.B., and so far at least, no other writer has been suggested as the author of *The Ten Pleasures*. To seek among the obscure writers is unprofitable, because *The Ten Pleasures* is obviously the work of an original, witty and vigorous mind. No mediocre A.B. could possibly have produced it. The fact that the publisher of the book cannot be traced and that the book appears to have been printed in Holland is in accordance with Aphra Behn's predicament. Negotiations with a London publisher through a third party would involve a strong possibility of her secret leaking out. She was too well-known a literary figure for such an experiment to ensure anonymity. Nothing then remained for her except to publish abroad. She had spent some time in Holland, and had friends there. All things considered it is not in the least surprising that she should decide to publish her book at The Hague or Amsterdam. Apart from the fact that it contains clues which point to Dutch publishing, there is another factor which strangely links *The Ten Pleasures* to Holland. The illustrations bound up in the copy of the 1621 edition of *Les Quinze Joyes* in the Bodleian Library indicate that this book is in some way related to the Dutch *De Tien Delicatessen des Houwelicks*. If these illustrations are contemporaneous with the 1621 edition or previous to it, then *De Tien Delicatessen* was a Dutch version of *Les Quinze Joyes*, and Aphra Behn's *Ten Pleasures* would most likely be based on the Dutch book. But there is no evidence whatever as to the date of *De Tien Delicatessen*, of which there appears to be no extant copy. There is, moreover, no means of ascertaining when these illustrations were bound up in the Bodleian copy of the 1621 edition of *Les Quinze Joyes*. It may have been done even a century later by some private owner of *Les Quinze Joyes* who considered the illustrations of *De Tien Delicatessen* applicable to the subject-matter of the French book. It is, indeed, quite possible that *De Tien Delicatessen des Houwelicks* was simply a Dutch translation of *The Ten Pleasures of Marriage*. It would not be the only translation of Aphra Behn's works published in Holland or in Germany.[7]

The Ten Pleasures must have been written by someone who knew French and who was familiar with French literature, because although there were numerous English translations of *Les Quinze Joyes, The Ten Pleasures* contains an allusion to the French poet Clément Marot, which would require more than a passing acquaintance with Marot's works. The reference probably alludes to the fact that in 1526 the Sorbonne condemned Marot and his poem *Colloque de l'Abbe et de la femme sçavante*. Mr Harvey in his introduction to *The Ten Pleasures* points out that Marot 'is not a 'stock figure' in English literary allusion, either learned or popular, and the fact suggests at least familiarity with the literature of other countries.'[8] Mrs Behn's mastery of the French language is proved by her excellent translation or rather adaptation of Fontenelle's *Entretiens sur la pluralité des mondes* as also her free paraphrase of the Abbé Tallemant des Réaux's *Voyage de l'Isle d'Amour.*[9]

But the person who wrote *The Ten Pleasures* must also have known some German, because in the second part of the book, *The Confession of the New Married Couple,* a High German doctor makes his diagnosis and his recommendations in High German. Aphra Behn must have learned Dutch, since she was considered a suitable person to send on a secret mission to Holland. It is, moreover, a very significant fact that the speech of the High German doctor in *The Ten Pleasures* contains a few misspellings due to Dutch.

Normally speaking, it might be suggested that a woman would not be likely to launch upon her fellow-women such a virulent attack as is to be found in part of *The Ten Pleasures.* Such a contention does not apply to such women as Aphra Behn. Not only was the Restoration attitude towards women entirely cynical, but Aphra Behn and her female followers were all the more relentless, because they themselves were outlawed by feminine society. It was comforting for them to mock at their more cautious sisters and to assert, self-justifyingly, that the courtesan, the wife and the *jeune fille bien élevée* were all sisters under the skin. Indeed (they cried) what is the difference between wife and mistress except that one has patented her claim to a man's protection and the other must rely solely on her own powers to retain it? When Mrs Pix could write as follows there is no room to doubt that these women writers sharpened their claws for their own sex:

Sir Francis: As for the Damosels, three sorts make a Bushel, and will be uppermost. First, there's your common Jilts will oblige every body.

Beaumont: These are Monsters sure.

Sir Francis: You may call 'em what you please, but they are very plentiful, I promise you; The next is your kept Mistress, she's a degree modester, if not kind to each, appears in her dress like Quality, whilst her ogling eye, and too frequent Debauches discovers her the youngest sister only to the first . . . The third is not a Whore, but a brisk, airy, noisy Coquette that lives upon treating, one Spark has her to the Play, another to the Park, a third to Windsor, a fourth to some other place of Diversion; She has not the heart to grant 'em all favours, for that's their design at the bottom of the Treats, and they have not the heart to marry her, for that's her design too, Poor Creature. So perhaps a year, or it may be two, the gaudy Butterfly flutters round the Kingdom, then if a foolish Citt does not take compassion, sneaks into a Corner, dies an Old Maid, despised and forgotten . . . The men that fit those Ladies are your Rake, your Cully, and your Beaux.[10]

In *Sir Patient Fancy* Aphra Behn puts into the mouth of Isabella these words:

Keeping begins to be as ridiculous as matrimony . . . The insolence and expense of their mistresses has almost tired out all but the old and doting part of mankind.

Indeed it would be difficult to exhaust the quotations from Aphra Behn's works which reveal her cynical attitude to women. In her *Lycidas, or the Lover in Fashion* (which is no mere translation, but rather a reply to Tanemant des Réaux's slight but graceful work) Aphra Behn makes her general attitude clear. Lycidas begins by condoling with Lysander on the death of his Aminte. Personally he takes such matters philosophically. He knows the game of love from A to Z, and considers it not worth the stakes. 'After you have heard,' he says, 'My account of the Voyage I made [to the Island of Love], with my more lucky one back again . . . you will by my Example become of my Opinion, (notwithstanding upon dismal Tales of Death and the eternal Shades), which is, that if there be nothing that will lay me in my Tomb till Love brings me thither, I shall live to all Eternity.'[11] Lysander speaks of love as if it were a mere devitalizing enslavement to women:

> I have seen a Man, handsom, well shap'd, and of a great
> deal of Wit, with the advantage of a thousand happy
> adventures, yet finds himself in the end fitter for a hospital
> than the Elevation of Fortune: And the Women are not
> contented we should give them as much Love as they give
> us (which is but reasonable) but they compel us all to
> Present and Treat 'em lavishly, till a Man hath consumed
> both Estate and Body in their service.

This is the subject of the Second Pleasure in *The Confessions of
the New Married Couple*. On his voyage to the Island of Love
Lycidas was accompanied by 'abundance of young Heirs, Cadets,
Coxcombs, Wits, Blockheads and Politicians, with a whole Cargo
of Cullies all, nameless and numberless.' He says:

> Heaven keep me from being a Woman's Property. There are
> Cullies enough besides you or I, Lysander. One would
> think, now that I, who can talk thus Learnedly and Gravely,
> had never been any of the number of those wretched,
> whining, sighing, dying Fops, I speak of, never been jilted
> and cozen'd of both my Heart and Reason; but let me tell
> you that think so, they are mistaken, and that all this Wisdom
> and Discretion I now seem replenish'd with, I have as
> dearly bought as any keeping Fool of 'em all. I was ly'd and
> flattered into Wit, jilted and cozen'd into Prudence, and, by
> ten thousand broken Vows and perjured Oaths, reduced to
> Sense again; and can laugh at all my past Follies now.[12]

He recounts that when he fell in love with Sylvia, a paragon
of beauty and grace, she

> found my Weakness and her own Power; and using all the
> Arts of her Sex, played the Woman all over: she wou'd be
> scornful and kind by turns, as she saw convenient, This to
> check my Presumption and too easy hope: That to preserve
> me from the brink of Despair. Thus was I tost in the Blanket
> of Love, sometimes up and sometimes down, as her Wit and
> Humour was in or out of tune, all which I watch'd, and
> waited like a Dog, that still the oftener kick'd would fawn
> the more. Oh, 'tis an excellent Art this managing of a
> Coxcomb, the Serpent has taught it to our Grandam Eve;
> and Adam was the first kind Cully: E're since they have kept
> their Empire over Men, and we have, e're since, been slaves.[13]

'Women,' says the author of *The Ten Pleasures*, 'are in effect of
less value than old Iron, Boots and Shoes, etc., for we find both

merchants and money always ready to buy these commodities.' There is no lack of evidence in Aphra Behn's accredited works that this was her view of women, and that she held downright views on 'the quarrelsome, crabbed, lavish, proud, opinionated, domineering and unbridled nature of the female sex.'[14]

To argue that *The Ten Pleasures* is so scathing a satire on women that no woman could possibly have written it is simply to demonstrate a touching but undeserved confidence in women's mutual loyalty. Such an argument collapses not only in view of the peculiar temper of Restoration women, but also because women of any age, in life or in print, tend to be more merciless towards each other than any man could be towards them. And yet it is interesting to observe that when a woman has rent her sex for the diversion of the men whom she proportionately praises or pities, some deep, primitive antagonism within her awakens, and drives her to execute a final volte face. She watches, as it were, the faces of men creased with laughter at her sardonic revelations of women, and then, unable to shed her own sex, she stands branded with the very brand she has forged for her sisters. She stands a self-confessed traitor, and she stands alone, having withdrawn momentarily from the objects of her scorn. Every man knows that a woman will deride other women up to the moment when he joins in her derision; then she turns swiftly and, by a curious metamorphosis, becomes the protagonist of her sex. A tamed lioness will lower her dignity by jumping through hoops and climbing on stools, and then, just when her keeper feels that she knows her place at last, she fells him to the ground with one contemptuous stroke of her paw. So it is with women, those 'Drawcansirs that maul both friend and foe.' So it was with Aphra Behn in *The Ten Pleasures*.

Mr Harvey in his introduction to the Navarre Society edition, says: 'The irony [of *The Ten Pleasures*] is less well sustained in the sequel, *The Confession of The New Married Couple*.' But this is not the main difference between *The Ten Pleasures* and *The Confession*. The fact is that whereas *The Ten Pleasures* is violently condemnatory of women and marriage, *The Confession* chiefly defends women and, showing that all marriages are not alike, pleads for reconciliation rather than divorce. The introduction to *The Confession* says: 'Of those [joys] we have before demonstrated unto you Ten Pleasant Tables: But because the Scale of Marriage may hang somewhat evener and not fall too light on the women's side, we shall for the Courteous Reader add unto them Ten Pleasures more.' In these additional pleasures a different point of view is very apparent, illustrated with innumerable touches which reveal a woman's mind. Many of the feminine grievances in *The Confession* concern matters of which a man would not be alertly conscious, as we shall see when we come to consider them in more detail. And it is worthy of careful note that whereas the *Quinze Joyes* and its English versions devote one episode only to satirizing the vagaries and extravagances which are represented as characterizing the expectant mother, no less than seven of the ten episodes in *The Ten Pleasures* are devoted to this subject. Since *The Ten Pleasures* depicts merely the first year in the life of a young married couple, it is obvious that the maeutic outlook supervenes at a very early stage, and it progresses with the most detailed and forthright consideration of every phase until the moment when the neighbours gather to celebrate the birth. If a man wrote *The Ten Pleasures,* he could surely have found a wealth of masculine grievances to depict without committing himself to describe the first married year almost entirely from an obstetrical point of view. Furthermore the feminine touch is evident in these descriptions. It is evident in the gusto, albeit the sardonic gusto, with which the author depicts these women deriving intense pleasure from their garrulous reminiscences of child-bearing, closing their ranks as they sit gossiping together, sinking their voices to mysterious whispers and raising them to dogmatic assertion, forming a temporary cabal against mere husbands, finding a brief unison in their common maternity. She despises the homely vulgarity of such seances, but she understands it; and she understands also the dogged strength which underlies the apparent weakness of the pettish, complaining, attitudinizing woman. That is why, when she has shown us these people she pulverizes them before our eyes. These chapters do not lend themselves to detailed exposition, but readers will find in them confirmation of the feminine authorship of this book.

For all the reasons, therefore, which we have mentioned, we believe that Aphra Behn wrote *The Ten Pleasures of Marriage and the Second Part, the Confession of the New Married Couple.* Let us see now how far she was indebted to the sources at her disposal. No doubt she was familiar with the original *Quinze Joyes* and with some of its English renderings, certainly with *The Batchelars Banquet*, but although she took from them the general, basic idea, *The Ten Pleasures . . . and the Confession* is in no sense a translation, paraphrase, or version of any of these works. It would be very simple indeed to show by collated columns that Aphra Behn's twenty pleasures do not adhere to the material or the sequence of the fifteen joys. One might expect that she would have given some characteristic twist to the fifteen joys and then added five joys or pleasures more. But this is not so. It is true that in the first ten pleasures there is the main principle of *Quinze Joyes* — that a married man is like a squirrel in a cage and that woman entraps and exploits him for her own selfish purposes, but Aphra Behn does not follow the material or the structure of the *Quinze Joyes* to illustrate this principle; instead she drives it home with ten sardonic pleasures which are ten nails in the coffin of a married man's happiness. Echoes from the *Quinze Joyes* are occasionally to be observed but they come and go as they will, and do not detract from the original character of *The Ten Pleasures*. Mr Harvey remarked that the letter at the end of *The Ten Pleasures* (first part) was a savage attack on women. So it is, but this letter is only an improved version of the preface to de la Salle's *Quinze Joyes*. For her letter (in which one friend asks another whether it is advisable to marry) Aphra Behn seems to have taken for her text these words in the preface of *Les Quinze Joyes* and of its translation *The XV Comforts:* 'The report is current of a famous Physician, Valere by name, who being ask'd by one of his Friends (that had the misfortune to be catched in the Nooze of Wedlock) whether he had done well in changing his condition of single Life, returned him this bitter, tho' true Answer; Friend (said he) could you not find some Precipice[15] to cast yourself from thence into the sea?' De la Salle's argument continues:

> It is certainly a greater Happiness for a Man to enjoy Freedom uncontroul'd, than to enslave himself for ever without compulsion . . . That man is unquestionably sense-less who enjoys his Freedom in the Vigour and Sprightliness of his youth, living in the stream of Wealth and the high Tide of Pleasure and Delight [who] throws himself into an Abyss of misery, confines himself to a person (a Wife) whose best qualification is Peevishness, forfeits his Freedom, Reason, Content, and Satisfaction and loseth his own to enslave himself to the Humour of another, and this too for

Life . . . Would not any rational creature judge him guilty
of Statute-madness, who being shewn the Loathsomeness
and Horror of a Dungeon, views the maigre and Ghost-like
Aspect of the famished Prisoner, hears the hideous Shrieks
and Groans of shackled Malefactors, the ratling noise of
whose heavy Irons is a Harmony only fit to drive a serious
Man out of his Wits; would not, I say, any Person gifted
with reason look upon him to be mad beyond the cure of
Drugs or Medicines, who shall . . . cast himself in a Goal
[*sic*] with a resolution never to be discharged, but to lie there
and perish . . . It is a Saying of the learned Scaliger, that a
Wife is a Hectic Fever never to be cur'd by any thing but
Death, nor can any wise man deny it.[16]

Aphra Behn's letter incorporates these views:

But the Tortures of Marriage are such a burthen, that I never
saw no man, let him be as couragious as he would, which it
hath not brought under the yoke of her Tyranny. Marry
then, you shall have a thousand vexations, a thousand
torments, a thousand dissatisfactions, a thousand plagues;
and in a word, a thousand sorts of repentings, which will
accompany you to your Grave.[17]

And there are more direct echoes in Aphra Behn's letter. She
says to the prospective husband: 'You shall never be at quiet till
you are in your grave.'[18] In *The XV Comforts* the pouting wife
says: 'I'm sure I shall never rest but in that place of undisturbed
Rest (the only Dormitory of Mortals) the Grave.'[19] *The XV Comforts*
says: 'Yet for all that is premention'd, I do not blame the State of
Matrimony (as now instituted by the Church) for beyond all
dispute Marriage is an Ecclesiastical and Religious tye.'[20] Aphra
Behn says: 'Yet I would not have you to believe, tho' I so much
discommend it that it is no waies usefully profitable. I esteem it
to be a holy institution ordained by God Almighty,' but, she adds,
'that which makes it bad is the woman in whom there is no good.'[21]

These quotations may convey a false impression of Mrs Behn's
indebtedness. She adhered to the general procedure of such
writings: she took such hints as were useful to her purpose, but
in the grip of her originality they become part of an entirely
different fabric. For example, she embodies the introduction of
the *Quinze Joyes* in a letter, but the episodes or pleasures which
constitute her book are quite individual and, from the point of
view of fictional development, very much superior. Although the

first three joys in de la Salle's work might be episodes in the same marriage, the remainder could not. But Aphra Behn, apparently with the idea of producing something which would approximate to an integral whole, rejects de la Salle's disjointed episodes, and in the first half of her book (the part entitled *The Ten Pleasures*) attempts to write a sequential narrative, beginning with the preparations for the marriage, recounting the events of the first year of married life, and ending with the picture of the young daughter growing up and being married in her turn. 'It is an early instance of the stringing together, in a connected narrative, of the material previously used only in short sketches or 'characters'; and so it is directly in the succession which in the end produced what is perhaps the most enduring and individual phenomenon in our language — the English novel.'[22] It is accepted that the character-sketches and episodic accounts given in the *Spectator* and the *Rambler* played an important part in the development of prose fiction, but such contributions were merely the culmination of a trend which had long given proof of its existence in such works as Thomas Overbury's *The Wife* (1614), John Earl's *Microcosmographie* (1628), Thomas Bastard's *Chrestoleras* (1598) and the Duchess of Newcastle's *CCXL Sociable Letters* (1664). These works, though most valuable for their embryonic delineations of character and for their scenes from real life, lacked a connecting thread. Indeed the *Spectator* and *Rambler* contributions were very loosely strung together, and as sequential narratives were in no way superior to *The Ten Pleasures*. An even more important contribution to the novel was the realism of *The Ten Pleasures*. Here there is no need for cautious hairsplitting as to the kind of realism involved. *The Ten Pleasures* and *The Confession* are a striking example of realism in a most artificial literary age. As Green, Breton, Nash and Deloney showed the England of their time, as the Duchess of Newcastle in *The Traveller* and in her *CCXL Sociable Letters* gave a glimpse of the uncorrupted side of Restoration life, so Aphra Behn takes us into the very heart of English middle-class life in the reign of James II. With complete fidelity, with immense energy, vivacity and colour she depicts for us the daily round of a young husband and wife. We know the details of their house, their furnishings, their clothes, their food, their customs, their friends, their servant problem, their money troubles, their quarrels and their reconciliations. We see the husband busy in the shop, or chaffering in the City or drinking with his cronies. When, flown with Dutch courage, he brings them home unexpectedly to supper we watch the wife bite her lips with temper, and we gather the fluent acidities of her certain lecture. Then the sun comes out again, and we see her in her finery going to market, followed by her hand-maid who carries a basket and the baby 'finically dressed'— a proud display for the neighbours. *The Ten Pleasures* and *The Confession* are an onlooker's account of Restoration bourgeois life, told with robustious humour and an astonishing facility of phrase. It is alive; it sweeps us along in a tide of vigorous words. It does not trouble itself with the subtleties of character, but it makes the stock characters of the husband and wife seem rich by virtue of their universality. They are as good as bread, as sound as ale, as pungent as an onion.

Mrs Behn, as we have said, took her general idea and some definite hints from the *Quinze Joyes* or its English versions, but this was not the end of her indebtedness. To *The Batchelars Banquet* she owes the style of *The Ten Pleasures,* that style which loses some of its intensity in the second part *(The Confession of the New Married Couple).* Whether or not Dekker was responsible for *The Batchelars Banquet,* it is characterized by the very same style as *Guls Horne-booke* which was Dekker's rendering of Dedekind's *Grobianus.* In *Guls Home-booke* and in *The Batchelars Banquet* Dekker maintained Dedekind's peculiar manner of writing which is known as Grobianism. The *Grobianus* consisted of a number of scenes not connected by a definite story, but giving an opportunity of describing various kinds of men and manners. It had for its subject bad manners reduced to a code, and its style consisted in a savagely sardonic agreement with all the idiocies described. The style of *The Batchelars Banquet* is an excellent example of Grobianism, and it is this self-same attitude which Aphra Behn adopts towards the objects of her satire. Any part of *The Ten Pleasures* might be quoted as an example. Let us take at random a passage from the First Pleasure. The wooing is successful. The parents have consented and the match is concluded. The wedding is at hand and all is bustle and preparation:

> Oh call the Bride, time will deceive us! The Semstress, Gorgetmaker, and Starcher, must be sent for, and the linnen must be bought and ordered for the Bridegroom's shirts, the Bride's Smocks, Cuffs, Bands and Handkerchiefs; and do

but see, the day is at an end again: my brains are almost addle, addle, and nothing goes forward: For Mrs Smug said she would bring linnen, and Mrs Smooth laces, but neither of them both are yet come. Run now, men and maids, as if the Devil were in you, and comfort yourselves that the Bride will reward you liberally for your pains.

Well, Mrs Bride, how's your head so out of order! Might not you now do (as once a Schoolmaster did) hang out a sign of a troubled pate with a Crown on it? How glad you'l be when this confusion is once over? Could you ever have thought that there was so much work to be found in it? But comfort yourself . . . it is not your case alone, to be in all this trouble, for the Bridegroom is running up and down like a dog, in taking care that the Banns of Matrimony may be proclaimed. And now he's a running to and again through the City to see if he can get Bridesmen to his mind that are capacitated to entertain the Bridesmaids and Gentleman with pretty discourses, waiting upon them and the rest of the Company. Besides that he's taking care for the getting of some good Canary, Rhenish and French Wines, that those friends which come to wish the Bride and Bridegroom much joy may be presented with a delicate glass of Wine. And principally, that those who are busy about the Bride's adornments may tast the Brides tears.

But really friends, if you come to tast the Brides tears now, tis a great while too soon: But if you'll have of the right and unfeigned ones, you must come some months hence.[23]

The Second Pleasure shows the young wife going to buy household stuff. The maid-servant goes with her and 'neighbour John, that good careful labourer must follow them softly with his wheel-barrow, that the things which are bought may be carefully and immediately brought home.'[24] Heart-burnings have begun. The husband is secretly distracted at his wife's extravagance, and she is displeased at the ingratitude of some of the wedding-guests. The Third Pleasure is in happier vein. The young couple walk daily abroad being entertained by their friends and travel into the country for their pleasure. The writer considers all these diversions with withering irony, and no wonder, because in the following seven Pleasures the husband is about to welter in a sea of troubles, no sooner breaching one wave than another takes his breath away. This part of the book is a very fine piece of sustained Grobianism, but although there is not really much occasion 'To make use of the gesture of turning up the whites of the eyes,' we must limit ourselves to two quotations. Some of the most notable effects are achieved by a deadly reduction of what appears unique to the commonplace. Mr Pecksniff's nocturnal quest for Sarah Gamp deserves its immortality, but not more so than this wretched husband's frantic predicament.

There's now no small alarm in the Watch. Who is there that is but near, or by the hand that is not set a work! Oh, was Dorothy the Semstress and Jane the Laundress now here, what a helping hand we might have of them! Where are now the two Chair women also, they were commonly every day about the house and now we stand in such terrible need of them, they are not to be found? Herewith must the poor Drone very unexpectedly get out of bed . . . having hardly time to put on his shoes and stockings . . . and it is nothing but hast, hast, hast, fetch the Midwife with all possible Speed . . .

Therefore without denial away the good man himself must to fetch the Midwife: for who knows whether or no she would come if the maid went; nay it is a question also, being so late in the night, whether she would come along with the maid alone, because she dwells in a very solitary corner clearly at th' other end of the City: (for, after a ripe deliberation of the good woman [the wife] the lot fell so that she made choice of this grave and experienced midwife).

Away runs the poor man without stop or stay, as if he were running for a Wager of some great concern. And though it be never so cold, the Sweat trickles down by the hair of his head, for fear he should not find the Midwife at home; or that perhaps she might be fetch out to some other place, from whence she could not come. And if it should happen so, we are all undone, for the good woman must have this Midwife, or else she dies; neither can or dare she condescend to take any other for the reasons afore mentioned . . . Be not discomforted although she doth thus unexpectedly force you out of bed, before you have hardly slept an hour, for you see there's great occasion for 't; and now is the time to show that you truly love your wife. This first time will make it more accustomary, the first is also commonly the worst. And if you be so fortunate that at the very first you happen to meet with this prudent and grave Matron Midwife, and do bring her to your longing-for dearly beloved Wife; yet nevertheless you may assure your self, that before you can arrive to have the full scope and height of this Pleasure you'll find some thing more to do: For the Midwife is not able alone to govern and take care of all things that must be fetched brought and carried to and again: therefore of necessity the friends must be fetched

with all the Speed imaginable, viz Sisters, Wives, Aunts,
Cousins, and several familiar good acquaintances must
have notice of it, and be defraied to come to her quickly
quickly, without delay: and if you do not invite them very
ceremonially, every one according to their degrees, it is
taken as no small affront.[25]

Expense now comes like an avalanche upon the unhappy
father; hordes of dictatorial women entrench themselves in his
house, and treat him like a worm. They enjoy themselves to their
hearts' content, gossiping and consuming incredible quantities of
food and drink. 'But stay a little, tomorrow or next day the Nurse
goes away. This seems to be a merriment indeed for then you'll
have an Eater, a Stroy-good, a Stuf-gut, a Spoil-all, and a Prittle-
pattler less than you had before.'[26]

So the narrative goes on, and the time is anticipated when the
little daughter is grown up:

Both you and her mother will reap an extraordinary
pleasure in seeing your daughter grow up in all manner of
comely and civil deportment, and that she begins to study
in the book of *French Manners and Behaviours*; and knows
also how to dress up her self so finically with all manner of
trinkum trankums, that all the neighbouring young
Gentlewomen, and your rich Nieces esteem themselves very
much honoured with the injoiment of her company; where
they, following the examples of their Predecessors, do by
degrees, instruct one another in the newest fashions, finest
Flanders Laces, the difference and richness of Stuffs, the
neatest cut Gorgets, and many more such Incombobs as
these. Nay, and what's more, they begin also to invite and
treat each other like grave persons, according as the
opportunity will allow them, first with some Cherries and
Plums; then with some Filbuds and Small Nuts; or Wallnuts
and Figs; and afterwards with some Chestnuts and new
Wine; or to a game at Cards with a dish of Tee; or else to eat
some Pancakes and Fritters or a Tansie; nay if the Coast be
clear to their minds to a good joint of meat and a Sallad. Till
at last it comes so far, that through these delicious conversations they happen to get a Sweetheart.[27]

In a word, another squirrel enters the cage to wear out his
distracted existence in the captivity he was too stupid to avoid.

The conclusion of *The Quinze Joyes* (written probably as a last-
moment attempt to appease feminine readers) appears to reverse

the author's ill-opinion of the female sex. We quote from *The XV Comforts of Rash and Inconsiderate Marriage* (1682):

> Nor on the other hand do I say it is ill done to Marry; but it is not well done certainly, for a man to be so Stupid and Insensible, as those we here discourse of apparently declare themselves to be, and so are enslaved with a self-procured Bondage. I would not willingly disoblige the Female Sex; nor indeed do I, if read without Prejudice, and rightly understood, the Contents of this Treatise, tending much to their Honour and Commendation, in all which Rencounters the Women win the day, come off triumphantly, and man is most shamefully worsted by the Weaker Sex: and 'tis but reason it should be so considering the wrongs that they suffer by the Oppression and Severity of their Husbands, by Violence, and without Reason; only because they are not of so Robustious Constitution, and are sent into the World with no other weapon but the Tongue, nor any other defence but their Chastity, though daily exposed to the crafty assaults of Wily Man: Nature have sent them so weakly arm'd into the World, it is a prodigious shame, that Man should so barbarously insult over them, who are so ready to serve and obey, without whose Society the World would soon be a Desart, nay Men could not, did not, nor cannot live happily.[28]

Possibly these words are sardonic in intention. At any rate, they did not placate the 'Person of Quality of the Female Sex' who, in the year following *The XV Comforts* replied with *The XV Real Comforts*. Whether or not it was possible for Aphra Behn to be influenced by this latter work, she may have taken the hint of feminine defence in the passage above quoted, and rallied to the cause of worthy wives as enthusiastically as she had pilloried the vapid opportunists.

In *The Confession of the New Married Couple* she parts company with those who asperse women and matrimony:

> Here they are cited to appear who display the married estate too monstrously as if there were nothing but horrors and terrors to be found in it. Now they would see how that Love in her curious Crucible, melteth two hearts and ten sences together. To this all Chymists vail their Bonnets, though they brag of their making the hardest Minerals as soft as Milk and Butter. This Art surpasseth all others.[29]

185

She applies herself to proving that it is not matrimony, but the abuse of matrimony which causes so much misery. Marriages made for money are foredoomed, and she flays the matchmakers 'who negotiate with a very Close intelligence in this sort of Flesh-Trade,' and who draw a commission on the good bargains they arrange:

> You, O Lovers, who seek to be Livry Men of the great Company, and aim to possess the pleasures of Marriage, have a care of the inchanting Voices of these crafty Syrens, because they intend to batter you upon the Scylla and Charibdis where the Hellish Furies seem to keep their habitation. These are the onely Occasioners of bad Matches, and such as raise a Scandal of that Estate, which at once affords both Pleasure, Mirth and Joy.[30]

The young couple in *The Confession* may or may not be identical with the young couple in the *Ten Pleasures*. They are a good-hearted pair, who set up a shop and are determined to live happy ever after. But alas! happiness does not come at the whistle of determination. They experience all the usual vicissitudes. We leave them at the end sunk in debt, short in temper, confused by the blows of life, wanting a divorce. Aphra Behn uses this couple to give continuity to her description of the storms which so often have 'the marriage-ship' on the rocks. She presents them to us as the average faulty but well-meaning husband and wife, and then, by a thousand examples, she shows us how, without love and with initial faults aggravated, men and women can make of marriage a hell upon earth. Now, however, it is the husband whom she lashes with scorpions. It is a curious fact that it is not the major vices which are shown as most objectionable in a husband. Aphra Behn does not greatly dwell, for example, on the loose livers who automatically outlaw themselves from the covenant of marriage. No, her purpose is to show the countless ways in which a man, although fundamentally sound, may be a maddening husband. In her writing there is all the stringency and the minute observation of exacerbated feminine nerves. She shows, in effect, that a wife's nerves, strung taut by her subservient position, may suffer exquisitely through the arrogance, stupidity or selfishness of her lord and master. How can she be supposed to acknowledge a superiority which, as often as not, is non-existent?

But nevertheless the imaginary authority of men, many times surges to such a height that it seems to them insupportable, to hear anything of a woman's contradiction, thinking that all whatsoever they do is absolutely perfect and uncontrollable.

The stingy husband is undoubtedly a sad affliction, and particularly to be abhorred when he calmly pockets his wife's dowry and then forces her to sue for every necessary farthing and to render an account of even the most trifling expenditure.

It is against all reason, that she, like a servant, should give an account to her husband, what, wherefore, or how that money is laid out; because the necessaries also for house-keeping are so many, that they are without end, name or number, and it is impossible that one should relate or ring them all into the ears of a Man.

The obvious solution must be that the wife become bursar because 'when men pay out anything, it goes out by great sums . . . this cannot be done with every pittiful small thing that belongs to housekeeping. Insomuch that the Husband can then, with all facility, demand what money is needful for his occasion from his wife.' Unfortunately, husbands feel that without the keys of the money-chest they are 'deprived of all their superiority, and like Men unmanned.' A woman with a stingy husband must face the prospect that, by a truly fearful deterioration, he may become a 'Peep in the Pot.' For such prying penuriousness there is practically no remedy. Jealous prying, however, is even worse. Such a husband does

nothing but pout, mumble, bawl, scold, is cross-grained and troubled at everything, nay looks upon his wife and the rest of his Family like a Welsh goat, none of them knowing the least reason in the World for it. In the meanwhile, he useth all means privately to attrap his wife; for to see that which he never will see; and at which he is so divellishly possessed to have a wicked revenge; nay, which he also never can see though he had a whole box-full of spectacles upon his nose; because she never hath, or ever will give him the least reason for it. In that manner violating loves knot, and laying a foundation of implacable hatred.

The best remedy in this case is for the wife to be 'a little light-hearted and merry-humoured.' Thus she can derive a certain amusement from the contemplation of these absurdities, 'but otherwise there is no greater Hell upon Earth.'

The husbands so far enumerated have all the faults of rigidity. There is, however, another class — the royal and ancient order of 'Whiffling Blades.' These are the tipplers, the gamesters, the roysterers, the resourceful fabricators of alibis; but they would need to adduce some better evidence than 'a multitude of lame excuses, before they can blind the eyes of a quick-sighted woman or pin it on her so far that she perceives not he seeks his pleasure from her in whom his whole delight ought to be.' Such men go about drinking, racketing and wasting their lives and their money. Their avocations afford them an excellent pretext for idleness, and it is enough to make any wife despair when she finds that whether her spouse is a physician, lawyer, exciseman, solicitor, merchant, or shopkeeper, his supposed duties are his best camouflage. Aphra Behn's description of this type of husband is really inimitable. She writes with the malicious humour of a woman who knows by heart all men's devices for playing truant. It is unbelievable that anyone but a woman could have written thus or given to her words so strong a sense of personal reinforcement. As a picture of Restoration London this part[31] of *The Confession* is very valuable. We bless the delinquents who lead us into the vivid, roaring life of coffee-houses, strong-water shops, fairs, horse-markets, coursing, pigeon-racing, cock-fighting, dog-fighting, bull and bear-baiting; although we cannot but agree these husbands are

> so dull-brained and so excessive careless, that if they had not the good fortunes to get notable sharp-witted young women to their Wives; they themselves would soon have been out of breath, and might now perhaps be found in the Barbado's or Bermoodo's planting Tabacco.[32]

Aphra Behn's great panacea for all matrimonial ills consists in mutual forbearance:

> It is the principallest satisfaction, and greatest pleasure in marriage, when a woman winks or passes by the action of her husband; and the husband in like manner the actions of the wife; for if that were not so, how should they now and then in passing by, throw a love-kiss at one another.[33]

There are crosses and dissatisfactions in every marriage, but still 'One pound of the hony of sweet love, can easily balance a hundred weight of that terrible and bitter Wormwood.'[34] And for a woman there is a particular pleasure which makes everything worth while:

> The Family must be well taken care of; going to market with the maid to buy that which is good, and let her dress it to your mind; and every Market day precisely, with the Maid neatly drest, and following you with a hand-basket, go to take a view of Newgate, Cheapside, and the Poultry Markets; and afterwards, when your got a little farther, then to have your Baby carried by you, neatly and finically drest up; and in hearing of it, whilst it is in the standing stool, calling in its own language so prettily Daddy and Mammy. O that is such an extraordinary pleasure, that where ever you go, what soever you delight in, all your delight is to be at home again in your shop, by your servants, and most especially (when you have it) to be by your baby.[35]

Domestic affairs, however, are not unalloyed bliss. One must take into account that much-abused tribe — the 'base-natured, lasie, tatling, lavish and ill-tongued servants . . . It was a much less trouble for Arion and Orfeus to charm all the senceless creatures both of Sea and Land in those daies, than it is for housekeepers to bring their servants to due obedience.' Jane, being dismissed for 'hair-brained' behaviour,

> runs to Goody Busie-body that hires out servants; where she makes no small complaint of her Mistresses insulting spirit; and asks whether she knows not of a hire for her by some housekeeping Batchelor or widower; because she understands the ordering of her work very well, is a special good Cook, and loves Children &c: Then she would leave her Mistriss, and tell her that her Aunt was very sick and lay dying, and that she would go thither.

Then, there is the maid who cannot be restrained from purloining food and drink, and the maid who refuses to postpone her outing,

> having gotten leave to go to church in the evening, tho she knows there are friends invited to supper, the children must be got to bed and all things set in good order . . . That it is, that makes them look like a Dog in a Halter, when they

189

cannot get leave on Sundaies to go agadding, and it is
a wonder they do not bargain for it when they hire
themselves.[36]

Some indeed do bargain thus, and depart for Church even if
the house were falling about the ears of the mistress, and this,
not because of extreme devotion, but 'really for no other end
than to catch some Tailor, Baker, Shoomaker, Cooper, Carpenter,
Mason or such like journey man.' Marriage is their object, even
though they may thereby exchange a plentiful livelihood for one
that is poor and wretched. Observe the vivid realism not only of
the foregoing, but particularly of this description of a soldier
courting a servant-maid. The soldier entreats the maid to marry
him, and she deliberates:

> In short, the Maid begun a little to listen to him (and so
> much the more because that very morning she had a falling
> out with her Mistress) and told him, she would take it into
> consideration. He answered her again, what a fidle stick,
> why should we spend time in thinking? We are equally
> matcht: a Souldier never thinks long upon any thing, but
> takes hold of all present opportunities, and it generally falls
> out well with him. But she drawing back a little, he saith, ah
> my dearest, you must take a quick resolution. *Behold there,*
> *yonder comes a Clod driving towards the Moon: I'll give you so*
> *much time till that be past by*; quick, for otherwise I must go
> and seek my fortune by another. Because a soldier neither
> wooes nor threatens long.

Mrs Behn does not understate the troubles which a wife may
find in marriage, that state in which sometimes husband, children
and servants are so many hornets about one's ears. Nevertheless,
she is sure that it is worth all its pains if it is a marriage of true
minds: 'Certainly to be of one mind may very well be said to be
happily married, and called a Heaven upon Earth.'[37] She has
some shrewd remarks to make as to the efforts of incompatible
couples to be divorced: 'Happy were those restless Souls, if they
did like the wise and prudent Chyrurgians, who will not cut off
any member, before they have made an operation of all
imaginable means for cure and recovery thereof; And that they
might the better excuse those of their adversary.'[38]

It would be difficult to over-stress the importance of *The Ten
Pleasures of Marriage and . . . the Confession of the New Married*

Couple as an example of 'plain, broad, humorous English realism,'[39] of that realism which, despite the indifference of aristocratic literary fashions, stoutly persisted in enduring from age to age. It is curious to note how aristocratic and popular genres, existing side by side and tending towards the same goal, refused for long to learn from each other and seemed each intent on working out its own destiny. The romantic genre had learned in a general way to tell a story, and when it considered reality at all, it sought it in the vivid pages of the Italian *novella*. Apparently it did not realize or was indifferent to the possibilities of stories fashioned from everyday life. On other hand, the popular school kept a tight hold on real life, but somehow, probably because its fullness bewildered them, they could not select and weave material into a sustained narrative. Bunyan was a tidal wave by which one must not measure the average advance, and even Bunyan was sustained by allegory. How long a period was to elapse before Bunyan's realism, characterization and narrative power were to be employed in depicting everyday life! In the days of Sydney the cleavage between aristocratic and popular prose fiction was complete. In Restoration times it was still evident, but the gap was lessening. Aphra Behn had a firm foot on either bank and, but for the need of enlisting the patronage of the leisured classes, we well know which foot would have followed the other. We have enumerated at the end of Chapter V the many ways in which she overtopped the fiction writers of her age. It remained only to prove her an English realist, and *The Ten Pleasures of Marriage, and . . . the Confession* proves that. It is the coping stone in her great achievement for English prose fiction. It is a characteristic of genius that its ideas find their full fruition in after-time, and it is illuminating to remember in this connection that Aphra Behn, poet, dramatist, novelist, satirist, translator, Aphra Behn of the prophetic inspirations, was a woman 'unlearned in schools.'[40]

Notes and References

1 See introduction (Navarre Society edn.), *The Ten Pleasures of Marriage*.
2 A poem of 12,103 lines.
3 *Nouvelle Biographie Universelle* (1859). See 'Antoine de la Salle.'

4 *The Batchelars Banquet* is included in the collected non-dramatic works of Dekker. See also J. J. Jusserand, *The English Novel in the time of Shakespeare* (1890), p. 339.

5 The Batchelars Banquet (ed. Wilson, 1929), Introduction.

6 Ibid.

7 E.g. *Oroonoko, traduit de l'Anglois de Mms Behn par P.A. de la Place* (Amsterdam, 1745); *Lebens-und Liebes-Geschichte des Königlichen Schlaven Oroonoko in West-Indien . . . Verteuscht durch M.V.* (Hamburg, 1709); *Oroonoko, ein Trauerspiel*, by W. H. Von Dalberg? or — Von Eisenthal? (1789).

8 *The Ten Pleasures*. Privately printed by the Navarre Society. Introduction by John Harvey.

9 *Lycidas, or the Lover in Fashion . . . His Voyage from the Island of Love* (1688).

10 Mary Pix, *The Innocent Mistress* (1697), Act 1.

11 *Works of Aphra Behn* (ed. Summers, 1915), vi, pp. 299 f.

12 Ibid., p. 300.

13 Ibid., p. 301.

14 *The Ten Pleasures*.

15 De la Salle used the word *fenestre*: 'Amy, n'avez vous peu trouver une haute fenestre pour vous laisser tresbucher en une rivière la teste devant?' (1607 edn., p. 11).

16 The version of the preface to *Les Quinze Joyes* given in *The XV Comforts of Rash and Inconsiderate Marriage* (4th edn., 1694).

17 Letter at the end of *The Ten Pleasures*.

18 Ibid.

19 *The XV Comforts*, 1st Comfort.

20 Ibid., Preface.

21 Letter, *The Ten Pleasures*.

22 *The Ten Pleasures* (Navarre Society edn.), Introduction by John Harvey, p. ix.

23 Ibid., pp. 19 f.

24 Ibid., pp. 26 f.

25 Ibid., pp. 77 ff.

26 Ibid., p. 122.

27 Ibid.

28 *The XV Comforts . . .* (4th edn., 1694), pp. 127 f.

29 *The Ten Pleasures . . . and the Confession of the New Married Couple*, pp. 152 f.

30 Ibid., p. 158.

31 *The Confession*, Fifth Pleasure.

32 Ibid., Sixth Pleasure, p. 218.

33 Ibid., Fifth Pleasure, p. 209.

34 Ibid., Fifth Pleasure, p. 213.

35 Ibid., p. 151.

36 Ibid., Ninth Pleasure.

37 Ibid., p. 152.

38 Ibid., p. 279.

39 'But there was that other side of the English genious to which Mrs Behn might have turned in her novels: the plain, broad, humorous, English realism which would so excellently have suited her temper.' V. Sackville-West, *Aphra Behn 1640–1689* (Representative Women Series, 1927), p. 76.

40 The Works of Aphra Behn (ed. Janet Todd, William Pickering, 1992), vol. I 'Poetry', 'To the unknown Daphnis on his excellent Translation of *Lucretius*'. p. 25.

Chapter VII

From 1689 to 1744

A cast-off Dame, who of Intrigues can judge,
Writes scandal in Romance — A Printer's Drudge!
Flushed with Success, for Stage-Renown she pants,
And melts, and swells, and pens luxurious rants.

(Savage, *The Authors of the Town, 1725*)

The example of Mrs Behn led a number of women to embark on professional writing, but it is not to be supposed that these, her immediate successors, made any notable contribution to the novel. While Defoe and Swift were establishing realism, these women rallied to the tattered banner of high-flown sentimentality, and avoided realism as if it were the plague. Mrs Manley and Mrs Haywood as exponents of the key-novel and the *novella* succeeded in debauching these types of prose fiction to an almost incredible extent. Their artificial and poisonous concoctions were doomed to perish by their very excesses, but they could not, in any case, survive the robust, eager life of Defoe's writings. In the stark daylight of Defoe's realism the Ismenias and Licentias stood revealed as raddled wantons, and all the whining fops melted away. Roxana was an honest trull compared with the silken decadence of the boudoirs. Not only so, but there was the growth of a conventional reading-public who would no longer subscribe to a cynical representation of love. Let there be transgressions certainly, but never unaccompanied by repentance. Eros is dead; so is Silenus and all the satyrs and nymphs. Robinson Crusoe falls on his knees and thanks God with unfailing regularity, and Moll Flanders, although she wallows in evil for about seventy years, always condemns her lapses in the most high-souled manner. The ethical focus returns to fiction. This new spirit of moral earnestness did not become marked, however, until the first two decades of the eighteenth century had passed. It is seen in the works of Mrs Barker, Mrs Davys, Mrs Aubin and the excruciating Mrs Rowe. But before we can arrive at this God-fearing and piously sentimental ground we must pass through noxious swamps. Here be crocodiles, here be stenches! Let us clench our teeth, hold our noses and advance.

We must journey half the way with Mrs Manley, that football of fortune. Fate kicked her down into the field at first. Thereafter she was the sport of many, and she gathered mud all the way. She was the daughter of Sir Roger Manley, who lost his fortune in the Stuart cause and did not regain it at the Restoration. He devoted himself to literary pursuits (he is involved in the mystery of *The Turkish Spy)* and paid little attention to his motherless children. At his death Mary Manley was left £200 and a share in the residue of his estate. It was fortunate for her that she also inherited a modicum of literary ability, because soon she was a pariah, living partly by her wits and partly by her pen. The man who brought her to these straits was her cousin, John Manley. She and her fortune were committed to his direction, according to her father's wish. John Manley decoyed her into a false marriage, his wife being then alive, and he used her money for his own purposes. When he deserted her, she was left, penniless and disgraced, to fend for herself, and thereafter it was a swift descent from bad to worse. She passed from one protector to another, endeavouring at the same time to earn some part of her living by her pen. In 1696, two years after she had been dropped by the notorious Duchess of Cleveland, and after she had passed the intervening time in obscurity, she published a volume entitled *Letters written by Mrs Manley.* This was reprinted in 1725 as *A Stage Coach Journey to Exeter,* and is worthy of note as a contribution to the epistolary form. In 1696 also Mrs Manley took to the writing of plays, two of which were produced within the year: *The Lost Lover; or the Jealous Husband* at Drury Lane, and *The Royal Mischief* at Lincoln's Inn Fields. In 1706, *Almyra, or the Arabian Vow,* a play based on *The Arabian Nights* was produced at the Haymarket, but before then Mrs Manley had hit on a much more remunerative form of writing. From gathering mud to throwing it is an easy transition. Mrs Manley collected filth with the relentless energy of a dredger, and aimed it with the deadly precision of a machine gun. It was her revenge on a condemnatory world. *The New Atalantis* was by no means a literary innovation. Even the ponderous Heroic Romance had often been made the vehicle for political and personal satire, as Barclay's *Argenis* and Lady Mary Wroath's *Urania* testified. With the decadence of the Heroic Romance it was increasingly used as a means of satirizing one's enemies, and in France this practice had attained great popularity, Bussy de Rabutin's *Histoire Amoureuse des Gaules* (1660) being the most outstanding of these works. Aphra Behn's *Love-Letters between a Nobleman and his Sister* (1683) are openly based on the *cause célèbre* of Lord Grey of Werk.

The New Atalantis, published in several different parts, was a heterogeneous mass of scandal aimed at well known people. The first part, *The Secret History of Queen Zarah and the Zarasians* (1705), chiefly attacked the Duchess of Marlborough. It was in two volumes. The second part, consisting also of two volumes, was *The Secret Memoirs and Manners of Several Persons of Quality, of both Sexes . . . From the New Atalantis, an Island in the Mediterranean* (1709). This was followed by a second edition including another part which also appeared separately as *Memoirs of Europe Towards the Close of the Eighth Century. Written by Eginardus, Secretary and Favourite to Charlemagne* (1710); and finally there appeared *Court Intrigues, in a Collection of Original Letters, from the Island of the New Atalantis* (1711).

Mrs Manley's writings were so libellous, and were so violently anti-Whig that she was arrested in 1709, together with the publishers and printers of *The New Atalantis*. She was admitted to bail, and was the following year discharged without punishment. In *Memoirs of Europe* she says in self-defence:

> Methinks 'tis hard, and I have often wondered at it why that Man shou'd be thought uncharitable, a Satyrist, or Libeller, who but repeats with his Pen what every Body fearlessly reports with their Tongue: Is it because the Reproach is more indelible? Let the Great take heed then how they give the Occasion; let 'em beware how they set to have Picture of their Vices made immortal. Do you believe the Liberty suffered at Athens, in their Dramatick Pieces, did not restrain several who were viciously enclin'd, fearful of seeing themselves represented? The Satyrist must be thought of use to his Country, tho' I can't forgive him that betrays the Weakness of his Friend, or any Secret that he happens to be

let into, of what Nature soever: or who, having been oblig'd, or receiv'd into Families, finds the defenceless part, and exposes their Foibles to the world; Those are meannesses below Contempt, scarce any can be guilty of 'em. I must always condemn the Person from whom Scandal first arises; he that gives a Man or Woman to the ruin of Tongues (perhaps yet young in Vice) and throws their Reputation to the Winds, to be torn and scattered by malignant Fame. I wou'd have every one tender even to repeat any thing disadvantageous of another, 'till he were very well assured not only of the Truth, but that the Mater of Fact were no longer a Secret; Nay, and even then, I wou'd have him distinguish between a Start, and a confirm'd Habit of Vice. We have all our Frailities, the Suppression of 'em is doubt-lessly meritorious; but the glorying in 'em, by an ostantatious long course of Evil, and refuging under the splendor of a great name and Quality, is something so abominable as must give Offence to every honest Man.[1]

But Mrs Manley was, in some cases, not merely repeating with her pen what everybody fearlessly reported with their tongues. Sunderland, at her trial, was so much at a loss to imagine the sources of her information that he asked her to reveal them. She refused, saying that perhaps she wrote under inspiration, but she admitted, when cornered, that inspiration could come from evil sources as well as from good. Mrs Manley's pose of moral indig-nation was really trying her readers too high. Her self-defence would have them believe that her scavengings were merely in the interests of public hygiene, but unfortunately the deliberate prurience of her writings makes her real purpose only too evident.

We are concerned here only with estimating *The New Atalantis* as a contribution towards prose fiction, therefore it is unnecessary to identify the objects of Mrs Manley's attacks, particularly since this information is so easily available in the keys which are appended to Mrs Manley's volumes, and has been summarized by several writers.[2] *The New Atalantis* is, on the whole, an end-lessly involved and an extremely dull book. The fact that the *double entendre* has died with the years, and has to be deliberately revived in our minds, before we can understand the references, makes the task of literary criticism all the easier. No longer vivified by the breath of scandal these volumes are now dead things. It must be very many years since decomposition first set in. By this time to make their acquaintance is like encountering a

skeleton. The wind blows through the grinning jaws with meaningless sound, the empty eye-sockets leer, a bony digit is placed
knowingly on what was once a nose. In vain: the foul insinu-
ations, the sneers, the grudges as now as dead as those whose
time they wasted. These scandals have found sanctuary in the
tomb, and it is strange that in recording them Mrs Manley
should at one stroke have secured for herself notoriety and for
her pen oblivion — both unending.

Who now reads *The New Atalantis* save those who endeavour to
trace the growth of the novel? Had this work been distinguished
by intelligent construction, a graceful style, or by wit, however
mordant, these qualities would suffice to triumph in a great
measure over the ephemeral nature of the subject. But actually
The New Atalantis is devoid of such characteristics. The construction
is execrable. It consists of endless conversations between vague
individuals, or rather monologues so long and so involved that
we forget the speaker, and are surprised when a question or a
reply reminds us of their existence. There is either no effort or no
ability to achieve verisimilitude.

For example, in *Memoirs of Europe* Horatio, immortal conqueror
of Iberia, deprived of his military command, wanders through
Europe, until near the river Neva he comes upon Solitude and
Sincerity between whom an extraordinary dialogue ensues. 'Well,
my dear,' says Solitude to Sincerity, 'Did I not prophecy to thee
aright? Did I not tell thee thou would'st return to me again,
that the world was unworthy of thee?' After which domestic
introduction Solitude in a prolonged harangue, exposes all the
hypocrisy of the world. The words are those of a scolding
woman, that is to say of Mrs Manley. Sincerity replies with an
encomium on Horatio, and he departs sped by the good wishes
of this egregious pair. But he has not travelled a league when
night overtakes him, and he discovers in the midst of that wild
and desolate country 'a sumptuous Tent (as it is the Custom in
that Country when Persons of Quality travel, because the Cabarets
are few and very ill provided), ostentatiously enlightened with a
vast number of white-Wax-Flambeaux.' He is invited to spend
the night in this magnificent 'Field Apartment,' and is entertained
by Merovius, Prior of Orleans. This entertainment consists in a
monologue of incredible length with which Merovius inveighs
against the corruption of politics and social life, particularly in

Sarmatia (England). Intermingled (there is no other word for it) with this diatribe is the story of Merovius' early passion for an idiot girl, a very disgusting and irrelevant episode. The monologue proceeds with a rambling description of the marriage of the Princess of Sarmatia (Mary) to the Prince of Illyria (William of Orange), and introduces secret notes, papist plots and counterplots, innumerable adulteries, all so confused, so wandering, hidden beneath such a weight of conceits and verbiage that it is extremely difficult to arrive at the author's intention, even if it were worth while. In the main narrative there is not one iota of humour and only an occasional touch of wit. Were Mrs Manley but content to be plainly abusive we should at least have the satisfaction of knowing exactly what she wished to say. But alas! some delusion of intellectuality betrayed her into an elephantine style, heavily sentimental, dully ironic, enlivened only by highly absurd bursts of ranting. As thus:

> View here, my Lord, said I, addressing the High-Priest, view the Fair, but Murther'd Honoria! Honoria! The Vertuous as well as charming! View her as the Trophy of Prince Alexis's Victory and Inconstancy! Honoria dy'd by her Lover's Infidelity!
>
> A Lover! who by holy and interchangeable Vows was sworn to become her Husband; having subdu'd her Heart, he wou'd have basely profited himself of the conquest by triumphing over her vertue; but finding the Heroick Maid set the Value upon it that she ought, he abandon'd what he should have worshipped, and from that moment thought no longer of Her, or of his Vows! Oh! Apostate to Love and Chastity! Thou did'st prepare thyself (after being engag'd by Oaths and solemn Imprecations to Honoria, in the sight of Juno the Awful Goddess, and Queen of Marriage-vows), thou did'st prepare, as all Sarmatia knows, to wed the Princess Emely! Oh! Unpresedented Perjury! Oh! inconsiderate Youth, to barter real Merit for glaring Titles. Oh! capricious God of Love, How wert thou so easily disgusted? . . . Behold her a Monument of Infidelity; it was the Arm of Treachery, and not her own that lifted the fatal Draught to her despairing Lip! It was Prince Alexis's Cruelty and Apostacy, that determin'd and gave her to swallow the stupifying Death! Revenge! Revenge! you immortal Powers! You that are ever excellent! Revenge upon his Name and Family, Honoria's Wrongs; take Possession of him all ye Furies! Seize him ye Infernal Powers! May his life be short and miserable, but may his hereafter Torments be never-ending.

Such rhetoric and indeed such punctuation is by no means rare in *The New Atalantis*, but even when the narrative takes a saner tone, it still suffers from the faults already indicated. There is a prurience which seizes upon and describes with voluptuousness every possible occasion of sensuality. Such writing is seducing without being seductive. Mrs Manley's idea of setting the stage for an amorous interlude is sublime in its vulgarity:

> The Duchess softly enter'd that little Chamber of Repose, the Weather being violently hot the Umbrelloes were let down from behind the Windows, the sashes open, and the Jessamine that covered 'em blew in with a gentle Fragrancy; Tuberoses set in pretty Gilt and China Posts, were placed advantageously upon Stands, the Curtains of the Bed drawn back to the Canopy, made of yellow Velvet embroider'd with white Bugles, the Panels of the Chamber Looking-glass, upon the Bed were strow'd with a lavish Profuseness, plenty of Orange and Lemon Flowers, and to compleat the Scene, the young Germanicus . . . in a lose Gown of Carnation Taffety, stained with Indian Figures, his beautiful long flowing Hair for then 'twas the custom to wear their own tied back with a Ribbon of the same Colour . . .

Equally unfortunate are the blowzy euphemisms with which she fondly hopes to raise her language to the true converse of the gods. 'The honey-moon' is 'The Hymenial Moon,' and when, for example, she wishes to say that the rascally crew willingly drowned so that their master should be saved, she says: 'The ignoble Crew willingly devoted themselves to the Seagreen Deity, to secure the Life of their Master.'

Mrs Manley did much better when she was vindictive without circumlocutions. Then by her very maliciousness she succeeds in driving home her blade very neatly. She says:

> I wou'd positively have some Method found out to acquaint all Women with their Decay. They should be told when they begin to be no longer charming, for they will never know it else: Nothing is so ridiculous as their carrying things to Extremity: they would joyn the Spring to Autumn, May to December, the two Ends of Time, in a True-love's Knot.[3]

And again, speaking of a paragon named Porcia who is married to a morose husband:

> Propetious Heaven! unloos'd the rugged Chain: He dy'd, she
> was no longer marry'd, left very young, very handsome, very
> rich, but very wise. The three former Qualifications drew
> Crowds of Adorers, the latter as dexterously dispersed 'em.[4]

Sometimes Mrs Manley achieves a pithy terseness:

> Surely you must have observed Julius Sergius: he began to
> sprout in your time; but, alas, his Growth is now past
> knowledge.[5]

And speaking of Maro (Addison), who has put himself under the
protection of Julius Sergius: 'Farewell, Maro, 'till you abandon
your artificial Patron, Fame must abandon you!' But most frequently Mrs Manley was not satisfied to attack one individual at
a time. She had to a very marked degree the power of hitting in
many directions at once. Possibly that multiple desire of wounding
largely accounts for the teeming confusion of her narrative style.
Here is a clear example of this savage irony, a double-edged and
(were it possible) double-pointed dagger of which every stab
goes home. She has been speaking of the abhorred Julius Sergius,
and his indiscriminate patronage of writers good and bad. Sapho
the younger is one of this number, a female writer who, we are
told, is bad in every sense of the word. But as for Lais!:

> Nor has another of the Sex forebore to intrude herself,
> Constantinople abounds in Pretenders of both kinds, the
> result of that Silence, which has invaded those who are truly
> Master of the Muses; but this Thing without a name, is only
> known by the permission Julius Sergius gave her to invoke
> him as a Patron; if she had any other Art of pleasing him, he
> had best conceal it, lest he make himself the laugh of those
> numerous Coxcombs, by whom her Address and Adulations
> have been so often rejected: Much good may it do you
> Sergius, with Lais's Charms, the Leavings of the Multitude.

Finally there is the neat comment on the lady who married a
profligate. He had already buried a Wife, to whom during her
life-time he had been consistently unfaithful. Mrs Manley says of
the second wife:

> She had the good fortune to fix, as well as to survive this
> wandering star, though it must be own'd, *that there are*

Follies like some Stains, that wear out of themselves among which,
Love is generally reckon'd to be one.

These triumphs of vindictiveness are, however, rare. For the
most part Mrs Manley seeks to maintain her readers' attention
simply by obscenity and slanderous *tours de force*. We see her
launch herself on the thin ice of contemporary scandal, and for
the remainder of the time we watch in shocked fascination her
intricacies, her convolutions, her daring unabated even when the
ice is cracking under her. She is a professional skater, trying by
reckless feats to gain the applause on which her bread depends.
Or perhaps it would be truer to say that she is the decayed
soubrette in a cheap music-hall, trying to achieve by lewdness
what she is unable to win by charm. But, alas! charm is unlimited
because unpredictable. Lewdness is an immense boredom, and
the more extreme the more boring, because there is no hope of
further variety. Hence it is that in her efforts to titillate Mrs
Manley is driven even into the ramifications of unnatural vice.
Mrs Manley's effort to exhaust exhaustion, to saturate saturation
point is her greatest mistake in the composition of *The New
Atalantis*. She cries 'wolf, wolf!' and that predatory animal appears
slavering for his prey. We observe him complete his horrible
meal, and depart, licking his chops. Before we have time to breathe,
the cry goes up again, the lupine repast is again consumed, and
another and another, until finally we are so bored with the
performance that no variety of wolfish meals, eaten singly or *en
masse*, could cause us a tremor of alarm or horror. That Mrs
Manley realized this difficulty is clearly shown in the following
passage, with which she stigmatizes a fellow-writer, without,
however, recognizing that her words are really a self-portrait:

> 'Tis a hard Task to be forced to be witty be one in never so
> opposite an Humour, but he has still Fire and Malice enough
> to do our Business. They call him in contempt a Bread-
> Writer a sorry (half Sasterce) fellow; but his pen is generally
> acceptable, he pleases those whom he stings; a commodious
> useful Hireling, stops at nothing, goes through thick and
> thin; He cants admirably, and pretends to Vertue, but is as
> ingrateful and unfair as one could desire. He'll lay on any
> Colours, and is so great an Artist, he can metamorphose in a
> Twinkling, the brightest Hero into a dirty Scavenger.

And yet, although in the main *The New Atalantis* has all the faults we have described, it is for one reason significant in the development of prose fiction. It is to be observed that Mrs Manley wove detachable stories into the framework of *The New Atalantis*. These are all modelled on the Italian *novella*, but are heavily laden with romantic superstructure. These inset tales seem superior to the seven stories, most of which she later adapted from Painter's *Palace of Pleasure*, and published under the title of *The Power of Love* (1720). But it is difficult to decide whether they truly are superior, or whether they merely achieve a kind of humanity in contrast with the scurrilous and unreal background. In *Secret Memoirs and Manners of Several Persons of Quality*, the story of the woman nailed dead to the gibbet is, however, really well told. The narrator is a country-woman, and it is interesting to note that the language put into her mouth is compatible with her station in life. Another tale worthy of mention is that of Charlot and the Duke.

The Duke, a widower and Charlot's guardian, designs her for marriage with his son, and does everything in his power to guard her innocence and to strengthen her mind against evil influences. She lives with the Duke's family about fifteen miles from the capital in a country-house to which the Duke sometimes comes 'to taste a rest from Power, a calm of Greatness, a Suspense of Business, a respiration of Glory.' One evening the company diverts itself with amateur theatricals; Charlot excels in the role of Diana, and the Duke, overcome by his delight in her performance, kisses her. This is the beginning of a passion which he is soon unable to curb. But the Duke is a statesman, and he is endeavouring to arrange for himself a marriage of international importance. He hopes to marry a Princess Dowager of a petty State, and therefore has no intention of making Charlot his wife. But he cannot renounce his passion for her. His struggle against the dishonour of his desires is very well described. He determines to make her his mistress, and immediately is confronted by the necessity of undermining that modesty in her which he has so laboured to strengthen. How to scale the ramparts he has himself erected? By giving her access to erotic books he gradually saps her spiritual health. He absents himself that she may feel his loss, and then returns to overwhelm her with caresses. She falls into a state of spiritual enervation. Now the least germ of immorality will be sufficient to undo her. In order that vitiation without may second the inward vitiation he removes her to Court, and her moral principles begin to totter. But now another effect of her reading and observation is a hindrance to the Duke:

> Charlot by this time had informed herself, that there were such terrible things as Perfidy and Inconstancy in Mankind; that even the very Favours [men] received, often disgusted; and that to be entirely Happy, one ought never to think of the faithless Sex. This brought her back to those Precepts of Virtue that had embellished her Dawn of Life.

Still, it was useless for the wheel to come full circle, while the Duke was there awaiting her at every point of the circumference. He could never have defeated her moral objections, but it only remained now for him to assure her of his constancy. She yields at last. She is happy for a while, although her liaison makes it necessary for her to live completely in seclusion. Her only guest and her sole confidant is a young Countess, a lovely widow. 'But Charlot could not escape her destiny.' The Duke becomes weary of her and enamoured of her friend. His political marriage fails of achievement, and, forsaking his ward whom he has taken such pains to seduce, he immediately marries the Countess who has never shown him any particular favour. The story has a moral, because the erring Charlot 'dy'd a true Landmark: to warn all believing Virgins from shipwrecking their honour upon (that dangerous Coast of Rocks) the Vows and pretended Passion of Mankind.' Mrs Manley adds a second moral which is a splendid example of practical cynicism: 'That no woman ought to introduce another [woman] to the man by whom she is belov'd.'

This story, which is after the style of the Italian *novella*, has obviously benefited by the *Princesse de Clèves* and the *Portuguese Letters*. The dissection of Charlot's mind, the struggle between inculcated principles and temptation, the description of her doubts, fears, hopes, desires, despairs; the tracing of every phase in the degeneration of innocent love into guilty passion — all this is very well done, and belongs to that trend in fiction which later found a notable exponent in Richardson. A more obvious result of the *Princesse de Clèves* is Mrs Manley's story of how the Lady of St Amant died for love. (This lady's husband dies, and she is deterred by scruples from marrying her lover.) As for the *Portuguese Letters*, we hear very occasionally in the diction of Mrs Manley's tales an echo of those profound outpourings, in scenes, alas! most alien to such accents. Once, we even have the exact words of the nun of Beja, that prior to the arrival of her lover she had only known people who were disagreeable to her.

There are many other inset stories in *The New Atalantis* none better than that of Charlot, and many worse. Some are borrowings or inventions, some are simply a medium for scandal.

In *The Power of Love* Mrs Manley borrows very largely from Bandello.[6] She does not justify unprincipled love as Mrs Behn had done, and seldom loses an occasion of moralizing. Like Congreve, she verbally indicates her dissatisfaction with the romantic tradition, and still, like Congreve, adheres to it. In *The Husband's Resentment* (first example) Desideria says: 'I must own myself perfectly weary of Groves and Purling Streams! I should never have liked the Life of a Shepherdess, tho' I had found never so many Corydon's to have endear'd it to me.' And in the introduction to *The Happy Fugitives*, Mrs Manley remarks:

> When we reflect upon these examples left us by Antiquity, as well in their Real as Fabulous Histories, we may observe that Love was quite another thing in the Souls of their Heroins, than it is now in ours. What Ariadne, Medea or Helen, as of old, do now leave their Fathers, Husbands and Country, to pursue the Fortune of their Lovers who were not always over grateful for the Favour? Fashions are changed! alas the Time! We speak only of Interest, Portion, Joyntures, Settlements, Separate Maintenance now-a-days! with other worldly considerations; which clearly proves, that Cupid has either blunted his Darts, or makes them of quite another sort of Stuff. Or, perhaps, he rarely concerns himself in modern Wedlock where Hymen officiates in his Robes, rather dip'd in Gall than Saffron! This Degeneracy causes us to look upon former Precedents without Complacency, as if we were unbelievers. The Constancy and Fortitude of Lovers in ancient Times, instead, of raising our Admiration, are called Stale, Romantick Stories, and the Legends of the Nursery: so easy is it to despise what we never mean to imitate. All this I very well understood when I set myself to draw forth of Obscurity the true History of our Happy Fugitives. There appears to me something so Heroick, so praiseworthy in their Passion and Perseverance, that however diffident I may be of the Success, from the different Taste of the present Age I have resolved to pursue the Undertaking.

But not only was she resolved to present the power of love, but resolved to present it in the romantic style. One instance will suffice to show how artificially she embroidered the direct, vivid tales in Painter. *The Happy Fugitives* describes the love of Alerane and Adelasia:

Painter's *Alerane and Adelasia:*

This good Prince had one daughter in whom nature had distributed her gifts in such wise, as she alone might have vaunted herself to attaine the perfection of them all, which ever had anything, worthy of admiration, were it in singularity of beauty, favour and courtesie, or in disposition and good bringing up. The name of this fayre Princesse was Adelasia.

Alerane:

This yonge Prince, besides that he was one of the fayrest and comliest gentlemen of Almaigne, had therewithal, together with Knowledge of armes, a passing skill in good sciences, which mitigated in him the ferocitie both of his warlike Knowledge, and of the nature of his countrey. His name was Alerane.

Mrs Manley's *The Happy Fugitives*:

The Princesse was the Favourite of Nature, who drew her extremely beautiful, with a Spirit full of Fire, a Greatness of Soul and Heart in which the God of Love took up his chiefest residence.

Alerane:

The young prince was distinguishingly handsome, called Hugo Alerane. He was formed to draw to him the Hearts of the Fair Sex, who doat on Beauty in their Lovers, much as their Lovers do in them; and are sooner surprised and caught by it, because it is more rarely found amongst them. The next Attractive in those Days of Chivalry, was Valour and Dexterity in Feats of Arms; in which Alerane outwent all his Contemporaries. He learnt these exercises with wondrous Ease, and performed them with infinite Applause! He was the Hero of the Age and the Pride of the Court! his Behaviour was Warlike in the Field; but in the Apartment, Civilised and Soft; so gentle and submissive to the Fair, that he subdued them all.

*When Adelasia heard that Alerane
had saved the Emperor's life:*

She no sooner cast her eyes
upon Alerane, but love which
had prepared the ambushe so
pierced her delicate breast as
he took possession of her . . .
Alerane by taking careful heed
to the looks which the Princess
continually did stealingly cast
upon him . . . assured himself
unfainedly to be beloved . . .
which caused him . . . to
beare unto her like affection.

*Alerane and Adelasia were both
deeply in love:*

A passion truly most
intollerable for a yonge
Princesse, as well because she
never had experience of sem-
blable sorow, as for her tender
age, and yet more for a natural
abashmente and shame, which
with the vails of honor doth
serve, or ought to serve for a
bridle to every Ladie covetous
of fame, or like to be the ornament or beauty of her race.

The fair Princess who was
born under an amourous Con-
stellation, found something so
worthy of her Heart in the
Merit and Person of Alerane
that she held herself excused
for that sweet Violence by
which she found it impossible
to withhold hers from him.
Love had, by Alerane's Beauty,
prepared the Toils, and so
entangled her Breast, that she
knew not how to extricate herself . . . Alerane, who was
under the Tuition of the same
Deity, learn'd Penetration from
him; he taught him to discover
the Distemper of the Princess
. . . As Alerane's Looks were
never from Adelasia he saw
those Glances which by Stealth,
she continually shot towards
him . . . Adelasia, floating on
a tempestuous Sea of Passion,
guided by a Master who is too
often pleased with the Shipwreck of those whom he
conducts; was withheld by
Shame and Modesty, which
like a Veil covers, or ought to
cover, the Desires of those
Virgins who would preserve
their Fame; and are to be either
The Ornament or Blemish of
their Race.

The superiority of Painter's version is quite clear in regard to
style, but it must be said that Mrs Manley endeavoured to particularize the characters, not, it is true, enough to give them
individuality, and yet sufficient to add to the probability of their

actions. Sometimes she effects some minor change in the structure of the story.

Among Mrs Manley's libellous works must be reckoned *Rivella,* her autobiography. The frontispiece has an extreme conventionality in marked contrast to the narrative which follows. We see stately houses well walled in from common life, trees growing in symmetrical rows and some courtly figures engaged in polite conversation. Unreal swans tower so high over the water as to seem poised on a mudbank, while over all a fantastic sun casts its mathematical beams. Here in Somerset House Garden, Sir Charles Lovemore (Lieutenant-General John Tidcomb) tells Mrs Manley's story to the young Chevalier D'Aumont, and this recital curiously combines egregious vanity and unintentional pathos. Take Lovemore's dissertation on Mrs Manley's writings:

> I have not known any of the Moderns in that point [amorous descriptions] come up to your famous Author of the *Atalantis.* She has carried the passion farther than could readily be conceived: Her Germanicus on the Embroider'd Bugle Bed naked out of the Bath; Her Young and Innocent Charlot transported with the powerful Emotion of a just kindling Flame, sinking with delight and Shame upon the Bosom of her Lover in the Gallery of Books . . . are such Representations of Nature, that must warm the coldest Reason . . . After perusing her Inchanting Descriptions which of us have not gone in Search of Raptures, which she everywhere tells us, as happy Mortals, we are capable of tasting. But have we found them, Chevalier, answered his friend? For my Part, I believe they are to be met with solely in her own Imbraces.

The Chevalier is inclined to agree with Lovemore, but as he has never seen Rivella, he cautiously demands an inventory of her charms. What follows is a strange mixture of truth and self-deception on the part of Mrs Manley: 'Is not this being a little too particular, answered Sir Charles, touching the Form of a Lady who is no longer young, and was never a Beauty? Not in the least, briskly reply'd the Chevalier, provided her Mind and Her Passions are not in Decay.' That they are not we may judge from this encomium:

> Speak to me of her eyes, interrupted the Chevalier, you seem to have forgot that index of the Mind: is there to be found in them, store of those animating Fires with which her writings are fill'd. Do her eyes love as well as Her Pen?

You reprove me very justly, answer'd the Baronet, Rivella would have a great deal of Reason to complain of me, if I should silently pass over the best Feature of her Face. In a Word, you have yourself described them; Nothing can be more tender, ingenious, and brilliant with a Mixture so languishing and sweet, when Love is the Subject of the Discourse . . .

But nothing will satisfy the exigent D'Aumont:

How are her Teeth and Lips, spoke the Chevalier? Forgive me, dear Lovemore, for breaking in so often upon your Discourse; but kissing being the sweetest leading pleasure, 'tis impossible a Woman can charm without a good Mouth.

He is assured that Rivella's mouth is unexceptionable. So the catechism proceeds, and we look beyond the words at the woman who penned them, the woman thus described by Swift two years previously:

Poor Mrs Manley . . . is very ill of a dropsy and sore legs; the printer tells me she is afraid she cannot live long. I am heartily sorry. She has very generous principles for one of her sort, and a great deal of good sense and invention; she is about forty, very homely and very fat.[7]

Here is Mrs Manley's description of herself:

Her Person is neither tall not short; from her Youth she was inclined to Fat; when I have often heard her Flatterers liken her to a Grecian Venus. It is certain, considering that disadvantage, she has the most easy Air that one can have; her Hair is of a pale Ash-colour, fine, and in a large quantity . . . But to do Rivella justice, till she grew fat, there was not I believe any defect to be found in her body: her Lips admirably colour'd; Her teeth small and even, a Breath always sweet. Her complexion fair and fresh; yet with all this you must be us'd to her before she can be thought thoroughly agreeable. Her Hands and Arms have been publickly celebrated: it is certain that I never saw any so well turned . . . her Feet small and pretty.

Small and pretty — those swollen, dropsical feet! Few things are sadder than a woman who knows, but will not own, that her day is done. So it is with this entire autobiography. It is the expression of a life, foolish, immoral, revengeful, brave.

We watch her juggling with words, talking feverishly on, building up an illusion of beauty, brilliancy and success, but we are no more deceived than she. She has ten years to live, she is poor, plain, middle-aged, alone, disreputable; but she is gallant. No one in her lifetime denied her that. It is not, however, merely for this reason that the history of Rivella has on us a peculiar effect of pathos. If we knew nothing of her actual circumstances, the effect would still be the same. It is only as to her writings that she believes her boasts. For the rest, she knows the truth, and we are conscious of the painful contrast between her words and her underlying mood. There is the sadness of her backward glance at youth, and her knowledge that never now can she extricate herself from the tangle of her life; there is her regret for what she was, and our regret for what she is. She has not even the happiness of being too stupid to see the ruin of her life. After the introduction Lovemore becomes a kind of *doppelgänger*, that better self that stands apart and watches her downward way.

> There are so many Things Praise and yet Blame-worthy in Rivella's conduct that as her Friend, I know not well how with a good Grace, to repeat, or as yours to conceal, because you seem to expect from me an impartial History. Her Vertues are her own, her Vices occasion'd by her Misfortunes.

Her father dies; her villainous cousin 'marries' her bigamously: the descent has begun. He goes on securely in respect and honour, becomes a Member of Parliament and Surveyor-General, but 'here begins Rivella's real Misfortunes: it would be well for her, that I could say here she dy'd with Honour, as did her Father . . . She told me all her Misfortunes with an Air so perfectly ingenuous, that, if some Part of the World who were not acquainted with her Vertue ridicul'd her Marriage, and the Villainy of her kinsman; I who knew her sincerity could not help believing all she said . . .' 'But Time,' says the *doppelgänger*, 'time which allays all our Passions, lessen'd the Sorrow I felt for Rivella's Ruin . . . her Wit and Gaiety of Temper return'd, but not her Innocence.' She loses caste, she is taken up and contemptibly dropped by the Duchess of Cleveland, against whose false accusations she successfully defends herself. After two years in the country two of her plays are successfully produced 'Behold another wrong Step towards ruining Rivella's character with the World: the incense that was daily offer'd her upon this Occasion by the Men of Vogue and Wit . . . I had still so much concern for Rivella that I pitied her Conduct, which I saw must infallibly center in her Ruin: there was no Language approached her Ear but Flattery and Persuasion to Delight and Love.'

Then follows her association with Sir Thomas Skipworth, recounted with unquotable indecency; and the complicated affair of Lord Montagu and the Monk family, which takes up so great a part of the narrative as to be out of all proportion. There is no doubt of the relish with which she narrates this scandalous intrigue. She becomes the mistress of Mr Tilly and probably of many others. She says that on his wife's death she refused to marry him. Be that as it may, he marries someone else. 'After that time, I know nothing memorable of Rivella, but that she seemed to bury all Thoughts of Gallantry in Cleander's Tomb.' This is not true, but it was the better self who made her stand her ground when three persons were arrested in reference to the *Atalantis:* 'She resolved to surrender herself into the Messenger's hands whom she heard had the Secretary of State's Warrent against her, so as to discharge those honest people from their Imprisonment.' She goes to Newgate, is tried and the case falls through. But Rivella is unchangeable. In 1712 she is the mistress of John Barber, the printer, and this liaison she maintained until her death. In 1714, in her very autobiography, despite her professed repentance for the *Atalantis,* she deprives her enemies of every shred of character, until we see them as thoroughly disreputable as herself, and her excuse is that 'she was become a misanthrope, a perfect Timon, or Man-Hater; all the World was out of Humour with her, and she with all the World.'

'But has she still a Taste for Love, interrupted young Monsieur D'Aumont? Doubtless, answered Sir Charles, or whence is it that she daily writes of him with such Fire and Force?' She knows the pity of 'appearing Fond at her Time of Day,' and is full of raillery against those ladies 'who sue when they are no longer sued unto.' She knows what her attitude should be, 'which is to say, knowing herself no longer young, she does not seem to expect the Praise and Flattery that attend the youthful . . . she converses now with our Sex in a Manner that is very delicate, sensible, and agreeable.' Yes, she understands that, but it is too late to be born anew. The past is never past: it is graven into our bodies and minds, and lives in our reactions to habitual stimuli. So it is that to the bitter end this woman remains the same. She sits at her desk scribbling libels, ogling the world out of her weary eyes. She waves a podgy hand at 'a Bed nicely sheeted and strow'd with Roses, Jessamines or Orange-Flowers, suited to the variety of the season.' Orange-flowers! Alas, Rivella!

By far the most prolific writer among Aphra Behn's female followers was Eliza Haywood. The daughter of a London tradesman named Fowler, she married at an early age the husband who soon abandoned her, and she then turned to quill driving to support herself and her two children. Whether her evil reputation was really deserved or was due merely to her key-novels is a point too difficult to determine. Swift considered her a 'stupid, infamous, scribbling woman.'[8] Walpole contemptuously refers to her as the counterpart of Mrs Behn.[9] Pope lashes her with scorpions in the *Dunciad*[10] (1728). In a note he describes her as one of those 'shameless scribblers who, in libellous memoirs and novels reveal the faults or misfortunes of both sexes, to the ruin of public fame or disturbance of private happiness.' Mrs Haywood's reply to this attack was the contribution of a few mild pages to *The Female Dunciad* (1729). Steele alone is credited with some good-natured remarks about Mrs Haywood. It is possible that he was well-disposed towards her, since one remembers his patience with Mrs Manley's alternate slanders and eulogies.

Eliza Haywood's imaginative writings include key-novels, sentimental *novelle,* cloak-and-sword intrigues, letters, pious effusions and two novels which make a really useful contribution to the school of domestic sentiment. In addition she was a translator, a successful playwright, and a 'poetess' (in the weakest sense of the word). She was the first woman to bring out a periodical for women — *The Female Spectator* (1744–1746) and *The Parrot* (1746) — lumbering and humourless productions, but nevertheless the forerunners of the modern spate of women's periodicals. She wrote for about thirty years, and her fictional works were extremely popular.

Her stories are mainly of three kinds: (a) the sentimentalized *novella;* (b) the key-novel; (c) the novel of domestic sentiment and of manners.

It is unnecessary to give a detailed account of her contribution to the first two genres of fiction. These types of story-telling were decadent in themselves, and were chiefly of importance in feeding the growing demands of the novel-reading public. Mrs Haywood wrote more than twenty sentimentalized *novelle* the first of which was *Love in Excess: or, the Fatal Enquiry* (1719–1720). This ran into six editions in four years. *The British Recluse: or, Secret History of Cleomira supposed Dead* (1722) represents the average level of Mrs Haywood's sentimentalized *novelle*. It consists of two stories connected in the slenderest and most improbable way. Two beautiful young ladies, Cleomira and Belinda, bruised and spent by the storms of life, happen to take refuge in the same boarding-house, where they mingle their tears and confidences. Cleomira, whose retirement from all human intercourse has earned her the name of the British Recluse, tells her story first.

This exquisite damsel, of excellent lineage and fortune, lives a very retired life with her mother in the country. One evening she is permitted to attend a ball in town, where she meets Lysander, whose beauty ravishes her at once into the seventh heaven of love. She returns home, and although she sighs, pants, burns and languishes, she manages to do so unknown to her mother, who is also unaware that an illicit correspondence is being carried on through the agency of Lysander's man-servant. Then, one morning, Lysander rides by Cleomira's window, and she is overwhelmed anew with the beauty of this paragon:

> At length he came, and with a Mien and Air, so soft, so sweet, so graceful, that Painters might have copied an *Adonis* from him, fit indeed to charm the Queen of Beauty. He was dress'd in a strait Jockey-coat of Green Velvet richly embroider'd at the Seams with Silver; the Buttons were Brilliants, neatly set in Fashion of Roses; his Hair, which is as black as jet, was ty'd with a green Ribband, but not so straitly but that a thousand little Ringlets stray'd o'er his lovely Cheeks and wanton'd in the Air; a crimson Feather in his Hat, set off to vast Advantage the dazzling Whiteness of his Skin. In fine, he was all over Charms! — all over glorious! and I believe it impossible for the most Insensible to have beheld him without adoring him! — What then became of me? — O God! how fruitless wou'd any Endeavours be to represent what 'twas I felt! Transported! — Ravish'd! — I wonder the Violent emotions of my *Soul* did not bear my Body out of the Window! O wou'd it had been so.

Such emotions could not fail to be observed by Cleomira's mother who confines her to her room, but: 'For many Days I did nothing but weep, and that in so violent a manner, that the servants, whom my Mother sent in to wait on me, apprehended I should fall into fits.'

No wonder that for two months the mother of this sentimental heroine rarely allows her out of her sight, but Cleomira escapes from this surveillance by having some dishonest people called Marvir appointed her guardians. She goes to live with them in town, and Mrs Marvir and her husband encourage the romance with Lysander, but they turn her away when the romance has dwindled to a mere seduction. Lysander turns away also to worship at another shrine, and Cleomira retires to the necessary seclusion of the country. While there she learns that her mother has died of grief at her unfilial behaviour. When she returns the Marvirs have swindled her out of the greater part of her fortune. She has no redress, as they threaten to expose her affair with Lysander if she should endeavour to call them to account. There is no end to Cleomira's misery; betrayed, deserted and fleeced, she now has to endure the news that Lysander — long since unfaithful to her — is about to marry a charming and virtuous friend of his. This news throws her into strong convulsions. She debates whether she will go to the house of this lucky lady to persuade her to relinquish her claims, or whether it would be better to remind Lysander that she herself should have first option on his matrimonial schemes. However, we are not surprised that in the true romantic convention, she pours all the passions of her soul into a letter: 'To the Inconstant, Ungenerous and Perfidious Lysander.' He replies with some terse remarks on the transitory nature of passion, and marries his lily-bud. Cleomira, whose vitals are now gnawed by all the vultures of Hope, Despair, Love, Passion, Remorse, Jealousy and Horror, decides to drown her sorrows in some liquid poison. Before she quaffs it, she writes another letter '*To the Dear Ruiner of my Soul and Body.*' 'A Draught of poison stands before me,' she writes, 'and the Moment I conclude this Letter, I take my Journey to that World, whence there is no return.' Having begged him not to make her sufferings the subject of ridicule (which was trying him rather high) she signs herself 'Only Yours, Cleomira.' But she muddles even her suicide. She awakens after a long sleep to find she has taken merely an opiate. Lysander on reading her letter, had expressed relief that, as she was dead, it needed no answer; upon hearing which Cleomira decides that she will live to scorn him ('Love alone shall die!'). She has finished with the follies of life, and betakes herself to the boarding-house, there to brood over her misfortunes.

Belinda, whom Cleomira meets in the boarding-house, is the daughter of a country gentleman. She was wooed by Worthly, a suitor of solid virtues. She was willing to marry him since her father wished it, and since, although she does not love him, neither does she love anyone else. Her father dies, and just when she is about to marry Worthly, a new adorer makes his appearance — Sir Thomas Courtal. One glance at this hero and Belinda is enslaved. She experiences 'A Mixture of Delight and Pain, a kind of racking Joy, and Pleasing Anguish.' She has 'drawn in an Infection at Eyes and Ears, which, mixing with my whole Mass of Blood was to poison all the Quiet of my future Days.' Belinda and Courtal, having gone through the formality of wooing in letters, meet in a wood. Fortunately for Belinda, Worthly intervenes. A duel is fought, and Worthly is fatally wounded. Belinda, overwhelmed with misery, flees to town, where one evening at the play she sees again her Adonis, but this time accompanied by his wife and mistress; and she learns that his real name is Lord Bellamy. On hearing this, the British Recluse exclaims that her deceiver and that of Belinda are one and the same — the composite seducer Lysander Courtal-Bellamy! With so much in common, it is only natural that a great friendship should spring up between these ladies, who resolve to spend their lives together in a house about seventy miles from London, 'sometimes bewailing their several Misfortunes, sometimes exclaiming against the *Vices*, sometimes praising the *Beauties* of their common Betrayer.'

Idalia: or, The Unfortunate Mistress (1723) is a curious discord, containing echoes of the *Portuguese Letters* and elements of the picaresque. As in *The British Recluse*, her efforts at revealing the heart of a woman in love result only in melodrama, although it must be said that *Idalia* has qualities which *The British Recluse* lacks. *Lasselia: or, The Self-Abandon'd* (1723) is the usual mess of pottage, this time served hot in an environment of court intrigue. Mrs Haywood's tempestuous emotions rarely become real, rarely identify themselves with individualized men and women. This melodramatic fustian bears a superficial resemblance to

Aphra Behn's worst novels, but without Aphra Behn's power and without her flashes of realism.

Of Mrs Haywood's key-novels one can only say that they are as scurrilous and as prurient as those of Mrs Manley, with similar flashes of mordant pithiness. The best known of these libellous works are *A Spy upon the Conjurer* (1725); *The Memoirs of a Certain Island Adjacent to the Kingdom of Utopia. Written by a Celebrated Author of that Country. Now Translated into English* (2 vols., 1725-1726); *Bath Intrigues* (1725); *The Secret History of the Present Intrigues of the Court of Caramania* (1727); *Eovaai* (1736); and *The Invisible Spy* (1754).

A Spy upon the Conjurer[11] is based, like Defoe's *Secret Memoirs of Duncan Campbell* (1732), on the occult powers of a certain Scotsman. But whereas Defoe was interested in the phenomenon of Campbell's prophetic powers, Mrs Haywood characteristically concentrated all her attention on the amorous intrigues which were likely to be confided to the fortune-teller. Her work consists of supposed confidences given to Duncan Campbell by various ladies whose secrets Mrs Haywood served up with her usual garnishing of passion.

To give a detailed account of Mrs Haywood's other secret histories would serve no useful purpose. They would, in Fuller's words, 'stain through the cleanest language I can wrap them in.' Speaking of *The Invisible Spy* (1754) written under the pseudonym *Exploralibus*, Mr G. F. Wicher says 'Love is still the theme of most of the anecdotes, no longer the gross passion that proves every woman at heart a rake, but rather a romantic tenderness that inclines lovely woman to stoop to folly.'[12] This criticism is wide of the mark. *The Invisible Spy* is an extremely distasteful book. Exploralibus, with a belt of invisibility and a recording tablet, spies on the habits of society. They are the habits of the farm-yard, grossly described. There is the merest pretence at unity of construction: the shadowy spy is far too unsubstantial to link the episodes together. *Eovaai* and *The Injured Husband: or, the Mistaken Resentment* have sufficient unity of plot to render them worthy of more detailed consideration. *Eovaai*, owing to its pseudo-oriental background, will find mention later. *The Injured Husband* may usefully be examined here since it possibly represents the fusion of the *histoire scandaleuse* and the sentimentalized *novella*, a coating of fiction rendering more lurid the less sensational colours of truth.

The Injured Husband; or, The Mistaken Resentment appears to be another secret history. In the preface, Mrs Haywood insists on defending herself against an alleged accusation that the story is a veiled account of certain events which happened in London a short time previously. She insists so much that one suspects her of cleverly stressing the fundamental truth of her narrative, although indeed the tale is so improbable in parts that, if it was substantially true, it must have been intricately embroidered by Mrs Haywood. The story concerns one Mme de Tortille and a pander called du Lache. Mrs Haywood wards off any accusation of satirizing an English lady of fashion by disclaiming any attack, and by putting on any possible accuser the onus of finding a shameful similarity between the iniquitous de Tortille and an English lady. Mrs Haywood still further safeguards herself by alleging that any man who sees this similarity must, like the infamous du Lache, be deep in the shameful secrets of this lady whom he endeavours to defend. Naturally guilt would prevent such a lady from self-defence, and fear of implication would muzzle any would-be defender, while all the time Eliza Haywood smugly enjoys this stalemate, and profits by it to write what was probably as scandalous a piece of libel as has ever soiled paper.

There is in this novel the same moral looseness which characterized the writings of Mrs Manley and Mrs Haywood: there is the same sentimentalized picture of innocent beauty, the same luscious descriptions of scenes which the author professes to abhor, but which she prolongs and enlivens in a way which makes her purpose only too clear. There is also the same attitude towards men as something ranging between suave lechers and charming, well-intentioned, but too amorous beaux, not weighed down by a 'soul much more refin'd than Man is ordinarily possess'd of.'

The middle-aged Baron de Tortille becomes enamoured of Mlle la Motte, an exquisite *demi-mondaine*, whose extravagant and ill-regulated life makes her grasp at the chance of marriage. She continues her old way of life, unknown to her besotted husband, who believes her to be an angel. But her many lovers are never valued once she has ensnared them, and she always wishes to conquer someone who seems beyond her reach. Such a one was Beauclair, whose engagement to marry the lovely and innocent Mlle Montamour would seem to ensure him against the wiles of the Baroness de Tortille. But this accomplished adventuress, by means of baseless slander spread about by her paid tools, manages to destroy Monsieur Beauclair's faith in Mlle Montamour. He writes bitterly to Mlle Montamour cancelling their engagement which he fears may prevent her from her pleasures, and then with masculine logic proceeds to take his own at the house of the Baroness. But it is Lethe he seeks more than love, and, from time to time, an inner conviction forcing him to reject belief in Mlle Montamour's baseness, throws him into mental conflict, and makes it necessary for the Baroness to entangle him further in her web of passion and deceit. She herself, having achieved her aim, begins to tire also and derives her chief pleasure not from Beauclair, who, after all, is not different from the throng of other lovers whom she entertains, but from a vindictive joy, in the humiliation of Mlle Montamour. However, it is Beauclair who seizes his chance of discontinuing the *affaire*. To her greater humiliation, an indiscreet letter of hers falls into the hands of her other lovers, who realizing that she has been playing one off against the other, desert her *en masse*. 'Wanting the Means of Vengeance on those who had occasioned it, her unavailing Rage recoil'd upon itself: She tore her Hair and Face, and bit her very Flesh in the Extremity of her Passion.' Her despair is all the greater since, the town ringing with her scandalous name, her husband comes to call her to account. Then with du Lache, her erstwhile pander, she decides to murder him and gain possession of all his property, with freedom to live as she wishes. Unfortunately for her, however, her bad luck persists, and the Baron escapes the daggers of her bravos, who, captured, admit their guilt and state her complicity. Meanwhile, Mlle de Montamour, ravaged with grief at the treatment she has received from her lover, enters a convent for the same reason as she would take a sedative. Beauclair discovers where she is. He is now convinced of her innocence, and cannot live without her. In his efforts to secure an interview with her he is as inventive of disguises as a small boy on a wet half-holiday: 'Sometimes he was thinking to disguise himself as a Cripple . . . another stratagem was to dress himself as a Woman . . . but this his Stature forbid.' Finally he decides to dress as a labourer. Thus disguised, he manages to catch a glimpse of his lady in the garden where she tunes her 'Guitter' and sings love ditties for which she would be expelled from any convent on the face of the earth. To cut a long story short, they are married on the day on which she was to have been professed, and the wicked Baroness swallows poison.

Mrs Haywood sinned against the improved artistic and moral standards of a later age, but she was well in touch with the fictional demands of her own period. She had, to a very considerable extent, the power of adapting herself to varying aspects of fiction, and it is to this opportunism that her only notable achievements are due. We have seen that she adhered to the established genres of the sentimentalized *novella* and the *histoire scandaleuse*. She responded also to tendencies which constituted the growing point of fiction. She contributed, as we shall see later, to the epistolary and oriental genres, but her most important contributions to the novel were more vitally adapted to the revolution which was taking place in fiction, both morally and artistically. Mrs Haywood is the chameleon of English novelists. In scurrility, in eroticism she had yielded an inch to no one — not even to Mrs Manley. Now, when she was forced to realize a new attitude in the reading public, she could strike her breast and cast her eyes heavenward with the best of them. It does not appear that her reformation was more than skin deep, because even in her period of moral earnestness, an occasional anonymous or pseudonymous work seemed to be the offspring of the old Haywood spirit. After all, what could be more natural than that Eliza, exhausted from playing the impeccable lady, should find private relaxation in blowing on her tea?

But she had become determined to be polite and impeccable, since she was determined not to starve. One imagines Mrs Haywood gritting her teeth at the contradictions of her lifetime. In her young days bawdy writers were sure of bread; now they were sure only of stones. For her own part, she had been stoned quite long enough. From 1728 until 1736 she had written almost nothing. From 1736 until 1742 she had written nothing at all. If she were ever again to please the public she knew that she must give them what they wanted. Well, so she would! She would roar them as t'were any sucking dove; she would roar them as t'were any nightingale. Mrs Haywood's first cooings were entitled *A Present for a Serving Maid* (1741). This emanated from a mind filled with Pamela. It is a worthless production, full of prudent sermonizing, but not unamusing if the reader cocks an ironic eye at the former Eliza Haywood. For example, it is not easy to remain serious when we hear the author of A *Spy Upon The Conjurer* warning young women against the wickedness of consulting fortune-tellers. In 1749–50 appeared *Epistles for the Ladies*, and in 1755 *The Wife, by Mira*, followed in 1756 by *The Husband*. These were in the vein of Mrs Rowe's heavy moralizing, and would have argued a transformed Mrs Haywood had she not shown the cloven hoof by her *Invisible Spy*, published pseudonymously in 1754. Despite such incidental lapses, she continued to follow the new moral conventions, and to attempt literary experiments. The influence of *The Spectator* is seen in her efforts to produce an imitation written especially for women.

But if Mrs Haywood had only trained her pen to moralize politely, she would have found that, to a writer, oblivion is even more fatal than being publicly stoned. Fortunately she was able to adapt herself to the new fashion in story-telling, and this adaptation was indeed a surprising achievement. Towards the end of Mrs Haywood's life a great change was evident in the conception of the novel, and it argues much elasticity of mind and unsuspected literary resource that she was able, even at the age of fifty-eight, to share in this new orientation, and actually to achieve her best works at a time when, if one were to dance at all, one must dance to the piping of Richardson, Fielding, and Smollett, with Dr Johnson as master of ceremonies. The day of stock vices and virtues was over. God's cheerful fallible men and women, with all their good intentions, failings, foibles and mannerisms now began to live within the covers of the English novel.

Mrs Haywood had no intention of being a wallflower. To interest the public it was necessary to abandon the old romantic extravagances and to depict real emotions, motives and characters. This she strove to do in *The Fortunate Foundling* (1744). At this time the Foundling Hospital in Lamb's Conduit had aroused much interest, and had given what might be called a foundling motif to some contemporary writings. Mrs Haywood's preference for tracing the fortunes not of one foundling but of two, shows us at once her greatest weakness as a novelist. She had long accustomed herself to the writing of short tales, and whenever she had attempted a longer narrative she had found herself unable to construct a unified plot. Then, as in *The Memoirs of a Certain Island*, she had endeavoured to string a number of disconnected anecdotes and stories on one loose thread; or, as in *The*

British Recluse, she had artificially united a double-barrelled story. Now, although she had seen how it might be done in *Pamela* and in *Joseph Andrews,* she did not find it easy to learn the technique, so she fell back on the expedient of having two foundlings, so as to bring her novel to the length now required by the reading public. The result was much what might be expected.

Mrs Haywood sets her story in the last quarter of the seventeenth century. In 1688 the foundlings are taken under the protection of a benevolent gentleman named Dorilaus. Louisa is simply another Marianne or Pamela; her virtue is equally impregnable and equally assaulted. Her trials begin when her guardian begins to pay her unwelcome attentions; they continue through her brief career as a milliner, and culminate when she becomes the companion of the indiscreet Melanthe. Louisa is a magnet for wicked men, and yet out of this evil came good, because finally the persecutions of a shocking rake win her the intervention of an honourable lover, who begs her to marry him. She refuses because of her inferior position, takes refuge in a convent, refuses to become a nun, and flees to Paris. There Dorilaus claims her as his own daughter, and, secure in her new status, she marries her lover.

The adventures of Horatio, Louisa's brother, are chiefly of a military nature. He leaves Westminster school to serve under Marlborough in Flanders. He is captured by the French, and later released to enter the service of the Chevalier. He falls in love with the beautiful Charlotte de Palfoy, and, so that he may speedily become rich enough to marry her, decides to serve under the King of Sweden. He wins a colonel's commission and some booty, but is taken prisoner by the Russians and cast into a dungeon at St Petersburg. Finally he succeeds in making his way to Paris. He too is claimed by Dorilaus, and he marries Charlotte.

The Fortunate Foundlings shows Mrs Haywood at the parting of the ways. The synopsis makes the faulty construction abundantly evident. Mrs Haywood may possibly have wished to contrast the sort of adventures likely to beset a young woman and a young man, but this does not excuse her from the necessity of correlation. Her attempts at unification are too slight. There is, nevertheless, a very considerable improvement in her handling of sensational incident. It is true that she still seems unable to resist introducing erotic scenes and spicy gossip, but she does not often yield to this temptation. She was beginning to learn that incident must be subordinated to plot.

The Fortunate Foundlings had been in the tradition of Marivaux and Richardson. *The History of Miss Betsy Thoughtless* (1751) and *Jemmy and Jenny Jessamy* (1753) belong also to the school of domestic sentiment, with an added flavour of the picaresque. *Betsy Thoughtless* is by far the best of all Eliza Haywood's novels. It achieves a greater unity of action, although there is an excess of incident. Mrs Haywood's concentration on events puts one in mind of Defoe, although, of course, she was incapable of his realism. Neither had she the power of painting a convincing background, nor of suggesting atmosphere. It is said that *Miss Betsy Thoughtless* gave Fanny Burney the idea of *Evelina*. A comparison of these two plots shows clearly the great fault in Mrs Haywood's construction. Fanny Burney knew how to prune away the superfluous, and to interweave her strands of narrative into a homogeneous whole. Mrs Haywood, even in this, her best novel, strings loosely together a number of detachable events. Betsy's adventures are so numerous and so diverse that they create a picaresque effect, and this characteristic is particularly to be observed in Betsy's bogus marriage to Sir Frederick Fineer and its sequel. Mrs Haywood's emphasis on the external is due to the fact that she was not capable of treating her material subjectively. Richardson and Fielding had depicted real emotions, motives and characters, but this was beyond the scope of Mrs Haywood, as indeed it was beyond most writers at that time. Her characterization is thin, and because she was unable to make action grow naturally from the inter-effects of personality, she was apt to stress mannerisms. This fault was also evident in Fanny Burney's novels, which achieved a far greater artistry in technique, but without penetrating the secret of real characterization.

Miss Betsy Thoughtless is a skittish young lady with a genius for involving herself in incriminating situations. At school she aids the flirtations of a precocious school-fellow. Later, her parents being dead, she goes to live with one of her guardians appropriately named Mr Goodman. This worthy gentleman, however, has a vicious wife, Lady Mellasin, who has bequeathed to her daughter Flora all the worst traits in her character. Betsy's morals are not undermined by this pernicious feminine influence — in fact, for a long time, she does not doubt the probity of Lady

Mellasin and Flora. But her commonsense is atrophied. She skims over the surface of life, not suspecting the treacherous currents. She does not suspect the guilty, and because she herself is innocent, it does not occur to her that she can fall under suspicion. But she does, and she has many adventures which she incurs by a magnificent indifference to appearances.

She begins her career as a ravisher of hearts at the ripe age of fourteen. Her first admirers are an honest youth called Saving, and Gayland, the profligate. Saving's father sends him to Holland, and all his letters to Betsy are intercepted. As she does not love Saving, his removal from her life does not affect her. She is caught up in a whirl of gaiety; fêted and flattered to such an extent that her reputation begins to be doubtful, although her innocence is really beyond question. She is invited to Oxford by her brother, and it is arranged that she shall be accompanied on her visit by Flora, that pert mind. The scene is set for a strenuous contest between these little scalp-hunters. At Oxford all is triumph until Betsy is insulted by a gallant who thinks she speaks his language. But Betsy is like a child who knows many words, but no meanings. There is a duel. The social temperature drops to zero, and the young ladies return to London. Betsy's ostracism in Oxford is soon forgotten in the adulation now showered on her by a multiplicity of suitors. There is the forthright sea-captain, the bogus Sir Frederick Fineer and many others, but Mr Trueworth is the sincerest lover, and unknown even to herself, Miss Betsy cares for him. She is so sure of him, however, that she takes a giddy pleasure in showing her power over him. He is not deterred by her apparent heartlessness, but one by one a succession of incidents, injurious to Betsy's good name, commences to undermine his faith in her. Lady Mellasin proves herself an evil woman, and her unfortunate husband dies shortly after her banishment from his house. Flora, by no means an innocent girl, falls in love with Trueworth, and by anonymous letters casts a cloud of scandal over Betsy, until at last Trueworth abandons his courtship, and marries Harriet Lovitt. Betsy now realizes that she loves Trueworth and her passion is increased by the knowledge that not only Harriet but also Harriet's sister find in Trueworth their ideal lover. Harriet's sister dies of her unrequited passion, and although Betsy is made of sterner stuff, she bids adieu to her old carefree, flippant life. She marries the first person to hand, who happens to be an avaricious, heartless, miserly youth called Munden. He not merely kills her pet squirrel, but refuses her pin money and finally is unfaithful to her — a variety of faults which secures him Betsy's contempt. Nevertheless, she bears with him until his death which, by a great stroke of fortune, soon intervenes. 'Nothing like death for cutting the Gordian knot,' Mrs Haywood seems to say, as with another timely stroke of her pen she kills Trueworth's wife. The lovers are happy at last in a marriage founded on respect and past sufferings; in a world where pet squirrels flourish undisturbed, and pin money flows like water.

In *Miss Betsy Thoughtless* Mrs Haywood goes with the anti-romantic tide:

> 'The deity of soft desires [said Mr Trueworth] flies the confused glare of pomp and publick shews; it is in the shady bowers, or in the banks of a sweet purling stream, he spreads his downy wings and wafts ten thousand nameless pleasures on the fond, the innocent and the happy pair.'
>
> He was going on, but she interrupted with a loud laugh: 'Hold, hold!' cried she, 'was there ever such romantick description? I wonder how such silly ideas come into your head? Shady bowers! and purling streams! Heavens, how insipid! Well,' continued she, 'you may be the Strephon of the Woods, if you think fit, but I shall never envy the happiness of the Chloe that accompanies you if these fine recesses. What, to be cooped up like a tame dove, only to coo, and bill, and breed? O, it would be a delicious life indeed.'[13]

Despite its shallowness, *Miss Betty Thoughtless* is a good story. There is no excess of moralizing, and our interest is easily won and retained by the energy and vivacity of the narrative. The novel was extremely popular with the English reading public, and was translated into French. This made it possible for Mrs Haywood to snap her fingers at critics who were less kind. For example, when the *Monthly Review* complained that *Miss Betsy Thoughtless* lacked 'those entertaining introductory chapters and digressive essays, which distinguish the works of Fielding, Smollett, or the author of *Pompey the Little*,' Mrs Haywood riposted in *Jemmy and Jenny Jessamy*, volume iii, chapter xviii, which, she said, 'contains none of those beautiful digressions, those remarks or reflections which a certain would-be critick pretends, are so distinguished in the writings of his two favourite authors; yet it is to be hoped, will afford sufficient to please all those who are willing to be pleased.'

In *Jemmy and Jenny Jessamy* Mrs Haywood did not maintain the standard she had reached in *Miss Betsy Thoughtless. Jemmy and Jenny Jessamy* consists of many little stories quite insufficiently connected by the slender motif of the mutual love of hero and heroine. Jemmy and Jenny are two pleasant young people whose parents have always intended them to marry. They are quite willing to fall in with this arrangement, but vanish to see a little of the world first. They are an affectionate, but very unromantic couple.

> Neither of them felt those impatiences, those anxieties, those distracting fears, those causeless jealousies, or any of those thousand restless sensations that usually perplex a mind devoted to an amorous flame: they were happy when they met, but not uneasy when they parted. He was not in the least alarmed on finding she was frequently visited by some of the finest gentlemen in town; nor was she at all disconcerted when she was told that he was well received by ladies of the most distinguished characters . . . yet that they did love each other is most certain, as will hereafter be demonstrated by proofs much more unquestionable *than all those extravagances: those raging flights, commonly looked upon as infallible tokens of the passion*: but which, how fierce soever the fires they spring from may burn for a while, we see frequently extinguish of themselves, and leave nothing but the smoke behind.[14]

Many instances of married infelicity and infidelity impress Jenny and Jemmy with the seriousness of the step they contemplate, and since each instance is followed by lengthy moralizing, the book has some characteristics of the tract. The wise Jenny gleans a lesson from everything that happens, and indeed Mrs Haywood makes the story subservient to this purpose. Jenny's moral soliloquies, although well reasoned, are far too sagacious for the fallible reader, and retard the story very seriously. Her views always express themselves according to a rigid formula. They fall into three parts, each introduced respectively by the phrases 'said she', 'continued she' and 'went she still on.' After a few such soliloquies, this Procrustean bed begins to creak loudly. There are at least ten stories of conjugal suffering, and one notable attempt by the villain Bellpine to alienate the lovers, who are, however, united in the end. Bellpine is quite a convincing villain. His deviousness in achieving his aim is well worked out. His final bid for Jenny's hand is, nevertheless, not in keeping with his former subtlety. Mrs Haywood foresees this objection, and explains that the deceiver is deceived by his own vanity. It is noteworthy that Mrs Haywood, despite her moral earnestness, considered gallantry in the hero quite compatible with his sincere love for the heroine. Jemmy Jessamy is a Tom Jones rather than a Sir Charles Grandison.

Mrs Haywood often indulges in romantic circumlocution, e.g., the wedding cake is 'the oblation to Ceres.' Sometimes a mist of romanticism obscures the sense altogether. What could Jemmy have meant by this postscript to a perfectly intelligible letter: 'P.S. If I have any friends among the intellectual world, I would petition them to haunt your nightly dreams with the shadow of me till propitious fortune throws the substance at your feet?' What a colourful thing life must have been when Lord Huntly, falsely accused of bigamous inclinations, thus expresses himself:

> 'Madam, I am pierced in too tender a part to stand upon punctilios — both my love and honour are wounded — gashed — mangled in a most cruel and infamous degree; and it is only from your ladyship's justice and humanity that I can hope a cure!'

But Mrs Haywood can turn a phrase with deft realism too, she speaks, for instance, of 'the tumultuous din, the smoak, the stench, the rugged stones of London.' And she can hit the truth sometimes with instinctive aim: 'Oh, why will men endeavour to persuade us we are goddesses, only to create themselves the pains of convincing us afterwards that we are but mortals'. She gives in a sentence the key to women's preoccupation with novels when she defines marriage: 'Marriage . . . is the great action of our lives . . . the hinge on which our happiness or misery, while we have breath, depends.'

Jenny is really a very sensible little creature — not so far from Jane Austen's idea of sense. But it is unfair to annihilate Mrs Haywood by the mention of Jane Austen's name. Jenny's adventures in Bath have only to be mentioned in the same breath as those of Catherine Morland to reveal Mrs Haywood's sins and omissions as a novelist. Jenny's exploits might just as well have taken place in Yorkshire. There is no background of assemblies and pump-room, no effort made to represent the fashion, the formality amid which Catherine Moreland later found such uncertain pleasure.

Mrs Haywood, in her lifetime, attempted many kinds of fiction, and is the link between the older school and the new. In this period of transition we find some curious examples of outworn types of story-telling, as for example the two novels of Mrs Arabella Plantin which appeared in 1727. These were *Love Led Astray: or, The Mutual Inconstancy;* and *The Ingrateful: or, The Just Revenge.* In the introduction to *Love Led Astray* Mrs Plantin makes a great show of opposing tales of 'obscure retreats' to those of 'the shining courts.' She says:

> I know that the name of a prince embellishes a story, and seems to interest a reader in it, tho' that pompous title is not always attended with all the gallantry which is often found in a private person; therefore I leave the Historians the choice of their illustrious name. I intend to confine myself to the passion of love, and as I am persuaded that a shepherd may in this point exceed the greatest king, I shall not go beyond the bounds of a forest to convince my readers of this truth.

What follows is an absurd travesty of the pastoral tradition. The shepherd Polemas who has no equal among the swains; the charming Cyparissa and the exquisite Lydippa form a triangle; cupids flutter incessantly in the background; even the sheep have an air of genteel simplicity, and go about wearing numberless knots of amaranth-coloured ribbon. There is a Country Ball for the feast of Pan, and the Nymphs go masked. They consult the oracle Apollo, although up to that moment no country has been designated as the background. *Love Led Astray is* a windy suspiration of forced breath. It is impossible to read it without one's lungs being tickled o' the sere. As for *The Ingrateful*, it is, if possible, even more deplorable. It begins: 'In Arcadia there lived a Gentleman.' But alas! too soon it transpires that he is really no gentleman at all, but a shocking deceiver. He befools the beautiful and wealthy Melissa to pay his debts before he marries her. Then he takes ship for Cyprus, and determines to marry a widow whose riches are beyond the dreams of avarice. When Melissa hears that the marriage day is appointed she sails for Cyprus, disguised as a man, and assassinates her recreant lover. This poignant and dramatic event is describes as follows:

> She was shewed into a Room, and Lysander soon sent to her. She approached him with a Letter in one Hand, and in the other a Dagger concealed, with which she stabbed him in the Breast, and had no sooner drew it from the Wound, but she struck it into her own Bosom. The cries which were occasion'd by the Wound, called in the Company, among whom was the designed Bride. Lysander had just Time enough to own his own Guilt and clear Melissa, she being Dead the moment she pierced her Heart.

Mrs Haywood's moral didacticism at the end of her life, as opposed to her earlier licentious writings, merely reflected the changed outlook which made itself felt in the second decade of the eighteenth century. Puritanism, though it had been out of power and therefore out of fashion, had not lessened its hold on the bourgeois section. Indeed the growing wealth of the middle class and its increased interest in refinements of life rapidly provided a reading public which, though it accepted the flashy at first, soon insisted on a supply which would suit its particular demands. There was for a while a transitional period, during which many writers tried to serve the old gods and the new by lurid pictures of vice which they were careful to condemn sanctimoniously, but an increasing spirit of conventional morality finally ousted the cult of indecency.

The popularity of such works as *Friendship in Death* (1728) by Mrs Elizabeth Rowe (1674-1737) shows how the tide had turned. This effusion reached its third edition in 1733, its fifth in 1738, and continued to be printed until 1816. It consisted of letters supposedly from the dead to the living, and the purpose was strongly evangelical. *Letters Moral and Entertaining* (1729-1733) gave much pious teaching with a sugar-coating of little stories, occasionally enlivened by dialogue. These letters were, to all intents and purposes, religious tracts. Some of these stories are reminiscent of the *novella* technique, some are pastoral in type. Mr Baker remarks on Mrs Rowe's 'idyllic painting of scenery in a manner afterwards followed by John Buncle.' Mrs Rowe's unctuous moralizing had that point of view later immortalized in the shrewd and shallow Pamela. Nevertheless her works in prose and verse earned her the respectful admiration of such men as Dr Watts, Klopstock, Wieland, Pope, Prior and Dr Johnson. These excellent men were willing to accord to piety an admiration which expressed itself as literary criticism. Pious mediocrity did not set their teeth on edge, and was indeed regarded as peculiarly womanly. When later Hannah More became the apotheosis of the Rowe tradition, she found her pedestal awaiting her.

Mrs Jane Barker belonged also to this female school of moral didacticism. In 1715, appeared *Exilius: or, the Banished Roman.* This was written not to win literary fame, but 'for the instruction of some young ladies of quality.' Mrs Barker considered that 'a learned lady was as ridiculous as a spinning Hercules.' Judged by this standard she is far from ridiculous; by any other she stands condemned. *Exilius* is a deplorable medley of hair-raising adventures in which female paragons incredibly become entangled. These heroines are all righteous, matter-of-fact prigs. They manage their lives by a sort of moral etiquette which is applied like a yardstick to everything from the interpretation of oracles to the regulation of suitors. And all the while they cant. These female Stigginses reappear in *A Patchwork Screen for the Ladies, or Love and Virtue Recommended* (1723) and *The Lining of the Patchwork Screen* (1726). Both works are collections of instructive novels. Mrs Barker claimed that the stories in *A Patchwork Screen* were 'related after a Manner entirely New,' but the method of narration is not in the least original. Like Mrs Rowe, but to a lesser extent, Mrs Barker was a popular writer. Her heroines exactly suited the current taste—from which it is clear that in creating Pamela, Richardson conformed to the prevailing conception of what a heroine ought to be.

Another novel which in its priggish outlook suggests Richardson, and which has the definite didacticism of Mrs Rowe, was published in 1724 by Mrs Mary Davys.[15] Amoranda, the heroine of *The Reformed Coquet,* is a wealthy and giddy young beauty who seems in danger of losing her head through the adulation of the fops who surround her. Her guardian chooses as her future husband a young nobleman, who loves Amoranda as much as he deplores her foolishness. He disguises himself as a friend of her guardian, and goes to live in her house in the role of an elderly advisor. He soon disperses her worthless suitors, saves her from compromising situations, and then reveals himself as her ideal lover. 'This,' says Miss Charlotte Morgan, 'is one of the earliest appearances in fiction of the perfect prig of which Sir Charles Grandison is the consummate example.'[16]

A fresher breeze blows through the works of Penelope Aubin. She was didactic, but she had the idea of enlivening her stories with unusual backgrounds. Obviously she was much influenced by Defoe and by records of travel. As a result, her narratives bring a new note of adventure into the novel. She was not an advocate of genteel morality. A staunch Catholic, it was her object to win her readers towards the Catholic point of view. She uses her stories to show that the vicissitudes and miseries of this world matter little if one's gaze is fixed on eternity: 'The virtuous shall look dangers in the face unmoved, and putting their whole trust in the Divine Providence, shall be delivered, even by miraculous means; or dying with comfort be freed from the miseries of this life, and go to taste an eternal repose.'[17] So that her characters may be sufficiently tried Mrs Aubin subjects them to the most extraordinary occurrences, of which one gains a sufficient idea from the long titles of her stories. For example: *The Life of Madam de Beaumont, a French Lady; who lived in a Cave in Wales about fourteen years undiscovered, being forced to flye France for her religion, and of the cruel usage she had there. Also her Lord's Adventures in Muscovy where he was a prisoner some years, with an Account of his returning to France, and her being discovered by a Welsh Gentleman who fetches her Lord to Wales, and of many strange accidents which befel them, and their daughter Belinda, who was stolen away from them and of their Return to France in the year 1718.*

In 1721, when this tale was published, there also appeared: *The Strange Adventures of the Count de Vinevil and his Family. Being an account of what happened to them whilst they resided at Constantinople. And of Mlle Ardelisia, his daughter's being ship-wrecked on the uninhabited Island Delos in the Return to France, with Violetta, a Venetian Lady, the Captain of the Ship, a Priest, and five Sailors. The Manner of their living. Their . . . Strange Deliverance . . .* This echo of *Robinson Crusoe* was followed a year later (1722) by another tale of shipwreck: *The Noble Slaves: or, The Lives and Adventures of Two Lords and Two Ladies upon a desolate Island.* Mrs Aubin made a determined attempt to imitate Defoe's realism, and in her best story, *The Life and Adventures of the Lady Lucy* (1726), she creates the impression of having been an eye-witness to certain happenings in the Williamite wars in Ireland, such as the sack of a castle after the Battle of the Boyne.

As a translator Mrs Aubin's choice lay with the wonderful. In 1726, before writing *Adventures of the Lady Lucy* she had rendered into English Pétis de la Croix's *History of Genghizcan The Great, First Emperor of the Antient Moguls and Tartars*. She also translated *The Illustrious French Lovers; being the True Histories of the Amours of Several French Persons of Quality* (1729). That interest in the Orient which led to the translation of *The History of Genghizcan* is very evident in her last original work, a picaresque novel, *The Life and Adventures of the Young Count Albertus, The Son of Count Lewis Augustus, by the Lady Lucy* (1728). The young Count, overwhelmed by his wife's death, tries by foreign travel to divert his mind from his grief. He encounters many people who narrate their life stories. Some of these inset stories are good, particularly the story of the old miser in Madrid, which is told with dramatic realism. Eventually the young Count becomes a Benedictine and goes as a missionary to China, where martyrdom awaits him.

Mrs Aubin is worthy of remembrance despite her obvious didacticism, in that she endeavoured to weave together romance and realism, and was, in however slight a degree, one of the early contributors to Oriental fiction. She is notable also in her adherence to the popular theme of the virtuous maiden pursued by the charming rake. Finally, she was one of the very few women who essayed the picaresque.

We have seen that Mrs Manley and Mrs Haywood sometimes showed a picaresque touch. This was evident also in *Letters written by Mrs. Manley*, (1696 republished as *A Stage Coach Journey to Exeter*, 1725), and in Mrs Haywood's *Bath Intrigues* (1725). Mrs Davy's *Merry Wanderer* also shows the picaresque influence. It has, by way of introduction to a story of intrigue, a picaresque description of various incidents in a journey, the unusual people encountered at an inn, and the miserly hospitality of a friend's house. Mrs Elizabeth Boyd united the picaresque and the tale of gallantry in a sorry concoction called *The Female Page* (1737). Its contents are indicated by its sub-title: *A Genuine and Entertaining History, Relating to some Persons of Destinction. Intermix'd with A Great Variety of affecting Intrigues in Love and Gallantry. Also the remarkable Letters that passed between the several Persons concerned.* Mrs Boyd in her preface alternates between suggesting and denying that her novel actually records the doings of certain well known people. She does not use the device of the key. The female page is a young woman who, besottedly in love with Duke Bellfont, dons male attire so that she may be near him in the guise of a page. It is unnecessary to describe all the voluptuous situations to which this masquerade and its discovery give rise. The story is written in a species of melodramatic blank verse, and is the dying gasp of the tradition of gallantry.

But the picaresque trend, so far from being extinct, was given a new lease of life by Fielding. *Joseph Andrews* (1742) and *Tom Jones* (1749) gave a great fillip to stories dealing with a varied succession of adventures — a vogue which Fielding's sister endeavoured to follow in the *Adventures of David Simple* (1744). Sarah Fielding's use of the picaresque medium was by no means a proof of sisterly admiration. On the contrary, she was one of Richardson's female adorers. Sarah Fielding sheltering under the wing of Richardson, and even acquiescing in his condemnation of that 'low fellow,' Henry Fielding, presents a curious anomaly. It seems fairly clear that she really considered Richardson a better writer than her brother, and yet her writings in part reflect some of Fielding's literary characteristics. She was dependent upon Fielding, with whom she lived. After his death she retired to Bath where she died in 1738.

David Simple, Sarah Fielding's best known work of fiction, is, strictly speaking, not a novel. It repays study as a peculiar mixture of influences, none of which appears to have been strong enough to triumph over the others. There is, therefore, no homogeneity, and the elements of Addison, Fielding and Richardson are separately recognizable from beginning to end. The book consists in the first part of a number of Addisonian essays, and in the second of a number of stories all loosely linked together by the ramblings of that cypher, David Simple. Its purpose is moral didacticism, and it achieves this sometimes by direct sermonizing, sometimes by satiric reflections on human life. It can most nearly be classified as picaresque, although of all the picaresque characteristics, it contains only the motif of wandering. Sarah Fielding had the gifts of an essayist, insight into character and an ironic view of life. She evidently wished to exert these in depicting various aspects of human society. It was thus, no doubt, that she stumbled into using the very genre most unsuited for her purpose. The picaresque novel, since it depicted the adventures of a light-hearted filibuster, dealt with externals, stressed incident and obtained its effects by giving a strong sense of varied and vivid reality. The picaro knew life from the drawing-room to the stews, and laughed to find the same failings and foibles in every grade of society. Even if it were his nature to reflect, he did not need to point the ironic lesson. The picaro's objective account of his experiences contains an implicit satire on life. It is evident that Sarah Fielding could not succeed in the picaresque medium. In the first place, as a decorous woman she had no intention of describing the exploits of a rakish adventurer, nor would her limited experience have allowed her to do so. Therefore, while choosing the picaresque genre for the sake of its variety, she at once determined to omit the picaro. Small wonder that the result is like a beefsteak pie without the steak. Furthermore, Sarah Fielding's attitude was subjective, her technique was direct and all her lessons fully explained in words. In the picaresque medium the satire was oblique and cumulative. Again, in the picaresque there was universality of outlook; *David Simple* consists more of a number of bird's-eye views.

Strong interest in the hero could alone have integrated the scenes and incidents in this book, but who could be interested in that cardboard figure, David Simple? David is a bloodless, moralizing sentimentalist. He wanders through the cities of London and Westminster in search of a true friend. 'This was the phantom, the idol of his soul's admiration. In the worship of which he at length grew such an enthusiast, that he was at this point only as mad as *Quixote* himself could be with knight errantry.'[18] David's sensibility is sorely tried in his wanderings, even to a great prodigality of tears and guineas which he expends on the unfortunates whom he continually encounters. His guilelessness is complete, and his ignorance of everyday facts so great that only a hair's-breadth saves him from being a bumpkin — and sometimes not even that. Since Sarah Fielding wished to pillory hypocrisy and selfishness, she could not allow the spotless David to take them in his stride as would the picaro. His blind innocence makes it necessary to explain everything to him constantly, and so as to provide an opportunity for social satire, he is made to ask innumerable obvious questions: 'David begged an explanation of what she meant by a toad-eater'; 'David begged her to let him know what she meant by *fine ladies*;' 'Pray,

Madam, what is the meaning of making a butt of anyone?' This transparency of purpose is very trying to the reader, but not more so than the awkward efforts of dialogue which Sarah boldly sets down as in a play.

Nevertheless, the incidents in themselves are recounted in a clear and telling style, and with the shrewd irony of one who views life detachedly. When David had been defrauded, and cast penniless on the world by his brother, Sarah Fielding ends the chapter thus: 'And there, for some time, I will leave him to his own private sufferings, *lest it should be thought I am so ignorant of the world, as not to know the proper time for forsaking people.*'[19]

The most interesting and praiseworthy aspect of Sarah Fielding's work is her effort to achieve reality in characterization. In view of the period at which she wrote, the following passage is very clear-sighted:

> I hope [she says] to be excused by those gentlemen who are quite sure they have found one woman who is a perfect *angel* and that all the rest are perfect *devils*, for drawing the character of a woman who was neither—for Miss Nancy Johnson was very good-humoured, had a great deal of softness, and had no alloy to these good qualities, but a great share of vanity, with some small spices of envy, which must always accompany it. And I make no manner of doubt, but if she had not met with this temptation she would have made a very affectionate wife to the man who loved her.[20]

Sarah Fielding was very much concerned with the interaction of human characteristics and motives. That she worked from within is very evident throughout the book, and one could quote many examples of this aim — in particular, perhaps, the story of Camilla and her stepmother. To Sarah behaviour is only a superficial stratum which more often conceals than exhibits the real man. We see, for example, that Mr Orgueil's good nature is a mere cloak for his extreme self-love. He is:

> One of a set of men in the world; who pass through life with very good reputations, whose actions are in the general, justly to be applauded, and yet upon a near examination their principles are all bad, and their hearts hardened to all tender sensations . . . The greatest sufferings which can happen to his fellow-creatures, have no sort of effect on him, and yet he very often relieves them; that is, he goes just

as far in serving others, as will give him new opportunities of flattering himself: for his whole soul is filled with pride, he has made a god of himself, and the attributes he thinks necessary to the dignity of such a being, he endeavours to have . . . When he knows any man do a dishonourable action, then he enjoys the height of pleasure in the comparison he makes between his own mind, and that of such a mean creature. He mentally worships himself with joy and rapture: and I verily believe, if he lived in a world, where to be vicious was esteemed praise-worthy, the same pride which now makes him take a delight in doing what is right . . . would then lead him to abandon himself to all manner of vice; for if by taking pains to bridle his passions, he could gain no superiority over his companions, all his love of rectitude, as he calls it, would fall to the ground. So that his goodness, like cold fruits, is produced by the dung and nastiness which surrounded it . . . He makes no allowance for the smallest frailties, and the moment a person exceeds, in the least degree, the bounds his wisdom has set, he abandons them, as he thinks they have no reasonable claim to any thing farther from him. If he were walking with a friend on the side of a precipice, and that friend was to go a step nearer than he advised him, and by accident should fall down, although he broke his bones, and lay in the utmost misery, he would coolly leave him, without the least thought of anything for his relief: saying, *if men would be so mad, they must take the consequence of their own folly*, Nay, I question, whether he would not have a secret satisfaction in thinking, that from his wisdom, he could walk safely through the most dangerous places, while others fell into them.[21]

On the other hand, there is Mr Spatter who imputes the worst motives to everyone, and appears to be most vindictive. But his ill-nature 'dwells no where but in his tongue,' and he has a soft and generous heart. David, not knowing that Spatter's spleen is a sort of defence mechanism, earnestly remonstrates with him, saying that the most he himself could do if he found a man capable of hurting him (unprovoked) was to avoid him:

'Indeed, Sir,' says Spatter, 'I am not of your mind; for I think there is nothing so pleasant as revenge: I would pursue a man, who had injured me, to the very brink of life. I know it would be impossible for me ever to forgive him, and I would have him live, only that I might have the pleasure of seeing him miserable.'

David was amazed at this, and said, 'pray, Sir, consider, as you are a Christian, you cannot act in that manner.'

> Spatter replied, 'he was sorry it was against the rules of
> Christianity, but he could not help his temper . . .'[22]

Spatter appears briefly, but he is the most interesting, because
he is the only live person in the book. Sarah Fielding's comprehension of character was sound, her aim was worthy of success,
but nevertheless, she failed to create real people. She had not the
ability to make her human beings objective. They are specimens
pinned down, and examined in the study. Even when we are
supposedly watching them in the Stock Exchange, at the play, in
the stage-coach, they are not alive; and we are always conscious
that what we see and hear has been filtered through the philosophic irony of Sarah Fielding's mind. Her minute dissections
seem to leave the component parts in their disintegrated state.
We are shown an aggregate of traits, but (with one minor exception) never a personality. The characters in the main stories are
all the more unconvincing because, instead of being presented in
action, the events in which they move are retailed to us at
second, and even at third-hand.

Still, there are glimpses of reality. For example, Cynthia
expresses independent views on education and marriage. She
thus describes her upbringing:

> If I was pleased with any book above the most silly story or
> romance, it was taken from me. For Miss must not inquire
> too far into things, it would turn her brain; she had better
> mind her needle-work, and such things as were useful for
> women; reading and poring on books, would never get me
> a husband. Thus was I condemned to spend my youth, the
> time when our imagination is at the highest, and we are
> capable of most pleasure, without being indulged in any
> one thing I liked; and obliged to employ myself, in what
> was fancied by my mistaken parents to be for my improve-
> ment, although in reality it was nothing more than what any
> person, a degree above a natural fool might learn as well in
> a very small time, as in a thousand ages. And what yet
> aggravated my misfortunes was, my having a brother who
> hated reading to such a degree, he had a perfect aversion to
> the very sight of a book; and he must be cajoled or whipped
> into learning, while it was denied me, who had the utmost
> eagerness for it.[23]

Such a young woman would hardly be likely to submit meekly
to arbitrary match-making. One may imagine then, the scene when

a country gentleman, with her father's consent, proposes marriage. He delicately expresses his offer as follows:

> Madam . . . I like your person, hear you have had a sober education, think it time to have an heir to my estate, and am willing, if you consent to it, to make you my wife; notwithstanding your father tells me, he cannot give you above two hundred pounds.[24]

He adds that, not being a nonsensical bore, he will not whine of love; he expects her to comply with his humours, rear his children, keep his house, and particularly provide for his love of good eating and drinking. Cynthia curtsies, and replies that she has no ambition to be his upper servant, but would be interested to know if, in return for all the offices allotted to her, he would, in addition to her food and lodging, think of giving her some small wages, 'that I might now and then recreate myself with my fellow-servants.'[25] The suitor departs, breathing fire, and Cynthia comments:

> I could not help reflecting on the folly of those women who *prostitute* themselves *(for I shall always call it prostitution, for a woman who has sense, and has been tolerably educated, to marry a clown and a fool)* and to give up that enjoyment which every one who has taste enough to know how to employ their time, can procure for themselves, though they should be obliged to live ever so retired, only to know they have married a man who has an estate.'[26]

David Simple fails because its form stresses a variety of external events while its purpose stresses a variety of character analyses, but still it merits recognition since her inward approach to character hit accidentally on what was to prove the growing point of the modern novel. In its own day this work was adjudged a success, so much so, in fact, that it was ascribed to Fielding. In a preface to the second edition he denies authorship, so that he may 'do justice to the real and sole author.' He praises his sister's book warmly and even says that it contains some touches that 'might have done honour to the pencil of the immortal Shakespeare himself.' Richardson wrote after Fielding's death: 'What a knowledge of the human heart! Well might a critical judge of writing say, as he did to me, that your late brother's knowledge of it was not (fine writer as he was) comparable to yours. His was but as the knowledge of the outside of a clock-work machine, while yours was that of all the finer springs and movements of the inside.'?[27]

Lack of money, and also, no doubt, genuine (though uncon-fessed) ambition drove Sarah Fielding into print again and again. She translated two books of Xenophon, the *Memorabilia* and the *Apologia*. With Jane Collier she wrote *The Cry* (1754). In 1757 appeared *The Lives of Cleopatra and Octavia*. This was reminiscent of Fielding's *Journey from this World to the Next*, but was too obviously didactic. Cleopatra and Octavia meet in the under-world, and tell their stories in rather a classical manner. *The History of the Countess of Dellwyn*[28] (1759) has a poorly connected plot, and is too heavily laden with moralizing. Still, it has touches of Henry Fielding's attitude and style. The story concerns a young woman who, dazzled by riches, marries a wealthy old lord. Ease and splendour soften her moral fibres, she yields to the temp-tations of a rake, is divorced by her husband, endeavours to marry again, but fails, and is abandoned to repentance and grief. Sarah Fielding's last novel *The History of Ophelia is* an echo of *Pamela*. A young lord carries off a lovely and innocent girl. She escapes his wicked intentions. He repents, and they are happily united.

It may be said that the women novelists who are the subject of this chapter achieved nothing much. In one sense it is true. The majority of their works were mediocre. Nevertheless, these women made a very useful contribution to the novel by their experiments with the various trends, and by their very fertility as novelists. The novel, after Aphra Behn's death, was in a transitional stage, feeling its way between, on the one hand, the romantic tradition and, on the other, the conception of realism in fiction which Defoe and Swift were building up. It was necessary during this critical period of evolution that the public appetite for fiction should be kept whetted, and that there should be sufficient novels to engross their interest, and to keep them from reverting to their former love of the drama. All that could be expected at this time was the ability to experiment. Even Defoe was only hammering out his own technique. Towards the end of this period the rise of the great novelists gave more difficult standards to imitate, and however weak were the women's first attempts, they rose to the challenge and, as we shall find, even-tually issued challenges of their own. The women here mentioned were, for the most part, merely hacks. They achieved results by trial and error, not by some intuitive spring towards the truth, but they prepared the way for the greatness to come. We shall see in the next chapter how much women contributed towards the growth of the epistolary form, so that, by the time Richardson used it, it was ready at his elbow.

Notes and Refernces

1 Mrs Manley, *Memoirs of Europe*, i, p. 254.
2 E.g. Lord Earnle, *Light Reading of our Ancestors* (1927), p. 175.
3 *Memoirs of Europe*, i, p. 262.
4 Ibid., 275.
5 Ibid., 276.
6 *The Fair Hypocrite* taken from Painter's *Duchess of Savoy* (45th novel). The *Physician's Stratagem* not identified in Painter, but obviously on the Italian pattern.
   The Wife's Resentment from Painter's *Didaco and Violenta* (42nd novel). *The Husband's Resentment*: example i: Painter's *Of a Lady of Thurin* (43rd novel); example ii: from Painter's *President of Grenoble* (58th novel). *The Happy Fugitives* from Painter's *Alerane and Adelasia*. *The Perjured Beauty*, based on the St Gregory legend, which gave Walpole the plot of his play *The Mysterious Mother*.
   (For these identifications see E. A. Baker, *History of the English Novel*, iii).
7 *Journal to Stella*, 28th January, 1712.
8 *Swift's Works* (ed. Scott), xvii, p. 430.
9 *Letters* (ed. Cunnigham), i, p. 251.
10 *The Dunciad*, Book 2, ii, pp. 157 ff.
11 For a detailed discussion of this work in relation to Defoe's *Secret Memoirs of Duncan Campbell* see G. F. Wicher, *Life and Romances of Mrs Eliza Haywood* (Columbia University Studies in English, New York, 1915).
12 G. F. Wicher, op. cit., p. 168.
13 Eliza Haywood, *The History of Miss Betsy Thoughtless*, (Intro. Dale Spender, 'Mothers of the Novel', Pandora, London, 1986), vol. ii, ch. viii, p. 196.
14 Ibid., ch. iv, *Jemmy and Jenny Jessamy*.
15 Mrs Mary Davys, an Irishwoman, was the wife of The Revd Peter Davys, or Davis, master of the free school at St Patrick's Dublin, after whose death she lived for some time at York. She knew Dean Swift. She afterwards kept a coffee-house in Cambridge, where she died. In addition to the novels mentioned in these pages she also wrote *The Lady's Tale* (written in 1700); *The Cousins; Familiar Letters betwixt a Gentleman and a Lady*; and *The Accomplish'd Rake, or the Modern Fine Gentleman, Being the genuine Memoirs of a certain Person of Distinction* (1756).

16 Charlotte E. Morgan, *The Rise of the Novel of Manners* (Columbia University Press, 1911), p. 70.
17 Preface to 'Adventures of the Lady Lucy' in *A Collection of Entertaining Histories and Novels designed to promote the cause of Virtue and Honour, Principally founded on facts and instructive incidents*, (3 vols., 1739).
18 Sarah Fielding, *The Adventures of David Simple* (ed. Malcolm Kelsall, Oxford University Press, 1987), Bk. i, ch. iii, pp. 26–27.
19 Ibid., Bk. i, ch. ii, p. 20.
20 Ibid., Bk. i, ch. v, pp. 37–38.
21 Ibid., Bk. i, ch. xi, pp. 72–73.
22 Ibid., Bk. ii, ch. iv, p. 95.
23 Ibid., Bk. ii, ch. vi, pp. 101–02.
24 Ibid., Bk. ii, ch. vi, p. 109.
25 Ibid., Bk. ii, ch. vi, p. 109.
26 Ibid., Bk. ii, ch. vi, pp. 109–10.
27 *Richardson's Correspondence*, i, 104. The critical judge was Johnson.
28 Mr E. A. Baker considers this the best of Sarah Fielding's novels.

Chapter VIII

The Epistolary Form Prior to 1740

When, in 1740, *Pamela* took England by storm, it seemed at first as if Richardson, by a miracle, had created an entirely new method in fiction. What he really did was by a stroke of genius, to crystallize certain tendencies which until then had been fluid. These tendencies had for a long time been increasingly evident, awaiting the mind which would gather them together, and evolve from them a work of art. To the evolution of *Pamela* went two tendencies of thought and one tendency of form. It is with the tendency of form that we are here concerned.

Richardson's choice of the epistolary form was not an accident. In fact, he had chosen the form before he realized that he was about to write a novel. That Richardson became a novelist was apparently fortuitous, but that he became an epistolary novelist was inevitable. It was inevitable because of his own particular bent, because of his subject, and because of a certain literary tradition.

His immediate object was to write, at the instance of two London booksellers, a small volume of *Familiar Letters* which were to unite elegance of style with the didactic purpose of showing 'how to think and act justly and prudently, in the common Concerns of Human Life.' He intended two or three of these letters 'to instruct handsome girls, obliged to go out to service, as we phrase it, how to avoid the snares that might be laid against their virtue.' With the idea of reinforcing his moral strictures he decided to recount the story of a servant-girl which he had heard some years before. This was the story of *Pamela*, which at once swept him away from his original purpose.

Richardson could have told his story directly, adopting the omniscient standpoint, as, for example, did Fielding, or he could have put the whole story into the mouth of the principal character as did Defoe, Swift, Marivaux, Goldsmith, Prévost, Thackeray and Charlotte Brontë. This latter way shares with the epistolary method the impossibility of giving a convincing portrait of the hero physically or mentally, without self-consciousness. The auto-biographical narrative, has, moreover, a peculiar disadvantage in that the flow of events in the life of the narrator is arrested while he recounts the past, and that the vividness one would expect from a personal relation is often lessened by the deflection of interest from the living narrator to the happenings he describes. This method, nevertheless, gives a wider point of view, and a more impersonal attitude than that possible in letters. The narrator may express his own thoughts, as it were, in soliloquy, without the embarrassment of confiding them to some particular indi-vidual. For Richardson, however, the epistolary form was the ideal medium. It exactly suited what he wished to express. All his life he had used letters to express his personality, and in his novels it was still his own personality which he was embodying in objective forms. Richardson was, in every sense, a most extraordinary man. As women ordinarily turned to letter-writing to give vent to their love of intimate outpourings and familiar gossip, and for the expression of views so often denied them in daily intercourse, so Richardson, that retiring and sedentary man, that unobtrusive egoist, had been a voluminous correspon-dent all his life long. Once the story of *Pamela* began to take shape in his mind, the peculiar suitability of the epistolary form must at once have become evident to him. It was the ideal medium for what he wanted to express. His mind was a hot-house within which a strange luxuriance of emotions fed on a sickly-sweet corruption, and grew out of all proportion in the vitiated air. It was an essential of his being, and consequently it was the habit of a lifetime, to observe minutely, to dissect every mood, impulse, reaction and motive, to magnify the emotions, and to luxuriate in sensibility. His method of describing external events was microscopic also. No detail was too minute for his observation, and he achieved his effects by tirelessly building up complete impressions from trifles light as air. Minuteness of external description could have been achieved without the epis-tolary form, certainly; but for the press and hurry of emotions, for the fluctuations of mood and sentiment, letters were a very apt medium. They constituted an eternal *now;* they gave a particular urgency to the events they described. They gave to Richardson's novels the tempo of a heart-beat. No more effective form could have been found for the tale of sensibility, because whereas human fears, hopes, excitements often appear baseless in retrospect, and not worth recounting, they appear of great import if recorded while the mind is still agitated.

The epistolary method had also very serious disadvantages, but it was not likely that Richardson would recognize them. It postulated always a confidant, and it offered no clue to the inner mind, except through revelations made to another. This led to such incredible confidences as those of Lovelace to Bellford; and even when the noblest sentiments were expressed, it gave a most distasteful self-consciousness to the utterances of the heroine or hero. Even if Pamela and Sir Charles Grandison had not been prigs, they would have been forced so to appear since it falls to their own tongues to express their own moral earnestness. But it was not for nothing that Richardson was called in his schooldays 'Serious and Gravity,' or that, when barely eleven years old, he addressed a letter full of Biblical reproof to a widowed lady of fifty. Richardson's purpose was didactic, and since he was not himself revolted by the pietistic mouthings of his principal characters, it was not likely that he would realize the disadvantage of a method which afforded no escape from explicit self-revelation.

Since the epistolary form satisfied Richardson's purpose of telling a story in such a manner as to emphasize sensibility and moralizing, and since letter writing was, in any case, his peculiar bent, it remains to show in how far there was a precedent for the epistolary novel, and to consider the contribution which letters, in one way or another, made towards the development of the novel.

When Richardson began his career as a novelist, letters, dialogues and character sketches had long been established in popularity, and were rapidly converging towards the enrichment of prose fiction. At that time letter-writing was a distinct accomplishment, and such people as Madame de Sévigné, Dorothy Osborne and Sir William Temple, Swift, Horace Walpole and Lady Mary Wortley-Montagu had made classic contributions to this literary genre. In the *Spectator*, the character-sketches had gradually lost their sharpness of outline, and ceased to be self-contained, becoming instead a continuous delineation of certain individuals who were no longer stock-types, but real human beings. These activities, however, were merely the culmination of similar literary efforts which had already been made for over one hundred years. Even in the days of the Pastoral and of the Heroic Romance letters were frequently interpolated in the narrative to afford variety or to concentrate interest on some crucial point of sentiment. It also became the custom to write collections of imaginary letters. These were used to essay character-sketches, to reflect a mood, describe an incident, or to suit various occasions or recipients. An early example was *A Poste with a Packet of Mad Letters* (1603)[1] by Nicholas Breton. In these there is as great variety as could well be imagined, ranging from various kinds of proposals, letters of advice, entreaty, expostulation, challenge to a duel, and a 'dissuasive from marriage.' In vol. 2, no. 153, Breton curiously anticipated Richardson. Most of Breton's letters have answers and in some cases there are two and even three letters and answers exchanged on the same subject.

In considering whether or not Richardson's use of letters was anticipated it is necessary not merely to ask whether some previous writers endeavoured to tell a story in letters but also to determine whether, before Richardson's time, anyone attempted in letters to delineate character or to describe scenes. Early in the seventeenth century many collections of character sketches appeared in the form of essays, notably *Character of Virtues and Vices* (1608) by Hall; Sir Thomas Overbury's *Characters* (1614); Nicholas Breton's *Characters upon Essaies Moral and Divine* (dedicated to Bacon) 1615; and again in 1616 Breton's *The Good and the Badde;* and John Earle's *Microcosmographie* (1628).

In the works already mentioned the epistolary genre had its nucleus. During the following century its growth was definitely aided by certain works which we are about to consider, and it will be observed that women ably assisted its development.

In 1664 the Duchess of Newcastle made a most notable contribution to the kind of writing which aimed at character sketches, and she even went further than the mere portrayal of character.

> Among the mass of her writings [says Jusserand] ideas are scattered here and there which are destined to live, and through which she anticipated men of true and real genius. To give only one example, she, too, may be credited with having anticipated Richardson in her 'Sociable Letters' *in which she tries to imitate real life, to describe scenes, very nearly*

to write an actual novel: 'The truth is,' she writes, 'they are rather scenes than letters, for I have endeavoured under cover of letters to express the humours of mankind, and the actions of man's life by the correspondence of two ladies, living at some short distance from each other, which make it not only their chief delight and pastime, but their tye in friendship, to discourse by letters as they would do if they were personally together.' Many collections of imaginary letters had, as we have seen, been published before, but never had the use to which they could be put been better foreseen by any predecessor of Richardson.[2]

Margaret Newcastle wrote letters as she wrote everything else, with complete spontaneity and forthrightness. 'In your last letter,' she says, 'you desired me to write some letters of complement as also some panegyricks, but I must entreat you to excuse me for my style in writing is too plain and simple for such courtly works; besides, give me leave to inform you, that I am a servant of truth and not of flattery . . . my mistress Truth, hath no need of such adornings, neither doth she give many words and seldom any praise . . . yet, howsoever, I being bred in her service from my youth, will never quit her till death takes me away.' This was the clear and vigorous sort of language through which reality might well shine.

An excellent example of characterization ironically incised against a contrasted background is to be found in the Duchess's description of the lady who has newly embraced Puritanism:

Yesterday Mrs P.I. was to visit me, who prayed me to present her humble service to you, but since you saw her she is become an altered woman, as being a sanctified soul, a spiritual sister, she hath left curling her hair, black patches are become an abomination to her, laced shoes and galoshes are steps to pride, to go bare-necked she accounts worse than adultery; fans, ribbons, pendants, necklaces, and the like, are the temptations of Satan, and the signs of damnation; and she is not only transformed in her dress, but her garb and speech, and all her discourse, insomuch as you would not know her if you saw her, unless you were informed who she was; she speaks of nothing but of Heaven and purification, and after some discourse, she asked me what posture I thought was the best to be used in prayer? I said I thought no posture was more becoming, nor did fit devotion better, than kneeling . . . for the scripture says from earth we came, and to earth we shall return; then she spoke of prayers, for she is all for extemporary prayers, I told her, that the more words we used in prayer, the worse they were accepted, for I thought a silent adoration was better accepted of God than a self-conceited babbling . . . with that she lifted up her eyes, and departed from me, believing I was one of the wicked and reprobate, not capable of a saving grace, so as I believe she will not come near me again, lest her purity should be defiled in my company, I believe the next news we shall hear of her will be that she is become a preaching sister.

Then there is her notable description of Sir N.G. who, in an effort to preserve his health, travels endlessly from place to place:

He stayes not anywhere for he is like a shadow, or a ghost, when you think it is so near as to speak to it, it straight appears afar off, or Vanishes away; and he is not onely in this City, but in every town, for he rides from town to town, as birds flie from tree to tree, and his onely business is for divertisement for health, so that his life is as if it rid Post; but let him ride from Death as far as he can, and do what he can to shun it, yet Death will meet him at his journeys end, and there arrest him and imprison his body in a grave, for Time hath laid an action of battery against him, and hath now three score and fifteen years summoned him to appear, but as yet he keeps out of sight, and will as long as he can, as we may perceive by his riding, and short stay in every place he comes to.

That there were Parnelas and Mr B.s within the knowledge of the Duchess is well seen in the following passage:

I am sorry Sir F.C. hath undervalued himself so much below his birth and wealth, as to marry his kitchen-maid, but it was a sign he had an hungry, or that he lived a solitary life, seeing no better company, or conversed not with women of quality; or else he had been too privately kind, and was loth to have it too publickly known; or he hath tried her virtue, and so married her for chastity . . . or else he married her for beauty, or wit, or both . . . But perchance Sir F.C. married his kitchen-maid in hopes she would make a nimble, and obedient which he might fear, one of equal birth might not be . . . Yet I write not this as believing he may not be happy in his choice, for 'tis likely the match may be more happy than honourable, and if he thinks it no disgrace, or cares not for disgrace, all is well for it only concerns himself, as having no parents living to grieve or anger, nor no former children to suffer by.

Of her many descriptions of living scenes, one must suffice —
her account of a winter city:

> If you were here in this city, now all the ground of the
> streets is covered with snow, you would see the young men
> and their mistresses ride in sleds by torch-light, the women
> and the men dressed antickly, as also their horses that draw
> their sleds and then every sled having a fair lady, at least to
> her lover's thinking, sitting at one end of the sled, dressed
> with feathers and rich clothes, and her courting servant like
> a coachman, or rather a carter, bravely accoutred, driving
> the horses with a whip, which draw the sled upon the snow
> with a galloping pace, whilst footmen run with torches to
> light them. But many of these lovers, not using to drive
> horses so often as to court mistresses, for want of skill over-
> turn the sled, and so tumble down their mistresses in the
> snow, whereupon they being in a frightened hast, take them
> up from that cold bed, and then the mistress appears like a
> pale ghost, or dead body in a winding sheet, being all
> covered with white snow; and the sled, when the mistress is
> seated again, instead of a triumphant chair, seems like a
> virgin's funeral herse, carried, and buried by torch-light;
> and her feathers seem like a silver crown, that usually is laid
> thereon, also the sled is drawn then in a slow, funeral pace,
> for fear of a second fall. By this custom and practice you
> may know, we have here recreations for every season of the
> year, and as the old saying is, that pride in winter is never
> cold, so it may be said, that love in winter is never cold;
> indeed, I have heard say, that love is hot, and to my
> apprehension it must be a very hot amorous love that is not
> cold this weather. But leaving the hot lovers in the cold
> snow, I rest by the fire-side, Madam.

> Your very faithful friend and servant.

Nor was the Duchess at a loss when words were needed to
express what was in her heart. There are her letters to that fourth
sister who was married to Sir Edmund Pye:

> Dear Sister Pye, — Distance of place, nor length of time
> cannot lessen my natural, or rather supernatural affection to
> you; for certainly my love for you is more than a sister's
> love, nay, such a love, as when I lived with you, it could not
> choose but be somewhat troublesome, by reason my love
> was accompanied with such fears, as it would neither let
> you rest, pray, nor eat in quiet. For though it was a watchful
> love, yet it was a fearful love, for I remember I have

oftentimes waked you out of your sleep, when you did sleep quietly, with soft breathing, fearing you had been dead; but oftener have I laid my face over your mouth, to feel if you breathed, insomuch as I have kept my self waking, to watch your sleeps, and as troublesome as I was to you concerning your feeding, as I was in your sleeping, for I was afraid that that which was to nourish you, should kill you. And I remember, I was so doubtful of every meat you did eat, as you were used to tell me, I was Sancapancha's doctor; neither could I let you pray in quiet, for I have often knocked at your closet door, when I thought you were longer at your prayers than usual, or at least, I did think the time longer; so as I could not forbear to ask you how you did, and whether you were well, and many the like impertinences which my extraordinary love troubled you with; and of which you are now quit, living so far asunder . . .

And again:

In your last letter you chid me for loving too earnestly, saying extreme love did consume my body and torment my mind, and that whosoever love to a high degree are fools; if so, Madam, I am as much a fool as ever Nature made for where I set my love, it is fixed like eternity, and is as full as infinite. My love is not fixed suddenly, for it takes experience and consideration to help to place it, both which have been my guides and directors to love you, which makes me love you much, and shall make me love you long, if souls die not.

Lyly had used letters in his *Ephues* (1579-1580) to indicate the mood of a character or to advance the plot. With the publication of the *Portuguese Letters* (1669) a new estimate of letters as an artistic medium dawned upon Europe. The earliest English version was that of Sir Roger L'Estrange, *Five Love Letters from a Nun to a Cavalier* (December 28,1677). For long these letters were supposed to be authentic. Now modern critics are inclined to ascribe them to Guilleraques, who claimed merely to have translated them. Be that as it may; we are concerned solely with the impetus which the *Portuguese Letters* gave to the growth of the epistolary form. The story is simple: During the reign of Louis XIV, France gave some desultory aid to Portugal against Spain. French volunteers went under arms to the Peninsula, and amongst their number was Noel Bouton, afterwards Marquis of Chamilly and St Leger. In the course of the intermittent campaign he became friendly with a young officer who belonged to an old and influential family of Beja in the province of Alemtejo. This officer had a sister who was a nun in the convent of Beja, and on one fatal day he went to visit her accompanied by his friend Chamilly. Mariana Alcoforado was entrusted to the convent when she was a child. She was professed at the age of sixteen. She was twenty-five when she saw and loved Chamilly—a young man of little intelligence and no scruples. Although Mariana is careful not to blame him for more than his share, his character is clearly to be read between the lines. He stands revealed a slight philanderer, a poor fool playing with a diamond as if it were a worthless piece of glass. One can almost regard compassion with the stupidity of this courtly dolt who meant to kindle a little blaze, only to find himself involved in a volcanic eruption. Well might she say 'You are more to be pitied than I.' Chamilly returned hastily to France, where he rose later to the highest dignity. St Simon tells us he was the best man in the world, the bravest and the most honourable, but he adds that no one after seeing him or hearing him speak could understand how he had inspired such an unmeasured love. Mariana lived to be eighty-three years. 'For thirty years she did rigid penance and suffered great infirmities with much conformity, desiring to have more to suffer.' So runs a statement supposed to have been signed by the scrivener of the convent.

Indeed, it is not easy to describe the *Portuguese Letters*. They are the outpourings of a mind bent upon self-torture, preying forever upon every detail of her fatal mistake and of her present position. She knows now too well her lover's unworthiness, and yet she cannot escape from the maze in which she is lost. She alternates between remorse, remonstrance, hopeless love, terrible longing, and a consciousness that she has within her something beyond man's contempt. She does not allow emotion to dull her moral sense. Truth is in her hand a merciless blade which she plunges into her bosom, with which she cuts out her heart and dissects it under our eyes. There is no self-pity. There is in the letters every possible fluctuation of mind and feeling:

> I conjure you to tell me why you set your heart on fas-
> cinating me as you did, when you knew very well that you
> were going to desert me? And why have you been so
> pitiless in making me wretched? Why did you not leave me

in peace in this cloister ? Had I done you any injury ? But forgive me, I impute nothing to you. I am in no state to think of revenge, and I only accuse the harshness of my fate. In separating us it seems to have done all the harm we could have feared. But our hearts can not be separated; love, which is more powerful than destiny, has united them for our whole life. If you take any interest in mine, write to me often . . . Above all, come to see me. Farewell, I cannot leave this paper; it will fall into your hands; would that I might have the same happiness. Alas! how insane I am! I see that this is not possible. Farewell! can write no more. Farewell, love me always, and make me suffer still more misery.

And then:

I realize that I deceived myself when I thought that you would act in better faith than is usual, because the excess of my love seemed to lift me above any kind of suspicion and to deserve more fidelity than is ordinarily to be met with. But the desire you have to betray me overmasters the justice you owe to all I have done for you . . . Ought I not to have foreseen that my happiness would come to an end, rather than my love? . . . You are more to be pitied than I. It is better to suffer all that I suffer, than to enjoy the languid pleasures that the women of France may give you. I do not envy your indifference and I pity you . . .

At least, remember me. I could content myself with your remembrance, but I dare not be sure of it. I did not limit my hopes to your remembrance when I saw you every day . . .

How much suffering you would have spared me if your conduct had been as indifferent the first few days I saw you as it has seemed to me lately, but who would not have been deceived . . . by such devotion, and who would not have thought it sincere? How hard it is to bring oneself to suspect the sincerity of those one loves! I see plainly that the least excuse is enough for you; and without your taking the trouble to make any, my love serves you so faithfully that I can only consent to find you guilty in order to enjoy the keen pleasure of justifying you myself . . . You were not blinded like me, why then did you let me fall into the state I am in? What did you want of all my ardent demonstrations which could only be importunate to you? You knew very well that you would not remain in Portugal; and why did you choose me here to make me so unhappy? You could certainly have found in this country some more beautiful woman, with whom you might have had as much pleasure since you were only in search of that; who would have loved you faithfully as long as you were in sight; whom time

would have consoled for your absence, and whom you might
have left without perfidy and cruelty. Such conduct is much
more that of a tyrant bent upon persecuting than of a lover
whose only thought is to please. Alas! why are you so pitiless
with a heart that is all your own? . . . What have I done to
be so unhappy, and why have you poisoned my life? . . .

What should I do alas! without all this hatred and all this
love which fill my heart?

But, though torn yet by her emotions, she is increasingly conscious of deep remorse:

I lived for a long time in an abandonment and idolatry
which fill me with horror now, and my remorse pursues me
without pity . . . I know very well that I am still somewhat
too concerned with my reproaches and your infidelity; but
remember that I have promised myself a more peaceful
state and that I will attain to it, or else that I shall take some
extreme measure against myself, which you will hear
without great distress. But I ask nothing more from you.
How foolish I am to repeat the same things so often! I must
leave you and think no more about you; perhaps even I
shall not write to you again. Am I obliged to give you an
exact account of all my varied emotions?

Gosse has said:

The extraordinary and at times the unique merit of the
Portuguese nun, as a letter writer, lies in the fact that, in the
full tempest and turmoil of her passion, she never yields to
the temptation of giving herself up to rhetoric, or rather that
whenever she does make a momentary concession to this
habit of her age, she doubles upon herself immediately and
is the first to deprecate such false flowers of speech.[3]

Coming in the age of French rhetorical extravagances, and
English stilted circumlocutions, the *Portuguese Letters* were at
once accepted as models of passionate sincerity. L'Estrange's
translation continued to be reprinted for fifty years, and
innumerable imitations poured from the printing presses. Most
of these were of no intrinsic value, but they were of importance
in that they showed an effort to express emotions and ideas in a
vivid and spontaneous manner.

Something of the strength, sincerity and despair of the
Portuguese Letters are echoed in Aphra Behn's *Love-Letters to a
Gentleman*. These documents, eight in number, were originally

251

published in the 1696 edition of the collected *Histories and Novels* and in subsequent editions form part of the introductory *Life and Memoirs*. They are supposed to be authentic, and have, indeed, all the signs of authenticity. To whom were they addressed? One cannot say with any definiteness. During Aphra Belm's lifetime it was usual to ascribe to her a vast number of lovers, and after ages accepted the legend enthusiastically, and even added to the multiplicity. Nevertheless, only one man is definitely known to have been her lover: John Hoyle, a lawyer of Grey's Inn and the Inner Temple. In Tom Brown's Letters *of Love and Gallants* there is a letter from Aphra Behn to Hoyle, remonstrating with him on his depraved way of life, and asking him in the name of 'Our past endearments' to clear himself, if possible, of the allegations made against him. This is not the letter of a woman in love, but of a kindly friend, so that if Hoyle was the object of Mrs Behn's *Love Letters to a Gentleman,* these must have been written at an earlier stage, before Hoyle stood branded as 'an athiest, a sodomite professed, a corrupter of youth and a blasphemer of Christ.' One thing at least is certain, that Aphra loved in vain, and that she suffered all the miseries of uncertainty, hope and longing. These letters do not attempt to tell a connected story, but they do record vividly and poignantly the emotions which agitate this woman's heart. They bear in every line the impress of the writer and of the mood, and even of the atmosphere in which they were written. They alternately plead and remonstrate. Some are written in a breathless hurry; some with all the weariness of a heavy heart:

> Though it be very late, I cannot go to Bed, but I must tell you I have been very good ever since I saw thee, and have been a writing, and have seen no Face of Man, or other Body, save my own People. I am mightily pleased with your kindness to me tonight, and 'twas I hope and believe very innocent and undisturbing on both Sides . . . If thou hast Love (as I shall never doubt, if thou art always as to-night) shew that Love I beseech thee; there being nothing so grateful to God, and Mankind, as Plain-dealing. Tis too late to conjure thee further: I will be purchased with Softness, and dear Words, and kind Expressions, Sweet Eyes and a Low voice.

Clearly, at this stage, Aphra's lover had sufficient interest in her company to make him appear all she believed. She expresses her sense of security in intimate little references to their friends and to places they have visited together:

> I stay'd after thee to-night, till I had read a whole Act of my new Play, and then he led me over all the Way, saying, Gad, you were the Man: and beginning some rallying Love Discourse after Supper, which he fancy'd was not so well received as it ought, he said you were not handsome, and called Philly to own it; but he did not, but was of my side, and said you were handsome; so he went on a While and all ended that concerned you. And this, upon my Word, is all.

But she cannot long deceive herself as to his attitude. Very well, then! If need be she will tear up her passion by the roots, while it is still possible: 'I grow desperate fond of you and would be used well; if not, I will march off. But I will believe you mean to keep your Word, as I will for ever do mine.' She tells him truly that her nature is proud and cannot bear his slights. But she does bear them, because she cannot help herself:

> For God's sake, make no more Niceties and Scruples than need, in your way of living with me: that is, do not make me believe this distance is to ease you, when indeed 'tis meant to ease us both of love . . . How could anything but the Man that hates me, entertain me so unkindly? Witness your excellent Opinion of me, of loving others; witness your passing by the End of the Street where I live and squandering away your time at any Coffee-house, rather than allow me what you know in your soul is the greatest Blessing of my Life. Your dear, dull, melancholy Company. I call it dull, because you can never be gay or merry where Astrea is.

And then, the end. He is not only unfaithful but he has the cruelty to tell her so, possibly with the desire to break with her completely:

> You left me to torments. You went to love, alone, and left me to love and rage, fevers and calentures, even madness itself. Indeed, indeed, my soul. I know not to what degree I love you; let it suffice I do most passionately, and can have no thought of any other man whilst I have life. No! Reproach me, defame me, lampoon me, curse me and kill me when I do. Farewell, I love you more and more every moment of my life. Know it and goodnight.

> Astrea.

Very different in type are Mrs Behn's *Love-Letters between a Nobleman and his Sister* (1683). These libellous effusions are based on a notorious scandal which had attracted great attention in England a short time previously. Lord Grey of Werk eloped with his sister-in-law, Lady Henrietta Berkeley. He was brought to trial on a charge of conspiracy on 23rd November, 1682. He appeared in court accompanied by his mistress and many of the powerful Whig lords. He was found guilty. Mrs Behn's 'fictitious gallimawfry'[4] is chiefly in verse. The key is given in preface. Lord Grey is Philander, Silvia is Lady Henrietta, and the Duke of Monmouth is Cesario. The *Letters* are merely romantic fustian, bristling with rodomontade. Nevertheless, the story is carried on partly in the letters, but principally by the postscripts, which are in prose. There are some prose letters also, which are important to the narrative.

Two notable letters in prose are from Cesario to the Count of _____, and from Melinda (Silvia's maid) to Philander. Melinda (who is in the lover's pay) describes very well how the wife discovers her sister writing a love letter to the husband. The wife suspects nothing, and jokingly insists on seeing it. Silvia passes it off by pretending that it is from the maid to her lover, Alexis, under the names of Silvia and Philander.

> To-day many ominous things have happened. Madam the Countess had like to have taken a letter writ to your Lordship to-day; for the Duchess —— of coming to pay her a visit, came on a sudden with her into my Lady's Apartment, and surprised her writing in her Dressing Room, hardly giving her time to slip the paper into her Comb-box. The first ceremonies being over, as Madam the Duchess does not use much, she began to commend my Lady's Dressing-Plate, and taking up the Box, and looking into it, saw the Letter, and laughing, cry'd, oh, have I found you making Love! At which my Lady, with an infinite Confusion, would have retrieved it but the Dutchess, still keeping her hold, cry'd—Nay, I'm resolved I'll see in what manner you write to a Lover, and whether your Heart is tender or cruel; at which she began to read aloud. My Lady blushed, and changed Colour a hundred times in a Minute; I almost died with fear; Madam the Countess in infinite Amazement; my Lady interrupting every word read by the Dutchess by Intreaties and Prayers, which served to heighten her Curiosity, being airy and young, regarded not the indecency to which she preferred her Curiosity; who laughing cry'd,

she was resolved to read it out, and find the Constitution of her Heart; when my Lady, whose Wit never fail'd her, cry'd, I beg you, Madam, let us have so much Complaisance for Melinda to ask her Consent in this Affair, and then I shall be pleased that you should see what Love I can make upon occasion. I took the Hint, and cry'd with a real Confusion — I implore you, Madam, not to discover my weakness to Madame the Dutchess, I would not for the World be thought to love so passionately as your Ladyship, in favour of Alexis, has caused me to profess, under the name of Silvia and Philander. This gave my Lady Encouragement, who began to say a thousand pretty things of Alexis, Dorillus' son, and my Lover, as your Lordship knows, and who is indeed no inconsiderable Fortune, for a Maid, only by your Lordship's Bounty enriched. After this my Lady took the Letter, and all being resolved it should be read, she did it herself, and turned it so prettily into burlesque Love, by her way of reading it, that Madam the Dutchess laughed extreamly.

There is no need to describe the rest of the story. The wife becomes suspicious and sets spies to observe the lovers. She appeals in vain to Silvia, who after struggling with herself, yields to Philander. Finally all is discovered and they elope.

In 1686 appeared an anonymous love-story in Letters, *Love's Posy*.[5] This is 'A collection of seven and Twenty Love Letters, both in verse and prose; That lately pass'd betwixt a Gentleman and a-very young Lady in France.'

In *Letters written by Mrs Manley* (1696) all the letters are from Mrs Manley to John Hoyle. They recount continuously all the main events of a stage-coach journey to Exeter. The narrative is quite free from the romantic tradition. There is much humour and realism, and considerable power of presenting character by a few deft touches. There is not much story, but continuity is established by the fact that the same characters speak from day to day, and that the travellers develop acquaintance with each other under our eyes.

Mrs Manley's references to the inns imply some customs which would be peculiar if true. She says 'They unmercifully set us to Dinner at Ten-a-Clock upon a great Leg of Mutton 'Tis the Custom of these Dining Stages to prepare one Day Beef, and another our present fare! 'tis ready against the coach comes.' On the whole, however, she does not take any trouble with background. 'I need say nothing to you of Salisbury Cathedral: If in a

Foreign Country, as the Lady in her Letters of Spain, I could entertain you with a noble description: but you have ever seen, or may see it; and so I'll spare my Architecture.'[6]

Mrs Manley atones for her scanty backgrounds by her racy descriptions of the people she meets on her journey. There is the landlord who is 'a perfect Beaux,' the 'Mrs Mayoress 'who 'now she is acquainted, has all the low, disagreeable Familiarity of People of her Rank,' and the two unfortunates who are so deplorably plebeian that they never before travelled by stage-coach. These last Mrs Manley savagely describes as follows:

> The two other Fellow-Travellers were never so promoted before, and are much troubl'd their Journey is to last no longer, and wish the four Days four Months. I hope every Jolt will squash their Guts, and give 'em enough on't: But they are proof against any such Disasters, and hugely delighted with what they are pleased to call Riding in State. After this ridiculous Account, you need not doubt but I am thoroughly mortified.

Then there is her excellent description of the foppish young lordling, his egregious vanity, his cocksure advances, all of which she ignores. Finally, determined to win her attention, he insists on giving an account of one of his love affairs. Mrs Manley very cleverly characterizes him by the words she puts into his mouth. His story, and his manner of telling it give us a complete picture of this self-opinionated young jackanapes. Mrs Manley is a keen observer and her humour has sometimes a vitriolic touch, that same touch which afterwards burned its way through the pages of *The New Atalantis*. She thus presents some new arrivals at an inn:

> . . . Presently saw alight a tall blustering, big bon'd raw Thing, like an over-grown School-Boy, but conceited above anything. He had an Appurtenance call'd a Wife, whom he suffer'd to get out as well as she cou'd; as long as he had layn with her, he did not think her worth the civility of his Hand. She seemed a Giant of a Woman, but very fine, with a right Citt Air. He blustered presently for the best lodging.

There are also present in the party several young females, quite lacking in attractions and in poise. To one of these 'awkward things 'the beau transfers his attentions —' a Gold-smith's Daughter with a tolerable face.' Mrs Manley strikes up an intimacy with a Mrs Stanhope, who confides in her some of her adventures. At Bridport, where the party spends the night, a friend of the beau's arrives, and greatly adds to the general interest. By the time Mrs Manley arrives at Exeter, the beau has returned to his allegiance, and sends her three foppish letters. But she remains unmoved. 'I can now with cold indifference shake Hands with all Things beyond this Solitude . . . I repeat with Stoical Pride — keep me, ye Bounteous Gods, my Caves and Woods in Peace: let Tares and Acorns be my Food.'

These letters of Mrs Manley, afterwards published as *The Stage Coach Journey to Exeter* (1725), are not only vividly alive and completely real in the experiences they recount, but the bustle and hurry of the journey are well suggested in remarks which are, as it were, asides: 'Tis now past 11, and they'll call us by two. Good Night; I am going to try if I can drown in Sleep that which most sensibly affects me—the cruel Separation we have so lately suffered.' And: 'The Trouts are just brought upon the Table, which are the only good thing here; they look inviting, and won't stay for cooling Compliments.' And even: 'I forgot to leave Orders with the Jew about the Chocolate: Pray, take care that it be sent me and excuse this trouble.'

In 1696, the same year as *Letters of Mrs Manley*, appeared Antony Hamilton's *Zénéyde*. This was an unfinished tale in letter form, but it cannot be said to add much, if anything, to the epistolary method, since it consists of one single letter. It is by the interchange of letters, or by a succession of letters from one person that an epistolary story should develop. A story told in a single letter differs from an autobiographical narrative only in the superscription. Nevertheless, that Antony Hamilton should decide to embody his story in a letter was evidence of the growing preoccupation with letters as a narrative form. It is strange that the French did not fully develop this genre of writing, although they far surpassed the English as letter-writers, and were enraptured by Richardson's novels when they appeared.

In 1702 appeared a work which still further anticipated Richardson: *The Lover's Secretary, or, The Adventures of Lindamira*, by Tom Brown. In twenty-four letters[7] Brown told an amusing and well-connected story, with much realism in characterization and background. Lindamira, a young lady of quality, gay but good, writes to her friend Indamora, who lives in the country, confiding in her all her love-affairs. Lindamira steers a safe course through the beaux and fops. She enjoys billets-doux as she enjoys visiting the playhouse, and she has a sound respect for her mother's advice. The last letter shows her at the end of her adventures and her trials, happily married to the faithful Cleomidon.

Early in the eighteenth century there appeared in the *Tatler* and *Spectator* short stories, romantic or domestic, either in one letter or in a series of letters. The story of Amanda *(Spectator,* no. 375, May 10, 1712) has been suggested as the original of Richardson's *Pamela,* although indeed, as we have seen, for example, in the Duchess of Newcastle's Letters, and shall see in Mrs Rowe's *Letters Moral and Entertaining* the story of *Pamela* was a commonplace, and it was Richardson's treatment which made it a masterpiece.

Perhaps another proof of the great popularity of letters, even in the beginning of the eighteenth century was the modernized version of Lyly's *Euphues* which appeared in 1718. under the title of *The False Friend and the Inconstant Mistress: an instructive Novel . . . displaying the artifices of the female sex in their Amours.* This book made its appearance not very long before *Pamela,* and it is cogent to observe that whereas in the text of the original *Euphues,* the interpolated letters appeared merely incidental, in the abbreviated version, these letters, all of which were retained, appeared very conspicuous in relation to the shrunken context. Jusserand observed that the table of contents in this modernized *Euphues* was quite Richardsonian. 'Here we find enumerated the many wise recommendations by which Lyly so long anticipated Richardson and Rousseau.'[8]

Mrs Haywood was in the main stream of this epistolary tendency. Her *Letters from a Lady of Quality to a Chevalier* (1724) were merely a loose translation of Edmé Boursault's *Lettres Nouvelles . . . avec Treize Lettres Amoureuses d'une Dame à un Cavalier.*[9] They tell a hackneyed story in the flamboyant style of gallantry, but as they did not originate with Mrs Haywood, they cannot be considered here. Far superior, in any case, is Mrs Haywood's own work: *Love-Letters on all occasions lately passed between Persons of Distinction* (1730). In letters XIII to XXXVI there is the story of Theano and Elismonda. The tale develops through the interchange of letters between the pair. In the first letter Theano, who has obtained 'the last favour,' reproaches Elismonda with her indifferent looks on the following day. Elismonda in reply states that her apparent coldness was due to her subsequent shame. To which explanation she adds this astounding remark: 'The Manner of my yielding admits of no Excuse, and leaves not the least Room to hope I can maintain any place in a Heart filled only with the most noble and refined Ideas.' Theano magnanimously forgives her for yielding to him, and has the noble and refined idea of visiting her that same evening. All goes well for a time, but soon the inevitable serpent raises a hissing head in this Eden. Armida, the friend with whom Elismonda lives, becomes jealous of her happiness and refuses to allow Theano's visits. 'In spite of the Secret which a reasonable Person would imagine must put her infinitely more in my power, than I can possibly be in hers, [she] has given me some Hints, that if I continue any Correspondence with you, she will expose me to the utmost censures of the ill-judging World.' Elismonda fears that, through seeing her seldom, Theano may grow indifferent to her. Theano replies reassuringly. Even the most venomous serpents cannot always remain poised to strike. Armida, 'the curst enemy,' will be away from home tomorrow, so Elismonda can meet Theano. But she fails to keep this appointment, because when the time came for the false Armida to set out on her expedition, she 'fell into a Spleen, fancy'd herself sick, undrest and went to Bed.' Elismonda fears Theano must have been very disappointed, but her apologies soon turn to furious recriminations when she hears that Theano also failed to keep the appointment. She now sees her sin, and leaves her avengement to Heaven. Theano, however, has a perfectly good excuse, and Elismonda decides that, after all, she is not a sinner, but a great romantic. Other obstacles now present themselves, and Elismonda fluctuates between ecstasy and despair, until at last the pair are reunited.

Despite the high-flown language, the story is vividly told. We feel impatience at the delays and the hindrances which beset the lovers, and this suspense is well maintained. The events are easily credible; in fact, they are commonplace, but their effect is out of all proportion to their importance. This is quite in keeping with the psychology of lovers. Mrs Haywood knows the Richardsonian trick of taking emotions and happenings at their very moment: 'I saw you but last Night . . . yet do I find already that I have utter'd but half the meanings of my soul . . . another soft adieu, but 't'will not be allowed; the Coach is ready, my Friends wait for me . . . and I but take its moment to remind you of your vows.' When Theano is called out of town we see how every stage of the journey increases Elismonda's fears, suspicions and anxieties. So it is with his return. He writes from every post-town, and as his haste swallows the miles which separate them, there is a convincing crescendo of excitement and emotion.[10]

It remains to consider the letters of Mrs Elizabeth Rowe in relation to the development of the epistolary form of novel-writing. *Friendship in Death, in twenty letters from the Dead to the Living* (1728) is nothing to our purpose. These are single letters on dreary subjects. They do not tell a story. Their didactic and pietistic intention is stated in the preface: 'The Drift of these Letters is, to impress the Notion of the Soul's Immortality; without which, all Virtue and Religion, with their temporal and eternal good consequences, must fall to the Ground.' *Letters Moral and Entertaining* (1729-1733) are equally bombastic and sententious. They are of import only in their bearing on the epistolary novel. These effusions are merely dressed-up tracts, and their morality is entirely prudential and self-conscious. It is, in fact, the morality of Richardson's novels. Some of these letters are mere sermonizing; some contain stories. Sometimes there is a sequence of letters on the same subject; sometimes a single letter is complete in itself. There are a number of single letters containing stories, as, for example, those describing an unhappy amour, a murder, and the love of Bellamour for Almeda. In some cases letters in the first part have a sequel in the second part of the volume. Mrs Rowe is occasionally willing to enliven her preaching with the art of the *novella,* and again her tracts sometimes take a pastoral turn, as in the three letters at the beginning of part two, *To Lady Sophia, from Rosalinda, relating the true occasion of her flying from France, and leaving her father's house in the disguise of a country girl* (with a sequel in the next part of the book).

Rosalinda, a staunch Protestant like her mother, flees the persecutions of her Papist father, who not only restricts her religious exercises but has, with the utmost villainy, arranged a splendid marriage for her with a French Catholic, Count Altomont. Aided by her mother, she runs away, and takes service in a Protestant household so purely religious that not only does the mistress give plentiful alms to the poor, but her children 'to mimick their mother gave away all the little treasure they had in their pockets to the beggars' children, and then fell acrying because she would not suffer them to pull off their own shoes and stockings, to give to some that were barebooted.' The master is so honest that he pays his servants every day. He is a farmer, but it would be mere vulgarity to assume that there were any pigs to be fed, cows to be milked, or potatoes to be dug on his land. 'A more agreeable situation cannot be imagined, nor a greater variety of Sylvan Scenes. The wide landscape round is all my Master's property; his snowy Flocks are ranging on the Hills, his grazing Herds lowing through the plains, the Mountains are crowned with the great Creator's Bounty and the Valleys made vocal with his Praises.' Rosalinda's unctuous humility rivals even that of Pamela. Pamela revelled in the proud dignity of being a servant; Rosalinda goes one better by glorying in 'my splendid distinction of being a head servant.' It was indeed a splendid distinction. No field work, no dairy work, even no house work sullies the lily-white fingers of this remarkable domestic, who spends her time rapt in high-souled ecstasies. 'But I am not always in the sublime. I sometimes descend to gather Cowslips and Daisies or pursue some gaudy Butterfly with my pretty Companions.' How heartily we believe her when she says 'I am as fine as any Shepherdess in an Opera!' We need scarcely record that, before long, a gentle youth sighs for her, and to him we consign her with a breath of relief.

Looking backwards at the writers who experimented with letters as a means of sketching character or telling a story, we observe with particular interest the women's contribution. We have seen that in her use of letters the Duchess of Newcastle anticipated Richardson. We have seen that Aphra Behn's *Love Letters to a Gentleman* gave sincere and vivid expression to varying emotions and moods. In *Love-Letters between a Nobleman and his Sister* she made a further advance in the use of the epistolary form. This is most evident in the scene where Silvia's maid, Melinda, pretends that she herself is the writer of Silvia's love-letter to Philander. As the quoted extract shows, this episode is described in the liveliest and most spontaneous manner. The dramatic quality, the interplay of wits, the suggestion of background and the urgency of the events narrated certainly anticipate Richardson's manner, and though the greater part of the book is in verse, the story does advance through the prose letters and postscripts. It is far from Richardson's use of letters, but it certainly points that way.

In the anonymous *Love's Posy* the story is carried on from letter to letter, but again the interpolation of verse constitutes an essential difference from Richardson's form. Nevertheless, *Love's Posy*,[11] like *Love-Letters between a Nobleman and his sister*, does lead towards the Richardsonian technique.

In *Letters written by Mrs Manley* the use of verse is eliminated and the epistolary form approximates to Richardson's use of it. In her use of letters, in her detailed realism, in the vivid delineation of scenes, Mrs Manley definitely anticipated Richardson. Her use of the road and its incidents suggests somewhat the attitude of Fielding.

There is no doubt that in *Love-Letters on all occasions* (1730), and particularly in the story of Theano and Elismonda, Mrs Haywood also shadowed forth Richardson's epistolary method of presenting the fluctuations of emotion and sentiment.

Mrs Rowe's significance as a forerunner of Richardson cannot be overlooked. Intrinsically her stories deserve no commendation: her characterization is of the most stereotyped; her backgrounds even when detailed are wooden; her moral standards are distasteful; her works are all devoid of the faintest ray of humour. In *Urania* there was a certain incongruity when the heroine entered a cave and found a love sonnet, but what are we to say to a hero who enters a house and finds a harpsichord, hymns and anthems, two atlases and a pair of globes? Despite all this, and not for the reasons that her own generation eulogized her, she is worth mentioning because she really did tell stories, not only in single letters, but in sequences of letters. And it was not only thus that she anticipated Richardson. She anticipated also his canting and self-interested morality and that sensibility which, whether gallant or righteous, had been steadily growing for a long time, and which the *Portuguese Letters* and later the powerful influence of Marivaux brought into prominence before Richardson took up his pen. These are the two tendencies of thought and the single tendency of form which went towards the evolution of *Pamela*. It is clear that women writers of fiction played their part in preparing the raw materials which Richardson excellently fashioned— so excellently, indeed, that his work was hailed as the first modern novel.

Notes and References

1 1603 is the earliest dated edition, but possibly this was not the first edition.
2 J. J. Jusserand, *The English Novel in the Time of Shakespeare* (1890), p. 378.
3 Sir E. Gosse, 'A Nun's Love Letters,' *Fortnightly Review*, no. 43 (1888), p. 514.
4 So Horace Walpole calls it in his *Royal and Ancient Authors*, iv, p. 4.
5 British Museum, no. 10910, aa. 22. Printed for J. Hindmarsh, p. 120.
6 Mrs Manley had in mind Mme La Mothe's: *The Ingenious and Diverting Letters of the Lady—Travels into Spain describing the Devotions, Mummeries, Humours, Customs, Laws, Militia, Trade, Diet and Recreations of that People, Intermixt with Great Variety of Modern Adventures and surprising Accidents.'* The second edition of this translation was in 1692. Detailed treatment of Mme La Mothe's book does not lie within our scope, since she belongs to French literature. There is no doubt whatever that she was a very important contributor to the development of the epistolary novel. The letters give a detailed description of all the towns on the route, the inns at which she stayed, the people she encountered on the way. Often there are inset stories (of the *novella* type) which are recounted to the lady by those whose plight seems to need self-explanation. Especially well told is the second story, the story of the Hermit, and the story of the haunted castle at Nios. The fault in Mme La Mothe's *Travels into Spain* is that nothing really happens to the lady herself, and that her journey is not much more than a convenient thread with which she strings her stories and anecdotes together. Her descriptions of scenery are a mere tabulation of facts; she mentions objects of interest with the assiduity of a Baedeker. In fact, this work is a kind of Heptameron-cum-guide book. *Travels into Spain* was extremely popular in England, the translation reaching its tenth edition in 1735.
7 228 duodecimo pages.
8 J. J. Jusserand. *The English Novel in the Time of Shakespeare* (1890), p. 141.
9 Second edition, Paris, 1699.
10 G. F. Wicher thinks otherwise. Speaking of the letters of Theano and Elismonda he says, 'in the course of the whole correspondence nothing more momentous happens than the lover's leaving town. Indeed, so imperceptible is the narrative element in Mrs Haywood's epistolary sequences that they can claim no share with the anonymous love story in letters entitled Love's Posy (1686), *Letters written by Mrs Manley* (1696) and *Adventures of Lindamira* (1702) . . . [in] the honour of having anticipated Richardson's method of telling a story in epistolary form.' But does anything momentous happen in *Letters written by Mrs Manley*? On the contrary, there is a far slighter and looser plot in Mrs Manley's Letters, if indeed the motif of journeying can be called a plot at all. Wicher also stresses the fact that Mrs Haywood never followed up the attempt she had made at epistolary narrative in Elismonda and Theano. What of it? Mrs Manley never

followed up her *Letters,* and Wicher does not consider that this lessened her claim as an anticipator of Richardson's use of the epistolary form. See G. F. Wicher: *Life and Romances of Mrs Haywood* (Columbia University Press, 1915), p. 11, footnote 18.

11 Mentioned here with the female contributors because there is the possibility that the writer was a woman.

Lucy Hutchinson (1620 ? - post 1675)
Hulton Deutsch Collection, London

Mary Robinson (1758 - 1800)
Hulton Deutsch Collection, London

Mary Wollstonecraft (1759 - 1797)
Hulton Deutsch Collection, London

Maria Edgeworth (1768 - 1849)
National Portrait Gallery, London

Frances Sheridan (1724 - 1766)
Hulton Deutsch Collection, London

Charlotte Smith (1749 - 1806)
Hulton Deutsch Collection, London

Fanny Burney (1752 - 1840)
National Portrait Gallery, London

Margaret Cavendish, Duchess of Newcastle (1623 - 1673)
Hulton Deutsch Collection, London

Anne, Lady Fanshawe (1625 - 1680)
Valence House Museum, Dagenham

Aphra Behn (c. 1640 - 1689)
Hulton Deutsch Collection, London

Jane Austen (1775 - 1817)
National Portrait Gallery, London

Mary Wollstonecraft Shelley(1797 - 1851)
National Portrait Gallery, London

VOLUME TWO

The Female Pen:
The Later Women Novelists
1744–1818

Foreword

This book is the second part of a work which was originally intended to be published in one volume entitled *The Female Pen*. The reader who has delved in English literature of the seventeenth and eighteenth centuries will not question the appositeness of the name, since he will recall that such was the term by which a woman writer was designated. The exigencies of war-time made publication in a single volume impossible. In 1944 appeared the first volume under the title: *Women Writers, their Contribution to the English Novel, 1621–1744.* Later impressions of this volume have the sub-title: *The Female Pen* — a sub-title which may now be taken to indicate both volumes.

I wish gratefully to acknowledge my indebtedness to Dr E.J. Thomas of Cambridge not merely for his generous advice and valuable criticism during the preparation of *The Female Pen*, but also for his faith and encouragement during long years of friendship. I am very much obliged to the Editor of the *Dublin Magazine* for his kind permission to include in this volume some pages (on the Irish Regional Novel and Maria Edgeworth), which had already appeared in the *Dublin Magazine*.

I desire also to express my gratitude to the Senate of the National University of Ireland for the grant made towards the cost of publishing this work.

B.G. MacCarthy

Chapter IX

The Oriental Novel

To Persia and Arabia and all the gorgeous East
I owed a pilgrimage for the sake of their magic tales.

(Nathaniel Hawthorne)

From France had come the classicism which closed like a vice on literary England during the eighteenth century. From France, cramped by its own restrictions, came a way of escape. It was not a full release; the prisoner did not throw off his fetters, leave his narrow cell, expand his lungs with fresh air, gaze his fill at the sky, and mingle with the common people. No, he found freedom in imagination, wild, colourful, romantic, fantastic, impossible, as far from reality as might be, yet satisfying. A magic carpet plied from the gorgeous East to fairyland. France turned from Boileau to Ali Baba and Mother Goose.

This dawning of Romanticism in France came from the East, and the first finger of light was seen in 1684, when Marana published his *L'Espion turc*. This was merely a pseudo-Oriental translation in letter form, wherein a disguised Oriental observes European society and politics, and comments thereon from an Eastern point of view. But the sun arose in all its splendour with Galland's translation: *Les mille et une Nuits, Contes Arabes*.[1] Thereafter the Oriental novel took its place among the recognized genres of French fiction. The reading public demanded more and more of these astonishing tales, and there at once appeared the translations by Pétis de la Croix: *L'histoire de la Sultane de Perse et des Vizirs, Contes turcs* (1707); and *Les mille et un Jours, Contes persans* (1710–1712). Galland and Pétis de la Croix had been to the East, and knew Oriental languages. Their translations were authentic, if bare. But soon many pseudo-translators tried their hand at

Eastern tales, the most facile and prolific being Thomas Simon Gueullette.[2] Thenceforward four main streams are observable in the flood of Oriental fiction which flowed from French pens, i.e. imaginative, moralistic, philosophic, and satiric.[3]

The English movement in Oriental fiction echoed the French movement, with certain notable variations, due, no doubt, to differing national characteristics. Galland's *Mille et une Nuits* was translated into English between 1704 and 1712, and it took even the most conservative English writers by storm. Johnson, Addison and Steele were enthusiastic, and their experiments gave to this new genre the necessary prestige. Whether they would have given the *Arabian Nights* so hearty a welcome if it had not come via France, is a question. Because, after all, this was not the first Oriental invasion of England, and previous borrowings, although they produced notable results, had never led to a literary movement.

Oriental influences in England go as far back as the eleventh century. We find descriptions of the wonders of India in Anglo-Saxon translations of legends concerning Alexander the Great. During the Middle Ages merchant-travellers like Marco Polo, missionaries, pilgrims and crusaders established a link with the East, and many Oriental tales came to England in this way, or else indirectly by way of Syria, Byzantium, Italy and Spain. In addition four great collections of Oriental tales were translated into Latin, the lingua franca of Europe: *Sendebar; Kalila and Dimna, or the Fables of Bidpai; Disciplina Clericalis; and Barlaam and Josaphat.* These influences produced in England such works as the fabliau of *Dame Sirez, The Proces of the Sevyn Sages*, Mandeville's *Voiage*, and Chaucer's *Squire's Tale*. In the sixteenth century, which was characterized by its eagerness for translations, there appeared the first English edition of the *Gesta Romanorum*, and the *Fables of Bidpai*. The earliest English translation of the Fables was entitled: *The Moral Philosophie of Doni . . . englished out of the Italian, by Thomas North* (1570). Other factors contributed towards intercourse with and interest in the Orient, e.g. Elizabethan voyages, the fall of Constantinople (1453), and the westward incursions of the Turks. In Painter's *Palace of Pleasure* we find several Oriental tales, and the drama also reflects this influence, as for example, *Tamburlaine, Soliman* and *Perseda*, and even, perhaps, the induction to *The Taming of The Shrew*. In the seventeenth century the translation of French Heroic Romances (many of which had Oriental heroes) and the activities of playwrights and Oriental scholars maintained some interest in the East.

Then came Sir Roger L'Estrange's version of *The Fables of Bidpai*, and the Latin translation by Edward Pococke of the Arabian philosophical romance, *Hai Ebn Yockdhan* (1671). The first English translation of *L'Espion turc*, by William Bradshaw, slightly edited by Robert Midgley, appeared 1687–1693.[4] There were other Oriental stirrings, such as Defoe's *System of Magic* (1726).

It is clear, therefore, that there was some precedent for the Oriental tale in England, and, no doubt, the eighteenth century impetus was due in England, as in France, to the fact that the *Arabian Nights* came at the psychological moment. In both countries the Oriental novel met with opposition as well as enthusiasm, and it was evident that classicism was making its last stand, and that Romanticism had determined to break away. 'The history of the Oriental tale in England in the eighteenth century might be called an episode in the development of English Romanticism.'[5]

Since the pseudo-Oriental novels showed varying character-istics, it may be as well to glance for a moment at the parent stem. The structure of the *Arabian Nights* is typically Oriental, consisting as it does in a great number of apologues, romances, fables and anecdotes intricately fitted into a loose framework. There is a rich confusion of life and colour, great diversity in events, detailed and vivid descriptions of Eastern customs, and the charm of Oriental names. All the interest is centred on the action, and the appeal to the imagination is unlimited, since magic may at any moment intervene.

In this wonderland fishes talk, hideous slaves become in a twinkling beautiful maidens, and terrible jinn appear from nowhere. Caverns contain gold, silver and rubies beyond the dreams of men. Sharkheaded monsters and alluring mermaids arise from the sea, and one may encounter dwarfs, and 'tremen-dous black giants, one-eyed and as high as a palm-tree,' or be caught up in an earthly convulsion when lightning tears the sky, 'followed by most tremendous thunder . . . hideous darkness . . . a dreadful cry . . . and an earthquake such as Asrayel is to cause on the day of judgment.' These descriptions and this use of magic give an effect of *naïveté*, and despite the appeal to the impossible, there is a sense of reality. The *Arabian Nights* really shows Eastern life as it might have been if freed from the limitations of physical laws. The characterization is very thin, generally a mere representation of stock-types, but by mysterious incidents, dramatic touches and the piling up of adventures the reader's interest is maintained. There is the charm of the story for the story's sake. A sententious element is apparent and yet, on the other hand, there is coarseness in many of the tales.

The period of the Oriental tale in England was roughly from the first English version of the *Arabian Nights* until about the year 1786. The English Oriental tales may, like the French, be classified according to imaginative, moralistic, philosophic and satiric types, but there is, nevertheless, a difference between the development of this Oriental movement in France and in England. Due, perhaps, to the fact that the fairy tales of Perrault reinforced the magic of the *Arabian Nights*, the movement began in France with great imaginative impetus, which soon gave way to the satirizing of human life and manners. This satiric school was the most powerful in the development of the Oriental tale in France. The moralistic tendency (set on foot by Marmontel) was less powerful, and its didacticism, as well as the *Contes licencieux* of such writers as Crébillon fils, hastened the decay of Oriental fiction.

In England, on the contrary, although the Oriental period began with imaginative stories, they were poor in quality and output,[6] and it was not until the very end that *Vathek* appeared to close the history of the Eastern tale in England with a blaze of glory. In the meanwhile, Dr Johnson, Hawkesworth, Addison and Steele saw in Oriental fiction a very good medium for philosophic and didactic purposes, and these were the predominant trends of the Oriental novel in England. Indeed, it was felt by the Johnsonian circle that only by such uses could such wild and exaggerated tales justify their existence. As for satire, it was in quality of a much narrower and slighter type than in France. It was concerned chiefly with conduct, and found its best expression in Goldsmith's *Citizen of the World*. Save for Horace Walpole's *Hieroglyphic Tales*, there is no original English parody in the oriental medium.

With one notable exception, women cannot be said to have made any notable contribution to Oriental fiction in England, although they attempted to follow three of the trends which we have enumerated. To the imaginative group belong Mrs Aubin, Mrs Pilkington and, in a sense, Clara Reeve. Mrs Aubin did not write an Oriental story. Her *Noble Slaves, or the Lives and Adventures of Two Lords and Two Ladies* (1722?) has a Spanish background and Spanish characters, but there are minor people in the story — Asiatics, who recount their adventures. Mrs Pilkington also, although her principal character was Asiatic, did not attempt a Eastern background. In *The Asiatic Princess* (1800) the heroine is Princess Merjee of Siam. Under the guardianship of an English lady and her husband, the Princess travels so that she may be more thoroughly educated. Her mentors moralize on the difference between Eastern and English customs, and seldom lose an opportunity to improve her mind with moral tales. There are references to the Eastern treatment of slaves and to suttee (the Indian custom which made the greatest appeal to English readers).

Although Clara Reeve did not make any original contribution to the Oriental genre, she had the judgment to publish in *The Progress of Romance*, a slightly modernized version of *Charoba*[7] which had been translated by Davies in 1672. This was one of the most interesting of all the imaginative Oriental tales and the direct source of Landor's poem *Gebir* (1798).

The only woman who attempted the satiric genre was Eliza Haywood, and a her satire was directed against people, her work is merely an *histoire scandaleuse* with a pseudo-Oriental background. In 1736 she published *The Adventures of Eovaai, Princess of Ijaveo. A Pre-Adamitical History. Interspersed with a great Number of Remarkable Occurrences, which happened, and may again happen, to several Empires, Kingdoms, Republics, and particular Great Men . . . Written originally in the Language of Nature (of later Years but little understood). First translated into Chinese . . . and now retranslated into English, by the son of a Mandarin, residing in London.* It was revised later as *The Unfortunate Princess, or the Ambitious Statesman* (1741). This tale was servilely dedicated to the Dowager Duchess of Marlborough: 'O most illustrious Wife, and Parent of the Greatest, Best and Loveliest! it was not sufficient for you to adorn Posterity with the amiableness of every virtue . . . '. One may well wonder how the Duchess swallowed such flattery from the woman who, some twelve years before, had pilloried her in *Memoirs of a Certain Island adjacent to the Kingdom of Utopia.*

271

In *Eovaai* Mrs Haywood happily sets herself to flay Walpole under the name of Ochihtou, Prime Minister of Hypotofa:

> This great Man was born of a mean Extraction, and so deformed in his Person, that not even his own Parents could look upon him with Satisfaction . . . As he was extremely amorous, and had so little in him to inspire the tender passion, the first proof he gave of his Art was to . . . cast such a Delusion before the Eyes of all who saw him that he appeared to them such as he wished to be, a most comely and graceful man . . .

She goes on to describe the hypocritical methods by which he won to power and encompassed 'the almost total ruin of both King and People.'

Eovaai begins with a fantastic account of the Pre-Adamitical world, and a very laboured description of how the book came to be written. The story at first is rather in the nature of a moral allegory, but Mrs Haywood finds this impossible to maintain, and soon draws upon her repertoire of scurrilous anecdotes, erotic situations and melodramatic adventures. In her key-novels she had, like Mrs Manley, frequently introduced some personified abstraction to act as *deus ex machina*. Now it was merely going a step further to employ the magical devices which the Oriental tale placed at her disposal. In *Eovaai* her use of magic was greatly exaggerated. As a writer, Mrs Haywood never learned the value of moderation.

The story of *Eovaai* is briefly as follows: the King of Ijaveo leaves to his daughter Eovaai a magical jewel on the keeping of which her happiness depends. One day, as she is admiring it in the palace garden, it is carried off by a little bird. Immediately misfortunes fall thick and fast upon Eovaai. Her quarrelsome subjects forsake her and her suitors turn away. The wicked Ochihtou, Prime Minister of the neighbouring kingdom of Hypotofa, has the worst designs upon Eovaai. By black magic he has gained ascendancy over his king and has instigated the banishment of the young prince. Now he uses the same means to satisfy his own desire for power and for the possession of Eovaai. By infernal agencies he conveys her to the court of Hypotofa, corrupts her mind, and is about to complete his domination of her, when a political crisis calls for his immediate attention. The Princess is saved by her good Genius, who enables her to see

Ochihtou as he really is and to escape to the kingdom of Oozaff, where his evil spells cannot pursue her. He kidnaps her, and again she escapes his evil intentions by substituting one of his former mistresses, who has been languishing under the shape of a monkey and whom she changes back into human shape. While Ochihtou is amorously employed, the populace storm the palace. Ochihtou is so enraged at the trick played upon him that he now changes his wretched mistress into a rat, and seizing Eovaai, carries her through the air to a neighbouring kingdom, which he intends to use as his base of attack against the rebels. He discovers by magic that the King of Hypotofa is now free from his evil spells, and he persuades Eovaai to return to Ijaveo with him so as to regain her kingdom. He transforms himself into a vulture and Eovaai into a dove, and flies with her to a wood where he again tries to complete his designs. She manages to break his wand, and just as he is about to scourge her, she is rescued by a splendid stranger. Ochihtou dashes out his brains against an oak, and Eovaai and the banished Prince of Hypotofa[8] (for such he is) are married, and rule happily their united kingdoms.

Mrs Haywood's story is not important in itself, because the background is weak even as a pseudo-Oriental effort, but chiefly because everything is subordinated to the purpose of a lampoon. The story is a political allegory hotly spiced with scandal and unrelieved by any philosophic or indeed moralizing purpose. Mrs Haywood was merely scavenging again—this time in a turban.

Women's best contribution to the Oriental tale was moralistic. In 1767 Mrs Frances Sheridan published *Nourjahad*, one of the best moralizing stories of the period. Her education had been limited to the ability to read and write, and, as we have already seen, this instruction was given in secret by her brother, very much against her father's wishes. By the time she wrote *Nourjahad*, her success as a novelist was already established by *Miss Sydney Bidulph* (1761), which won the warm admiration of Dr Johnson, and which was translated by Prévost under the title of *Mémoires d'une jeune dame*.[9]

Nourjahad[10] was meant for the first of a series of instructive moral tales which the author meant to dedicate to the Prince of Wales. Translations from Marmontel[11] and Thomas Parnell's poem, *The Hermit*, had already shown that didactic purpose and imaginative treatment could be fused with excellent results. With Marmontel the word moral referred chiefly to manners, but Addison, Steele and Hawkesworth were concerned with questions of conduct. It is in this latter sense that *Nourjahad* is a moral tale.

When Schemzeddin, the wise young prince, mounted the throne of Persia, it was necessary for him to appoint a new ministry. He strongly wished to advance to the office of 'First Minister' a young man of about his own age, who had been bred up with him from infancy, and whom he loved. But Schemzeddin had a sense of responsibility towards his people and, before taking any decisive step, he consulted the aged councillors of the late Sultan. With one voice they vetoed the appointment of Nourjahad, advancing as their various reasons that he was too young, too avaricious, too pleasure-loving, and was, moreover, irreligious. Schemzeddin requires proofs, but they retort that these faults, though not yet obvious, are in Nourjahad's nature and need only an opportunity to show themselves. Schemzeddin turns in displeasure from these advisers, but their words linger in his mind. He determines to test Nourjahad and, choosing a moment of friendly relaxation, he asks him what he would wish for, if he could have anything he desired. Nourjahad replies that he would wish for inexhaustible riches and everlasting life in which to enjoy them. His doubts thus confirmed, the Sultan angrily upbraids him, but Nourjahad, now seeing his hopes of advancement vanishing, tries to persuade him that he merely spoke in jest. Schemzeddin accepts this explanation without enthusiasm, and Nourjahad retires, cursing his unguarded tongue. He spends the remainder of the night and all the next day torturing himself with regrets and despair. Night falls again, and Nourjahad falls into an exhausted sleep. He awakens to behold a vision. It is his guardian Genius, who offers him anything he may wish for. Nourjahad repeats the wish he had expressed to Schemzeddin. The Genius warns him that happiness may not follow, and says that if he should grievously offend the Prophet, he will be punished by falling into a sleep that may last even for a hundred years. Nourjahad persists in his wish despite the warning of the Genius, who yields at last. Nourjahad is now immortal and rich beyond the dreams of men. He is so stunned at his good fortune that he spends days in planning glorious schemes of living and neglects to make his peace with Schemzeddin, who enraged casts him off, but permits him to keep his house as a gift. Nourjahad rejoices at permission to keep the house because all his treasure is stored in a vault in the garden. He surrounds himself with splendour and with every possible means of gratifying the senses and, sunk in this luxurious existence, remains for some months indifferent to the outside world. He is particularly happy in loving and being loved by Mandana, the most beautiful and gentle in all his seraglio. Then one evening, carried beyond all reason by excessive pleasures, Nourjahad so far forgets the law of the Prophet that he drinks to excess. When he awakens from sleep, it is only to discover that he has been asleep for over four years and that Mandana has died in giving birth to his infant son. Nourjahad is overwhelmed with grief at the loss of Mandana, and the possession of a son does not greatly comfort him. But he has to face an eternity of life so he must forget, if he is to avoid an eternity of sorrow. He wishes to travel, but the Sultan decrees that, though he may remove to a house in the country, he shall be a prisoner within his own grounds. Thus doomed to narrow limits of life, Nourjahad plunges into more complete debauchery than before. Finally, having exhausted every pleasure, he casts about for some new diversion, and decides on playing at being Mahomet in Paradise surrounded by the houris. The ladies of his seraglio are as unfit for this role as he is for that of the Prophet, but he does not shrink from the final impiety. All is prepared, and he retires to rest a little before the excesses to come. When he awakes it is to find that he has slept for forty years. His beautiful slaves are withered hags. His trusted major-domo is dead. His son has robbed him of all the money in his coffers and stolen away out of Persia forever. The Sultan, now very old, still is bent on Nourjahad's captivity, but he is permitted to return to his house at Ormiz. This Nourjahad does, and so embittered and disillusioned is he that now he can find amusement only in cruelty. Finally he stabs an old slave and laughs while she welters in her blood. After a night's debauch he goes to rest. When he awakens he finds that he has been asleep for twenty years. The Sultan has just died. His son rules in his stead. The city is in mourning for twenty days. Nourjahad is now so overwhelmed by the nothingness of earthly pleasure, so weary of losing everyone whom he has ever known or loved, that his heart changes and he repents. He bids his servant to go about the city giving alms. But this is contrary to the commands for public mourning, and his servant is condemned to death. He himself is given a chance to escape the death sentence by bribery, but he is tired of the power of money and he cries to Mahomet to take back his gift. No blow falls. Instead, he learns that he has been the victim of a benevolent hoax. Schemzeddin, during the short space of fourteen months, has made him imagine that he has experienced the joys and sufferings of a hundred years. His sleeps were due to soporifics, not magic; his wealth, his slaves were merely lent by Schemzeddin. The Genius was the gentle Mandana who was happy to have a share in redeeming him. Now, purified and wise, he has his reward in Mandana, and in the office of First Minister to Schemzeddin who loves and trusts him.

This charming story is excellently constructed, and the magical effects are most ingeniously and convincingly suggested and reasonably explained. The moralizing is not in the least overdone. Indeed, throughout the action the reader is left to gather the moral for himself, and it is only stated explicitly at the end. The background is like the background of all these pseudo-Oriental tales, an Eastern setting as imagined by an eighteenth-century mind — without glamour, but illuminated by the serene light of reason. The conversation is spirited; the interest is very well sustained. All the time we remain in suspense as to the impending punishment of Nourjahad's evil deeds — either by the deep slumbers into which he falls, or by the displeasure of Schemzeddin. There is a satisfying sense of justness in the course of events. The style is graceful, dignified and flexible. The moral is expressed in Schemzeddin's final speech to Nourjahad:

> I now discovered with joy, that thou hadst entirely divested thyself of that insatiable love of pleasure to which thou hadst before addicted thyself, and that thou no longer didst regard wealth, but as it enabled thee to do good. Only one trial more remained. 'If,' said I, 'his repentance be sincere, and he has that heroism of mind which is inseparable from the truly virtuous, he will not shrink at death, but, on the contrary, will look upon it as the only means by which he can obtain those refined enjoyments suited to the divine part of his nature, and which are as much superior in their essence as they are in their duration, to all the pleasures of the sense.
> I made the trial — the glorious victory, O Nourjahad, is thine! By thy contempt of riches, thou hast proved how well

thou deservest them; and thy readiness to die, shows how
fit thou art to live.

Very much inferior to *Nourjahad* is *Dinarbas* by Ellis Cornelia
Knight (1790). Miss Knight, a companion to the Princess Charlotte,
had the temerity to attempt a continuation of Johnson's *Rasselas*,
a task in which she failed, not merely in degree but in
conception. *Rasselas*, as the finest philosophic novel of the
English Oriental School, would have been very difficult indeed
to equal, even if it lent itself to continuation, which it did not. But
Miss Knight, apparently not understanding its philosophic content,
continued *Rasselas* in moralistic vein. *Rasselas* had for its subject
the vanity of human wishes, the impossibility of happiness
except through serenity and patience, which Johnson thought
could be attained only by integrity and knowledge. Rasselas reared
in the Happy Valley is the optimist brought up in unreality. In
contact with actual life he finds that 'human life is everywhere a
state in which much is to be endured and little enjoyed.' There
is no free choice of one's lot in life. We are enmeshed in circumstances. Rasselas finds that nobody is happy — neither the
simple shepherd, nor those who make pleasure their pursuit, nor
hermits, nor sages. Even the illusion of happiness found in the
past is a source of misery. One can endure life only by inner
harmony of spirit. Indeed 'the choice of life is become less
important. I hope hereafter to think only on the choice of eternity.' Though differing in treatment, *Rasselas* and *Candide* (which
were published almost simultaneously) have much the same
philosophic content.

Of the return of Rasselas to Abyssinia Johnson said: 'It is a
conclusion in which nothing is concluded.' No doubt, he referred
to the impossibility of making some final pronouncement on the
riddle of life, but Ellis Cornelia Knight may have found in this
remark the germ of her intention to write a sequel. At any rate,
her purpose sprang into being when she read in Sir John
Hawkins's life of Dr Johnson: 'The writer had an intention of
marrying his hero, and placing him in a state of permanent
felicity.' She says: 'This passage suggested the idea of the
continuation now offered with the greatest diffidence, to the
reader, and without any thought of a vain and presumptuous
comparison; as every attempt to imitate the energetic stile, strong

imagery, and profound knowledge of the author of *Rasselas*, would be equally rash with that of the suitors to bend the bow of Ulysses.'

She begins at the point where the returning travellers reach Abyssinia. They are held up on the frontier, as war has been declared between Egypt and Abyssinia, and their approach from Egypt is regarded with suspicion. Rasselas with his sister Nekayah, her attendant Pekuah, and Imlac, the poet and philosopher, are taken to a nearby fortress by Dinarbas, the young warrior in charge of the frontier guard. The Governor of the fortress (Amalphus, father of Dinarbas) entertains the party and listens with belief and interest to an account of their travels. The travellers do not acknowledge their identity, but suggest that they are known at the Abyssinian court. A messenger is sent to verify this statement, and meanwhile Rasselas determines to try a military life, partly as an experiment in living, and partly to avoid the company of Zilia, the daughter of Amalphus, who is too charming, too wise and altogether too perfect for his peace of mind. He departs with Dinarbas on a military expedition, and returns after some weeks, having acquitted himself so well that his friendship with Dinarbas is firmly established.

If Rasselas is in danger of loving Zilia, Dinarbas is already in love with Nekayah, who unknown to herself returns his affection. But all is thrown into confusion when the Egyptians attack the fortress. Rasselas is captured and Dinarbas left for dead. He is not dead, however. In the midst of the funeral oration he gives signs of life, and is soon restored. He pays court to Nekayah, who discloses to him that she is the daughter of the Emperor of Abyssinia, and that Rasselas is his fourth son. Nekayah says that, although she loves him, their fates must remain apart.

All this time Rasselas has remained a prisoner in the hands of the Egyptians. He is rescued and brought back to the fortress, where a command awaits him from his father. He is bidden to succeed the Emperor, who is now too old to rule, but first he must subdue his rebellious brothers. This he does. Eventually he marries Zilia. Nekayah marries Dinarbas and all live happily ever after in the Happy Valley.

But did Johnson consider marriage 'a state of permanent felicity', as Sir John Hawkins seems to aver? Johnson said in *Rasselas*: 'Marriage has many pains, but celibacy has no pleasures.'

That is the extent of his claim for marriage in an imperfect world. Miss Knight evidently felt that two marriages would produce a greater amount of happiness than one, and gracefully ignored the question of ratio. She ignored also, or she did not understand, that the return to the Happy Valley might be regarded as a return to unreality, and consequently as a defeat. Or is it, after all, the happiest philosophy to cultivate one's garden and to shut one's ears to the still sad music of humanity? Miss Knight was not preoccupied with reflections on mankind as a whole. She moralized about the life of an individual, and she believed that the sum of good outweighs the sum of evil: 'Youth will vanish, health will decay, beauty fade, and strength sink into imbecility: but if we have enjoyed their advantages, let us not say there is no good because the good in this world is not permanent.'

The philosophic theme in Johnson's novel prevents one from dwelling on the slightness of the characterization and the lack of a convincing Oriental atmosphere. *Dinarbas* brings us down to earth, and since we are asked to interest ourselves in the lives of certain individuals, we are entitled to expect that they should be convincingly characterized. One can rise to the personifying of symbols, but one cannot sink to the marriage of cyphers. It is true that none of the Oriental tales of eighteenth century England had more than a shadowy background and thin characterization; but when, as in *Dinarbas*, love is the main subject described, then we have the final unreality — the love-making of abstractions. Miss Conant says that the value of *Dinarbas* is not literary but historical, that it is an evidence of the desire to moralize everything, even the philosophical tales.[12] But we do not know that Miss Knight deliberately chose to moralize. Indeed it seems that she wrote a moralistic tale because philosophy was beyond her scope.

An example of the persistence into the nineteenth century of the moralizing, pseudo-Oriental tale is Maria Edgeworth's *Murad the Unlucky* (1804). This story is sheer edification from beginning to end, and lacks the more imaginative touches of *Nourjahad*, but it is well told. The Sultan of Constantinople debates with his vizier whether fortune or prudence does more for men. The Sultan believes that human success depends on luck, but the vizier is of opinion that there is no such thing as luck, and that success is always the result of prudence, and misfortune merely the natural punishment of imprudence. Wandering one night through the moonlit city, as in the days of Haroun Alraschid, the Sultan and his vizier observe the life around them, and the vizier suggests that the solution of their argument may be found in listening to the stories of two brothers whose fortunes have been so different that one is called Saladin the Lucky and the other Murad the Unlucky. Murad is convinced that he was born under an unlucky · star, and by many instances endeavours to show that he has always been dogged by an evil fate, but Miss Edgeworth ingeniously words his narrative in such a fashion as to show that prudence has always offered him a way of escape, which he was always too blind to see. Murad's imprudence is not a reckless disregard for the sensible course, but a stupid inability to recognise it. To mark the moral Maria Edgeworth provides the contrast of Saladin's prudent management of his opportunities, and she even shows how differently each brother acted in the self-same predicament. Murad is fooled by a crafty Jew into buying a chest of second-hand clothes which really come from plague-ridden Smyrna. Murad sells the clothes at a profit, and thus unwittingly spreads the plague throughout Grand Cairo. But Saladin, to whom the Jew previously offered the chest, recognized the suspicious circumstances, and positively refused to have anything to do with so doubtful a bargain. Saladin's prudence wins him respect, honours, riches and true love. Murad's imprudence renders him destitute and miserable — a pariah abandoned by men who fear his ill-luck as a contagion. The moral is summed up thus:

> Had Murad possessed his brother's discretion, he would not have been on the point of losing his head, for selling rolls which he did not bake: he would not have been kicked by a mule, or bastinadoed for finding a ring: he would not have been robbed by one party of soldiers, or shot by another: he would not have been lost in a desert, or cheated by a Jew: he would not have set a ship on fire: nor would he have caught the plague, and spread it through Grand Cairo . . .

The catalogue of folly continues, and long before it ends we are quite convinced of the lesson Maria Edgeworth wishes to convey. She not only hits the nail on the head, but keeps on hitting it long after it is driven home, so eager is she to penetrate our human ignorance with her moral point.

The story is well told in clear, economical prose, But it suffers from its extreme didacticism. English novelists had not yet learnt that, though art may teach obliquely by its own symbolism, it must never be subordinated to mere pedagogy. It was a just retribution that the nearer fiction came to direct teaching, the farther it was from developing its own particular technique and from realizing its own destiny.

With the exception of *Vathek*, the pseudo-Oriental novel in England was a peculiar phenomenon of that age. It was the dawning of Romanticism, which might have been expected to stimulate and enrich the imagination. Instead, its light was, for the most part, diverted into the school-room to aid the teaching of pious copybook maxims. This moralistic genre, despite its obvious limitations, was a safe medium for the female pens, who could not fall into disrepute by such activity. The women who thus moralized had the satisfaction of being in the main stream of the pseudo-Oriental movement in fiction, and one of them, at least, held her own with the best of such writings. *Nourjahad* is a definite achievement in an interesting phase of the English novel.

Notes and References

1 *Les mille et une Nuits, Contes arabes traduits en français par M. Galland* (Paris, 1704–1717).
2 Four of his collections were translated into English under the following titles: *Chinese Tales, or The Wonderful Adventures of the Mandarin Fum-Hoam* . . . (1725); *Mogul Tales, or The Dreams of Men Awake; being Stories Told to Divert the Sultanas of Guzarat, for the Supposed Death of the Sultan* (1736); *Tartarian Tales or a Thousand and One Quarters of Hours* (1759), and *Peruvian Tales Related in One Thousand and One Hours by One of the Select Virgins of Cuzco to the Inca of Peru* . . . (1764, 4th edn.?). The last named collection is worthless.
3 This is the classification made by Miss M. P. Conant in her distinguished treatise, *The Oriental Tale in England in the Eighteenth Century* (Columbia University Press, 1908).
4 Mary Manley maintained that the English version was written by her father (Sir Roger Manley). J. M. Rigg, in *D.N.B.*, says it is 'practically certain that the first volume of the letters was composed not by Manley, but by Marana; and it is at least very probable that the Italian was the author of the remainder of the work.' See *D.N.B.* Life of Robert Midgley.
5 M. P. Conant, *The Oriental Tale in England In the Eighteenth Century* (Columbia University Press, 1908), Introduction, p. viii.

6 It may be cogent to observe that Perrault's *Contes de ma mère l'oye* was not translated into English until 1729.

7 *The History of Charoba* extracted from *The History of Ancient Egypt, translated by J. Davies, 1672, from the French of Monsieur Vattier, written originally in the Arabian tongue by Murtadi.*

8 Possibly a reference to the Young Pretender.

9 Part of it was also dramatized under the title: *L'habitant de la Gaudaloupe.*

10 Dramatized by Sophia Lee.

11 E.g. *The Watermen of Besons,* and *Friendship put to the Test.*

12 M. P. Conant, op. cit., p. 104.

Chapter X

The Novel of Sentiment and of Sensibility

A sufficient quantity of Slobbering and
Blessing, and White Handkerchief Work.

(G. L. Way, *Learning at a Loss*, 1778)

Certain striking features of the novels of eighteenth century
women may be said to be due to the general characteristics of the
time. The fiction of this century was a curious reflection and
denial of contemporary life and thought. It was a reflection of the
conventions which a certain level of society chose as the framework of its human and artistic existence, but this framework not
only excluded, but tacitly denied all that lay outside its deliberate
limitations. It was an age of paradoxes: a period of apparent
hypocrisy, but of actual self-deception; a period of earnest ethics
divorced from moral principles; a period of philosophic sententiousness which took no thought of social conditions; a period of
complacent sensibility, but of the most callous obduracy. It was
an England of salons and illiteracy; of thundering divines and
pluralism; of languid beaux and highwaymen. The upper stratum
of society prided itself on an exquisite sensibility which, however, was invulnerable to the sufferings of the less fortunate.
Ladies whose hearts were wrung by the beauty of a snowdrop or
the indisposition of a pet bird were unmoved by social injustices,
by the iniquitous law which hanged children for theft, or by the
squalid horrors of the prison system. Class distinctions in England
at that period were completely rigid. The middle class scorned
the lower class and was in turn scorned by the privileged class. It
was a ladder of condescension which one climbed feverishly for the
pleasure of looking down. That Christianity did not bridge the gulf
is well seen in the letter of the Duchess of Buckingham to Selina,

Countess of Huntingdon. Speaking of the Wesleyan preachers, her Grace says 'Their doctrines are most repulsive and strongly tinctured with impertinence and disrespect towards their superiors, in perpetually endeavouring to level all ranks and to do away with all distinctions. It is monstrous to be told you have a heart as sinful as the common wretches that crawl on the earth. This is highly offensive and insulting, and I cannot but wonder that our Ladyship should relish any sentiments so much at variance with high rank and good-breeding.' Such, in brief, was the social background which the novel ignored, transmuted or partly revealed.

In considering the Oriental novel and the growth of the epistolary genre we have already touched on certain aspects of eighteenth century fiction. It would be profitable to take a cursory glance at the factors which chiefly influenced the women writers.

In the first place, one cannot fail to be struck by the extraordinary popularity of the novel during the eighteenth century. For some time the growing wealth and power of the middle classes had made it possible for them to share more fully in the amusements of the leisured, and had therefore resulted in a great increase in the reading public. The predilections of so large a class of readers were obviously worth considering, and soon in the greater output of novels we observe a deliberate effort to give the middle classes the sort of pabulum they preferred. But it happened that this economic factor was reinforced by an unpredictable circumstance — by a spontaneous flowering in fiction. When Fielding, Richardson, Sterne and Smollett, for one reason or another, chose the novel as their medium, a new era opened for English fiction, for these men by their genius not only set it firmly on its feet, but raised it to a new level and showed its claim to be recognized as a branch of literary art. This achievement led to great fictional activity but, for a considerable time, had no effect on the quality of subsequent novels. A ceaseless tide of fiction flowed from the printing presses, but the vast majority of these works were worthless and had very little relation to the aims of the Great Four. A number of causes contributed to this lack of succession. It would scarcely be wise to assert that, after Fielding and Richardson, no writer of equal calibre was left to carry their ideas into effect, but it is certain that if such existed they were unwilling to express themselves in fiction. This is easily understood because, though the great novelists had shown that fiction was a branch of literary art, this claim was far from being admitted, and the novel continued to be the pariah of the arts even at the beginning of the nineteenth century. Those who did write fiction seemed unable to grasp the conception and the technique of such works as *Tom Jones* and *Clarissa Harlowe*. This was partly due to their lack of ability, and partly to the difficulty of analyzing the artistic subtlety which produces a great literary work. It is true that Fielding, the finest novelist of his age, not content with embodying his artistic principles in his novels, actually enunciated them in his prefaces, but if they were not beyond the comprehension, they were quite beyond the power of the average writer. Fielding was the first to conceive that all of life, focused with benevolent irony, might be made to live through the personality and behaviour of characters involved in a carefully woven plot. In vision, in perspective, in construction and in characterization this differed so much from the old desultory aims and methods that a mediocre novelist could not be expected to take so great a leap. A further deterrent was that readers considered Fielding 'low'. Smollett more justly earned the same judgment. Sterne's fictional aim and his subtle sensuality eluded them, but they delighted in his sensibility. Goldsmith's classic simplicity had too fine a flavour for their palates. It was Richardson who really went home to their hearts—not because they realized his greatness as an artist, but because he had so much in common with their outlook and again because, in a general sense, he was more easily imitable.

To understand eighteenth century tastes in fiction one must remember that the reading public was composed of people who had never relinquished the old romantic tradition. It was a middle class public, three quarters of which were women. Thus the bourgeois and the feminine outlook reinforced each other in the reaction against coarseness, in the preoccupation with conventional morality and in a strong bent towards emotionalism. By the second half of the century these were the strongest traits in fiction. They found in Richardson their greatest exponent, and gained from his works an added impetus. But Richardson, the master craftsman, succeeded in manipulating these tendencies in conformity with artistic proportion; his followers, for the most part mere apprentices, sadly lacked this ability. Consequently the influence of Richardson, of Marivaux, and partly of Sterne gave rise to a great accumulation of futility with only an occasional contribution of value. This was the school of sentiment and sensibility, and we shall see later that sensibility also found expression in the Gothic novel. But it was a real sensitiveness to human sufferings, with a determined effort towards amelioration, which gave rise to the *tendenz* group of novelists.

Sensibility, the peculiar boast of the eighteenth century, had many aspects. It differed from sentiment mainly in degree. Sentiment is, in a sense, the norm of feeling. Sensibility was an excessive vulnerability to feeling. It arose from an idealization of spiritual delicacy. It eventually perished of its own falsity. In its career it exhausted every variety of aim, form and degree. Sensibility did not merely value emotion in itself as a proof of the sensitive nature. It substituted emotion for thought and laid great stress on arriving at a truth instinctively. Mary Wollstonecraft says: 'It is the result of acute senses, finely fashioned nerves, which vibrate at the slightest touch, and convey such clear intelligence to the brain, that it does not require to be arranged by the judgment.'[1] This was sensibility at its healthiest — an exquisite susceptibility to emotion by which one felt one's way through life, by which one lived at the highest possible level. Sensibility made one 'tremblingly alive'; without it one merely existed in 'a vegetative state.'[2] It was the great ideal of eighteenth century novelists and an essential characteristic of all heroines and heroes. Every opportunity for a display of sensibility was seized upon with avidity, and the plot was even deliberately framed so as to involve the characters in the greatest possible number of tribulations. Joy and happiness were at once felt to offer little scope for sensibility. Suffering as a bottomless abyss in which a human being might fall forever — or an eternal winepress in which the victim might forever yield the essence of his soul. This explains the popularity of novels which, like *Sydney Bidulph*, earned the reproach that they caused their readers too much suffering. 'Whether it be that the mind abhors nothing like a state of inaction, or from whatever cause, I know not, but grief itself is more agreeable to us than indifference; nay, if not too exquisite, is in the highest degree delightful; of which the pleasure we take in tragedy, or in the talking of our dead friends, is a striking proof. We wish not to be cured of what we feel on these occasions; the tears we shed are charming — we even indulge in them.'[3] And again: 'Pleased with the tender sorrow which possessed all my soul, I determined to indulge it to the utmost.'[4] This cult of suffering was the inevitable result of the deification of sensibility, and however it may have been strengthened or developed by the influence of Marivaux, Prévost, Madame Riccoboni and others,[5] it seems logical to suppose that the English novel of sensibility, like the French novel of sensibility, would have arrived by much the same path at similar plots of endurance and trial.

Sensibility, however, has other aspects than those of suffering. It may be aroused not only by affection but by love, romantic or dutiful, and also by the poor and the unfortunate. Few of these novels are without at least one incident of charitable succour. Albany in Fanny Burney's *Cecilia* is the incarnation of this philanthropic impulse. Yet there is never a direct reference to the actual conditions of social neglect and injustice. Poverty is a sentimentalized circumstance introduced to give sensibility another outlet; and the poor are always presented from the standpoint of patronage — humbly submissive to their fate and fulsomely grateful for the life-giving crust. There was need for a Mary Wollstonecraft to tell with stark abruptness the sordid story of a servant girl.

Beauty was another delightful irritant of sensibility — whether of a face, a book, or a scene. In *Camilla* the Oxford student reading Thomson's *Seasons* in a bookshop exclaims, cries out, beats his forehead and finally bursts into tears. He is not insane, but commendably sensitive. Nature became, with the growth of the century, an increasing source of sensibility, but it was rarely nature unadorned. Scenery and the elements were sentimentalized, stage-managed and used romantically to echo a mood or to arouse retrospective emotion. This is an aspect of sensibility which we find most fully exploited in the Gothic novel.

Even morality was only sensibility in another guise — sensibility in this sense meaning moral sensitiveness, roughly the equivalent of conscience. In the words of Mrs Brooke:

> Women are religious as they are virtuous, less from principles founded upon reasoning and argument, than from elegance of mind, delicacy of moral taste, and a certain perception of the beautiful and becoming in everything. This instinct, however, for such it is, is worth all the tedious reasoning of the men.[6]

This is a view which Hannah More also expresses in her poem on *Sensibility*.[7]

But apart from the enervating waste of emotion and the lack of balanced judgment, apart from the hairsplitting fastidiousness which, says Mrs Arlbery in *Camilla*, 'refines away' its own happiness, sensibility was damned by its egoism. Even if it had given rise to greater artistry in fiction it would not have been possible to forgive its complacence at its own capacity for feeling — this subordination of all things to that exquisitely sensitive soul whose sensibility it is their only function to arouse.

> Of this danger the majority of eighteenth-century writers cannot have been much aware: they give themselves away too handsomely. Again and again we find that enormity of self-gratulation with which the weeper at once luxuriates in the beguiling softness of tears and compliments himself on his capacity for shedding them, seeing in his mind's eye not only the object of his attention, but himself in a suitable attitude in front of it.[8]

The modern reader of eighteenth century fiction sometimes feels caught in a nightmare in which seduced girls, dying parents, families starving in garrets, begging negroes, unctuously repentant sinners, white-haired clergymen and innocently prattling children clutch with their pale fingers a naked heart from which they wring streams of — tears. It is a world in which intensely cultivated emotion finds unrestrained expression. Speech becomes rodomontade, and action, passing rapidly through every phase of convulsive behaviour, reaches the limit of human endurance and is intermitted. Thus the characters sob, groan, scream, beat their breasts, tear their hair, fall into a frenzy, rave and become insensible. Tears are the only safety valve, and never did the 'vater-vorks', scorned by Sam Weller senior, operate with such torrential force. The slightest tremor of feeling opens the floodgates. Indeed Mackenzie's *Man of Feeling* was a dam of which the sluice gates were never shut. The liquidity of Mr Villars in Thomas Bridges's *Adventures of a Banknote* shows the extent to which fiction lacked a sense of humour. We read that 'tears cours'd one another down his manly cheeks and form'd a rapid current o'er his garments.'

Implicit in sensibility there appears to have been some notion of focusing the attention on the inner man. But writers, lacking insight or unable to cope with the minutiae of character and motive, found it easier to enlarge everything to many times its natural size. Yet even such an explanation is too merciful, because the falsity is not merely of scale, but of kind. Even allowing for extreme exaggeration, the fiction of sensibility has little or no relation to reality. Prior to 1740, writers had concerned themselves with external life and padded their narratives with a multiplicity of exciting adventures. Now, since it had been demonstrated that fiction could be written from within, the lesser novelists of the eighteenth century could not be deterred from what they fondly believed to be an internal treatment. The result was unreal and inartistic to the last degree. False notions of nobility and villainy precluded characterization; orgies of melodrama in plot and style completed the artificiality. It was an unnatural, an hysterical and even a morbid school of fiction. It died of exhaustion accelerated, no doubt, by continuous cardiac haemorrhage. Jane Austen laughed heartlessly over its corpse.

This period of the English novel was marked by a great influx of women writers. Indeed their proportion was almost equal to that of the women readers. Many reasons co-operated to cause this determined invasion of the lists. In the first place, the epistolary form was easy, and the domestic novel brought fiction into the field of feminine experience. The cult of sentiment and sensibility was so effeminate and the trend of moral earnestness so decorous, that women, without relinquishing their delicacy, could compete with the men writers. As a matter of fact, the supposed feminine pre-eminence of imagination and feeling gave the women such an advantage that some of the male hacks wrote under the pretence of being women. 'We suspect,' wrote the *Critical* (in April, 1778) of the *Memoirs of the Countess D'Anois*, 'that Madame la Comtesse may be found in some British garret, without breeches, perhaps, but yet not in petticoats.'[9]

Another factor which encouraged many women was that the general standard of fiction was low, and was rendered still lower by the money-making devices of the publishers, the book-sellers, and the circulating libraries, which were generally either in league, or actually under the same ownership. The libraries brought novel-reading within the competency of a far greater number of people, the majority of whom were quite uncritical, and it became a very profitable business to cater deliberately for this easily satisfied public. The ready market for rubbish had naturally a debasing effect on fiction, which was still further prostituted by the popularizing of the many-volume novel. This mercenary scheme involved novelists in a despairing effort to fill three, four or even five volumes. So gullible and so unfailing was the public that libraries frequently changed the name of a novel and put it into circulation again, while publishers brought the faking of editions to a fine art. There is no doubt that the book trade had, at that time, a grievous effect on fictional development, since it made it possible for the merest scribblers to make a living out of their wretched effusions. This was a benefit to the untalented woman writer, but was far from aiding women's contribution to the novel, which must be judged only by sifting the good grain from the chaff.

The standard of criticism applied to the novel in the eight-eenth century was a further encouragement to the female pen. Didacticism was regarded as the only justification of the novel; moral teaching was indispensable, and if the novel could also be made the vehicle for general information (such as history or geography), it would then serve the added purpose of sugar-coating the pill of education, which readers, especially females, would otherwise find unpalatable. It was essential that the novel should be both interesting and probable so that it might be able to teach convincingly. General information was, no doubt, beyond the scope of women novelists, but earnest morality was their forte, and their refined imaginations already disposed the critics in their favour. Indeed the critics were much inclined to be indulgent to the 'British fair', so long as she wrote from a legitimate motive and was sufficiently humble. To venture safely into print a woman should be either morally didactic, dilettante or distressed. Any such reason, explained with extreme diffidence and self-depreciation, would win the critic not to soften, but to abstain from applying, the canons of criticism. This uncritical indulgence came particularly into play if the writer penned her tale at the bedside of a bedridden mother, or was the sole support of an invalid husband and nine children. But the super-ficiality of such chivalry became apparent at the slightest deviation from the apologetic code. Literary ambition in a woman was regarded as an impertinence and led to terrible scourgings. It was considered indelicate for a woman to write her name on the title page—a taboo which was carefully observed, although sometimes we find that a signed preface is not considered inconsistent with a title page that admits nothing. Clara Reeve, that spirited spinster, wrote her first book at forty, and withheld her full signature until she was in her sixtieth year. Very often authorship was an open secret, but it was supposed to remain unacknowledged nevertheless. No reader of Fanny Burney's diary can ever forget her acute sensibility on the subject of her authorship. She was entertained and fêted by the great only because she was the writer of *Evelina*. It was her passport to the most learned and aristocratic circles, yet if anyone mentioned *Evelina* in her presence she was overwhelmed by the indelicacy. Congratulations on her achievement she regarded as a most shocking display of coarseness. This was the attitude sanctioned by the critics. They were not kind to women novelists because they were women—only because they were humble, which, it was hoped, they would continue to remain. Reviewers were ever on the alert for the slightest sign of female self-importance. If a woman, to remain anonymous, put 'Author of—' on the title page she was withered. But there was a worse offence: the innocent use of the editorial plural once drew upon a woman novelist the jeer: 'We suppose the lady is pregnant, and her unborn child shares her emotions.' Still, there must have been women even then who in their hearts resented, more than scoffings, the insulting magnanimity which forgave them their novels in view of their sex. It was an attitude which encouraged mediocrity and crushed real worth.

Although the influx of women into the field of fiction during the eighteenth century happened, for the reasons we have noted, to produce little that was of value nevertheless even the trashy level of their work has a certain interest. It is interesting because it enables us to trace their conception of womanhood and their attitude to life. What emerges is a dead level of conventionality with occasional outbursts of the feminine point of view. Women's conventions were prudential, narrow and superficial. They provided for every contingency of behaviour with the most minute forethought, and absolved women from any need of understanding or reflection. The 'principling' which was the great essential of women's upbringing had little to do with fundamentals, and consisted merely of a set of intricate rules for the preservation of chastity. These taboos appear to have induced a rather distasteful sex-consciousness; womanly delicacy seems chiefly to have implied a complete absence of respect and confidence between the sexes and a defensive rampart of hypocrisy on the part of the women. But it is represented as intuitive integrity and a watchful and scrupulous virtue. Women who were so unfortunate as to fall from virtue always died, generally from a decline, bitterly repentant. Sometimes they are allowed to live long enough to show the earnestness of their reformation, but generally not, in case they should contaminate the community. A modest young woman never loves until the man has declared himself. She should never aim at learning, which would only unsex her and ruin her chances of a husband. All women should have an exquisite fineness of perception and feeling. They should be meek, compassionate, patient and forgiving, particularly wives, who owe the deepest submission to their husbands whether or not such submission is deserved. This is a very brief summary of the women novelists' views. It is at once apparent that they are masculine views. They are to be found in the men's novels. The women novelists who expressed them had, in any case, been reared according to such beliefs. It would be a nice point to determine how much of this ideal of womanhood was imposed on them by men, and how much was a web of high-flown theory which women had been spinning for ages in an unconscious effort to build up a self-respecting pattern of life despite the arbitrary, contradictory and sometimes humiliating circumstances which limited them. No doubt they had listened so long to soporific pronouncements that they really believed them. Effective propaganda does achieve such results; and certainly, at that period, men's comfort and supremacy depended on the credibility of this pseudo-philosophy for soft feminine brains. Now and then, in these women's novels, a spark leaps up for a moment to throw light on the untouched question of the women *per se*. Sometimes there is even a tiny blaze. Then we return again to women echoing the masculine ideal of women. Even the very air of physical delicacy (which gave men of that period a feeling of superior strength) was made by female novelists the essential of every heroine. But it must be said that women took an unintended revenge by evolving a hero who was most elegantly delicate in every way. He was as pure as the driven snow; had perfect manners; dressed charmingly; wrote beautiful verse and frequently swooned.

Still, despite the valueless flotsam that lay thick upon the stream of female fiction during the eighteenth century, the current flowed on and gathered force. Passing from Addison's England to that of Johnson, we note a definite change in women's prestige. In Addison's time it was a fact that 'in the female world, any acquaintance with books was distinguished only to be censured.'[10] Those were the days 'when a woman who could spell a common letter was regarded as all-accomplished. Now [said Johnson] they vie with the men in everything.'[11] When Richardson was in his glory it was for women the greatest privilege to be admitted to the circle at Northend. By the time *Evelina* appeared women had their own salons. Johnson's broadminded encouragement of female talents had no small share in developing this new attitude. Richardson had surrounded himself with women because they 'listened to him implicitly and did not venture to contradict his opinions.'[12] Johnson's circle consisted of men and women, and the women enjoyed something bordering on equality. But now there were circles where women reigned supreme, either for learning, wit, elegance, or individuality. Of these the greatest was Mrs Montagu, 'Queen of the Blues'. Other stars in this firmament were the bookish Mrs Carter; the ugly and good-natured Mrs Chapone; the flighty and fashionable Mrs Vesey; the elegant Mrs Crewe and Mrs Boscawen; Mrs Thrale, the vivacious bourgeoise; Mrs Cholmondeley and Mrs Walsingham, both great wits; the social Mrs Ord and others of less note. Uniquely apart, not competing in learning, wit, fashion, or hospitality, was the ageless Mrs Delany. In the last quarter of the century these were names to conjure with, so that Fanny Burney well might say: 'Now that I am invited to Mrs Montagu's, I think the measure of my glory is full.'

Before the great army of female novelists had entered the field of sentiment and sensibility, while yet they were only sharpening their pens for conquest, a woman novelist scored a spectacular triumph. It was the happy fate of Charlotte Lennox, at the beginning of her career, to be publicly crowned with laurels by Dr Johnson himself. The scene has been well preserved for us in the vinegar of one Hawkins, a pompous gentleman whose powers of revelry were precluded by a 'raging tooth'. One spring evening in the year 1751, a merry party assembled at the Devil Tavern near Temple Bar. It consisted of sixteen members of the Ivy Lane Club, who came at the bidding of Johnson to honour Charlotte Lennox's first novel, then either just published or issuing from the press. The authoress was kept in countenance by the presence of her husband and a lady-friend, and by the wish of the genial lexicographer it was an 'all night sitting'. First there was an 'elegant' supper, of which the *pièce de résistance* was a 'magnificent hot apple-pye' stuck with bay-leaves — a graceful reference to the volume of poetry that Mrs Lennox had already published. Then, after a suitable invocation, the coronation took place, and thereafter the company made merry until morning with talk and laughter which flourished, for the most part, on no stronger liquids than tea and coffee. Some few back-sliders there were from this plan of non-alcoholic high spirits; but Johnson needed no intoxicant but the exuberance of his own verbosity, and at five o'clock his face still shone with meridian splendour. When St Dunstan's clock was striking eight, the literary revellers, weary and dishevelled, issued forth into Fleet Street. Mr Hawkins withdrew to nurse his tooth and his disapproval, and the queen of the evening went home, her brain reeling with exhaustion and fame.

Charlotte Lennox was the daughter of Colonel James Ramsay, reputed to be the Lieutenant-Governor of New York. When she was fifteen she was sent to England to live with an aunt who, when she arrived, was either dead or mad. Then her father died and she had to support herself. She was befriended by Lady Rockingham, was turned away for some supposed love affair, and was taken up for a while by the Duchess of Newcastle. She attempted the stage and was (says Walpole) a 'deplorable actress'. An unfortunate marriage caused her to commence author as a means of support. For over forty-three years she continued to write poems, novels, plays and translations but, despite her outstanding success at one period, she ended her days in penury. Latterly she was supported partly by the Literary Fund and partly by the Hon. George Rose who also paid her funeral expenses. It was a strange declension from the triumph at the Devil Tavern to that poor and lonely death-bed in Dean's Yard, Westminster — a life of effort ending merely in a defeated sigh.

Charlotte Lennox's first novel was *The Life of Harriot Stuart*, which was published in December, 1750. This was a tale centring on the flight of the heroine from marriage with a hated suitor. There are hairbreadth 'scapes from redskins, pirates, ravishment and other perils; and there are the usual misunderstandings between the true lovers who are finally united. In this novel (as in her last novel, *Euphemia*) Mrs Lennox drew on her memories of American life, but the background also changes to England and France. Harriot Stuart scarcely merited Johnson's celebrations, and indeed it brought its author at least as much notoriety as fame, since in it she pilloried Lady Isabella Finch[13] in a manner so obvious that it aroused much resentment in society.

But however opinion may have varied about Charlotte Lennox's first novel, with her second she took the reading public by storm. *The Female Quixote*, which appeared in 1752, is this writer's strongest claim to literary remembrance. Not only Johnson, but Richardson and more especially Fielding were loud in their praises. The book ran into a second edition in three months, and continued to be published up to 1820. It was translated into German, French and Spanish.[14] *The Female Quixote* is an imitation of *Don Quixote*, that is to say that Charlotte Lennox, like Cervantes, satirized the old style of romantic fiction. Charlotte Lennox had chiefly in mind the novels of Mlle de Scudéry and her followers.

Lady Arabella, the Female Quixote, is the daughter of a nobleman who, through disgust at the injustice of the court, quitted it for a life of complete retirement in the country. Absence of human companionship and endless reading of Heroic Romances have caused her to create for herself a fantastic world peopled with characters who live according to an astonishing code. In this realm of heroic romanticism all the heroines are young, beautiful and virtuous, and time is powerless to impair these qualities. The men are of two kinds: heroes who are generally princes in disguise, and who in every vicissitude remain princely; and villains who devote themselves to foul emprises with an astounding assiduity. They never cease to plot against the heroines, and are everlastingly carrying them off, but this they must do so as to give the heroes an opportunity of rescuing the distressed fair ones, generally in the nick of time. Nothing could be more selfless than these services. The heroines live on a system of payment deferred. If the hero is sufficiently valourous, sufficiently devoted, and sufficiently pure-souled, he may with luck win his lady at the end of a quarter of a century. Meanwhile the most he can hope for is her negative toleration. At the slightest offence she will immediately wish his death, whereupon it is understood that he will at once be stricken down. To live in disobedience to such a command would be an unthinkable impertinence, and if the human frame does not spontaneously dissolve, then the hero must deliberately destroy it. If, however, at the last moment, when the hero is actually expiring, the lady should change her mind and command him to live, his physical system will immediately respond, and make it possible for him to return to his duties there and then. There are no duties in this Never-Never country save those connected with love and beauty; adoring beauty, serving beauty, rescuing beauty. As to love, it is the direct antithesis of eroticism; it is known chiefly as a lack:

> It is to be all made of sighs and tears . . .
> It is to be all made of faith and service . . .
> All made of passion and all made of wishes;
> All adoration, duty and obedience,
> All humbleness, all patience, and impatience,
> All purity, all trial, all observance.

The hero may (indeed he must) love, but he must never dare to insult the heroine by a declaration. In fact, that he should centre his affections on a lady is considered so gross in its implications that twenty years of purgatory are all too little as a preface to elysium. If the goddess so served were not infallible and perfect, then the whole code of chivalry would fall to the ground; but she is infallible and, as a consequence, completely autocratic.

Such are the fantasies with which Arabella is obsessed, but her father's death and his wish that she should marry her cousin, Charles Glanville, force her to face reality, or rather force her to decide between two possible realities: the actual world of men and women, and the world of the Heroic Romance. She must either abandon the world of the Heroic Romance or force others to share it with her. Her efforts to impose its code on the outer world are the subject of the novel.

It is to be expected that all sorts of absurdities would result from Arabella's obstinacy, and one of Mrs Lennox's first problems was how best to explain Arabella's persistence in quixotism. She had to choose between making Arabella an idiot or an autocrat. She made her an autocrat. One questions her decision, because it is necessary for a heroine to be lovable, and, on the whole, idiots are more lovable than autocrats. Still, Arabella's high-handedness is relieved by an unconscious childishness, and by her complete innocence, generosity and lack of affectation. These qualities in her are marked by contrast with the sophisticated, envious, husband-hunting flirts with whom she is brought into contact.

The strongest chain of continuity in the story is the love of Charles Glanville which, though tried almost to breaking, still holds firm. Arabella alighting on the terra firma of everyday life interprets everything by the standards of romance. The gardener lurking about suspiciously because he plans a theft, the idle gallant staring curiously at Arabella's antique style of dress, are to her disguised noblemen with the worst intentions, awaiting only the opportunity to carry her off. She believes that every male cherishes a secret passion for her and this induces in her such active resentment that several of them are forced to tell her the simple truth: that they never for a moment thought of loving her. She leaves her country estate and goes to Bath and then to London, but the life around her never impinges on her consciousness. Her beauty, social position and riches win a certain amount of tolerance for her eccentricity, and therefore her *idée fixe* is not dislodged. Finally, after she has thrown herself into the river to escape being ravished by some men who have never even noticed her existence, Charles Glanville believes that the time has come for drastic action. He sends a learned clergyman to reason with her, and this logical appeal to her common-sense effects what no amount of ridicule could achieve. All ends happily with her marriage to Glanville.

The humour of *The Female Quixote* arises from the conflict of the romantic and the everyday code of behaviour, and it is very well sustained throughout. For example, there are the conversations between Miss Glanville the vapid, sophisticated and calculating flirt, and Arabella the intelligent, the unspoiled, but the bizarre. Highly amusing indeed is their interview after Arabella has (as she thinks) barely escaped abduction by a disguised nobleman (who is really the gardener).[15] But still better are the cross-purposes between this ill-assorted pair on the subject of the adventures which beautiful ladies cannot escape, and of the favours which they may grant to their adorers. A favour to Arabella means not actually wishing the death of a presumptuous lover or, at the very most, a ribbon from the lady's sleeve. By the word favour Miss Glanville understands what Mrs Manley's school politely termed 'the last favour'. Arabella, thinking to compliment Miss Glanville, says that she is sure she must have had many adventures, by which she means being carried off by men of 'unbridled passions' and, of course, always being rescued opportunely by honest princes in disguise. Unfortunately, to Miss Glanville the word adventure connotes the exploits of the adventuress:

> 'Whence comes it, cousin [says Arabella] being so young and lovely as you are that though you questionless, have been engaged in many adventures, you have never reposed trust enough in me to favour me with a recital of them?'
> 'Engaged in many adventures, Madam!' returned Miss Glanville, not liking the phrase: 'I believe I have been engaged in as few as your ladyship.'
> 'You are too obliging,' returned Arabella, who mistook what she said for a compliment; 'for, since you have more beauty than I, and have also had more opportunities of making yourself beloved, questionless you have had a greater number of admirers.' 'As for admirers,' said Miss Charlotte, bridling, 'I fancy I have had my share! Thank God, I never found myself neglected; but, I assure you, Madam, I have had no adventures, as you call them, with any of them.' 'No, really,' interrupted Arabella, innocently. 'No, really, Madam!' retorted Miss Glanville, 'and I am surprised you should think so.'

Arabella then cites the case of Mandana who had thousands of adventures, and who so enslaved the great Cyrus that he could refuse nothing she asked, even to the freeing of great number of Jews whom he had taken captive.

> 'Well,' said Miss Glanville, 'and I suppose she denied *him* nothing he asked; and so they were even.'
> 'Indeed but she did though,' resumed Arabella; 'for she refused to give him a glorious scarf which she wore, though he begged for it on his knees.'
> 'And she was very much in the right,' said Miss Glanville, 'for I see no reason why a lover should expect a gift of any value from his mistress.'
> 'Doubtless, ' said Arabella 'such a gift was worth millions of services and had he obtained it, it would have been a glorious distinction for him: however, Mandana refused it;

and severely virtuous as you are, I am persuaded you can't help thinking that she was a little too rigorous in denying a favour to a lover like him.'

'Severely virtuous, Lady Bella!' said Miss Glanville, reddening with anger. 'Pray what do you mean by that? Have you any reason to imagine I would grant any favour to a lover?'

'Why, if I did, cousin,' said Arabella, 'would it derogate so much from your glory, think you, to bestow a favour upon a lover worthy of your esteem, from whom you had received a thousand marks of a most pure and faithful passion, and also a great number of very singular services?'

'I hope, Madam,' said Miss Glanville, 'it will never be my fate to be so much obliged to any lover, as to be under a necessity of granting him favours in requital.'

'I vow, cousin,' interrupted Arabella, 'you put me in mind of the fair and virtuous Antonia, who was so rigid and austere, that she thought all expressions of love were criminal, and was so far from granting any person permission to love her that she thought it a mortal offence to be adored even in private.'

Miss Glanville, who could not imagine Arabella spoke this seriously, but that it was designed to sneer at her great eagerness to make conquests, and the liberties she allowed herself in, which had probably come to her knowledge, was so extremely vexed at the malicious jest, as she thought it, that, not being able to revenge herself, she burst into tears.

Arabella is overcome by amazement and solicitude, and begs to know how she has offended: 'You have made no scruple,' answered Miss Glanville, 'that you think me capable of granting favours to lovers: when Heaven knows, I never granted a kiss without a great deal of confusion!'[16] A kiss! Arabella is appalled— a kiss, when the chaste Mandana, the virtuous Statira, the wise Antonia felt themselves compromised if, after having been served in humility and with terrific feats of derring-do for long years, they went so far as not to wish the death of their faithful knights!

Arabella reads the erring one a long lecture with Mandana as her text, and points the moral with insulting comparisons to the 'inconsiderate Julia, who would receive a declaration of love without anger from anyone, and was not over-shy any more than yourself, of granting favours almost as considerable as that you have mentioned.' We are not surprised to learn that Miss Glanville, having dried her tears, sits silently swelling with rage, and is restrained only by the hope of revenging herself later—a vain dream, because Arabella's beauty and fortune centre on her all the masculine attention. Nor is there even any hope that Arabella's peculiar views may lead her into humiliating situations as, though she is constantly involved in misunderstandings, that haughty visionary either fails to observe any cause of embarrassment, or else autocratically considers that she is unfortunate in encountering people who lack nobility of spirit.

It has been suggested that Mrs Lennox attributed Arabella's conversion to her interview with the learned divine simply to compliment Dr Johnson, who is supposed to have written that chapter;[17] and it has been said[18] that it would have been more natural if Arabella's experiences had forced her gradually to realize that her views were fantastic. This would indeed have been more reasonable, but Arabella is modelled on Don Quixote, and he also was characterized by invulnerability to the opinion of others. When the Knight of the Silver Moon has him at his mercy, the prostrate Quixote still asserts that Dulcinea del Toboso is the finest lady in the world. It is true, however, that Arabella's whims are carried too far; that her declamations, peppered with examples from the French romances, are altogether too long-winded, and that there are too many improbable incidents. These are criticisms which, at first glance, might be supposed to apply also to Don Quixote, but in Cervantes' book such points are merely superficial, whereas in Mrs Lennox's they are the essential matter of the novel. It may be said in Mrs Lennox's defence that there were special difficulties in satirizing a female Quixote. Cervantes' knight could wander where he would in search of adventure: Arabella was forced to find her adventures wherever she happened to be and, although the scene changes, her immediate circumstances do not, because the conventions require that she should be accompanied everywhere by an entourage of her nearest relatives. Don Quixote could initiate romantic emprises as the spirit moved him. Arabella could merely give romantic interpretations to the actions of others (the one exception being when, to escape imaginary ravishers, she jumps into the river—an incident which seriously jars one's ideas of probability). This is one of the points made by Fielding in his long and favourable review of *The Female Quixote*.[19] The surprising thing is not merely that, in some minor respects, he should find *The Female Quixote* better than *Don Quixote*, but that he should seriously compare these works. It is true that he stresses the superiority of Cervantes, but even with Fielding as a precedent, no sensible person could think of comparing Cervantes and Charlotte Lennox. One was a genius. The other was a clever wit. One, intending to write a satire, achieved an immortal work of art: the other, intending to write a burlesque — wrote a burlesque. The greatness of Cervantes (as Heine so finely suggests) lies in the symbolism of the haggard knight and his serving-man who 'so constantly burlesque and yet so wonderfully complement each other, so that together they form the one true hero of romance — these two figures give evidence of the poet's artistic taste and of his intellectual profundity.' They represent the spiritual and the material — both aspects of life, in short; and they represent also the fusion of the ideal and the common, of the aristocratic and of the popular element, from which sprang the modern novel.[20]

Clara Reeve[21] made the point that the romances satirized in *The Female Quixote* had ceased to be read about forty years before Charlotte Lennox wrote. Fielding[22] also supports this view. But he finds Glanville a very well-drawn character, whereas really no claim can be made for the characterization in this novel. Austin Dobson[23] stresses this opinion, and says, in addition, that the tale has not lived on because of the absence of real background. Macaulay's words in this regard are worth quoting: ' [*The Female Quixote*] has undoubtedly great merit when considered as a wild, satirical harlequinade; but, if we consider it as a picture of life and manners, we must pronounce it more absurd than any of the romances which it was designed to ridicule.'[24] It is as a satirical harlequinade that we must consider it, and it was this aspect which attracted a great train of imitators.

Spurred on by the success of *The Female Quixote*, Mrs Lennox published a third novel in 1758. *Henrietta* begins by securing our interest at once:

> About the middle of July, 17—, when the Windsor stage-coach with the accustomed number of passengers was proceeding on its way to London, a young woman genteely dressed, with a small parcel tied up in her handkerchief, hastily bolted from the shelter of a large tree near the road; and calling to the coachman to stop for a moment, asked him if he could let her have a place.

301

This is Henrietta Courteney, running away to London from her aunt's house.

Henrietta is the daughter of an earl's younger son who has married beneath him. Her mother was the child of an officer's widow. Hence Henrietta is poor and proud, and most obtrusively honest. She is befriended by her aunt who, however, is estranged by Henrietta's refusal to marry an aged peer, or alternatively to enter a convent. She refuses the peer on sentimental grounds, and the convent on religious grounds, since she is not a Catholic. She believes that she will be either married or immured against her will—hence her flight. Through a confusion of address, she takes lodgings in London at a questionable house, and attracts the attentions of the dangerous Lord B— whose passion and worldliness are foiled by her purity and poverty. Seduction and marriage being both out of the question, he still longs, but continues to negotiate for the daughter of a wealthy parvenu merchant. Henrietta, like Pamela, becomes a servant. She refuses to be a companion, and extols the dignity of honest service compared to dependence. But her real reason is that she wishes to spite her rich relatives who have ignored her. ('What a triumph would be mine if any of my relations should happen . . . to behold me in the character of Miss Cordwain's servant!'[25]) As few mistresses could live up to the beauty, the exalted sentiments and the open superiority of this unusual lady's maid, she is passed from one to another, still refusing to be parted from coronet or apron. Lord B—'s endeavours to make her his mistress are repulsed with fluent scorn. Henrietta goes to Paris with Miss Bellmour who employs her as a maid, but at once promotes her to the position of companion and confidante. Miss Bellmour is toying with the notion of yielding to her love for a married man. The journey to Paris is in the nature of a virtuous retreat, but it needs Henrietta's most didactic moralizing to keep her mistress firm in this attitude. Meanwhile two young men attach themselves to Miss Bellmour and Henrietta, Melvil (really a duke's son) and Freeman (really Henrietta's long-absent brother). Melvil adores Henrietta and she truly loves him, but holds back because of her inferior position. Melvil is so prostrated by his love that the doctors take a serious view, and, to help his recovery, Courteney comes to his sister, whom he has not recognized, and suggests that she yield to Melvil. He discovers whom it is that he is trying to ruin and is horrified. Miss Bellmour, tired of virtuous isolation, summons her lover. Henrietta accompanies her brother and Melvil to England. Her aunt repents of her injustice and gives Henrietta a dowry. Henrietta and Melvil are married.

The Richardsonian touches in this story are apparent[26] but it is to be observed that, unlike Richardson, Charlotte Lennox does not make her heroine forgive all her enemies. On the contrary, Rousseauistic punishment is rigorously assigned to every culprit. Lord B— marries his wealthy plebeian and is miserable. 'The sight of the charming Henrietta renewed his passion. Tortured with remorse, disappointment, and despair, he had recourse to the bottle, and fell an easy sacrifice to intemperance.' Miss Bellmour is forsaken by her lover and enters a convent, where she dies of 'grief, remorse and disappointment.' The younger Mr Damer (a married man who had been attracted by Henrietta) 'found in the incessant clamours of a jealous wife a sufficient punishment for his treacherous designs on Henrietta.' 'Every branch of the Courteney family made frequent advances towards a reconciliation with the marchioness and her brother: but, generous as they were, they had too just a sense of the indignities they had suffered from them to admit of it; and in this steady resentment they had, as it usually happens with successful persons, the world on their side.' These are the last words of the novel, and it is easy to recognize in them the stifled wishes of Charlotte Lennox herself. She had endured slights from the rich and noble, and it had left in her a steady resentment without hope of outlet.

Henrietta is not merely righteous and oppressed. She is a minx. Witness, for example, her interview with the foolish old baronet whom her aunt wishes her to marry.

> In Sir Isaac Darby, age was contemptible as well as unlovely; he wanted to be young, in spite of time; he talked and laughed aloud; he strutted about the room; he adjusted his bag [-wig], for he was dressed up to five and twenty; he hummed a tune; I sat staring with astonishment at him . . . Since I was obliged to stay, I would draw some amusement from the ridiculous scene before me. I know not whether it was from any particular archness in my looks just then, (for I had composed my countenance to a kind of forced gravity) or whether the old man was at a loss in what manner he should form his address, but it is certain that all his confidence

> seemed now for the first time to forsake him, and he sat
> silent during several minutes, stealing a glance at me every
> now and then; while I with a formal air, played my fan and
> increased his confusion by my silence.[27]

Finally the unfortunate man summons up a little courage and attempts to take her hand, 'which I withdrew as hastily as if a snake had touched it.' So the scene progresses, Henrietta mercilessly playing with her aged suitor as a cat with a mouse.

The characters in *Henrietta* are types, not individuals. There is much energy, vividness and acute observation. There is no humour, but rather an attitude of acid criticism, chiefly exerted on the *nouveaux riches* and on the nobility who are shown as haughty and heartless, willing to lower their pride only for money. Still, despite its superficiality and its crudities, this is an interesting novel — immensely superior to *Harriot Stuart*, Mrs Lennox's first attempt at this kind of fiction. The *Monthly* and the *Critical* both hailed it as the best novel that had appeared for some time.

Thereafter Mrs Lennox published two more novels: *Sophia* which first appeared in *The Lady's Museum* (1760–61) and *Euphemia* (1790). Sophia is a great reader, very reflective and very pious. Her effect on men is startling: '"Angelic creature!" exclaimed Sir Charles, with his eyes swimming in tears.' Mrs Gibbon, in this novel, is worth mentioning for her resemblance to Mrs Malaprop. ('She declared she would never have any *collection* with such vulgar creatures . . .' 'You see, Madam, what affluence your commands have over me.') *Sophia* is a sorry failure. *Euphemia* is little better. This latter novel is in epistolary form. In its efforts at sentimentalizing scenery and its complications as to the identity of a lost child, it suggests the influence of Mrs Radcliffe's *The Castles of Athlin and Dunbayne* which had appeared one year previously.

The difference between sentimentalism and sensibility in fiction is chiefly one of degree and, since many writers are, in their various works, now sentimental and now deliberately emotional, it would be impossible to group them according to the amount of feeling expressed. The most one can say is that, with the growth of the century, sensibility became more exaggerated. This was probably due to the fact that French sensibility gradually reinforced English sensibility. In Richardson's novels sensibility was merely incidental, the aim being to inculcate morality through stories of domestic life and manners. With Sterne, sensibility was little more than an unctuous camouflage for sensuality. As time went on, the idea of sensibility for its own sake became predominant on both sides of the Channel, and French writers appear to have given greater scope to the cult of feeling by stressing themes of adventure rather than of domesticity. A flood of French and English translations soon made it difficult to distinguish indebtedness either in regard to national characteristics or particular individuals, and it is perilous to claim that a novelist deliberately modelled his work on that of some French or English writer, since he might possibly be influenced simply by general tendencies which it would be difficult to trace to their true source. For these reasons it seems best, in discussing the principal women writers of this period, not to attempt to group them according to sentiment or sensibility, or to claim definitely that they were influenced by specified authors. It would appear more advisable to consider their works in roughly chronological order. On the whole, the mid-century novels are sentimental and the crescendo of sensibility grows with the years, but even this guide is merely rule of thumb.

The Miss Minifies (to use the contemporary plural) were well-known writers in their day, particularly Susannah Minifie (1740?–1800) who married John Gunning, brother of the famous Gunning sisters. Before her marriage she had written novels in collaboration with her sister Margaret (author of *The Count de Poland*, 1780). These first novels, including *The Picture*, *Family Pictures* and *The Cottage*, are in letter-form, poor in construction and unduly sentimental. In 1763 appeared *The Histories of Lady Frances S— and Lady Caroline S—*, similar to the works above mentioned in form, structure and tone. The epistolary medium is clumsily used. Sometimes the principal characters do not describe their own experiences, which fall to the pen of a third party. This may have the advantage of giving a more objective view but, were that the author's intention, it would have been better to drop the epistolary form altogether. There is the familiar double-barrelled plot in which two stories are forced disjointedly into one denouement. The story of Lady Frances S— is the better. Lady Frances suffers keenly at the hands of her jealous mother and her weak father. She is befriended by her uncle, at whose house she meets Worthley, a devoted but impecunious lover. Refused her parents' consent, Lady Frances secretly marries the man of her choice. Her marriage is discovered and she is banished from her parents' house. The other story concerns Lady Caroline S—. We are told at first that she is dead, but we do not believe this, and look forward confidently to the final identification by means of a strawberry mark. We see the humble Miss Dalton, daughter of the Duchess of S—'s waiting-woman, living with her grandfather, a Somerset parson. We see her pursued by Lord Ormsby who is making his first experiment in seduction. Ormsby abducts Miss Dalton, is confounded by her shining virtue, repents and thoroughly enjoys his repentance even to the extent of taking his sister and a friend to visit Miss Dalton, who is on the verge of brain-fever and a decline through the delicacy of her situation. The visiting ladies are charmed with the beauty, humility and magnanimity of Miss Dalton. Indeed she refuses to marry Lord Ormsby because it would demean him. But virtue has its reward. The Duchess's waiting-woman confesses on her death-bed that she substituted her own infant for the infant Caroline. Caroline lives yet as Miss Dalton and may be identified not indeed by a strawberry mark, but by a cherry mark which is equally convincing. Lord Ormsby now woos Miss Dalton in a garnet suit, 'the coat richly laced with a gold point d'Espagne, the waistcoat entirely covered with a net of gold thread.' She yields. The Duchess, after an attack of smallpox, sees the vanity of maternal jealousy and, happy at recovering one daughter, forgives the other.

Despite its obvious faults, there are points of interest in this novel. Miss Dalton is one of those prodigies so beloved by the newer school of women novelists: she combines much learning with a decent humility. The feminine point of view is also evident in the description of Mr Martin, the sporting lout. This character who, through Lord Newminster (in Mrs Smith's *Desmond*) develops into John Thorpe in *Northanger Abbey*, deserves a closer scrutiny. Miss Hamilton (whom he hopes to marry) describes him thus:

> a person you have often remark'd, for a bluntness, which tho' he does not say anything to offend, yet his boisterous manner keeps you in continual dread.— He enters a lady's drawing-room with the same ease he would his kennel; and seems to consider it as no other being always attended by a number of his four-footed friends, whom he familiarly

introduces to you; and indeed appears more conversant in their language, than that of any intelligent Being . . . This gentleman has lately honour'd me with an offer to be at the head of his pack; but I should have so many rivals that upon my word I cannot accept it. At present there is a Pointer and Greyhound, that he says tenderer things to, than to me, tho' not his wife.—This unaccountable creature tells me, whenever I reject him, that he can follow a chase twenty years, and will not pay me a worse compliment than he should to a fox or a stag.[28]

The brutality of Mr Martin can only be realized in relation to the feminine ideal of a hero at that period—such a man, for example, as Mr Worthley shows himself when pleading with the uncle of Lady Frances to help him obtain the consent of her parents. Mr Worthley throws himself on his knees in soul-piercing agony. When he succeeds in speaking, his words are 'hardly articulate, his manly eyes full of tears, full of imploring sweetness, lifted up to my uncle, as to his judge, whose mercy he petitioned.'[29]

But however much women novelists might subscribe to the sentimentalized conception of hero and heroine, they are very frank as to the minor women characters. In particular they dislike a gathering of women, and are adepts at describing the pettiness and the complacent spitefulness of women's gossip. Miss Hamilton's account of such a seance[30] is the most realistic part of this novel. Fanny Burney herself could not have been more acute. Susannah Gunning's best work[31] is *The Memoirs of Mary* which was published in 1793. In the interval between this novel and *The Histories of Lady Frances S— and Lady Caroline S—*, she had published two novels: *Barford Abbey* in 1768, and *Anecdotes of the Delborough Family* in 1792. *Barford Abbey* is a pleasing story, dealing with the misunderstandings and final happiness of true love. Her marriage in 1798 interrupted the composition of *Anecdotes of the Delborough Family* which she completed after her separation from her worthless husband, John Gunning. When Gunning turned his daughter out of the house for plotting to marry the man she loved, Mrs Gunning followed her. Soon afterwards his intrigue with Mrs Duberly led to litigation. He was obliged to pay the injured husband £5,000 damages. Thereafter he and his mistress retired to Naples where he died in 1797. These events (called by Walpole the 'Gunningiad') are recounted obliquely in *The Memoirs of Mary*. It may have been the sincerity of Mrs Gunning's feeling which made this her best novel. It has received scant praise, but in the opinion of the present writer, at any rate, it is one of the best of the lesser novels of this period. It is narrated in a spirited, graceful, and effortless style. There is no straining after elegance—almost an entire absence of sentimentality, and no sensibility at all. Compared to Mrs Brooke, for example, Mrs Gunning is a strong-minded writer.

Mary Montague is the beloved grand-daughter of Lady Auberry who rears her in the seclusion of her country estate. At the age of eighteen, according to the will of her father, she goes to live with the Duke and Duchess of Cleveland, who are connections of hers. She is beautiful, amiable and ingenuous. She soon has scores of suitors and becomes the toast of the season, but she is enmeshed in a deep-laid conspiracy to deprive her of her legitimacy and of her fortune. Mary Pleydell, the daughter of Lady Auberry, had married secretly to avoid her father's anger. Her husband had been obliged to sail at once with his regiment for America, and fell in battle shortly afterwards. Mary Montague is the fruit of this marriage. Her mother died a few days after the birth, and Lady Auberry has the child brought up secretly until Lord Auberry dies, when she brings her home and openly acknowledges her. By her father's will, Mary Montague is to inherit her father's property, but a relative, Sir Ashton Montague, conspires to disinherit her. Her cousin, the young Lord Auberry, had been engaged to her a few years before she came to London, but he was parted from her by a letter purporting to be in her handwriting, she remaining in entire ignorance of the reason for his withdrawal, and supposing that he had jilted her. These are the cross-currents which undermine the happiness of her life in London society. Mary knows nothing except that Sir Ashton Montague is always at her elbow, sinister and cryptic, with veiled allusions to her past engagement to Lord Auberry; and that Lord Auberry, studiously rude, and flaunting in her face his flirtations with such women as the loose Mrs Oxburn, yet hisses in her ear that he will never renounce his claim to her.

Meanwhile Mary is wooed by Henry Lexington, the nephew and heir of the Duke of Cleveland. She returns his love. They become engaged, but they are parted by the jealous scheming of Lord Auberry. Lexington goes abroad, and the plot against Mary culminates when her parents' marriage certificate and her father's will, carefully preserved by Mary's grandmother, are stolen through the machinations of Sir Ashton Montague. Nameless and penniless, Mary is scoffed at by those who envied her triumphs. But, at that moment, Lexington returns, discovers the plot which parted him from Mary and renews his addresses. By a great stroke of fortune, Sir Ashton Montague meets with a fatal accident and makes a death-bed confession. At a ball given by the Duchess of Cleveland the radiant Mary enters on her husband's arm. The Duchess announces their marriage, and all the ill-wishers are forced to feed on their own bitterness.

Lady Auberry's words to the friend who weeps at Mary's loss of name and fortune, sum up the attitude towards sensibility which this book expresses:

> These emotions, my child . . . are a sort of cannibals, that will feed on our own vitals, if we do not contend against them; let us then conquer these enemies, that will otherwise conquer us, and leave us neither sense nor reflection to baffle our misfortunes, or fortitude to support them.[32]

Speaking of Lord Auberry, who appears to resent the fact that his termination of their engagement has not sent her into a decline, Mary says:

> I have no doubt that he expected I should exhaust my whole life in performing funeral obsequies to the memory of his departed vows. Perhaps too, his sanity is piqued and himself injured, in his opinion, in finding me a rational woman rather than a despairing, forsaken heroine There are mistakes which might easily be adjusted, whenever his Lordship condescends to bestow a moment's serious reflection on what he was, what he is, and what I am.[33]

And she goes on to say that she has had the good fortune not merely to be taught how to sing, draw, paint, and speak languages, but also 'how to distinguish between honour and dishonour; how to be firm as well as yielding; how to be the guardian of my own repose.' 'To be the guardian of my own repose'! This is precisely the attitude of Jane Austen's rational heroines.

The Memoirs of Mary is the least sentimental work of this group of women novelists. Elizabeth Bonhote[34] seems to have patterned her Rambles of Mr Frankley on Sterne's *Sentimental Journey* and her other novels adhere to the accepted view of feminine behaviour. *Olivia, or the Deserted Bride* shows a dutiful and long-suffering wife freed by her husband's death to make a happier second marriage. In *Darnley Vale*, Mrs Bonhote works out the theory that a woman parted by treachery from her first lover can be entirely happy in a second attachment, even when she realizes how she has been tricked. In *Bungay Castle* some Gothic touches are blended with descriptions of Mrs Bonhote's own neighbourhood. Another writer intent on depicting domestic morality was Maria Susannah Cooper, author of *Letters between Emilia and Harriet* (1762); *The School for Wives* (1763); and *The Exemplary Mother, or Letters between Mrs Villars and her Family* (1769). Mrs Woodfin's *The History of Sally Sable* (1758) introduces the theme of incest, which may have owed some of its popularity to Prévost's literary influence. It transpires that Sally Sable is the natural daughter of one of the rakes who pursue her. This is the best of Mrs Woodfin's novels,[35] the rest of which do not merit particular mention.

By far the best writer of the school of sensibility was Mrs Frances Sheridan whose *Miss Sydney Bidulph* (1761) is in the direct line of succession from Richardson. Richardson, indeed, encouraged Mrs Sheridan as a writer, and he it was who arranged for the publication of this novel. Its reception amply justified the enthusiasm which Richardson had expressed when he first read it in manuscript. It was highly praised by reviewers, and received the warmest commendations from such people as Dr Johnson, Lord North and Charles James Fox. In the year following its appearance, an adaptation of *Miss Sydney Bidulph* was made into French by Prévost and published under the title *Mémoires pour servir à l'histoire de la vertu. Extraits du Journal d'une Dame.* In 1762 a German translation appeared, and later it was again translated into French by René Robinet.

Sydney Bidulph is on the point of marrying her brother's friend, Faulkland, when it is discovered that he has seduced and deserted a young girl named Miss Burchell. Sydney and her mother at once break off the match, and shortly afterwards Sydney marries a Mr Arnold. She is an exemplary wife and devotes herself to rearing her two children, but the happiness she manages to derive from her married life is destroyed when she learns that her husband is intriguing with an adventuress named Mrs Gerrarde. This woman is actually Miss Burchell's aunt, and she it is who bargained with Faulkland for delivering up her niece to him. Arnold not only refuses to part with Mrs Gerrarde, but turns Sydney out of his house under the pretence of believing that she is encouraging Faulkland. Griselda that she is, Sydney agrees to give up her claim to her children, and goes to live with her mother. Faulkland concocts a pretty scheme for clearing Sydney's name and making it possible for her to be with her children again. He kidnaps Mrs Gerrarde under the pretence that he is smitten with her charms. Arnold is therefore forced to believe that Faulkland, so far from thinking of Sydney, is determined to win Mrs Gerrarde. This point is driven home by a letter which Faulkland cleverly induces Mrs Gerrarde to write to Arnold, explaining that Sydney is innocent. Arnold repents, and his repentance is the deeper because he is now penniless as a result of Mrs Gerrarde's extravagances. The magnanimous Sydney forgives her husband, who dies shortly afterwards, leaving her to bring up her children on £50 a year. She again refuses to marry Faulkland and persuades him to marry Miss Burchell, who actually had not been innocent, but already all too experienced, when he was drawn in by her aunt and herself. This Faulkland later discovers to his cost.

Meanwhile Sydney and her children are pitifully poor. Her brother, Sir George, disgusted with her obduracy towards Faulkland, and under the influence of his selfish wife, ignores her. She is rescued from her distress by a West Indian relative who proves her good genius. This kinsman, because he appears to be destitute, is badly treated by Sir George. Sydney, on the contrary, treats him with all the generosity her poor circumstances permit. He is fabulously wealthy, showers money on her and makes her his heiress. Finally comes the day when Faulkland, who has been living with his wife in Ireland, bursts into Sydney's house to tell her that he has found his wife in adultery, and that, in shooting her lover, he has accidentally killed her also. He begs Sydney to marry him, threatening to commit suicide if she refuses. Her brother and her benefactor both support his entreaties, and Sydney yields. They marry and flee to the Continent. Then it transpires that Faulkland's erring wife is not dead, after all. Faulkland dies, and Sydney, worn out by misfortune and hoping for death, quietly resigns herself to the task of bringing up her daughters and Faulkland's son by his irregular union with Miss Burchell.

The second part of *Miss Sydney Bidulph* describes the romantic complications which arise between these young people, chiefly through the scheming of Audley, a cynical villain.

This brief outline of Mrs Sheridan's novel testifies to the appositeness of Dr Johnson's famous criticism that he doubted if the author should have made her readers suffer so much. The motif of endless misfortunes suggests the influence of Madame Riccoboni; and the many-volume convention was an added reason for the undue protraction of the story. Indeed the necessity for spinning out the plot appears to have been chiefly responsible for the divagation and discursiveness which are too apparent in this novel. Condensed, it could have gained greatly in strength. Mrs Sheridan could have omitted her adventitious stories and shortened her sub-stories. She frequently made the mistake of concentrating interest on what should have been merely incidental. For example, when Sydney repeats the account given her by Sir George of Faulkland's deed in Ireland, her narrative is far too detailed. Mrs Sheridan ignored the fact that Faulkland's past adventures are far less exciting than his present distracted state.

There are many interesting aspects in *Miss Sydney Bidulph*. There is a stressing of sensibility and endurance. Each of these qualities increases the other, and both unite to wring the heart of the heroine. Still, Sydney neither goes mad nor falls into a decline, but survives until her daughters are of marriageable age. Another point worth noting is that, in general, Mrs Sheridan subscribes to the accepted standards of feminine status and behaviour, and yet, in some respects, most strikingly presents the feminine point of view. In fact, the pivotal point of this story essentially represents a woman's judgement on an issue which, until that time, had not been raised in fiction. Before Mrs Sheridan, women writers had not required that the hero should be guiltless of seducing innocence. In *Miss Sydney Bidulph* this claim is made, but a single standard of morality is not applied. Faulkland is exonerated when it is discovered that Miss Burchell was guilty before she met him. Mrs Sheridan does not judge immorality *per se*, but only in relation to its victim. Nevertheless, it was an advance on the code of gallantry and on the code of casual sexual adventure which sheltered women were supposed to take for granted in their men-folk.

But it was not merely in moral outlook that Mrs Sheridan struck a feminine note. In her presentation of a woman's mind, with its characteristic moods and impulses, there is much that indicates a woman's insight. When the excellent Lord V— pays court to Sydney's daughter, Cecilia, she will have none of him, and makes short work of every argument which a family friend makes in his favour. Yes, he is handsome, very accomplished, extremely well-bred and perfectly good-tempered: his morals are unexceptionable.

> She turned her eyes at me with so arch a look, that I could scarce refrain from laughing. 'I know nothing to the contrary, Madam,' —'Has he not a fine estate?'—'I do not want money, Mrs B—.'—'Of a considerable family, and noble rank?'—'I desire not titles either.' —'What then do you desire, Cecilia?'—'Only to please myself;' and she shook her little head so, that all the powder and the curls in her hair fell about her face . . . And yet she has her hours of sadness. 'For what, my dear?'—'Oh, you'll know all in time,' in a low voice, as she curtseyed to take her leave; and down she flew like a lapwing.[36]

Cecilia has vivacity, charm and depth; she is a 'bewitching little gypsy,' in marked contrast to her sister Dolly who is a young woman of the greatest sensibility. Dolly is far too full of maidenly delicacy. She is too grave, too prone to tears and swoons. Both sisters love young Faulkland. Dolly feeds on her emotions which so rend her that, when Faulkland's dislocated shoulder is being set, she faints away twice although she is in a distant part of the house. On the contrary, Cecilia candidly avows her love to Faulkland—surely the first woman in fiction thus to take the initiative. '"I always thought you loved me," said she, "yet, Faulkland, you should have spoken first, and spared me the pains of extorting a confession from you."' Faulkland comments:

> What a noble frankness was here! how unlike a woman! no affected confusion, no pretty coyness, after such a declaration! Amazed, overwhelmed, and penetrated to the soul, I fell at her feet, and grasping her knees, with the action of a madman—'Oh, Cecilia' cried I, 'dare I believe my senses?'[37]

But Faulkland, in a moment of pity for Dolly, has already given her his vows. Now he engages himself to Cecilia whom he really loves. Their marriage ceremony is interrupted by Dolly's distraught reproaches, and Faulkland fights and kills the man who has played on his weakness and used him as a catspaw. This is the end of Audley, a most interesting villain with a sense of humour. Audley is determined to marry either Cecilia or Dolly, because both have splendid fortunes. Personally he prefers Cecilia because she is spirited. Dolly, he says (with an echo of *The Female Quixote*):

> would do mighty well to be the mistress of a Don Bellianis, or a Sir Launcelot, who could afford to waste seven years in strolling up and down the world, without either meat or drink, in order to prove his constancy; and after that, would think himself fully paid, if he were allowed to brush his beard (which he had vowed never to shave till he saw her again) on her lily-white hand through the grated window of some enchanted tower.[38]

But Cecilia loves Faulkland, so Audley concentrates his energies on winning this bread-and-butter miss, undeterred by the fact that he has a wife already. He kidnaps her and releases her unharmed, hoping that the compromising circumstances will force her to marry him. His death cuts the tangle he has so cunningly devised. Audley's philosophy of evil is summed up in the declaration:

> Of all devils, I hate a penitent devil: What a noble figure does Satan himself make, as he is described in the sixth book of Milton, where he boldly defies the whole artillery of Heaven! And what a sneaking rascal does he appear in the fourth book, where just like Faulkland, he recapitulates his woes, and bemoans his lost estate.

Truly excellent is the hypocritical account which he gives Dolly of his efforts to persuade her relatives that she was constrained by illness to spend the night in his house. Poor Dolly is innocent, but he has spread too clever a net. His arguments, his deceptions, his sophistries, his deliberate forcing of her into a corner until there appears no possibility of escape except through lies and a patched-up marriage with him — here is a fine crescendo of subtle and cynical villainy. At the thought of the coil of falsehood to which she must lend herself, Dolly stopped short, striking her forehead with her hand. 'Oh, Lear, Lear!' whispered the sardonic Audley, 'beat at this gate that lets the folly in, etc.'[39]

Though Mrs Sheridan owed much to Richardson's influence and something to French sensibility, these debts are merely incidental — not more than any author owes to the literary atmosphere of his period. *Sydney Bidulph* is an original, vivid, and charming book. It is, above all, human. Mrs Sheridan never forgets that she is dealing with people of flesh and blood; and (as with her description of Lady Grimston[40]) she can make them live before our eyes.

Sensibility exercised in a sequence of misfortunes and generally doomed to final misery is also the theme of Mrs Brooke, Mrs Griffith, Helen Maria Williams and Mary Robinson. But, as they had neither the power nor the individuality of Mrs Sheridan, there is little escape in their novels from an excess of that fatality which governs lovers in the works of Prévost and Mme Riccoboni.

Mrs Brooke (1724–1789), daughter of a clergyman named Moore, and wife of the chaplain to the forces at Quebec, was much influenced by Mme Riccoboni. In fact, she translated into English, in 1764, Mme Riccoboni's *Milady Juliette Catesby*. Prior to that time (in 1763), appeared anonymously *The History of Lady Julia Mandeville*.

Henry Mandeville is reared to expect only £700 a year. He loves his relative, Lady Julia, and considers his chances hopeless. Actually there is an amiable conspiracy between the fathers that the young couple shall marry and so compensate for a flaw in the succession of the family title. But Henry and Julia are kept in ignorance of this design, so that the idea of carrying out a family plan may not destroy the possibility of their falling in love. They keep their love a secret while Henry seeks to improve his fortunes. There is a rumour that the rich Lord Melvin is intended to be Julia's husband. The parents prepare lavishly for the marriage of Julia and Henry, whose secret attachment has become known to them, but these unexplained preparations seem to confirm Henry's suspicions of a rival. He becomes distracted and insists on engaging Lord Melvin in a duel. He is slain and Lady Julia survives him only by a few hours. Prévost is echoed in the descriptions of their deaths, in the awful spectacle of the lovers lying side by side in their coffins, in the despair of their parents and friends. There is a rather interesting suggestion of Gothic terrors in the passage which describes Lady Anne Wilmot's walk in the shrubbery, while the lovers lie dead:

> Pleased with the tender sorrow which possessed all my soul, I determined to indulge it to the utmost; and revolving in my imagination the happy hours of cheerful friendship to which that smiling scene had been a witness, prolonged my walk till evening had, almost unperceived, spread its gloomy horrors round; till the varied tints of the flowers were lost in the deepening shades of night.
>
> Awaking at once from the reverie in which I had been plunged, I found myself at a distance from the house, just entering the little wood go loved by my charming friend; the very moment increasing darkness gave an awful gloom to the trees. I stopped, I looked around, not a human form was in sight. I listened, and heard not a sound but the trembling of some poplars in the wood. I called, but the echo of my own voice was the only answer I received; a dreary silence reigned around; a terror I never felt before seized me; my heart panted with timid apprehension; I breathed short; I started at every leaf that moved; my limbs were covered with a cold dew; I fancied I saw a thousand airy forms flit around me; I seemed to hear the shrieks of the dead and dying: there is no describing my horrors.[41]

This is a very disappointing novel. The story is clear and closely linked, but there is no characterization, except possibly for the witty and vivacious Anne Wilmot who is a fascinating widow with a kind heart and an ironic turn of mind. Her flirtations, capricious moods and railleries are amusing, but too often overdone ('O mon Dieu! what do I see coming down the avenue? Is it in women to resist an equipage? Papier maché—highly gilded—loves and doves—six long-tailed grey Arabians. By all the gentle powers of love and gallantry, Fondville himself!').[42]

In *Lady Julia Mandeville* the descriptions of nature and of country life were so idealized as to be pastoral. In *The History of Emily Montague* (1769) Mrs Brooke, drawing on her knowledge of Canada, achieves some very good effects. This is one of the better aspects of a desultory novel which extends over four volumes a tale which might have been compressed into two. The events are slight. The obstacles to the true love of heroine and hero are all due to their own sensibility or that of others. The macabre element, however, is happily absent. The story is prolonged not only by the complications of sensibility, but by disquisitions on love, marriage, education, colonial politics and scenery. This latter subject is of value since descriptions of nature were all too rare and too unreal in English fiction up to that period. Mrs Brooke's descriptions in Emily Montague are very little idealized, sometimes not at all, and are easily visualized. The best known scene is the breaking-up in spring of the bridge of ice over the St Lawrence.[43] Very fine also is the description of the Falls of Montmorenci in winter, and there are innumerable other shorter descriptions which show in Mrs Brooke the ability to observe closely and to reproduce faithfully. For example:

> The rock on the east side, which is first in view as you approach, is a smooth and almost perpendicular precipice, of the same height as the fall; the top, which a little over-hangs, is beautifully covered with pines, firs, and ever-greens of various kinds, whose verdant lustre is rendered at this season more shining and lovely by the surrounding snow, as well as by that which is sprinkled irregularly on their branches, and glitters half melted in the sunbeams: a thousand smaller shrubs are scattered on the side of the ascent, and, having their roots in almost imperceptible clefts of the rock, seem to those below to grow in air . . . The torrent, which before rushed with such impetuosity down the deep descent in one vast sheet of water, now descends in some parts with a slow and majestic pace; in others it seems almost suspended in mid air; and in others, bursting through the obstacles which interrupt its course, pours down with redoubled fury into the foaming bason below, from whence a spray arises, which freezing in its ascent, becomes on each side a wide and irregular frozen breast-work; and in front, the spray being there much greater, a lofty and magnificent pyramid of solid ice.[44]

And there are such delightful spring touches as: 'Tis amazingly pleasing to see the strawberries and wild pansies peeping their foolish heads from beneath the snow.'[45]

In this novel sensibility is the ideal. ''Tis the magnet which attracts all to itself: virtue may command esteem, understanding and talents admiration, beauty a transient desire; but 'tis sensibility alone which can inspire love.'[46] Emily Montague is the typical heroine of sensibility, whom we shall meet again in the pages of Mrs Radcliffe:

Without being regularly beautiful, she charms every sensible heart: all other women, however lovely, appear marble
statues near her: fair; pale (a paleness which gives the idea
of delicacy without destroying that of health), with dark hair
and eyes, the latter large and languishing, she seems made
to feel to a trembling excess the passion she cannot fail of
inspiring: her elegant form has an air of softness and languor,
which seizes the whole soul in a moment: her eyes, the most
intelligent eyes I ever saw, hold you enchain'd by their
bewitching sensibility.[47]

The role of Belle Fermor resembles that of Anne Wilmot in
Lady Julia Mandeville. She is a foil for the extreme sensibility of the
principal characters. These minor personages, though not well
drawn, are at least refreshing and lend a sense of reality. Emily
Montague, despite its looseness of plot, is preferable to *Lady Julia
Mandeville* because the story is more natural and the background
much more interesting.[48]

Like Mrs Sheridan, Elizabeth Griffith[49] was Irish. She first won
the attention of the reading public by *A Series of Genuine Letters
between Henry and Frances* (1757) — the actual letters which passed
between her and Richard Griffith prior to their marriage. In 1769
she and her husband published two companion novels in letters:
The Gordian Knot by Richard Griffith, and *The Delicate Distress*
by Elizabeth.

The Delicate Distress consists of graceful letters in which a
number of stories are loosely strung together. The main narrative
describes the complications which arise when the Marchioness
d'Aumont, once loved by Lord Woodville, tries to regain her
hold over him during the first year of his marriage. He really loves
his wife, and yet is extremely fascinated by the Marchioness. He
alternates between resistance and weakness, and finally determines
to join the *femme fatale* in France. A fall from his horse hinders his
plans, and in the serious illness that follows, his wife, who has long
suspected and now knows all, heaps coals of fire upon his head.
They are united more fully than ever, and the wicked Marchioness,
intent on other victims, passes out of their lives. Slightly linked
with this central theme are various peripheral stories. The chief
of these are the story of Lord Seymour and Charlotte; the story
of Lady Harriet Hanbury; the story of Lucy Straffon; the story of
Lady Somerville; and the story of the Ransfords.

Sensibility and delicacy are the keynotes of this novel. We do not find, however, the exaggeration and artificiality which these terms too often connote in eighteenth century fiction. Sincerity is apparent in Mrs Griffith's style, and her outlook is thoughtful and generous. Speaking of Miss Fanning who has alienated the affections of Sir William Lawson, the husband of her benefactress, Lady Straffon says:

> Had she been led astray, by an agreeable young man, I could have pitied, nay, perhaps, have loved, and even esteemed her; for I am not such an Amazon in ethics, as to consider a breach of chastity, as the highest crime, that a woman can be guilty of; though it is, certainly, the most unpardonable folly; and I believe there are many women, who have erred, in that point, who may have more real virtue, aye, and delicacy too, than half the sainted dames, who value themselves on the preservation of chastity; which, in all probability, has never been assailed. She alone, who has withstood the solicitations of a man she fondly loves, may boast her virtue; and I will venture to say, that such an heroine will be more inclined to pity, than to despise, the unhappy victims of their own weakness.

She goes on to speak of acidulated and complacent virtue:

> There is no character, I so heartily abominate, as that of the outrageously virtuous. I have seen a lady render herself hateful, to a large company, by repeating, perhaps a forged tale, of some unhappy frail one, with such a degree of rancour, and malevolence, as is totally inconsistent, with the calm dignity of real virtue.[50]

Gentleness and magnanimity Mrs Griffith holds to be the best equipment for life, enabling one to bear all trials and vexations with self-respecting dignity. It is by gentleness that erring husbands are to be reclaimed. It is by magnanimity that treachery is to be repaid. When Sir James Miller jilts Lucy Straffon (because she insists on being inoculated against smallpox!), he marries Miss Nelson, and is soon as deep in debt as his wife is in infidelity. Lucy considers his vices justly punished, but is so grateful to him for leaving her free to marry Lord Mount Willis, that she insists on giving him an allowance anonymously. 'I formerly looked upon him, with horror and aversion; I now consider him as my benefactor; and the saving him from the miseries of extreme poverty will relieve my mind, from a sort of mental debt.'[51]

To Mrs Griffith sensibility chiefly means refinement of feeling:

> There is everything to be expected from sensibility, and delicacy, joined; but, indeed, I have scarce ever known them separated, in a female heart. Refined manners are the natural consequences of fine feelings, which will, even in an untutored mind, form a species both of virtue, and good breeding, higher than anything that is to be acquired, either in courts, or schools.[52]

Still, the emotional tempests and all the external phenomena of sensibility are strongly evidenced in this novel. When Lord Seymour's adored Charlotte takes her vows as a nun, he says:

> How I got out of the convent, I know not: my senses vanished, with her.— I was fifteen days delirious, and but for the officious kindness of Wilson, should not now feel those poignant agonies, that rend my heart.[53]

When Charlotte failed to win the recognition of her unnatural parents 'she threw herself on the ground, and washed it with her tears.'[54] When Lady Harriet Hanbury learns from her supposed fiancé, Captain Barnard, that he has married another, she treats him with frigid contempt, but later pays for this resolute self-control:

> The heroism of my conduct towards Captain Barnard, had flattered my pride, and kept up my spirits, while he was present, but I was no sooner alone, than I felt all the weight of my misfortunes; and the agitation and distraction of my mind, threw me into convulsions. My maid had immediate help for me, but all the art of the best physician in Paris, could not restore my senses for fifteen days.[55]

The History of Lady Barton (1771) is a very poor novel indeed. It begins in so vague and unconnected a way that several letters pass before we understand the general setting. The plot is straggling and shows no planning. It is interrupted by inset stories of a length out of all proportion to the main narrative. Not only are the minor tales inset in the principal story, but they are also inset in each other like Chinese boxes. For example, the story of Mrs N— is inset in the story of Maria, which is inset in the

320

story of Lady Barton. The use of letters is evidently a mere adherence to a literary fashion, since the peculiar advantages of the epistolary medium are not applied. Nothing could be more mechanical than the manner in which, for instance, the long inset story of Mrs Walter is continued from letter to letter, the correspondent quoting it verbatim in the first person. The main narrative shows a sorely tempted lady being true to a husband whom she does not love, and rejecting a man whom she adores. In all awkward situations Lady Barton, a victim of extreme sensibility, becomes unconscious and remains so for hours. There is an accouchement of which the contingent circumstances are completely incredible. There is no characterization. The hero and heroine are exquisitely sensitive paragons; Hume is meant to be a gay gallant worth reclamation; Colonel Walters is a villain of the deepest dye. There is not one convincing touch of human nature, incident or surroundings from beginning to end. The style is prosy and sententious. Tears gush in torrents. The moral is that one must not marry without love: 'It must be the joining of hearts, not hands, that can insure the marriage *rights*—I don't misspell the word—and the woman who stretches out an *empty hand*, at the altar, but mocks the institution; and, if I may hazard the boldness of the expression, becomes *guilty*, before her *crime*; receives an antepast of misery, and puts her trust in miracles, for safety.'[56] All the scenes which are supposed to be vital are absurdly melodramatic: 'Hear me, Sir, while I call Heaven to witness, that Lord Lucan never solicited a criminal indulgence from me! and that my heart has never yet admitted a thought which could reflect dishonour on my husband.'[57] Parents lament that they must, because of undutiful children, 'sink with sorrow to the grave'. A daughter, pressed to marry in obedience to her mother's wishes, on threat of that mother's decease, bathes the bosom of this exigent parent with her flowing tears, and cries out: 'O take me, sacrifice me, do what you will with me. I will not be a parricide! But give me time to conquer this poor heart, and tear my L—'s much loved image from my breast.[58] No wonder that this victim's sufferings have serious results. 'For five days I continued in a state of mental annihilation, the return of my reason, was like the appearance of an ignis fatuus, it glimmered, and vanished, several times, as if unwilling to return to the wretched habitation which it had forsaken.'[59]

But although Mrs Griffith adhered to the masculine notion of womanhood, there are occasional glimpses of the feminine point of view. In speaking of the educational advantages denied to women she deplores that the most mediocre man is given, as a matter of course, opportunities beyond the reach of the most gifted woman, but she finds consolation in the reflection that academic learning and character-training are two distinct things: 'The greatest blockheads I have ever known, have been bred in college — Neither absurdity nor meanness prevent a man from becoming a master of language, nor of arriving at a competent knowledge in any particular branch of science.'[60]

The male attitude towards female frailty does not meet with serious opposition in fiction until Mary Wollstonecraft and Mary Hays hit back. The established view was that even the seducer has the right to condemn on moral grounds the woman he has seduced. This inconsistency finds its apotheosis in Hugh Kelly's *Memoirs of a Magdalen; or, the History of Louisa Mildmay* (1767). The Magdalen, who was the affianced of the hero, Sir Robert Harold, yields to him before the marriage ceremony. He writes: 'I have succeeded, fatally succeeded, with this amiable wretch, and both of us must bid adieu to happiness forever.' Only after she has undergone severe and prolonged penance does he take the risk of marrying this woman he has ruined. Mrs Griffith puts the mild reply into a man's mouth: 'We first take pains to destroy the foundation of every female virtue, modesty; and are then surprised to find the superstructure totter.'[61]

The sensibility in Mrs Griffith's novels seems to reflect French influence. Incidentally it is interesting to note in the association of Margarita and Hume[62] an echo of *Manon Lescaut*. Margarita, who has betrayed Hume, and who is now living with a supposed brother, has only to smile at him with ineffable sweetness to win him into the toils again.

Mrs Griffith's last novel,[63] *The Story of Juliana Harley* (1776), also dealt with domestic cross-currents. It is the story of a forced and loveless marriage between a sensitive woman and a clod. It bears out Mrs Griffith's view that marriage without love is legal prostitution.

It remains to mention Helen Maria Williams and Mary Robinson, who are alike in several respects. Both wrote highly emotional novels, both were poetesses, both were supposed to have some connection with the Della Cruscans,[64] and (though it is a matter of no literary import) both had strayed from the path of morality. Helen Maria Williams was a fervent believer in the doctrines of the French Revolution. In fact she was imprisoned in the Luxembourg by Robespierre and narrowly escaped being guillotined for her connection with the Girondists. Her political writings involved her in controversies, and drew upon her condemnation as 'a woman whose lips and pen distil venom'; 'whose wretched pen has long been accumulating on itself disgrace after disgrace.' As the words of a political opponent, these judgments need not be taken too seriously. While in Paris, Miss Williams lived with John Hurford, and some say with Imlay, circumstances which would have caused Fanny Burney to refuse her acquaintance, had she known them when they met at an evening party. Just before that meeting, Miss Williams had published, in 1782, *Edwin and Eltruda*, a legend in verse, and Fanny objected strongly to her air of self-opinionation. She lives for us in Fanny's words: 'A pretty girl rather, but so superfinely affected that, tho' I had the honour of being introduced to her, I couldn't think of conversing with her.'[65] In 1771 Miss Williams published *Anecdotes of a Convent*, a series of letters which tell a straggling story. In 1790 appeared *Julia, a novel interspersed with some poetical pieces*. This story (which has for its background eighteenth-century England) has nothing to recommend it.[66] According to the author, it is intended 'to trace the danger arising from the uncontrouled indulgence of strong affections . . . When disapproved by reason, and uncircumscribed by prudence, they involve even the virtuous in calamity.' This prepares one for strong meat, whereas nothing could be more etiolated than the love-story which follows. After tacking backwards and forwards repeatedly among the first chapters, we finally gather that Julia, a paragon of virtue and beauty, is beloved by Frederick Seymour, who is engaged to marry her cousin Charlotte. He marries Charlotte, but continues to love Julia with increasing passion and despair. These emotions he expresses by following her with his eyes and sitting near her. When he is in a very unbridled frame of mind, he plots to be alone with her so that he may hint his hopeless love, as thus: 'Oh, may every felicity attend you! — may you be happy, when the grave shall have covered my despair, and my heart may retain no longer these sensations, which are interwoven with my existence.' From such speeches Julia shrinks with terrified propriety. She invariably hastens from the room saying that she will conceal herself henceforth in some unknown asylum. These lawless dallyings continue for two volumes.

Julia is purer than the driven snow and of the most delicate sensibility. She is always reading the Bible to her old grand-mother; making camlet gowns for the poor; rescuing worms from heedless feet, birds from cats, and flies from bowls of water. She is undoubtedly a noble character. She is very intellectual too, and constantly composes elegant verses which we are never spared. She is tremblingly alive to scenery, particularly at sunset, and she knows the charm of a Gothic ruin, especially if it should have a Gothic gate.[67] Indeed it is when her party is looking at a *snail's nest* in a Gothic abbey that a huge stone almost falls on her, and precipitates her into the arms of Frederick. He keeps his head, however, contenting himself with saying: 'The reflection that I have been the instrument of your preservation, I shall ever cherish as the most delightful that can occupy my mind.'[68] Having struggled gamely to strangle his fatal partiality, he dies of fever. His ravings would melt the heart of a stone. Julia soothes his last moments; Julia breaks the news to Charlotte, whose son has just been born. Thereafter Julia, who refuses to marry, lives with Charlotte and devotes her time to the improvement of Seymour's son; but the memory of her repressed love for Seymour still embitters her life, which otherwise might have been fortunate and happy.

The only parts of this novel which have any link with reality are the descriptions of other women, particularly of venomous gossips. There is a card-party at Mrs Chartres', which is certainly drawn from Miss Williams's experience. The description of Mrs Melbourne is also acute. This lady is generally morose and ill-humoured to her family.

> The only seasons memorable for Mrs Melbourne's tender-ness were when any of her connections or family were ill. She was then the most courteous creature existing, and began to love them with all her might, as if she thought there was no time to lose, and that she must endeavour to crowd such an extraordinary degree of fondness into the short space which was left, as might counterbalance her neglect or

unkindness through the whole course of their lives. The way to make her regard permanent was to die.[69]

Miss Williams translated a number of works from the French among them *Paul and Virginia* (1796); and Xavier de Maistre's *The Leper of the City of Aosta* (1817). *The History of Perourou, or the Bellows-maker* (1801), on which Lytton based his *Lady of Lyons*, was said to be original. Dr Baker believes that she must have adapted it from the French.[70]

Mary Robinson, actress, author, and royal mistress, was of Irish descent. She received her earliest education in the school kept in Bristol by the sisters of Hannah More. Her father, the captain of a whaler (whose family name of McDermott had been changed by a forebear into Darby) appears to have taken only an intermittent interest in his family. He deserted them for long periods, and Mary's upbringing was very haphazard. Her story is too well-known to need repetition. When she, 'the exquisite Perdita', became paralyzed, she could no longer rely on love, and she returned to those notions of literary fame which had occasionally attracted her since childhood. She published a quantity of poetry and several novels,[71] all highly coloured with sensibility, one an epistolary novel on the Fanny Burney pattern. Space makes it necessary to confine ourselves to examining only one of Mary Robinson's novels—*Vancenza, or the dangers of credulity* (1792).

This is a very romanticized tale couched for the most part in effusive euphemisms. There is a mingling of the elements of titled romance, Gothicism, and incest. Amid the wild and glowing beauty of Vancenza in Spain stands the castle of Vancenza, dating back to the twelfth century. This Gothic pile is the seat of Count Vancenza who lives there in the most perfect happiness with his sister, the Marchioness de Vallorie, her daughter Carline, and Elvira, 'an illustrious orphan'. Elvira has every qualification for being a heroine—beauty, goodness, exquisite sensibility and mysterious parentage. It needs only the advent of men into this Eden to set in train all the raptures, misunderstandings, villainies and tortures which beset any heroine worthy of the name. It happens that the Prince of Almanza is injured while hunting and conveyed to Vancenza. Elvira loves him at first sight and so transparently that her secret is an open book to the Duke del

Vero, who is powerfully attracted by her. The Prince departs in ignorance of the conquest he has made, but del Vero, secretly lingering in the neighbourhood of Vancenza, determines to pursue his own designs, which do not include marriage to a nameless orphan of no fortune. Pretending to be Almanza, he serenades Elvira and asks her to meet him at daybreak at the cottage of an old woman who is a retainer of the Vancenza family. With trembling reluctance she keeps the appointment, and is so overcome by the sight of the Prince's cloak thrown carelessly on a bench that 'her tottering limbs just supported her to the door, she sunk upon the green sod at the threshold and fainted.' When she recovers she finds kneeling before her the Duke del Vero. She is filled with rage, shame, self-reproach, pride, and the spirit of insulted virtue. She prepares to wither him, but he insolently tells her that Almanza loves another, and makes it clear that he, del Vero, will hold over her her indiscretion in coming secretly to meet him. Elvira soon sees the mistake of exposing herself 'to the artifice of an abandoned libertine' when del Vero prepares to carry her off there and then. But virtuous indignation triumphs. Pushing him from her with a look of scorn she says resolutely: 'I am above reproach.' She then walks firmly to the castle, but is delirious within a few hours. She recovers, but 'the icy hand of torpid, melancholy chilled the vital source that fed her being while her fine eyes darted their paly lustre, like the expiring lamps that glimmer in the arches of a sepulchre.' She keeps her secret, and nobody knows why she has changed. To divert her the family decides to go on a visit to Madrid. There Almanza falls in love with her, and del Vero troubles her with his minatory attentions. Carline is privately wooed by the Marquis Petrozi, who is an impostor, a gamester and a rake. When Count Vancenza hears Petrozi's real character, he withdraws his family coldly from the acquaintanceship. Petrozi, in revenge, tries to abduct Carline, but is foiled by Vancenza, whom he slays. His sister, Carline and Elvira return home, and there, having discovered (in Gothic circumstances) a manuscript which reveals that Almanza is her half-brother, Elvira dies.

There is really no characterization in this novel. Almanza is a woman's hero. His eyes beam with sensibility; his chestnut hair curls beautifully. He wears a scarlet hunting dress, bordered with sable, a cloak with a brilliant star, and a hat of black velvet with a white plume. Nowadays we should call him a musical-comedy Prince.

Unreality is but too evident also in Mary Robinson's language. Elvira 'enveloped her fair form in a robe of muslin'; the trees are 'the venerable vistas'; the grave is 'the narrow pallet of eternal repose'. 'The villages were crowded with rustics engaged in a variety of gambols.'

But however smothered by high-falutin' nonsense, there is sincere feeling for scenery, and it is evident also that Mary Robinson had taken the Gothic hint from Mrs Radcliffe. When Elvira leaned out of her window at night:

> All was cold and turbid; not a glimmering star shot forth its feeble rays through the thick clouds that hovered over the forest. The screech-owl, hid within her solitary dwelling, pierced with her horrid shrieks the ear of night; the winds moaned along the battlements, and the long windows rattled round the castle. She stood aghast . . .[72]

When Almanza returned to Vancenza after the Count's death, he found the outer gate unbarred:

> The great court yard was covered with long grass, and the Gothic hall unoccupied by its usual train of domestics. He proceeded through the long gallery; the setting sun cast a gloomy light through the painted windows, the portraits of the family, for many generations, still decorated the damp walls, covered with faded tapestry. His footsteps echoed as he passed along; Elvira heard them as she entered from the terrace; her heart palpitated with apprehension that some supernatural being occasioned the unusual sound.[73]

Mrs Robinson's novels are a curious mixture of vulgarity, ignorance, and poetic feeling. She can sum up Gothic splendour in one excellent phrase: 'moth-eaten magnificence', and yet she constantly uses words without understanding their meaning. Her conception of intense emotion may be gleaned from her description of Elvira's death (mostly in capitals and with double marks of exclamation as finger-posts to tragedy), and yet with the lyrical spirit of Romantic poetry she tells us that, when the Prince heard the dread news, he shrank 'like a blasted flower that meets the fervid lightning'.[74]

We have been careful to show the faults of that group of women writers who followed the trends of sentiment and of sensibility, but we have endeavoured also to make clear the peculiar value of their contribution. It lay in these women's growing consciousness that female novelists should use a female pen, that with their increasing hold over the reading public they need no longer subscribe to a masculine attitude in fiction. We have already seen a growing individuality in the women's novels — a tendency to write as women. This was the aspect which came fully into view in the novels of Fanny Burney.

Notes and References

1 Mary Wollstonecraft, *Posthumos Works*, i, *The Cave of Fancy*, pp. 135 f.
2 Mrs Frances Brooke, *The History of Emily Montague* (4 vols., Garland Press, New York, 1974), vol. i, p. 83. Sir George Clayton is a dreadful example of this insensitive nature.
3 Mrs Frances Brooke, *The History of Lady Julia Mandeville* (*British Novelists* edn., 1820), xxvii, p. 35.
4 Ibid., p. 201.
5 Mr James Foster (in 'The Abbé Prévost and the English Novel', Publications of the *Modern Language Association of America*, vol. xlii, no. 2, June, 1927) states definitely that at this period French fiction exerted a strong influence on English fiction. He says that Mmes de la Fayette, d'Aulnoy, de Tencin, Riccoboni and de Genlis, and particularly Marivaux and Prévost, all animated by sensibility, had a most powerful and far-reaching effect on the English novelists. He claims that Prévost and his disciples (of whom Baculard d'Arnaud was one) prolonged the epoch of sensibility in the English novel, and showed that, when the Richardsonian gamut of domestic sufferings was exhausted, a wider field of sensibility was to be found in adventurous perils, this aspect of sensibility finding cumulative expression in the Gothic romance. In addition to a detailed exposition of these views, Mr Foster gives an account of the numerous English translations of the French writers mentioned and traces the influence of Prévost and his followers on individual English novelists of this period. As against Mr Foster's opinion there is the opinion of George Saintsbury (Introduction to H. Waddell's translation of *Manon Lescaut*, 1934, p. xxviii):

> Mr James Foster . . . has collected a mighty list of translations and suggested a mightier one of imitations inspirations and the like. I confess that I think he has altogether over-rated the Abbé's influence on individuals . . . Prévost influenced those who influenced nobody. I can myself see very little resemblance to him in Mrs Sheridan's *Sydney Bidulph* and still less in Mrs Radcliffe anywhere, while he

certainly may have any share in Miss Lee's rubbishy *Recess* that anybody chooses to assign to him. I desire not to be in the least impolite to Mr Foster, but I think that he and all his school are much too fond of assuming direct 'imitation', 'influence', 'origin', etc., when there is merely coincidence or at most similar influence of period and fashion.'

6 *The History of Emily Montague*, op. cit., vol. ii, p. 225.

7 Prefixed to her *Sacred Dramas* (1782).

8 J.M.S. Tompkins, *The Popular Novel in England*, 1770–1800 (1932), p. 101.

9 Dr J.M.S. Tompkins makes this point and adds that 'there is evidence that eight years earlier the fraud was already an old and paying one.' See *The Popular Novel in England, 1770–1800*, p. 120.

10 *Boswell's Life of Johnson* (ed. Hill), vii, p. 107.

11 *Diary of Madame d'Arblay*, i, p. 160.

12 *Boswell's Life of Johnson* (ed. Hill), v, pp. 395 f.

13 For full details see Miriam R. Small *Charlotte Ramsay Lennox* (Yale University Press, 1935). Lady Mary Wortley Montagu's letter to the Countess of Bute expresses 'great surprise and indignation'.

14 The earliest translation was into German: *Don Quixote im Reifrocke* (1754), published at Hamburg and Leipzig. The French translation appeared in 1773, second edn. 1801, the Spanish translation (by Don Bernardo Maria de Calzada) appeared in 1808.

15 Charlotte Lennox, *The Female Quixote: Or, The Adventures of Arabella*, (Intro. Sandra Shulman, 'Mothers of the Novel', Pandora, London, 1986), Bk. ii, ch. x, pp. 107 f.

16 Ibid., Bk. ii, ch. ix, p. 99.

17 See Miss M. R. Small, *Charlotte Ramsay Lennox* (Yale University Press, 1935) for a detailed discussion of Johnson's supposed authorship of chapter eleven (book 9), the penultimate chapter of *The Female Quixote*. This point was first raised by The Revd J. Mitford in the *Gentleman's Magazine*, August, 1843.

18 Ibid., p. 82.

19 *Covent Garden Journal*, March 24, 1752. Johnson may also have written a review of The *Female Quixote* in the *Gentleman's Magazine*, March 1752, xxii, p. 146. So, at any rate, suggests Dr Birbeck Hill in his *Life of Johnson* (1887), i, p. 367.

20 *Prose Writings of Heinrich Heine* (1887), p. 261 f.

21 Clara Reeve, *The Progress of Romance* (Colchester, 1785), part 2, p. 6.

22 *Covent Garden Journal*, March 24, 1752.

23 Austin Dobson, *Eighteenth Century Vignettes* (Nelson), pp. 89 f.

24 Macaulay, *Critical and Historical Essays*, 'Diary and Letters of Madame d'Arblay'.

25 Charlotte Lennox, *Henrietta* (*Novelists Magazine*, vol. xxiii), Bk. iii, ch. vi, p. 88.

26 Dr E. A. Baker says that this is not a Richardsonian novel. He says it is rather in the spirit of Fielding, but that the model was not Fielding, but Marivaux's *Marianne*. This may be so, but since *Henrietta* reflects so many influences, and none with fidelity, it is a point beyond proof.

27 Op. cit., ch. iii, pp. 39 f.
28 *The Histories of Lady Frances S— and Lady Caroline S—* (1763) ii, pp. 120 f.
29 Ibid., ii, pp. 7 f.
30 Ibid., i, p. 67.
31 The following is a list of Susannah Gunning's novels:
　　(a) *The Histories of Lady Frances S— and Lady Caroline S—* (4 vols. 1763). In collaboration with her sister Margaret.
　　(b) *Barford Abbey*, a novel in a series of letters (2 vols., 1768), anon.
　　(c) *Anecdotes of the Delborough Family* (5 vols., 1792).
　　(d) *Memoirs of Mary* (5 vols., 1793).
　　(e) *Delves; a Welch Tale* (2 vols., 1796).
　　(f) *Love at First Sight: a novel from the French*, with alterations and additions (5 vols., 1797).
　　(g) *Fashionable Involvements* (3 vols., 1800).
　　(h) *The Heir Apparent*, revised and augmented by her daughter, Miss Gunning (3 vols., 1802). In association with her sister she also wrote *The Picture*, *Family Pictures* and *The Cottage*.
32 *The Memoirs of Mary* (3rd edn., 1794), iv, pp. 146 f.
33 Ibid., iii, pp. 43 f.
34 Elizabeth Bonhote (1744–1818), wife of Daniel Bonhote, solicitor of Bungay, wrote the following:
　　(a) *Rambles of Mr Frankley by his Sister* (1773), published anonymously, translated into German at Leipzig, (1773). It describes the characters seen during rambles in Hyde Park.
　　(b) *The Parental Monitor* (1788). A series of moral essays written for her children's guidance.
　　(c) *Olivia, or the Deserted Bride* (1787).
　　(d) *Darnley Vale, or Amelia Fitzroy* (1789).
　　(e) *Ellen Woodley* (1790).
　　(f) *Bungay Castle* (Minerva Press, 1797).
　　(g) *Feeling, or Sketches from Life, a Desultory Poem* (Edinburgh, 1810); anon .
35 Mrs Woodfin's other novels are:
　　(a) *The Auction* (1759).
　　(b) *The History of Miss Harriot Watson* (1763).
　　(c) *The Discovery, or Memoirs of Miss Marianne Middleton* (1764).
36 *Miss Sydney Bidulph* (*Novelists Magazine*, xxii), p. 298. (Published in 1987 by Pandora, London with an introduction by Sue Townsend, in the 'Mothers of the Novel' series.)
37 Ibid., p. 323.
38 Ibid., p. 325.
39 Ibid., p. 360.
40 Ibid., p. 33.
41 *The History of Lady Julia Mandeville* (*British Novelists* edn., 1820), xxvii, p. 201.
42 Ibid., p. 35.
43 *The History of Emily Montague* op. cit., vol. iii, pp. 22 ff.
44 Ibid., vol. ii, pp. 74–76.

45 Ibid., vol. iii, p. 42.
46 Ibid., vol. i, p. 83.
47 Ibid., vol. i, pp. 40–41.
48 Mrs Brooke's other novels are:
(a) *The Excursion* (1777). It describes the adventures of Maria Villiers, an impulsive young poetess whose 'wild and Pindaric virtues,' warm heart and social inexperience lead her into difficulties which are worked out in a conventional way. Dr J. M. S. Tompkins says that she 'is the nearest approach to a female Tom Jones (*mutatis mutandis*) that could have been offered.' (*The Popular Novel in England, 1770–1800*, p. 169). On page 118 of this work the date of *The Excursion* is given as 1771, obviously a misprint.
(b) *The History of Charles Mandeville* (1790); a sequel to her first novel. Of this there is no extant copy.
   Dr E. A. Baker points out that *Memoirs of the Marquis de St Forlaix* was not an original work, but merely translated from the French by Mrs Brooke (1770). See *H.E.N.*, v, p. 146.
49 Lived 1720?–1793.
50 *The Delicate Distress* (1769), ii, pp. 112 f.
51 Ibid., ii, p. 101.
52 Ibid., ii, p. 105.
53 Ibid., i, p. 29.
54 Ibid., i, p. 181.
55 Ibid., i, p. 92.
56 *The History of Lady Barton* (1771), ii, pp. 116 f.
57 Ibid., ii, p. 149.
58 Ibid., iii, p. 79.
59 Ibid., ii, p. 162.
60 Ibid., ii, p. 202.
61 Ibid., ii, p. 195.
62 In *The History of Lady Barton*.
63 She edited *A Collection of Novels selected and revised* (1777) from the works of Mrs Behn, Mrs Aubin and Eliza Haywood.
64 Dr E. A. Baker says that Helen Maria Williams actually preceded the Della Cruscans, but that Mary Robinson did probably belong to the coterie (*H.E.N.*, v, p. 150).
65 *The Early Diary of Frances Burney, 1768–1778* (ed. Bohn) ii, p. 302.
66 Dr E. A. Baker says: 'But it is in *Julia* . . . that the poetess lets herself go, not only in the verses. The tragic story of Julia's love for the man whom she did not meet till too late, of his death through his impassioned response to her more sober affection, followed by that of his wife, is told with a certain power, and if the sentiments are excessive, they are at any rate sincere, and, further, Helen Maria could bring out character. The scene is laid in fifteenth-century Spain and so a quasi-historical colour is imparted.' (*H.E.N.*, v, p. 151) Dr Baker's statements as to the background of the novel and the death of Seymour's wife are probably misprints. Miss William's poems are as washy as her novel. They are eight in number; chiefly

on such subjects as birds, famous poets, the Bastille, and Hope. Only three have any bearing on love: no. 3, a formal idyll; no. 7, in which peace is said to be found only in the grave; and no. 6, in which the faithful woman sadly addresses the man who loves another. Even these poems are all most discreet and mild.

67 *Julia* (1790), i, p. 192.
68 Ibid., i, p. 199.
69 Ibid., ii, p. 11.
70 E. A. Baker: *H.E.N.*, v, p. 151.
71 Mary Robinson's fictional works are:
(a) *Celadon and Lydia* (printed in 1777, together with a poem called 'Captivity').
(b) *Angelina* (1796).
(c) *The False Friend*, a domestic story (1799).
(d) *Lyrical Tales* (1800).
(e) *Effusions of Love*, n.d. (purporting to be her correspondence with the Prince of Wales).
(f) *Vancenza, or the dangers of credulity* (1792).
(g) *Walsingham, or the Pupil of Nature*, a domestic story (2nd edn. 1805). Twice translated into French.
(h) *The Natural Daughter?*
72 *Vancenza, or the dangers of credulity* (1792), i, p. 61.
73 Ibid., ii, pp. 70 f.
74 Ibid., ii, p. 125.

Chapter XI

The Domestic Novel — The Novel of Manners

For a young woman's work I look
upon it to be really Wonderful.

(Dr Burney)

At the end of January, 1778, the London reading public was thrown into high excitement by three small volumes published anonymously. Walpole read them in his Gothic retreat; Dr Johnson and Mrs Thrale read them at Streatham; Sir Joshua Reynolds refused to lay them down for sleep or food; Burke forgot to go to bed and was still reading at daybreak. Sheridan, Gibbon, Windham, and even the envious Cumberland, read and wondered. The Blues read and talked profoundly. The circulating libraries circulated at a feverish rate. Lowndes was besieged by eager queries as to the authorship of this new novel. And the first murmurs grew into a shout of triumph for *Evelina*.

Meanwhile at Chesington Hall, near Epsom, the anonymous author was just recovering from pneumonia and heard the first clarions of fame only by letter. Could the literary pundits, the great artists, the politicians, the learned ladies, the fops, the beauties, the society hostesses all clamouring for an opportunity to lionize and monopolize the author of *Evelina* — could they but glance now into the old Samuel Crisp's parlour, they would (like Mrs Cholmondeley a few months later) start back, exclaiming in consternation: 'It can't be — I don't believe it! no, you are an impostor!' But it is true. This young girl pouring short-sightedly over her sister's exuberant letters — this sallow, sharp-nosed, mousey-haired, round-shouldered, insignificant young girl is the author of *Evelina*. This is Fanny Burney — about to burst from her chrysalis and to become a butterfly. But one cannot spend one's

333

life as an obscure caterpillar and suddenly adapt oneself to the glory of the wings. Fanny Burney's overwhelming shyness made public adulation somewhat of an ordeal, but that her family should realize her capabilities was an unmixed joy. Fanny Burney's diaries naively record many of her first intimations of success, but none with greater happiness than those which concern her recognition by her own family. Scott loved to think of Fanny Burney dancing round the mulberry tree in Samuel Crisp's garden when she heard that Dr Johnson had praised *Evelina*, but better still is the picture of Susan Burney listening outside her father's door at seven o'clock in the morning while Dr Burney reads *Evelina* aloud to his unsuspecting wife — every detail of their laughter and their emotion being written post-haste by the faithful Susan to Fanny at Chesington. Best of all is the scene when Fanny's cousin, the flippant, witty, happy-go-lucky Dick Burney, discovers that she is the author of *Evelina*. He suspects that she knows the author and presses her to tell — never dreaming, of course, of the actual truth. She says finally that she will write the name on a piece of paper, but first exacts a vow of secrecy. He places his hand upon his heart and promises by his honour that he will be faithful; nay, he will even kneel down and swear never to tell a living soul. But at that moment, finding himself observed by Miss Humphries who is also in the room, he holds himself absolved from this mock-heroic detail. Fanny's courage fails, and she writes, not her name, but the cryptic words 'no man'. She hands the scrap of paper to her cousin. 'He read it with the utmost eagerness — but still did not seem to comprehend how the affair stood, till he came to the window — and then, I believe, my countenance cleared up his doubts.' He gazes at her speechlessly, colours violently, and then, having somewhat recovered himself 'he came again to me, and taking my hand, said: "I believe I must now kneel indeed!" and drawing me to the fire, he actually knelt to me.'

Dick Burney kneeling to Fanny; Dr Burney's amazed discovery of Fanny's secret five months after *Evelina* had appeared; even Samuel Crisp, who should have guessed, dumbfounded at this extraordinary achievement of his Fannikins — such reactions have a double significance. They prove that Fanny's intimates, like the rest of the world, had rated her too poorly in the past and now rated her too highly.

To estimate the influence of Fanny Burney's environment on her artistic development, it is necessary to refer briefly to the Burney family. On her father's side she came of a family called Macburney, probably of Irish origin but long settled in Shropshire. The Macburneys had possessed a considerable estate, but by perversity and extravagance had reduced themselves to poverty. When Fanny Burney's grandfather, James Macburney, made a run-away marriage with an actress from Goodman's Fields, his father had retaliated by marrying his cook, willing all his property to Joseph, the cook's son, and cutting off James with a shilling. Joseph, however, was in the end no better off than James, for he squandered his patrimony and was forced to earn his living as a dancing-master. James dropped the Mac from his name, and became a portrait painter at Chester. Here was born, by a second marriage, his son Charles Burney, the father of Fanny Burney.

Charles Burney had a considerable talent for music, but a far greater talent for friendship. He early secured the powerful patronage of Fulke Greville, but relinquished it that he might be free to marry. He became an organist and a teacher of music, and worked so hard that he was compelled, after a few years, to seek a less exacting post and healthier air. These he found in King's Lynn, where he remained for ten years and where Fanny was born.

There was nothing in the least brilliant about Fanny Burney's earlier years. In fact, an observer would have considered her a dull child. She was extremely shy and silent, and had such difficulty in learning the alphabet that at eight years old she was still unable to read. Her brothers and sisters called her a dunce, but her mother had no fears for Fanny who showed herself quick-witted in observing people and in inventing games of make-believe. In 1760 the Burney family returned to London and the following year Mrs Burney died. From that time onward, that is from the age of nine, Fanny Burney's education rested entirely with herself. Of formal education she never had more than some casual instruction in reading and writing, given by a brother or a sister. It is impossible to say why Fanny Burney was denied the educational advantages enjoyed by her sisters. The reasons suggested are not at all convincing. When Hetty and Susan were sent to France, Fanny was kept at home lest she might be tempted to become a Catholic, her affection for her Catholic grandmother being supposed to render her more vulnerable to Catholicism than were her sisters. When Charlotte was later sent to school in Norfolk, Fanny was still kept at home, and this time no other reasons can be suggested than that she was sensitive, and that she was devoted to her father. Devoted indeed she was in the true sense of the word, and as Macaulay has said: 'Her father appears to have been as bad a father as a very honest, affectionate and sweet-tempered man can well be. He loved his daughter dearly; but it never seems to have occurred to him that a parent has other duties to perform to children than that of fondling them.' There is a kind of fantastic humour in the reflection that if Fanny Burney had not so warmly loved her father and her grandmother she might have become a much better novelist. She might perhaps, through education, have developed her mental powers, and acquired a standard of literary judgment. And later, she might have resisted her father's mistaken advice, refusing to abandon her pen for the privilege of becoming a court drudge. Such hypotheses, however, do not lend themselves to proof and must be balanced by what we know of Fanny Burney's character and abilities. Fanny Burney was not more neglected than were the children of Haworth Parsonage. The education of the Brontës had little or nothing to do with their fugitive periods at Cowan Bridge and elsewhere; and they were in their twenties before they went to Belgium—fully developed and self-sufficient. But Charlotte and Emily Brontë were born with powers which 'little Burney' never possessed, and which she would have feared even to imagine. The Brontës were born mature; Fanny Burney died a precocious child. In the visible, tangible possibilities of learning, what was there in Haworth which was not in Poland Street? In each house there was a neglectful father and an extensive library. In Poland Street there was a very happy family and constant intercourse with the most interesting and brilliant people of the age. In Haworth there was a consumptive family, an atmosphere of melancholy and terror, a violent father, a sinister brother, and a sodden graveyard giving on to the storm-swept moors. The children of Haworth found their reality in books. Fanny Burney found hers in her father's drawing room. The children of Haworth read with intuitive genius. When Fanny Burney read, she read like a numbskull. Witness her criticisms of works which she read in her teens. In spite of the erasures and emendations which she made towards the end of her life (when she had

336

learned the opinions of others) one can decipher in the early diary that *The Vicar of Wakefield* did not interest her in the least. Indeed, she was tempted to throw the book aside. 'I began it with distaste and disrelish, having just read the elegant letters of Henry — the beginning of it, even disgusted me — he mentions his wife with such indifference.'[1] There is, nevertheless, a change for the better half way through the first volume. Then 'I was, as I may truly express myself, *surprised into tears* — and in the second volume I really sobb'd.'[2] This method of determining literary value by the tearfall[3] was a characteristic of the period, and was particularly to be expected of one whose favourite book was Sterne's *Sentimental Journey*. She says: 'Insensibility, of all kinds, and on all occasions, most moves my imperial displeasure.'[4] In keeping with this extreme delicacy of emotion is her criticism of Caius Marius in Plutarch's *Lives*. 'There is a something, a *je ne sçais quoi*, in Plutarch's *Lives* that draws one's attention, and absolutely prevents me leaving off.' But she does not really enjoy herself until she comes to Caius Marius: 'Brutal! inhuman! savage! execrable wretch! *Man* I cannot write — Good God! how shocked, how unaffectedly shocked I am to find that such a *human* brute could ever really exist . . . When he entered Rome — I really trembled — shuddered at the recital of his actions.' And she adds ingenuously 'you may have perceived that I am very earnest and warm in whatever interests me — not of a philosophick or phlegmatick turn.'[5] When Fanny Burney wrote these criticisms she was about sixteen years. She was twenty-one when her brother-in-law Rishton, read Spenser's *Faerie Queen* aloud to Maria and herself. She recorded the fact, and gave her judgment as follows: 'He is reading Spenser's *Faerie Queen* to us in which he is extremely delicate, omitting whatever to the poet's great disgrace, has crept in that is improper for a woman's ear. I receive very great pleasure from this poem in which there is an endless fund of ingenuity and poetry.'[6]

It is not in the least unjust to refer to these youthful essays in criticism, because Fanny Burney never reached a higher level of judgment. She must, however, have realized later her lack of critical insight, because in the *Diary and Letters* one cannot but observe how she eluded every effort to draw her into a discussion on books. When Johnson sought to delve into her mind she hedged constantly, and steadfastly refused to utter a single syllable which might reveal her ignorance, playing 'dear little Burney' with all her might, until Johnson gave her a fatherly hug and called her his 'little toadling'. But sometimes he returned to the attack. One day he says (though very kindly) that he believes she does not care for reading, because he has never seen her with a book in her hand. She meets the accusation by taking a book from behind a cushion in her chair where she says she has hidden it lest anyone might think her affected. Johnson dropped the subject. Good honest man! he could not be supposed to divine that Fanny's affectation really lay in pretending to hide under an appearance of womanly ignorance, knowledge which she certainly did not possess. If indeed she wished to clear herself of the suspicion of pedantry, she had only to voice the vacuous judgements which she wisely confided to — Nobody. Then would Johnson in stentorian tones have silenced her forever with a tremendous 'Madam!'

Much has been said as to the value of Fanny Burney's diaries and correspondence. Their importance as a vivid and detailed picture of her time is indisputable, but they are still more interesting as a record of her mind. They provide an explanation of all her literary works because they fully show her evolution. To her diaries, to her sister Susan and to Samuel Crisp, Fanny Burney confided her inmost thoughts. In Samuel Crisp's friendship she was particularly fortunate, because he was exactly the sort of mentor to aid the development of her mental powers. Crisp was a man of wide literary interests, an excellent critic, and so completely a recluse that he had time and to spare for Fanny Burney. His retirement from social intercourse was generally ascribed to the failure of his tragedy *Virginia*, and there is no doubt that this misfortune never ceased to rankle, but poor health would, in any case, have confined him to his retreat at Chesington. He was, perhaps, the most intimate friend of the Burney family, and Fanny was his especial favourite. From the age of nine she claimed him as her other 'Daddy', and she poured out to him by letter everything that was of importance in her life. Had she been of an enquiring or thoughtful disposition, she might, through Crisp's guidance, have found depth and cultivation. He would have been an excellent confidant for ideas and reflections which she might have been too self-conscious to communicate to her family. But she seems to have been completely free from the long thoughts and obstinate questionings of youth. It does not appear that Crisp had any influence on her development. Fanny's letters to Crisp were merely a transcript of her diary, and her diary was simply a minute record of all the objective life that eddied around her.

Since Fanny Burney had the mind of a newspaper reporter with a keen sense of the ridiculous, it was fortunate for her that she lived in such a maelstrom of events, albeit merely social events. The Burney ménage was the perfect environment for such talents, because a ceaseless tide of life flowed swiftly in at the front door swirled through the drawing room and music room, and so out again. Not such a tide as moving seems asleep, but the most charming, shallow, babbling, frothy stream in the world. The Burneys' social position was peculiar. It was, so to speak, negative or neutral. Dr Burney's talents, his versatility and his spontaneous charm attracted to his musical evenings people who belonged to the most various backgrounds. Many belonged to a social stratum much higher than his own. Many, drawn by his mild Bohemianism, were artists. Many had in other ways achieved fame, popularity or notoriety. They came to listen to the music, to meet each other, to be able to say that they had been there. Dr Burney's 'evenings' became a fashion. These assemblies in Poland Street were heterogeneous and even cosmopolitan. There were people of title, people of the *ton*, visiting Grand Dukes, singers with temporary husbands, painters, actors, composers, explorers, bishops, generals, admirals, ambassadors, human curiosities such as Omiah, the South Sea Islander. Indeed, to 'the silent, observant Miss Fanny' they were all human curiosities. Her shyness in company left her the freer to look on, and caused the people and incidents before her to imprint themselves vividly upon that sensitive photographic film which served her as a brain. She never tried to imagine what went on in the minds of those by whom she was surrounded. Like a child, her interest was caught and held by what the senses could perceive. She never looked beyond externals. Grief, love, beauty, remorse, evil, idealism, despair — unless they had their obvious outward signs they were all one to Fanny Burney. And, because she had no key to human character, she saw life always as a pageant or a masquerade. In her earlier life she could enjoy nothing without feeling impelled to relate it, and so she set down all she saw or heard either in her diaries or letters. These show to a very marked extent her ability to record scenes vividly and to report long conversations verbatim. They show also most of the weaknesses which were later to become so apparent in her novels. In one of the prefaces in *Tom Jones* Fielding had said that the true discerner is he who can distinguish the fine shades of human personality. Such distinctions were always quite beyond Fanny Burney. In the masquerade of life she could recognize the villain by his moustache, the *ingénue* by her downcast eyes, the fop by his affectation, the miser by his clutching fingers, the vulgarian by his bad manners. Because she could not understand the growth or the diversity of human characteristics, the subtleties which give a great range of variety even to one single trait, she was unconsciously driven to find diversity in peculiarity. She had no taste for ordinary scenes, or for ordinary people. She preferred everything to be strongly marked, strongly contrasted, verging on the grotesque. She was most in her element in describing some gathering of unusual people—Omiah with his quaint broken English, the giant Orloff (reputed to be the murderer of the Czar, and the lover of the Czarina) with his portrait of the Czarina hanging about his neck; Bruce of Abyssinia with his periodic abdominal convulsions; Miss W—, the moron. Even Garrick is shown to us only when he is being temperamental, when he is acting a dozen parts in a moment and sweeping through the house like a whirlwind. We never hear a lively description of Daddy Crisp, or of Susan or of any other normal individual. She never recounts any of Johnson's conversations except those which were eccentric or which eulogized herself. She must have heard some excellent talk in her intercourse with some of the finest intellects of the age. She never records it. The letters and diaries only present life to us photographically, with the emphasis on the ludicrous or on the unusual, and with a selectivity that is merely prudish or egotistic. There is no depth of feeling anywhere to be observed. Fanny Burney professed an absorbing love for music. Did she feel it, or was she simply mimicking the interests of a musical household? She devotes many pages to the divine singing of the Agujari, and if she was sincere we must assume that in the following words she strained every nerve to describe it:

> Such a powerful voice!—so astonishing a compass—
> reaching from C in the middle of the harpsichord to *two*

notes *above* the harpsichord!—Every tone is so clear, so full, so charming!—Then her *shake*—so *plump*—so true, so open! It is as strong and distinct as Mr Burney's upon the harpsichord. Besides its great power, her voice is all sweetness, and when she pleases, all softness and delicacy. She sings in the highest style of taste and with an *expression* so pathetic, that it is impossible to hear it unmoved. She does the greatest difficulties to be given to her with all the ease and facility that I could say: 'my dear Daddy!'[7]

Such is the shallow jargon with which Fanny Burney records an experience which (we are to believe) stirred her very soul. But she can give an excellent description of the Agujari's first visit, her appearance, her mannerisms and her conversations. At once she pounces on the Agujari's most obvious characteristic: 'Her excessive vanity was perpetually betrayed'[8] and she imprints the Agujari on our minds by stressing her foreign tricks: her reputed husband, Signor Colla; her nickname of La Bastardini ('from some misfortune that preceded her birth'[9]); and the story that she was 'mauled when an infant by a pig, in consequence of which she is reported to have a silver side.'[10]

But if Fanny entirely fails to convey the beauty of the Agujari's voice, she can make us see Omiah, the South Sea Islander, singing a native song. He and his song are so bizarre that she is at her best describing them:

Nothing can be more *curious* or less *pleasing* than his singing voice; he seems to have none; and *tune* or *air* hardly seem to be aimed at; so queer, wild, strange a *rumbling of sounds* never did I before hear, and very contentedly can I go to the grave, if I never do again. His *song* is the only thing that is *savage* belonging to him. The story that the words told, was laughable enough, for he took great pains to explain to us *the English* of the song. It appeared to be a sort of trio between an old woman, a young woman, and a young man. The latter two are entertaining each other with praises of their merits and protestations of their passions, when the old woman enters, and endeavours to *faire l'aimable* to the youth; but as she cannot boast of her *charms*, she is very earnest in displaying her *dress* and making him observe and admire her taste and fancy. Omiah, who stood up to *act* the scene, was extremely droll and diverting by the grimaces, *minauderies*, and affectation he assumed for this character, examining and regarding himself and his dress with the most conceited self-complacency. The youth then avows his passion for the nymph; the old woman sends her away, and, to use Omiah's own words, coming to offer *herself*, says: 'Come! *Marry me.*' The young man starts as if he has seen a viper, then makes her a bow, begs to be excused and runs off. Though the singing of Omy is so barbarous, his actions, the expression he gives to each character, are so original and so diverting, that they did not fail to afford us very great entertainment of the *risible* kind.[11]

If the Burney 'evenings' were the training ground for Fanny Burney's observations, the diary and letters were an admirable preparation for her fictional works. They contain many rough drafts of situations and characters later employed in the novels. In fact, the first two novels were the natural culmination of those powers which found outlet and development in her journals. *Evelina*, however, was not merely the outcome of the diary. It was a story which had been long maturing in Fanny Burney's mind. Indeed it even had a literary ancestor in the cremated *Caroline Evelyn*. This was a novel which Fanny wrote in her early youth and which she burned with all her other manuscripts when she was about sixteen, in obedience to her stepmother, who strongly disapproved of scribbling young ladies.

Caroline Evelyn was the daughter of a French barmaid and a young gentleman who, when making the grand tour with his tutor, insisted on contracting this very unsuitable marriage. He died shortly afterwards, confiding his child to the care of his tutor, a clergyman named Villars. When Caroline had grown up, Mr Villars allowed her to visit her mother in Paris, who through a second marriage had become Madame Duval. Caroline secretly married a rake, Sir John Belmont. He returned with her to England, deserted her, and repudiated the marriage. She died at the birth of her daughter, who, disowned and therefore considered illegitimate, was brought up by the good Mr Villars at Berry Hill, Dorset.

It is clear that such a story had great possibilities of continuation, and long after Fanny Burney had burned the manuscript of *Caroline Evelyn*, her mind continued to dwell on the fate of Caroline Evelyn's daughter. This child, who took the name of Evelina Anville, was most curiously situated. As the obscure ward of a country parson, she was safe and happy enough, although her life was shadowed by the slur of illegitimacy. But, if she were ever to make her entrance into the outer world, it seemed inevitable that she should suffer for the social inequality of her ancestors. She stood between two worlds — the exclusive society in which, as her father's daughter, she had a right to move; and the lower world of petty tradesmen, in which she had relations through her vulgar grandmother, Madame Duval. But she could advance no claim on society, unsupported by her father; and her indeterminate background and her isolation caused her to be ignored and slighted, or else pursued by rakes who considered her fair game. Even against these odds, her innate refinement, beauty, and innocent charm might have triumphed, were it not for the impertinent intrusion of her vulgar relations and the domineering claims of Madame Duval. This was the situation which exercised the mind of Fanny Burney and which developed into the novel *Evelina*.

It is easy to see that such subject-matter was admirably suited to Fanny Burney's powers. It offered to her keen dramatic sense a great variety, indeed a succession of conflicting circumstances and personalities, greatly heightened throughout by continual contrasts. It offered to her sense of the ridiculous all the incongruities of behaviour and of mannerisms which are the proper field of comic writers. Again, the vogue for the epistolary form exactly suited Fanny Burney, who already for so many years had conveyed by letters, to Crisp and others, the most vivid and circumstantial account of life around her. Crisp had called her his little 'anecdotemonger', but she had been far more than that. She had not been content with describing isolated incidents, preferring always to weave together all the events of some particular occasion, and, when ten or twelve quarto pages did not suffice for the narration, continuing it spontaneously from letter to letter. Nothing could have been more natural to Fanny than the epistolary form. For *Evelina* she needed only to make a more prolonged effort and, instead of recounting actual happenings, to invent them. Perhaps, indeed, it would be truer to say that instead of recounting actual happenings, she wrote down imaginary events which she had thought out a long time previously and which had become so familiar to her that the characters lived in her mind, talked, acted and fulfilled their appointed ends without conscious prompting. This maturing, one might also say this autonomy of the characters, left Fanny the letter-writer, almost as free to describe as when she wrote to Crisp. She could still obey the advice he had once given her, when she had feared lest her epistolary style might be too careless and trifling:

> You cannot but know that *trifling, that negligence, that even incorrectness*, now and then in familiar epistolary writing, is the very soul of genius and ease; and that if your letters were to be fine-labour'd compositions that smelt of *the lamp*, I had as lieve they [travelled elsewhere]. So no more of that, Fanny, and thou lov'st me. Dash away, whatever comes uppermost, and believe me you'll succeed better, than by leaning on your elbow, and studying what to say.[12]

And again: 'There is no fault in an epistolary correspondence like stiffness and study ... The sudden sallies of the imagination, clap'd down on paper, just as they arise, are worth folios.'[13] The truth of these remarks is seen by comparing the letters of Mr Villars with the other letters in Evelina. In Mr Villars's letters Fanny leant very heavily on her elbow and the result is grandiloquent sermonizing which, although it reduced eighteenth century readers to floods of tears, is most wearisome to the modern mind.

But the rest of the novel is by no means wearisome. Even by present-day standards it is still worth reading by virtue of a certain quality. In its own day it was like champagne. It came out with a sudden explosive energy. It went to the heads of the reading public, blinding them to its faults. Let it blind us too, for the moment. Later we shall discover its defects in sober sadness, but we must not begin by doing so, or we shall never understand why England went mad over *Evelina*. To judge *Evelina* justly and to understand the furore it caused it is necessary to limit our minds to what had previously been written. *Evelina* appeared at an opportune moment when the public was weary of the school of feeling and extreme sentimentality, and before the Gothic novel had come into power. The four great novelists had left a volume of work which had been imitated, but never equalled. Fanny Burney triumphed because she did not try to imitate them. She may have imagined that she was imitating Richardson since she used the epistolary form and presented the story of a young girl, as told by herself, but we shall see that, in outlook and method *Evelina* was quite individual. Naturally one does not attempt to compare Fanny Burney to 'the four great wheels' of the novel, but it is useful to consider that, within its own limits,

Evelina showed aspects not hitherto apparent in fiction, and excellences peculiar to itself. Fielding's novels depicted life with a deep, ironic, benevolent insight, but their emphasis was on the picaresque, and they were (though rather unjustly) considered coarse. Richardson, by the exercise of his imagination, created a sort of reality within his own mind, but he did not write from direct observation, and, although he analysed the emotions in great detail, he viewed the human heart through the distorting lens of sensibility. The moral code in his novels was prudential, and they were clouded by a covert eroticism by comparison with which Fielding's novels were robustly clean. Smollett was simply a more sophisticated Defoe. In powers of external portraiture and absence of the subjective Fanny Burney rather resembled him, but most of Smollett's characters were brutal and lewd, and his estimate of human nature was low. Sterne was a slyly sensual sentimentalist. Salacious innuendo was inextricably woven into the fabric of his writings. Like Smollett, he was unable to construct a plot, although indeed, Smollett's roughly-strung succession of episodes seems a master-stroke in architectonics in comparison with the indolent confusion of *Tristram Shandy*. Goldsmith's domestic novel came nearest to the view of life which now interested the female novelists, and its idealism set it apart from the maculate writings of the great men; but the *Vicar of Wakefield* was too consciously didactic. When *Evelina* came out, it must have been apparent to reflective readers that in depth and scope it fell short of the classic novels, but they did not seriously attempt a comparison. It was enough for them that *Evelina* differed in several important respects from all that had gone before — and this so markedly that it must be hailed as something new.

It was new, not because all its constituents were hitherto unknown, but because they were combined in an unusual way. It was new also because its aim had not previously been attempted. By some stroke of genius Fanny Burney limited the aim of *Evelina* so exactly to her own powers that her success appeared to argue a concentration and not (as it was) a straining of ability to its fullest extent. This aim Fanny Burney states as follows:

> To draw characters from nature, though not from life, and
> to mark the manners of the times, it is the attempted plan of
> the following letters. For this purpose, a young female,
> educated in the most secluded retirement, makes at the age

of seventeen, her first appearance upon the great and busy stage of life; with a virtuous mind, a cultivated understanding, and a feeling heart, her ignorance of the forms, and inexperience in the manners of the world, occasion all the little incidents which these volumes record, and which form the natural progression of the life of a young woman of obscure birth, but conspicuous beauty, for the first six months after her *Entrance into the World*.[14]

This aim perhaps, does not seem ambitious, and yet it had never before been achieved. Male novelists had shown themselves able to create minor women characters convincingly, e.g. acidulated spinsters, redoutable matrons, adventuresses and serving-maids, but they had always failed to create a convincing heroine. For obvious reasons, their heroines were generally high-souled and sentimental creatures.[15] The female novelists mentioned in the preceding chapter did not free themselves from this man-made convention, and though Eliza Haywood makes Betsy Thoughtless anti-sentimental, she goes to the other extreme and creates merely a pert minx. But Evelina is real, and it is important to note that she is not only a real woman, but she is really young.

It has often been said that Evelina was Fanny Burney herself at seventeen. The shy Fanny could well remember the timidities and the self-consciousness occasioned by her first ball, her first admirer, her first feelings of attraction; perhaps, for all we know, her first love. How easy it was for her to enter into the predicaments of Evelina! She had not experienced a tenth of them, but she had a feeling of oneness with her heroine which helped her to imagine how she herself would have behaved under such circumstances. This feeling of personal reinforcement is strongly evident in the book, and we cannot even say that *Evelina*'s delicacy of sentiment and acute sense of propriety are peculiar to herself, since we know that they were very evident traits in Fanny also ('Poor Fan is such a prude!' her father used to say).

That shyness which was a continuing characteristic of Fanny Burney is represented in Evelina as being due to her rusticity and inexperience. When Evelina is permitted to go with Mrs Mirvan and her daughter, Maria, on a short visit to London, she is involved in countless new experiences, some pleasurable, some not, but all very interesting because they are so vividly described that to us, also, they seem to be happening for the first time. Not only is Fanny Burney the first to create a convincing heroine, but she is the first writer to show us real life through a woman's eyes. She even catches for us that state of mind (between sharp-cut clarity and delicate illusion) in which a young girl first views the world. It is this spirit of youth which constitutes the greatest charm in *Evelina*. In no preceding novel is it to be observed. Fielding had exuberant energy; Smollett had 'raw-boned high spirits'; Richardson had, at times, a kittenish playfulness; but neither they nor any other writer, prior to Fanny Burney, infused the breath of spring into a novel. *Evelina* reminds one of a young lamb or a young puppy-dog—all awkwardness, enthusiasm, friendliness, all mistakes, but very much alive and rather pathetic. No doubt it was this ingenuous *élan* which took the great men of the age by storm and closed their eyes to the serious defects.

Another revolution which Fanny Burney effected can best be recognized by a comparison of Pamela and Evelina. Richardson had professed to show a young girl's reactions to a certain set of circumstances. But this young girl is not real and she is not pure-minded. Her sense of values has nothing to do with morality. Indeed she is so unnaturally overwhelmed by social distinctions that she thinks the vicious Mr B. far better than she is herself simply because he is richer. Her character is summed up in the incident when Mr B., all else failing, brings himself to marry her, and at the ceremony says: 'I take thee, Pamela, for my wedded wife'; the self-seeking little toady curtsies and says: 'Thank you, sir!' Women readers did not revolt against that scene because it was in accordance with a male convention in fiction to which they were accustomed, but it is certain that no woman could have invented an episode so degrading to the self-respect of her sex. The complications with which Richardson besets Pamela are the complications a certain type of man would envisage. They all centre in ideas of pursuit and possession. *Evelina* represents a different point of view. There are plots against Evelina's virtue, but these are a minor question. Her main difficulties have to do with the conflicting social circumstances in which she is entangled. She is ignorant of how to behave. She is shy, confused, makes innumerable mistakes. For all her beauty she lacks self-confidence. This is an aspect never presented before *Evelina*—a young girl as she is to herself, not merely as she appears to men. Up to then, in fiction, a beautiful woman was supposed to be invulnerable to uncertainties of social procedure. She would not have wondered whether a dress suited her, or have lost her glow merely because she was conscious of dowdy clothes. She would never have needed to find courage and poise in a new style of hairdressing or a new cap. She was never gauche. She had no doubts as to etiquette. But Fanny Burney knew that beauty and self-possession, beauty and tact are not necessarily the same thing. Evelina's mingled delight and fear in her preparations for her first ball reveal perfectly the mind of an inexperienced girl:

> We are to go this evening to a private ball, given by Mrs Stanley, a very fashionable lady of Mrs Mirvan's acquaintance. We have been *a-shopping* as Mrs Mirvan calls it, all this morning, to buy silks, caps, gauzes and so forth.
>
> The shops are really very entertaining, especially the mercers; there seem to be six or seven men belonging to each shop; and every one took care by bowing and smirking, to be noticed. We were conducted from one to another, and carried from room to room with so much ceremony, that at first I was almost afraid to go on. I thought I should never have chosen a silk: for they produced so many, I knew not which to fix upon; and they recommended them all so strongly, that I fancy they thought I only wanted persuasion to buy everything they showed me. And indeed, they took such trouble, that I was almost ashamed I could not.
>
> At the milliners, the ladies we met were so much dressed, that I should rather have imagined they were making visits than purchases. But what most diverted me was, that we were more frequently served by men than by women; and such men! so finical, so affected! they seemed to understand every part of a woman's dress better than we do ourselves; and they recommended caps and ribbands with an air of so much importance, that I wished to ask them how long they had left off wearing them.
>
> The despatch with which they work in these great shops is amazing, for they have promised me a complete suit of linen against the evening.
>
> I have just had my hair dressed. You can't think how oddly my head feels; full of powder and black pins, and a great cushion on the top of it. I believe you would hardly know me for my face looks quite different to what it did before my hair was dressed. When I shall be able to make use of a comb for myself I cannot tell; for my hair is so much entangled, *frizzled* they call it, that I fear it will be very difficult.

I am half afraid of this ball to-night; for, you know, I
have never danced but at school: however Mrs Mirvan says
there is nothing in it. Yet I wish it were over.[16]

Better still is Evelina's description of the ball. There is excellent
comedy in the contrast between her outward seeming and her
inmost thoughts. She appears a heart-subduing beauty, while
inwardly she is little more than an awkward child. The confusion
and misunderstandings which result from her ignorance of social
forms are highly amusing, all the more so since, even when her
partners finally consider her 'ignorant or mischievous', or 'a poor
weak girl', they are still very far from understanding what is going
on in her mind. She has summed them all up to a nicety and her
vivacious descriptions of her adventures would be hard to better.
These are her reflections while waiting for the first dance to begin:

> The gentlemen, as they passed and repassed, looked as if
> they thought we were quite at their disposal, and only
> waiting for the honour of their commands; and they saun-
> tered about in a careless indolent manner, as if with a view
> to keep us in suspense . . . and I thought it so provoking,
> that I determined in my own mind that far from humouring
> such airs, I would rather not dance at all, than with any one
> who should seem to think me ready to accept the first
> partner who would condescend to take me.
> Not long after, a young man, who had for some time
> looked at us with a kind of negligent impertinence, advanced
> on tiptoe towards me; he had a set smile on his face, and his
> dress was so foppish that I really believe he even wished to
> be stared at; and yet he was very ugly.
> Bowing almost to the ground with a sort of swing, and
> waving his hand with the greatest conceit, after a short and
> silly pause, he said: 'Madam' — may I presume — and stopt,
> offering to take my hand. I drew it back, but could not
> forbear laughing. 'Allow me, Madam,' continued he, affec-
> tedly breaking off every half moment, 'the honour and
> happiness — if I am not so unhappy as to address you too
> late — to have the happiness and honour.'[17]

Evelina refuses, saying she believes she will not dance at all, but
changes her mind when Lord Orville offers himself as her partner.

Lord Orville, the hero of the novel, is merely a 'condescending
suit of clothes',[18] but for some inscrutable reason he attracts
Evelina, possibly because he is handsome and because his

manners and morals are impeccable. She slips unconsciously into loving him, but it is long before he discloses his intentions. Her peculiar lack of family and background, her vulgar relatives, rival suitors, and a variety of accidents which cause her to appear indiscreet despite her innocence — all conspire to delay his proposal of marriage. They are happy in the end, but only after many weary months, during which Evelina vainly tries to understand the fluctuations in his attitude towards her. We have seen that the women writers of the school of sentiment and sensibility sometimes touched on the aspect of women's passivity before the puzzle of men's minds and intentions. With Fanny Burney this aspect is made the pivotal point of a novel. It was Jane Austen who brought this motif of passivity to its full perfection, but even in Fanny Burney's novels we have that tragicomedy of woman observing a man's attitude to her, her secretly responsive hopes, his inexplicable withdrawal, and the impossibility of showing that she cares, or of asking for the explanation to which she is entitled. When in *Camilla*, for example, that finicking prig, Mandlebert, blows hot and cold for five volumes, Fanny Burney puts into the mouth of Mrs Arlbery this very trenchant protest against such a quibbling code of honour:

> Mandlebert is a creature whose whole composition is a pile of accumulated punctilios. He will spend his life in refining away his own happiness; but do not let him refine away yours. He is just a man to bewitch an innocent and unguarded young woman from forming any other connection, and yet, when her youth and expectations have been sacrificed to his hesitation . . . to conceive he does not use her ill in thinking of her no more, because he has entered into no verbal engagement. If his honour cannot be arraigned of breaking any bond . . . what matters merely breaking her heart?[19]

Jane Austen shows one woman revolting against the feminine convention of dignified acquiescence, and asking her erstwhile lover why he has suddenly changed. Jane did this to indicate that the convention was a necessary one; and she proves it by showing the young man feigning consternation that Marianne could so have 'misunderstood' him. Marianne has no weapon against that blank disclaimer, although she knows quite well that there is an unstated reason for the change. That is the attitude of

Fanny Burney, fully developed in Jane Austen. Another aspect for the first time presented by Fanny Burney and driven home with all Jane Austen's power, is that money and social position often load the dice against beauty and love. It had never been admitted before, although Smollett shows his heroes as eager fortune-hunters. Smollett's heroes, however, return in the end to the beautiful and pure heroine, whose love outweighs the heaviest money-bags.

One notes, also, another important point on which eighteenth-century women-novelists firmly differed from men. Beauty and virtue are the philosopher's stone in the men's novels. Tom Jones may go a-roving from Sophia, but he will return when he is weary of folly; she cannot really lose him if she is beautiful and good. Women knew that beauty and virtue were no talisman, and that one might retain both, without winning happiness. Nor did they account it happiness to await the magnanimous return of the prodigal. Fielding, Smollett, and Richardson take it for granted that the woman is ready to take back the young hero after a thousand amorous adventures. Not so Mrs Brooke and Mrs Sheridan, and not so Fanny and Jane. Fanny and Jane never marry vice to virtue. If the young man sows wild oats, then he must eat bitter bread. That is the woman's attitude.

'To draw characters from nature . . . and to mark the manners of the times' was a part of Fanny Burney's aim, but those abilities which made her so pre-eminently a recorder of manners were most calculated to defeat her purpose of characterization. Her powers of observation were, as we have seen, very acute, but she had no insight. Hazlitt says:

> Madame d'Arblay is . . . a mere common observer of manners . . . There is little in her works of passion or character, or even manners in the most extended sense of the word, as implying the sum-total of all our habits and pursuits; her forte is in describing the absurdities and affectations of external behaviour, or the manners of people in company. There is little other power in Madame d'Arblay's novels than that of immediate observation.[20]

Evelina is Fanny Burney's best novel not only because, as Hazlitt has said, it was her shortest, but also because its subject-matter was least likely to expose her superficiality. Life through

351

the eyes of a girl of seventeen is vivid, refreshing and amusing, but it is not deep, and therefore the lack of depth in *Evelina* might be considered in keeping with the writer of the letters. Some of Fanny Burney's studies in manners are, however, extremely clever. She was most successful with vulgar characters, and her best portraits are those of Evelina's shopkeeper cousins, the Brangtons, and Mr Smith, their lodger.

Evelina's grandmother, the ex-barmaid, Madame Duval, introduces her to the Brangtons, who are at once summed up with withering shrewdness, as follows:

> The relations to whom she was pleased to introduce me, consisted of a Mr Brangton, who is her nephew, and three of his children, the eldest of which is a son, and the two younger are daughters. Mr Brangton appears about forty years of age. He does not seem to want a common under-standing, though he is very contracted and prejudiced: he has spent his whole time in the city, and I believe feels a great contempt for all who reside elsewhere.
>
> His son seems weaker in his understanding, and more gay in his temper; but his gaiety is that of a foolish, overgrown schoolboy, whose mirth consists in noise and disturbance. He disdains his father for his close attention to business, and love of money; though he seems himself to have no talents, spirit or generosity, to make him superior to either. His chief delight appears to be tormenting and ridi-culing his sisters; who, in return, most heartily despise him.
>
> Miss Brangton, the eldest daughter, is by no means ugly; but looks proud, ill-tempered, and conceited. She hates the city, though without knowing why; for it is easy to discover that she has lived no where else.
>
> Miss Polly Brangton is rather pretty, very foolish, very ignorant, very giddy, and, I believe, very good-natured.[21]

The Brangtons are deplorably bumptious and impertinent, and quite look down on Evelina because she is country bred, though they themselves know little more of London that the environs of their shop at Snow Hill. Madame Duval's intro-duction is so brutally phrased as to make it appear that Evelina's mother 'went astray'. Evelina is so shocked at this suggestion that young Brangton becomes dimly aware that something is wrong! 'If aunt pleases,' said young Mr Brangton, 'we'll talk o' somewhat else, for Miss looks very uneasylike.' His sisters, however, have no misgivings in returning to a subject which absorbs their crude wonder: 'In a few minutes, Miss Brangton, coming suddenly up to her sister, exclaimed, "Lord, Polly, only think! Miss never saw her papa!" "Lord, how odd!" cried the other, "Why, then, Miss, I suppose you wouldn't know him?"' And when Evelina finally runs from the room, they insist on following, to comfort her and bring her back! They question her acutely as to what she has already seen in London, and when it appears that she has not been to the Tower their contempt is great. When she is forced to confess that she has, nevertheless, 'seen such a thing as an opera', it occurs to them that it might be worth their while to see one also, 'for once, for the curiosity of the thing'. They arrange to take Evelina to the opera, riding rough-shod over her objections. The Brangtons at the opera is really an inimitable piece of writing. Their squabbles over money, the cheese-paring of Mr Brangton who takes them to the gallery, pausing to beat down the price of every box-office on their upward way: the confusion of Evelina who is dressed for the pit, and the added misery of knowing she is observed by her friends in that part of the house: the crass comments of her companions who talk and titter through every act — all are presented to the life, and Mr Brangton's final comment sums up perfectly the family point of view: 'As for me,' said Mr Brangton, 'they've caught me once, but if ever they do again, I'll give 'em leave to sing me to Bedlam for my pains: for such a heap of stuff never did I hear: there isn't one ounce of sense in the whole opera, nothing but one continued squeaking and squalling from beginning to end.' No wonder that Dr Johnson revelled in these characters and used the word Brangton to connote a vulgarian ('One would take you for a Brangton, sir' he roars at Boswell, when that unfortunate is being more heavy-handed than usual. 'A Brangton, sir? What is a Brangton?' 'Where have you lived, sir, and what company have you kept not to know that?').

Even better than the Brangtons is Mr Smith, whom Hazlitt calls 'an exquisite city portrait', and whose 'vulgar gentility' delighted Johnson. When Mr Smith enters, the Misses Brangton fall into ecstasies and beg Evelina to remark his 'smart air'. They consider that he has 'very much a *quality look*'.

> 'Come,' cried he, advancing to us, 'you ladies must not sit together; wherever I go I always make it a rule to part the

ladies.' And then, handing Miss Brangton to the next chair, he seated himself between us.

'Well, now, ladies, I think we sit very well. What say you? for my part I think it is a very good notion.'

'If my cousin likes it,' said Miss Brangton, 'I'm sure I've no objection.'

'O,' cried he, 'I always study what the ladies like—that's my first thought. And indeed, it is but natural that you should like best to sit by the gentlemen, for what can you find to say to one another?' 'Say!' cried young Brangton: 'O, never you think of that, they'll find enough to say, I'll be sworn. You know the women are never tired of talking.' 'Come, come, Tom,' said Mr Smith, 'don't be severe upon the ladies: when I'm by, you know I always take their part . . .'[22]

'Well, Mr Smith is always in such spirits!' said Miss Brangton.

'Why, yes, Ma'am, yes, thank God, pretty good spirits; I have not yet the cares of the world upon me: I am not married,—ha, ha, ha!—you'll excuse me, ladies—but I can't help laughing!'[23]

Such portraits support the truth of Mr Christopher Lloyd's sound criticism:

> Miss Burney was the first novelist to make the ordinary incidents of everyday life significant and interesting. She realized, perhaps unconsciously, a truth which critics have always seen—that one of the chief, if not the true, pleasures of art is the pleasure of recognition. In this way she founded the realistic but polite novel of manners and led the way for that much greater artist, Jane Austen.[24]

But Fanny Burney's portraits are not always so recognizable. Too many of her characters are caricatures. One cannot but remark that Fanny Burney had no fineness of conception, and that her lack of judgement betrayed her into many vulgarities. This lack of good taste is the plague spot in Fanny Burney, and to it we may trace all the worst faults in her writings. It shows itself always in a want of restraint, in the deplorable way in which she always tended to exaggerate, whether it was a character, an emotion, or a style. As to character, it is seldom that she can invest an individual with a mannerism, and then let him behave like a human being. No, he must become an idiosyncrasy masquerading as a human being. This preference for caricature verging on the grotesque is certainly vulgar. It is the same impulse that drives a crowd to pay its penny for a sight of the pig-faced lady. Not only are Fanny Burney's exaggerated characters always displaying the same mannerism — they are always expressing it in the very same words. Captain Mirvan and Madame Duval, for example, are forever quarrelling. The Captain is always damning Frenchies and lauding Britons. Madame Duval is always-saying 'Ma foi' and using an unchanging farrago of bad grammar for broken English. Indeed the scenes between this pair are so brutal that they were not approved even by the age for which they were written. They were not necessary to the plot and are in the worst possible taste. We are shown a lout shaking and beating a grandmother, making her the subject of the most savage jeers and horseplay, throwing her in the mud and tying her by her feet to the bough of a tree so that she is unrecognizable for filth. Her face plastered with a mixture of mud and tears; her wig is gone; her voice, from screaming, has become like an animal's howl; she tears the ground with her hands. In this state she is laughed at by the servants, who are in the conspiracy. Fanny Burney does not present this as a disgusting business. She implies that the Captain is a great, rough schoolboy — no more. Then there is the occasion when Madame Duval spits in the Captain's face, and when he tells her that, if she were not so old and ugly, he would spit back; and again the scene where the Captain, to insult a fop, brings in a monkey dressed as a beau and is so overwhelmed with merriment when the monkey bites off a piece of the fop's ear, that he rolls on the floor, shouting with laughter. No wonder that Mrs Montagu expressed her amazement that 'so delicate a girl could write so boisterous a book.' Even allowing for the liberty with which the century indulged in practical joking, the horseplay in *Evelina* is quite shocking. Captain Mirvan (who, incidentally, is not at all like a sea-captain, but rather resembles a brutal country squire) did not find favour with the reading public, but Fanny Burney was unrepentant. She says: 'The more I see of sea-captains, the less reason I have to be ashamed of Captain Mirvan, for they have all so irresistible a propensity to wanton mischief, to roasting beaus, and detesting old women that I quite rejoice I showed the book to no one 'ere printed, lest I should have been prevailed upon to soften his character.'[25] This aspect of the demure, sensitive and prudish Miss Burney would be surprising did we not remember that she helped to bait the poor moron, Miss W—, and was openly convulsed with laughter at her efforts to sing. Even when Miss W—'s host and bear-leader takes a tablespoon and thrusts it down the front of her dress, while she is singing, Fanny Burney is only the more amused. Indeed she seizes the opportunity later to make Miss W— sing again, for the pleasure of laughing herself sick. This was the paragon whose ladylike decorum at Windsor impressed even 'the sweet Queen'!

But it is when Fanny Burney tries to plumb the depths of passions and of pathos that her lack of restraint most betrays her. Characters which, until then, seemed flesh and blood suddenly seem to be transmuted into cardboard. They rant and rave, beat their breasts and liquidate themselves into a pool of tears. All fustian—and there is rarely even a credible cause for these mock-heroic typhoons. For example, one cannot accept as natural Evelina's attitude towards her father. Sir John Belmont had treated her mother abominably. But for Mr Villars's kindness, Caroline might have died in a ditch, and Evelina might have begged her bread in the gutter; nevertheless, this dutiful young woman quivers with eagerness at the possibility that her father may relent. She says: 'My imagination changes the scene per-petually: one moment I am embraced by a kind and relenting parent, who takes me to that heart from which I have hitherto been banished, and supplicates, through me, peace and forgive-ness from the ashes of my mother!—at another, he regards me with detestation, considers me as the living image of an injured saint, and repulses me with horror!'[26] When at last they meet the scene out-herods Herod. Sir John cries inarticulately: 'My God! does Caroline Evelyn still live!' And in a few minutes he adds: 'Lift up thy head—if my sight has not blasted thee! Lift up thy head, thou image of my long lost Caroline.' Far from suggesting that the loss was self-imposed, Evelina embraces his knees. '"Yes, yes," cried he, looking earnestly in my face, "I see, I see thou art her child! she lives—she breathes—she is present to my view!—Oh, God, that she indeed lived!—Go, child, go," added he wildly starting, and pushing me from him: "take her away, Madam—I cannot bear to look at her."' With which, and having offered to plunge a dagger in his heart to serve her, he rushes from the room, crying that his brain is on fire. Evelina's intervention when Macartney is about to commit suicide is in the same tone. She bursts into the room, exclaiming: 'O, Sir! have mercy on yourself!'

The guilty pistols fell from his hands, which disengaging from me, he fervently clasped, and cried: 'Sweet Heaven! is this thy angel?' Encouraged by such gentleness, I again attempted to take the pistols; but with a look half frantic, he again prevented me, saying: 'What would you do?'

'Awaken you,' I cried, with a courage I now wonder at, 'to worthier thoughts, and rescue you from perdition.'[27]

Although, in general, the style of *Evelina* is simple and vivacious, there are glimpses of that pretentious pedantry which was later to prove Miss Burney's undoing:

'During the childhood of Evelina, I suggested a thousand plans for the securing of her birthright; but I as many times rejected them. I was in a perpetual conflict, between the desire that she should have justice done her, and the apprehension that, while I improved her fortune, I should endanger her mind. However, as her character began to be formed, and her disposition to be displayed, my perplexity abated . . . Then did I flatter myself, that to follow my inclination, and to secure her welfare, was the same thing, since, to expose her to the snares and dangers inevitably encircling a house of which the master is dissipated and unprincipled, without the guidance of a mother, or any prudent and sensible female, seemed to me no less than suffering her to stumble into some dreadful pit, when the sun is in its meridian.'[28]

She cannot say in plain English: 'To stumble into some dreadful pit in broad daylight.' It must be 'when the sun is in its meridian.' The euphuistic pomposity which was to weigh her later writings to the ground was already beginning to grow. Her aspirations towards Johnsonese, too, are even now to be observed. With careful balancing of thought against thought, of word against word, Fanny Burney writes that it had been Villars's intention to bestow Evelina 'upon some worthy man, with whom she might spend her days in tranquillity, cheerfulness, and good humour, untainted by vice, folly, or ambition.'[29] And Madame Duval is 'too ignorant for instruction, too obstinate for entreaty, and too weak for reason.'[30]

In 1782, four years after *Evelina*, appeared *Cecilia*. It was written after a certain amount of hesitation, and against the advice of Samuel Crisp. He appears to have felt that his young protégée could never equal what she had already achieved, and that an inferior work would only lower her prestige. Above all, he warned her not to force herself to further composition: 'It was not "hard fagging" that produced such a work as *Evelina*. It was the ebullition of true, sterling genius. *You wrote it because you could not help it — it came, and you put it down on paper*,' Fanny herself felt that 'but for pecuniary advantages, it would be better to write no more.' She seems to have been overwhelmed by the apparent impossibility of repeating her triumph. Indeed, she says: 'I have already, I fear, reached the pinnacle of my abilities, and therefore to stand still will be my best policy.' The wonder with which she was regarded gave her perhaps a sense of unreality. She had no feeling of continuous life with the prodigy who wrote *Evelina*, and she must have believed that, if she were to equal that achievement, it would need a herculean effort. She made a herculean effort, which, since she lacked judgment, meant that she exaggerated everything. She used too large a canvas; she introduced too many eccentrics; she heightened the melodrama; she revelled in the vulgar scenes. Instead of adhering to the epistolary form and to her light-hearted style, she used the ordinary novel form and expressed herself in Johnsonese. The unsuitability of Dr Johnson's language for a domestic novel of manners does not appear to have struck her.

Cecilia has an elaborate plot, the pivot of which was so unconvincing that Crisp implored Fanny to give it up. She refused. His objection was obviously well founded because the novel appears to depend on an improbable and unreasonable situation. Cecilia Beverley inherits a large fortune on condition that, if she should marry, her husband should take her name. She falls in love with Mortimer Delvile, the heir of an ancient family, and he with her. Delvile's parents oppose the marriage, the very mention of which particularly enrages his father. Mortimer is torn between love and filial devotion. Cecilia suffers intensely and the action moves in a crescendo of drama. Mrs Delvile grows to love Cecilia and wishes to yield, but feels that it is impossible. Mr Delvile remains uniformly implacable. Finally Cecilia consents to a secret marriage, but the ceremony is interrupted by a mysterious voice, and she refuses to be married on that day or any other. Mortimer now falls into a state of extreme anguish. There is a tremendous scene between the mother, the son and Cecilia, and Mrs Delvile is so overwhelmed that she cries: 'My brain is on fire', rushes from the room and bursts a blood vessel. This is the scene around which Fanny Burney avowedly wrote the novel, and which nothing would induce her to abandon. It made contemporary readers ill with emotion. Now it merely makes one yawn. With Mrs Delvile's consent the lovers marry. Mortimer keeps his treasured surname, and all might have been well, had not Miss Burney insisted on introducing further complications. Mortimer fights a duel and finds it necessary to flee the country. Cecilia's marriage is discovered and her fortune is claimed by the next heir. She seeks refuge with Mortimer, but jealousy causes him to misinterpret a situation in which she is innocently involved. He spurns her, and she goes mad and runs about the streets. It is all very distressing, but happiness awaits them in the end.

Ingeniously woven into this main theme is the subsidiary plot dealing with the Harrels. These are friends of Cecilia's with whom she lives for some time in London and who involve her in many difficulties and misunderstandings. Mr Harrel is a weak scoundrel who gambles away all his money, and then, by threats of suicide, repeatedly blackmails Cecilia into 'lending' him money. She is even driven to borrowing money from Jews. Mrs Harrel is a brainless and heartless woman, and there is a great deal of amusement in the manner in which this irresponsible couple fluctuate between despair and frivolity. As often as not Mr Harrel spends the morning sharpening his razor for self-slaughter, only to sally forth at night with Mrs Harrel to a ball or a rout, leaving the impoverished Cecilia aghast at their volatile insensibility. Harrel really does commit suicide at last, blowing his brains out at Vauxhall, almost in the presence of some of his creditors whom he first entertains to supper, with liberal quantities of champagne. This Vauxhall scene has been much praised by some, notably by Mrs A. R. Ellis whose critical prefaces to *Evelina* and *Cecilia* are, in general, so interesting that one cannot in this instance quite pass over her remarks, although they are undoubtedly too eulogistic. She says:

> Surely all that leads up to [Harrel's] end, and the chapter which completes it, are the finest parts of the book. In the self-importance of Mr Hobson and the servility of Mr Simkins, amid the awful merriment in the box at Vauxhall, there is something not unlike the great dramatists of the sixteenth century.[31]

The characterization in *Cecilia* shows in excess that tendency toward caricature which was observable in *Evelina*. Macaulay[32] has shown the distinction between writers who can discriminate the fine shades of human character and those who concentrate on exhibiting what Ben Johnson called humours. Such humours exist and are therefore within the province of art, but as they are infrequent in human life, so they should be infrequent in any work which professes to be a representation of human life. The writer who shows genius in representing humours can claim a place among the classics, but it must be a lower place than that of writers who give a balanced view of human character. He goes on to say:

> If we have expounded the law soundly, we can have no difficulty in applying it to the particular case before us. Madame d'Arblay has left us scarcely anything but humours. Almost every one of her men and women has some propensity developed to a morbid degree. In Cecilia, for example, Mr Delvile never opens his lips without some allusion to his own birth and station, or Mr Briggs without some allusion to the hoarding of money; or Mr Hobson without betraying the self-indulgence and self-importance of a purse-proud upstart; or Mr Simkins, without uttering some sneaking remark for the purpose of currying favour with his customers, or Mr Meadows, without expressing apathy and weariness of life, or Mr Albany, without declaiming about the vices of the rich and the misery of the poor; or Mrs Belfield, without some indelicate eulogy on her son; or Lady Margaret, without indicating jealousy of her husband. Morrice is all skipping, officious impertinence, Mr Gosport all sarcasm, Lady Honoria all lively prattle, Miss Larolles all silly prattle. If ever Madame d'Arblay aimed at more, we do not think she succeeded well.
>
> We are, therefore, forced to refuse Madame d'Arblay a place in the highest rank of art; but we cannot deny that, in the rank to which she belonged, she had few equals, and scarcely any superior. The variety of humours which is to be found in her novels is immense; and though the talk of each person separately is monotonous, the general effect is not monotony, but a lively and agreeable diversity. Her plots are rudely constructed and improbable, if we consider them in themselves. But they are admirably framed for the purpose of exhibiting striking groups of eccentric characters, each governed by his own peculiar whim, each talking his own peculiar jargon, and each bringing out by opposition the

oddities of all the rest. All probability is violated in order to bring Mr Delvile, Mr Briggs, Mr Hobson, and Mr Albany into a room together. But when we have them there we soon forgot probability in the exquisitely ludicrous effect which is produced by the conflict of four old fools, each raging with a monomania of his own, each talking a dialect of his own, and each inflaming all the others anew every time he opens his mouth.

But a plot subordinated to the purpose of exhibiting humours cannot really be defended, and the inevitability of each humour and its particular jargon is wearisome in the extreme. The final impression is that stated by Walpole: 'Her great fault [is] that her characters are never allowed to utter a syllable out of character, which is unnatural.' The same point arises when one considers Fanny Burney's classification of the *ton*. She very cleverly groups the society of the day according to the affectations displayed. There are the Insensibilists, the Jargonists, the Voluble, the Supercilious, and later the Ennuyés. Each group has its particular idiom, and when we first hear them speak we are most amused. But boredom very quickly supervenes when we find that we can always anticipate what each type is going to say.

Before we pass on to Fanny Burney's other novels, it may be as well to mention a criticism of Macaulay's with which we find it impossible to agree. He says:

> Madame d'Arblay was most successful in comedy, and indeed in comedy which bordered on farce. But we are inclined to infer from some passages, both in *Cecilia* and *Camilla*, that she might have attained equal distinction in the pathetic. We have formed this judgement, less from those ambitious scenes of distress which lie near the catastrophe of each of those novels, than from some exquisite strokes of natural tenderness which take us here and there by surprise. We would mention as examples, Mrs Hill's account of her little boy's death in *Cecilia*, and the parting of Sir Hugh Tyrold and Camilla, when the honest baronet thinks himself dying.[33]

Mrs Hill's 'little boy' (who was really seventeen) would have been affecting if his mother had not interlarded all her conversation with references to him, but he haunts every sentence with such persistency that we are tempted to hail him with 'Art there, old mole?' As for Sir Hugh Tyrold, his utterances are usually so imbecile that when, for a single paragraph, he deviates into sense, the effect is out of all proportion to the actual value of the incident. As an example of Fanny Burney's more ambitious efforts at pathos, one cannot forget Albany's visit to Cecilia when she is believed to be dying. He makes his entrance (as the author terms it) 'accompanied by three children, two girls and one boy, from the ages of four to six, neatly dressed, clean and healthy.' He apostrophizes Cecilia, and begs her to look at the objects of her bounty. Cecilia continues to die, but Albany cannot be deterred from making an oration. He bids the children kneel ('Come, little babies, come! . . . lift up your innocent hands . . .') and thus addresses the unconscious figure:

> Sweet flower! untimely cropt in years, yet in excellence mature; early decayed in misery, yet fragrant in innocence! Gentle be thy exit . . . Look at her, sweet babes, and bear her in your remembrance . . . She departs the envy of the world while yet no guilt had seized her soul, and no remorse had marred her peace. She was the handmaid of charity, and pity dwelt in her bosom! her mouth was never opened but to give comfort; her footsteps were followed by blessings! Oh, happy in purity, be thine the song of triumph! — softly shalt thou sink to temporary sleep — sublimely shalt thou rise to life that wakes for ever!'
> He then got up, took the children by their little hands, and went away.[34]

It is with reluctance that one comes to speak of Fanny Burney's later novels,[35] *Camilla* (1796) and *The Wanderer* (1814). In themselves they are not worth mentioning because they are in no sense a contribution towards the English novel. Nevertheless, because they present a curious problem in the literary career of Fanny Burney, they may be briefly considered. One may begin by saying outright that these two novels are as futile as they could well be. *The Wanderer* is generally held to be the worse, but it is a point not worth determining.[36] What really matters is that these novels reveal an incredible deterioration in the author's powers. *Cecilia*, despite its ambitious scope, had not reached the level of *Evelina*, but in aim and in general characteristics the two novels are alike. On the contrary, *Camilla* and *The Wanderer* might almost be the work of a changeling. There is an occasional echo of the old love of humours, in such characters as Sir Sedley

Clarendel and Mrs Arlbery, but for the most part there is an immense gap between the work of the earlier and the later periods. Where, in the later period, is the keen observation, the striking caricature, the rapid, even abrupt sequence of events, the really excellent dialogue, the vivacity and the sense of the ridiculous? If Fanny Burney had retained even this last characteristic she would never have published her last two novels. For what do they contain except the trifling misunderstandings of maudlin nonentities, couched in depraved Johnsonese? Horace Walpole, until then an enthusiastic admirer of Fanny Burney, threw up his hands at *Camilla*, which he said was 'a deplorable book'.

It was well that Dr Johnson was not alive to see what his style became in the hands of Madame d 'Arblay. Inflated with sensibility, deadened by the weight of magniloquent euphuisms and liberally peppered with vulgarisms and grammatical errors, it was a travesty enough to make the good man turn in his grave.[37] But Madame d'Arblay had no hesitation in twisting language to her ill-conceived uses. Indeed she took herself so seriously that she most frequently coined words. 'Surely,' she wrote (somewhat earlier), 'I may make words at a loss, if Dr Johnson does'—and this despite her incomplete grasp of English and total ignorance of Latin. She had, after a few Latin lessons from Johnson, refused further tuition on the grounds that 'to devote so much time to acquire something [Latin] I shall always dread to have known is really unpleasant.' Trusting thus in her own intuition, she evolves a style of which this extract is a fair example: 'The tide of youthful glee flowed jocund from her heart, and the transparency of her fine blue veins almost showed the velocity of its current.'[38] And again: 'The bird . . . made whatever evolutions were within the circumference of his limited habitation, with wonderful precision.'[39] In the midst of such pretentiousness she does not scruple (as Mrs A. R. Ellis points out) to use 'me' in the nominative case, adjectives as adverbs, and such expressions as 'to stroam' ('to roam'), 'he made up to' ('he approached'), and 'he made off' ('he went away').

Writing, no doubt, with one eye on 'the sweet Queen' to whom *Camilla* was dedicated, Madame d'Arblay no longer aimed to amuse. Her brain was paralysed by the necessity for extreme refinement and decorum, and in her efforts to sift her material, she was left only with the veriest trifles for her subject. The motif is the love and misunderstandings of Camilla and Edgar Mandlebert. These misunderstandings hinge on the most negligible points. Again and again Camilla promises Edgar to avoid some trifling amusement. Again and again her resolution is overthrown not so much by the strength of the temptation as by a concatenation of circumstances. Unfortunately Edgar always discovers these lapses. For example, he find that she has taken part in a raffle, and that she has been so unwomanly as to attend an exhibition of performing monkeys. Still, he never despairs of helping her to acquire 'the modesty of retired elegance, and the security of established respectability'. Sometimes he withdraws in disapproval, but it is always possible to win him back by asking his advice. Once, for example, a delicate situation is created when Sir Sedley Clarendel, observing her pity for a bullfinch which is ill-treated by its trainer, buys the bird and sends it to her. For the moment, she keeps the bullfinch 'sooner than render [Sir Sedley's] humanity abortive', but she is so overwhelmed by the impropriety that she feels it necessary to ask Edgar's advice, even though he is in a mood of pained aloofness. She looks forward to 'the approaching conference with almost trembling delight'. She loves him with the most quivering sensibility and with the most delicate decorum, but Edgar is evidently determined that she shall, by long trial, fit herself for the true duty of wifehood, which Madame d'Arblay thus defines (in the case of Mrs Tyrold): 'Had this lady been united to a man whom she despised, she would yet have obeyed him, and as scrupulously, though not as happily, as she obeyed her honoured partner. She considered the vow taken at the altar to her husband, as a voluntary vestal would have held one taken to her Maker; and no dissent in opinion exculpated, in her mind, the least deviation from his will.'[40] But indeed the standard of feminine behaviour and propriety makes *Camilla* incomprehensible to a later age. Who could pretend to understand a period when to kiss the hand of a lady was a vile liberty? Bellamy, a fortune-hunter, feigns a passion for the mis-shapen but kindhearted heiress, Eugenia, who is intended, by her uncle, to marry Clermont. Clermont remains travelling on the Continent, and has no notion of the honour which awaits him. Madame d'Arblay thus describes the shocking affair:

Bellamy suddenly took the opportunity of [Eugenia's] being out of sight of all others, to drop on one knee, and passionately seized her hand, exclaiming: 'O, Madam! . . .' When hearing an approaching step, he hastily arose; but parted not with her hand till he had pressed it to his lips.

The astonished Eugenia, though at first all emotion, was completely recovered by this action. His kneeling and his 'O Madam!' had every chance to affect her; but his kissing her hand she thought a liberty the most unpardonable. She resented it as an injury to Clermont, that would risk his life should he ever know it, and a blot to her own delicacy, as irreparable as it was irremediable.[41]

It is curious to recall that Jane Austen praised *Camilla*, and to contrast with that judgment her uncompromising statement that, for heroines, 'pictures of perfection make me sick and wicked'.[42] Jane, like the rest of Madame d'Arblay's public, could not forget the joy she had found in the early novels of Fanny Burney, and no doubt forgave much because she had loved much. *Camilla* had a huge sale; so had *The Wanderer*, but one cannot think of either work without repeating the words of Sir Sedley Clarendel: 'O, a very crush! a cannon ball would be a butterfly in the comparison.' Though *The Wanderer* was her last novel, *The Memoirs of Dr Burney* show the depths to which her style of writing finally sank. Thus she describes how her father met his second wife:

Six heartless, nearly desolate, years of lonely conjugal chasm, had succeeded to double their number of nearly unparalleled conjugal enjoyment — and the void was still fallow and hopeless! — when the yet-very-handsome-though-no-longer-in-her-bloom Mrs Stephen Allen, of Lynn, now become a widow, decided, for promoting the education of her eldest daughter, to make London her winter residence.

What happened to the genius which, despite its limitations and faults, was yet apparent in *Evelina*? How can one explain not merely the decline of Fanny Burney's powers, but her apparent metamorphosis from a genius into an idiot? Her years at Court, however miserable, could not surely have changed her into an entirely different person. Her lack of education could not be directly responsible for her later style, since her first style, when she had not more education, was her best. Speaking to Hannah More of *Camilla* Walpole said: 'Alas! [Madame d'Arblay] has reversed experience . . . this author knew the world and penetrated characters before she stepped over the threshold: and now she has seen so much of it, she has little or no insight at all.'[43] Johnson, who died before the rot set in, speaks in almost identical terms of *Evelina*: '*Evelina* seems a work that should result from long experience, and deep and intimate knowledge of the world. Miss Burney is a real wonder.What she is, she is intuitively.'[44] There appear to be only two possible solutions to the problem of Fanny Burney's later writings. It may be that her first impetus of inspiration died, or that by deliberately changing her aim and methods of composition she destroyed her literary powers. Hazlitt held this latter view. He says, in reference to *The Wanderer*:

> We are sorry to be compelled to speak so disadvantageously of the work of an excellent and favourite writer; and the more so, as we perceive no deal of talent but a perversion of it. There is the same admirable spirit in the dialogues . . . as in her former novels, but they do not fill a hundred pages of the work; and there is nothing else good in it. In the story, which here occupies the attention of the reader almost exclusively, Mme d'Arblay never excelled.[45]

It is true that Hazlitt's opinion would seem to be supported by the fact that, though Fanny Burney's diary becomes rather dull during the Court period, it still contains lively and vivid descriptions (e.g. her meeting with the king during his madness, and Goldsworthy's amusing talk). It is also true that from the moment she went to Court, Fanny Burney seems to have become ashamed of being a novelist — so much so, indeed, that she racks her brains for some other way of describing *Camilla*: 'I own I do not like calling it a novel; it gives so simply to the notion of a mere love story that I recoil a little from it. I mean this work to be sketches of character and morals put into action — not a romance.'[46] Novels were still in low repute, and she who had been privileged to mix the royal snuff could no longer allow herself the freedom of a private person. In *Camilla*, at any rate, she wrote to please her patron, and she did not write in vain. Her Majesty allowed the three elder princesses, aged respectively thirty, twenty-eight, and twenty-six to read *Camilla*, without first censoring it. If Madame d'Arblay sold her genius for a mess of patronage, verily she had received her reward.

But however great her snobbishness, her desire for dignified decorum, had Fanny Burney retained her first impetuous inspiration, she could not, one believes, so stem and check it that, from

366

a sparkling spring, it became a stagnant pool. It seems more likely that, by the time she wrote *Camilla*, her youthful powers had waned and there was nothing to take their place — not even the judgment by which she could truly have compared her later and her earlier productions. We have already said that Fanny Burney died a precocious child. We should have said rather that, when she died, she had already experienced that strange eclipse which precocity so often suffers. Youthful prodigies very frequently become stodgy adults. So it was with Fanny Burney. When life weighed her down, when she could no longer remain a carefree onlooker, when it became necessary to struggle and to endure, then it seemed that what had lent her wings had been little more than youthful spirits. A light heart may go all the way in life, but it rarely goes far in literature. There comes the time when exuberance and excess of energy no longer imperiously seek expression, when the shallow nature can no longer feed on external impressions because they are no loner pleasurable. Such minds must either flit over the surface of life or go under. Fanny Burney went under at Windsor, and when she came to the surface again she had become — the prosy Madame d'Arblay.

Still, she had fulfilled her literary destiny. She had written one novel which, although it was superficial, was great. It was great because, in some respects, it excelled the technique of previous novels, and because it projected new and important aims in fiction; because it marks the point at which the feminine movement in fiction comes fully into view, and because it aided the development of Jane Austen and Maria Edgeworth. Fanny Burney's mental development is not unlike the evolution of the silk-moth. The silk-moth begins as an insignificant caterpillar of unpromising appearance. At this stage of its life it occupies itself entirely with preparations for its future activities. Then comes the inevitable moment; it begins to spin out of itself a thin fibre of silk, and it continues to spin thus out of its being until it has enveloped itself completely in this cocoon. Then, spent and exhausted, it remains hidden within its own creation which has cost it such vital energy. So did Fanny Burney lie hidden while *Evelina*, which she spun out of the substance of her life, engaged the public attention. But the silk worm never spins again; it change entirely; grows wings; emerges from its hiding place a beautiful white moth. It flutters about a little, mates and dies. So did Fanny

Burney. *Evelina* is her only lasting achievement, and it would have been better for her fame if she had never attempted any other.

Notes and References

1 *The Early Journals and Letters of Franny Burney*, (ed. Lars E. Troide, Claredon Press, Oxford, 1988), vol. i, Journal 1768, p. 12.
2 Ibid, vol. I, Journal 1768, p. 12.
3 Mrs A. R. Ellis coins this witty and useful word.
4 *The Early Journals and Letters of Franny Burney*, op. cit., vol. i, Journal 1768, p. 25.
5 Ibid., vol. i, Journal 1768, pp. 26–27.
6 Ibid., vol. i, Teign Month Journal 1773, p. 299. When Mme d' Arblay revised this diary with a view to publication, she changed the words 'ingenuity and poetry' to 'invention and fancy'.
7 Ibid., vol. ii, Journal 1775, p. 155.
8 Ibid., vol. ii, Journal 1775, p. 77.
9 Ibid., vol. ii, Journal 1775, p. 74 (note 24).
10 Ibid., vol. ii, Journal 1775, pp. 98–99.
11 Ibid., vol, ii, Journal 1775, pp. 196–97.
12 Ibid., vol. ii, Journal 1775, pp. 107–08.
13 Ibid., vol. i, Journal 1773, p. 320.
14 *Evelina: Or, The History of a Young Lady's Entrance into the World* (ed. Edward A. Bloom, Oxford University Press, London, 1968), Preface, p. 7–8.
15 Fielding's Sophia Western is sensible, but she does not count as she is not really a heroine — merely an anchor for Tom Jones.
16 *Evelina . . .* , op. cit., pp. 27–28.
17 Ibid., pp. 28–29.
18 So Hazlitt once called him. See Christopher Lloyd, *Fanny Burney* (1936), p. 127.
19 Fanny Burney, *Camilla: Or, a Picture of Youth* (ed. Edward A. Bloom and Lilian D. Bloom, Oxford University Press, 1983), vol. iii, Bk. vi, ch. xii, p. 484.
20 See Hazlitt, *Lectures on the English Comic Writers*, 'Madame d'Arblay'.
21 *Evelina . . .* , op. cit., pp. 67–68.
22 Ibid., p. 186.
23 Ibid., p. 188.
24 Christopher Lloyd, *Fanny Burney* (1936), p. 75 f.
25 *Diary and Letters of Madame d'Arblay* (ed. Dobson), i, p. 375
26 *Evelina . . .* , op. cit., p. 130.
27 Ibid., pp. 182–83.
28 Ibid., p. 126.
29 Ibid., p. 127.
30 Ibid., p. 127.
31 A. R. Ellis, Preface to *Cecilia* (1882 edn.) p. 13.
32 Macaulay, *Critical and Historical Essays*, 'Diary and Letters of Madame d'Arblay', pp. 601–604.

33 Ibid., p. 605.
34 Fanny Burney, *Cecilia* (Intro. Judy Simons, Virago Classics, London, 1986), pp. 894–95.
35 During this later period Fanny Burney's play *Edwy and Elgiva* was produced (21 March, 1795). This was one of the three historical tragedies which she roughly sketched at Windsor. On leaving the court she arranged her notes, but thought no further about them until the impending birth of her child made it necessary for her to raise money. Kemble and Sheridan, when approached, at once decided to produce the play, giving her no time for revision. The play had a very strong cast, Kemble and Mrs Siddons taking the leading parts. It was a miserable failure. Mrs Siddons wrote to Mrs Piozzi: 'There never was so wretched a thing as Mrs d'Arblay's Tragedy . . . The Audience was quite angelic and only laughed where it was impossible to avoid it.' When one reflects that *Edwy and Elgiva* was written in very bad blank verse, and that Elgiva, murdered at the beginning of the last act, had to lie prostrate on the stage for twenty minutes, it is clear that its chances of success were poor. This was Fanny Burney's second attempt at the drama, her play *The Witlings* (1779) being, adjudged so like Molière's *Femmes Savantes* that it was not produced, lest it should appear a mere imitation. Actually Fanny Burney had never read Moliere's play.
36 In an article in *E.L.H. A Journal of English Literary History*, December 1938, entitled 'An Unpublished Burney Letter', Mr W. B. Gates finds *The Wanderer* 'considerably more interesting than *Camilla* and not nearly so worthless as Macaulay and Mrs Ellis would have us believe.' (footnote 8, art. cit.) But a very useful point in this article is that Mr Gates has listed together all the contemporary reviews on all Fanny Burney's novels. This appears not to have been previously done.
37 Speaking of Madame d'Arblay's later style, Macaulay says: 'Nothing in the language of those Jargonists at whom Mr Gosport laughed, nothing in the language of Sir Sedley Clarendel, approaches this new Euphuism.'
38 *Camilla* . . . , op. cit., vol. i, Bk. i, ch. i, p. 13.
39 Ibid., vol. iii, p. 401.
40 Ibid.. vol. i, Bk. i, ch. i, pp. 13–14.
41 Ibid., vol. i, Bk. ii, ch. x, p. 127.
42 *Letters of Jane Austen* (ed. Brabourne, 1816), ii, p. lxxxiv.
43 *Works of Horace Walpole* (5 vols., folio, 1798) i, p. 623. Letter to Hannah More dated August 29, 1796.
44 *Diary and Letters of Madame d'Arblay* (ed. Dobson) i, p. 247. It is worth noting that Johnson must have thought Fanny Burney younger than she is, when she wrote *Evelina*. His words were part of a conversation with Mrs Thrale, in which they were comparing Pope's *Windsor Forest* with *Evelina*. Pope was sixteen when he began *Windsor Forest* (1704) and twenty-five when he finished it (1713).
45 *Edinburgh Review*, 24 (February 1815), pp. 320–338.
46 Letter to Susan Burney.

Chapter XII

The Gothic Novel

Sonitus terroris semper in auribus.

The gothic novel was at once a part of the Romantic Revival and a prolongation of the cult of sensibility. One characteristic of the Romantic movement was that writers turned to bygone ages for imaginative scope. Early in the eighteenth century this new interest had shown itself in poetry and in essays. Antiquarian research in mediaeval poetry and romances increasingly attracted attention, and even led to such impositions as MacPherson's Ossian and Chatterton's luckless forgery. But although this interest in literary antiquities was a notable aspect of the new orientation, it was not strong enough in itself to kindle the Romantic spirit, and it soon became evident that the architectural approach to medievalism was to prove the main channel by which olden times were to influence modern literature. A Gothic cathedral or more particularly a Gothic castle was the nucleus of great imaginative activity. Such a building could not be considered without reference to the people whose lives centred therein, and nothing was more natural than to weave about it ideas of human life and thought, and to make it the background for events which might be supposed to have occurred within its walls.

Although the impetus to this kind of story-telling was first evidenced in poetry, novelists did not long delay in seizing upon inspiration so suited to their craft. It was an escape from the gamut of domestic themes, and offered an almost unlimited freedom of invention. It was necessary only that the events described should be such as might be expected to happen in a Gothic castle — the interpretation of verisimilitude depending merely on the author's fancy.

Nowadays when such writers as Sigrid Undset bring to the writing of historical fiction not only artistic conception, but the perfect accuracy of an archaeologist, it is somewhat difficult to realize the insouciance with which the Gothic writers set themselves to depict the life of ancient days. It was not that they ignored, but that they did not conceive the essentials of a historical novel. Prior to Scott, nothing had been written which could with any justice be called a historical novel. *The Castle of Otranto* contained historical elements, but it cannot be claimed as an historical novel. Still less can this claim be advanced for Sophia Lee's *Recess*, unless one is satisfied to accept as a historical novel a tale without the slightest historical verisimilitude woven around certain historical personages. It does not even seem possible to credit Sophia Lee with the originality of introducing historical characters, as there is little room to doubt that she got the idea from Prévost, and modelled *The Recess* on *Cleveland.*

But even if writers of the English Gothic school had known enough to reproduce the real life of ancient times, they would not have done so, because they would have been profoundly shocked at its lack of refinement. Julia Kavenagh treats this point very well. She remarks that Walpole, the English Gothic school, and even Scott followed the only feasible plan in presenting to the finical reading public only a romantic and polite picture of bygone days, but she stresses the fact that theirs was a very bad method, because in giving a romanticized version of the past they omitted 'the rudeness, and with it the breadth and geniality of those wonderful times.' She continues:

> Our ancestors have been shown to us with singular capacities for bloodshed, because we could bear this, our humanity not having progressed in proportion to our delicacy; but of their joyousness of that mad mirth which went hand in hand with deeds heroic or terrible, of that roughness which pervaded every rank of society, we have not been told. The knight has been clothed in modern gentleness, politeness, and refinement, and in that smoothing down of features offensive to the modern taste, the largeness, that great characteristic of the Middle Ages, and perhaps the greatest, the manly and noble frankness, have been irremediably lost.[1]

The Gothic novel stressed terror—a twofold terror compounded of physical dangers and the more paralysing fear of the supernatural. The proportion and degree of these two elements constituted the main difference between the English, German and French schools. Prévost's power of creating an atmosphere of sinister gloom, his mysterious and bloody incidents, foreshadowed the main elements of the Gothic novel, and Baculard d'Arnaud's charnel-house conceptions strongly influenced one group of novelists. In Germany the tale of terror developed by contact with the folklore of gnomes, spirits and diabolism. Schiller's *Die Rauber* (1781) and his *Der Geisterseher* (1789) represent the aspects of brutality and supernaturalism which became the most outstanding characteristics of the *Schauerroman*. The German conception of the novel of terror became the chief influence during the later English period, of which 'Monk' Lewis and Maturin are the most outstanding writers. Lewis's violence and obscenity show one side of the German influence carried to excess. Maturin's *Melmoth* shows what genius can make of a supernatural legend. But Maturin's psychological technique sets him apart from other Gothic novelists who, as a rule, did not trouble themselves with the intricacies of character. Of the women writers only Mary Shelley was influenced by the German school, and then only by its ghostly elements. The other women novelists with whom we are concerned belong to the earlier period of English Gothicism which found its best expression and, in a sense, its origin in Mrs Radcliffe.

The popularity of terror as a literary theme during the second half of the eighteenth century led to enquiry as to the cause of such enjoyment and as to the technique by which terror should be presented so as to produce pleasurable effects. Edmund Burke considered that 'whatever is qualified to cause terror, is a foundation capable of the sublime'[2] and this because terror rouses the mind to exercise its strongest faculties. Such expense of energy is pleasurable in itself. Miss Aikin explained 'the strange luxury of artificial fear'[3] as being due to the reader's feeling of curiosity. She held that stimulation of curiosity not only made a terrible story pleasurable, but brought imagination and feeling into full play. Suspense maintains the mind in full activity and 'the pain of terror is lost in amazement.'[4] Dr Nathan Drake[5] did not enquire why fear is 'welcome' and why it is 'salutary' for the reader. He was interested in determining how best to manipulate the terrible so as to produce the most pleasurable results, without dependence on the supernatural. He believed that Mrs Radcliffe's balancing of beauty and suspense was the most effective way of making pleasure overcome the painful sensations induced by the narrative. Such views approached from different angles the fundamental interest in the Gothic novel.

However much the Gothic novel may have aided the evolution of the historical novel, it seems clear that the Gothic novelists merely played at reproducing the past. That they did not burden themselves with the task of historical accuracy greatly simplified their labours. They had only to expand their minds in the direction of antiquity, to unleash their imaginations. The term 'Gothic' was abstracted from its architectural connotation. It was loosely used to designate some bygone period, not necessarily the Middle Ages, and was even protracted by Mrs Radcliffe to include the year 1758. A Gothic novelist kept well in mind such general notions of antiquity as were common property. These were his historical boundaries, and within them loomed the Gothic castle, rich with hints for the development of the story. In itself this mighty stronghold was a visible commentary on contemporary social conditions. It had been built to withstand the sieges of men and time, and by its very construction it implied the determination to defy and to exert force. Dizzying battlements, dark and winding stairways, dark dungeons, instruments of torture, groans and gouts of blood, secret passages with many a suggestion of spectral life, ghostly music, tapestries which sway with the wind and which betray the secret watcher or the assassin—this was the stuff of the Gothic novel. This was the stuff of romance. No wonder that minds long shackled to sensible themes cast reason to the winds, and played the Gothic game of make-believe — a game in which anything might happen so long as one began with 'Once upon a time'. This flight from the present into the past was really a romantic quest — an effort to discover strange aspects of beauty, to give a loose to the restlessness, the curiosity, and the sense of wonder which excessive normality had stifled. At best the Gothic novel was a blending of beauty and terror. It was an attempt to convey by story-telling 'the tempestuous loveliness of terror'.[6] This is why in such novels as Mrs Radcliffe's we find not merely patches of beauty which relieve the tension, but very often an intermingling of beauty and fear. Fear is the element which transmutes this loveliness, or loveliness is the element which makes this terror bearable. And both viewed in the perspective of antiquity take on a variety of quickly-changing shapes. Antiquity is the Gothic moonlight which shadows or illumines everything. It creates beauty and it is beautiful in itself. It is to stress antiquity that we are always shown a Gothic building in decay. This emphasis on dilapidation marks not only the contrast between then and now. It gives also a sense of tradition outbraving the ravages of time. In the Gothic castle ancestors gaze down from their portraits in the gallery — nay, they even step down out of their frames, as in Otranto. Tattered banners rustle on the walls of the banqueting hall. And this castle, these portraits and these banners are usually first shown to us at sunset — a symbolism which at once suggests a dying glory and a romantic splendour.

That the Gothic novel was a part of the Romantic Revival is not more apparent than that it was a development of the cult of sensibility. Indeed one might consider it as the last resource of authors seeking some new irritant for emotion. The gamut of domestic distresses was exhausted, and, as we have already seen, English novelists, like their French brethren, turned to that wider field of sensibility which dealt in dangerous adventures and tragic strokes of fate. Here were already the elements of suspense and peril which were so prominent a feature of the Gothic tale. The key to the relationship of the Gothic novel and the novel of sensibility is the heroine. This trembling girl who now endures every variety of horror is the very same who formerly suffered more normal vicissitudes. The events described in a Gothic story are enough to harrow up the spirit of a brave man, but it is always a trembling girl who has to endure them. Thus the fullest effects of terror and anxiety are achieved. We gain our knowledge of these dread adventures through the perception of the heroine. As we read, we become identified with her, and since her sensitiveness is extreme and her reactions intense, we are caught up in a mounting wave of sensibility. This heroine is always friendless, often ignorant even of her parentage, and her isolation makes her sufferings all the more exquisite:

> Un coeur isolé, forcé de se replier sur lui-même, de se parler, de se répondre, de se nourrir, si l'on peut s'exprimer ainsi, de sa propre substance, en acquiert plus de ressort et d'énergie dans ses mouvements. Il n'est point de faibles

oscillations pour une âme solitaire: tout y porte de violentes secousses.[7]

But though the persecuted heroine is extremely sensitive, she is not weak. She may weep and swoon but she does not succumb. Indeed she cannot succumb if the story is to continue. Neither can she yield to tyrannous demands, because it is essential that the state of tension be maintained. This necessity of reconciling strength and weakness forced the novelist to trim his sails. He compromised by making the heroine not defiant, but firm. She will not yield to oppression so as to end it, but he feels the oppression in every lacerated nerve. This, of course, is quite possible, but the reader is afflicted with a sense of improbability when he observes this shrinking girl not merely enduring inescapable terrors, but deliberately incurring them. Well might Jane Austen burlesque the well-worn sequence of the heroine who, despite extreme nervousness, insists on adventuring into a deserted wing, listens behind the arras to the foul lots of bloody men, and sits up all night to read, by the light of an expiring lamp, a manuscript found under the most sinister circumstances. Whether or not the author realized this inconsistency, he could scarcely avoid it, if he was to maintain a ceaseless onslaught of terror. The fitness of such a purpose does not appear to have given these novelists pause, and no doubt even the sensitive Mrs Radcliffe would have been overwhelmed with surprise had she been confronted with such arguments as Swinburne later advanced against the tale of terror. Speaking of Wilkie Collins's novels, Swinburne said: 'The suggested or implied suffering of such poor innocent wretches, the martyrdom of perpetual terror and agony inflicted on the shattered nerves or the shaken brain of a woman or a girl, is surely a cruel or a painful mainspring for a story or a plot.'[8]

We have been speaking of Gothic fiction at its peak, so as to examine its main characteristics. It would be well to refer very briefly to some of the main evidences of its evolution. Prior to *The Castle of Otranto* (1764), which was avowedly the manifesto of a new genre of fiction, Gothic touches had shown themselves from time to time in English fiction, notably in Smollett's *Ferdinand, Count Fathom* (1753) and to a lesser extent in Leland's *Lonsord, Earl of Salisbury* (1762). In *Ferdinand, Count Fathom* there is definite proof that Smollett had chanced upon the Gothic idea, and upon the very technique which Mrs Radcliffe later employed. Smollett aimed at nothing more than to enliven his picaresque tale with some new kind of adventures—horrible and mysterious events which he depicts with great vividness. He creates an atmosphere of terror and employs all those properties which were to become so dear to the school of Gothic novelists. Like them, he appeals directly to the innate superstition in his readers, plays on their nerves by hinted horrors and keeps them in taut suspense. Darkness and solitude are the constituents of his atmosphere. In the description of the Count's journey through the dark forest there is a suggestion of the Gothic treatment of nature. Having aroused fear and anticipation, Smollett makes our flesh creep by means of unburied corpses, robbers, owls screeching in ruined battlements, a midnight visit to a chapel lighted only by a glimmering taper, a spectre, a heroine who sleeps at the end of a long gallery and who hears in the still watches the ghostly music of an aeolian harp. Smollett later explains away all his mysteries, as did Mrs Radcliffe.[9]

The Castle of Otranto was a contribution to the Gothic and also to the historical novel. Which was really Walpole's aim? In his preface he states that it is his intention to unite the imagination and invention in old romances with the probability of modern fiction, and he justifies his introduction of the supernatural by claiming that it was necessary for verisimilitude: 'Belief in every kind of prodigy was so established in those dark ages, that an author would not be faithful to the manners of the times who should omit all mention of them.'[10] But the superstitious element in his tale was so ill-conceived that it contradicts instead of establishing the appearance of veracity. Walpole's supernatural phenomena appeal only to the risible faculty. The plumed helmet is really too large even for the most voracious reader to swallow, and the three drops of blood would have done better to issue from any part of Alfonso's statue than the nose. Such a sanguinary effusion calls merely for a doorkey, and the terror it inspires in the onlookers merely adds to the ludicrous effect. Nor is the supernatural giant a more fortunate invention. This double appeal to our fear seems to cancel itself out. Enormous ghosts do not terrify. The more a ghost retains the proportions of humanity, the more it is driven home to us that here is one who has been what we are, and who has gone where we must surely follow. That is the terror on which the skilful narrator of ghost-stories relies. And it is amusing to consider that whereas Walpole's supernatural fails in its effect, Mrs Radcliffe's mysterious suggestions impress and terrify so much that we are indignant when she explains them away. Who would not prefer to dwell in Otranto rather than in Udolpho? The blood on the turret-stairs in Udolpho is much more frightful than Alphonso's nasal effusion, even though the one had a harmless explanation and the other denoted ghostly vengeance. The sword which at Otranto weighed down one hundred men was slight by comparison with the strange light which flickered on the sentry's spear on Udolpho's battlements. The ghostly portrait of Manfred's grandfather is far less appalling than the veiled picture which Emily St Aubert dared to view. Did Walpole introduce the historical merely as a background for his tale of terror? Or did he use the supernatural merely as a stimulus to his readers — to key them up to the imaginative state which would enable them to live vicariously in his medieval tale? Whatever was his purpose, Otranto fails as a Gothic novel and is not much more successful from a historical point of view. Its best contribution to Gothicism is the character of Manfred, whose dark passions drive him onward to his doom.

Clara Reeve (1729–1807), the daughter of a clergyman resident at Ipswich, came under the influence of *The Castle of Otranto*, but she quarrelled seriously with Walpole's method of introducing the marvellous. She says:

> The opening excites the attention strongly: the conduct of the story is artful an judicious; the characters are admirably drawn and supported; the diction polished and elegant, yet with all these brilliant advantages, it palls upon the mind . . . and the reason is obvious; the machinery is so violent that it destroys the effect it is intended to excite. Had the story been kept within the utmost verge of probability, the effect had been preserved, without losing the least circumstance that excites or detains the attention.
>
> For instance; we can conceive, and allow of, the appearance of a ghost; we can dispense with an enchanted sword and helmet; but then they must keep with the limits of credibility.[11] A sword so large as to require a hundred men to lift it; a helmet that by its own weight forces a passage through a courtyard, into an arched vault big enough for a man to go through; a picture that walks out of its frame; a

skeleton ghost in a hermit's cowl;—when your expectation
is wound up to the highest pitch, these circumstances take
it down with a witness, destroy the work of imagination,
and instead of attention excite laughter.[12]

This is excellent criticism; worthy, in fact, of the author of the
Progress of Romance (1785). What follows is an excellent prognos-
tication which, although she voiced it, she herself did not take
seriously. She says hat she decided to attempt a work upon the
same plan, on which she would avoid Walpole's defects: 'But
then I began to fear it might happen to me as to certain trans-
lators and imitators of Shakespeare: the unities may be preserved
while the spirit is evaporated.'[13] These words exactly describe
The Old English Baron.

Published, in 1777, under the title of *The Champion of Virtue, a
Gothic tale*, this novel reached a second edition the following year,
and was named *The Old English Baron*. Neither title is apt. There
are so many champions of virtue in this story that one cannot
well distinguish the one Miss Reeve had in mind. As for the
second title, it does not refer to the principal character, and is
useful only to indicate contrariwise the chief faults of this novel.
In a word, the setting is not sufficiently old, the characters are too
aristocratic and the hero is too excessively of the type which Miss
Reeve mistakenly considered English. Edmund (for this is the
paragon's name) is like the bespectacled and earnest young
curate so dear to the comedian's heart. He is too good, too long-
suffering and too humble. Our difficulty is not the belief that he
has blue blood in his veins, but the belief that he has any blood at
all. He has all the virtues, but no vigour. He wins through all his
difficulties simply by being harmless—an affecting but rather
improbable circumstance. We see him first as the lowly Edmund
Twyford, a peasant lad of unknown parentage, a servant in the
house of Baron Fitz-Owen. But we at once recognize in him the
young heir, whose parents have been foully murdered. He is
loved by the Baron and the Baron's son William, the Baron's
daughter Emma, the chaplain, Father Oswald, and an old
retainer, Joseph, as well as by all the servants and country folk.
He is hated by the Baron's son Robert, and by two villains who
do all they can to disgrace him in war and malign him in time of
peace. He is finally challenged to sleep in the haunted room.
Phantoms haunt his slumbers, and emit groans from underground,

like Hamlet's father; but Edmund's strength is as the strength of ten because his heart is pure.

He solves the riddle of his birth, bids Emma an enigmatic farewell and seeks the help of Sir Philip Harclay, a knight so benevolent that his castle is something between Chelsea Royal Hospital and a home for decayed gentlemen. On hearing that Lord Lovel, Edmund's wicked uncle, murdered Edmund's parents, Sir Philip Harclay decides to engage this caitiff in single combat. Haughty challenges ensue and finally they take the field, Sir Philip determined to wring a confession from his opponent.

> The lists were cleared, and the combatants began to fight. They contended a long time with equal skill and courage at length Sir Philip unhorsed his antagonist. The judges ordered that either he should alight or suffer his enemy to remount; he chose the former, and a short combat on foot ensued. The sweat ran off their bodies with the violence of the exercise. Sir Philip watched every motion of the enemy, and strove to weary him out, intending to wound, but not to kill him unless obliged for his own safety.
>
> He thrust his sword through his left arm, and demanded whether he would confess the fact. Lord Lovel, enraged, answered he would die sooner. Sir Philip then passed the sword through his body twice, and Lord Lovel fell, crying out that he was slain.
>
> 'I hope not,' said Sir Philip, 'for I have a great deal of business to do with you before you die.'[14]

This business-like method of inquisition succeeds. Lord Lovel is banished to the Holy Land. Edmund is reinstated, Emma becomes his wife, and the moral is 'the over-ruling hand of Providence, and the certainty of Retribution.

Clara Reeve's story is cursed with all the faults of its qualities. The plot is clear, but it is only too clear; there is not much sentimentality, but there is far too much commonsense; it is moral, but it is too moralizing; it does not exaggerate the marvellous, but it reduces the marvellous to the commonplace. Clara Reeve's horrors arouse no fear.[15] Her ghost groans, and it is no more than if a harmless old gentleman cleared his throat; it appears in blood-stained armour and we perceive nothing amazing; it speaks and, despite its words, we feel that it is only making a polite reference to the weather. Its skeleton is found tied neck and heels in a buried chest. We attend the exhumation and are as unmoved as if we watched a gardener transplanting lettuce. Indeed Edmund himself is most philosophic, not to say absent-minded, as to the remains of his murdered parents. With much difficulty he finds and reassembles their skeletons. Then we observe him enter into his inheritance, and become affianced to the fair Emma. All is happiness and joy:

> After they had refreshed themselves and recovered from the emotions they had sustained on this interesting occasion, Edmund thus addressed the Baron: 'On the brink of happiness, I must claim your attention to a melancholy subject. The bones of both my parents lie unburied in this house; permit me, my honoured lord, to perform my last duties to them, and the remainder of my life shall be devoted to you and yours.' 'Certainly,' said the Baron, 'Why have you not interred them?'[16]

He might well ask.

Clara Reeve published, in 1793, a historical novel called *Memoirs of Sir Roger de Clarendon*. This dealt with the most important events in the reigns of Edward III and Richard II. It was her intention to weave a romantic tale around the historical facts. Her facts are correct, but there is no historical atmosphere, and this story, like *The Old English Baron*, is a cold and commonplace production. In 1788 appeared another Gothic attempt: *The Exiles, or Memoirs of the Count of Cronstadt*. This was based on two of Baculard d'Arnaud's novelettes.[17] Cronstadt was the gloomy and self-doomed character who so often figures in Gothic tales, and probably was the inspiration for Harriet Lee's *Kruitzner*. Indeed Cronstadt takes for a time the name of his servant Albert Kreutzer, a fact which may have influenced Harriet Lee in the choice of her hero's name. In addition to the novels which we have mentioned, Clara Reeve wrote two stories of her own period: *The Two Mentors* (1783) and *The School for Widows* (1791). Like all her fictional compositions, these were deliberately didactic, the latter envisaging a sort of educational Utopia. Clara Reeve's influence on Harriet Lee is really her best claim to remembrance. She had not the temperament for Gothic fiction which required vivid and almost unbridled imagination both in creating atmosphere and in inventing and employing elements of terror. Clara Reeve writing a Gothic novel calls up a picture of a maiden lady in elastic-sided boots, endeavouring to control a mustang.

Far more important was the contribution made by Harriet Lee (1757–1851) and her elder sister Sophia (1750–1824). These women really caught the Gothic spirit, and are amongst the most notable writers who aided its development in fiction. They were daughters of the irascible John Lee, author and actor. Years before his death in 1781, they had taken to the writing of novels and plays, partly, no doubt, because of an inherited flair, and partly because their father's continual quarrels with theatre managers made it necessary for them to supplement the meagre family finances. On the death of their father, the sisters opened a school in Bath, where they had amongst their pupils one Anne Ward of whom, as Mrs Radcliffe, we shall hear much more presently.

Many claims have been made for Sophia Lee's first novel, *The Recess* (1785). Her sister Harriet called it 'the first English Romance that blended interesting fiction with historical events and characters, embellishing both by picturesque description. *Cleveland*, written as I believe, by the Abbé Prévôt, had precedence of all.'[18] Various critics since that time have agreed in substance with Harriet's assertion, and it has been suggested that *The Recess* gave hints for *Kenilworth*. Scott may possibly have been attracted by the idea of writing a historical novel on the more personal aspects of Elizabeth's reign. Genius can find an inspiration in the most unexpected and even worthless material. That *The Recess* is worthless there is little doubt. It is historical only in the sense that its background is Elizabeth's reign. Raleigh, Essex, Leicester, Sir Philip Sidney and his sisters, and the two rival queens are integral parts of the story. Sophia Lee represents that Mary Queen of Scots, believing Bothwell dead, secretly married the Duke of Norfolk during he imprisonment in Bolton Castle. There is much plotting to release Mary and finally, through the agency of the Regent Murray, Elizabeth discovers the truth. Norfolk is arrested. Meanwhile twin daughters are born to Mary and, as she wishes to conceal a marriage which would cost her husband his life, she causes them to be secretly conveyed away. Norfolk's sister, Lady Scroope, arranges that the children shall be cared for in some subterranean quarters formerly the refuge of persecuted priests, and known as the Recess. Bothwell reappears; and Norfolk, deprived thus of any legal connection with Mary, is released, but further plotting leads him to the block. Mary's twin daughters,

Mathilda and Ellinor, reach maturity in their gloomy retreat, and though they have never once seen the sun, they are, when the story opens very lovely young women. With their mother's beauty they inherit her fatality, and it is not long until they are involved as deeply as she in love and political intrigue.

Mathilda, the elder, encounters the Earl of Leicester by a strange accident and wins his heart. He marries her and takes her and her sister Ellinor to Kenilworth. To escape Elizabeth's wrath the marriage is concealed, but she is not deceived, and carries them off to the court so that she may have them under supervision. The story now splits into two strands, narrating Mathilda's adventures as the wife of Leicester and Ellinor's as the beloved of Essex. Elizabeth is the villain of the piece, and by every means in her power she destroys the happiness of the lovers. Mathilda and Leicester eventually flee to France where he is slain. She is decoyed to the West Indies, persecuted by wicked lovers, and imprisoned for long years, but she at last returns to England with Leicester's child.

Meanwhile Ellinor has been parted from Essex. Elizabeth discovers the secret of the sisters' birth and, under threat of executing Essex, forces Ellinor to sign a confession that their royal pretensions are imposture. To make assurance doubly sure, Elizabeth forces Ellinor to marry Lord Arlington who is too stupid for intrigue. Thereafter Ellinor's reason gives way and, after the execution of Essex, she becomes quite demented. Mathilda, after many trials, the greatest of which is the poisoning of her daughter, dies at last.

Sophia Lee makes no attempt to create the atmosphere of Elizabethan times, or to reproduce the customs or language of the period. She forestalls criticism thus: 'I make no apology for altering the language to that of the present age, since the obsolete stile . . . would be frequently unintelligible.' Evidently she also considered her readers incapable of understanding the outlook and the behaviour of the Elizabethan age, and felt it necessary to make her characters conform to eighteenth century fictional standards. Indeed it is probable that she was honestly unaware of any differences in relation to period, and was unconscious of the anomaly of an Elizabethan age peopled with etiolated beings and speaking the jargon of sensibility. An anaemic Raleigh goes on polite tours around the world; so languishing a Sidney could never have fought at Zutphen; Drake, had she presented him, would have played croquet, but never bowls. That Sophia Lee could have thought her Essex consistent with his fate shows how far she was from estimating the quality of her work. Otherwise she would have known that such a nincompoop could never have achieved the dignity of decapitation. Elizabeth alone lives, and she only because Miss Lee outraged her own feelings to create her. No sensible reader would give one such Elizabeth for a wilderness of Ellinors.

From beginning to end this novel is bathed in tears. Though sometimes the self-dissection is accurate, it is devitalized by an extreme lack of restraint. When presenting the emotions, Sophia Lee makes Pelion and Ossa like a wart. One might quote in proof of this by opening any of the three volumes at random. For example, there is the occasion when Leicester and Mathilda are captured and imprisoned by a vengeful villain from whom nothing is to be feared but dishonour and death. This really beggars description.

From a humorous point of view it is a pity that space does not permit us to give some of Ellinor's adventures in Ireland. Miss Lee sees no reason to doubt that in Elizabeth's reign Scotland was a Hesperides peopled with refined and benevolent men, while Ireland, on the contrary, was inhabited by beings who in 'their language, manners, and lives' resembled the 'inhabitants of the Torrid Zone'. Ellinor falls into the hands of 'Tiroen', a villainous savage with the most dishonourable intentions. Tiroen lays his plans, but Ellinor, several moves ahead of him, thoughtfully provides herself with laudanum which she induces him to quaff as a love-pledge. Ellinor in relating this incident is so reminiscent of a spinster aunt that one cannot resist quoting:

> I was one evening alone in the tent allotted to me . . . when Tiroen approached me unawares — his complexion was flushed with wine, and his eyes and air showed a determination at which my nature shuddered — no longer regarding decorum or respect, his manners made me in a moment sensible I had deferred taking my laudanum too long. An idea, at which I have never ceased to wonder, suggested itself to my mind; and while fluctuating between the possible and impossible, I a little soothed the boisterous wretch at whose profligate vows I trembled . . . convinced by the tenor of his discourse and conduct, that I could

escape his licentious purposes only by feigning an intention of yielding to them, I smoothed my agonised features into a smile which almost stiffened me into a convulsion, and complained of thirst—a glass of water stood by, of which I drank—inclination no less than gallantry made him insist on pledging me . . . He eagerly swallowed the beverage. Sleep had before hovered over his eyelids; it was now forerun by stupefaction.[19]

Yet, though rarely, this fustian is sometimes relieved by such a passage as describes the escape of Mathilda, Leicester and their friend, Rose Cecil, to France:

We ascended the deck, and seating ourselves in a little boat lashed to it, every fear, every hope seemed suspended, and the present all our lives for which any had a sense. The gentle breezes only played upon the white sails, and the vessel cut with a safe and pleasant motion, through those green waves whose points the full moon exquisitely silvered, as breaking they gave life to the stillness of the night. I turned my eyes with the sweetest satisfaction from my love to my friend, from my friend to my love; the same mild orb delicately illumin'd either face . . . These sacred pauses in life, which lovers only know, invigorate the soul, as sleep does the body, and alone can enable us to sustain the past and coming ill.

That Sophia had not Harriet's ability as a novelist was proved by *The Canterbury Tales* which appeared in 1797. This was a collection of stories planned by Harriet who wrote most of them, Sophia contributing *The Two Emilys* and *Pembroke*. *The Canterbury Tales* are of the novella type, most of them suffering from undue condensation. The subject matter is generally domestic and sentimental, and often shows a democratic spirit unusual in days when readers dearly loved a lord. The stories are very uneven in technique. In many of them time is badly managed, notably in *Montfort* and *Constance*. ('And what is become of Constance? Nine years are past—nine long years, in about as many lines. This is going full speed indeed! Patience, courteous reader! The ensuing years will perhaps creep a snail's pace.') But despite the faultiness and improbability of some of these stories, there is much evidence of originality, of realism. One observes in such fiction a sure instinct to develop a technique equal to its conceptions. For example, there is the spirit of experiment in which

Harriet Lee begins *Constance* with conversation, then explains the background and works in the characters. The characterization is usually convincing, sometimes achieved with crisp deftness.

The best of Harriet's domestic stories is *The Landlady's Tale*. This bears the impress of the supposed narrator. It is told with convincing power and complete naturalness. Mary, a shop-girl, is betrayed by Captain Mandeville, an army officer whom the landlady describes as follows: 'He was one of those rattling sparks, Sir, who dash on in life without looking to the right or the left, through a long lane of the maimed and the blind, whom they have made so; till, being come to their journey's end, they are obliged to cast their eyes back, and see the sad spectacle of human misery.'[20] When Mary is deserted by Mandeville she goes to his native place, discovers he is married, and bears her child, which dies. At the same time Mandeville's wife has a child, and she dies soon afterwards. Mary offers herself as nurse to the baby son, and lives at the Hall. Mandeville returns, persecutes her with his demands, and threatens to have her dismissed without a character. On an impulse she rushes to the nursery, bundles his son into her arms, walks to Newcastle and takes ship for London. There she lives until the boy is twelve years old, and then goes to Weymouth. She and the boy are taken in by Mrs Dixon, the landlady, who engages Mary as a seamstress. The death of her father calls Mary from home and in her absence Mandeville, now a Member of Parliament, comes to stay at Mrs Dixon's. He little knows that under the same roof is his son, now aged seventeen. This youth, Bob, falls under the bad influence of Mandeville's groom, and agrees to 'borrow' some of Mandeville's valuables, and to pawn them so as to raise money for betting. They are sure they can return the articles in time to avoid detection, but they are wrong. Mandeville exonerates the groom and all the blame falls on Bob, who is shipped to Botany Bay. Mary returns and, distracted at what has happened, tells Mandeville that he has ruined his own son. Mandeville falls into a fit. All efforts to free the boy are vain, but he frees himself by dying on the outward voyage. Mary's reason becomes impaired; Mandeville's health remains enfeebled, and public censure forces him to leave Weymouth.

Of the dignified pathos which characterizes this story, one brief example must serve. When Mary was in despair,

After turning her thoughts a thousand ways in search of
comfort, she found no gleam of it but in the idea of going
back to her own village. She had been innocent—she had
been comparatively happy there. She believed she should
find something to love, and Mary could not live without
loving something.[21]

The three Gothic stories in *The Canterbury Tales* are all by
Harriet Lee. They are *Constance* (the Frenchman's tale), *Lothaire*
(the old woman's tale), and *Kruitzner* (the German's tale).

Constance is a good story told with animation. The heroine is a
beautiful and innocent girl who lives with her godparents in a
cottage on the Marquis of Valmont's estate in Languedoc. Her
loveliness attracts the attention of the Marquis and his guests
and, to avoid them, it is arranged that she shall be sent to some
friends in Dauphine. But Constance is more in love than she
knows with one who calls himself Valrive, a servant of the Valmont
household, but who is actually the Chevalier de Valmont. She
agrees to say farewell to him in a little house in the forest, but is
kidnapped and taken to a château of the Marquis of Valmont.
Some three months later the Marquis arrives, but his dishonourable
attentions are in abeyance as he is a fugitive from the Revolutionaries. Constance's effort to escape is described with Gothic
effect. Her fears, her midnight explorations of the grim château
are exciting. She accidentally comes upon an emaciated prisoner
in the castle dungeon — the rightful Marquis of Valmont who has
been incarcerated for almost a century, and this despite the fact that
he is not above forty years of age. The arrival of the *sans-culottes*
frees both him and Constance. She discovers that he is her father.
He dies, and Constance after many vicissitudes marries her lover.

Kruitzner is not only the best of Harriet Lee's Gothic stories,
but the best of all her writings. The story begins with the arrival
at an obscure town in Silesia of a man, his wife and their son.
This man is Kruitzner who, from the moment of his appearance,
impresses the villagers with a sense of mystery. Kruitzner's
illness detains these strangers in this little backwater, although
they wish to press forward on their journey. They are miserably
poor, and the Intendant of the Prince de T— (who has his own
purposes to serve) allows them the use of an empty house near
the Palace. A junta of village schemers sets itself to spy on
Kruitzner and to discover his secret.

The secret they so long to discover would not disappoint them, for the family sheltered in the dilapidated house was destined for strange adventures and had already felt the hand of fate. Kruitzner, whose real name was Siegendorf, was the heir of Count Siegendorf of Bohemia, disowned for the licentiousness of his private life and for his incapacity and indifference in defence of his country. Thus disgraced, he went into Saxony where he continued his profligate course until he saw and loved Josephine Michelli, the daughter of a poor scientist. At first he is ideally happy, but soon memories of his high birth and all that he has lost torture him, and he pours out the whole story to his wife and her father. They are amazed; and Michelli is alarmed lest in Kruitzner's new desire for reconciliation with his father he may be prepared to abandon Josephine. He resents also the way in which Kruitzner has deceived him, and they quarrel. Kruitzner, in his anger, makes another of his fatal decisions and, at once putting it in action, sets out secretly for Bohemia with the object of making a personal appeal to his father. On the way he communicates with the old Count who, in response, arranges to have an allowance paid to Kruitzner, but forbids him to return to Bohemia until he has redeemed the name of Siegendorf. Determined to reform, Kruitzner continues his journey home-wards, but at Cassel his good intentions break down before the argument of a full purse and opportunity. He again falls into evil ways and spends all he has, even the money he left in Hamburg for his wife and son. His father hears of his dissipations and renounces him forever.

From that day forth Kruitzner's nature undergoes a change. He believes himself deeply wronged by his father, and he withdraws into himself to feed upon his own bitterness. When the old Count offers to take Kruitzner's little son, Conrad, and to rear him for succession to the title and estates, Kruitzner cannot refuse, although this offer is the final proof that he himself has been disinherited.

Years elapse, and Kruitzner and his wife continue in poverty while their son grows into manhood. But there is a secret pretender to the estates in Bohemia, the cold and avaricious Stralenheim who, on the death of the old Count, reveals his real nature. He contests Conrad's legitimacy, and claims his inheritance. Conrad leaves Bohemia; Kruitzner and his wife try to reach it.

Stralenheim seeks Kruitzner to destroy him. All their ways meet at the remote village in Bohemia where Kruitzner's illness has detained him. There are spies, searches, evasions, a secret passage, a theft and finally a murder — the murder of Stralenheim. A Hungarian, who disappears immediately after the murder, is suspected of the crime, but there is no real proof. Kruitzner, freed of Stralenheim's evil pursuit, returns to Bohemia and succeeds to his inheritance, but his son's strange remoteness of manner and his reluctance to live at home afflict Kruitzner with a fear that he himself will know the sufferings of a father who watches, but cannot reclaim, a wayward son.

Finally, it transpires that Conrad was the murderer of Stralenheim. Conrad is killed in a skirmish, and is not long survived by his parents. Kruitzner rests at last, after a weary cycle of error and expiation.

Kruitzner is a story which suffers from compression. Reading it is like entering a house where great things are toward; we are enveloped in an atmosphere of intrigue; we see people hastily passing to and fro, talking together, going out, re-entering. We have been given a hint of what is happening, but so rapidly that it is with difficulty we take in the complicated plot. But the character of Kruitzner is the focal point. That is so finely conceived, so minutely dissected, driven home to us with such living force that it gives reality and coherence to the involuted story. Kruitzner is an egoist of turbulent passions, cursed with all the morbidity of introversion. He has a consciousness of fatality which sets him apart, invests him with strange and sinister individuality, and gives a gloomy grandeur to his tragic life. Kruitzner should have been born in the fury of a storm when earth and sky were convulsed with demoniac rage. He carries with him his own dark atmosphere, and the deadly lightning of his will brings ruin to himself and to those around him. He has depths easily stirred to good or evil, but moving in obedience to some law of his own nature. He errs, and he is so embittered against himself for his mistakes that he perversely continues in courses that can lead only to destruction:

> It is the wrong we commit against ourselves that corrodes
> and most bitterly envenoms the heart; that we receive from
> others sometimes displays its noblest faculties, either by the
> act of repelling or enduring the evil. [Kruitzner] owed half

his faults and almost all his miseries to a secret tearing consciousness of error, which he never permitted to rise into reformation.[22]

After he has forfeited his father's affection and the respect of his country, he is for a while redeemed by the love and goodness of his wife. But not for long. Soon thoughts of what he has thrown away break the tranquillity of his days, and he deceives himself with the idea that it is remorse which disturbs him and which urges him to a reconciliation with his father. It is not remorse.

> The radical fault of his character was yet far from being extirpated: for whether under the influence of virtuous or illicit passions, whether revelling in the courts of princes, or living in the bosom of frugality and temperance, it was self and self only, that had hitherto guided all his actions; and even at a crisis, when he was willing to believe that final duty and honour gave rise to his returning sensibility, it was strangely compounded of that pride and self-love the avenging angel had not yet wrung out his heart.[23]

Even when he has ruined his life, he is not willing to live in the future of his son Conrad. It rankles within him that Conrad will have what might have been his own. And yet he loves his son, and yields him up to his grandfather with relief at the thought that this child, at least, will come into his own. No wonder that a heart devoured at the same moment by pride, remorse, envy, love and bitterness can never for a moment find peace.

The end of *Kruitzner* is finely conceived. The Count, reinstated in his honours and possessions, is still gnawed by the remembrance of the means he has employed, and by doubts of his son's nature which too much appears to resemble his own. Nor is he spared the final horror of finding that Conrad has put into action the very deed which his own mind had secretly contemplated. He has to endure the misery of having begotten an instrument for the performance of those dreadful promptings from which his own mind recoils in horror. His punishment is not merely remorse for his own sins, but responsibility for that of his son. The suffering he inflicted on his father is as nothing to what he himself has now to endure.

Harriet Lee set herself the task of making us understand the nature of Kruitzner, and how he precipitated and endured the events of his life. At the same time she claims our sympathy for him. That she succeeded in achieving these purposes gives her the right to be considered as a most valuable contributor to English fiction. We have in Kruitzner not merely Gothic mysteries, but the mysteries of a soul. Hartley Coleridge says of it: 'The motif—a son predestined to evil by the weakness and sensuality of his father, a father's punishment for his want of rectitude by the passionate criminality of his son, is the very key-note of tragedy.' Byron read this story when he was about fourteen, and it affected him powerfully: 'It made a deep impression on me,' he says, 'and may, indeed, be said to contain the germ of much that I have since written.' In 1821 he dramatized it under the title of *Werner, or the Inheritance.*

In *Kruitzner* there is a very sparing use of Gothic para-phernalia. Indeed of external adjuncts there is little more than a ruined house and a secret passage. The real action is in the mind. There is a steady growth of suspense, fear, and mental torture. Harriet Lee did not need the rack of the Inquisition. She knew that a certain kind of nature tortures itself, and she introduced outside forces merely to tighten the screw. The result is Gothic in the psychological sense. Kruitzner is in excelsis a Gothic hero—a figure of isolated and tormented grandeur.

Another woman who aided the development of the Gothic novel was Mrs Charlotte Smith (1749–1806). Poverty drove her to commence author, and she brought to her work a great natural talent and no education. Her schooling, such as it was, ended at the age of twelve. At fifteen she was forced by her step-mother into a marriage which was distasteful to her, and which proved a disastrous failure. Her worthless husband involved her in many misfortunes, even in imprisonment, and she was forced to support not only her twelve children, but their irresponsible father. These were the circumstances of a writer who provided Mrs Radcliffe with some valuable hints, and who made a signal contribution towards the development of the Gothic novel.

Her first works were a volume of poems, and a translation of *Manon Lescaut* (1786). In 1788 appeared her first novel *Emmeline, the orphan of the castle*. This story of domestic sensibility is not worth recounting from a Gothic point of view. Except for the formal background of the castle, and some hints of sentimental landscape, it has no Gothic characteristics. This love of romantic scenery is very important. Rousseau and such writers as Madame de Genlis[24] may have prepared the way by popularizing harmonious landscapes, but to Mrs Smith must go the credit for adding this most prominent trait to the Gothic novel. There is no doubt that it was from Mrs Smith that Mrs Radcliffe derived this very interesting aspect of Gothicism. In Charlotte Smith's second novel *Ethelinde, or the Recluse of the lake* (1789) the Cumberland setting is carefully elaborated, but it is in *Celestina* (1791) that we find awe and beauty mingled in the true Gothic proportions. Here also, in the descriptions of the Pyrenees, we find proof of Mrs Radcliffe's indebtedness.

Celestina is a curious mixture of tendencies. It unites the elements of domestic sensibility, doctrinal didacticism and Gothicism. The plot is loose and straggling with several inset stories given at a length out of all relation to their importance. These are: the story of Jessy and Cathcart, the story of Mrs Elphinstone and the story of the Count de Bellegarde. This latter tale has the Pyrenean background which Mrs Radcliffe used three years later in *The Mysteries of Udolpho*. Both women obviously used the same source: Ramond de Carbonnières' *Observations faites dans les Pyrénées* (1789), but it seems more than probable that Mrs Radcliffe turned to de Carbonnières after she had read *Celestina*. Charlotte Smith's instinct as a novelist gauged the value of the Frenchman's descriptions. The might and splendour of the mountains, the glaciers, the torrents, the gloomy pine forests, the little valleys like oases in this rugged isolation, the swirling mists, storm, thunder and lightning, the hollow cry of the vulture, awe and fear — in adapting all these to the purposes of fiction Mrs Smith anticipated Mrs Radcliffe. Here, too, is the half-ruined castle on an airy summit, the nearby convent and the story of cruel wrongs, imprisonment, plotting Jesuits, and pitiful maidens forced to take the veil. None of it, of course, is presented with Mrs Radcliffe's artistry of suspense and mystery, but the paraphernalia are there. It is notable that Mrs Smith here arrives also at a suggestion of that chiaroscuro technique which Mrs Radcliffe had already employed, and which she was later to bring to a fine art. Mrs Smith may have taken the hint from Mrs Radcliffe's previous novels, or may simply have followed closely Ramond de Carbonnières' contrasted use of the storm and peril of the mountains and the peaceful security of the valley. Indeed the Vallée de Luron (to which Willoughby comes after his dangerous wanderings) suggests to Mrs Smith the words applied by Rousseau to a similar spot among the rocks of Meillerie: 'Il semblait que ce lieu désert dût être l'asyle de deux amants échappés seuls au bouleversement de la nature.' Such exquisite moments of happy security Mrs Radcliffe always gave her persecuted lovers, before she sent them relentlessly forward on the dark path of their fate.

But it was not only in her use of nature that Mrs Smith sounded the Gothic note. The Count of Bellegarde's castle, situated on a height with masses of ruined fortifications, is unmistakably Gothic:

> The gate of the castle, and all beyond the moat . . . was yet entire, as were the walls within its circumference, bearing everywhere the marks of great antiquity, but of such ponderous strength, as time alone had not been able to destroy . . . The towers, at each end, rose in frowning grandeur, above the rest of the building; and having only loops, and no windows, impressed ideas of darkness and imprisonment, while the moss and wall-flowers filled the interstices of the broken stones and an infinite number of birds made their nests among the shattered cornices, and half-fallen battlements, filling the air with their shrill cries.[25]

The interior of the castle is no less romantic:

> An immense hall, barbarously magnificent; it was roofed with beams of oak, and the sides covered with standards, and trophies of armour, the perishable parts of which were dropping to pieces. The narrow Gothic windows were filled, not with glass, that admitted the light, but with glass, painted with the achievements of the family; mingled with the heads of saints and martyrs.[26]

No wonder that 'Willoughby as he marched gravely along, through the long galleries, and across the gloomy hall, fancied himself a knight of romance, and that some of the stories of enchanted castles, and wandering adventures, of which he had been fond in his early youth, were here realized.'[27]

Desmond, an epistolary novel which appeared in 1792, is again a mélange of the same tendencies which were evident in *Celestina,* but in *Desmond* the doctrinal didacticism is so shameless that the book is less a novel than a social and political tractate. The domestic framework sets forth the love of an idealistic young man for Geraldine, the patient wife of a wastrel named Verney. Verney's wretched behaviour reaches the limit when he tries to decoy his wife into becoming the mistress of the Duc de Romagnecourt. She manages to evade this situation. Then she hears that her husband has been seriously wounded near Avignon, and hastens to join him. On the way she has a terrible adventure in an inn which is really a house of call for robbers. She is rescued in the nick of time by Desmond who has followed her to France and unobtrusively watched over her. They take refuge in the Count d'Hautville's Gothic castle, which, although the embers are still glowing on the hearth, seems deserted. The gloom, their fears, their discovery of a man's cap pierced by a bullet and covered with blood, the mysterious sounds of low breathing, their final discovery of a hideous man — one of a troop organized by d'Hautville for the defence of the castle against the revolutionaries — all arouse curiosity and fear. It transpires that the Count d'Hautville has gone to Italy and the garrison become outlaws. Eight of the bandits are out marauding when Geraldine and Desmond arrive. On hearing this, Desmond has the draw-bridge raised and prepares to defend the castle against the robbers should they return while he and Geraldine are still there. They get safely away to Avignon, however, and do all in their power to nurse Verney back to life. But Verney, with a singular tact, dies repenting all his misdeeds and recommending the sorely-tried lovers to marry — which they do.

Arising from a description of the estate of Montfleuri, there is a reverie of Desmond's which blends the two main elements of Mrs Radcliffe's Gothic conception. Here Charlotte Smith unites the romantic loveliness of nature and of terror, and creates about them a widening sense of the strangeness of human existence. She says:

> I know this betrays a very Gothic and exploded taste, but such is the force of early impressions, that I have still an affection for 'the bowed roof' — the cathedral-like solemnity of long lines of tall trees, whose topmost boughs are interlaced with each other . . . But I account for my predilections, by the kind of pensive and melancholy pleasure I used to feel, when in my childhood and early youth, I

walked alone, in a long avenue of arbeal, which led from a very wild and woody part of the weald of Kent, to an old house my father, at that period of my life, inhabited. I remember the cry of the wood-peckers or the yaffils, as we call them in that country, going to roost in a pale autumnal evening, answered by the owls, which in great numbers inhabit the deep forest-like glens that lay behind the avenue. I see the moon slowly rising over the dark mass of wood, and the opposite hills, tinged with purple from the last reflection of the sun, which was sunk behind them.— I recall the sensations I felt, when, as the silver leaves of the aspins trembled in the lowest breeze, or slowly fell to the ground before me, I became half-frightened at the increasing obscurity of the objects around me, and have almost persuaded myself that the grey trunks of these old trees, and the low murmur of the wind among their branches, were the dim forms, and hollow sighs of some supernatural beings; and at length, afraid of looking behind me, I have hurried breathless into the house.[28]

The best of all Mrs Charlotte Smith's novels is *The Old Manor House* (1793). Once again the elements which most interested her are apparent, but they are more evenly balanced, and they are not, as formerly, merely collateral, but are fused in the greater part of the story. In her previous novels there had really been no characterization, although there had been the ability to sketch the minor characters with a few touches of realism or malice. These portraits, however, were merely external, but in *The Old Manor House* Mrs Smith shows herself interested in human reactions and motives. The character of Mrs Rayland is most effectively and consistently drawn. She dominates the action of the story, not only during her lifetime, but even after her death, since the mystery which surrounds her will causes the involvements in the second part of the novel.

Mrs Rayland, the owner of Rayland Hall and its extensive estates, is a rigid autocrat whose greatest pleasure lies in the power which she derives from her illustrious ancestry and her great wealth. Her only relatives are a family called Somerive who live a few miles away and whom she despises because they are descended from a branch of the family which has repeatedly demeaned itself by misalliances. Mrs Rayland has it in her power to do as she wishes with all her property and, by her arrogance and grudging condescension, she keeps the Somerives in a state of perpetual suspense as to her intentions. The profligacy of the elder son, Philip, alienates her sympathies from him; and Orlando, the younger son, who is her favourite, seems to have the best chance of succeeding to her property. Mrs Rayland, however, does not commit herself as to her intentions, and Orlando has to be content with frequenting Rayland Hall and awaiting her pleasure. This he does, not so much for selfish motives as for the benefit of his needy family. But a complication arises from the presence at Rayland Hall of Monimia, the orphan niece of Mrs Lennard, the housekeeper. Orlando falls deeply in love with Monimia. The necessity for keeping their affection a secret from Mrs Rayland leads to midnight meetings, to which they come through a secret passage and a ghostly chapel. With much power Charlotte Smith shows that, though Mrs Rayland is an inflexible autocrat, she is being watched silently and rapaciously by Mrs Lennard and Pattenson, the butler, both of whom are interested in feathering their nests, and who would oust Orlando from favour if they could. Mrs Lennard's motives are very well dissected. We are shown that she is fiercely opposed to the love of Orlando and Monimia because, if Orlando does not become heir, the estate will probably be split up, and Mrs Lennard in that case would get a much smaller legacy. Pattenson hates Orlando because he foolishly suspects him of intriguing with one of the maids whom Pattenson himself hopes to seduce, and because Orlando's mysterious movements around Rayland Hall at night seem to menace Pattenson's secret commerce with smugglers. Pattenson has some unexplained hold over Mrs Lennard which makes it necessary for her to placate him when their interests clash. All these separate motives of intrigue are most skilfully interwoven, and it is against this background of fear, spying, ruthlessness and self-interest that the guileless Monimia and Orlando pursue the course of true love. Although Mrs Rayland plays with Orlando as a cat with a mouse, her hard nature softens towards him, and although she dissimulates her affection and her intentions, it becomes clear that he has a very good chance of becoming her heir.

At this juncture an elderly admirer of one of Orlando's sisters, for reasons of his own, wishes him out of the way, and offers him a commission in the army. Mrs Rayland, who comes of a martial line, encourages Orlando to accept, and he has no choice but to go, thus leaving Monimia to the tyranny and restraint of Mrs Lennard, who has the strongest suspicions of their secret understanding. After enduring many terrible adventures in the American war, Orlando escapes from the red Indians who are his captors, and with great difficulty gets back to England. He finds his father's house in the possession of strangers, his father dead and his mother and sisters grone without a trace. Rayland Hall is shut up, and he learns that, by Mrs Rayland's will, it now has passed with all the rest of the property into the possession of an avaricious clergyman called Dr Hollybourn. Mrs Lennard has taken her legacy and married a scheming rascal young enough to be her son. Monimia is nowhere to be found. The rest of the novel deals with Orlando's efforts to find her, to help his family and to bring to light Mrs Rayland's last will, which is in his favour. He succeeds in all these undertakings, and the story ends with a full measure of justice for all the characters.

In setting, in its mysterious or brutal events, and in its use of scenery *The Old Manor House* is Gothic. Rayland Hall provides the architectural background necessary to a Gothic tale. When Orlando first sees Monimia, it is 'by the faint light which the old gothic casements afforded at that hour of the evening.'[29] Their secret interviews involve breathless moments like an eternity when they steal down the winding staircase from the turret, feeling their way in the inky darkness, hearts racing madly at every sound which may denote human spies or ghostly hauntings. Very interesting as an exposition of Mrs Smith's use of terror is the incident when Orlando and Monimia, in the study at midnight, see a face at the window. We are told at once that it is a human face, but we are kept in suspense as to the origin of the voice which, when they are returning to the turret through the chapel, pronounces in the deathly silence the words 'Now, now!' This supernatural effect is later explained away — a fact which shows that, in the use of terror, Mrs Smith and Mrs Radcliffe were in agreement. The difference in their Gothic technique lay only in the degree and frequency of the appeal to the reader's fears. Mrs Smith possessed to a very marked extent the power of creating a ghostly and terrible atmosphere, and her use of nature resembled Mrs Radcliffe's not only because it was romantic, but also because Mrs Smith, like her more famous contemporary, brought to her descriptions a lyrical gift. Not only does she, like

Mrs Radcliffe, continually interpolate poems throughout the narrative, but she gives us sometimes prose lyrics, in which the poetic intention is all the more clearly marked by the repetition of a motif. Mrs Radcliffe had done this in *The Romance of the Forest* (1791). In *The Old Manor House* we find a similar kind of composition. When Orlando bade farewell to his native country-side before going to America: 'The night was overcast and gloom; chill and hollow the wind whistled among the leafless trees, or groaned amid the thick firs in the dark and silent wood; the water-falls murmured hollow in the blast, and only the owl's cry broke those dull and melancholy sounds, which seemed to say — "Orlando, you will revisit these scenes no more!"' These valedictory words run like a refrain through the chapters which lead up to Orlando's actual departure. The misery of his family, his father's illness, the destitute state of Monimia, his own uncertain fate — 'all combined to sink and depress him and again to lend to the well-known paths he was traversing, horrors not their own, while every object repeated: "Orlando will revisit these scenes no more!"'[30] In Rayland Hall 'he traversed the library, yielding to these tormenting thoughts; and, by the light of the solitary candle he had set down in the window seat, every thing appeared gloomy and terrific. Every object and every sound seemed to repeat the sentence that constantly occurred to him —"Orlando will revisit this house no more."'[31] When, many months later, he returned to Rayland Hall:

> The sight of the many well-known objects on his way — every tree, every shrub, recalled to his mind a thousand pleasing ideas; and as he passed hastily through the fir wood, where in a dreary night of December he had last parted from Monimia . . . he compared his present sensations with what he had at that time felt, and laughed at the superstitious impression given him then, and on some former occasions, by the gloom of the winter sky — when he fancied that, in the hollow murmur of the breeze, he heard, 'Orlando will revisit these scenes no more!'[32]

Monimia is just such a heroine as Mrs Radcliffe's Emilys and Adelines, and her fearful predicament in the main resembles theirs. For example, in the turret room:

> As I lay, listening of a night to the howling of the wind in the great melancholy room at the end of the north gallery,

where I was locked up every night, I have frequently started at the visions any fancy raised; and as the dark green damask hangings swelled with the air behind them, I have been so much terrified as to be unable to move or summon to my recollection all the arguments . . . against super-stitious fear—Then too I have been glad to hear the rats as they raced around the skirting boards, because it convinced me there were some living creatures near me, and helped me to account for the strange noises I sometimes heard . . . Good God! how weak I was to add imaginary horrors to the real calamities of my situation.[33]

The domestic element in *The Old Manor House* is worth noting. There is an echo of *Evelina* in the descriptions of Orlando's rela-tions who are in trade. Dr Hollybourn and his egregious daughter are in the same vein, and we have a further example of this aspect in Isabella's humour at the expense of her foppish old wooer, General Tracy. The practice of tilting at purse-proud cits had long been established in the novel, and it is amusing to reflect that Mrs Smith's democratic sympathies led her, in this regard, to make common cause with the snobbish tradition in fiction which had ever mocked at bourgeois crudities.

Charlotte Smith is one of the most interesting writers of her time. In her effort to unite the Gothic, domestic and *tendenz* genres she attempted the impossible, yet, as a reflection of the chief trends in the second half of the eighteenth century, her novels repay careful examination. Their chief value lies in their Gothic aspect. That Charlotte Smith and Mrs Radcliffe had the same conception of Gothicism is quite clear, and Mrs Smith's best claim to remembrance rests in the fact that she provided Mrs Radcliffe with some of the raw materials of the Gothic craft.

To see the possibilities of a trend in fiction, and to choose for its development the most effective materials and technique was the peculiar achievement of Mrs Radcliffe. What had been hinted sporadically by others became her entire theme, and the instruments which they had fingered experimentally she used with the certitude of genius. Thus she gains the credit of initiating the most characteristic type of English Gothic fiction.

Mrs Radcliffe was more fortunate than many of her sister-novelists. She wrote not under financial compulsion, but simply to while away the hours when her husband's editorial duties took him daily from home. She had had the usual smatterings of polite education and the usual feminine taste for novel-reading. She was of a most sensitive and retiring disposition, and found in the exercise of her imagination the pleasure which more gregarious women find in social intercourse. What began, no doubt, in day-dreams, in a fireside game of make-belief, soon took form as her pen set down the strange adventures which grew within her mind.

Mrs Radcliffe's first novel *The Castles of Athlin and Dunbayne, an Highland story* (1789) merited the severe criticisms of the *Critical*[34] and the *Monthly*.[35] The *Critical* bluntly stated that she knew nothing about the Highlands, and the *Monthly* found her wonders 'insipid, if not disgustful'. That book contained some of the Gothic paraphernalia of secret passages and supernatural hints, but it is clumsy and unconvincing. Somewhat better, although still quite undistinguished, was *The Sicilian Romance* (1790). The motif is pursuit. The story might be summed up in Keats's lines:

Ages long ago
These lovers fled away into the storm.

Mrs Radcliffe's lovers begin their flight at an early stage of the story, and continue to be pursued until the end. The action takes place towards the close of the sixteenth century. The Marquis of Mazzini marries as his second wife Maria de Vellorno, a beautiful and unscrupulous woman. They live mainly at Naples, returning only once a year to their Gothic castle at Mazzini. Here live Emilia and Julia, the Marquis's two daughters by his first wife. Julia is loved by a young man called Hippolitus de Vareza, but this earns her the hatred of her stepmother who hopes to enslave Hippolitus. To avoid a forced marriage with a libertine, Julia determines to elope. She gets safely away, but Hippolitus is struck down at the moment of escape. He is taken by his servants to his ship which lies waiting. Then follow, on the one hand, the pursuit and evasion of Julia; on the other, the terrible experiences of those who try to solve the mystery of the haunted wing of the castle of Mazzini. It appears later that the Marquis's first wife is imprisoned in a subterranean chamber in this wing. Julia's flight takes her, amongst other places, to a convent of monks with an annexe of nuns, all under the rule of an Abate. Here she finds

Hippolitus's sister, a nun who dies of consumption with great pomp before the high altar at midnight, surrounded by all the nuns and monks. This is a foretaste of the pseudo-Catholic procedure with which Mrs Radcliffe astounds us in her later novels. Julia escapes from this peculiar ecclesiastical ménage, finds Hippolitus (who is not dead after all), and the pair continue to be pursued through a maze of caverns, forests, subterranean passages, and vaults opening only by a spring lock on the outside, until they arrive back at the castle of Mazzini. Here they rescue Julia's mother. The Marquis dies of poison. Maria de Vellorno stabs herself, and all ends happily.

The plot of this novel is confusing and weak. The general atmosphere is one of extreme sensibility. There is a deliberate striving for exquisite beauty in effects which always seem meretricious. Anachronisms are many but no seasoned reader of Gothic fiction will cavil at pianofortes and 'sophas' towards the close of the sixteenth century. Mrs Radcliffe's device of tricking us into false alarms is very evident.

In comparing these first totterings with Mrs Radcliffe's balanced stride in *The Romance of the Forest* (1791), one observes a great advance in technique. *The Romance of the Forest* shows for the first time Mrs Radcliffe's power to unite and sustain the elements of beauty and terror. For these elements, as they take form in this novel, Mrs Radcliffe appears to have been to some extent indebted to Charlotte Smith. As we have already seen, Mrs Radcliffe found in *Celestina* (which had just appeared) not merely an indication of a valuable source of scenic descriptions, but also very useful hints as to the employment of these sources. A second debt which Mrs Radcliffe owed to Charlotte Smith has been suggested by Miss C. F. McIntyre. Mrs Radcliffe stated that she found La Motte's story in Guyot (or Gayot) de Pitaval's *Causes Célèbres*. Miss McIntyre believes that Mrs Radcliffe's source as actually Charlotte Smith's *Romance of Real Life*.'[36]

The events of Mrs Radcliffe's take take place in France during the seventeenth century. The story opens with the predicament of Pierre de La Motte who, to escape imprisonment, flees from Paris with his wife. They are benighted near a ruined house and, on seeking shelter, are given the alternative of taking away with them an unknown girl called Adeline, or of sharing her doom. Naturally they choose to live, and they take Adeline under their protection. They continue their journey until their carriage breaks down in a lonely part of the forest of Fontanville, and they see before them dark towers rising above the trees. This is the Abbey of St Claire—the perfect example of a Gothic ruin in which lurks every possible terror. The travellers decide to shelter there for the night, but the morning brings delay, and delay gives time for the conclusion that here more than anywhere should they be safe from discovery. But these fugitives, already involved in the web of their own difficulties, soon find that the Abbey is a perilous refuge. There are secret trapdoors, dungeons, a skeleton, a rusty dagger and a parchment revealing a tale of cruel wrong. There are also the cross-purposes of human behaviour, chiefly instigated by a wicked marquis who, in pursuing Adeline with his vicious attentions, little guesses that she is the niece whom he has ordered to be assassinated. Adeline makes repeated efforts to escape and succeeds at last. She is finally united to her faithful lover, Theodore, and her villainous uncle swallows poison.

In this, as in Mrs Radcliffe's other novels, there is really no characterization. In fact, for the most part, Mrs Radcliffe weaves her story about the same stock types. Adeline in *The Romance of the Forest* becomes Emily in *The Mysteries of Udolpho* and Ellena in *The Italian*. Madame La Motte becomes Madame Cheron in *Udolpho* and the Marchesa di Vivaldi in *The Italian*. Theodore becomes Valancourt in *Udolpho* and Vivaldi in *The Italian*. There are always precisely the same honest and garrulous maid and man-servant, the direct descendants of Bianca and Jaquez in *Otranto*. Only in the creation of Schedoni did Mrs Radcliffe penetrate beneath the surface of character and motive.

The method of working on the reader's nerves by mysterious suggestions and by suspense comes fully into view in *The Romance of the Forest*. For example, Adeline's reading of the parchment is protracted for three chapters by such devices as the sudden extinguishing of the light, or an ungovernable access of fear which makes it impossible for her to continue. All the circumstances connected with the reading of this parchment (the howling of the wind, the moving of the arras, the voice whispering Adeline's name) exemplify what Scott calls the 'dressing up of the very phantom by which we are to be startled.'[37] But Mrs Radcliffe's conception of terror had nothing in common with the rude shocks of the German school. It was rather an extreme sensibility to impending danger and a sense of isolation by which one reached an ineffable mood. When La Motte approached the Abbey of St Claire he was conscious of this upsurging of emotion which had its source in a profound apprehension of beauty, of antiquity, and of the mystery of human existence. Thus he felt when he entered

> the chapel of the Abbey, here the hymn of devotion had once been raised, and the tear of penitence had once been shed; sounds, which could now only be recalled by imagination—tears of penitence which had long since been fixed in fate. La Motte paused a moment, for he felt a sensation of sublimity rising into terror—a suspension of mingled astonishment and awe! He surveyed the vastness of the place, and as he contemplated its ruins, fancy bore him back to past ages.[38]

It is *The Romance of the Forest* which first brings home to us the appositeness of Scott's criticism that 'Mrs Radcliffe has a title to be considered as the first poetess of romantic fiction.' Her descriptions of the forest of Fontanville have a wild and dewy freshness which puts us in mind of the forest of Arden. In Fontanville the birds are always singing; flowers spring beneath our feet; it is eternal spring—the springtime of a poet's fancy. And Mrs Radcliffe not merely gives lyrical descriptions of nature but actually, in the account of Clara and her lute,[39] proves that her mind sought the movement and the form of lyric poetry. This passage is far too long for quotation, but with some omissions it could easily be arranged to show the growth of the lyrical thought, and the development of the motif which runs through it and gives it unity:

> I have been playing all day on my lute under the acacias by the lake . . .
>
> She at length found herself, she scarcely knew how, beneath her beloved acacias by the side of the lake . . .
>
> I fear I should again have forgotten them while I played on my lute on the banks of the lake . . .
>
> The evening was still, and uncommonly beautiful. Nothing was heard but the faint shivering of the leaves, which returned but at intervals, making silence more solemn, and the distant murmurs of the torrents that rolled among the cliffs. As she stood by the lake, and watched the sun slowly sinking below the Alps, whose summits were

tinged with gold and purple; as she saw the last rays of light gleam upon the waters whose surface was not curled by the lightest air, she sighed. 'Oh! how enchanting would be the sound of my lute at this moment, on this spot, and when everything is so still around me!'

She went to fetch her lute and 'returned with the instrument to her dear acacias, and beneath their shade continued to play till the surrounding objects faded in darkness from her sight. But the moon arose, and, shedding a trembling lustre on the lake, made the scene more captivating than ever . . . She was perfectly enchanted "no! nothing was ever so delightful as to play on the lute beneath her acacias, on the margin of the lake, by moonlight."'

This is the imagery and the rhythm of lyric thought, and it is notable that in the last sentence she gathers up and weaves together the elements of her conception.

Mrs Radcliffe's descriptions of nature would lead one to expect great things of her poetry, but alas! her interpolated poems are worthless in themselves and absurd in their settings. And so we are faced with the riddle of this woman who could in prose write of flowers seen at daybreak 'while the dew yet hung glittering on their leaves'; and yet who, desiring a poetic expression of the same idea, perpetrates a luxuriantly futile sonnet which begins:

'Soft silken flower that in the dewy vale . . .'

Mrs Radcliffe should have been a poet, but she failed as a poet. She finds expression in prose, but her attitude to nature is not that of a prose writer. It is not merely a reflection of the romantic vogue. It is the result of her temperament. Not only, in common with such writers as Mrs Smith, does she use nature excessively to reflect individual moods, but she elaborates her descriptions of nature out of all proportion to the story. Such a prose poem as that of Clara and her lute is an excrescence in a novel, and yet if she had detached it and given it poetic form it would at once have become a sickly platitude. It was Mrs Radcliffe's misfortune that, like Hamlet (and how she would have enjoyed such a comparison!), she was poised between two worlds. She had not made M. Jourdain's discovery that what is not verse is prose, and what is not prose is verse. She is the supreme example of genuine literary power misdirected for want of education. Any one of her novels contains a thousand testimonies of this fact. All her novels constitute a depressing avalanche of proof. Her style is the style of a poet gone astray. It is the style of one who had not subjected herself to intellectual discipline. There are no bones and sinews, and far too much soft flesh. Had she been censured for this in the beginning, she might have rectified it, but, unfortunately, to the school of sentiment and sensibility an excessive billowing of the emotions did not appear an error of taste. Thus the period in which she wrote gave the added impetus of approval to the defects of Mrs Radcliffe's style. Perhaps she was aware of her lack of education for she is continually straining after cultural effects. She is everlastingly enumerating statuary and paintings. In the words of a contemporary writer:

> She affects in the most disgusting manner a knowledge of languages, countries, customs, and objects of art of which she is lamentably ignorant. She suspends tripods from the ceiling by chains . . . . She covers the Kingdom of Naples with India figs . . . and she makes a convent of monks a necessary appendage to a monastery of nuns . . . Whenever she introduces an Italian word it is sure to be a gross violation of the language. Instead of making a nobleman's servant call him *Padrone* or *Illustrissimo*, she makes him address him by the title of *Maestro* which is Italian for teacher.[40]

This critic is prejudiced against novels of terror and particularly against their high-priestess; therefore his condemnation is too pitiless. Yet in Mrs Radcliffe's novels we are too often afflicted with pretentiousness. For example, we hear that 'in the cool of the evening, the ladies took the fresco along the banks of the Brenta';[41] and that 'the *Lagune* soon displays a gay scene of innumerable little barks, passing from terra firma with provisions.'[42] Then again, our acceptance of the following passage depends on whether we believe that cows sip: 'Under the shade of the oak and chestnut, herds of cattle were grazing. Groups of them, too, were often seen reposing on the banks of the rivulet, or laving their sides in the cool stream, and sipping its wave.'[43] And it is not only in such ways that Mrs Radcliffe reveals her weakness. In *The Sicilian Romance* there is a description of midnight festivities in the woods which is either naive or vulgar, according to one's point of view. The woodland vistas are hung with variegated lamps; collations are spread under the trees; music touched by unseen hands breathes around, the musicians being concealed in the most embowered spots so as to elude the eye and strike the imagination. Nothing meets the gaze but beauty and romantic splendour. All is mirth and melody, and 'Julia seemed the magic queen of the place'. This romantic effusiveness is Mrs Radcliffe's most evident fault. It is not enough that the heroine finds herself amongst beautiful surroundings. No, it must be at sunset (or sunrise), the perfume of flowers must rise as an odorous exhalation, the birds must warble in the shimmering air, the trees must sigh in unison: the mountains must rise majestically in the background and the music of an aeolian harp must be heard in the distance. If the heroine is near the sea, then a single sail must glide gracefully over the polished surface of the water, and a luminous star glow with effulgence in the serene of heaven. One would suppose that even an author's economy would prevent the discharge of all this ammunition at once, but Mrs Radcliffe has no hesitation in producing the same effects over and over again. She will vary the background, or the order of her images: the trees may sigh before the birds warble, or the star may glow before the flowers exhale their perfume . One part of this programme, however, remains immutable: the music of the aeolian harp must always be heard at the last. It is the aesthetic apex — the thinnest, highest note of all the tight-strung play on our emotions.

But it is not only in scenic descriptions that Mrs Radcliffe ignores the aesthetic possibilities of a disciplined imagination. There is in *The Romance of the Forest* an incident which proves that the nature which Mrs Radcliffe knew was not human nature. When Theodore La Luc is going to be executed he asks his friends to spend the last night with him in his cell, and they do so. Now, apart from any consideration as to the likelihood of this incident, it is highly improbable from a psychological point of view. No man would so lay himself open to a protracted ordeal of farewell. Indeed, even Mrs Radcliffe is struck by the difficulty of filling in this painful period. She says: 'The night was passed in embarrassed conversation; sometimes interrupted by long fits of silence, and sometimes by the paroxysms of despair.'[44] The final interview between Theodore and his relatives takes place next morning. La Luc (his father, an aged clergyman), Clara (his sister) and Adeline (his beloved) come to say good-bye. It is impossible to describe the orgy of emotion that ensues. The father preaches a sermon; they all invoke heaven, and talk about their hearts at great length. Swoons are almost uninterrupted by consciousness and the sufferers are nearly drowned in their own tears. Dry-eyed despair, heroism without heroics did not occur to Mrs Radcliffe, and she arouses in us something like contempt when, having dragged us through these puling farewells, she reprieves the prisoner at the last moment. Nothing but death could decently follow the scene in the prison cell.

It must not be imagined that these criticisms are aimed at lowering Mrs Radcliffe's literary prestige. On the contrary, it is precisely because she had genius that it has seemed necessary to determine the explanation of those inequalities so apparent in her novels. Genius is natural bent developed to the fullest capacity. Lack of education certainly impedes such development, however much that bent may succeed in expressing itself merely through its own strength. It was really more by the strength of her natural impulse that Mrs Radcliffe succeeded. In 1863 Julia Kavenagh asked what might have been the literary result 'had Ann Radcliffe been John Radcliffe and received a vigorous and polished education.' And the answer seems to be that then surely Ann Radcliffe would have lived on, not merely through her influence on the minds of great men, but in her own writings; not merely as the half-forgotten initiator of a phase of fiction, but as the creator of some imperishable beauty in verse or prose.

Mrs Radcliffe was unaware that beauty is created chiefly through an impassioned control of inspiration. Nevertheless, she did, with practice, perfect the better aspects of her work, although she was not sufficiently conscious of her faults to eradicate them. The two last novels published during her lifetime are certainly her best.

The Romance of the Forest established Mrs Radcliffe as a successful novelist. *The Mysteries of Udolpho* (1794) reinforced her fame. The story begins slowly and takes some time to get really under way. Monsieur St Aubert, a gentleman of Gascony, is left on the death of his wife with failing health and fortunes. His one comfort is his daughter Emily. It becomes necessary for him to travel for the sake of his health, and, accompanied by his daughter, he journeys towards Provence, only to die on the way. Emily, poor in everything but the love of a young soldier named

Valancourt, goes to live with her aunt, Madam Cheron, who despises her for her poverty and discourages Valancourt's suit. Soon Madam Cheron abandons her widow's weeds to marry the mysterious Italian, Count Montoni, who boasts a palace in Venice and a castle at Udolpho. To Venice they repair. Montoni shows the cloven hoof from the first moment of his married life, and proves a tyrant not only to his wife but to Emily. Her he endeavours to force into an unsuitable marriage, but before he can complete his design he has made Venice too hot to hold him, and flees to Udolpho, taking with him his wife and Emily. At this point the interest of the story really begins. In the mountain stronghold of Udolpho, Montoni is lord of all. Too late his wife discovers that he is really a penniless ruffian who has married her only for her money. She refuses to sign over her possessions to him, and dies tormented but unyielding.

Emily is now alone in what is virtually a robbers' stronghold — driven almost to madness by spectral voices, apparitions, bloody scenes and insulting attentions. Her unwelcome Venetian suitor, Morano pursues her to Udolpho and makes several efforts to abduct her, but is foiled by Montoni who has now formed the idea of taking for himself Emily's estates. Emily steadfastly refuses to sign a document of surrender, but is made to yield by Montoni's threat to abandon her to the insults of his subordinates. Then, by a wonderful stroke of luck, she escapes from Udolpho.

Here the interest of the story becomes moribund, although it gasps on for twenty chapters or more. Emily reaches France and is given refuge in another castle which soon becomes as haunted as Udolpho. While Emily's sojourn at Château-le-blanc was peaceful, it provided a welcome contrast to the horrors at Udolpho. Mrs Radcliffe always provides her heroine with such tranquil respites. But the repetition of the ghostly motif at Château-le-blanc is inartistic. Udolpho has already exhausted the reader's nerves to such an extent that these fresh mysteries fail to arouse any response. Furthermore, Mrs Radcliffe's method of bringing Emily to Château-le-blanc is extremely awkward. We see Emily, escaped from Udolpho, safely embark for France, and are then forced to endure two chapters describing the Villefort family, the quarrels of Monsieur with his wife, and the mawkish raptures of his daughter Blanche, fresh from her convent school. We are even condemned to endure a lamentable poem of sixteen stanzas entitled *The Butterfly and his Love*, composed by this soulful young creature, before we see Emily's ship approaching, and witness her arrival at Château-le-blanc. Possibly our thwarted disgust at these irrelevancies is a proof of our interest in Emily, but if Mrs Radcliffe created this interlude to heighten our suspense, she was sadly mistaken, because these chapters would certainly be 'skipped' by the unconscientious reader.

These are the weaker aspects of the novel. Its perfections are far greater than its faults. The journey to Udolpho is a crescendo of majestic scenery and human premonition so interwoven that they create a single effect of mounting awe. As the travellers climb higher and higher into the Apennines, among the dark pine forests and dizzy precipices, they are awed by sensations of dreadful sublimity. Emily's mind is oppressed by strange foreboding. She is entirely without a friend and she is powerless. Thus Mrs Radcliffe describes the first view of Udolpho:

> Towards the close of day, the road wound into a deep valley. Mountains whose shaggy steeps appeared to be inaccessible, almost surrounded it. To the east a vista opened, and exhibited the Apennines in their earliest horrors; and the long perspective of retiring summits rising over each other, their ridges clothed with pines, exhibited a stronger image of grandeur than any that Emily had yet seen. The sun had just sunk below the top of the mountains she was descending, whose long shadow stretched athwart the valley, but his sloping rays, shooting through an opening of the cliffs, touched with a yellow gleam the summits of the forest that hung upon the opposite steeps, and streamed in full splendour upon the towers and battlements of a castle that spread its extensive ramparts along the brow of a precipice above. The splendour of these illumined objects was heightened by the contrasted shade which involved the valley below.
>
> 'There,' said Montoni, speaking for the first time in several hours, 'is Udolpho.'
>
> Emily gazed with melancholy awe upon the castle, which she understood to be Montoni's; for, though it was now lighted up by the setting sun, the gothic greatness of its features, and its smouldering walls of dark grey stone, rendered it a gloomy and sublime object. As she gazed the light died away on its walls, leaving a melancholy purple tint, which spread deeper and deeper, as the thin vapour crept up the mountain, while the battlements above were still tipped with splendour. From these, too, the rays soon

faded, and the whole edifice was invested with the solemn duskiness of the evening. Silent, lonely and sublime, it seemed to stand the sovereign of the scene, and to frown defiance on all who dared to invade its solitary reign. As the twilight deepened, its features became more awful in obscurity, and Emily continued to gaze, till its clustering towers were alone seen rising over the tops of the woods.[45]

Speaking of this description, Scott says that if six artists endeavoured to embody it on canvas, the result would be six pictures entirely dissimilar to each other, and yet all authorized by Mrs Radcliffe's printed words. Scott compares the description of Udolpho with Mrs Radcliffe's description of Hardwicke ruins, which she wrote with her eye on the object. He contrasts the precision of this latter description with the romantic glamour of Udolpho, which he considers 'a beautiful effect-piece', and he emphasizes that in accuracy and realism Mrs Radcliffe's descriptions are inferior to those of Mrs Smith. Nevertheless, it was the poetic alchemy of Mrs Radcliffe's mind which intoxicated Byron with the magic of a Venice which she had actually never seen,[46] and which inspired the unforgotten stanzas on Venice in *Childe Harold*.

Lewis himself stated that The Mysteries of Udolpho had influenced him in writing *The Monk* (1795). There is a possibility that Mrs Radcliffe found in this otherwise distasteful book some hints for the chief character in *The Italian* (1797); and it seems possible also that she influenced by Schiller's *Der Geisterseher*.

Apart from the deliberate incorrectness of the historical background into which Mrs Radcliffe was betrayed by her animosity towards Catholicism, *The Italian* is the best of all her novels. But Mrs Radcliffe's attitude towards Catholicism is so typical of the Gothic school that it deserves a few words of literary criticism. One cannot do better than quote in this connection the remarks of a sound and temperate commentator. She says:[47]

> The dealings of the literary men of Protestant England in the eighteenth century with the institutions of the Roman Catholic Church are little disingenuous. They are very conscious of the picturesque attractions of convents, of celibacy, confession and penance; they are seduced by the emotional possibilities of the situations that can be based on these usages; but they seldom fail to make it quite clear that they regard the usage as superstitious and irrational and, if they did, there was not wanting a critic to blame this

'attempt to gloss over the follies of popery or to represent its absurdities as sacred'.[48]

In her earlier novels Mrs Radcliffe had shown anti-Catholic bias coupled with a complete ignorance of Catholic beliefs. These misrepresentations might have been made unsuspectingly, but such a plea cannot be entered for *The Italian*. In *New Observations on Italy and its Inhabitants*, which was a source book most lavishly used by Mrs Radcliffe, Grosley makes light of the Roman Inquisition, distinctly stating that when he was in Rome, in 1758, the Inquisition had passed no capital sentence for over one hundred years . He continues: 'Everything there is transacted in private by spiritual and pecuniary penalties.' Did Mrs Radcliffe, who drew so heavily on Grosley, accept these statements? She did not. On the contrary, she defiantly dates *The Italian* exactly at 1758. She says: 'It was in that very year that Vivaldi in the vaults of the Inquisition heard the thrilling groans of the tortured and was bound by masked familiars on the rack.'[49]

Scott's remarks as to the authenticity of Mrs Radcliffe's background would seem to indicate that, when the canons of literary criticism run counter to ingrained prejudice, literary criticism is cast to the winds. He says: 'We have been told, that in this beautiful romance [*The Italian*] the customs and rules of the Inquisition have been violated; a charge more easily made than proved, and which, if true, is of minor importance, because its code is happily unknown to us.' In a word, it was unnecessary for Mrs Radcliffe to know what she was talking about, and it was unnecessary for Scott to possess enough knowledge of the Inquisition to be able to judge the verisimilitude of her novel.

The plot of *The Italian* opens with the Marchesa di Vivaldi's violent opposition to the proposed marriage of her son and one Ellena, whose birth is obscure. The Marchesa is supported in her opposition by her confessor, the mysterious and terrible Schedoni. The death of Bianchi, Ellena's aunt, leaves the young girl quite unprotected, and makes Vivaldi all the more determined to marry her. Ellena, however, is carried off by masked men, and confined in the Convent of the Black Penitents. Here she is treated with rigorous contempt by the stately abbess, but not more so than the unfortunate nuns, all of whom are racked by secret sufferings and treated like convicts in a particularly inhumane prison. Vivaldi succeeds in finding Ellena at the very moment when she is being forced to take the veil. He helps her to escape. They evade many dangers and throw dust in the eyes of their pursuers. Ellena takes refuge in an Ursuline Convent at Celano.

Meanwhile the Marchesa di Vivaldi is passing through a storm of passionate resentment at the attitude of her son. Schedoni skilfully plays on her feelings, and, at a moment when her mood might have softened, he sedulously aggravates her pride and anger until he has wrought her to his purpose, which is the murder of Ellena. The subtlety with which he works upon her temperament and mood shows that Mrs Radcliffe at last understands the interplay of character. Schedoni is like a cat playing with a mouse. Detailed arguments at length give place to broken-off phrases which suggest the murder, but avoid plain speech. Schedoni finally manoeuvres the Marchesa into imagining that the idea is hers, not his. The next day, at the Church of San Nicoli, she is led deeper into the toils, and she authorizes him to do the deed which he offers himself to perform. Her acquiescence, her sudden fear of the course to which she has committed herself, and of Schedoni in whose power she must henceforth be — these are excellently shown. At the last moment she postpones the final decision. Schedoni is disappointed, but does not despair. He sets in motion the machinery of the Inquisition, and Vivaldi and Ellena are both found and taken into custody. There is a tremendous scene in which Vivaldi is examined by the chief Inquisitor. Ellena is taken to a lonely house by the sea, where Schedoni comes to murder her. At the very moment when his arm is raised to strike, he observes that she is wearing a miniature of himself, and recoils in horror at the idea that he has attempted to kill his own daughter.

Ellena is not really the daughter of Schedoni. She is his niece. Schedoni, really the Count Ferando di Bruni, has a past stained with many crimes. Having caused his elder brother to be assassinated, he married that brother's wife, but stabbed her when he feared she would detect his crime. This unfortunate woman survived, however, and lived on in the Convent of the Black Penitents long enough to meet Ellena, the child of her first husband. Schedoni, at the last, poisons himself in prison. The Marchesa di Vivaldi dies repentant, and Ellena and Vivaldi marry.

Of the many magnificent descriptions in this novel we must omit all save that of Schedoni, and that which leads up to the appointed murder at Spalatro's lonely house by the sea. Thus for the first time we see Schedoni, a being who resembles Milton's Satan, a further development of Kruitzner, a fore-runner of Byron's sinister heroes:

> His figure was striking, but not so from grace; it was tall, and, though extremely thin, his limbs were large and uncouth, and as he stalked along, wrapt in the black garments of his order, there was something terrible in its air; something almost superhuman. His cowl too, as it threw a shadow over the livid paleness of his face, increased its severe character, and gave an effect to his large melancholy eye, which approached to horror. His was not the melancholy of a sensible and wounded heart, but apparently that of a gloomy and ferocious disposition. There was something in his physiognomy extremely singular, and that cannot easily be defined. It bore the traces of many passions which seemed to have fixed the features they no longer animated. An habitual gloom and severity prevailed over the deep lines of his countenance; and his eyes were so piercing, that they seemed to penetrate, at a single glance, into the hearts of men, and to read their secret thoughts; few persons could support their scrutiny, or even endure to meet them twice. Yet, notwithstanding all this gloom and austerity, some rare occasions of interest had called forth a character upon his countenance entirely different and he could adapt himself to the tempers and passions of persons whom he wished to conciliate with astonishing facility.[50]

The scene between Ellena and Schedoni on the sea-shore is finely conceived; the scene in which Schedoni comes to murder Ellena and makes his terrible discovery surpasses anything that Mrs Radcliffe wrote. This entire chapter is perfectly sustained. There is the rising tide of fear and evil, the altercation between Spalatro and Schedoni, with its turgid dialogue hinting at horrors, and culminating in the words: 'Give me the dagger'. Mrs Radcliffe, that lover of Shakespeare, found this inspiration in *Macbeth*. 'You forget,' says Schedoni, threatening Spalatro, his reluctant minion, 'You forget that I know you; you forget the past.'

> 'No . . . I remember it too well; I wish I could forget; I remember it too well. I have never been at peace since. The bloody hand is always before me; and often of a night,

when the sea roars, and storms shake the house, they have come, all gashed up as I left them, and stood before my bed! I have got up, and run out upon the shore for safety.'

'Give me the dagger,' said the confessor after a long pause; 'Take up the cloak and follow to the staircase. Let me see whether your valour will carry you so far . . . Give me the dagger.'

'You have it already, Signor.'

'True,' said the monk, 'ascend softly or our steps may awaken her.'

'You said I was to wait at the foot of the stairs, signor, while you —'

'True, true, true!' muttered the confessor, and had begun to ascend, when his attendant desired him to stop. 'You are going in darkness, signor, you have forgotten the lamp' . . . Schedoni took it angrily, without speaking, and was again ascending, when he hesitated, and once more paused. 'The glare will disturb her,' thought he, 'it is better to go in darkness.' Yet—he considered that he could not strike with certainty without a light to direct his hand.[51]

This chapter not only excels in the vivid urgency of the action, but reveals also a psychological insight which ordinarily Mrs Radcliffe was very far from possessing. She shows Schedoni in the grip of the ruthless determination which has devoured his life — the determination to win power by any means. But this deed which he contemplates is more appalling than any he has already perpetrated, and his meeting with Ellena on the shore has awakened in him the unusual feeling of pity. Pity and ambition struggle within him, and he betrays this inner tumult by his abrupt and contradictory commands, his hesitations, and his assumed stoicism. Mrs Radcliffe thus gives us the clue to his thoughts:

The emotions of his mind were violent and contradictory. At the very instant, when his heart reproached him with the crime he had meditated, he regretted the ambitious views he must relinquish if he failed to perpetrate it, and regarded himself with some degree of contempt for having hitherto hesitated on the subject. He considered the character of his own mind with astonishment, for circumstances had drawn forth traits, of which, till now, he had no suspicion. He knew not by what doctrine to explain the inconsistencies, the contradictions, he experienced, and, perhaps it was not one of the least that in these moments of direful and

conflicting passions, his reason could still look down upon
their operations, and lead him to a cool though brief
examination of his own nature. But the subtlety of self-love
still eluded his inquiries, and he did not detect, that pride
was, even at this instant of self examination, and of critical
import, the master spring of his mind.[52]

It is not merely for the reasons we have stated that *The Italian*
is Mrs Radcliffe's best work. In structure also it is far superior to
her other writings, and most of its terrors have the advantage of
being real. Mrs Radcliffe's method of creating mysteries only to
explain them away ended by exasperating the nerve-racked
reader. Schedoni and Spalatro could not be explained away, and
the reader, sharing vicariously in Ellena's dangers, does not feel
that he has been deliberately fooled.

After *The Italian*, Mrs Radcliffe wrote no more for a considerable time. Her public had grown weary of being tricked by false
alarms, and criticism became more audible. Furthermore the
market was flooded by an immense crowd of imitators, who
fastened only on such sensational parts of Mrs Radcliffe's technique as were imitable. Terror was divorced from beauty; terror
was divorced from virtue; and Mrs Radcliffe had the misery of
observing the degeneration of the novel she had initiated. It
was but too easy to confuse the originator with her self-styled
disciples and to attribute to Mrs Radcliffe's influence the egregious
works of those who were incapable of understanding her aim.
There is proof that Mrs Radcliffe was hypersensitive to the acid
criticisms now launched against the Gothic novel. She withdrew
more and more from a publicity which she had never coveted
and which now became most painful to her. When she again
took up her pen, it was to attempt a historical novel. This had 'all
the faults of the historical novel before Scott, and none of her
own merits.'[53] She devoted much time to studying in old sources
the social background of Henry III's reign. The result of these
researches was *Gaston de Blondeville*, written in 1802 and published
posthumously. Since Mrs Radcliffe was so dissatisfied with this
novel that she left it unpublished during the remaining twenty-
one years of her life, it would not be just to criticize it seriously.
In *Gaston de Blondeville* Mrs Radcliffe deliberately abandons the
elements of her characteristic type of fiction. Her romantic descriptions are no more; sensibility is eliminated; and her peculiar

414

technique of creating terror from trifles is cast aside in favour of a real ghost. This flat-footed apparition alarms far less than the tiniest mouse scurrying in the wainscot of Udolpho. Mrs Radcliffe's historical data stick out through the skin of her narrative, and on this sorry steed she jerks her weary way through the forest of Arden—a forest not a revelation of primeval beauty as at Fontanville, but simply a large number of trees growing close together.

Mrs Radcliffe must be judged not merely by her works, but by their influence. Turning one's eyes from the more sensational aspects of the Gothic novel which have produced such a spate of modern 'thrillers', one can find evidence of the more subtle elements, handed down to us through such writers as Maturin, Godwin, Ainsworth, Hawthorne, Poe and Henry James. These owe much to other sources than Mrs Radcliffe, and no doubt many of them would have repudiated the notion of being indebted to her, however indirectly, but it must be remembered that it was, nevertheless, Mrs Radcliffe who gave the tale of terror its first real impetus in England. More interesting still was her influence on poets. She helped to turn Scott's attention to the past; she kindled the imagination of such men as Byron. It was her fate that greater minds than her own should fully express her half-articulate inspirations. With all her faults (and they are great) Mrs Radcliffe deserves to be remembered amongst these who have permanently influenced English literature.

Of the many women who followed the Gothic vogue only one other deserves mention. Mary Shelley, influenced by German ghost stories and by the vague scientific notions current at the time, determined to write a tale which would terrify her readers. This intention was the result of a competition proposed by Byron to while away an evening at Lake Leman. At first Mary Shelley could not hit upon a subject. Then she had a dream which she embodied in Frankenstein (1818).[54] The story is so well-known that it is unnecessary to outline its plot. The most glaring fault in its structure is due to the fact that, having begun 'It was on a dreary night in November', Mrs Shelley later inserted four predatory chapters. The theme of the mechanical monster too great for his creator to control gave ample scope for frightful adventures. This monster, oppressed by his isolation among human beings who fear and hate him, becomes a satanic character, terrible in his pride and malignancy. There are queer echoes of Godwin and Mary Wollstonecraft in the protracted account of his education, and in the evil effects upon him of humanitarian doctrines. This aspect of Frankenstein links it to the *tendenz* fiction of this period, which must be considered briefly in the following chapter.

Notes and References

1 Julia Kavenagh, *English Women of Letters* (1863), i, p. 242.
2 *Inquiry into the Sublime and Beautiful* (1756).
3 See *Monthly*, November, 1794 on 'The Mysteries of Udolpho'.
4 J. and A. L. Aikin, *Miscellaneous Pieces in Prose* (1773).
5 Dr Nathan Drake, *Literary Hours* (1798).
6 Shelley's poem *On the Medusa of Leonardo da Vinci*.
7 So Baculard d'Arnaud describes an isolated soul. His words apply very well to the Gothic heroine. See Baculard d'Arnaud, Preface to *Euphémie, ou L'Triomphe de la Religion* (Paris, 1768).
8 See A. C. Swinburne, *Studies in Prose and Poetry* (1894).
9 The fragment *Sir Bertrand*, included in J. and A. L. Aikin's *Miscellaneous Pieces of Prose* (1773), shows the appositeness of Godwin's remark that tales of terror have a sort of resemblance to nursery tales. *Sir Bertrand* is *The Sleeping Beauty* as one might imagine it in a nightmare.
10 Preface to 2nd. edn. of *The Castle of Otranto*.
11 Scott, in his *Life of Clara Reeve*, disagrees with her objections to the *The Castle of Otranto*. He says: 'If we are to try ghosts by the ordinary rules of humanity we bar them of their privileges entirely. For instance, why admit the existence of an aerial phantom and deny it the terrible attribute of magnifying its stature? Why admit an enchanted helmet and not a gigantic one?' The reasons suggested on page 137 seem a possible answer to Scott's argument.
12 Clara Reeve, *The Old English Baron* (ed. James Trainer, Oxford University Press, 1977), Preface, p. 4.
13 Ibid., Preface, p. 5.
14 Ibid., p. 100.
15 See Julia Kavenagh's sound criticism (*English Women of Letters*, 1862) i, p. 239.
16 *The Old English Baron*, op. cit., p. 144.
17 See E. A. Baker, *H.E.N.*, v., p. 180. Clara Reeve's borrowings were from Baculard d'Arnaud's *The History of Count Gleichen* (so called in the English translation), 1785, and d'Almanzi, *Anecdote françoise* (1776), apparently never translated. Dr Baker says that Prévost's *Doyen de Killerine* probably gave to Clara Reeve's book 'as much of the tone and atmosphere as Baculard's two stories .'
18 Harriet Lee and Sophia Lee, *The Canterbury Tales* (Intro. Harriett Gilbert, 'Mothers of the Novel', Pandora, London, 1989), Preface, p. xviii.

19 Sophia Lee, *The Recess: Or, A Tale of Other Times* (Foreword J.M.S. Tompkins, Intro. Devendra P. Davenport, Arno Press, New York, 1972), vol. iii, pp. 72–75).

20 *The Canterbury Tales*, op. cit., 'The Land Lady's Tale: Mary Lawson', p. 283.

21 Ibid., 'The Land Lady's Tale: Mary Lawson', p. 306.

22 Ibid., 'The German's Tale: Kruitzner', p. 179.

23 Ibid., 'The German's Tale: Kruitzner', pp. 138–39.

24 E.g. her *Adèle et Théodore* (1782).

25 Charlotte Smith, *Celestina* (1791), iv, pp. 220 f.

26 Ibid., iv, p. 224.

27 Ibid., iv, p. 231.

28 Charlotte Smith, *Desmond* (ed. Dublin, 1792), i, pp. 104 f.

29 Charlotte Smith, *The Old Manor House* (ed. Anne Henry Ehrenpreis, Intro. Judith Philips Stantan, Oxford University Press, 1989), vol. iii, ch. vii, p. 305.

30 Ibid., vol. ii, ch. xiii, p. 236.

31 Ibid., vol. iii, ch. i, p. 253.

32 Ibid., vol. iii, ch. vii, pp. 304–05.

33 Ibid., vol. iv, ch. ix, pp. 475–76.

34 See *The Critical Review*, September 1789.

35 See *The Monthly Review*, September 1789.

36 See C. F. McIntyre: *Ann Radcliffe in relation to her time* (Yale University Press, 1920), pp. 51–58.

37 *Mrs Radcliffe's Novels* (ed. Ballantyne, 1824), Scott's prefatory memoir, p. xxiv.

38 Ann Radcliffe, *The Romance of the Forest* (Oxford University Press, 1986), ch. xi.

39 Ibid., ch. xxi.

40 Note appended to a letter on 'Terrorist Novel Writing' in *The Spirit of Public Journals* (1797), i, p. 323.

41 Ann Radcliffe, *The Mysteries of Udolpho* (ed. B. Dobsée, notes by Frederick Garber, Oxford University Press, 1992), vol. ii, ch. xvii, p. 214.

42 Ibid., vol. ii, ch. xviii, p. 224.

43 Ibid., vol. ii, ch. i, p. 167.

44 *The Romance of the Forest*, op. cit., ch. xxi.

45 *The Mysteries of Udolpho*, op. cit., vol. ii, ch. xviii, p. 226.

46 At the time when Mrs Radcliffe wrote Udolpho she had not visited the countries with which she was so familiar. Miss C. F. McIntyre and Dr J. M. S. Tompkins have made most valuable discoveries as to the sources on which Mrs Radcliffe drew. Acting on a suggestion in the *Diary of a Lover of Literature*, Miss McIntyre traces Mrs Radcliffe's description of Venice and of the voyage up the Brenta to Mrs Piozzi's *Observations and Reflections made in the course of a journey through France, Italy and Germany*. Dr Tompkins reinforces Miss McIntyre's opinion, and adds to more sources used by Mrs Radcliffe in Udolpho: Ramond de Carbonnières' *Observations faites dans les Pyrénées* (1789) and P. J. Grosley's *New Observations on Italy and its*

Inhabitants (English translation, 1794). The evidence in Grosley's case is conclusive, in de Carbonnières' a strong probability can be established. Dr Tompkins also suggests the influence of Arthur Young's *Travels in France* and Henry Swinburne's *Journey from Bayonne to Marseilles*, the latter appearing as a supplement to the second edition of *Travels through Spain* (1787). Dr Tompkins believes that it is probably Mrs Smith's *Celestina* which stimulated Mrs Radcliffe's interest in the Pyrenees and which turned her attention to de Carbonnières' book. De Carbonnières had just that spirit of lyrical romanticism which would appeal to Mrs Radcliffe. Miss Tompkins notes that, though Mrs Radcliffe certainly drew on Grosley, she avoided his less romantic touches and preferred always to give an idealized version of what he described. Dr Tompkins gives a most detailed account of Mrs Radcliffe's debt to Grosley, showing how Emily St Aubert followed Grosley's route into Italy and experienced on the way many incidents which Grosley describes. At Udolpho we come to Mrs Radcliffe's greatest debt to Grosley: the incident of the veiled picture. Grosley describes (vol. i, p 205) that in Ravenna, at the Benedictine Church of St Vital, he was shown the waxen image of a woman, representing the horrors of the grave by such details as a devouring worm, lizard and toad. This was exactly the sort of material to suit Mrs Radcliffe's purpose. *The Italian* also shows Grosley's influence.

See C. F. McIntyre: *Ann Radcliffe in relation to her time* (Yale University Press 1920), and J. M. S. Tompkins: 'Ramond de Carbonnières, Grosley and Mrs Radcliffe' (*Review of English Studies*, July, 1929).

47 J. M. S. Tompkins, *The Popular Novel in England, 1770–1800*, (1932), p. 274 f.
48 See *Critical*, March 1792, on Mrs Robinson's *Vancenza.*
49 See J. M. S. Tompkins, 'Ramond de Carbonnières, Grosley and Mrs Radcliffe' (*Review of English Studies*, July, 1929).
50 Ann Radcliffe, *The Italian: Or, The Confessional of the Black Penitents* (ed. Frederick Garber, Oxford University Press, 1981), vol. i, ch. ii, pp. 34–35.
51 Ibid., vol. ii, ch. ix, pp. 230–33.
52 Ibid., vol. ii, ch. ix, p. 225.
53 George Saintsbury, in Cambridge History of English Literature, xi, p. 301, footnote.
54 Mrs Shelley also wrote:
    (a) *Valperga, or the life and adventures of Castruccio, Prince of Lucca* (1823).
    (b) *The Last Man* (1826).
    (c) *Perkin Warbeck* (1830).
    (d) *Lodore* (1835).
    (e) *Falkner* (1837).

Chapter XIII

The Didactic Novel

Our unsexed female writers now instruct, or confuse, us and themselves in the labyrinth of politicks, or turn us wild with Gallick frensy.

(Mathias, *Pursuits of Literature*)

I know that the earth is the great Bridewell of the Universe.

(William Godwin, *Fleetwood*)

The difference in aim between *tendenz* and other kinds of fiction, during the eighteenth century, was the difference between sensitiveness and sensibility. Sensibility had luxuriated in trumped-up causes of emotion In the *tendenz* novel there was real sensitiveness. It was in closer contact with the facts of life, and took cognizance of real aspects of human suffering. Such aspects became increasingly evident towards the end of the century, and the output of *tendenz* fiction grew in proportion. Many reasons contributed towards this preoccupation with social and political problems. Social neglect might truthfully be regarded as a characteristic of eighteenth-century England. The criminal code, the prison system, the conditions of the working class, the lack of adequate educational and medical facilities for the poor, the neglect of the aged and infirm, the misguided and cruel treatment of the insane — these for a long time had needed reform, but now such miseries were aggravated by the enclosure of common land, and by the beginnings of the industrial revolution. Increasing discontent was fanned by the new spirit of democratic enquiry which made itself felt in England during the American War of Independence and the early phases of the French revolution. Radicals were inflamed by the spectacle of France embattled

against class distinctions and invidious privilege. The reflections
of philosophers were based on the theories of Voltaire and
Rousseau. One might have supposed that only faith and courage
were needed to bring the ideal of justice to earth. It followed that,
if a political conception of justice could be realized, justice could
be established as the foundation of human existence. It seemed
(as it still seems) as if all the evils of life might be banished by the
application of just principles. Justice was a flaming sword by
which the hydra-headed monster of oppression and suffering
might be slain, and a new era of freedom might dawn. Nothing
is more intoxicating than an ideal. In this divine intoxication it
seemed possible to assert that men are born equal and free.
Starting from these premises lovers of freedom, that is to say
lovers of justice, developed an argument which could be applied
to all forms of human bondage. Of these the bondage of civilization seemed responsible for all the miseries of civilized society,
and the life of the natural man alone seemed to offer the conditions of a free and harmonious existence. Social grievances
seemed to arise from the assertion of baseless privilege, and so
this declaration of the human being's right to justice had many
facets. It sought to abolish the prerogative of rank and wealth,
the traditional privileges of institutions whether political, social,
or ecclesiastical; it abhorred the slave trade; it anathematized
the endless bondage of the poor. Certain women extended the
argument of justice to their own sex, and showed that the subjection of women was no less flagrant than any other aspect of
traditional injustice. On all these fronts the wordy battle raged,
and the philosophic champions of justice ingenuously imagined
that because their arguments were irrefutable those who profited
by power and privilege must be convinced, and therefore must
yield. Every literary means was employed to drive home the
principles of justice, and the novel, because of its popular appeal,
was regarded as an excellent means of propaganda.

But unfortunately propaganda and art neither propose the
same aims nor employ the same means. Art may teach, but only
obliquely, and, however much it may convey some judgment of
life, it seems certain that this result must be incidental to its
purpose. The philosophic novelists used fiction as a convenient
means of expression and were not primarily concerned with the
artistic possibilities of the novel. It was, therefore, to be expected

that their contribution to fiction would be meagre. They did a service to the novel by introducing the wider issues of human life, but we cannot estimate the value of their contribution by the value of their philosophic ideas. Fiction may (and, it may be contended, should) suggest the abstract, but it is inherent in the technique of the novel to use life as its symbolic medium. It is only by such means that fiction may teach. To reduce the characters in the novel to mouthpieces for doctrine, or to puppets whose behaviour must prove some philosophic contention is to negate the purpose of fiction. Those who achieved success as didactic novelists did so only when, in obedience to an artistic impulse, they created real people and involved these characters in a plot which, while it bore out the didactic purpose, was yet compatible with human existence. In a word, success in didactic fiction is possible only when the writer succeeds in reconciling the didactic purpose with the technique of art.

John Moore of *Zeluco* fame, although he had seldom lost a chance of exposing the errors of human society, was, nevertheless, chiefly interested in the psychological aspects of his novels. Robert Bage, Thomas Holcroft and William Godwin had a more doctrinal purpose. Their novels reveal at once the individuality and the strength of their inspirations, and the weakness due to their didactic aim. Bage and Holcroft unquestioningly used the epistolary form, which was, in fact, quite unsuited to their kind of story-telling, and yet, by the power of their convictions and by flashes of realism, they compensated in part for their too obvious pedagogy. Godwin's *Caleb Williams* (1794), that peculiar mixture of sociology and Gothicism, is in a sense a masterpiece; but its power is due not to its sociological purpose, but to its use of suspense and terror.

There were opposing tendencies influencing the attitude of women novelists towards *tendenz* fiction. They had thrown themselves wholeheartedly into moral didacticism not only because it was moral, but because its serious purpose pleased their earnestness. Now the novel of doctrine offered further scope for teaching, but unhappily the social and political problems involved were regarded either as beyond women's ability, or as a most unsuitable field for feminine speculation. Thus it was that few women took sides in the vexed questions which now cloaked themselves in fiction. Not many women indeed could have vindicated

political interests as did that lady who incurred the disapproval
of Robespierre. He asked witheringly: 'Since when have women
interested themselves in politics?' And he was answered: 'Since
they have become liable to be guillotined.' Mrs Smith's reply is
as convincing, though less deadly:

> Women, it is said, have no business with politics. Why not?
> Have they no interest in the scenes that are acting around
> them, in which they have fathers, brothers, husbands, sons,
> or friends, engaged? Even in the commonest course of
> female education, they are expected to acquire some know-
> ledge of history; and yet, if they are to have no opinion of
> what is passing, it avails little that they should be informed
> of what has passed, in a world where they are subject to
> such mental degradation; where they are censured as affecting
> masculine knowledge if they happen to have any under-
> standing; or despised as insignificant triflers if they have
> none.[1]

In *Desmond*, as we have already seen, Mrs Smith used the
novel form as a mere frame-work for her political views. Still, she
struck some shrewd blows through the mouths of those dramatis
personae whom we must hesitate to designate as characters. She
despises the corruption of party politics, the arrogance of ancient
titles, the insolence of 'mushroom nobility' and the ignorant
pretentions of the new rich. The conversation between General
Wallingford and Lord Newminster concerning the French
Revolution and its repercussions in England is most amusing.
Mrs Smith manages very skilfully the constituents of comedy in
this scene. We listen to the inveterate prejudice and stupidity of
these self-appointed critics, each reinforcing the bellowing of the
other, to the accompaniment of Mrs Fairfax's ladylike lamentations.

> 'Rot the people,' cried the noble Peer: 'I wish they were all
> hanged out of the way, both in France and here too. What
> business have a set of blackguards to have an opinion about
> liberty, and be cursed to them? . . . By Jove, Sir, I'd set fire to
> their assembly, and mind no more shooting them all, than if
> they were so many mad dogs.'[2]

But alas! too soon these glorious imbecilities are reduced to
the level of actual controversy by Desmond's address on the evils
of the feudal system.[3] Later we are given the queasy views of the
church dignitary: "Tis an uneasy thing, a very uneasy thing, for a

man of probity and principles to look in these days into a newspaper. Greatly must every man be troubled to read . . . wrath of heaven . . . perfidious and irreverent people . . . They have done the most unjust and wicked of all actions in depriving the church of its revenues.'[4] This Doctor of Divinity blusters and browbeats at the slightest effort to take the opposite view ('I won't argue, I won't commit myself, nor endeavour to convince a person whose principles are, I see, fundamentally wrong'); and, when a quiet man who opposes him scores several points, the Doctor swells with rage, crying: 'I don't know who that person is, but he is very ignorant, and very ill-bred.'[5]

At the beginning of *Desmond*, Mrs Smith makes her characters sufficiently alive to rebut the suggestion that they are merely pegs on which to hang her arguments. They are, of course, merely types, but they are presented *en ronde* and, without being in the least individual, they are human. They look and speak as such types look and speak in real life. It is for that reason that their statements do not appear a deliberate pattern of didacticism, but are the natural expression of their opinions and prejudices, that is to say of the opinions and prejudices of their caste. This touch of humanity, however, soon vanishes and we are left with a trackless waste of doctrine.

Mrs Smith went far in her revolutionary doctrines, but she did not really apply the principle of freedom to women. It was reserved for Mary Wollstonecraft to throw down the gauntlet for her sex. She was not the first to see in education the best way of raising the status of women. Mary Astell, a hundred years before, had made a reasoned plea for women's education, but Mary Wollstonecraft had views undreamt of by the gentle Mary Astell. That we are here concerned simply with Mary Wollstonecraft's contribution to fiction restricts this to the barest summary of her life and of her epoch-making book *The Vindication of the Rights of Woman*, and yet it is only through the knowledge of these that we can interpret her attempts at fiction.

Mary Wollstonecraft was the eldest daughter of a most unhappy marriage. Her mother was an Irish woman of good family. Her father, the son of a wealthy manufacturer in Spitalfields, started out in life with £10,000, but soon reduced his children to beggary and his wife to despair by his profligacy and tyranny. Mary's childhood burned into her mind squalid scenes of drunkenness, violence and domestic misery. This helps to explain her distrust of marriage and her corroding consciousness of women's subjection. The poverty in which the family lived made schooling impossible. She picked up what learning she could in the midst of household drudgery and everlasting migration from place to place in obedience to her father's whims. She had always had to contrive some sort of livelihood for herself and her family. After her mother's death, she no longer had a home and turned to governessing as a means of support. Her employer, Lady Kingsborough, is the original of Mary's 'fine lady' in the Vindication — her conception of what a woman should not be. No doubt, life as she saw it at Mitchelstown Castle was vapid and heartless, but her pride and her loneliness as a dependent must have added to her feeling of isolation. It was not merely the minor tragedy of a lonely governess: it was the consciousness of mental powers undeveloped and failing to find expression; it was the consciousness of youth, beauty and capacity for emotion withering unused. But Mary was not long to remain in this servitude. Lady Kingsborough, jealous of her daughter's affection for the governess, found an occasion to get rid of her, and Mary went to try her literary fortunes in London. At this point she really began to live as a woman and as a writer, but she brought to this new life the memories of the old. Her struggles, her generosity to her useless and disloyal sisters, her removal to Paris and her life with Imlay are too well known to need elaboration. The *Vindication* coupled with her unsanctified union drew upon her horrified condemnation. Her attempts at suicide and her marriage with Godwin offered the public further sources of criticism. Her death released her from the struggle of trying to solve the problems of woman's emancipation and woman's happiness.

The Vindication of the Rights of Woman caused the chivalrous Walpole to stigmatize the author as a 'hyena in petticoats', a 'philosophic serpent'. To the modern reader it appears a gallant but rather badly written statement of obvious facts. To Mary Wollstonecraft's contemporaries it was a shocking proclamation of revolt not merely against men's authority, but against female propriety. Indeed Mary deliberately attacked the superficiality of feminine conventions. She wished them to abandon the pernicious cult of sensibility, the 'deluge of false sentiments and overstretched feelings', the narrow opportunism of their upbringing. Rousseau had denied women the power of reasoning, and had stated that works of genius were beyond their capacity. He had recommended that 'all the ideas of women . . . should be directed to the study of men.' 'Educate women like men', said Rousseau, 'and the more they resemble our sex the less power will they have over us.' This training for the seraglio disgusted Mary Wollstonecraft. She replied: 'This is the very point I aim at. I do not wish them to have power over men; but over themselves.'[6] In education she saw the key to this self-government. Through education women might realize their mental powers, and share in the wider possibilities of life. Women's economic dependence on man induced in them a hypocritical attitude and an undue preoccupation with emotions. And what of the women who, for one reason or another, were cast upon their own resources? Education would, at least, give them a means of self-support. Women should purify their hearts. They should develop a sense of dignity. They should remember, said Mary, that until now they had never had a chance to show what they might become: 'Men of genius and talents have started out of a class, in which women have never yet been placed.'[7] Since Mary Wollstonecraft disliked novels, it is curious that she should have attempted to become a novelist. She may have done so simply because she believed in the didactic power of fiction, or she may have sought in such writing to express, and thus to rid herself of, the memories which preyed upon her. Fiction, however, was not her medium. Hers was a philosophical, though not always a logical, mind. She had not the novelist's gift of creating characters and weaving a pattern of life. All her attempts at fiction are thinly veiled autobiography, and since the circumstances of her life had aroused in her a strong sense of women's grievances, her fragments of fiction are strongly polemical. Indeed, by a curious anomaly, it is in the main this propagandist purpose which galvanizes her stories into life. The character who represents herself lives by the impassioned sincerity of her sufferings and her beliefs. Other characters only come to life when they are impassioned by their theories or by their wrongs. These crude and confused outpourings are not really novels, and yet there are grim patches of reality, sudden glimpses of power which make it impossible to dismiss Mary Wollstonecraft as a novelist. There is occasionally a passage which shows the style which she might have achieved, had she lived long enough to find a mental outlook which would have permitted her to remember without agony, and to fight against social injustice without sacrificing artistic principles.

Mary Wollstonecraft's first attempt at story-telling was *The Cave of Fancy* which she began in 1787, and never finished. This is a strange mixture of morbid reminiscence and philosophic deliberation. It begins in Johnsonian style, and seems to have an echo of *Rasselas*. A sage, who lives in a hut and has control over spirits, adopts a child whose mother has been drowned in a ship-wreck, and decides to educate her. One branch of her education is by means of a variety of stories and characters presented to her in the Cave of Fancy. Then follows a specimen of these stories, which begins: 'My mother was a most respectable character, but she was yoked to a man whose follies and vices made her ever feel the weight of the chain. The first sensation I recollect, was pity.' That is Mary's youth. There is a blending of identifiable incidents and inventions, and here appear the chief constituents of her later novels. We hear of an unhappy love affair, of a marriage to a family benefactor, undertaken to please her mother. A consciousness of unusual gifts and dreams of a great love are here expressed for the first time. 'I was afraid of the unmarked vacuity of common life'.[8]

> I grasped a mighty whole and smiled on the king of terrors; the tie which bound me to my friends he could not break, the same mysterious knot united me to the source of all goodness and happiness. I had seen the divinity reflected in a face I loved; I had read immortal characters displayed on a human countenance and forgot myself while I gazed.[9]

Mary, a Fiction (1788) is a further development of the same theme — the theme of Mary's life. There are scenes from her childhood, presentation of the characters of her father, mother and elder brother. Her friend, Fanny Blood, here appears as Ann, and there is a description of Mary's journey to Portugal and of Fanny's death. The rescue during the storm at sea is autobio-graphical also. Mary wrote this novel before meeting Imlay. It is evidently the work of one in great mental distress. The heroine reveals a pressing need to be understood and loved, a need which is frustrated by her mother's preference for her elder brother, by Ann's passive acceptance of her affection, and by her lover's death. She ends by dragging out her life with a husband to whom she has been joined in a marriage of convenience. The concluding words show her anticipating death with a sense of relief.

The Wrongs of Woman; or Maria, a Fragment[10] develops Mary Wollstonecraft's subject more fully, and brings into prominence her arguments against women's subjection. At the opening of the story we find Maria in a private asylum where her husband has caused her, though sane, to be confined. One of the attendants, called Jemima ('she had only a claim to a Christian name, which had not secured her any Christian privileges'), impressed Mary as a person who might help her to escape. She convinces Jemima of her sanity. Meanwhile she becomes interested in a fellow prisoner called Henry Darnford, and is soon assured that he, like herself, is the victim of an intrigue. He lends her books in which political theories are expounded. Through Jemima's help, he visits her, and tells her the story of his life, in which Imlay's is partly embodied.

Jemima's story is not an echo of anything in Mary's own life. It is an accumulation of misery designed to show the injustices which a woman might endure. Jemima's father seduced her mother. They were both servants in a rich house. The erring woman was dismissed in disgrace. The man was slightly reproved and allowed to keep his position. Jemima is born at the expense of her mother's life. Her father marries, and Jemima is apprenticed to one of her step-mother's friends who keeps a slop-shop in Wapping. There she endures the harshest treatment. At the age of sixteen, the unwilling victim of her master's brutality, she is thrown into the street by her jealous mistress. Nothing remains but the life of the streets, which she describes with a grim ferocity. She finally becomes the mistress of a literary man. He dies. She is friendless again. Want of a character prevents her from getting domestic employment, and she cannot sew well enough to support herself by needlework.

> At last I got recommended to wash in a few families, who did me the favour to admit me into their houses, without the most strict enquiry, to wash from one in the morning till eight at night for eighteen or twenty pence a day. On the happiness to be enjoyed over a wash-tub I need not comment; yet you will allow me to observe, that this was a

> wretchedness of situation peculiar to my sex. A man with
> half my industry, and, I may say, abilities, could have
> procured a decent livelihood.[11]

She hurts her leg, suffers from the wretchedness of the hospital
system, and is dismissed scarcely able to stand and with nowhere
to go. She is refused a piece of bread by a householder who bids
her go to the workhouse. She does, and this is her comment:
'What are the common run of workhouses, but prisons, in which
many respectable old people, worn out by immoderate labour,
sink into the grave in sorrow, to which they are carried like
dogs.'[12] After she has spent some time in the workhouse, she is
offered the position of attendant in an asylum, which she accepts,
although she knows the cruelties to which she will become a
party. 'What should induce me to be the champion of suffering
humanity? Who ever risked anything for me? Who ever acknowledged me to be a fellow-creature?'[13]

Then follows Maria's narrative, written for the future information of her infant daughter. Maria is Mary Wollstonecraft, and
again we have a presentation of her youth, this time fully elaborated. It is a terrible indictment of her father and of her elder
brother, 'the deputy tyrant of the house'. There is a poignant
description of her mother's death. She tells of the long months of
watching by her mother's bed; of her brother's neglect of this
mother who adored him. Mary describes her mother's last
moments:

> I shall not dwell on the death-bed scene, lively as is the
> remembrance of the emotion produced by the last grasp of
> my mother's cold hand; when blessing me, she added, 'A
> little more patience, and all will be over!' Ah! my child, how
> often have these words rung mournfully in my ears — and I
> have exclaimed — 'A little more patience, and I too shall be
> at rest.'[14]

Maria marries George Venables to escape from a home made
unbearable by the authority of her father's servant mistress.
Venables turns out a drunken profligate. (Possibly Mary
Wollstonecraft drew him with her eye on Bishop, the husband of
her sister Eliza). A benevolent uncle (for whom alas! there was
no parallel in Mary's family) supplies Maria with money which
her husband invariably seizes. Here Mary Wollstonecraft lashes

the law by which a husband owned all his wife's property, and might even (as did Venables) force a lock to get at her money.

> On the other hand, a mother could not lawfully snatch from her unwilling husband even enough to keep her children alive. 'When such laws were framed, should not impartial law-givers have first decreed . . . that the husband should always be wiser and more virtuous than his wife, in order to entitle him, with a show of justice, to keep this idiot or perpetual minor, for ever in bondage?'[15]

Venables finally tries to compromise his wife with one of his friends so that he may blackmail him. In a similar situation Charlotte Smith shows the wife evading the danger, but still considering it her duty to care for her husband. Mary Wollstonecraft shows Maria at once leaving her husband forever. At this juncture Maria's rich uncle dies, bequeathing all his money to Maria's little daughter and appointing Maria as guardian. Baulked of his hopes, her husband has her kidnapped and imprisoned in an asylum. He keeps the child, this being within his legal rights. While in the asylum Darnford becomes Maria's lover. They escape. Her husband sues Darnford for seduction. Darnford is obliged to leave England on urgent business, but Maria fights the case alone. In court she vindicates women, and states their grievances. The judge condemns her attitude, and the story breaks off here. A few notes indicate a possible end. Darnford deserts her. She hears that her child is dead and determines on suicide. Jemima enters with her child who has merely been hidden by the vengeful Venables, and Maria decides to live for her daughter's sake.

It is a very badly constructed novel, too obviously intended as a fictional supplement to the *Vindication*, but apart from its bearing on doctrinal fiction, it had aspects of reality which had been too long ignored by the women novelists.

Another feminist novel-writer who drew upon herself a storm of protest was Mary Hays (1760–1843). Without Mary Wollstonecraft's greatness of mind, she appears, like her, to have been obsessed by painful aspects of life. But whereas Mary Wollstonecraft dwelt on unhappy episodes in her life and made them the starting point for a wider feminist protest, Mary Hays appears to have suffered from frustration. Her novels are case books of morbid psychology, and however much she dissociated herself from her first heroine, Emma Courtney, that she could ever have conceived such a character testifies to her own abnormal outlook. *The Memoirs of Emma Courtney* (1796) describe the predicament of a young woman who, having singled out a man whom she considers suitable to mate with one of her high powers, cannot induce him to marry her or even take her as his mistress. She pursues him with the most terrifying determination, but in vain, and she makes a marriage of convenience with a man to whom she is indifferent. Nevertheless, she still loves the first-chosen, and has the melancholy satisfaction of soothing his dying hours, a transaction which enrages her long-suffering husband. Emma resents her husband's attitude as unreasonable tyranny, and considers her morbid sufferings and the circumstances which cause them as 'the unnatural and odious result of a distempered and unnatural civilization'. Mary Hays seemed unable to understand that the problem she presented had nothing to do with the state of society.

The Victim of Prejudice (1799) had, on the contrary, a reasonable thesis. The book does not, however, convey a reasonable impression partly because of the exaggeration of the story by which the thesis is to be proved, and partly because it is told in the manner of sensibility. This high-flown style of telling terrible truths is grotesque.

Mary, the heroine of the novel, is the daughter of a woman who, betrayed and abandoned by a man of fashion, falls into evil ways and dies on the scaffold.[16] Mary grows up under the benevolent care of a philosophic gentleman called Ramond, and is idyllically happy until she arrives at the age of love. Her beauty subjects her to the odious attentions of the profligate Sir Peter Osborne, but she is consoled by the respectful adoration of William Pelham, a young man of ancient family and ample fortune. Mary and William are deeply in love, but William's father, furious at the prospect of such a misalliance, orders his son to travel abroad for two years. He departs, but first solemnly promises Mary that they will marry when he returns. Mary is full of forebodings that 'he will imbibe the contagion of a distempered civilization', and that he will, therefore, become *a man of the world* (a phrase always used in italics). No sooner is William safely out of the way than Sir Peter Osborne becomes more resolute than ever in his pursuit, particularly when Mary's guardian dies and she is left alone and helpless. He decoys her to his house and ruins her. She refuses all his offers of 'reparation', and rushes into the street. By a great coincidence she meets William, now returned from Paris, and long since become 'a man of the world'. He breaks the news that he has married another, and she refuses with the wildest indignation his suggestion that they forget everything except their love. In vain does William argue that she cannot now stand alone; in vain he 'hinted that society would, with inexorable malignity, hunt me from its privileges; that with a mind peerless and unstained, I should yet suffer all the penalties of guilt, without possible appeal or redress.' Mary's 'spirit still triumphs in conscious rectitude.'

She endeavours to find work, but soon discovers that her unfortunate story causes the women to condemn and the men to pursue her. Still, she refuses to change her name, since she is guilty of no crime. Her betrayer endeavours to ensnare her again. He has her imprisoned for debt, involves her in all kinds of miseries, deprives her of every comfort and refuge, but fails to secure his ends. At the conclusion of this novel, we leave her dying of consumption and hoping for death.

The myth of the betrayed woman conveniently dying of a decline had long persisted in fiction. Mary Hays tore it to pieces, and asserted the need for a single standard in morality. This was a theme which engaged the attention of Mrs Inchbald and Mrs Opie. Mary Hays's treatment destroyed the effectiveness of her argument for the woman innocent but ruined. That it had great artistic possibilities was superbly proved long afterwards in *Tess of the d'Urbervilles*.

Mary Hays's high-flown exaggerations were sufficiently absurd to provoke a burlesque, which duly appeared as *Memoirs of Modern Philosophers* (1800). In this amusing book Elizabeth Hamilton[17] set herself particularly to satirize Mary Hays, and seldom lost an opportunity of tilting also at Godwin. She has no quarrel with Mary Wollstonecraft, regretting only that she so much over-stated her case.

The company of modern philosophers has its leader in the arch-villain Vallaton, who poses as a French revolutionary of good family. He is really a gutter-rat reared in a stew of vice, and his most respectable avocation has been that of a barber. The

431

disciples of this plausible rogue are Mr Glib, the rascally chemist; the befuddled Mr Myope; the Goddess of Reason, a French adventuress who has followed Vallaton from France, and Miss Bridgetina Botherim. Bridgetina, that dwarfish little egoist, that arrogant and absurd country bumpkin, is enchanted with the new philosophy and rants its pretentious jargon from morning till night, to the mingled admiration and misery of her unfortunate mother, whose pastry is so much better than her grammar. Bridgetina, though hideous, is particularly enthusiastic about the philosophic tenet by which a woman may pursue the man she loves — not simply await his approach supinely. She pursues two men with perfect safety, as her face is in itself a padlock to her virtue. Not so the unfortunate Julia, the beloved daughter of the invalid Captain Desmond. She is beguiled by Vallaton's sophistries, so that she revolts against her parents, considers herself victimized even by the mention of honourable suitors, and flees to London with Vallaton. In due time he deserts her. She is found by her friends, but she has taken poison and dies. Vallaton goes to France with the Goddess of Reason who, when she tires of him, betrays him to the guillotine. Bridgetina, who is present at Julia's deathbed, is galvanized into sanity and goes home with her mother, her reform being the more firmly established by a candid friend who informs her that only by her ugliness has she escaped Julia's fate.

This brief outline of the plot makes it clear that Elizabeth Hamilton employed two methods of discrediting the revolutionary philosophers. She began by heaping ridicule upon them, but soon engaged herself in serious contradiction of their arguments. At first she manipulated the plot merely to expose the evils which resulted from a practical application of such pernicious views. Her efforts to reconcile burlesque and explicit moral teaching are naturally unsuccessful, and the best parts of the story are those in which she appeals to our sense of humour. Her comic effects are greatly heightened by her malicious trick of putting into the mouths of her unreasonable characters the very words of Godwin and Mary Hays. Such theorists arouse her laughter by their lack of proportion and by their intense and declamatory style. Indeed she finds in their beliefs the crowning proof that they are humourless. Bridgetina says: 'The energies of philosophical authors are all expended in gloomy masses of tenebrific shade. The investigators of mind never condescend to make their readers laugh.'[18] Mrs Hamilton's philosophers can never be cornered in argument. They always take refuge in such redoubtable phrases as 'infinite causation', 'perfectibility' and 'the fable of superstition'. They have no use for goodness unless it flows 'from a conviction of general utility pursued through the maze of abstract reasoning.' They constitute a Hottentotian Society which aims at leaving forever 'the corrupt wilderness of ill-constituted society, the rank and rotten soil from which every finer shrub draws poison as it grows.'[19] Life among the Hottentots is the ideal of these reformers. When Bridgetina is dunned by tradesmen she sighs to be where such vulgarians would not intrude upon her towering fancy, 'but each congenial Hottentot, energizing in his self-built shed, would be too much engrossed by forming projects for general utility, to break in upon my repose.'[20]

Bridgetina is the splendidly idiotic heroine of this burlesque. Having imbibed Godwin's principles from the loose leaves that wrap up her mother's snuff, her 'ardent sensibility' led her back to novels.

> As I read each sweet, delicious tale, I reasoned, I investigated, I moralized. What! said I to myself, shall every heroine of all these numerous volumes have a lover, and shall I remain 'a comfortless, solitary, shivering wanderer in the dreary wilderness of human society.' I feel in myself the capacity of increasing the happiness of an individual; but where is he? Does he live in this town? Have I seen him? How shall I find him? Does his breast sympathize with mine? An idea of young Gubbles came across my mind. Yes, said I, it must be he! I heaved a convulsive struggling sigh. Tears half delicious, half agonizing, gushed in torrents from my eyes. O Gubbles! Gubbles! cried I, my importunate sensibilities, my panting tenderness, are all reserved for thee![21]

Bridgetina, undeterred by torrential rain, went at once to the chemist's shop where Gubbles was employed. He was there 'looking into the mouth of an old woman who sat upon the floor to have a tooth pulled out. The attitude was charming; the scene was interesting; it was impressive, tender, melancholy, sublime. My suffocating sensibilities returned.' Bridgetina throws herself into a chair and bursts into tears. Gubbles, quite staggered at her peculiar behaviour, plies her with hartshorn. She believes that he is deeply moved. 'The tenderness of Gubbles inspired the most delightful hope. "The delicious poison circulated through every vein." I gave myself up to the ardent feelings of a morbid imagination.' Within a week Gubbles has married the young woman with whom he has been 'walking out'. Bridgetina transfers her tumultuous affections to Dr Henry Sidney. She knows he loves her because once when she got stuck on a stile 'Henry sprung to my assistance, and with manly energetic fervour tore my petticoat from the stump in which it was entangled.' She perceives that it is with his that her mind was formed to mingle and that he is henceforth the arbiter of her fate. But what is that mysterious reserve that seals his lips? She determines to pursue him more assiduously than ever.

This was Mrs Hamilton at the top of her bent. The more one enjoys such a method of attack, the more one must regret that she did not sustain it throughout her novel. Julia's story is dull, and Mrs Hamilton's direct moralizing has really no place in a work of fiction.

In Godwin's group of philosophic enthusiasts was one woman who found it possible to be doctrinal without abating her femininity. This was the charming and gifted Elizabeth Inchbald. She subscribed to Rousseau's view of civilized society, but avoided the opinions of the extremists. The fact that she was a devout Catholic insulated her against those theories of sexual liberty by which other 'philosophesses' were held to have unsexed themselves, but, in any case, it was in her nature to maintain a moderate attitude. She had no ungovernable passions. She was not repressed. She had no grievance against men. On the contrary, she greatly enjoyed their admiration and she understood their outlook. It was Mrs Inchbald's fortune to be beautiful and beloved, irreproachable, highly talented, and moderately well-off. Because she was a happy woman she was essentially sane and sweet-tempered. Indeed the converse would be equally true. And added to her charm and equability was a most engaging simplicity of manner. These traits characterized her not merely as a woman, but as a novelist. From the day when as Elizabeth Simpson, she had determined to become an actress, and ran away from her father's farm in Suffolk, it had been necessary for her to support herself. An impediment in her speech made it impossible for her to make a success of the stage, but her good looks secured her engagements. She continued to act even after her marriage to Inchbald, a needy actor. Her husband's death two years later threw her completely on her own resources, and to eke out her slender earnings she took to writing plays. These were successful, but it is on her achievement as a novelist that her fame depends.

A Simple Story (1791)[22] was Mrs Inchbald's first achievement in fiction—an achievement insufficiently praised in its own time and even since. By the very simplicity of its aim it avoided alike the hysterical and complicated plots of sensibility, and the unnatural adventures of the Gothic tale. It took for its theme the relations of a little group of people whose reactions create the real interest of the narrative. They are no paragons: 'They are human creatures who are meant to be portrayed . . . and where is the human creature who has not some good qualities to soften, if not to counterbalance his bad ones?'[23] In characterization, in its directness, in the surprising modernity of its tone, this is an unusual novel. Its structure, however, is very faulty. The story consists of two parts separated by a lapse of seventeen years.

Miss Milner, a lovely, flighty but good-hearted girl, falls in love with Dorriforth, her guardian. When Dorriforth succeeds to the family title and becomes Lord Elmwood, he considers it his duty to marry. He knows nothing of Miss Milner's affection, and intends to marry (without any feeling but respect) a lady who has been suggested to him as a suitable wife, when Miss Woodley (the confidante of Miss Milner), grieved for her friend's secret misery, tells Dorriforth the truth. He realizes that he loves Miss Milner and their marriage is arranged. But it is Miss Milner's fate that she must ever play with fire, and she cannot give up the fashionable amusements which Lord Elmwood condemns, or forbear arousing his jealousy. There are frequent quarrels and Lord Elmwood breaks the engagement and determines to travel abroad. At the last moment they are reconciled and married. For four years they are perfectly happy. A daughter is born. Then Elmwood goes to inspect his estates in the West Indies. His return is delayed, and Lady Elmwood, doubting his love for her, and weary of waiting, returns to the frivolous life, and takes a lover. When Elmwood comes home, he casts off his wife and even his daughter Mathilda. After some years of repentance Lady Elmwood dies.

The second part of the story deals with the reconciliation of Lord Elmwood with his daughter. Mathilda falls in love with her cousin, Rushbrook, Lord Elmwood's heir. They succeed in winning Elmwood's consent to their marriage, and all ends happily.

By a moral introduced in the penultimate paragraph, Mrs Inchbald proclaims that her object was didactic. She says that she wished to show that Miss Milner's misfortunes were the result of an improper education, and she contrasts the superior character of Mathilda who was reared in the 'school of prudence, through adversity'. Actually, however, the main narrative seems so free from a didactic intention that, if Mrs Inchbald had such a purpose at the beginning, one would say that she lost sight of it when she was caught up by the human interest of her story. The inartistic addition of Mathilda's vicissitudes may have been inspired by the intention of establishing a didactic contrast. On the other hand, it may have arisen because Mrs Inchbald did not know when to stop, or because she wished somehow to make a happy ending. One must remember that, simply because she failed in structure, there is an inartistic gap of fifteen years in *Nature and Art*. The general impression created by *A Simple Story* is that Mrs Inchbald first wrote Miss Milner's part of the story, and then introduced the didactic purpose as an afterthought. Mrs Inchbald represents that education at a boarding school was responsible for the faults in Miss Milner's character. In fact, Miss Milner's faults are those of temperament which education could scarcely change unless it could make her anew. Throughout the novel Mrs Inchbald shows Miss Milner impulsively acting from the depths of her nature, not from some superficial stratum of worldliness or custom. Indeed, in many cases, her wilfulness and frivolity are defensive — either to cloak her real feelings, or because her real feelings sting her into a perverse defiance. When, for example, Lord Elmwood does not come to the opera, but spends the evening with Miss Fenton whom he contemplates marrying, Miss Milner allows the rake, Lord Frederick Lawnley, to escort her to her carriage — not because she likes him, but because she is 'piqued — heart-broken — full of resentment against the object of her uneasiness, and inattentive to all that passed'; because she 'thought this the moment to retaliate'. That is the sort of reaction, common to women and to men alike, with which education has nothing to do. Not only does Miss Milner not care for this particular rake; she has an aversion to all rakes: 'What! love a rake, a man of professed gallantry! impossible! To me a common rake is as odious as a common prostitute is to the man of the nicest feelings. Where can be the joy, the pride, of inspiring a passion which fifty others can equally inspire.' And yet Sir Frederick Lawnley is the very rake with whom Miss Milner, years later, was unfaithful to her husband. This heroine has many facets to her nature. She is affectionate, generous to an enemy, free from pettiness. Yet she is unwise in her impulses, and she runs 'a course full of perils, of hopes, of fears, of joy, and at the end of sorrows; all exquisite of their kind, for exquisite were the feelings of her susceptible heart.' She is indeed no paragon, but Mrs Inchbald, although she stresses the necessity for prudence and self-control, has no use for paragons. Such a one is Miss Fenton, very evidently despised by Mrs Inchbald because she has no heart. Mrs Inchbald has courage enough to explode the fallacy that women felt love only after they had been solicited in marriage. Miss Milner, with no apparent hope of a return from Dorriforth, cries out: 'I love him with all the passion of a mistress, and with all the tenderness of a wife.'[24]

So excellently has Mrs Inchbald mixed the elements in Miss Milner that we debate her character and motives as if she were (as she is to us) a living person. Mrs Inchbald meant us to do this. She used in fiction the dramatic technique of presenting behaviour and allowing us to draw our own inferences. She says: 'The reader must form a judgment of the ward of Dorriforth by her actions — by all the round of great or trivial circumstances that shall be revealed.'[25]

Mrs Inchbald shows her dramatic instinct in fiction, but she avoids melodrama. Only when Miss Milner, to prevent a duel, pretends to love Lawnley is there any exaggeration, and then it is deliberate. For the rest there are no high-flown ebullitions, no explosions of rodomontade. When feelings are tense they relieve themselves in action, often of the most trivial kind. When Dorriforth imperiously forbids Miss Milner to keep her evening engagement there is a painful silence. Then 'Mrs Horton rose from her chair — moved the decanters and fruit round the table — stirred the fire — and came back to her chair again before another word was uttered. Nor had this good woman's officious labours taken the least from the awkwardness of the silence, which, as soon as the bustle she had contrived was over, returned in its full force.'[26] By such touches (and there are many of them) Mrs Inchbald shows her acute observation of life, and her familiarity with those 'bits of business' which would relieve such awkward moments on the stage.

The other characters in the Miss Milner's story are as interesting as she herself. Dorriforth is stern and gentle; slow to love; loving greatly when his heart is given; but his love betrayed turns to hatred. Despite his goodness there are in his nature 'shades of evil'. Sanford is a strange compound. In Miss Milner's frivolous days he sets himself to mortify her. Indeed he even seems to persecute her, but his intention is to destroy her vanity, and when at last he believes in her sincerity, he is generous. He it is who reunites Miss Milner and Dorriforth, and when Miss Milner has fallen from virtue he succours her. Miss Woodley is a complete departure from the type of old maid which, up to that time, was a convention in fiction. Fielding and every other had presented an old maid as a thwarted fury oozing bitterness at her single state, and ever hoping to marry no matter whom. Miss Woodley is very plain and very good-natured — a loyal friend to beauty in distress. She could always discover a virtue 'although of the most diminutive kind', and, for all her meekness, she has courage enough for the most difficult situations.

In *Nature and Art* (1796) Mrs Inchbald postulates that natural education is superior to formal education. To prove this contention she presents two brothers; Henry and William, who in character and fortunes are a complete contrast. Henry, who has a happy knack with the violin, fiddles his way into a livelihood and helps to support his brother who, unable to find employment, decides to continue his studies at a university. In due time a great man, delighted with Henry's fiddling, is induced to give William a living of £500 a year. William climbs to affluence, marries for money and position and becomes a heartless snob. He ignores Henry and Henry's plebeian wife.The brothers quarrel. Henry's wife dies shortly afterwards, and he goes abroad taking his son with him. He is captured by savages, but years later his son (also named Henry) escapes to England with a letter consigning him to the care of his uncle William. He is reared with his cousin (also named William). Again Mrs Inchbald presents the contrast of simple good-nature and sophisticated self-seeking, and in this latter case her contention is more strongly enforced because the two youths have had a very different upbringing. The elder Henry and William do not really support Mrs Inchbald's thesis at all, because they were reared and educated side by side until about the age of twenty. The wide divergence between their characters cannot be ascribed to William's sojourn at the university, since it was apparent before he went there. Mrs Inchbald tells us that both were educated at a grammar school. She shows us that from the beginning William was moody, proud, selfish and ungrateful, and that Henry was sunny, affectionate, spontaneous and ingenuous. Had she reasoned out this part of the story, she would have been forced to admit that the contrast between William and Henry was due, not to education or environment, but to their very different dispositions. The younger Henry, however, reared without any formal education, is an excellent argument in favour of Rousseauism, and throughout he reasons remorselessly on the anomalies, shams, and abuses of the civilized society in which he comes to live. The younger William's mechanical acceptance of established conditions and his easy parroting of conclusions which he has never questioned appear cheap. His superficial religion and semblance of morality have no connection whatever with his daily life, which is governed entirely by self-interest and self-indulgence. Henry, on the contrary, learns with wonder that there is a God, and another world; and, untrammelled by social clap-trap, he applies these religious principles to the world without him and within. Henry's enquiring mind, directed to the social inequalities and injustices which prevail, gives Mrs Inchbald a very good opportunity to flay the selfishness, the toad-eating and the supercilious patronage of the rich, and the defencelessness of the poor. In her view the poor are in much the same category as the natural man — both are free from the stale and pernicious ideas which pervert the rich.

For the purpose of social satire Mrs Inchbald's style is really admirable. It is direct, terse, pithy and ironic. For example, it would be hard to better her description of the manner in which William, the purse-proud dean, received the news that Henry's wife is dead. William and his wife Lady Clementina have never recognized this honest creature's existence, but —

If Henry's wife were not fit company for Lady Clementina, it is to be hoped that she was company for angels; she died within the first year of her marriage, a faithful, an affectionate wife, and a mother.

When William heard of her death, he felt a sudden shock; and a kind of fleeting thought glanced across his mind, that — 'Had he known she had been so near her dissolution, she might have been introduced to Lady Clementina; and he himself would have called her sister.'

That is (if he had deemed his fleeting idea), 'They would have had no objection to have met this poor woman for the last time; and would have descended to the familiarity of kindred in order to have wished her a good journey to the other world.'[27]

And again, this description of the relations between the dean and Lady Clementina:

If the dean had loved his wife but moderately, seeing all her faults clearly as he did, he must frequently have quarrelled with her; if he had loved her with tenderness, he must have treated her with a degree of violence in the hope of amending her failings; but having neither personal nor mental affection towards her, sufficiently interesting to give himself the trouble to contradict her will in anything, he passed for one of the best husbands in the world.[28]

Mrs Inchbald's use of dialogue is trenchant and sardonic. One almost commiserates the smug dean subjected to the pitiless inquisition of his young nephew. When Richard the coachman is turned away, Henry puzzles over his uncle's form of dismissal: 'You shall never drive me again.' The omniscient and superior cousin William elaborates: 'Richard is turned away; he is never to get upon our coach-box again, never to drive any of us any more.'

'And was it pleasure to drive us, cousin? I am sure I sometimes pitied him: it rained sometimes very hard when he was on the box; and sometimes Lady Clementina has kept him a whole hour at the door all in the cold and snow: was that pleasure?'

'No,' replied young William.

'Was it honour, cousin?'

'No,' exclaimed his cousin with a contemptuous smile.

'Then why did my uncle say to him, as a punishment, "he should never —"'

440

The dean hastily intervenes to explain the relations of rich and poor:

> 'The poor are born to serve the rich.'
> 'And what are the rich for ?'
> 'To be served by the poor.'
> 'But suppose the poor would not serve them?'
> 'Then they must starve.'

But, when cornered, the dean says that the poor will be rewarded in the world to come, and reveals under further questioning that in the world to come all persons are equal.

> 'But cannot this world try to be as good as that?'
> 'In respect to placing all persons on a level, it is utterly impossible; God has ordained it otherwise.'
> 'How! Has God ordained a distinction to be made, and will not make any himself?[29]

By far the best part of the novel deals with William's seduction and desertion of the cottage-girl, Agnes Primrose. His sensuality and heartlessness, her deep love, humility, weakness and self-torture are finely traced. To him it is a casual adventure broken off to contract an ambitious marriage. When eventually it is proved that he is the father of her child, it involves him in no censure. The suffering and disgrace are all hers, and everything conspires to degrade her further. Finally, after long years of misery and wrongdoing, she is arrested for robbery and on the day of her trial is brought before the learned judge — her seducer, William. Eighteen years, which have brought her to the depths, have raised him to his eminence. It is a scene which has been greatly praised and which is too well-known to need quotation. Its intensity of feeling, its sense of fate, its contrasts, its pathos, its restraint make this a memorable achievement in the history of English fiction. When William puts on the black cap to condemn to death the woman for whose mis-spent life he is responsible, this gesture is intended to represent the triumph of worldly corruption over untutored simplicity, of riches over poverty, of masculine privilege over woman's defencelessness. It is the coping stone of Mrs Inchbald's didactic and artistic purpose.

Mrs Amelia Opie (1769–1853) inherited her father's radical principles, and his active interest in such social works of mercy as visiting hospitals, workhouses and prisons. She was friendly with Horne Tooke and an admirer of Mary Wollstonecraft. Both Holcroft and Godwin had wished to marry her. She was also on very good terms with Mrs Barbauld, Mrs Siddons, the Duc d'Aiguillon and other French emigrants. By the time Mrs Opie commenced author, the French Revolution had reached a stage which damped, if it did not entirely quench, the fervour of English sympathizers. Mrs Opie's novels, written during this revulsion of feeling, are anti-Revolutionary. Her didactic purpose is primarily moral, and her interest in social questions is chiefly a prolongation of those earnest principles which eventually caused her to become a Quaker. She stresses the necessity of Christian education, condemns the slave-trade and opposes the outlawry of women fallen from virtue. She teaches through domestic portraiture, and her novels reflect her own generosity and gentle charm. She had a pleasant, simple narrative style, and was particularly praised in her own day for her pathos, but she had not a sure touch, and, by comparison with Maria Edgeworth, she appears mediocre.

Her first novel, *Father and Daughter*, appeared in 1801. The story begins well:

> The night was dark—the wind blew keenly over the frozen and rugged heath, when Agnes, pressing her moaning child to her bosom, was travelling on foot to her father's habitation.
> 'Would to God I have never left it!' she exclaimed, as home and all its enjoyments rose in fancy to her view

This is Agnes Fitzhenry who a few years before had eloped with the fascinating villain, Captain Clifford. Marriage had never been his intention, but he deluded her with promises and intercepted her appeals to her father, so that she remained with him, and her dependence was all the greater when her child was born. When, however, she learns that Clifford has deliberately foiled her efforts at reconciliation with her father, she determines to return home. She finds that her father has gone mad through grief at her behaviour, and resolves that his restoration to reason and his forgiveness will be the sole object of her life. Braving public opinion, she settles down in her own town and earns her living by needlework. She wins respect from people of her own class whose friendship she had forfeited, and love from the poor who knew her charity and sympathy. In due time she makes a home for her father, but he recovers his reason only for a few moments before he dies. He pardons and blesses her, and, overwhelmed by the event, she dies a few hours later. They are buried in the same grave. Clifford, disappointed in a childless marriage, owns his son and makes him his heir. The moral is explicitly stated at the end:

> Peace to the memory of Agnes Fitzhenry! — and may the woman who, like her, has been the victim of artifice, self-confidence, and temptation, like her endeavour to regain the esteem of the world by patient suffering, and virtuous exertion; and look forward to the attainment of it with confidence! But may she whose innocence is yet secure . . . tremble with horror.[30]

Mrs Opie followed up the success of *Father and Daughter* with *Adeline Mowbray; or, the Mother and Daughter* (1804). This is the best of her novels. It is based on the life of Mary Wollstonecraft which it treats with sympathetic understanding. Considering the rigid morality of the age, the sex of the writer and the nature of her subject, it speaks well for Mrs Opie that she recognized Mary Wollstonecraft's sincerity and her essential clean-mindedness. Adeline Mowbray's story differs in detail from Mary's, but in general outline it is meant to be the same. Adeline, reared by a theorizing mother, puts into practice the false doctrines with which her brain has been filled. She falls in love with the revolutionary philosopher Glenmurray, and considers that marriage would be a betrayal of his principles and hers. He loves her sincerely and does not wish to expose her to public censure, but she insists on dispensing with a ceremony which she considers quite meaningless. They go to Lisbon and are happy for a time, but soon realize that ostracism must be the penalty of their illegal union. Glenmurray dies, and Adeline's miseries increase a hundred-fold. For the sake of her daughter, she marries Berrendale, as bad an argument for marriage as could well be. He is selfish, miserly and unfaithful, and constantly afflicts her with references to his generosity in marrying a 'kept woman'. Finally he deserts her. Mrs Mowbray had, from the beginning, cast off Adeline not merely for her association with Glenmurray, but because Adeline had unfortunately attracted the attentions of a profligate who had (bigamously) married her foolish mother.

Mrs Mowbray, influenced alike by real horror at her daughter's repudiation of marriage and by jealousy, had vowed that she would never forgive her until she saw her disgraced and on her death-bed. She repents this vow, but when she does find Adeline, she is on her death-bed. The reconciliation is complete and Adeline consigns her child to her mother's care.

A good example of Mrs Opie's simple pathos is the occasion when the dying Adeline, accompanied by her little daughter, returns to her old home. It seems to her that she will never live to see it, that she cannot endure the emotions which arise within her.

> At length, however, she did reach it! and the lawn before Mrs Mowbray's white house, her hayfields, and the running stream at the bottom of it burst in all their beauty on her view—'And this is my mother's dwelling!' exclaimed Adeline; 'and there was I born; and near here—' shall I die, she would have added, but her voice failed her.
>
> 'Oh ! What a pretty house and garden!' cried Editha in the unformed accents of childhood; 'how I should like to live there!' The artless remark awakened a thousand mixed and overpowering feelings in the bosom of Adeline; and after a pause of strong emotion, she exclaimed, catching the little prattler to her heart—'You shall live there, my child! — yes, yes, you shall live there!'
>
> 'But when?' resumed Editha.
>
> 'When I am in my grave,' answered Adeline.
>
> 'And when shall you be there,' replied the unconscious child, fondly caressing her: 'pray, mamma — pray be there soon!'[31]

But Mrs Opie does not always achieve this simplicity. Although this novel is most sensible in outlook, there are many evidences that the melodramatic exaggerations of sensibility still survived. Adeline goes mad for six months after Glenmurray's death. When she fears lest she may infect her child with smallpox, she runs frenzied around the streets; is found by an acquaintance whom she does not recognize; is put to bed muttering incoherently, bled and drugged. She remains unconscious until the following morning. When Adeline hears that her mother inveterately hates her, she horrifies Glenmurray by shrieking frantically and continually: 'She detests me!'

There is in this novel a considerable ability in the presentation of the characters. On the whole, these are not individual, but

Mrs Opie draws on a fount of humanity or on a knowledge of human nature, so that we are constantly pleased with touches of reality which give these types a convincing appearance of life. Dr Norberry, although he wipes away too many unobtrusive tears, is a creature of flesh and blood. He is good-natured, tactless, and faithful. He finds women a mass of contradictions and is nearly always defeated in his arguments with them, particularly by his wife and daughters.

The moral of the story is emphasized in Adeline's final retraction of all her mistaken views. Though her marriage has failed, she no more thinks that an argument against marriage 'than the accidental bursting of a musket would be for the total abolition of fire-arms.' She considers marriage a necessary contract, so that passion may give place to affection and affection may devote itself to the family. Through Dr Norberry, Mrs Opie repeatedly expresses her pity and admiration or the misguided Adeline— that is for the misguided Mary Wollstonecraft. Her opinion is summed up finely in the words: 'What a glorious champion would this creature have been in the support of truth, when even error in her looks so like to virtue.'[32]

In *Adeline Mowbray* Mrs Opie spoke out on such subjects as duelling and the slave-trade. In her subsequent works of fiction she concentrated chiefly on personal ethics. *Temper* (1812) is really a wretched novel. Every incident in the plot is framed so that a moral may be drawn from it, and the reader is never credited with ability to glean the moral for himself. The lesson is driven home endlessly with sledge-hammer sermonettes. *Temper* is a tract in three volumes showing the pernicious effects of this passion throughout three generations. The text is given in the front page: 'A horse not broken becometh headstrong, and a child left to himself will be wilful.' Mrs Opie's other works consist mainly of short tales, unequal in quality.[33]

Hannah More was another of the women writers who strove by means of fiction to inculcate morality and to counteract subversive Jacobin doctrines. Since it cannot be said that she contributed anything to the art of fiction, and since her stories are nearer to direct pedagogy than to literature, it would serve no useful purpose to consider them in any detail. She and her sister, aided by private subscribers and by committees, published and circulated all over England an immense number of tracts and tales intended to disinfect the minds of the lower and middle classes from the disease of democratic thought. To aid the circulation of these propagandist works, they were sold at a price which undercut competitors. *Coelebs in search of a Wife, comprehending Observations on Domestic Habits and Manners, Religion and Morals* (1809) cannot be taken seriously. We are asked to contemplate this characterless prig, this sententious vacuum, while he scours England for one who might be worthy to marry him. To endure his interviews with hopeful parents and marriageable daughters, one must laugh. The best of Hannah More's other works are *Tales for the Common People* and *Stories for Persons of the Middle Classes*, both published in 1818. These are characterized by shrewd commonsense, with an occasional glimpse of humour. Hannah More attracted a large reading public for which, as her tales and stories indicate, she provided specialized fare. Whether she succeeded in preventing the common people from perusing the fiction intended for their betters must remain a question.

Maria Edgeworth (1767–1849) was the greatest of the didactic moralists. She belonged to an English Protestant family which since the reign of Henry VIII had been landed proprietors in County Longford. Her father, Richard Lovell Edgeworth, was a broad-minded and kindly man whose imagination was as limited as his energies were immense. His greatest interest was in education (an earnestness which was fostered by his friendship with Thomas Day) but he also had a literary bent; amused himself with mechanical experiments; sat in the Irish House of Commons, where he spoke for the Union but voted against it; administered his estate with benevolence; married four wives and reared a huge family. Indeed the Edgeworth family were a happy and self-sufficient commonwealth, all apparently intent on being amiable and useful, and all loyally owning allegiance to their genial and self-assured parent. It would, one imagines, have been dashing to his vanity had he dreamt that only as a parent would he escape oblivion — only as the parent of Maria Edgeworth, who was hailed as one of the literary lions of her day.

Maria loved her father to the verge of idolatry. From him she inherited her literary powers, and it was he who directed their aim. It was his object that in her life and writings she should be 'amiable, prudent, and of *use*.' Whether Richard Edgeworth helped or hindered his daughter's development as a writer is a controverted point. If he was responsible for her extreme utilitarianism, if he was responsible for her neglect of her best fictional gift, then he certainly was her evil genius. But, after all, in determining responsibility, we must remember that Maria was not merely under his influence, she was of his blood. By heredity and training she appears to have become his second self — the extension of his own personality. His advice seems almost always to have coincided with her own views, and she tells us of the help he gave her in plot-construction — a point in which she was weak. His part in her work went far beyond mere encouragement. During his lifetime he actually supervised her writings. First he required a preliminary outline of the story.

> Then he would in his own words fill up my sketch, paint the description, or represent the character intended, with such life, that I was quite convinced he not only seized ideas, but that he saw with the prophetic eye of taste the utmost that could be made of them . . . When he thought that there was spirit in what was written, but that it required great correction, he would say, 'Leave that to me; it is my business to cut and correct — yours to write on.'[34]

It was not his business, but whether his interference aided or crippled her powers is a point very difficult to determine. For example, his decisions to kill off King Corny and to spare the life of the reformed Lady Delacour (in *Belinda*) were sad errors. Against them must be set his contributions to *Patronage* and to *Ormod*. But one cannot forget that although Maria agreed with his utilitarian view of fiction, she did once have the impulse to write 'for fun', and the resultant work (written without her father's supervision) was her best. Whether the impulse returned and was stifled by Richard Edgeworth's passion for didacticism we shall never know. Can genius be stifled ? Does an eagle voluntarily fold its wings and walk?

From her youth Maria Edgeworth found her duty and her pleasure in teaching, whether it was the instruction of her little brothers and sisters or of the wider circle reached through her writings. Her first attempts at narrative, made at about the age of twenty, were the 'wee wee stories' which she wrote on a slate to please the younger children at Edgeworthstown. Soon she attained her first successes in print. *The Parent's Assistant* (1796–1800) and *Early Lessons* (1801–1815) were children's stories. *Moral Tales* (1801) were meant for young people of a more advanced age. In 1804 appeared *Popular Tales* specially written for middle-class readers. These volumes are the key to Maria Edgeworth's view of life and to her fictional technique. She evidently believed that God had ordained the differences in the social order, and that only by doing one's duty in one's appointed sphere could happiness be attained. Her tales and novels were simply fables by which to make platable her moral teaching. She was so certain, for example, of the difference between the bourgeois and the upper-class mind that, like Hannah More, she considered it necessary to devise a suitable approach to each. Her *Popular Tales* are all unassuming cheerfulness and industry. *Fashionable Tales* expose unfeeling frivolity and extravagance, and stress the need for accepting the responsibilities of wealth and exalted station. Unlike Mrs Inchbald, she never doubts the justice of the social order. When, for example, in *The Absentee* she shows a whole community groaning under the heel of oppression she appeals merely for a just exercise of power. She does not question that one man should have such power over the lives of others. Her own social position made such reflections impossible. Her views on morality are equally superficial, whether in her children's stories or in those intended for the grown-up. It is the child's duty to be good, amiable and useful. If he fulfils this duty he will be happy not only in avoiding the penalty of wrong-doing, but in the rewards invariably given to virtue. The naughty child can be reformed, but until reformation is achieved he must suffer not merely the penalty of disturbing the normal pattern of life, but active punishments also. So that the reader may not confuse good and evil, so that the issue may always be clear, there are no 'mixed characters ' among the children of Miss Edgeworth's pen. Simple Susan is a really good little girl. Lazy Lawrence is undoubtedly a bad boy. Their behaviour makes happiness and reward as inevitable for the one as unhappiness and punishment are for the other. The Edgeworths evidently held that, since their tales for children were meant to instruct, this simplification was necessary. They were not concerned with amusing the young, and either discounted or were unaware of the child's wish to hear stories simply for the stories' sake — to read not of paragons and pariahs, but of children like himself; to find food for the imagination in tales of magic and wonder. Fairies were banned at Edgeworthstown because they could not enforce moral principles and did not admit of rational explanation. It was the Edgeworth principle that everything should be explained with complete thoroughness. After all, Richard Edgeworth had published in 1802 a monstrous little book entitled *Poetry Explained for Young People*. The same rational outlook which deprived children of fairies deprived adults of romance, of all that is mysterious and unpredictable in human existence. In the stories intended for mature people Maria Edgeworth still offers the same simplified pattern. She avoids 'mixed characters' with all the moral earnestness that drove her to reject Mrs Inchbald's Rushbrook on the score that he told a lie. Since this simplification negated the knowledge and experience of maturity, it sinned grievously against art. To judge Maria's novels we must abandon the standards of reality and deliberately adopt the Edgeworth outlook. We must willingly become citizens of a world which we know does not exist — a schoolroom world where everything is reduced to clear, bright, cheerful sanity, where the good and industrious child wins the prize and the naughty, selfish child stands in the corner. To do Maria Edgeworth justice within the narrow limits of this her chosen myth we must at least suspend our disbelief.

When we do so, some really good qualities become apparent. It is true that her plots are weak not only because they are devised to point a moral, but even in resourcefulness. In this respect she tells us that she owed most to her father, and that, in fact, he invented the story of *Patronage* and told it aloud in installments before she wrote it. Still, passing over the question of construction, there are aspects that deserve praise. She had the narrator's gift of securing interest. We read her shallow stories and swallow her specific for happiness as a hypochondriac might swallow quack medicine — not because we believe, but because it seems so easy and infallible. These obvious motives, these issues capable of only one interpretation, these natures which know themselves and which are never puzzled or thwarted by irreconcilable impulses — because they are presented with charm and wit we can find pleasure in watching this mimic show. There is often an exuberance, a vivacity which gives these puppets a convincing appearance of life. In the lower social strata we are always conscious that it is the benevolent lady of the manor who pulls the strings. No 'small farmer' ever talked like Farmer Grey, despite the letter of testimony which Maria appends as a footnote. But in her stories of fashionable life she is at her ease. It was a life with which she was familiar, and therefore in conversation and social behaviour there are no false notes. Indeed the conversation of her worldlings is unusually excellent in its suavity and in its delicate and malicious fencing. This was a higher social level than the world of Jane Austen's heroines, but, like Jane Austen, Maria quarrels with the heartless snobbery and manoeuvring of such people. Maria, however, seriously sets herself to reform these worldlings. Jane simply laughs them out of existence. But Maria does poke fun at sensibility, notably in *Angelina, or l'amie inconnue*, in *Emilie de Coulanges*, and in *Patronage* where she tilts at Rosamund Percy. Maria is a votary of commonsense. So was Jane Austen, but Jane's commonsense and her instinct for the ludicrous could never have allowed her to reduce the whole of life to a tract. Jane's commonsense was the reasoning of a satiric genius; Maria's was the blind earnestness of a second-rate mind.

Maria Edgeworth was the first of the regional novelists. *Castle Rackrent*, *The Absentee*, *Ennui* and *Ormond* show that she was most successful in writing of the Irish life she knew. Nevertheless, since she never doubted the justice of the social order, it may be doubted whether she was qualified to become the national novelist of a country in which the social order was no natural growth, but an unnatural imposition. Ireland in the early nineteenth century was a dual Ireland locked in mutual and deadly opposition. It was entering on the last phase of that struggle which had continued down the ages. For centuries there had existed side by side two separate peoples, two separate racial traditions, two languages, two literatures, two codes of law, two ways of life and thought — all utterly irreconcilable. Time had resolved the struggle externally into a social system consisting of two strata, an alien system superimposed upon the native system. It had been possible to disrupt the Irish pattern of life, to break the sense of continuity with the past and to condemn the native Irish to a general level of poverty and illiteracy. Yet Irish remained the habitual speech of a very large number of the people and indeed was spoken up to the outskirts of Dublin city. Not only so, but there was still a remnant of the Gaelic school of writers. Out of that conflict had grown the Anglo-Irish dialect. The people who used it still conserved their ancient music, poetry and legends (transmitted by oral tradition), and their old customs, now dim in origin.

From these two classes, therefore — the Ascendancy class and the native Irish class — the Irish novelists of the nineteenth century must emerge, and their interpretation of that material would depend on their particular experience and point of view. One would expect two different kinds of Irish novel: that which dealt with Ascendancy life and with the peasants in relation to their masters; that which dealt with the life of the common people and with the masters in relation to the oppressed. In fact these two schools of fiction came into existence. The cultural advantage lay with the more educated class. Nevertheless, it was certain that the more Ascendancy the tone of the novel the more it would approximate to English life, since the higher the level of Irish society the fewer Irish characteristics were to be expected. But the descendants of the old Irish people were intensely themselves, and as such could not fail to be a rich source of inspiration to the novelist, an unworked mine of speech and behaviour. Yet who could write of the simple people of Ireland? Only those who were near enough to know them; if possible, one of themselves; someone who shared their daily life, their speech, their outlook, who realized their sources of action and re-action. Could such a man have the necessary equipment of education, and if he had not, what kind of novel would result? Time would tell. Meanwhile a writer emerged, as was most natural, from the class which had the greatest access to culture. Maria Edgeworth turned her eyes to the contemporary Irish scene.

Maria Edgeworth belonged to the Ascendancy class. There were other factors which diminished her opportunities of giving a true picture of Irish life. She came to Ireland at the age of sixteen. Since she had been reared in England, she brought to Ireland a set of values which could not apply in a very different state of society. In addition, her privileged social position did not help her to establish contact with that class of people which constituted the majority of the population. For these reasons she remained, despite her kindliness, an outsider. Yet the air she breathed was Irish air and she was impelled to write of Ireland. In 1800, the year of the Act of Union, there appeared her first novel, *Castle Rackrent*. This she wrote 'for fun' and without her father's supervision. It was her only work free from didacticism and her greatest achievement—facts which should have given her food for thought had she realized them.

Castle Rackrent records the annals of the old Irish family which, from one generation to another, pursues the rollicking way to perdition. It is told through the lips of an ancient retainer, Honest Thady—a character whom Maria draws from a steward on the Edgeworth estate. She says that she grew so accustomed to this steward's dialect that she could think and speak it without effort. That this was so is abundantly evident in the facility with which this vivid narrative flowed from her pen. The other three Irish novels contain much that is of value, much too that is worthless. The alternation between her natural bent and her deliberate didacticism is well seen in *Ormond*.[35] One moment we are in the wild domain of the Black Isles, observing with delight the uproarious nobility of King Corney; the next, there is Ormond snivelling (there is no other word for it) his repentance for having unwittingly intervened between Moriarty and his coquettish Peggy. It must truly be said, however, that Sir Ulick O'Shane is not merely a ruffian in black and white. Miss Edgeworth shows us that Sir Ulick justified to himself his own opportunism and knavery. His epitaph, spoken by one of the grave-diggers, represents her own view: 'There lies the makings of an excellent gentleman—but the cunning of his head spoiled the goodness of his heart.' As for King Corney, he was 'the true thing and never changed'. This hard-drinking, practical, daring, generous creature has about him something of the rugged splendour of those kings who won and retained power by their own strength. When he dies (killed by the intervention of Richard Edgeworth) the real interest of the story dies with him. He revenged his untimely end by dwarfing the rest of the characters and making the virtuous and sententious folk seem very mawkish.

But there are in Maria Edgeworth's novels curious evidences of myopia. In *Ennui* she uses the rebellion of 1798 really as a means of relieving Lord Glenthorne's sense of futility. The plot of the United Irishmen (to make Glenthorne their leader or, alternatively, to kill him) would seem to indicate a degree of impulsiveness unusual even among the native Irish. And what are we to say to a writer who, having explained that the Clonbrony estate has been drained dry by the infamous agent, yet shows the incognito Lord Colambre being lavishly entertained in the cottage of the Widow O'Neill. He sups on bacon and eggs, potatoes, milk and butter; and there would have been a chicken had there been time to prepare it. He breakfasts on white bread, tea, cream, butter and eggs. Truly such hospitality is little calculated to show the evils of absenteeism.

Rebellion and famine, 'the state of the country'— of these Miss Edgeworth was aware. They did not induce her to change her chosen tone, but finally they caused her to give up writing of Ireland. In 1834, in a letter to her brother in India, explaining why *Helen* was not an Irish novel, Maria Edgeworth made this most illuminating remark: 'It is impossible to draw Ireland as she is now in a book of fiction— realities are too strong— party passions are too violent to bear to see, or care to look at their faces in the looking glass. The people would only break the glass and curse the fool who held the mirror up to nature.' One remembers that the Lady of Shallot could no longer spin when one glance at reality shivered her mirror to atoms. Even if Maria Edgeworth were not unable, it seems certain that she was unwilling to include in her novels any analysis of Irish life. The *Edinburgh Review* of 1831 says in regard to her Irish works: 'We are not sufficiently told the influence of circumstances upon the national character, nor what in each individual is natural and what the result of his opinion. There is a careful avoidance of political topics, the bearing of which upon Irish society is too marked and important to be altogether omitted.' In so far as politics represent the impact of history upon human life they could scarcely be omitted from the Irish novel. Unless the writer showed the causes which underlay rack-rents, evictions, tithe-proctors, hedge-schools and secret societies, then Irish figures in fiction would appear as meaningless as marionettes, acting without autonomy, out of no causation, dancing convulsively in response to the controlling finger. It was this cautious refusal to touch the roots of Irish life which led to the superficial growth of what may be called the Irish colonial novel. Its greatest exponents were the witty Lever and the farcical Lover.

The relation between Maria Edgeworth's picture of Irish life and the real life which surrounded her is essential to an estimate of her art, but her Irish stories carried conviction to those who did not fully know Ireland, and proved an inspiration to Scott[36] and to Turgeniev. Scott indeed had more claim to be styled a national novelist than had Maria Edgeworth, since he presented the people of his country as an integral whole, without that squinted vision which results from closing one eye. It was, of course, a simpler matter for him, because Scotland was not divided by an abnormal stratification.

A detailed examination of all Maria Edgeworth's fictional work is beyond the scope of this work, nor would such an examination add anything essential to the general criticisms we have offered. Still we may spare a little space for a brief outline of some of the stories which we have not already mentioned. These may all be loosely classified as tales of fashionable life. In 1801 appeared *Belinda*, which begins very interestingly after the manner of Fanny Burney, but soon dwindles into moral teaching and improbability. Belinda, like Evelina, makes her entrance into society under difficult circumstances. She is entrusted to the brilliant and worldly Lady Delacour who, in a negligent way, is her sponsor in the marriage market. Lady Delacour is a very unhappy woman who tries by perpetual gaiety, flirtation and social triumph to forget the failure of her married life and the horror of being (as she erroneously believes) the victim of cancer. The locked room where she keeps her medicines excites her husband's jealousy, and leads to complications in which Belinda is involved. That gentle paragon[37] has fallen in love with Clarence Hervey who at first affronts her pride, more crudely indeed, but still in much the same way as Darcy offends Elizabeth Bennet. He comes to love her, but does not feel free to propose because a foundling whom he has reared according to Rousseauistic principles wishes to marry him out of gratitude. Belinda then imagines herself in love with a Creole, but these tangles, introduced to protract the course of true love, are unravelled in the end.

Lady Delacour is at her best in her moods of defiant brilliance. It is a theatrical brilliance, but it greatly impressed contemporary readers. A much-praised scene is that in which Lady Delacour, who believes herself dying, imagines even the faithful Belinda to be her enemy. But Lady Delacour redeemed and reunited to her husband does not hold our interest. Maria would have done better had she adhered to her first intention of making her die.

There is plenty of humour in this novel, and much excellent dialogue. Maria Edgeworth well knew the different varieties of fool, and she amuses herself with portraying the weak but good-natured Lord Delacour and the malicious numbskull, Sir Philip Baddely. Sir Philip's proposal to Belinda, undertaken merely so as to make 'Clary look blue', is very diverting. It gives rise to such a rejection scene as previous novelists had described, and which was to become the climax of *Pride and Prejudice*. But Darcy and Elizabeth were deep in love and understanding. Between Sir Philip and Belinda there was only vanity and distaste.

Leonora (1806) was considered to be Maria Edgeworth's retort to Madame de Staël's *Delphine*. It is supposed to have been written with the hope of pleasing the Chevalier Edelcrantz, whose proposal of marriage Maria felt obliged to refuse. *Leonora* is a novel in letters, which resembles in subject Elizabeth Griffith's *The Delicate Distress*. In 1809 appeared the first series of *Tales of Fashionable Life*, comprising *Ennui, The Dun, Manoeuvring* and *Almeria*. The second series (which appeared in 1812) consisted of *Vivian, The Absentee, Madame Fleury* and *Emilie de Coulanges*. *Ennui* is a most wearisome book, relieved only by the amusing description of Lord Glenthorne's journey to his estate in the west of Ireland. The plot unrolls itself at first in so desultory a manner that it seems to be merely an essay on ennui relieved by anecdotes and slices of Baedeker. When the plot thickens it befuddles us with such improbabilities as the discovery that the humble Christy O'Donoghue is the real Lord Glenthorne. The question of absenteeism is prominently treated. *The Dun* is a homily on the injustice of not paying one's debts. *Manoeuvring* shows a cunning woman defeating by her deviousness the very aim she wishes to achieve. *Almeria* is the story of a vulgar heiress casting off the friends of her obscure days for fashionable people who sneer at her. Her social climbing brings upon her the heavy punishment of lonely spinsterhood. *Vivian*, which Scott greatly admired, is the life-story of a domestic Hamlet.[38] His vacillations involve himself and others in much misery. Evidently daunted by the difficulty of strengthening his will, Maria causes him to be killed in a duel.

The Absentee shows the injustice of landlords who live away from their estates on rents extorted from the harassed tenantry. In *Ennui* McLeod, the honest agent, is contrasted with the rascally agent Hardcastle. In *The Absentee* that pitiless schemer, Nick Gerraghty, is the villain of the piece. The Clonbronys live in London because Lady Clonbrony wishes to shine socially. She is willing to return to Ireland only when she is forced to realize that she is the butt of those fashionable people whom she has so abjectly tried to cultivate. Her son Lord Colambre, who has seen for himself the misery of the people on the Clonbrony estate, persuades his parents that by living at home they will secure their own happiness and that of their tenants. Lord Colambre's sudden visit to Clonbrony is, despite its improbabilities, the most interesting part of the story. The scene where he reveals himself to his tenants and to the tyrannical Gerraghty has been compared by Macaulay to the recognition scene in the Odyssey. This might have been a really good Irish novel, but it is spoiled by its didacticism. The narrowness of Maria's moral code is but too apparent in the fact that, though Colambre loves Grace Nugent, he is prepared to abandon her because she is supposed to be illegitimate. But Grace Nugent is proved to have been born in wedlock, and her reward is marriage with Colambre and the privilege of spending her fortune in the rehabilitation of the Clonbrony estate. Another instance of Maria's wish to eat her cake and have it is that, although she wrote *Harrington* as a vindication of the Jews, she finds it necessary, at the last moment, to disclose that her heroine is not a Jewess, but 'a Christian — a Protestant'. She lacks the courage to abide by the consequence of her didactic thesis, and constantly disappoints us by dishonestly twisting the plot to escape the issue she has deliberately raised.

There is nothing much to be said of her remaining stories. *Patronage* has the same faults and the same good qualities as the other novels. It is shamelessly didactic and employs throughout the device of contrast which made her fiction so diagrammatic. *Madame Fleury* tells how a charitable lady is saved from the guillotine by those who have benefited by her benevolence. *Emilie de Coulanges* cleverly exposes the essential egoism in sensibility. *Helen*, written years after her father's death, shows a great falling off in power.

In summing up Maria Edgeworth's literary achievements one is forced to discount much of the praise assigned to her by over-generous critics. At every point she appears to have been incapable of the best. It is said that she excelled as a writer of children's stories and as a didactic novelist, and also that she showed much facility in the use of the short story form. The last claim only can one admit without reservation. The first depends on whether children prefer Frank and Rosamund to Brer Fox and Brer Rabbit or *Treasure Island*. The claim of didactic pre-eminence is in itself sufficient to range a novelist on a lower artistic level. The question of her Irish sketches remains. Her interest in local colour was secondary to her didactic purpose except in one single work—*Castle Rackrent*, on which must be based her surest claim as a novelist. Her greatest achievement lies in the fact that, although she had no clearly conceived intention and had imagined no corresponding artistic form, her novels did suggest the idea of regionalism to later writers.

A Scottish counterpart of Maria Edgeworth was Susan Ferrier (1782-1854). Like Scott, she had kept a half-written novel in a drawer for years, but *Waverley* was published four years before *Marriage* appeared. Susan Ferrier was not a follower of Scott. Her novels contain in general the same constituents as those of Maria Edgeworth. They are tales of fashionable life, blending a delineation of Scottish manners with a didactic purpose. But within this similarity there was a very considerable difference between the Irishwoman and her Scots sister of the quill. Susan Ferrier was much less didactic and had a far greater grasp of reality than Maria Edgeworth. She had a strong and satiric mind, but she lacked Maria Edgeworth's sympathetic tolerance. Both had plenty of wit and humour, but Maria's was mellow: Susan's was malicious and even pitiless. Maria presented 'characters', but despite their individual modes of thought and behaviour they are too essentially human to be called eccentric. Susan's 'characters' are a delight, but it must be admitted that they are often caricatures. In this she resembled Fanny Burney, as Maria resembled Fanny Burney in her portraits of the rich and noble. Like Maria, Susan Ferrier was weak in plot-invention, but whereas Maria was led away chiefly by her didacticism, Susan (also digressing and dwindling into pedagogy) was becalmed by her intense pleasure in vivisecting her eccentrics. She holds up, indeed she frequently forgets, the plot while for her own diversion and ours she carefully oils her originals and as carefully disposes them on the gridiron for roasting.[39] They were originals in more senses than one. It was Susan Ferrier's method to draw such characters from the life, and this was evidently the reason why she delayed so long in publishing her first novel, and remained, even after her initial triumph, always rather hesitant in venturing into print.

Marriage (1818) grew from Susan's realization of the rich harvest of humour to be gained by introducing an English society belle into the household of a Scottish laird. Since a frivolous butterfly like Lady Juliana would never voluntarily exile herself in a Scottish glen, Susan Ferrier invented circumstances which would force her to do so. Lady Juliana refuses to marry the wealthy old duke of her father's choice, and elopes with Harry Douglas who is dependent on his army pay. He is suspended for being absent without leave; she is disowned by her father, and nothing remains but to take refuge with Harry's father — the Laird of Glenfern. Everything goes badly from the moment of their arrival. Lady Juliana is merely a pettish child, who makes not the slightest effort to disguise her horror at the dreary residence and farouche manners of her new relations. There are three long-chinned spinster aunts: Miss Jacky, the sensible woman of the parish; Miss Grizzy who is merely distinguishable from nothing; and Miss Nicky who as an individual is non-existent. There are also 'five awkward purple girls' — Harry's sisters, at the sight of whom his highbred wife 'gave way to the anguish that mocked control.' All these worthy creatures are quite unconscious that they are the abomination of desolation. They shower kindness on dear Harry's wife. When, as most frequently happens, she simulates a faint to express her nausea at her surroundings or at some Scottish phenomenon such as the pipes, the spinster ladies dose her with potent herbal brews, or revive her with a bowl of greasy cockie-leekie soup. Then again there is the terrific Lady MacLoughlin who speaks unvarnished truths and strides rough-shod over all mealy-mouthed efforts at politeness. Never is this more evident than when the ladies of Glenfern, accompanied by Lady Juliana, array themselves in their richest attire and set out for Lochmarlie Castle in acceptance of an invitation from Lady MacLoughlin. When they arrive they find they are not expected, and they are grimly received by Lady MacLoughlin who 'regarded the invaders with her usual marble aspect, and without moving either joint or muscle as they drew near.'

> 'I declare—I don't think you know us, Lady MacLoughlin,' said Miss Grizzy in a tone of affected vivacity, with which she strove to conceal her agitation.
>
> 'Know you!' repeated her friend—'humph! Who you are, I know very well; but what brings you here, I do not know. Do you know yourselves?'
>
> 'I declare—I can't conceive—' began Miss Grizzy; but her trepidation arrested her speech, and her sister therefore proceeded—
>
> 'Your ladyship's declaration is no less astonishing than incomprehensible. We have waited upon you by your own express invitation on the day appointed by yourself; and we have been received in a manner, I must say, we did not expect, considering this is the first visit of our niece, Lady Juliana Douglas.'
>
> 'I'll tell you what, girls,' replied their friend, as she still stood with her back to the fire, and her hands behind her; 'I'll tell you what—you are not yourselves—you are all lost—quite mad—that's all—humph!'[40]

A violent quarrel ensues, but the matter is cleared up when Lady MacLoughlin says that though she may have mentioned Tuesday in her letter she really meant Thursday. When Miss Grizzy meekly says that Tuesday was the day she read in Lady MacLoughlin's letter, that redoubtable woman closes the subject by declaring: 'How could you be such a fool, my love, as to read it any such thing? Even if it had been written Tuesday, you might have had the sense to know it meant Thursday. '

But unfortunately for the reader, he is soon dragged away from these delights to starve on moralizing. Following the usual didactic pattern, Miss Ferrier presents us with a strong contrast to the petulant Lady Juliana. In the person of Mrs Douglas we are shown that an Englishwoman may be happy on a Scottish estate, and may find happiness in marriage, even though duty has forbidden her to marry the man of her own choice. Thence the scene shifts to London. Lady Juliana leaves in the care of Mrs Douglas, Mary, one of her twin daughters, and takes with her Adelaide. Before long Lady Juliana's brainless behaviour ruins her husband's prospects, and he goes on foreign service.

She and Adelaide find refuge in her brother's home. After a lapse of years we are presented with the contrast between Mary and Adelaide; the one a most wearying miracle of sententiousness and sensibility, the other a languid young worldling. The didactic purpose works itself out to a suitable conclusion, but there is no dearth of amusing characters, and in addition we make the acquaintance of the inimitable Mrs Macshake and Dr Redgill.

Susan Ferrier's second novel, *The Inheritance* (1824), was far better than her first. Its plot is more skilfully devised, and we are again entertained with diverting character studies. The inheritance is the earldom and estates of Rossville to which the heroine, Gertrude St Clair, comes as heiress presumptive. In due time she succeeds, but soon an American imposter called Lewiston claims that she is really his daughter. She finds it impossible to refute his lying assertions, but the loss of the title and property rids her at least of her false lover Colonel Delmour. She marries her true lover who later becomes Lord Rossville.

Amongst the many excellent characters in this novel the best of all is Miss Pratt:

> In the hum-drum society of a dull county, what a relief to the weary soul to have some person to be weary of! To have a sort of bag-fox to turn out, when fresh game cannot be had, is an enjoyment which many of my readers have doubtless experienced. Such was Miss Pratt—everybody wearied of her, or said they wearied of her, and everybody abused her, while yet she was more sought after and asked about, than she would have been had she possessed the wisdom of a More, or the benevolence of a Fry. She was, in fact, the very heart of the shire, and gave life and energy to all the pulses of the parish. She supplied it with streams of gossip and chit-chat in others and subject of ridicule and abuse in herself.[41]

Miss Pratt is the particular *bête noire* of the pompous and finical Lord Rossville, whose feelings she unwittingly lacerates by her every word and deed. The climax is reached when she arrives at his mansion in a hearse, the only convenience she can find to carry her through a snowstorm. Her nephew, Anthony White (whom she always quotes, but who never gives proof of his existence), seems to be the ancestor of Sarah Gamp. Miss Pratt is a character whom Jane Austen would have gladly owned. Another excellent personage is Uncle Adam, said to have been drawn from Susan Ferrier's father, but having, as Saintsbury suggests, prophetic touches of no less a person than Carlyle. Uncle Adam is related to Gertrude St Clair through her mother—and this more plebeian side of the family offers such gems of characterization as Lilly Black, and Major and Mrs Waddell whose bridal tour can never be forgotten.

Miss Ferrier's third novel, *Destiny* (1831), shows an increasing power of plot-construction, but a falling off in vivacity. There is a greater seriousness in tone and a more marked didacticism, yet the old satiric spirit is still evident in such portraits as that of the odious McDow. *Destiny* was Susan Ferrier's last published work and though she could have continued to profit by her popularity as a writer, it speaks well for her strong critical sense that she knew when to retire. Her literary reputation stands in some respects lower than Maria Edgeworth's, in some respects higher. She made a valuable contribution to Scottish fiction. Her power of satiric characterization was great—great, that is to say, until we compare it with the artistic subtlety of Jane Austen.

Notes and References

1 Charlotte Smith, *Desmond* (Dublin, 1792), Preface, p. iii.
2 Ibid., vol. i, p, 37.
3 Ibid., vol. i, p. 40.
4 Ibid., vol. i, p. 47
5 Ibid., vol. i, p. 48.
6 *The Works of Mary Wollstonecraft* (eds. Janet Todd and Marilyn Butler, assistant ed. Emma Rees Mogg, William Pickering, London, 1989), *A Vindication of the Rights of Woman*, vol. v, p. 131.
7 Ibid., *A Vindication of the Rights of Woman*, vol. v, p. 146.
8 Ibid., *The Cave of Fancy*, vol. i, p. 203.
9 Ibid., *The Cave of Fancy*, vol. i, p. 205
10 Published posthumously in 1798.
11 *The Works of Mary Wollstonecraft*, op. cit., *The Wrongs of Woman: Or, Maria*, vol. i, pp. 116–17.
12 Ibid., *The Wrongs of Woman: Or, Maria*, vol. i, pp. 118–19.
13 Ibid., *The Wrongs of Woman: Or, Maria*, vol. i, p. 119.
14 Ibid., *The Wrongs of Woman: Or, Maria*, vol. i, p. 132.
15 Ibid., *The Wrongs of Woman: Or, Maria*, vol. i, pp. 149–52.
16 This, like Mrs Opie's *Brother and Sister*, was an echo of Agnes Primrose in Mrs Inchbald's *Nature and Art*.
17 Her other works of fiction were: *Translation of the Letters of a Hindoo Rajah* (1796) and *The Cottagers of Glenburnie* (1808). This latter work, which preceded Waverley is written to inculcate in the working classes a love of industry and orderliness. To stress her didactic point, Mrs Hamilton presents with grim realism the ignorance, squalor and misery too often found in the villages she knew. It is well worth

noting that her rustic dialogues are in the Scottish vernacular.

18 Elizabeth Hamilton, *Memoirs of Modern Philosophers* (3rd edn. 1801), ii, p. 77.

19 For this quotation Mrs Hamilton wickedly appends the footnote 'See *Caleb Williams*.'

20 Elizabeth Hamilton, *Memoirs of Modern Philosophers* (3rd. edn. 1801), iii, p. 143.

21 Ibid., ii, p. 89.

22 Written in 1777.

23 The words actually occur in *Nature and Art* (ch. viii), but they are more applicable to *A Simple Story*.

24 Elizabeth Inchbald, *A Simple Story* (ed. J.M.S. Tompkins, new Intro. Jane Spencer, Oxford University Press, 1988), p. 72.

25 Ibid., p. 15.

26 Ibid., pp. 28–29.

27 Elizabeth Inchbald, *Nature and Art* (1796), ch. vi.

28 Ibid., ch. xv.

29 Ibid., ch. xiii.

30 Elizabeth Opie, *Father and Daughter* (9th. edn., 1824), pp. 231 f.

31 Amelia Opie, *Adeline Mowbray: Or, The Mother and Daughter* (Intro. Jeanette Winterson, 'Mothers of the Novel', Pandora, London, 1986), p. 227.

32 Ibid., p. 93.

33 I.e. *Simple Tales* (1801), *Temper, or Domestic Scenes* (1812), *Tales of Real Life* (1813), *Valentine's Eve* (1816), *New Tales* (1818), *Tales of the Hearth* (1820), *Madeline* (1822).

34 *Black Book*, p. 142.

35 In regard to Richard Edgeworth's contribution to this novel Maria writes: 'The following parts of *Ormond* were written for me by my dear father in his last Illness: The death of King Corney . . . the whole of Moriarty's history of his escape from prison . . . also the meeting between Moriarty and his wife, when he jumps out of the carriage the moment he hears her voice.' (*Black Book*, p. 229) These interpolations are certainly well written, but although they equal Maria's average writing, they are not comparable to the best of her Irish sketches.

36 See 'General Preface' to 1829 edn. of Scott's novels; also the original edition of *Waverley*.

37 Maria Edgeworth herself speaks of 'the cold tameness of that stick or stone, Belinda'. Yet she continued to present such heroines, e.g. Grace Nugent, Helen, Miss Annaly.

38 So Julia Kavenagh calls him (*English Women of Letters*, 1863, vol. ii, p. 159).

39 Saintsbury uses this amusing metaphor (*Essays in English Literature*, 1780–1860, 2nd. series, 1895, p. 170).

40 Susan Ferrier, *Marriage, A Novel* (ed. Herbert Foltinek, Oxford University Press, London, 1977), p. 105.

41 Susan Ferrier, *The Inheritance* (Intro James E. M. Irvine, Three River Books, Bampton, Oxfordshire, 1984), p. 82.

Chapter XIV

Jane Austen

Genius should be judged only by its peers, and not merely by those of equal, but of similar powers. It is because such juridical conditions are impossible that literary criticism fails in proportion to a writer's greatness. How humbly then must critics of Jane Austen approach the mystery of her art, asking pardon (like the clumsy headsman) before proceeding to hack to pieces what they could never create. For when all has been said, when every tittle of evidence has been adduced, when her brain and her heart have been weighed and dissected, how far have we progressed towards the secret of her unique power? While we are fumbling through the post-mortem the elusive spirit mocks us where we cannot follow.

Jane Austen's genius was unique not merely in its peculiar essence, but in what one can only term its spontaneous maturity. Dispensing with the evolutionary stages of childhood, it sprang fully armed into the arena of letters. Although her artistic powers developed, her mental attitude at the age of fourteen is the same as it was at forty. There is evidence that at times her artistic balance was disturbed by the strength of her ethical convictions, but such waverings were only partial and momentary. They never caused a complete lack of poise, and they were always followed by a return to equilibrium so triumphant as to prove more than ever the insistence of her inspiration. Were she of a cold, impassive nature it would have been easier for her to maintain an invincible uniformity, but actually she was possessed of such intense energy as to make it impossible for her not to think and feel strongly. It is this energy of mind and heart which gives such vitality to her novels, and this force is all the more dynamic for being controlled and directed by an acute judgment. Jane Austen seems to have been born with a fine sense of values, and with an instinct for proportion which gave her mind its characteristic bent. 'To the soul is given intelligence and that delectation that cometh from the contemplation of truth.' This is the delectation which absorbed her life and which her articulateness offers to us with all the perfection of art. Truth, or sanity, or 'commonsense'—call it what you will—it was for this she hungered, for this that, even as a child, she felt impelled to reject all that was false in literary symbolism, and to forge for herself an appropriate technique. Jane Austen's 'commonsense' does not connote a bread-and-butter philosophy. Despite crass misunderstanding and reiteration, it does not mean the exclusion of beauty and romance from life, and the substitution of worldly wisdom. By 'common-sense' Jane Austen meant the repudiation of uncontrolled emotionalism, of grandiose clap-trap and melodrama, of hypocrisy and self-deception. It is a word which has been used so often in a narrow and utilitarian sense that we are disinclined to give it its positive value. Jane Austen's passion for 'commonsense' was a passion for reality—a mordant dissatisfaction with false standards of life. At first it was the falsity of novels which aroused her. Then, no longer content with showing the discrepancy between real life and literary misrepresentations, her attention was caught and held by the illusions and deceptions of human beings. A real world in which no one faced reality—in which each man spun for himself a cocoon of delusion; a world with no positive set of values since every mind was a separate kingdom; a world where bodily solitude and mental communion were equally impossible, where no man understood his neighbour nor even himself—a jostling, lonely, selfish, kindly, mean and noble world; a mad world—Jane Austen sharpened her quill.

Literature has grown out of the revolt against some aspect of life or of art. Emily Brontë was a rebel chained in the outer darkness of earthly life, trying to free herself by terrific convulsions of the spirit. Jane Austen was a rebel who freed herself by laughter, and, because she was not a fool, the laughter was ironic. The individual confronted by a majority holding an opposite opinion must either yield or resist. If he resists it cannot be merely a passive preference for his own view. It must be a direct negative, taking some tinge from the dissenter's feeling of isolation—an attitude of rebellion expressing itself in slashing attack, or more subtly transmuted into a feeling of superiority. It is the sense at once of rightness and of isolation which gives the ironic outlook.

Jane Austen was thus a dissenter. She did not subscribe to the delusions of life; neither could she tolerate literary flights from reality. The romanticists did not quarrel with the limitations of stunted minds and sordid aims. They simply took refuge in another world, and in fiction their efforts to express their romantic conceptions resulted in wild exaggeration. It was not in Jane Austen's nature to take fire from the Romantic Revival. She not merely evaded, but she deliberately repudiated it. Her interest was in human life as she knew it — an inexhaustible mine, and one very little worked. And it was not merely the romanticists' avowed flight from reality which she disowned, but the deplorable tradition of the Heroic Romance, which in itself had been sufficiently bad, but which, when vulgarized to suit middle-class tastes, had become quite shocking from an aesthetic point of view. The deification of emotionalism which evinced itself as sensibility was a further phenomenon of insincerity and lack of proportion. The novel which resulted from this blend of Heroic tradition, bourgeois taste and pseudo-introspection was a deplorable affair; the Gothic novel was a romantic illusion with sensibility as its plague-spot; the didactic novel was a prostitution of art. All ignored or distorted everyday life. No wonder that Jane Austen, with gales of ironic merriment, brought these pasteboard erections to the ground. Yet she owed them something. The characteristic outlook which led her to revolt was strengthened and clarified by these proofs of unreality taken to excess. On the other hand, these fictional exaggerations were partly responsible for the rigidity with which she denied herself emotional expression in her novels. She was like a sensitive woman in a house of mourning who, nauseated by noisy grief and melodramatic ebullitions, bites her lips and determines to show no emotion at all. 'I detest jargon of every kind [says Marianne in *Sense and Sensibility*] and sometimes I have kept my feelings to myself, because I could find no language to describe them in but what was worn and hackneyed out of all sense and meaning.'[1]

The attitude of amused detachment which was instinctive with Jane Austen (and which appears most strongly in those of her letters preserved by Cassandra) led her inevitably to fashion a corresponding technique. The ironic focus not only allowed, but necessitated the reticence of the author. However pleasing this reticence may have been when she set herself to expose exaggerated styles of fiction, she must have found it essential in the delineation of emotions and sentiments. It was a means of avoiding personal statements on subjects towards which her discretion, shyness, or her own personal experiences dictated an indirect approach. The aloofness thus secured by the ironic approach was reinforced by Jane Austen's use of the dramatic technique. But it must be said that although one may unravel the causes underlying her use of her particular technique, it is certain that she did not consciously reason out her choice of instruments, but instinctively fashioned the medium of story-telling most suited to her temperament. In a word, her sensitiveness sought the defence of irony, and irony gave to her mind a particular attitude which achieved its aim by characteristic means.

Jane Austen's use of the ironic focus, reinforced by the dramatic technique, involved a particular choice of material and certain manipulations of this subject-matter. One would expect the ironic mind to be mainly interested in human relationships, in the inter-play of motive and behaviour which constitutes the eternal comedy of life. Since Jane Austen was supremely an artist it followed that she would keep within the limits of her experience. They were narrow limits—a 'little bit (two inches wide) of ivory.' The daugh-ter of a country parson at the end of the eighteenth century was almost entirely restricted not merely to her immediate surround-ings, but to her own social class. Jane Austen did not feel cramped by such limitations. Indeed she says: 'Three or four families in a country village is the very thing to work on.'[2] In *Pride and Prejudice* she explains why such material is sufficient.

> 'I did not know before [says Bingley to Elizabeth] that you were a studier of character. It must be an amusing study.'
> 'Yes, but intricate characters are the most amusing. They have at least that advantage.'
> 'The country,' said Darcy, 'can in general supply but a few subjects for such study. In a country neighbourhood you move in a very confined and unvarying society.'
> 'But people themselves alter so much, that there is some-thing new to be observed in them forever.'[3]

Jane Austen as a little girl rolling down the green slope at the back of Steventon rectory, Jane Austen the gay butterfly leading a cotillion, Jane Austen with but a month to live—at every stage there is evident her absorption in human behaviour and her minute dissection of motive and mannerism; at every stage she delivers judgement in tones that are gently mocking or coldly merciless. She has been too often blamed for the searing quality of her criticisms, which are adduced as proof that she had no heart. The truth seems to be that she had a heart which repudiated scornfully all that was evil, pretentious, hypocritical or poisonously silly. She had an ideal of inner harmony—to be achieved by honesty, sanity and self-control—and against those who fell short of these principles her judgments were launched with all the added impetus of feeling. But good-natured foolishness she treated gently, as witness Mrs Jennings and Miss Bates. It is not easy to reconcile the impulses of a sensitive heart and a relentless mind. Jane Austen had a mind which deprived itself of all the comforts of illusion, which obliged her to face the facts about herself and others, and to relate every word and action to the general sum of personality. As she says of Anne Elliot engaged in ruthless self-examination: 'One half of her should not always be so much wiser than the other half.' It was not merely that Jane Austen judged with pitiless justice. She observed with a selectivity, a minute realism and an analytic force which exactly served her dispassionate purpose. In her letters (which, as the direct account of actual events, are most valuable in this connection) there are many instances of her razor-keen perception. For example, in describing a ball, she says:

> There were very few beauties, and such as there were were not very handsome. Miss Iremonger did not look well, and Miss Blount was the only one much admired. She appeared exactly as she did in September with the same broad face, diamond bandeau, white shoes, pink husband, and fat neck. The two Miss Coxes were there: I traced in one the remains of the vulgar, broad-featured girl who danced at Enham eight years ago; the other is refined into a nice composed-looking girl, like Catherine Bigg. I looked at Sir Thomas Champneys and thought of poor Rosalie; I looked at his daughter and thought her a queer animal with a white neck.[4]

The words are mordant, but it is not the words which matter, but the kind of perception which they record. As the angle of vision or an effect of lighting makes a familiar object seem strange, so does Jane Austen's individual point of view find unending novelty in the human scene around her. She withdraws, viewing it from such a standpoint that the objects of her observation are no longer the people whose personal history and manners she knows by heart. In this perspective they take on new aspects—aspects as curious as that of Miss Champneys who suddenly appears sub-human—a queer animal with a white neck. The power that, by a trick of focus, could find new appearances in solid bodies could never be at a loss for novelty in the instability of human behaviour, for it is true that 'Nobody ever feels or acts, suffers or enjoys, as one expects.'[5] Revolution and war, great movements, religious, social, political and literary—all the wider issues of life flowed by her, while she viewed under the microscope one single drop from a stagnant pool. Under the lens of her genius this drop became a microcosm teeming with the most varied and interesting forms of life.

The ironic technique[6] employed by Jane Austen narrowed her chosen field still further. As a satirist she was confronted not merely with the novelist's usual problem of presenting human life, but of presenting it in such a way as to imply critical comment. The satirist's first duty is to maintain the ironic tone throughout—a task which calls for the most impeccable artistry. To do so he must preserve what one may call the unity of satire, introducing only such characters as lend themselves to satiric treatment or at least serve to show others in a satiric light. He must be very sparing in the use of background, of nature, or of any other factor which might divert the attention from the human involvement which is being portrayed. He must avoid direct expressions of emotion which must be suggested by understatement rather than by exposition, by silence rather than by speech, by the hints offered in word and deed. Even behaviour should not often express a direct reaction, but rather, skipping a link or two, should represent a stage in the sequence of thought which must serve as a clue to the first cause. In a word, the ironic focus, working by undertone and understatement, requires subtlety from both author and reader, and this exigence partly explains why Jane Austen's novels have taken so long to come into their own, and why even now they tend to remain caviare to the general. They are works for the mental gymnast—a fact which she herself fully realized. She says: 'I do not write for such dull elves as have not a great deal of ingenuity themselves.' The necessity of securing the reader's active co-operation is rendered more acute by Jane Austen's use of the dramatic method. The ironic focus is not in itself a sufficient smoke-screen for the writer who wishes to keep his own views to himself. Ironic comment is a form of disguise easily penetrated by the reader, who has only to follow the satiric finger-post; but the dramatic method renders the author completely unobtrusive, and gives the characters an apparent autonomy. It involves still further subtlety, however, requiring from the writer the most carefully balanced relation between words and action, thought and speech. In dialogue especially it calls for the skill of a virtuoso. To succeed in a medium compounded of satiric and dramatic technique is to reach the highest peak of artistry in fiction. It calls for the most exquisite minuteness and forethought in planning and execution, for those tiny and perfect strokes by which so little seems achieved after the most patient and unwearying care. Such an aim had never before been projected, and, except perhaps by Flaubert, has never been fulfilled since. That Jane Austen evolved such a medium and succeeded in it sets her apart as the most consummate artist in English fiction. Her triumph was all the greater, and was all the less realized, because hers was the art which conceals art. To the unobservant, to those accustomed to a wider canvas and more lurid and sweeping brush-work this 'Chinese fidelity' this 'miniature delicacy'[7] appeared, as to Mme de Staël, 'vulgaire'. To Charlotte Brontë (whose great difference in temperament drove her to inimical comment) the Austen novels were merely 'an accurate daguerrotyped portrait of a commonplace face', but the judgment of succeeding generations may well be summed up in the saying of an excellent critic:[8] 'Jane Austen, Jane Austen and life, which of you two has copied the other?'

But although from the beginning Jane Austen saw the goal which she must reach, she achieved her purpose only by the most patient labour. Her youthful efforts and unfinished sketches serve to show the development of her art. This child had no particular educational advantages beyond what was usual among gentlefolk. Since her boarding-school period began at the age of seven and ended when she was nine, she could not have 'scrambled herself' into much learning, particularly as the school-mistress, Mrs Latournelle, a jovial old lady with a cork leg, was chiefly occupied with giving out clothes for the wash, ordering dinner, and discoursing on play-acting and the private lives of actors. As The Revd George Austen was a scholarly man, it would seem that Jane's real education was gained between the years of nine and sixteen which she spent under his care. But the time which Mr Austen could spare from his duties as a clergyman was chiefly devoted to the education of his three sons and of such pupils as he took into his house. It does not seem probable that Jane and Cassandra could have received much deliberate instruction, but life at Steventon rectory was an education in itself. The Austens were a good-humoured, affectionate and lively race, inheriting from both sides of the family a tradition of culture and wit. They were omnivorous readers especially of novels and plays, very sociable, and on excellent terms with a large circle of relatives and friends. Steventon was emphatically not a place to rust the intellect, and a touch of cosmopolitan brilliance was introduced when the Comtesse de Feuillide, a niece to Mr Austen, made frequent visits to Steventon and finally took refuge there when widowed by the French Revolution. In this exhilarating atmosphere the young Jane Austen found all that was needed for the growth of her particular mental powers. She seems to have read a good deal in an ill-regulated way, but certainly not as much and not with such clearly defined benefit as certain critics[9] would have us suppose. One cannot praise a school of criticism which believes that Jane Austen found her real inspiration in books and which observes in her plots and in her style resemblances to practically every author whom she is known to have read. It is impossible to agree with the statement that Jane Austen 'wrote books because she loved books, and for no other reason. She did not study human nature, but loved men and women; and her realism sprang from loyalty to her friends.'[10] One must regard with reserve the facility with which there are found in Jane Austen's novels imitations of Dr Johnson's style and identifiable traces of Richardson and Fielding. Her debt to Fanny Burney has been magnified out of all proportion to the truth. Jane Austen loved Fanny Burney's novels, lavishing such praise on *Camilla* that only her obvious sincerity makes one take her seriously. Why she so greatly admired the worst of the Burney novels, when she might have chosen *Evelina*, is a mystery beyond solution. Jane Austen was attracted to Fanny Burney because the elder writer concentrated on themes of domestic life and manners. She purloined from *Cecilia* the three words 'Pride and Prejudice'. On the slight foundation of this trifling debt and of Jane Austen's generous praise there has been based a large and elaborate superstructure of obligation which she is supposed to owe to Fanny Burney. Similarities of speech and situation have been adduced to prove her indebtedness. It has even been found possible to recognize a fundamental likeness between the plot of *Cecilia* and of *Pride and Prejudice*, whereas none exists beyond the well-worn fact that high-born families dislike marrying outside their own caste. If the use of this theme establishes a debt, then Jane Austen is indebted to the hundreds of novelists who employed it before her. Human life can provide only a certain number of entanglements and juxtapositions; the English language can provide only a certain number of words in which to express them. These are the resources of the novelist, and his chance of originality is limited to the selection and arrangement of incidents, the individuality of his interpretation, and the form and style he chooses to employ. In all these essentials Jane Austen resembles Fanny Burney as much as a racehorse resembles a pony — no less and no more. It has been suggested that Jane Austen's sense of values 'might be described as Richardson's corrected by Fielding.'[11] With the first part of this statement one cannot agree. It is true that in *Mansfield Park* she departs from the ironic method to moralize directly — a fault in her art for which an admirer might wish to blame some outside influence. But the criticism is not made in a fault-finding sense. It maintains that '*Mansfield Park* is Richardsonian through and through; Sir Thomas Bertram has the unmistakable Grandisonian stamp. Darcy and Mr Knightley, in other novels, show marks of the same origin. Richardson, admittedly, would never have drawn them as they stand; they are Richardsonian with radical differences.'[12] These differences are indeed so radical that they seem to negate Richardson's influence. His notion of morality was certainly not Jane Austen's, and his sensibility was precisely what her fastidious taste rejected with scorn. Neither can one really claim that 'she is like Richardson in her registration of the minutest details of mannerism and behaviour'. Richardson's was the realism of the bookish man — achieved by the sedulous accumulation of minu-tiae. Jane Austen's was the realism of Crabbe, though not exerted on the subjects which absorbed Crabbe's interest. And again, though Jane Austen, like Richardson, is concerned with the 'annotation of the scarce perceptible, but significant and often decisive impulses of the heart', her conception of emotions and sentiments is not his, and her method of suggestion does not appear to owe him anything. For the rest, influenced perhaps by the epistolary vogue, or perhaps by the fact that Richardson and Fanny Burney had been its greatest exponents, Jane Austen twice essayed the letter-form. *Lady Susan* is a failure which she left unrevised and unexpanded. The first draft of *Elinor and Marianne* was also in letters, but Jane Austen soon realized that through such a medium she could never express what she wished to convey, and she abandoned the epistolary form for ever. No more striking evidence can be adduced as to the essential difference in inspiration between Jane Austen and those writers to whom she is supposed to have owed so much. With Fielding she really had much in common — not his wide field, not his bold freedom of speech, but, to a most marked degree, his attitude. Allowing for the difference in sex, that is to say for the difference in scope and in experience, Jane Austen is the feminine counterpart of Fielding. Like him she is an ironic humourist, like him she curls her lip at everything spurious. In her writings, as in his, a depth of feeling gives force to the deliberate moderation of each measured word. Each rejoices in the endless variety of human nature, and finds in affectation 'the only source of the true ridiculous.'[13] Each finds his pleasure in marking 'the nice distinction between two persons actuated by the same vice or folly.' Each views the human tangle with detachment, and metes out justice according to a sense of values so profound as to ensure to their novels the abiding trait of universality.

Among the many opinions which Jane Austen shared with Fielding was the view that 'true nature is as difficult to be met with in authors, as the Bayonne ham and Bologna sausage is to be found in the shops.'[14] Jane Austen appears to have held this conviction from the time when she was old enough to read a novel. Instead of the imitations which are usually the young author's stock-in-trade, her early writings are rollicking burlesques of every type of contemporary fiction. With complete nonchalance this girl not yet fifteen points an unerring finger at all the improbabilities and absurdities which marred the novels of her day. It begs the question to say that *Love and Friendship* is 'a criticism and reproduction, of art—not of life.'[15] It is a criticism of art by comparison with life, and that involves a judgement of the standard applied. G. K. Chesterton called *Love and Friendship* 'a satire on the fable of the fainting lady'. Like all the rest of Jane Austen's precocious efforts, it is much more than this, attacking as it does not only sensibility, but also the Gothic tale, and especially such survivals of the old Romantic tradition as still contributed to the unreality of fiction. Laura, as a heroine of sensibility, must have a mysterious or highly complicated origin: 'My Father was a native of Ireland and an inhabitant of Wales; my Mother was the natural daughter of a Scotch Peer by an Italian Opera-girl—I was born in Spain and received my Education in France.' She describes, in the style of the romantic novelette, that in her mind 'every Virtue that could adorn it was centred; it was the rendez-vous of every good Quality and of every noble sentiment.' One can picture the wicked glee of the youthful satirist as she twists the stale jargon: 'A sensibility too tremblingly alive to every affliction of my friends, my Acquaintance and particularly to every affliction of my own, was my only fault, if a fault it could be called.' Isobel is an excruciating example of that self-conscious prudery which believes the whole world scheming against female virtue:

> Isobel had seen the world. She had passed 2 years at one of the first Boarding schools in London; had spent a fortnight in Bath and had supped one night in Southampton.
> Beware my Laura (she would often say) Beware of the insipid Vanities and idle Dissipations of the Metropolis of England; Beware of the unmeaning Luxuries of Bath and of the striking fish of Southampton.

The hero typically preserves an unmeaning incognito. He is one Lindsay, whose name for particular reasons must be concealed under the name of Talbot. Here Jane hits off excellently the moth-eaten situation of cruel father and love-lorn son:

> 'My father, seduced by the false glare of Fortune and the Deluding Pomp of Title, insisted on my giving my hand to Lady Dorothea. No never exclaimed I. Lady Dorothea is lovely and engaging; I prefer no woman to her; but know Sir, that I scorn to marry her in compliance with your wishes. No! never shall it be said that I obliged my Father.'
> We all admired the noble Manliness of his reply.

Sir Edward's comment is Jane's: 'Where Edward in the name of wonder (said he) did you pick up this unmeaning gibberish? you must have been studying novels, I suspect.'

The dependence on unnecessary change of scene for diversifying the novel, and a suggestion of the picaresque element are not forgotten. Edward Lindsay quits his father's house in Bedfordshire for his aunt's in Middlesex, and though he is a tolerable proficient in geography, finds himself in South Wales. After his immediate marriage to Laura, he sets off with his bride to Middlesex. No sooner have they arrived there than the unrelenting father is announced, and the defiant couple flee to M—, the seat of Edward's dearest friend, Augustus. They come just in time to witness the arrest of Augustus for the theft of money which, before his marriage to Sophia, he has 'gracefully purloined from his unworthy father's Escritoire'. Edward goes to comfort his friend in prison, and Laura and Sophia, alarmed at his prolonged absence, order a carriage and set out for London at breakneck speed, inquiring of every decent-looking person they pass 'if they had seen my Edward', but driving too rapidly to permit of any reply. Sophia flinches at the prospect of visiting Augustus in prison; they return to Wales, and then decide to go to Scotland. It is an echo of a thousand romantic wanderings, and is scarcely more unreasoning

The recognition scene, a *sine qua non* of the ink-spattering novelist and an important ingredient even in the works of Fielding and the better writers, provided Jane Austen with an excellent target. Laura and Sophia are about to set off on another stage of their frantic Odyssey when 'a coroneted coach and 4' enters the inn-yard, and an old gentleman descends. 'At his first appearance my sensibility was wonderfully affected and e'er I had gazed a 2nd time, an instinctive sympathy whispered to my heart, that he was my Grandfather.' No sooner have they embraced than the venerable peer catches sight of Sophia and exclaims 'Another Granddaughter'. A moment later a beautiful young man appears, and 'Lord St Clair started and retreating back a few paces, with uplifted hands, said, "Another Grand-child! What an unexpected Happiness is this! to discover in the space of 3 minutes, as many of my Descendants"'—whereupon a fourth enters and Lord St Clair hastily retreats before this flood of relatives.

Every aspect of sensibility is travestied. Laura finds Dorothea lacking in 'interesting Sensibility' and 'amiable sympathy' because, when they meet for the first time, Dorothea does not confide any of her secret thoughts, or ask for similar confidences. The meeting of Edward and Augustus is so affecting that Sophia and Laura faint alternately on a sofa. All records are exceeded when these sensitive females come unexpectedly upon their husbands 'elegantly attired but weltering in their blood'. Sophia shrieks and faints upon the ground. Laura screams and instantly runs mad.

> Beware of fainting fits [says the expiring Sophia] . . . Though at the time they may be refreshing and agreeable yet believe me they will in the end, if too often repeated, prove destructive to the Constitution . . . Beware of swoons Dear Laura . . . a frenzy fit is not one quarter so pernicious; it is an exercise to the Body and if not too violent, is I dare say conducive to the Health in its consequences—Run mad as often as you chose; but do not faint.

Jane Austen parodies Fanny Burney's affected superlatives in *The Young Philosopher*, which is stuffed with such phrases as 'softness the most bewitching' and 'vivacity the most striking'. The ravings of Laura sound suspiciously like Cecilia's frenzy fit: 'Talk not to me of Phaetons . . . Give me a violin . . . Beware ye gentle nymphs of Cupid's Thunderbolts, avoid the piercing shafts of Jupiter . . . They told me Edward was not Dead; but they deceived me—they took him for a cucumber—.' There is a very clever distinction between the self-dramatization which impels Sophia to post to Newgate, and the selfishness which makes her decide at the last moment not to overpower her delicacy by the sight of Augustus in durance. The Radcliffian cult of scenery is mocked in that passage which describes the place chosen by Laura and Sophia for meditation: 'A grove of full-grown Elms sheltered us from the east—. A Bed of full-grown Nettles from the West—. Before us ran the murmuring brook and behind us ran the turnpike road.' And the use of nature to echo and exacerbate the anguished mood is inimitably caricatured when Sophia is unable to endure the summer sky because it reminds her of her Augustus's blue satin waistcoat striped with white. The other sketches in Jane Austen's juvenilia carry on this exuberant burlesque of fiction. Melodrama, improbability and emotional flaccidity are stressed throughout. Nothing is forgotten— not even the blank-verse prose of the sentimental school:

'Yes I'm in love I feel it now
And Henrietta Halton has undone me.'

Sometimes one can distinguish the very novel which she has in mind. Miss Jane's story (second letter) is plainly reminiscent of Susannah Gunning's *Memoirs of Mary*. But some of these early writings are interesting not merely because they reveal the assured aptness of Jane Austen's critical judgement, but also because they present in embryo situations and characters which later she incorporated in her novels. When Lady Greville arrogantly summons Maria Williams to the door of her coach where, despite a cold wind, she interrogates her, we have a foretaste of Lady Catherine de Burgh and Elizabeth Bennet. In the description of Maria chaperoned to her first dance and patronized by the élite there is a hint of *The Watsons*.

Another early work which shows Jane Austen as an experimenter is *Lady Susan*, supposed to have been written between 1792 and 1796. It is the story of an adventuress told in letters, without comment ironic or otherwise. Since we are completely admitted into Lady Susan's unscrupulous plans, there is no suspense and no subtlety. The only benefit which might be derived from such treatment — the reader's satisfaction in knowing more than the victims of Lady Susan's schemes — is negated in this case, because Lady Susan has such a bad reputation that, without understanding precisely what is afoot, all the other characters agree in expecting the worst. They exchange letters recounting their various impressions, and some variety is achieved by this changing of focus, but it is all flat-footed and overdrawn. Lady Susan's delight in describing her wicked intentions reminds one of the moustached villain exultantly flicking his boots with a riding-crop. The burlesques of Jane Austen's early teens are in direct line with her mature method, since broad satire may be refined by subtlety. *Lady Susan* lacks satire and wit, and serves to show how undistinguished a writer Jane Austen might have been had she continued to dispense with these essentials of her art. But, in fact, she was so conscious of the ineffectiveness of this method that she brought *Lady Susan* to a hastily conceived conclusion, and made no effort to polish it for publication. It appeared in print only in 1871, when Austen-Leigh made it an addition to his memoir of his aunt.

It is not easy to trace in Jane Austen's novels the exact sequence of her development as a writer, since they were not published in the order in which they were written and since she was continually revising the manuscripts which accumulated for want of a publisher. By about 1795 she read aloud to the family at Steventon a story in letters called *Elinor and Marianne*. From this she turned to *Pride and Prejudice*, which she began in October, 1796, and completed in August, 1797—a period of ten months. The title she first intended for the novel was *First Impressions*. She was then twenty-one years of age. In November, 1797, *First Impressions* was offered to Cadell by The Revd George Austen and refused by return of post. Within that same month Jane began to rewrite *Elinor and Marianne* in its present form, and later decided to call it *Sense and Sensibility*. *Northanger Abbey* was certainly first composed in 1798. It was originally known to Jane Austen's family as *Susan*; then it became, by the changing of the heroine's name, *Miss Catherine*, and owes its permanent title to Henry Austen who arranged for its posthumous publication. Although no consistent line of artistic differentiation can be drawn in the period of her mature creativeness, it is convenient to consider her activities in relation to her various places of residence; and certain breaks in output due to migrations or experiences seem to sanction this superficial division. In what we may call the first phase Jane Austen, working at Steventon, accomplished that amount of literary composition to which we have just referred. In the spring of 1801, she removed with her family to Bath. Her unhappiness at leaving her old home was increased that summer when, during a holiday in Devonshire, she was romantically involved with a young man who died shortly afterwards. It was a blow with which the loving Cassandra could all the more fully sympathize since her own fiancé had died in San Domingo in 1797. During the three years of the Austens' residence at Bath, Jane revised *Northanger Abbey* which was offered to Crosby and Sons of London in 1803. The manuscript was purchased for £10, and put into a drawer where it remained until it was bought back some years later.

The period between 1803 and 1811 is generally regarded as a gap in Jane Austen's creativeness, and, despite some argument as to her activity during this time, one cannot deny that it shows a great slackening in productiveness at least, if not in effort. Since *Northanger Abbey* had already been written in full, the work of revision cannot have been great. *The Watsons*, possibly also written during these years, is only a partial outline of a novel, and even if, as has been suggested, *Lady Susan* also belongs to this period, it is too brief and too unsatisfactory to be worth serious consideration. The manuscript of *The Watsons*, which contains many erasures and alterations, as in some parts the watermark '1803' and in others '1804'—evidence which seems to establish the time of composition. The manuscript of *Lady Susan* bears the watermark '1805' but, as it is beautifully written, the probability is that it is merely a fair copy of some earlier effort. This view is reinforced by the quality of the work which ranges it with the *Juvenilia*. Whether because of uncongenial surroundings, or of depression still further accentuated by the death of the beloved Mrs Lefroy in December, 1804, and of The Revd George Austen in January, 1805, it seems clear that between 1803 and 1811 Jane Austen virtually laid down her pen.

In 1805 the Austens removed to Southampton. In 1809, Edward, the second son (who had inherited the property of a distant relative, and had taken his family name of Knight), offered a home to his mother and sisters, and thenceforward they lived in the little cottage at Chawton which was to see the second spring of Jane's creative power. Here, in the security of a settled background, she wrote, between February, 1811, and August, 1816, *Mansfield Park*, *Emma* and *Persuasion*. She also began, but never finished, *Sanditon*. Before undertaking these new subjects, however, she set herself to revise *Sense and Sensibility*, which was published by Egerton at the author's own financial risk. It was by no means a sensational success, but that it had at last seen the light was sufficient stimulus to renewed effort, and Jane turned to the revision of *Pride and Prejudice*, which appeared in 1813. Thereafter it was easy to secure publication and *Mansfield Park* came out in 1814, to be followed in 1816 by *Emma*. Her other writings appeared only after her death.

Since *Sense and Sensibility* was Jane Austen's first mature work, it is helpful to consider it before the more brilliant novels which succeeded it. It has excellences equal to her greatest writings and faults which appeared again in her weakest—*Mansfield Park*. It would be unprofitable to seek, like some of Jane Austen's critics,[16] for parallels between the characters and situations in Jane Austen's novels and her human experience. They exist, but are not so close as to allow more than a few identifications of detail, and no possible identification of character or circumstance. This is a great solace to those who claim for her the highest level of creativeness, and not merely the reproductive imagination of, for example, a Charlotte Brontë. But although Jane Austen transmuted her experience, one would expect to find among her characters some recurring symbol of her own personality and some echo of her own life. These may be guessed in *Sense and Sensibility*, as in some of the other novels, but they may never be established.

Sense and Sensibility is to some extent a diagrammatic story with a forthright moral, which somewhat disturbs the fine balance of satire. It is a blow aimed at once against a literary fashion and against the self-indulgent emotionalism which that literary fashion deified. It was Jane Austen's intention to show that self-control was the basis of that harmony which self-indulgence destroyed. At this stage, at least, she seems to have had a view of living which, though it coincided with Christian ethics, need not necessarily have been identified with it. She had a high and even an austere standard of human behaviour, but in this earlier period it appears to have been more concerned with aesthetics than with theology. If one were to formulate the impressions gained from the majority of her writings, one would say that to her life was a bitter fruit with a sweet kernel, a thorn-thicket enclosing a green dell, a noisy tumult through which one could win to an inner peace. In her view the bitterness, the wounds and the confusion of life are due to a lack of sanity — to a fecund illusion which throughout man's days never ceases to bring forth a brood as fatal to his own happiness as it is to that of the world. It is the illusion of self-importance which so warps the judgment that either man can never see reality, or if for a moment he should glimpse it, must frantically spin some veil to obscure it if possible from his own eyes, but particularly from his neighbours. In *Sense and Sensibility* Elinor stands for clear-eyed sanity, and when self becomes insistent she steadily maintains the just proportion between the importance of her personal trials and the general scheme of things. This cannot be done without exertion, and that is why exertion is the basis of Jane Austen's creed. Once we cease to exert control over our egoism it spins a web which blinds and fetters us, and ends by isolating us from the power or even the wish to see the truth. This is to live in a false twilight instead of in the unequivocal light of day. If one must suffer through the delusions of others (and one must), at least, says Jane Austen, let us be free from self-delusion: let there be peace and harmony within. But not all of man's evasions are harmful. Many are indeed merely foolish and sometimes so naive as to be lovable. The serious framework of Jane Austen's novels is forged from such deceptions as threaten happiness; the humour depends on the clash of foibles and on those misunderstandings which arise from the irreconcilable preoccupations of the various characters. Both aspects of Jane Austen's conception are clearly shown in *Sense and Sensibility*.

The love affairs of Marianne and of Elinor are both based on deception. Willoughby engages the affection of Marianne without a thought of returning it—through 'selfish vanity', in fact. He deceives Mrs Smith on whom his worldly expectations depend and, when the necessity for decision arises, he abandons Marianne. She, on the other hand, despite the fact that Willoughby never makes a declaration and that his conduct is entirely equivocal, cherishes the happy delusion that he intends to marry her. Elinor, not knowing that Edward Ferrars is secretly engaged to Lucy Steele, permits herself to find in his attentions sufficient promise to allow her love of him to grow unchecked. In one respect there is not much to choose between Edward Ferrars and Willoughby, although Jane Austen seems to justify the one and rigorously condemns the other. Edward Ferrars's interest in Elinor was so marked as to secure to her the jealous dislike of his mother and sister. If he was not a deliberate deceiver, it is certain that he was not behaving like an engaged man. His general character was unstained by such behaviour as Willoughby's towards Brandon's ward, but his integrity and his sedate manner made his unwarranted interest in Elinor all the more dangerous to her peace of mind, since from him such attentions were far more credible than those of the volatile Willoughby. Elinor was deluded as to Edward Ferrars's freedom, but not as to his love for her. Marianne was deluded as to Willoughby's love, but he was bound by no prior engagement—only by his own avarice. In his weak way he seems to have grown to care for Marianne, yet he savagely repudiates her claims and marries a wealthy shrew. Edward Ferrars does not care a jot for Lucy Steele, yet he prefers to be disinherited rather than to break his honourable engagement. Jane Austen is careful to mark these differences, and that we may not blame Edward for outgrowing his love for Lucy Steele, she is shown as a mean opportunist who has been actuated throughout only by a determination to make a brilliant marriage.

480

The difference between Elinor and Marianne is shown in the way in which each reacts to her unhappy love affair. Marianne luxuriates in her agony. Her sufferings involve all those who love her in great unhappiness, and also in the deepest embarrassment, since she makes not the slightest effort to hide her feelings. Her prostration drives such warm-hearted friends as Mrs Jennings to conclude that Willoughby had engaged himself to marry her, and Elinor, who considers it necessary to clear him of having broken his word, has the added misery of explaining that Marianne has never been engaged. The high-flown tradition by which lovelorn maidens fall into a decline is deliberately shattered by Jane Austen's careful explanation that Marianne's illness has resulted from a careless indifference to wet shoes.

Against the foolishness of the one sister is set the sensitive self-respect and balanced sincerity of the other. Elinor always endeavours to be just, to admit the claims of others and to conceal her own misery. She is supported by those fundamentals, 'good principles and good sense'. Never turning from fact even when it is most painful, she can be surgically truthful, as when she sets herself to show Marianne the exact value of Willoughby's confession. 'Fancy must not be led astray by tenderness'; Marianne, in forgiving Willoughby, must not be softened into loving him again, or into preserving an idealized memory of him which might lessen her hopes of happiness with Brandon. Willoughby's charm must not obscure his selfishness, and his abject confession must not be attributed to real contrition with a purpose of amendment. 'At present,' says Elinor, 'he regrets what he has done. And why does he regret it? Because he finds it has not answered towards himself. It has not made him happy.' Marianne's lips quiver, but she sees all that has happened in its true light, and she resolves to amend those faults of her own which have been largely responsible for the whole wretched business. Her resolutions are fully expressed in chapter 43 — a chapter which is too didactically explicit.

The balance between Elinor's judgment and her emotions is well preserved. Her feelings, however repressed, surge up with a force of which the reader is all the more conscious because of the restrained narrative. When Edward, whom she believes married to Lucy Steele, is seen coming up the garden path, Elinor moves away and sits down. 'He comes from Mr Pratt's purposely to see us. I will be calm; I will be mistress of myself.' The family waits in silence until he enters. He explains. Elinor hears that Lucy Steele has married Edward's brother. 'Elinor could sit it no longer. She almost ran out of the room, and as soon as the door was closed, burst into tears of joy.'

So perfectly are the other characters drawn that each deserves a most detailed examination. Space, however, allows only a brief and general treatment. In this novel we find the first of Jane Austen's inimitable portraits of fools. Mrs Dashwood is a charming and faulty creature—one of those foolish mothers who are presented with such skill. Good-natured, emotional and undiscriminating, she is an older Marianne. She is well-bred, and although she delights in sentimental dreams for her children, she is incapable of the brazen manoeuvring of the thick-skinned Mrs Bennet. Mrs Jennings at first appears merely a common and comfortable woman, but she soon wins the heart by her warm-hearted generosity. Her matter-of-fact philosophy is summed-up in her efforts to soothe Marianne's broken heart with a glass of Constantia wine. The elder Miss Steele is a vulgar and stupid upstart whose garrulous revelations nullify the cautious scheming of her sister. Lucy Steele is a crafty and heartless climber. She fears Elinor's power over Edward Ferrars, and shrewdly appeals to those very qualities of honour and magnanimity which she herself lacks. The interview with Elinor in the shrubbery is a triumph of subtlety and self-control on both sides. No example of the ironic situation in which Jane Austen delighted can surpass the dinner-party at the house of Mrs Ferrars. This arrogant dowager and her daughter set themselves to freeze and to ignore Elinor who, they believe, is secretly engaged to Edward. For Edward nothing will satisfy them but a great match with, for example, the much discussed Miss Morton whose superlativeness is summed up in the words: 'Miss Morton is Lord Morton's daughter.' To mark their coldness to Elinor the Ferrars ladies shower attentions on Lucy Steele, unconscious of her secret claim to be treated as a prospective relative. Lucy Steele rejoices in her success with Mrs Ferrars, thinking that it will pave the way to her happy reception into the family and little dreaming that, when her engagement comes to light a few days later, she will be abused until she faints, and turned out of the house. Meanwhile she hugs herself not merely at being singled out for preference, but because she is delighted at Elinor's humiliation. The complexities of the unwitting Mrs Ferrars, confronted with two potential daughters-in-law, and choosing to be gracious to the more dangerous and more unsuitable is high comedy with a sharp sting of retribution at the tail. It is characteristic of Elinor that she is not unhappy or agitated at the behaviour of these mean-spirited people. She merely despises them. It is a scene in which every character unconsciously reveals himself. The famous conversation between John Dashwood and his wife as to the provision that might be made for Mrs Dashwood and her daughters is another splendid example of dramatic self-revelation. Each maintains to himself and to the other a semblance of generous consideration for the widow, while Jane Austen mercilessly directs our gaze into their selfish and penurious hearts.

Jane Austen has often been accused of stressing too much the theme of husband-hunting. A realist could scarcely have avoided such an aspect at a period when matrimony was not merely a woman's choice, but, practically speaking, her only profitable career. 'Single women have a dreadful propensity for being poor, which is one very strong argument in favour of matrimony.'[17] *Pride and Prejudice*, more than any other Austen novel, is concerned with matrimonial scheming. The circumstances of the Bennet family are admirably planned to emphasize the importance of this issue. Five portionless girls must make some provision for their future before their father's small property will pass by the law of entail to their cousin, Mr Collins. If they do not realize the urgency of getting married, their mother realizes it for them, and applies herself to husband-catching with a blatancy which almost defeats her ambition. That power of conserving family resemblances for which Jane Austen has been praised is nowhere more strikingly exercised than in her portrayal of the Bennets. Elizabeth and Jane are their father's daughters; Lydia and Kitty are their mother's. The negligible Mary seems a blend of her father's sobriety and her mother's stupidity. She is a sententious dullard—a development of the moralizing Julia Millar.[18] Mr and Mrs Bennet might be considered an elaboration of the slightly-sketched Palmers, if one could imagine Mr Palmer ceasing to snub his vacuous wife, allowing her to take command and withdrawing into a cynical passivity. It is certain, at any rate, that Mr Bennet's cynicism, like Mr Palmer's rudeness, arises from a defeated sense of being unequally yoked. Mr Elton (in *Emma*) suffers no change of disposition, although his wife is not merely silly but also a spiteful and underbred snob. This is because Elton is the male equivalent of Mrs Elton, and he requires no defence mechanism to get through his life with her. Mr Bennet, having married a pretty face, finds himself saddled until death with a garrulous and insensible vulgarian. He has sufficient detachment to see this joke at his own expense and, to lessen his feeling of failure, he generalizes that the world is simply a large home for the feeble-minded in which a few sane people suffer for their lack of conformity. Because he sensitively continues to feel ashamed of his wife's lack of sense he sometimes directs at her sarcasms of which she can make neither head nor tail. It is not because Mrs Bennet's people were in trade that she is vulgar. Her brother, Mr Gardiner, is 'a sensible, gentlemanlike man'. Mrs Bennet is vulgar for the same reason as Lady Catherine de Burgh — because she has a coarse-grained mind. Jane Austen never meant to show vulgarity as the stigma of any particular class. It seems to have been her view that vulgarity is like the wind which bloweth where it listeth. The predicament of the two elder Misses Bennet resembles, without the disadvantage of caricature, the predicament of Evelina. Their eligible suitors become faint-hearted at the sight and sound of Mrs Bennet and her hoydenish younger daughters. It is perhaps to widen the gap between Elizabeth and her lover that Jane Austen made Mrs Bennet so impossible and Darcy so proudly fastidious. But he is not merely fastidious; he is arrogant and a snob, and this makes him a distasteful character — to the present writer at least. He begins by being abominably rude to Elizabeth, and becomes conscious of her attractions only because she treats him with cool and sparkling scorn. He falls in love against his will, a backhanded compliment which testifies at once to Elizabeth's charm and unsuitability. Perhaps the strongest proof of her love for him was that she brought herself to forgive the implied insult. It was very clever of Jane Austen to arrange that Darcy's sister should have intended to run away with Wickham, and so provide Darcy with an excellent reason for not holding Elizabeth disgraced by Lydia's behaviour. Darcy is too concerned with cautious considerations to be likable. He is too self-assured, too invulnerable in his pride, rank and wealth. The measure of our resentment against this Cophetua is the satisfaction with which we watch Elizabeth refuse his proposal in terms which humble him to the dust. True, it is not his former attitude towards her which brings upon him her vehement condemnation. For a long time there has rankled within her a deep resentment of his open scorn for the less creditable members of her family. She knows their faults, but they are nevertheless her own flesh and blood. Such feelings, however, are as nothing compared to her anger at the sufferings which Darcy's interference has inflicted on Jane. And indeed the more one thinks of Darcy's unhesitating decision to prevent Bingley's proposal to Jane, and of Bingley's lap-dog acquiescence, the more one is assured that these reluctant lovers needed more castigation than they ever got. Elizabeth has been criticized for having too sharp and ready a tongue. Those who hold this view have evidently made no attempt to fill in the details of intonation and look which the dramatic method can only hint. If one accepts Jane Austen's words as to Elizabeth's way of neutralizing her spirited sallies, one can be in no doubt of her inescapable charm: 'There was a mixture of sweetness and archness in her manner which made it difficult for her to affront anybody; and Darcy had never been bewitched by any woman as he was by her.'[19] Elizabeth's circumstances made it necessary for her to be perpetually *en garde*, and the brilliant deftness of her parries and ripostes was due not only to her quicksilver temperament, but because she was fighting, not indeed for her life, but for her happiness and self-respect. Never is her nervous skill so curiously displayed as when she takes the field against the lumbering Lady de Burgh—the young David trying to find a vulnerable spot in an extremely pachydermatous Goliath. With what power does Jane Austen make us feel the inequality of these combatants—on the one side rank, arrogance, and brutal stupidity, on the other worldly insignificance and all the indomitable spirit of a cool brain and a stout heart. In regard to Lydia Bennet a critic has said: 'The whole treatment of Lydia conclusively removes Jane Austen from the modern realists. She is neither oppressed by ethics nor determined upon naked truth. The episode never develops into a problem.'[20] It does not become a problem, because there was nothing in the least mystifying in Lydia's elopement, which Jane Austen treated with her usual sense of proportion. Lydia's condemnation by those characters whom Jane Austen presents as the most valuable is entirely in accordance with sound ethical principles. Lydia is shown throughout as a brainless little animal, and so we can scarcely feel surprised when through a lack of training, her sensuality gets the upper hand. When Wickham refuses to marry her she is quite satisfied to remain with him without benefit of clergy. When he is bribed into marrying her, she comes flaunting home to queen it over her sisters, generously offering to get husbands for them all before the winter is over. 'I thank you for my share of the favour,' said Elizabeth, 'but I do not particularly like your way of getting husbands.' Mrs Bennet, forgetting the method in the accomplished fact, is overjoyed at having a daughter married, and especially that daughter whom she best understands. There is no problem in Jane Austen's shrewd but incidental treatment of Lydia Bennet. The treatment is incidental because Lydia is a minor character in the plot; because in any case her fate is not in the least tragic. She had lost nothing that she valued. She was not even immoral—she was amoral. Why should one use a two-handed sword to decapitate a butterfly?

The immortal Mr Collins is so well-known as to need merely a passing glance. In him the delusion of self-importance is a mono-mania, and yet he is as craven a sycophant as ever drew breath. One can reconcile these contradictions only by recalling that he had spent the greater part of his life under the guidance of an illiterate and miserly father. This subjection had left in him an instinct to cower to those in authority over him, or to those who derived their importance from sources which, because he had always lacked them, he regarded with awe. Wealth and power could always secure the subservience of Mr Collins. Because he had been used to nothing, his moderate success in life went to his weak head and 'made him altogether a mixture of pride and obsequiousness, self-importance and humility.' He marries, as he does everything else, to please his patroness. It is no mean achievement of Jane Austen's that she makes it possible to retain our respect and liking for Charlotte Lucas after she became Mrs Collins. Poor plain Charlotte must find her security in this bumptious oaf. No wonder Elizabeth cries out in horrified amazement. And Charlotte sums up her reasons in the words: 'I am not romantic, you know; I never was. I only ask a comfortable home.' When Elizabeth visits her at Hunsford she finds that Charlotte's comfort consists in seeing as little as possible of her husband. For the most part we are too busy laughing at Mr Collins to bother much as to whether a sound heart may not, after all, be his. We feel that we have not undervalued him when we come to his spiteful letter on Lydia Bennet's elopement. Still, he is a harmless creature in comparison with Bingley's sisters, those nettles in the path of Elizabeth and Jane Bennet.

Pride and Prejudice is, in every respect, a masterpiece. Its closely woven plot, the *élan* of its development and the minute perfection of its characterization show nowhere an unsure touch. Whatever it may have owed to the author's later revision, there is not the slightest evidence of patching. Indeed the sustained brilliance and energy of this novel leave no room to doubt that it was composed in one creative outburst, and owed to second thoughts merely the polishing of its wit. That Jane Austen realized her own *tour de force* is evident in her words of pretended self-depreciation:

> The work is rather too light, and bright, and sparkling; it wants shade; it wants to be stretched out here and there with a long chapter of sense if it could be had; if not, of solemn specious nonsense, about something quite unconnected with the story; an essay on writing, a critique on Walter Scott, or the history of Buonaparté, or something that would form a contrast, and bring the reader with increased delight to the playfulness and epigrammatism of the general style.[21]

Pride and Prejudice was to Jane Austen her 'own darling child', and she rightly considered Elizabeth Bennet 'as delightful a creature as ever appeared in print.'[22]

Northanger Abbey, like *Sense and Sensibility*, suffers somewhat from a double aim. It is not easy to maintain an even balance in a work which satirizes a school of fiction and endeavours at the same time to present a faithful picture of human life. In *Northanger Abbey* the plot and, in one instance, the characterization are so governed by the intention of burlesquing the Gothic romance[23] that there appears to be a lack of verisimilitude. Catherine Morland is sufficiently simple and credulous to accept Gothic mysteries as gospel-truth, and to expect a Gothic building to enforce such circumstances as were inevitable in Gothic novels. Her intrusive curiosity, a parody of Mrs Radcliffe's Emilys and Elleanas, is quite in keeping with her childishness, but General Tilney is really not convincing. He is made to behave outrageously because some Montoni must be provided for Catherine in her role of Emily. Since his behaviour must spring from some circumstance which links it with the normal plot, it is explained as being due to the discovery that Catherine, after all, is only a penniless nobody. But however great his disappointment and however vile his temper, it does not seem probable that he would turn a young girl out of his house at a moment's notice, and make it necessary for her to return home unprotected in the common stage-coach. At that period the necessity for chaperonage would make such an enforced journey an outrage against the conventions. It was an improbable outrage, but it was the best Jane Austen could do in subjecting Catherine to a tyranny which would establish a parallel with Gothicism and which, at the same time, would seem to arise out of the everyday life portrayed.

Elizabeth Bennet's commonsense and self-reliance, her pleasure in long, muddy walks, set her apart from the heroine of romance. Catherine Morland establishes an even greater contrast. The first chapter of *Northanger Abbey*[24] is really a sardonic essay on the absurdities of the conventional heroine. It vigorously presents all the reasons which would make it impossible that anything of the slightest importance could happen to this insignificant young creature. She is the child of ordinary, respectable parents. In her earlier years she was very plain, and even when she begins to curl her hair and to gain some colour and plumpness her looks are not at all above the average. 'She could never learn or understand anything before she was taught, and sometimes not even then.' She has not the slightest ability in music or drawing, and up to the age of fifteen 'loved nothing so well in the world as rolling down the green slope at the back of the house.' She is a most unpromising focus for romance. At the age of fifteen her love of dirt and romping gave way to an inclination for finery. 'From fifteen to seventeen she was in training for a heroine; she read all such works as heroines must read to supply their memories with those quotations which are so serviceable and so soothing in the vicissitudes of their eventful lives.' Alas! the parish contained not one lord, not one foundling, not one man of unknown origin. 'But when a young lady is to be a heroine, the perverseness of forty surrounding families cannot prevent. Something must and will happen to throw a hero in her way.'

In choosing Henry Tilney as the hero for such a heroine Jane Austen showed her usual sense of fitness. He is an attractive and sensible young clergyman, wise and kind enough to see her honest worth, not too brilliant for her timid inexperience. He marries her because he has grown sincerely attached to her, but 'I must confess that his affection originated in nothing better than gratitude; or, in other words, that a persuasion of her partiality for him had been the only cause of giving her a serious thought. It is a new circumstance in romance, I acknowledge, and dreadfully derogatory of a heroine's dignity; but if it be as new in common life, the credit of a wild imagination will be at least all my own.'[25]

The lets and hindrances which impede this denouement are very skilfully devised. There are no real dangers; indeed there are no real difficulties, but only such a concatenation of circumstances as would seem difficult to a young girl who has left home for the first time. That Catherine's chaperon, Mrs Allen, should be kind, but rather self-engrossed is a good stroke, because it deprives her of that helpful support which would have blown away her troubles like thistledown. It is Catherine's ingenuousness which makes a little tangle seem a complicated web; and it is because of her ingenuousness that this tangle falls apart. She weaves no counter-plots; she watches each encompassing strand with troubled eyes, and because she is so simple and trusting Henry Tilney becomes the hero that she imagined him to be. For her he faces that dragon, the General, and this heroine without beauty, or brains but with an unassuming charm which is very lovable — lives happily ever after. The success of her entire lack of strategy is in strong contrast to the failure of Isabella Thorpe's selfish manoeuvring.

Mansfield Park was the first of those novels written in Jane Austen's later period. When she commenced it (in 1811) she was nearing her forties, and she had remained comparatively inactive for eight years. Of her actual experiences during that interval we know a little. Of her mental reactions we know practically nothing. One can only say that in *Mansfield Park* there is an unaccustomed sobriety and a temporary change of focus. The extent of this difference can best be judged by comparing *Mansfield Park* with the preceding novels—not merely with the exuberance of *Pride and Prejudice*, but also with the spirited irony of *Northanger Abbey* and *Sense and Sensibility*. This latter novel had shown Jane Austen not yet arrived at perfect equilibrium, wavering at times towards didacticism, but, by relaxing into her instinctive attitude, finding her true poise. In *Mansfield Park* this ironic poise is lost almost entirely. It is exerted only in the portrayal of the minor characters, such as Mrs Norris and Lady Bertram. The plot and the main dramatis personae are fashioned and directed from the standpoint of moral earnestness. Nor is this the only surprise in Jane Austen's fourth novel. She offers to us in Fanny Price very much the sort of heroine whom she had formerly derided. Fanny Price is a young woman of exquisite sensibility who alienates our sympathies from the first. She is too much of a 'creep-mouse'; she is too prim and juridical; she is too completely the sweet, suffering saint. Her physical delicacy is almost as extreme as her mental delicacy. She is above all things unfitted to be a poor dependent. She must have a horse because walking exercise tires her. If she pulls roses or walks a mile or so in the sun, she becomes so prostrated that she needs to be revived with a glass of wine. She has no vivacity, no youthful spirits. She is slighted and overlooked by the Bertram family, but not with deliberate unkindness. It seems as if her meekness at least as much as her dependence causes her to be set at naught. Even a poor relation need not have been so colourless. She might have been many times more cheerful than she was without overstepping the bounds beyond which poor relations may not presume. Indeed so thin-skinned and frail a poor relation could not fail to arouse in her wealthy connections an unsalutary sense of power, and to incur more bullying than might otherwise have been her share. In fact, except for Mrs Norris who was a mean and cowardly oppressor, the others at Mansfield Park were not so much unkind as self-engrossed. They were not a whit more self-engrossed than Sir Walter Elliot and his eldest daughter Elizabeth, nor was Fanny much more ignored and ill-used than Anne Elliot. 'Anne, with an elegance of mind and sweetness of character, which must have placed her high with any people of real understanding, was nobody with either father or sister; her word had no weight, her convenience was always to give way—she was only Anne.' Fanny Price, by her uncle's ruse sent back for a while to her home in Portsmouth, is a sore trial. She finds her mother 'a partial, ill-judging parent, a dawdle, a slattern, who neither taught nor restrained her children.' Her father is a coarse man given to tippling and swearing. The children are boisterous and unmanageable. Every time the door bangs Fanny's temples ache. She pines for Mansfield. 'After being nursed up at Mansfield, it was too late in the day to be hardened at Portsmouth.' She cannot eat hash and pudding with half-cleaned knives and forks, and is constrained to defer her heartiest meal till she can send her brothers in the evening for biscuits and buns. One cannot be expected to have much patience with a girl who droops in luxurious surroundings because she is a dependent, and who, in the equality of her own home recoils in fastidious horror at its crudities — and still droops. It does not increase our respect for her that at Portsmouth 'the men appeared to her all coarse, the women pert, everybody underbred.' It is to be feared that she was not merely a snob, but a self-righteous prig. Her strictures on private theatricals are staggering to the modern mind, particularly when we remember that there were private theatricals at Steventon. Fanny's moral reflections on every situation pall upon us, and in one instance they appear unfeeling. When Tom Bertram is very ill and threatened with consumption, her sorrow is exceeded by her perturbation at his spiritual unpreparedness: 'Without any particular affection for her eldest cousin, her tenderness of heart made her feel that she could not spare him, and the purity of her principles added a keener solicitude, when she considered how little useful, how little self-denying his life had (apparently) been.'

Throughout the novel Fanny and the earnest Edmund drive home every moral explicitly. Maria and Julia Bertram are foils for Fanny. Their selfishness, flamboyance and ungoverned passions provide a strong contrast with Fanny's selflessness, unobtrusiveness and quiet firmness. We foresee that Maria will wreck her marriage, but Julia's elopement is ill-judged on Jane Austen's part. It is improbable that the two sisters should elope at the same time, and still more improbable that Julia should elope with Yates, who is merely a chattering monkey. At Mansfield, during the week of the theatricals, she had not shown any marks of favour that would prepare us for such a violent preference later. Yates at Mansfield provides some very amusing comedy and is the necessary agent for the introduction of the play-acting virus, but it can only have been through Jane Austen's desire to limit the number of her characters that he is shown as the partner of Julia's flight. Julia Bertram was a fine-looking girl with a large fortune. Failing to secure Crawford, she had really no reason to go from the sublime to the ridiculous. She is made to elope so as to mark the evil fruit of that indulgence which the lethargic Lady Bertram and the adoring Mrs Norris have accorded to the sisters. But, in fact, Maria's behaviour is presented so direfully that we cannot be expected to feel further shock at the second elopement.

The characters of Mary and Henry Crawford do not seem to be consistent. They are a worldly, frivolous and fascinating pair. We are told at the beginning that their principles are not sound. Mary Crawford, however, is so good-natured that she makes a point of being attentive and comforting to Fanny when that meek creature is snubbed by Mrs Norris. She does not show herself capable of bad taste and even her slighting observations on clergymen are made before she is aware that Edmund intends to take orders. It is very surprising, therefore, towards the end of the story to find her behaving with an insensibility that is really shocking. When Tom Bertram is supposed to be dangerously ill, Mary Crawford writes to Fanny to enquire whether she can rely on Tom Bertram's being in a decline, and to hint broadly that nothing could be more fortunate because then Edmund would inherit, and she could marry Edmund without relinquishing her intention of making a wealthy marriage. Referring to Tom Bertram's grave condition she says:

> I need not say how rejoiced I shall be to hear there has been any mistake, but the report is so prevalent, that I confess I cannot help trembling. To have such a fine young man cut off in the flower of his days, is most melancholy. Poor Sir Thomas will feel it dreadfully. I really am quite agitated on the subject. Fanny, Fanny, I see you smile and look cunning, but upon my honour I never bribed a physician in my life. Poor young man! If he is to die, there will be two poor young men less in the world; and with a fearless face and bold voice would I say to anyone, that wealth and consequence could fall into no hands more deserving of them.[26]

How could such a perceptive young woman have supposed that the loyal and conscientious Fanny could smile and look cunning over the imminent death of a young man with whom she had been reared, and to whose family she owed everything? Mary Crawford could certainly have hoped for Tom Bertram's death, but her worldly sense could not have allowed her to express such hopes to a member of the Bertram family.

Henry Crawford's character seems to fluctuate unconvincingly. At first we see him as a vain and rather unscrupulous philanderer. Then, when Fanny's indifference piques him, his sole happiness seems to depend on making her his wife. Her poverty and her unpresentable family do not deter him, and when he visits Portsmouth he is as determined as ever to persevere in his suit. Nevertheless, the next thing we hear is that he has eloped with Maria (now Rushworth's wife). Had he ever had a serious feeling for Maria, one could imagine that Fanny's coldness might make him yield to the temptation of Maria's accessibility, but Jane Austen explicitly states that while flirting with both of the Bertram sisters, he concentrated on Maria only because, as she was then engaged, he need not be supposed to have any intentions. Even when he elopes with Maria he still loves Fanny. If Jane Austen meant to convey that Maria had for him a physical attraction to which he yielded, she should have made this clear. Or rather, since she had a strong objection to such themes, she should have formed some other motive. To state the circumstances and avoid the explanation merely lays her open to the charge of inconsistent characterization.

These are the faults of *Mansfield Park*. It has many compensatory aspects. Mrs Norris's self-justifying meanness is inimitably sketched. There are some well-managed descriptions of background, as, for example, the economy and vividness with which Jane Austen makes us visualize the ever-changing hues of the sea at Portsmouth. We hear the waves dashing against the ramparts. We smell the salt. Her power of minute realism is forever established in the much-quoted passage which describes the sordid home of the Prices.[27] But Fanny's prim eulogy on the evergreen[28] is a bad lapse, and her rhapsody on the beauty of night[29] is even worse. Such outbursts of lyrical feeling are precluded by the ironic focus, which, although much neglected in this novel, is still sufficiently in use to render such emotional expression out of place.

Mansfield Park was, on the whole, a departure from Jane Austen's characteristic outlook and method. In *Emma* she returns triumphantly to the same level of achievement as *Pride and Prejudice*. With a resilience all the more surprising in a woman of thirty-nine, she regains not the extraordinary vivacity of *Pride and Prejudice*, but a sufficient degree of high spirits to restore her to her normal sense of proportion. She had always had strong moral principles firmly governed by the exigencies of her art. In *Sense and Sensibility* the governance was not fully established. In *Mansfield Park* it was in partial abeyance, due to some experience which so increased her moral earnestness as to impel her to that direct expression which her particular technique could not sanction. *Emma* shows her again in the full mastery of her powers.

Fanny Price was a heroine so dear to Jane Austen that she even calls her in the context 'My Fanny'. She does not seem to have doubted Fanny's claim to a favourable reception. On the other hand, she believed that Emma was a heroine whom nobody but herself would like very much. In one sense, perhaps this is true. Many critics have voiced their disapproval of Emma's self-assurance and snobbery. But the temperament of the critic can never be discounted in his criticisms, and some there are who find Emma far more lovable than Fanny. Fanny was humble, but she was convinced that her judgments were sound; and, of course, they were sound because they were based on unimpeachable moral principles. Emma was self-opinionated, and she was convinced that her judgments were sound, but they were completely mistaken in every case, because they were based only on inexperience and intolerance. This difference is the key to our strong preference for Emma. If we must have youthful infallibility — always a grievous affliction to the less assured adult—then we prefer an infallibility at which we can laugh. We can not only endure, but hugely enjoy Emma's vaunting cocksureness because we know that her house of cards will come crashing about her. Fanny's impregnable fortress is founded on a rock, and that is not likely to endear her to poor wandering mortals who bide the pelting of the pitiless storm. We love Emma because she is not wise, because we know that her blundering progress will bring her to a salutary realization of her own shortcomings. We cannot love Fanny because she is too wise. It is perhaps unjust, or perhaps merely in keeping with some law of compensation, that in this world wisdom must be its own reward, and that we reserve our love for the foolish and the faulty.

Emma is in structure probably the most perfect of the Austen novels. An excellent critic has summed up the substance of this work in the words 'The heroine in her wrong-headed folly spins six separate, interlacing, circles of delusion. On this highly formalized base the characters move to and fro with a naturalness that defies description.'[30] Emma's insistence on organizing the lives of those around her is the mainspring of the action, and the humour lies in the comparison of Emma's misconceptions with the characters and circumstances as they really exist. Never did Jane Austen present with such unerring skill reality and delusion, and it required no little ingenuity to weave together such people and such events as might move towards their own aims without shattering too soon the fantasy which Emma has based on them. There are points at which illusion and reality impinge upon each other. Poor simple Harriet is forced to realize that the eligible suitors designed for her by Emma have other plans. Emma is forced to realize that Mr Elton has mistaken her efforts to secure him for Harriet, as efforts on her own behalf, and again that Frank Churchill's sedulous attentions to her were designed merely to cloak his secret engagement to Jane Fairfax. If these discoveries caused real suffering, we should be unable to see Emma's delusions in a comic light, but Jane Austen is careful to emphasize that the good-natured Harriet has so indefinite a character that she is ready to love any kind and personable man, and does not suffer unduly in transferring her affections. Emma is insulated against Frank Churchill's charm by her unrealized love for Mr Knightley. It is beyond doubt, however, that if Harriet is too simple and trusting to resent Emma's interference in her life, we are much inclined to resent it for her. Jane Austen provided for this attitude by giving it an outlet in Mr Knightley. Mr Knightley's sanity is throughout offered as the antidote to Emma's irrational perverseness, and he never hesitates to reprove her as strongly as she deserves. But though he sees her faults very clearly, he loves her for her essential goodness of heart. He knows that her arrogance and intolerance will eventually be corrected by experience, that they arise from a hasty lack of judgement, and not from a lack of generosity. Emma's attitude to the Martins really is very distasteful. She scorns them because they belong to the farming class — too low for her intimacy and too high for her patronage. With the whole weight of her own prestige and personality she crushes Harriet's obvious wish to marry Robert Martin, and forces her to repay the kindness of his mother and sisters with the most unfeeling rudeness and ingratitude. Emma's attitude is that of her class and period. That she should have imposed it on Harriet was shocking from every point of view; because Harriet was a weak character, and became merely the instrument of Emma's snobbish cruelty; because Harriet was illegitimate and therefore, as Knightley points out, really the inferior of Robert Martin; because Harriet had only a pretty face to recommend her, and almost completely lacked personality and intelligence — circumstances which made it highly desirable that she should gain the protection of some honest man as soon as possible. But Emma comes to repent her behaviour sincerely, and it is an ironic comment on human nature that she begins to realize the enormity of her mistake only when it affects herself. Misinterpreting Emma's mysterious hints that a far more eligible suitor will console her for Elton's contempt, Harriet directs her ready affections towards Mr Knightley. Then and only then does Emma see the absurdity of those pretensions with which she has inspired her simpleton protegée. Then she is only too glad to hear that Harriet will willingly turn to the rejected Robert Martin, and withholds her former threat that such a misalliance must cut her off from Hartfield for ever. Other shocks help to explode her opinionation. She finds that from the first she has misjudged everyone and misunderstood every happening — these blind stupidities recoiling upon her and stinging into life her dormant commonsense. She has put herself in a false position with Elton, whose resentment at her refusal of his proposal causes him to marry at once. Emma must show to the upstart Mrs Elton more courtesy than she otherwise would, lest the Eltons should suppose that her coldness was due to envious disappointment. She must even, as an unmarried lady, give precedence to Mrs Elton in company. She has flirted with Frank Churchill. Now she must bear the sympathy of those who believed her in love with him. She has confided to Frank Churchill humorous suggestions that Jane Fairfax's mysterious depression is due to the fact that she is in love with a married man. Now she finds that Frank Churchill and Jane Fairfax share a confidence from which she has been excluded, and that he has enjoyed a humorous aspect of which she was unconscious. She now realizes that her hints as to Jane Fairfax's love-sickness were in the worst of taste. In a fit of nervous instability, brought on by the jarring moods and ominous silences of the unhappy picnic party, she was flippantly rude to the humble and kindly Miss Bates. Mr Knightley's authoritative reprimand sends her in shame to make her peace. It is characteristic of Emma that, once she realizes her mistakes, she feels them deeply and tries at once to make reparation.

Dramatic dialogue is so much the substance of the Austen novels that it would be invidious to single out for praise any particular passages, but the use of dramatic monologue to forward the action is well worth noting. On the occasion of the strawberry party at Donwell, the garrulous Miss Bates, in a disjointed stream of remarks, expresses what the rest of the party might be taken as saying if they had not been too busied in eating fruit. Again, at the ball Miss Bates, by her spontaneous flood of comments, gives us a lively picture of the arriving guests, their greetings, their small-talk, and all the stir and bustle of circulating refreshments. She bridges the gap between the arrival of the firstcomers and the opening of the ball. In *Persuasion*,[31] Admiral Croft, walking through the streets of Bath with Anne Elliot, is made to achieve the same purpose.

The lesser characters in *Emma* repay as full consideration as that afforded to the heroine. Frank Churchill who seems, but is not, boyishly ingenuous; Jane Fairfax who seems not, but who is, sensitively upright; the valetudinarian Mr Woodhouse and his true daughter Isabella; the gentle and motherly Mrs Weston, the pushing Eltons — all live as vividly and as completely as if they were our nearest neighbours, all reveal themselves so surely that, if they were silent, we could invent speeches for them. We could predict how they would act in any situation. Is there, after all, a higher criterion of the art of fiction?

Jane Austen's heroines are the victims of some social or financial disadvantage. Emma, the rich and consequential heiress, is the victim of her own illusions, and is shown thoroughly humbled at the end. In *Persuasion* the heroine is at a disadvantage which, because it seems almost insuperable, arouses from the first our anxious sympathy. It is not poverty, or obscurity or a flaw in character which deprives Anne Elliot of happiness. It is because of one mistaken decision in the past that her future seems devoid of hope. When, years before the story opens, Anne refused to marry Wentworth, it was due not to a want of love, but because she feared lest an early marriage might impede his career. She was influenced by the over-persuasion of Lady Russell, who altogether disapproved of a union which seemed to offer nothing but poverty. When it is too late, Anne realizes the undying quality of her love. 'She had been forced into prudence in her youth, she learned romance as she grew older.' The return of Captain Wentworth, rich, distinguished, and apparently quite indifferent, accentuates her love, her pain and her consciousness of having irrevocably ruined her life. Loneliness and isolation are the keynote to

Persuasion. It is an autumnal symphony which, above the mono-tone of waning beauty, weaves every moment of pain and longing with the motif of endurance. There is a great deal of endurance in Jane Austen's novels — silent, polite, well-bred endurance, that patience which, she says, is synonymous with hope. Endurance can wait for better times, or even survive without them. Even at the worst, suffering wears itself out and that is hope, however forlorn. Anne Elliot, like Jane Austen's other heroines, cannot have the luxury of grieving alone. Indeed not only is such withdrawal considered a selfish indulgence, but we are told that human society offers the kind of solitude most suitable to a disturbed mind. Anne's 'spirits wanted the solitude and silence which only numbers can give.'[32]

Of all Jane Austen's novels none contains the intensity of emotion which pulses through *Persuasion.* It is expressed by indirection, by short dramatic sentences, by staccato repetitions, by sudden phrases or gestures which reveal only in such momen-tary release the crescendo of feeling that has been silently growing. When Wentworth, after the eight years' parting, enters the crowded breakfast-room at Kellynch, only a bow and a curt-sey pass between the former lovers. When the room has emptied and Anne is alone: '"It is over! It's over!" she repeated to herself again and again, in nervous gratitude. "The worst is over."' When she hears that Wentworth is freed by Louisa Musgrave's marriage to Captain Benwick, 'she had some feelings which she was ashamed to investigate. They were too much like joy sense-less joy!' In Bath, when she meets Wentworth unexpectedly in the street, he shows confusion because by that time he has begun to love her anew. She is less agitated because she has so long been accustomed to loving him secretly, and because already she suspects, even more than he, that the miracle has been performed and that his heart has returned to its allegiance. 'She had the advantage of him in the preparation of the last few moments. All the overpowering, blinding, bewildering, first effects of strong surprise were over with her. Still, however, she had enough to feel! It was agitation, pain, and pleasure; a something between delight and misery.[33]

The stages by which Wentworth passes from coldness to love are excellently planned. At first he has a heart for any pleasing young woman who can catch it, but Anne Elliot is not out of his thoughts when he more seriously describes his ideal of womanhood as being 'A strong mind, with sweetness of manner.' After the first meeting she has the humiliation of hearing that he found her so much altered that he would not have known her again. Still, he is hyper-sensitive to her presence. He shows in various ways a desire to spare her annoyance or fatigue. The conversation in the nut-hedge proves that he is inwardly dwelling with puzzled resentment upon the past. At Lyme the fresh breeze gives bloom to her cheek and a glow to her eyes; she is stared at by a gentleman who seems to admire her exceedingly. 'Captain Wentworth looked round at her instantly in a way which showed his noticing of it. He gave her a momentary glance, a glance of brightness, which seemed to say: "That man is struck with you, and even I, at this moment, see something like Anne Elliot again."'[34] Thereafter fate conspires for Anne. She secures his admiration by her behaviour on the Cobb, but since the shrewd Jane Austen doubted man's willingness to worship an ideal woman with a faded face, she gives to Anne Elliot 'a second spring of youth and beauty' and two admirers, the more dangerous of whom arouses in Wentworth a fine rage of jealousy. Thenceforward the outcome is inevitable.

In this, as in all Jane Austen's other works, she avoids describing the lovers' *éclaircissement*. Such scenes could not fail to be very emotional and could not be treated by her reticent method. In the first draft of *Persuasion* she showed Anne and Wentworth coming together in an actual interview. Then, dissatisfied with what she had written, she planned a far more subtle method of reunion. In the famous scene with Captain Harville, Anne in discussing Captain Benwick's engagement, reveals her own heartfelt convictions on the eternal constancy of women, their way 'of loving longest, when existence or when hope is gone.' Wentworth overhears, and answers her in a letter which declares his fervent devotion. It is perhaps the supreme example of Jane Austen's triumph over the difficulty imposed upon her by her art.

The softer tone of *Persuasion* has led some critics to suggest that, had Jane Austen lived, she would have brought to her writings less irony and more heart. One can only say that Sanditon, left unfinished at her death, is a return to her more characteristic mood of brilliant satire. In her beginning was her end.

The chronicler of women's achievement in fiction must pause somewhere, and nowhere perhaps more fittingly than with Jane Austen. It would, perhaps have been more satisfying to go on and to show that what Jane Austen left unsaid about the passions Emily Brontë expressed with terrifying power—thus proving that women may claim not only the highest artistic level in fiction, but also the most profound depth and the most unshackled freedom of conception. These two women, each supplying what was deficient in the other, are the true apex of English fiction. Nobody has ever reached, much less surpassed, the perfection of Jane Austen's art; nobody has ever crossed the threshold of Emily Brontë's genius.

But one cannot rest on such an apotheosis without a backward glance, without hailing that vast army who, through some hunger of the body or of the spirit, enlisted under the tattered banner of the female pen. They come, brave and hardy as ever out of the past, pushing aside the cerecloths of time and prejudice and obloquy which have shut them from men's eyes. They press around, showing their scars and their achievements, crying like George Sand riding madly through the storm: 'Here we are! Here we are! It is our turn to be judged!' Who can doubt in surveying that great multitude, who can doubt in weighing their varied campaigns and victories, that these were no sporadic camp-followers but a united army advancing doggedly towards their objective. We have stressed their disabilities so that their feats may appear in their true light. These were women who not merely contributed to the development of English fiction, but who had to fight for their right to contribute. We have judged them not in relation to their opportunities, but by the standard which men, with every advantage on their side, established. It is because this standard of judgment had to be applied, that this book[35] traces as background the fictional movement as a whole, and considers, sometimes even in detail, the men's contribution. If this background, this scaffolding, were neglected the work of the women novelists would appear merely as an occasional phenomenon, and not, as it was, an inevitable, sequential and highly characteristic movement, tending always to the moment when, having discarded the male standards by which at first they were governed, the women would choose their own canvas, their own point of view and their own technique. They can claim to have attempted almost every genre of fiction, to have enriched many and to have initiated some of the most important. They can boast that the nearer fiction came towards their characteristic outlook and subject-matter the nearer it came to reality. And they can add that it was women who were largely responsible for giving fiction this orientation, since only thus could they ever hope to make their own peculiar contribution. Fighting then on their own home territory, who could withstand them, when the long tradition of courage and genius culminated in an Austen and a Brontë? To the memory of that great band of women who contributed to the development of English fiction, a woman and a lover of English fiction, humbly offers this record of the female pen.

Notes and References

1 *Sense and Sensibility*, (ed. Peter Conrad, Everyman, London, 1992), vol. i, ch. xviii, p. 97.

2 *Letters of Jane Austen*, (ed. Peter Conrad, Everyman, London, 1991), vol. i, ch. ix, p. 35.

3 *Pride and Prejudice*, ch. ix.

4 *Letters of Jane Austen* (ed. Brabourne, 1884), i, p. 242.

5 Ibid., i, p. 371.

6 See Lord David Cecil, *Jane Austen* (Cambridge University Press, 1935). This brilliant monograph is the finest dissection of Jane Austen's art which has appeared.

7 Expressions used by Charlotte Brontë.

8 The Revd Dr Montague Summers. 'Jane Austen: An Appreciation', *Royal Society of Literary Transaction* (1918), xxxvi, p. 33.

9 Clara Linklater Thompson and R. Brimley Johnson.

10 R. Brimley Johnson, *A New Study of Jane Austen*, p. 4 (published in the same volume as *Jane Austen: A French Appreciation*, by Léonie Villard, 1924).

11 E. A. Baker, *H.E.N.*, vi, p. 64.

12 Ibid., p. 63.

13 Henry Fielding, Introduction to *Joseph Andrews*.

14 Henry Fielding, *Tom Jones*, Bk. i, ch. i.

15 R. Brimley Johnson, *A New Study of Jane Austen*, p. 37 (published in the same volume as *Jane Austen: A French Appreciation* by Léonie Villard, 1924).

16 E.g. Clara Linklater Thompson, whose volume on Jane Austen is permeated with such attempted proofs and parallels.

17 *The Letters of Jane Austen* (ed. Brabourne, 1884), ii, p. 296.

18 See *The Female Philosopher* (*Love and Friendship*, ed. G. K. Chesterton, 1922).

19 *Pride and Prejudice*, op. cit., vol. i, ch. x, p. 43.

20   R. Brimley Johnson *A New Study of Jane Austen*, p. 40 (published in the same volumes *Jane Austen: A French Appreciation* by Léonie Villard, 1924).

21   J. E Austen-Leigh, *Memoir of Jane Austen*, (1871). Letter to Cassandra from Chawton, February 4, 1813.

22   Ibid., letter dated January 29, 1813.

23   In *Sense and Sensibility* Edward Ferrars opposes the Gothic notion of scenery: 'I like a fine prospect, but not on picturesque principles. I do not like crooked twisted, blasted trees, I admire them more if they are tall, straight, and flourishing. I do not like ruined, tattered cottages. I am fond not of nettles, or thistles, or heath blossoms. I have more pleasure in a snug farmhouse than in a watchtower—and a troop of tidy, happy villagers, please me better than the finest banditti in the world' (op. cit., vol. i, ch. xviii, p. 98).

24   In regard to the consistency of Jane Austen's mental attitude, it is interesting to compare this chapter with *Love and Friendship* and again with her *Plan of the Novel* written in 1816 (included in J. E. Austen-Leigh's *Memoir of Jane Austen*, Oxford, 1926).

25   *Northanger Abbey*, (ed. Peter Conrad, Everyman, London, 1992), vol. ii, ch. v, p. 243.

26   *Mansfield Park*, (ed. Peter Conrad, Everyman, London, 1992), vol. iii, ch. xiv, pp. 433–34.

27   Ibid., vol. iii, ch. xiv., p. 439. The passage begins: 'She was deep in other musing . . .'

28   Ibid., vol. ii, ch. iv, p. 209.

29   Ibid., vol. i, ch. xi, p. 113.

30   Elizabeth Jenkins, *Jane Austen* (1939), pp. 248 f.

31   *Persuasion*, vol. i, ch. viii, pp. 63–72.

32   Ibid., vol. i, ch. x, p. 89.

33   Ibid., vol. ii, ch. vii, p. 175.

34   Ibid. vol. i, ch. xii, p. 104.

35   This final summing-up refers to the entire work *The Female Pen* which, owing to the exigencies of war-time, it was impossible to publish in one volume. The first part of *The Female Pen* appeared in 1944 under the title *Women Writers: their Contribution to the English Novel, 1621–1744*.

Original Bibliography

Abbreviations: *D.N.B.* = *Dictionary of National Biography*; *H.E.N.* = Dr E. A. Baker's *The History of the English Novel*.

Unless otherwise stated, London is the place of publication.

An Index to the biographical and obituary notices in the Gentleman's Magazine, 1731–1780, 1891.
Biographical Dictionary of Living Authors, 1816.
Cambridge History of English Literature, 14 vols., 1907–16.
Dictionary of National Biography, 1885 ff.
Halkett and Laing, *A Dictionary of anonymous and pseudonymous Literature*, Edinburgh, 1882–88.
Julleville, L. Petit de, *Histoire de la langue et de la littérature française*, Paris, 1896–99.
Manuel de bibliographie biographique et d'iconographie des Femmes célèbres . . . par un vieux bibliophile, Turin, Paris, 1892.
Watts, R., *Bibliotheca Brittanica*, 1824.

Adams, O. F., *The Story of Jane Austen's Life*, Chicago, 1891.
Apperson, G. L., *A Jane Austen Dictionary*, 1932.
d'Arnaud, Baculard, *Les Amans malhereux, ou le Comte de Comminge*, Paris, 1766.
    Euphémie, Paris, 1768.
Austen-Leigh, J. E., *Memoir of Jane Austen*, Oxford, 1926.
Austen-Leigh, M. A., *Personal Aspects of Jane Austen*, 1920.
Bailey, John C., *The Continuity of Letters*, Oxford, 1923.
    Introduction to Jane Austen, Oxford, 1931.
Baker, E. A., *The History of the English Novel*, 10 vols., 1924–39.
    ed., *Aphra Behn's Novels*, 1905.
    and Packman, James, *A Guide to the best Fiction, English and American, including Translations from Foreign Languages*, 3rd edn., 1932.
Baker, Reed and Jones, *Biographia dramatica*, 1812.
Ballard, George, *Memoirs of Several Ladies of Great Britain*, Oxford, 1752.
Barry, F. V., *Maria Edgeworth, Chosen Letters*, with an introduction by F. V. Barry, 1931.

Bassi, Emelia, *La Vita e Opere di Jane Austen e George Eliot: studi inglesi*, undated.

Beer, H. A., *English Romanticism*, 1899.

Bell, H. W., ed., *Letters of a Portuguese Nun*, 1901.

Bernbaum, Ernest, 'Mrs Behn's Oronooko', *Kittredge Anniversary Papers*, 1913.

    'Mrs Behn's Biography a Fiction', *Modern Language Association of America*, xxviii, 1913.

    The Mary Carleton Narratives, 1663–1673; a missing chapter in the history of the English Novel, 1914.

    'The Drama of Sensibility: a sketch of the history of English sentimental comedy and tragedy, 1696–1780', *Harvard Studies in English*, vol. 3, 1915.

    A Guide through the Romantic Movement, 1930.

Birkhead, E., 'Sentiment and Sensibility in the eighteenth century Novel', *Essays and Studies of the English Association*, vol. xi, 1925.

    The Tale of Terror; a Study in Gothic Romance, 1921.

Bissell, F. O., 'Fielding's Theory of the Novel', *Cornell Studies in English*, vol. 22, New York, 1933.

Block, Andrew, *The English Novel, 1740–1850; a Catalogue including Prose Romances, Short Stories and Translations of foreign Fiction*, 1939.

Boas, F. S., 'Richardson's Novels and their Influence', *Essays and Studies of the English Association*, vol. 2, 1911.

Bonnell, H. H., *Charlotte Brontë, George Eliot, Jane Austen*, 1902.

Brabourne, Lord, ed., *Letters of Jane Austen*, 2 vols., 1884.

Bradley, A. C., 'Jane Austen', *Essays and Studies of the English Association*, vol. 2, 1911.

Brown, The Revd Stephen J., *Ireland in Fiction*, Dublin, 1916.

Buchan, John, 'The Novel and the Fairy Tale', *English Association Pamphlet*, 1931.

Burton, R. E., *Masters of the English Novel*, New York, 1909.

Butler, Harriet J. and Edgeworth, H., *The Black Book of Edgeworthstown and other Edgeworth Memoirs, 1585–1817*, 1927.

Canby, H. S., *The Short Story in English*, New York, 1909.

Cecil, Lord David, *Jane Austen*, Cambridge, 1935.

    Early Victorian Novelists, 1934.

Chesterton, G. K., *The Victorian Age in Literature*, Home University Series.

Church, Richard, *Mary Wollstonecraft Shelley*, Representative Women, 1928.

Cibber, Theophilus, *Lives of the Poets of Great Britain and Ireland*, 5 vols, 1753.

Collins, A. S., *Authorship in the Age of Johnson, being a Study of the relation between Author, Patron, Publisher and Public, 1726–1780*, 1927.

    'The Growth of the English Reading Public in the eighteenth century', *Review of English Studies*. July–Oct., 1926.

    The Profession of Letters: a Study of the Relation of Author to Patron, Publisher and Public, 1780–1832, 1928.

Conant, M. P. *The Oriental Tale in England in the eighteenth century*, New York, 1908.

Cornish, F. W., *Jane Austen*, English Men of Letters, 1913.

Crosse, W. L., *The Development of the English Novel*, New York, 1899.
The Life and Times of Laurence Sterne, 3rd edn., New Haven, 1929.

Dawson, W. J., *The Makers of English Fiction*, 1905.

Disraeli, Isaac, *Curiosities of Literature*, 3 vols., 1849.

Dobson, Austin, *Eighteenth Century Vignettes*, 3 vols., 1892–96.
Samuel Richardson, 1902.
Fanny Burney (English Men of Letters), 1903.
ed., *The Diary and Letters of Madame d'Arblay*, 2 vols.
ed., *Evelina*, 1904.

Dowden, E., *Studies in Literature*, 1789–1817, 1878.
New Studies in Literature, 1895.

Downes, John, *Roscius Anglicanus*, 1709.

Doyle, J. A., *Memoir and Correspondence of Susan Ferrier*, 1898.

Drew, E. A., *The Modern Novel: some Aspects of Contemporary Fiction*, 1926.

Dunlop, J. C., *History of Prose Fiction* (revised edn.), 1896.

Ellis, A. R., Critical prefaces to: *Early Diary of Frances Burney, 1768–1778* (ed. Bohn, 2 vols., 1907); *Cecilia* (1882); *Evelina* (1881).

Elswood, Mrs, *Memoirs of the Literary Ladies of England*, 2 vols., 1843.

Elton, O., *A Survey of English Literature*, 6 vols., 1912–28.
The Augustan Age, 1899.

Ernle, Lord, *The Light Reading of our Ancestors; Chapters in the Growth of the English Novel*, Oxford, 1921.

Esdaile, Arundell, *A List of English Tales and Prose Romances printed before 1740*, 1912.

Fairchild, Hoxie Neale, *The Noble Savage: a Study in Romantic Naturalism*, 1928.

Firth, C. H., ed., *Memoirs of Colonel Hutchinson*, 1885.
ed. *Life of William Cavendish*, 1886.

Forster, E. M., *Aspects of the Novel*. 1927.

Foster, James R., 'The Abbé Prévost and the English Novel', *Publication of The Modern Language Association of America*, vol. xlii, 1927.

Garnett, R., *The Age of Dryen*, 1895.

Gates, L. E., *Studies and Appreciations*, New York, 1900.

Gates, W. B., 'An Unpublished Burney Letter', *Journal of English Literary History*, Dec., 1938).

Genest, John, *Some Account of the English Stage*, 10 vols., Bath, 1832.

George, W. L., *The Intelligence of Woman*, 1917.
A Novelist on Novels, 1918.

Gerwig, G. W., *The Art of the Short Story*, New York, 1909.

Gildon's Langbaine, *The Lives of the Poets*, 1699.

Gosse, Edmund, *Seventeenth Century Studies* (2nd revised edn.), 1885.
ed., Thomas Nash's *The Unfortunate Traveller*, 1892.
'A Nun's Love Letters', *Fortnightly Review*, 43, 1888.

Grabo, C. H., *The Technique of the Novel*, New York, 1928.

Grainger, J., *Biographical History of England*, (3rd edn.), 1779.

Gregory, Allene, *The French Revolution and the English Novel*, 1915.

Grierson, H. J. C., *The First Half of the Seventeenth Century*, 1906.

Gryll, M. R. G., *Mary Wollstonecraft Shelley*, 1938.

Hamelius, Paul, 'The Source of Southern's *Fatal Marriage'*, *Modern Language Review*, vol. iv, 1909.

Hamilton, C. M., *Materials and Methods of Fiction*, New York, 1909.

Hamilton, Catherine J., *Women Writers: their Works and Ways*, 1893.

Hare, Augustus, *The Life and Letters of Maria Edgeworth*, 2 vols., 1894.

Harrington, G., *Nugae Antiquae*, 3 vols., 1779.

Harrison, F., *Studies in Early Victorian Literature*, 1895.

Hazard, Paul, *L'Abbé Prévost et l'Angleterre: étude critique sur 'Manon Lescaut,'* Paris, 1929.

Hazlitt, William, *Lectures on the English Comic Writers* (3rd edn.) 1841.
Review of Fanny Burney's *Memoirs of Dr Burney*, *Edinburgh Review*, 24 Feb., 1815.

Heine, Heinrich, *Prose Writings*, 1887.

Hentch, Alice A., *De la Littérature didactique du moyen age s'adressant spécialement aux femmes*, Cahors, 1903.

Hill, Constance, *Jane Austen, her Homes and her friends*, (3rd edn.) 1923.
Maria Edgeworth and her Circle in the Days of Bonaparte and Bourbon, 1910.
The House in St Martin's Street, 1907.
Juniper Hall, 1904.
Fanny Burney at the Court of Queen Charlotte, 1912.

Horner, Joyce, 'Women Novelists, 1688–1797', Smith College Studies in Modern Languages, vol. xi, nos. 1–3).

Hunt, Leigh, *Men, Women and Books*, 1847.

Hutchinson, The Revd Julius, *The Memoirs of Colonel Hutchinson*, 1810.

Jack, A. A., *Essays on the Novel as illustrated by Scott and Jane Austen*, 1897.

Jacobs, Joseph, *Literary Studies*, 1895.

James, Henry, *Partial Portraits*, 1888.

Jeaffreson, J. C., *Novels and Novelists from Elizabeth to Victoria*, 1858.

Jenkins, E., *The Cavalier and his Lady*, 1872.

Jenkins, Elizabeth, *Jane Austen*, 1938.

Jerrold, W. and C., *Five Queer Women*, 1929.

Johnson, R. Brimley, *The Women Novelists*, 1918.
Novelists on Novels, 1928.
Jane Austen: her Life and Critics, 1930.
Fanny Burney and the Burneys, 1926.

Jusserand, J. J., *Literary History of the English People* (new edn.), 1926.
The English Novel in the time of Shakespeare, 1890.

Kavenagh, Julia, *English Women of Letters*, 2 vols., 1863.

Killen, Alice M., *Le roman terrifiant ou le roman noir de Walpole a Ann Radcliffe, et son influence sur la littérature française jusqu'en 1840*, Paris, 1924.

Krutch, J. W., *Five Masters: Boccaccio, Cervantes, Richardson, Stendhal, Proust*, 1931.

Lang, Andrew, *History of English Literature from Beowulf to Swinburne*, 1912.

Langbaine, Gerard, *An Account of the English Dramatic Poets*, Oxford, 1691.

Lanier, S., *The English Novel and the Principles of its Development*, New York, 1891.

Lasserre, Pierre, *Le Romantisme français: essai sur la révolution dans les sentiments et dans les idées au XIXe siècle*, 1919.

Lathrop, H. B., *The Art of the Novelist*, 1921.

Lawless, Emily, *Maria Edgeworth*, English Men of Letters, 1904.

Leavis, Q. D., *Fiction and the Reading Public*, 1932.

Lloyd, Christopher, *Fanny Burney*, 1936.

Lodge, E., *Portraits of Illustrious Personages of Great Britain*, 12 vols., 1835.

Longueville, T., *The First Duke of Newcastle-on-Tyne*, 1910.

Lovatt, Robert and Hughes, Helen, *The History of the Novel in England*, 1933.

Lower, M. A., ed., *Lives of the Duke and Duchess of Newcastle*, 1872.

Lubbock, P., *The Craft of Fiction*, 1921.

Lussky, A. E., *German Romanticism*, 1932. (Translation of *Deutsche Romantik* by Oskar Walzel, 2 vols., 1918.)

Macaulay, Thomas Babington, *Critical and Historical Essays*.

McIntyre, C. F., *Ann Radcliffe in relation to her time*, New Haven, 1920. *Horace Walpole and the English Novel*, 1764–1820, 1934.

Mais, S. P. B. *Books and their Styles*, 1920.

Malden, S. F. *Jane Austen*, Famous Women, 1889.

Marshall, Julian, *Life and Letters of Mary Wollstonecraft Shelley*, 2 vols., 1889.

Masefield, Muriel, *Women Novelists from Fanny Burney to George Eliot*, University Extension Series, 1934.

Masson, David, *English Novelists and their Styles*, Cambridge, 1859.

Mathias, Thomas J., *The Pursuits of Literature*, 1798.

May, Marcel, *La Jeunesse de William Beckford, et la genèse de son 'Vathek,'* 1928.

Meakin, A. M. B., *Hannah More*, Eminent Women, 1911.

Meres, Francis, *Palladis Tamia*, 1598.

Mitton, G. E., *Jane Austen and her Times*, 1905.

Moore, F. F., *The Keeper of the Robes*, 1912.

Moore, Virginia, *Distinguished Women Writers*, New York, 1934.

More, Paul Elmer, *The Drift of Romanticism*, 1913.

Morgan, C. E., *The Rise of the Novel of Manners: Fiction between 1600 and 1740*, New York, 1911.

Morley, Edith, 'Fanny Burney', *Essays and Studies of the English Association*, no. 60, April 1925.

Nicol, J. R, Allardyce, *Restoration Drama, 1660–1700*, (2nd edn.) 1928.

Nichols, John, *Illustrations of the Literary History of the Eighteenth Century*, 1817.

Overton, G. M., *The Philosophy of Fiction*, New York, 1928.

Painter, William, *The Palace of Pleasure*, ed. Jacobs, 3 vols., 1890.

Parrish, M. L., *Victorian Lady Novelists*, 1933.

Paterson, A. H., *The Edgeworths*, University Tutorial Press, 1914.

Patterson, Richard Ferrar, *Six Centuries of English Literature*, 6 vols., 1933.

Perry, B., *Study of Prose Fiction*. New York, 1902.

Phelps, W. L., *Essays on Modern Novelists*, New York, 1910.

Pollock, W. H., *Jane Austen, her Contemporaries and herself*, 1899.

Praz, Mario, *The Romantic Agony* (trans.), 1933.

Prestage, E., ed. *Letters of a Portuguese Nun*, 1903.

Railo, Eino, *The Haunted Castle: a Study of the Elements of English Romanticism*, 1927.

Raleigh, Sir Walter, *The English Novel*, 1894.

Rawlence, Guy, *Jane Austen*, Great Lives, 1934.

Reeve, Clara, *The Progress of Romance*, 1785.

Reynaud, Louis, *Le Romantisme; ses origines anglo-germaniques*, 1926.

Rhydderch, David, *Jane Austen: her Life and Art*, 1932.

Rickert, Edith, trans. of *Lays of Marie de France*, ed. Nutt, 1901.

Roquefort, J. B. de, ed., *Works of Marie de France*, 2 vols.

Rossetti, Lucy Madox, *Mrs Shelley*, Eminent Women, 1890.

Sackville-West, V., *Aphra Behn, 1640–1689*, 1927.

Sadleir, Michael, 'The Northanger Novels; a Footnote to Jane Austen'. (*Essays and Studies of the English Association*, no. 68, Nov. 1927)
  Introduction to 1927 edn. of *The Heroine* by Eaton Stannard Barrett.

Saintsbury, George, *The English Novel*, 1913.
  A History of Criticism and Literary Taste in Europe, Edinburgh, 1900.
  A Short History of French Literature, Oxford, 1882.
  A History of the French Novel, 1917.
  A History of Elizabethan Literature, 1887.
  A History of Nineteenth Century Literature, 1780–1895, 1896.

Scott, Sir Walter, *Lives of Eminent Novelists and Dramatists*, 1835.
  ed. *Mrs Radcliffe's Novels*, Ballantyne, 1824.

Seeley, L. B., *Fanny Burney and her Friends*, 1890.

Sheavyn, Phoebe, *The Literary Profession in the Elizabethan Age*, Manchester, 1909.

Simonds, W. E., *Introduction to the Study of English Fiction*, New York, 1911.

Singer, G. F., *The Epistolary Novel: its origin, development, decline and residuary influences*, 1933.

Small, Miriam R., *Charlotte Ramsay Lennox*, Yale, 1935.

Smith, G. B., *Poets and Novelists*. 1875.

Smith, Goldwin, *Life of Jane Austen*, Great Writers, 1890.

Soet, Frans de, *Cavalier and Puritan in the seventeenth century*, Delft, 1932.

Stephens, Sir Leslie, *English Literature and Society in the Eighteenth Century*, 1904.
  A History of English Thought in the Eighteenth Century, 2 vols., 1876.
  Hours in a Library, 1874.

Stoddart, F. H., *The Evolution of the English Novel*, New York, 1900.

Stokoe, F. W., *German Influence in the English Romantic Period*, 1788–1816, 1926.

Summers, Montague, 'A Great Mistress of Romance: Ann Radcliffe, 1764–1823', *Royal Society of Literature*, vol. xxxv.
  ed., *Works of Aphra Behn*, 1915.

'The Source of Southern's "The Fatal Marriage" *Modern Language Review*, April, 1916.

'Jane Austen: an Appreciation', *Royal Society of Literature Transactions*, vol. xxxvi, 1918).

Thackeray, W. M., *The English Humorists of the Eighteenth Century*, 1853.

Thomson, Clara L., *Jane Austen: a Survey*, 1929.

Tieje, A. J., 'The Theory of Characterisation in Prose Fiction prior to 1740', *University of Minnesota Studies in Language and Literature*, 1916.

Tinker, C. B., *Dr Johnson and Fanny Burney*, 1912.

Tompkins, J. M. S., *The Popular Novel in England*, 1770–1800, 1932.

'Ramond de Carbonnières, Grosley and Mrs Radcliffe', *Review of English Studies*, July 1929.

Tourtellot, A. B., *Be Loved no More*, 1938.

Trahard, Pierre, *Les maitres de la sensibilité française au XVIIIe siècle*, 2 vols., 1931–32.

Tucker, T. G., *The Foreign Debt of English Literature*, 1907.

Tuckerman, B., *A History of English Prose Fiction*. New York, 1891.

Turberville, A. S., *English Men and Manners in the Eighteenth Century: an illustrated narrative*, 1926.

Upham, A. H., 'Lucy Hutchinson and the Duchess of Newcastle' (*Anglia*, vol. xxxvi, 1912).

Verschoyle, Derek, *The English Novelists*, 1937.

Villard, Leonie, *Jane Austen: a French Appreciation* (trans.), 1924.

Walford, L. B., *Twelve English Authoresses*, 1892.

Walker, H., *The Literature of the Victorian Era*, Cambridge. 1910.

Walpole, Horatio, *A Catalogue of the Royal and Noble Writers of England*, ed., Parks, 5 vols., 1806.
Works, 5 vols., 1798.

Ward, A. W., *History of English Dramatic Literature*, 3 vols., 1899.

Warren, F. M., *The History of the Novel previous to the Seventeenth Century*, New York, 1911.

Warren, George, *Impartial Description of Surinam*, 1667.

Wharton, Edith, *The Writing of Fiction*, 1925.

Whincop, Thomas, *Scanderbeg* (with appended list of dramatic authors covering period until 1747).

Whitmore, Clara, *Women's Work in Fiction from the Restoration to the Mid-Victorian Period*, New York, 1910.

Wicher, George F., *Life and Romances of Mrs Eliza Haywood*, New York, 1915.

Wieten, A. A. S., *Mrs Radcliffe: her relation towards Romanticism with an appendix on the novels falsely ascribed to her*. Amsterdam, 1926.

Wilson, F. P., ed. *The Bachelor's Banquet by Dekker*, 1929.

Wright, James, *Historia Histrionica*, 1699.

Woolf, Virginia, *The Common Reader*, 2 vols., 1925.

Zimmern, *Maria Edgeworth* (Eminent Women), 1883.

Supplement to Original Bibliography

(recent reprints of primary texts cited and works not previously cited in text)

Astell, Mary, *The First English Feminist Reflections on Marriage and Other Writings*, ed. Bridget Hill, Gower, London, 1986.

Aubin, Penelope, *The Adventures of the Prince of Clermont, and Madame de Raveza* (trans. from French), Bell, London, 1722.

The Life and Adventures of Lady Lucy, E. Golding, Dublin, 1753.

The Life, Adventures and Distresses of Carlotte Dupont, and her Lover Belanger, A. Lemoine, London, 1800.

A Collection of Entertaining Histories and Novels, designed to promote the cause of virtue and honour . . ., D. Midwinter, London, 1739.

The Life and Adventures of the Young Count Albertus, the son of Count Lewis Augustus, by the Lady Lucy, J. Darby, London, 1728.

The Life and Amorous Adventures of Lucinda, E. Bell et al., London, 1722.

The Life of Madame de Beaumont, a French Lady, E. Bell et al., 1721.

The Noble Slaves, Nicholas Van Riper, New York, 1814.

The Strange Adventures of Count de Vineuil and his family, E. Bell et al., London, 1721.

The Welcome: a poem to his Grace the Duke of Marlborough, John Morphew, London, 1708.

The Masquerade; or, the Humourous Cuckold.

Austen, Jane, *The Complete Novels*, Oxford University Press, 1994.

Emma, ed. Ronald Blythe, Penguin, London, 1985.

Catherine and Other Writings, ed. Margaret Anne Doody and Douglas Murray, Oxford University Press, 1993.

Pride and Prejudice, ed. Tony Tanner, Penguin, London, 1985.

Persuasion, ed. W. Harding, Penguin, London, 1985.

Sense and Sensibility, ed. Tony Tanner, Penguin, London, 1986.

Northanger Abbey, ed. John Davie, Oxford University Press, 1990.

Lady Susan; The Watsons; Sanditon, ed. Margaret Drabble, Penguin, London, 1974.

Mansfield Park, ed. Tony Tanner, Penguin, London, 1985.

Selected Letters: 1796–1817, ed. R.W. Chapman, Oxford University Press, 1985.

Jane Barker, *The Entertaining Novels of Mrs Jane Barker*, 3rd edn., Bettesworth et al., 1736.

Exilius: Or, The Banished Roman, E. Curll, London, n.d.

The Lining of the Patchwork Screen; Designed for the Further Entertainment of the Ladies, Bettesworth, London, 1726.

Poetical Recreations: Consisting of original poems, songs, odes, etc., Benjamin Crayle, London, 1688.

Love Intrigues: Or, The History of the Amours of Bosvil and Galesia, as related to Lucasia, in St. Germain Garden, E. Curll, London, 1713.

A Patchwork Screen for the Ladies; Or, Love and Virtue Recommended, in a Collection of Instructive Novels, E. Curll, London, 1723.

Behn, Aphra, *Love Letters Between a Nobleman and his Sister*, introduction by Maureen Duffy, Virago, London, 1987.

Oroonoko, The Rover and Other Works, ed. Janet Todd, Penguin, London, 1992.

The Lucky Chance: Or, The Alderman's Bargain, ed. Fidelis Morgan, Methuen, London, 1984.

Five Plays, introduction by Maureen Duffy, Methuen, London, 1990.

Selected Writings, Greewood, New York, 1970.

The Works of Aphra Behn, ed. Montague Summers, Bloomsbury, New York, 1967.

The Works of Aphra Behn, vol. 1: Poetry, ed. Janet Todd, Pickering Masters Series, Pickering and Chatto, London, 1992.

The Complete Works of Aphra Behn, vol. 2: Love Letters Between a Nobleman and his Sister, ed. Janet Todd, Ohio University Press, 1993.

Novels of Mrs. Aprhra Behn, Greenwood, New York, 1970.

Abdelazar: Or, The Moor's Revenge, Music Press, New York, 1947.

Two Tales: The Royal Slave and the Fair Jilt, Folio Society, London, 1953.

Bonhote, Elizabeth, *Darnley Vale: Or, Emelia Fitzroy*, W. Lane, London, 1789.

Ellen Woodley, William Lane, London, 1790.

Ungay Castle, a Novel, printed for William Lane at the Minerva Press, London, 1796.

Olivia: Or, Deserted Bride, W. Lane, London, 1786.

The Fashionable Friend, A Novel, J. Potts, Dublin, 1774.

Feelings: Or, Sketches from Life — a Desultory Poem with Other Pieces.

The Parental Monitor, 3rd edn., W. Lane, London, 1796, reprinted in Boston, 1823.

The Rambles of Mr. Franklin, 4 vols., T. Beckett and P. A. Dehandt, London 1772–76 (repr. William Lane, at the Minerva Press, London, 1797).

Brooke, Frances, *The History of Emily Montague*, Garland, New York, 1974.

Rosina, W. Simpkin and Robert Marshall et al., London, 1820.

Fanny Burney, *Cecilia: Or, Memoirs of an Heiress*, Virago Modern Classics, Virago Press, 1986.

Evelina: Or, The History of a Young Girl's Entrance into the World, ed. Edward A. Bloom, Oxford University Press, London, 1970.

The Journals and Letters of Fanny Burney, 10 vols., Clarendon Press, Oxford, 1972–1982.

The Wanderer: Or, Female Difficulties, ed. Margaret Anne Doody et al., Oxford University Press, 1990.

Camilla, eds Edward A. Bloom and Lillian D. Bloom, Oxford University Press, 1983.

Cecilia: Or, Memoirs of an Heiress, eds Peter Sabor and Margaret A. Doody, Oxford University Press, 1988.

Edwy and Elgiva: A Tragedy, ed. Miriam Benkovitz, Shoestring Press, Hamden, 1987.

Clifford, Lady Anne, *The Diaries of Lady Anne Clifford*, ed. D.J.H. Clifford, Alan Sutton, Stroud, 1990.

>*Lives of Lady Anne Clifford Countess of Dorset, Pembroke and Montgomery (1590–1676) and of her Parents, Summarized by Herself*, Hazell et al., London, 1916.

Mary Davys, *The Works of Mary Davys: Consisting of Plays, Novels, Poems and Familiar Letters*, H. Woodfall, London, 1725.

>*The Reformed Coquet* bound with *Familiar Letters Betwixt a Gentleman and a Lady* and *The Mercenary Lover: Or, The Unfortunate Heiress* (Eliza Haywood), Foundations of the Novel Series no. 42, Garland Press, New York, 1974.

>*Familar Letters Betwixt a Gentleman and a Lady*, introduction by Robert A. Day, University of California Press, Los Angeles, 1955.

>*The Self-Rival*, London, 1725.

>*The Northern Heiress: Or, The Humours of York*, printed by H. Meere for Bettesworth et al., London, 1716.

>*The Fugitive*, G. Sawbridge, 1705.

>*The Accomplished Rake: Or, Modern Fine Gentleman*, printed 1727.

>*The False Friend: Or, The Treacherous Portuguese*, T. Astley, London, 1732.

Maria Edgeworth, *The Absentee*, eds W.J. McCormack and K.M. Walker, Oxford University Press, 1988.

>*Castle Rackrent*, ed. George Watson, Oxford University Press, 1982.

>*Castle Rackrent and Ennui*, introduction by Marilyn Butler, Penguin, London, 1993.

>*Letters for Literary Ladies, to which is added an Essay on the Noble Science of Self-Justification*, Everyman, London, 1993.

>*Ormond: A Tale*, Appletree Press, Belfast, 1992.

>*Maria Edgeworth in France and Switzerland: Selections from the Edgeworth Family Letters*, ed. Christina Colvin, Oxford University Press, 1979.

>*Belinda*, introduction by Eva Figes, Pandora Press, 1986.

>*Letters from England 1813–1844*, ed. Christina Colvin, Oxford University Press, 1971.

>*Old Poz* (1893), *Helen* (1924), *Harrington* (1924), *Ennui*, Garland, New York, 1978.

Fanshawe, Lady Anne, *The Memoirs of Anne, Lady Halkett and Anne, Lady Fanshawe*, ed. John Loftis, Clarendon Press, Oxford, 1979.

Ferrier, Susan, *Marriage*, introduction by Rosemary Ashton, Virago Modern Classics no. 202, Virago Press, London, 1986.

>*The Works of Susan Ferrier*, E. Nash and Grayson, London, 1929.

>*Destiny: Or, The Chief's Daughter*, introduction by Lady Margaret Sackville, E. Nash and Grayson, London, 1929.

>*The Inheritance*, Three Rivers, Bampion, 1984.

Fielding, Sarah, *The Adventures of David Simple*, ed. Malcolm Kelsall, Oxford University Press, 1987.

>*The Correspondence of Henry and Sarah Fielding*, ed. Martin C. Battesten and Clive T. Probyn, Clarendon Press, 1993.

>*The Cry, a New Dramatic Fable*, introduction Malcolm Kelsall, Scholars' Facsimilies and Reprints, New York, 1986.

Bibliography

The Governess: Or, Little Female Academy, introduction by Mary Cadogan, Pandora Press, London, 1987.

The History of Ophelia, Garland Press, New York, 1974.

The History of the Countess of Bellwyn, A. Millar, London, 1789.

The Lives of Cleopatra and Octavia, Garland Press, New York, 1974

The History of Betty Barnes, J. Fleming, London, 1770.

The Story of the cruel giant Barbico, the good giant Benefico, and the little pretty Dwarf Mignon, Mein and Fleming, Boston, 1768.

Gunning, Susannah, *Barford Abbey*, Garland Press, New York, 1974.

A letter from Mrs Gunning, addressed to His Grace the Duke of Argyll, 3rd edn., London, 1791.

Hamilton, Elizabeth, *The Cottagers of Glenburnie: A Tale for the Farmers' Ingle-Book*, Garland Press, New York, 1974.

The Illustrious Lady: A Biography of Barbara Villiers, Countess of Castlemaine and Duchess of Cleveland, Hamish Hamilton, London, 1980.

Letters Addressed to the Daughter of a Nobleman on the Formation of the Religious and the Moral Principle, ed. Gina Luria, Garland Press, 1974.

Hays, Mary, *Memoirs of Emma Courtney*, introduction by Sally Cline, Pandora Press, London, 1987.

The Victim of Prejudice, introduction by Terence Allen Hoagwood, Scholars' Facsimiles and Reprints, New York, 1990.

Letters and Essays, Moral and Miscellaneous, introduction by Gina Luria, Garland Press, New York, 1974.

Appeal to the Men of Great Britain in Behalf of Women, introduction by Gina Luria, Garland Press, New York, 1974.

Haywood, Eliza, *The History of Miss Betsy Thoughtless*, introduction by Dale Spender, Pandora Press, London, 1986.

Bath Intrigues: Four Letters to a Friend, introduction by Simon Varey, Augustan Reprint Society no. 236, Los Angeles, 1986.

A Present for the Servants from their Ministers, Masters and Other Friends And a Present for a Servant-Maid, Garland Press, New York, 1985.

The Plays of Eliza Haywood, ed. Valerie C. Rudolph, Garland Press, New York, 1983.

Four Novels of Eliza Haywood, introduction by Mary Anne Schofield, Scholars' Facsimiles and Reprints, New York, 1983.

Masquerade Novels of Eliza Haywood, introduction by Mary Anne Schofield, Scholars' Facsimiles and Reprints, New York, 1986.

Life's Progress Through the Passions: Or, The Adventures of Natura, Garland Press, New York, 1975.

The Fortunate Foundlings, Garland Press, New York, 1974.

The History of Jemmy and Jenny Jessamy, Garland Press, New York, 1974.

Hutchinson, Lucy, *Memoirs of the Life of Colonel Hutchinson Governor of Nottingham by his Widow Lucy*, Oxford University Press, 1973

Inchbald, Elizabeth, *A Simple Story*, ed. J.M.S. Tompkins (1967), with new introduction by Jane Spencer, Pandora Press, London, 1988.

A Mogul Tale: A Farce in Two Acts, E.M. Murden, New York, 1827.

Lover's Vows: A Play in Two Acts (J. West, Boston, 1799), repr. Louisville, 1965.

Inkle and Yarico: An Opera in Three Acts, D. Langworth, New York, 1806.

Knight, Ellis Cornelia, *Dinarbas*, ed. Ann Messenger, Early Women Writers 1650–1800 no. 2, 1993.

Lee, Harriet, *The Canterbury Tales*, introduction by Harriet Gilbert, Pandora Press, London, 1989.

Clara Lennox: Or, The Distressed Widow, J. Adland, London, 1797.

Constantia de Valmont, a Novel, M. Carey, Philadelphia, 1799.

The Errors of Innocence, Burnet, Dublin, 1786.

The Mysterious Marriage: Or Hardship of Roselia, A Play in Three Acts, C. G. and J. Robinson, London, 1798.

The New Peerage: Or, Our Eyes May Deceive Us, W. Watson, Dublin, 1788.

The Three Strangers: A Play in Five Acts, Laymen, London, 1825.

Lee, Sophia, *The Recess, or a Tale of Other Times*, reprinted with new foreword by J.M.S. Tompkins and introduction by Devendra P. Varma, Arno Press, New York, 1972.

Lennox, Charlotte, *The Female Quixote: Or, The Adventures of Arabella*, Pandora Press, London, 1986.

Henrietta, Garland Press, New York, 1974.

Sophia, Garland Press, New York, 1974.

Manley, Mary, *The Novels of Mary Delarivier Manley*, ed. P. Kvster, Scholars' Facsimiles and Reprints, New York, 1971.

The Adventures of Rivella: Or, the History of the Author of the Four Volumes of the New Atalantis, 2nd edn., London, 1715.

Almyna: Or, The Arabian Vow, a Tragedy, W. Turner et al., London, 1707.

Court Intrigues, John Morphew, London, 1711.

Mrs Manley's Dramatic Works (includes *The Royal Mischief; Lucius, the First Christian King of Britain; The Lost Lover: Or, The Jealous Husband; Almyna: Or, The Arabian Vow*), London, 1696–1717.

Translation of the Secret History of Queen Zarah, and the Zarazians, A. Le Verbineux, Oxford, 1771.

Mrs. Manley's History of her own Life and Times, 4th edn., E. Curll and J. Ramberton, London, 1725.

Letters Written by Mary Manley, 2nd edn., R. B., London, 1713.

Memoirs of Europe, J. Morphew, London, 1716.

A Modest Inquiry into the Reasons of the Joy Expressed by a Certain Set of People upon the Report of Her Majesty's Death, J. Morphew, London, 1714.

The Power of Love: in Seven Novels. 1. The Fair Hypocrite, 2. The Physician's Strategem, 3. The Wife's Resentment, 4 and 5. The Husband's Resentment, in two examples, 6. The Happy Fugitive, 7. The Perjured Beauty, C. Davis, London, 1741 (first printed for J. Barber, 1720).

The Royal Mischief, a Tragedy, R. Bentley et al., London, 1696.

Secret Memoirs and Manners of Several Persons of Quality, of Both Sexes, John Morphew, London, 1709, reprinted 1770.

A Stage-Coach Journey to Exeter, Cadell and Davis, London, 1815.

Bibliography

A True Relation of what Pass'd at the Examination of the Marquis de Guiscard, at the Cock-pit, the 8th March 1710–11., J. Morphew, London, 1711.

A True Relation of the Several Facts and Circumstances of the Intended riot and tumult of Queen Elizabeth's Birthday, John Morphew, London, 1711.

More, Hannah, *Strictures on the Modern System of Female Education*, 1974.

Slavery, a Poem, T. Cadell, London, 1788.

Hints Towards Foming the Character of a Young Princess, 4th edn. T. Cadell and W. Davies, 1809.

The Book of Private Devotion, 25th London edn., D. Appleton, New York, 184–.

Newcastle, Margaret Duchess of, *The Life of William Cavendish, Duke of Newcastle to which is added the true Relation of my Birth, Breeding and Life*, ed. C.H. Firth, John Nimmo, London, 1886.

Sociable Letters, Scolar Press, Menston, 1969.

Poems and Fancies, Scolar Press, Menston, 1972.

Opie, Amelia, *Adeline Mowbray: Or, the Mother and Daughter*, introduction by Jeanette Winterston, Pandora Press, London, 1986.

The Father and Daughter: A Tale, Grove and Son, Southwark, 1845.

Pix, Mary, *The Inhumane Cardinal*, introduction by Constance Clark, Scolars' Facsimilies and Reprints, New York, 1984.

The Plays of Mary Pix and Catherine Trotter, ed. Edna L. Steeves, Garland Press, New York, 1982.

Pilkington, Laetitia, *Memoirs of Mrs. Laetitia Pilkington, 1712–1750*, Routledge, London, 1928.

Radcliffe, Ann, *The Mysteries of Udolpho*, ed. Bonamy Dobrée, notes by Frederick Garber, Oxford University Press, 1992.

The Italian: Or, The Confessional of the Black Penitents, a Romance, ed. Frederick Garber, Oxford University Press, 1971.

A Sicilian Romance, ed. Alison Milbank, Oxford University Press, 1993.

Gaston de Blondville: Or, The Court of Henry III keeping Festival in Ardenne, a Romance, Arno Press, New York, 1972.

A Journey Made in the Summer of 1794 through Holland and the Western Frontier of Germany, Anglistica and Americana Series no. 121, Geog Olms, 1975.

The Romance of the Forest: Interspersed with some pieces of Poetry, Oxford University Press, 1986.

The Castles of Athlin and Dunbane, A Highland Story, foreword by Frederickk Shroyer, Arno Press, New York, 1972.

Robinson, Mary, *Memoirs of the Late Mrs. Robinson*, ed. Mary Elizabeth Robinson, Cabden-Sandersen, London, 1930.

Walsingham: Or, The Pupil of Nature, introduction by Peter Garside, Routledge and Thommas, 1992.

Lyrical Tales, Woodstock Books, Oxford, 1989.

Ainsi la Vie, a poem, J. Bell, London, 1790.

Angelina, a Novel, printed for the author, London, 1796.

The Beauties of Mrs. Robinson, H. D. Symonds, 1791.

Captivity, a poem and Celadon and Lydia, a Tale, T. Beckett, London, 1777.

Elegiac Verses to a Young Lady on the Death of her Brother . . ., J. Johnson, London, 1776.

The False Friend: A Domestic Story, T.N. Longman and O. Rees, London, 1799.

Hubert de France, a Romance of the Eighteenth Century, Hookham and Carpenter, London, 1796.

Impartial Reflections on the Present Situation of the Queen of France; by a Friend to Humanity, John Bell, London, 1791.

The Lucky Escape, London, 1778.

Memoirs of the Late Mrs. Robinson, Whittaker et al., London, 1830.

Mrs. Mary Robinson, Written by Herself, The Grolier Society, London, 191–.

Modern Manners; A poem in two cantos, printed by the author, London, 1793.

Monody to the Memory of Sir Joshua Reynolds, J. Bell, London, 1792.

Monody to the Memory of the Late Queen of France, T. Spilsbury, London, 1793.

The Poetical Works of Mrs. Mary Robinson, R. Phillips, London, 1806.

Reeve, Clara, *The Old English Baron, a Gothic Story*, ed. J. Trainer, Oxford University Press, 1979.

Plans of Education with Remarks on the Systems of Other Writers, Garland Press, New York, 1974.

The Champion of Virtue, W. Keymer, Colchester, 1777 (new edition, A. Clough, London, 1795).

Destination: Or, Memoirs of a Private Family, printed by T. Burnside for Burnet et al., Dublin, 1799–1800.

Edmund: Orphan of the Castle, a Tragedy in Five Acts, R. Faulder et al., London, 1799.

The Exiles: Or, Memoirs of the Count de Cronstadt, 2 vols., P. Byrne et al., Dublin, 1789.

The Fair Impostor, a Novel, 2 vols., T. Hookham et al., London, 1792.

Fatherless Fanny: Or, A Young Lady's First Entrance into Life, T. Kelly, London, 1821.

The Progress of Romance, through Times, Countries and Manners, Garland Press, New York, 1970.

Rosa, The Orphan: Or, The Danger of Female Life, W. Nicholson & Sons, Wakefield, n.d.

The School for Widows, a Novel, T. Hookham et al., London, 1844.

The Two Mentors, A Modern Story, J. Mawman, London, 1803.

Rowe, Elizabeth, *The Works of Elizabeth Rowe*, 4 vols., J. & A. Arch, London, 1796.

Devout Exercises of the Heart, in Meditation and Soliloquy, Prayer and Praise, n.p., 1937.

An Expostulatory Epistle to Sir Richard Steele Upon the Death of Mr. Addison, W. Hinchcliffe, London, 1720.

Friendship in Death, Bennett, Plymouth, 1814.

The History of Joseph: A Poem in Ten Books, J.T. Buckingham, Boston, 1815.

The Hermit: A Poem, Philadelphia, 1753.

Letters Moral and Entertaining, 2nd edn., S. Powell and E. Exshaw, 1735.

The Miscellaneous Works in Prose and Verse, of Mrs. Elizabeth Rowe, J. Buckland, London, 1772.

Philomela: Or, Poems by Mrs Elizabeth Singer, E. Powell for E. Exshaw, Dublin, 1738.

Poems on Several Occasions, John Dunton, London, 1694.

The Poetical Works of Mrs. Elizabeth Rowe, Suttaby, Evance and Fox, London, 1820.

Sheridan, Frances, *The Plays of Frances Sheridan*, ed. Robert Hogan and Jerry C. Beasley, University of Delaware Press, Newark, 1984.

The Memoirs of Miss Sidney Bidulph, introduction by Sue Townsend, Pandora Press, London, 1987.

Shelley, Mary, *The Last Man*, new introduction by Brian Aldiss, Hogarth Press, London, 1985.

History of a Six Week's Tour, Woodstock Books, Oxford, 1989.

Frankenstein: Or, The Modern Prometheus, ed. M.K. Joseph, Oxford University Press, 1992.

Collected Tales and Stories, ed. Charles E. Robinson, John Hopkins Press, Baltimore, 1976.

The Journals of Mary Shelley, 1814–1844, eds. Paula R. Feldman and Diana Scott-Kilvert, Clarendon Press, Oxford, 1987.

The Letters of Mary Wollstonecraft Shelley, ed. Betty T. Bennett, vol. 2 'Treading the Unknown Path', John Hopkins Press, Baltimore, 1983.

An Historical and Moral View of the Origin and Progress of the French Revolution and the Effect it has Produced in Europe, Scholars' Facsimilies and Reprints, New York, 1975.

Letters to Gilbert Imlay, English Literature Series no. 33, M.S.G. Haskell House, 1971.

Smith, Charlotte, *The Old Manor House*, ed. Anne Henry Ehrenpreis, new introduction by Judith Phillips Stanton, Oxford University Press, 1989.

Marchmont, Scholars' Facsimilies and Reprints, New York, 1989.

Montalbert, Scholars' Facsimilies and Reprints, New York, 1989.

Emmeline, The Orphan of the Castle, introduction by Zoë Fairbanks, Pandora Press, London, 1988.

Beachy Head, Green Piers Press, Wisborough, 1985.

Elegiac Sonnets, (1789), repr. of 5th edn. with new introduction by Jonathan Wordsworth, Woodstock Books, Oxford, 1992.

The Poems of Charlotte Smith, ed. Stuart M. Curran, Oxford University Press, 1993.

Desmond, a Novel, introduction by Gina Luria, Garland Press, New York, 1974.

The Young Philosopher, a Novel, introduction by Gina Luria, Garland Press, New York, 1974.

Williams, Helen Maria, *Memoirs of the Reign of Robespierre*, Hamilton, London, n.d.

The Young Philosopher, a Novel, introduction by Gina Luria, Garland Press, New York, 1974.

Williams, Helen Maria, *Memoirs of the Reign of Robespierre*, Hamilton, London, n.d.

    Letters Written in France, introduction by Jonathan Wordsworth, Revolution and Romanticism no. 1, Woodstock Books, Oxford, 1989.

    Paul and Virginia, Woodstock Books, Oxford, 1989.

Wollstonecraft, Mary, *Mary; Maria; Matilda*, ed. Janet Todd, Penguin, London, 1992.

    Collected Letters of Mary Wollstonecraft, ed. Ralph M. Wardle, Cornell University Press, Ithaca, 1980.

    Mary Wollstonecraft's Original Stories, introduction by E.V. Lucas, H. Froude, London, 1906.

    Original Stories from Real Life, Woodstock Books, Oxford, 1990.

    Political Writings, ed. Janet Todd, Pickering and Chatto, London, 1992.

    A Short Residence in Sweden, Norway and Denmark, Harmondsworth: Penguin, 1987.

    A Vindication of the Rights of Woman, Everyman, London, 1992.

    The Works of Mary Wollstonecraft, eds. Janet Todd and Marilyn Butler, assistant ed. Emma Rees-Mogg, 7 vols. William Pickering, London, 1989:

    vol. 1, *Mary, A Fiction; The Wrongs of Woman: Or, Maria; The Caves of Fancy*.

    vol. 2, *Elements of Morality; Young Grandison*.

    vol. 3, *Of the Importance of Religious Opinions*.

    vol. 4, *Thoughts on the Education of Daughters; The Female Reader; Original Stories; Letters on the Management of Infants' Lessons*.

    vol. 5, *A Vindication of the Righs of Men; A Vindication on the Rights of Women; Hints*.

    vol. 6, *An Historical and Moral View of the French Revolution; Letters to Joseph Johnson; Letter Written in Sweden, Norway and Denmark; Letters to Gilbert Imlay*.

    vol. 7, *On Poetry; Contribution to the Analytical Review, 1788–1797*.

    A Wollstonecraft Anthology, ed. Janet Todd, Polity Press, Cambridge, 1089.

Index